Hobson Library

Keesing's Guide to the Mid-East Peace Process

KEESING'S GUIDE TO THE MID-EAST PEACE PROCESS

by

Lawrence Joffe

Cartermill
Publishing

Keesing's Guide to the Mid-East Peace Process

Published by Cartermill International Ltd
Maple House, 149 Tottenham Court Road, London W1P 9LL

Telephone: (0171) 896 2424
Facsimile: (0171) 896 2449

First Published 1996.

A catalogue record for this book is available from the British Library.

ISBN 1-86067-009-1

Typeset in 9/10pt Times New Roman; headings in Univers bold.
Printed and bound in Great Britain by Bookcraft (Bath) Ltd., Midsomer Norton, Somerset

Contents

For my beloved parents, Hyam and Vivienne

'Behold, I extend peace like a river,
and the honour of nations like a mighty stream'
   Isaiah 66:12, Hebrew Bible

'Blessed are the peacemakers,
for they shall be called the children of God'
   Matthew 5: 9, New Testament

'If thy enemy incline toward peace,
do thou also incline toward peace'
   Sura VIII:61, Koran

'The essence of peace is in bringing together two opposites.
Never panic . . . when you see two parties who are totally antagonistic . . .
Indeed, it is the crux of the wholeness of peace,
to attempt to bring peace between two opposites'
   Rabbi Nachman of Bratzlav, Likutei Ha'Moharan, Part A necessary good

Acknowledgements

I am extremely grateful to so many people who helped and encouraged me during the writing of this book, and without whom I know it could not have been finished. Space does not permit me to mention everyone. However, I feel I must thank in particular: Ram Aviram, Elise Redstone and Mark Faber at the Israeli Embassy in London; Afif Safieh, Chief Delegate of the PLO in London, and Mr Samara; Ahmed El-Ibrashy, head of the Egyptian Information Centre in London; Bassam Asfour, Director of Information at the Embassy of the Hashemite Kingdom of Jordan; staff at the Lebanese, Norwegian and American Embassies; The World Bank Press Office in Washington D.C.; Prof Efraim Karsh of King's College, London; Helen Davis and staff at BIPAC, and CAABU; Dr Ghada Karmi at SOAS; and Dr Joel Peters at the Royal Institute of International Affairs. I made extensive use of the marvelous library at SOAS (London University's School of Oriental and African Studies), and the Warburg Institute Library, where I work. I drew heavily from the following sources: Keesings Record of World Events, the Jerusalem Report magazine, the Guardian, Al-Ahram International, the Independent, Time magazine, the Jewish Chronicle, Journal of Palestine Studies, MEED, Middle East International, Palestine Times and BBC Radio 4; not to mention several excellent books on the subject of Mid-east peace including PANARAMA's biographies of Palestinians. In addition, I used a number of Websites on the Internet, including: Israeline, the Israel MFA Peace Gopher, the Al-Quds news-server, the US Department of State gopher (DOSFAN), University of Texas Middle East Studies, WSU Friends of Palestine, FT server, Palestine Homepage, and Netserver for the Hashemite Kingdom of Jordan. To my family and friends, thank you for all of your constructive criticism and support, especially to my father for his wise insights and tireless readings of the text and to my mother for her unofficial press-cuttings service! Thanks also to Dr John Harper at Cartermill, who commissioned me to write this book; and above all, to my publisher, Kevin Blyth, and my editor, Shane Hooper, for their remarkable patience, guidance and necessary good humour.

Introduction

On Sept. 13 1993, an event took place which only a week earlier would have seemed beyond the dreams of the most imaginative photo-montage artist. Yasser Arafat, Chairman of the Palestine Liberation Organization (PLO), and Yitzhak Rabin, Prime Minister of Israel, sworn enemies, were shaking hands on the lawn of the White House in Washington DC. At a stroke, Israel and the PLO had – in theory at least – turned from mortal foes to potential allies.

Just over two years later, another event occurred, if anything more surreal. On Nov. 4, 1995, Yitzhak Rabin was gunned down at a huge peace rally in Tel Aviv. What most shocked Israelis was the fact that the assassin, 27-year-old Yigal Amir, was not an Arab, but a fellow Jew, a man who saw in the burgeoning Arab-Israeli peace process a threat to his vision of the Jewish state. And while the Israeli right joined in the chorus of outrage at the first assassination of an Israeli leader, many on the left (including Leah Rabin, the late prime minister's widow) accused the right of generating the atmosphere of hatred which led to Rabin's murder.

With bitter irony, Yitzhak Rabin achieved almost as much in death as in life. For the first time, King Hussein of Jordan and President Hosni Mubarak of Egypt visited Israel, to attend his funeral in Jerusalem. The foreign ministers of Oman and Qatar were there too, even though their states have yet to officially recognize the existence of Israel. Three days later, Yasser Arafat made his first official visit to Israel, to pay his condolences to Leah Rabin. Some called it a glimpse of what a future regional peace might be. With Shimon Peres, the main architect of Israel's peace policy, as acting prime minister surely the momentum would now be unstoppable? More sobre voices, however, noticed that the enemies of peace, amongst both Jews and Arabs, were unrepentant. The challenge was how to galvanize the broad centre to take the risk for peace.

To many observers, Benjamin Netanyahu's victory over Peres in the May 1996 Israeli elections proved that the risks for peace were indeed too big. Now, once again, the whole region was asking whether the peace process would finally unravel. For the first time in six years the Arab League convened a summit of leaders in Cairo to address the issue. Others, however were less certain. The question to them was which aspect of Netanyahu would prevail: the candidate who promised not to surrender an inch of territory for peace, or the post-election statesman who called on Israel's Arab neighbours to join in a new drive for peace 'without preconditions'?

Between 1948 and 1993

The handshake between Rabin and Arafat in 1993 had important echoes for each leader personally, but it also served as a symbol of their respective peoples and their intertwined histories. The wars of 1947–49 and 1967 were watersheds in the lives of both men. As a lieutenant-colonel in the Israeli Defence Forces, Rabin had played a key role in helping the new-born State of Israel survive its War of Independence. At 26 he had been entrusted with negotiating a post-war armistice with Egypt. Then, as Israeli chief of staff in 1967, he had led Israel to a victory which in less than a week quadrupled the Sate's land mass.

Arafat was involved in gun-running for Palestinian forces in the 1947–49 war, a conflict which Palestinians still regard as a nadir in their history, and one which sent a majority of them into exile. After the Arab defeat in 1967, their feeling of humiliation led directly to Arafat assuming control of the PLO. Under his direction, the Arab world, and indeed a majority of the UN General Assembly, hailed the PLO as 'the sole representatives of the Palestinian people'. But in the face of the organization's persistent use of terrorism, and its seemingly implacable opposition to the existence of the Jewish state, successive Israeli governments refused to have anything to do with it. Murmurings of change on both sides led to a plethora of peace initiatives over more than two decades, but ultimately these yielded nothing of substance.

The year 1993, by contrast, was meant to mark a new beginning for both men and both peoples. No longer did the old 'zero-sum equation' apply, whereby one side's gain meant the other side's loss. Now that mutual recognition was a reality, they strove for peace together. The gist of the deal (known as Oslo 1 after the secret negotiations in Norway which led to the breakthrough) was a plan to withdraw most Israeli forces from the Gaza Strip and Jericho in the West Bank. In their place would be a Palestine National Authority, staffed largely by PLO officials.

If 'Gaza-Jericho First' proved a success, Palestinians would acquire more land, greater democracy and increased authority over their daily lives. Israel, now free of a hostile subject population, would be able to foster new ties with its Arab neighbours (including a reborn Palestinian entity), and so at last win acceptance in the Middle East. The really difficult issues – Jerusalem, final borders, settlers and refugees – have been postponed till permanent status talks. In theory, by this stage the two sides would have built up a reservoir of trust and co-operation large enough to overcome even these potential obstacles.

Dreams and realities

In practice, however, the deadweight of history, and the legacy of years of conflict, have blighted the 'peace process'. Oslo 1, born of such goodwill and amidst such euphoria, has apparently delivered less than it initially promised. Oslo 2, the Interim Agreement sealed by another Arafat-Rabin handshake in Washington two years later, on Sept. 28, 1995, was a much less euphoric affair, even though the implications were much greater.

Perhaps expectations had been too high. Certainly, they were different for the two parties involved. Writing in the New York Review of Books, Israeli Professor Avishai Margalit explained that what Palestinians wanted most from peace was full independence, whereas what Israelis wanted was real security. To many Palestinians a state of their own, genuinely independent of Israel (both politically and economically), still seems a distant dream. And in the two years since the first Washington signing, the number of Israelis killed in terrorist attacks has increased, contrary to the original predictions. The 140,000 Jewish settlers in the 'occupied territories' feel particularly threatened. Once they were seen as 'heroes' by the ruling *Likud*, as they developed *Eretz Yisrael*; now they were depicted as impediments to peace (a view obviously deepened after one of their sympathizers killed Rabin). Settlers realize that the upshot of Palestinian autonomy must mean a smaller role for them, despite all the special protection and consideration given to them in Oslo 1 and 2. In the end it might mean their forced departure from the area.

Optimists hoped that Oslo 2 might be the germ of a future and long-lasting peace. It will extend Palestinian authority to most of the rest of the West Bank. Once again there is a timetable (for redeploying troops, releasing Palestinian prisoners from Israeli jails, and preparing for elections to a Palestinian Council). But have the leaders learnt from their past mistakes, and this time build a sense of common purpose? And in the light of Rabin's killing, can they marginalize extremists and still be able to tackle the difficult issues which will arise in the 'final status talks'?

Defining 'the Middle East conflict'

The Israeli-Palestinian issue is just one, albeit crucial, aspect of the Arab-Israeli dispute. That dispute is, in turn, just one facet of Middle East politics. There are a welter of issues – the battle between rich and poor Arab states; and within states, between often beleaguered governments and 'the street'; and the ideological battle for supremacy between liberalism, pan-Arabism and Islamic fundamentalism. Sometimes disputes echo ancient rivalries, such as Arabs versus Persians, or Sunni versus Shi'ite Muslims, both seen in the eight-year-long war between Iran and Iraq. Over and above this, the Middle East has served as a cockpit for superpower rivalry (between France and Britain in the inter-war years, and between the USA and the USSR from 1945 to 1989). The oil-producing nations have their own rivalries – when united they have wreaked havoc on the rest of the world (as in the 1973 oil boycott following the Yom Kippur War); when divided, they have boiled over into vicious intra-Arab wars (as in Iraq's annexation of Kuwait in 1990, which led to the Gulf War of 1991).

In so many different ways these myriad issues are interrelated. Furthermore, the reality of today's political actions often hark back to earlier conflicts, many of which occurred outside the Middle East. For instance, Arab political rhetoric is replete with images of the loss of Muslim Spain in 1492, or memories of the Crusader conquests of the Middle Ages. Likewise, the recollection of Jewish powerlessness in the face of the Nazi Holocaust forms a psychological backdrop for much of Israeli politics.

Main phases of the dispute

Nonetheless, the Israeli-Palestinian issue is regarded (rightly or wrongly) as being at the centre of international concern about the Middle East. It is possible to define the main phases of the dispute as follows:

- The return of Zionist Jews to Palestine coinciding with the growth of Arab nationalism
- The demise of the Ottoman Empire and the period of British Mandate rule (1920–48) The failure of partition plans in the 1930s and 1940s
- The post-war creation of the state of Israel and birth of Palestinian refugee problem (1947–49)
- The rebirth of Palestinian politics under the PLO (1964 to present)
- The military victory of Israel in 1967 and its acquisition of occupied territories
- The electoral victory of Likud in Israel in 1977, and the government's support for settlements
- The change in PLO, from terrorism and maximalism, to compromise and a two-state solution
- The peace between Israel and Egypt in 1979, which broke Israel's regional ostracization
- The changes in Israel due to the Lebanon War (1982) and the Palestinian intifada (1987)
- The Gulf War and the path to peace at Madrid (1991)
- The return of Labour to power in Israel (1992)
- The Oslo accords and the Israel-PLO breakthrough with the Gaza-Jericho First plan (1993)
- The Jordan-Israel peace treaty (1994)
- The plan to extend Palestinian interim self-government to the rest of the West Bank (1995)

The significance of 1967

Ironically, the events of 1967 planted the seeds for the solution on the White House Lawn. The war had radically altered the dispensation in the Middle East. Israel now occupied territories which it believed afforded them security against future attack. Yet the existence of a hostile Palestinian population there, themselves largely refugees from the earlier war of 1947–49, was to lead to an uprising, the *intifada* of 1987, which forced Israel to reappraise its foreign policy. Those same events in the late 1980s also led the PLO to consider seriously for the first time a historic compromise – a Palestinian entity (maybe in time a state) on part of the land they claimed.

Of course, much has happened between 1967 and now. Up to 140,000 Jewish settlers, encouraged especially by *Likud*-led governments between 1977 and 1992, have planted deep roots in the 'occupied territories'. On a psychological level, this phenomenon encouraged some Israelis to believe that these human 'facts on the ground' precluded any territorial surrender to Arabs.

The new phase – Madrid, Oslo and beyond

Throughout the 1970s and 1980s a huge range of peace plans were considered. Apart from a few limited agreements (such as the ceasefire after the 1973 war, and Egypt's 'separate peace' with Israel at the Camp David talks), these largely failed to touch on the central vexed issue of Israel and the Palestinians. Only in October 1991 at the Madrid peace conference did the right conditions come together. For various reasons (which the book will outline), Madrid failed to solve the central issue, of Israel and the Palestinians. Hence the breakthrough of Oslo and the Washington White House signing ceremony. However, the process begun in Madrid and followed up in Moscow and Washington is continuing, with varying degrees of success, in two broad areas. These comprise Israel and each of its neighbours in separate bilateral talks; and the quieter (but in many ways more successful) multilateral talks, which deal with intra-regional issues that had never been addressed before in such a strategic way.

The four most dramatic achievements which arose out of the Madrid peace talks process were:

- The Oslo accords – mutual recognition between PLO and Israel for the first time
- The peace treaty between Jordan and Israel
- The plan to extend Palestinian autonomy from Gaza and Jericho to the rest of the West Bank
- The vision of a new Middle Eastern economic dispensation, as expressed at the Casablanca summit in 1994 and Amman summit of 1995.

The Oslo accords also broke the taboo of mutual recognition between Israel and the PLO. It was signed in Washington and is currently unfolding in the shape of Palestinian autonomy and Israeli troop withdrawal. The treaty with Jordan, by contrast, was more expected and altogether less problematical. Even so, it promises to herald a new era of economic and ecological co-operation. At the time of going to press, Israel and Syria are seriously engaged in trying to resolve the Golan issue, after which, it is hoped, relations between the two major Middle Eastern rivals will be normalized. This, in turn, will pave the way for Israel to sign a peace treaty with Lebanon (which is currently very dependent on Syria). If all this comes about, Israel will finally be at peace with all its immediate neighbours. Furthermore, it is hoped, the Palestinian people will feel that their national aspirations have at last been addressed, and that a new and happier future for them is just beginning.

The essence of the peace process

Since the Madrid conference in 1991, the crucial principle of mutual recognition has been established. Both the PLO and Arab states have publically committed themselves to peace with Israel (although the means towards achieving this, and the nature of the peace, is still a matter of debate). Israel in turn has for the first time recognized the legitimacy of the PLO. More abstractly, it has accepted that it is part of the Middle East region, and once peace is secured, wishes to participate in dealings with its neighbours. In short, the essence of the Arab-Israeli dispute has changed from one of competing ideologies, each denying the other its legitimacy, to one of implementing real agreements and managing practical problems.

There is another important change between today's negotiations and past attempts at reaching a comprehensive Middle East peace, although this one is more open to interpreta-tion – namely, the Israeli-Palestinian question appears to be less and less the central issue governing Israel's relations with Arabs, and is increasingly one (albeit arguably the most important) of many issues.

Among the phenomena to be considered in this book are:

- The way Israeli-Palestinian peace has facilitated a broader Arab-Israeli peace
- Other issues outside the immediate 'question of Palestine'
- Influence of immigration to Israel
- Terror and its control
- The mechanisms of maintaining peace
- The mechanisms of new Palestinian authorities
- Regional issues covered by the multilateral talks

Outline of the book

The purpose of this book is not to pass judgement on the peace process (that would be premature, particularly with changes taking place daily). Rather, it seeks to provide readers with the resources to make their own assessment. It is hoped that readers will be able to access information by a variety of means. At the same time, it is essential to place the peace process in some historical context. After all, the Oslo accord/ Washington agreement may never have taken place without the earlier talks which began in Madrid in October 1991. And those talks in turn reflect a long pedigree of peace attempts dating back to the beginning of the conflict. Furthermore, it is important to see how the Israeli-Palestinian dispute fits into the broader picture of Middle Eastern and even global politics. For without the end of the Cold War and without the realignment of forces represented by the Gulf War, the circumstances favouring peace may have had to wait for decades.

Part One, Historical Background, outlines the background to the current negotiations, in terms of the histories of each of the main participating parties at Madrid in 1991. The Israeli-Palestinian conflict is considered in its geographical context. Following this, there is a short overview of the occupied territories, a separate chronology dealing with Palestinian political movements since 1948, and a general chronology charting the rise of Islam amongst the Arabs of the Middle East. Separate histories are then presented of the other Arab countries involved in the peace process (Egypt, Jordan, Syria and Lebanon). However, considering ever-changing borders and vast population movements, there is considerable overlap between these chronologies.

Part Two, The Peace Process, brings brings history up to date with an investigation of the structure and timetable of the peace process itself. It also provides a checklist of what has actually been achieved, and where problems lie. In addition, this section also deals separately with the two major strands of talks: Bilateral talks between Israel and her neighbours; and Multilateral talks involving much of the Middle East region

Part Three, The Nations Involved – Contemporary Status, presents current profiles of the peace talks participants (Israel, the frontline states of Jordan, Lebanon, Syria and Egypt, and the Palestinian Authority) in more detail. This section provides their 'vital statistics' (in terms of population, land size, capital city and so on), and describes their political systems and parties, current leadership, political issues and economic status.

Part Four, The Main Players – Biographies, includes a list of biographies of the main figures involved in the peace process, both for and against, arranged alphabetically. A list of the individuals by country appears at the end of the section.

The book concludes with an index which should help the reader find a particular fact or area of interest as quickly as possible.

Part Five, Current Developments and the Future, summarises the central issues at stake in the 'final status talks', and gives more information about important recent developments. The last chapter ends with an overview of the 1996 Israeli elections, and considers the implications of the results for the peace process.

Interim Agreement (Oslo 2) 28th September 1995

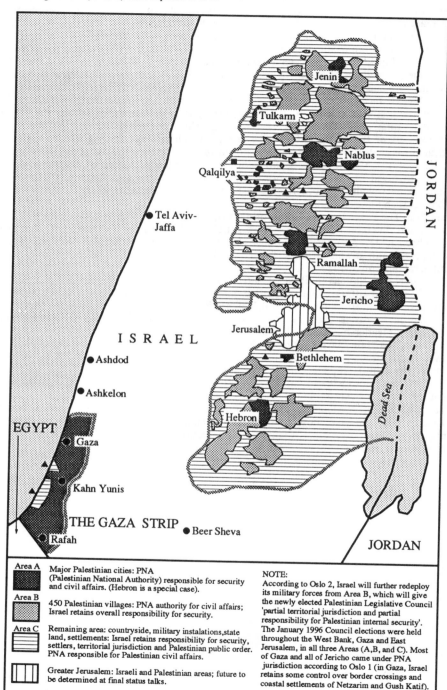

Area A — Major Palestinian cities: PNA (Palestinian National Authority) responsible for security and civil affairs. (Hebron is a special case).

Area B — 450 Palestinian villages: PNA authority for civil affairs; Israel retains overall responsibility for security.

Area C — Remaining area: countryside, military instalations,state land, settlements: Israel retains responsibility for security, settlers, territorial jurisdiction and Palestinian public order. PNA responsible for Palestinian civil affairs.

Greater Jerusalem: Israeli and Palestinian areas; future to be determined at final status talks.

▲ Major Israeli settlements

NOTE:
According to Oslo 2, Israel will further redeploy its military forces from Area B, which will give the newly elected Palestinian Legislative Council 'partial territorial jurisdiction and partial responsibility for Palestinian internal security'. The January 1996 Council elections were held throughout the West Bank, Gaza and East Jerusalem, in all three Areas (A,B, and C). Most of Gaza and all of Jericho came under PNA jurisdiction according to Oslo 1 (in Gaza, Israel retains some control over border crossings and coastal settlements of Netzarim and Gush Katif).

1   15 km

PART ONE

HISTORICAL BACKGROUND

Chapter 1   Israel and Palestine

Today's dispute between Israel and the Arabs does not date back much further than a century. Its origins lie in the clash between two historical trends which arose at roughly the same time: **political Zionism**, which inspired Jews to begin returning to the area in substantial numbers; and **Arab nationalism**, expressed as opposition to 'colonialism', whether Ottoman or Western. Hence the conflict is essentially between two peoples who both claim the same territory, variously known as Palestine, the Holy Land, or the Land of Israel (in Hebrew, *Eretz Yisrael*).

The area in question is really quite small. The State of Israel itself covers 20,770 sq km, which is slightly larger than New Jersey. All the additional 'occupied territories' amount to 7,460 sq km, of which the West Bank accounts for 5,860 sq km, Gaza for 360 sq km and Golan Heights 1,240 sq km. What makes the Israel-Palestine issue so compelling to the world is:

- its strategic situation – located at the nexus of three continents;
- its spiritual richness, as a home to three great monotheistic religions – Judaism, Christianity and Islam.

Israel is the only Middle Eastern country without a Muslim majority and with a Western-style democratic system. Indeed, it is doubly unique as being the only Jewish state in the world. Yet for almost 2,000 years the Jewish people were only minimally represented in Palestine or the Land of Israel, even though it commanded a central focus of their faith. And despite the extraordinary waves of Jewish immigration to Israel this century, from literally every continent, most Jews still remain in the Diaspora.

While the current Arab–Israeli dispute is a comparatively recent phenomenon, its emotional roots run deep. In order to understand the conflict better, it is necessary to consider earlier history and issues:

- The historical claims of Jews to the Land of Israel
- The historical claims of Muslim and Christian Arabs to the same area
- The 2,000-year-long history of Jews in the Diaspora and the anti-Semitism which they suffered
- The role of great power rivalry over the Middle East in general and Israel/Palestine in particular.

Many events occurred outside the geographical ambit of Israel–Palestine, but played an important role in shaping both the psychology and history of the conflict there (for instance, the birth of Islam in the Arabian Hejaz, the expulsion of Jews and Muslims from Spain in 1492, the Nazi Holocaust of 1942–45). The Israeli–Arab regional dispute can be viewed alongside the Palestinians' own story of dispossession and possible reclamation of statehood. The dispute makes little sense unless seen in the context of the Cold War, changing post-war economic circumstances, and the struggle for the leadership in the Middle East between Arab nationalists, Pan-Arabists, leftists, secularists and fundamentalists.

The chronology below considers the Israeli–Palestinian conflict in its geographical locus. Events which occur outside the historical region of Israel–Palestine are put in italics.

From Canaan to Israel

The old question 'Are Jews a religion or a race?', is ultimately unanswerable. Some suggest that both aspects – faith and ethnicity – inform Jewish identity. Another school speaks of Jewish 'peoplehood', the idea being that the course of history has endowed Jews with a common sense of identity, even if they live in widely dispersed communities. Indeed, over the centuries, distinct Jewish communities have arisen (notably, the *Ashkenazim* of central and eastern Europe, and the *Sephardim* of Spain and later North Africa). But, despite some differences in customs and physical appearances, they share a basically identical set of core beliefs and religious traditions (in terms of liturgy, festivals and dietary laws). Zionism determined to restore a Jewish sense of nationhood, grounded in the soil of their ancestral land, Israel – a political identity which they had lost 2,000 years earlier. More controversially, some Zionists sought to solve the old conundrum of Jewish identity, by redefining the House of Israel in the modern era as 'a nation like other nations'.

Judaism itself is less problematic to define. It was the first of the three great monotheistic religions (the others being Christianity and Islam). Judaism's essential belief concerns the unity of God and the unity of His creation. Furthermore, it believes mankind was created 'in God's image', and was given the gift of free will, with the corresponding obligation to improve the world. Following from this, Judaism set out an ethical code of conduct (shared by other faiths and peoples in varying degrees since biblical times); and certain customs that are particular to Jews. In the Jewish tradition, this message was revealed to the Jewish people at Sinai; it was a unique honour, but also obliged them to be 'a light unto the nations' and obey God's decrees. Thus Judaism encapsulates both universalism, and a particular role for the Jewish people. But this Jewish 'chosen-ness' has often been misinterpreted, and arguably led to the anti-Semitism (hatred of Jews) which has coloured so much of post-biblical Jewish history.

While Judaism is a revealed religion, in practice it has developed over time. Rabbinical authority was based on the power to teach the law, as derived from the Bible, and as interpreted in the later *Talmudic* tradition. After the destruction of the Temple and the dispersal of the Jews into the Diaspora, rabbis kept the old faith alive and, with it, a keen sense of Jewish identity. Over time, there were a series of backlashes against the established rabbinate, out of which emerged new forms of Jewish expression. By the 19th century these included Reform, Reconstructionist and Liberal Judaism; and also secular expressions of Jewish identity, like the *Maskilim* ('enlightment' followers), Yiddish playwrights, and political Zionists.

The Old Testament of the Bible (known also as the *Torah* or, more strictly speaking, the *Tanakh*) can be regarded as the primary source for Jewish people's historical attachment to the Land of Israel. However, the further back one travels in time, the less sure one can be about the accuracy of the dates of events (bearing in mind that the Bible is fundamentally a religious and not an historical treatise). By the advent of Christianity, which was born in the land of Israel/Palestine, there are other historical sources: Roman authors, the works of the Romano-Jewish historian, Josephus Flavius, and, several centuries later, Islamic scholars. Here the dates are more certain, but even so the authors were writing to a particular agenda; hence it is, to say the least, difficult to arrive at a truly 'objective' depiction of events.

A word about nomenclature

In the Bible the Jewish people are called by different terms at various stages of their history: Children of Abraham (whom most Jews see as their progenitor), Hebrews (also the language of Jews), Israelites (after the time of Jacob) and Jews (*Yehudim*). The latter word derives from the tribe of Judah, one of the two remaining tribes of the initial 12 after the Assyrian conquest of Israel in 720 BC.

The Jewish calendar dates history from the Creation, while Muslims date history from the departure of Muhammed from Medina. However, this book uses the conventional Western formulation BC ('before Christ') and AD (meaning 'after Christ'). To avoid a Christian gloss, this is sometimes rendered as BCE and CE ('before the common era' and 'common era'); but the author has chosen to use the BC-AD system because of its widespread familiarity to English-speaking readers.

Note: events of significance outside the Middle East are in italic type.

Year	Event
8000 BC	Evidence of the world's first walled city in Jericho
3200 BC	Appearance of Canaanite civilization in Palestine
17th cent BC	The age of the Patriarchs: Abraham, Isaac and Jacob
	Abraham of Ur (in present-day Iraq), the first true believer in the one God according to the Bible, is called on to father a new nation in Canaan (later, Land of Israel or Palestine)
13th cent BC	Exodus from Egypt, return to Land of Israel

12th cent BC	Israelite settlement of the Land of Israel; they conquer or absorb most of the inhabiting Canaanite tribes, and set up a first rudimentary government ruled by religious 'Judges'
c. 1020 BC	Monarchy established; Saul is the first King of Israel
c. 1000 BC	Jerusalem becomes capital of King David's kingdom; Battles against the Philistines (whence is derived the name, Palestine) on coastal plain
c. 960 BC	King Solomon builds the First Temple in Jerusalem
c. 930 BC	The Kingdom divides into two: Israel in the north and Judah in the south
722–720 BC	Assyrians crush Israel; ten of the 12 tribes are sent into exile
586 BC	Babylonians (successors to Assyrians) conquer Kingdom of Judah; Jerusalem and the First Temple are destroyed; remaining Jews exiled to Babylon
538–515 BC	First Return from Babylon allowed under Persian rule; Temple rebuilt
mid-5th cent BC	Second Return – period of Ezra and Nehemiah
332 BC	Alexander the Great of Macedonia conquers land and institutes Hellenistic rule
166–160 BC	Maccabean Jewish Revolt against Hellenistic rule
142–129 BC	Jewish autonomy under Hasmonean dynasty
129–63 BC	Hellenic authority withers; Hasmoneans achieve Jewish independence in new Kingdom
63 BC	Roman army under Pompey (from Egypt) takes Jerusalem; institutes 400 years of Roman imperial rule over the Holy Land, which they rename 'Palestrina'
37 BC – 4 AD	Rule of King Herod, a pro-Roman monarch of Judea
4 BC	Birth of Jesus Christ in Bethlehem; a century later Christianity becomes a distinct religion
66 AD	Jewish revolt against Rome

Living in the Diaspora

The end of Jewish statehood marks the beginning of the Diaspora, a Greek word meaning dispersal. By the time of the Muslim conquest of Palestine, there were still about 300,000 Jews in the land. But most lived outside, having been drawn to Jewish communities established along the Mediterranean rim in earlier centuries. The institution of the synagogue and rabbinical council (*Sanhedrin*) filled the void left by the destruction of the Temple. Babylon (today's Iraq) became the spiritual hub of Judaism for years, where rabbis codified the Oral Law. Later, some Jews went to Spain where they became known as *Sephardim*; others travelled north, to central and later eastern Europe. Ethnologists speculate that this latter group, the *Ashkenazim*, may have absorbed non-Semitic converts into their ranks. Whatever the case, all Jews kept Hebrew as their language of prayer, although in everyday affairs they spoke local tongues, or Judaized vernaculars (Yiddish amongst the *Ashkenazim* and Judaeo-Arabic and *Ladino* amongst the *Sephardim*). As Christianity spread throughout Europe, Jewish minorities were often persecuted on religious grounds. This trend intensified during the Crusades, when Jews were confined to ghettoes and subjected to pogroms, or expelled (as in England in 1290). Generally, Jews were better protected under Islamic rule, and some flourished as doctors, scholars and traders (Moorish Spain is the best example). But from time to time they, too, became the scapegoats of popular unrest and were confined to separate quarters, sometimes known as *mellahs*. Eventually, the Enlightenment and French Revolution allowed European Jews to enter civil society. A number prospered, finding a happy medium between their faith and their nationality. Some became famous outside the confines of the Jewish community, such as Baruch Spinoza, Karl Marx, Felix Mendelsohn, and Benjamin Disraeli. Others, however, suffered a crisis of identity, either disappearing as Jews through assimilation into the host culture, or retreating in the face of a revivified anti-Semitism, especially in the Russian Empire. By the latter half of the 19th century, Jews who could no longer find solace in religious orthodoxy sought a way out through a variety of often revolutionary political expressions – socialist, republican, anarchist, Marxist, and increasingly Zionist.

70	Destruction of Jerusalem and Second Temple (Josephus estimates one million Jews die)
73	Last stand of Jews at Massada, a mountain fortress next to the Dead Sea
132–135	Shimon Bar Kokhba leads abortive uprising against Rome; his failure prompts strict Roman clampdown on Jewish activities and spurs flight into the Diaspora. Tacitus estimated that 600,000 Jews died in the rebellion

Jewish Exile and Arab Palestine

(See also overlapping chronologies – Rise of Islam, Syria, Jordan, Egypt – in following chapters)

Year	Event
c. 210	Jews complete the Mishnah (codification of Oral Law)
313–636	Byzantine (Orthodox Christian) rule in Palestine
c. 390	Depleted Jewish community completes Jerusalem Talmud (commentary on Mishnah)
636	Beginning of Muslim Arab rule in Palestine (four years after Muhammed's death)
691	Construction of Dome of the Rock in Jerusalem
709–717	Construction of Al-Aqsa Mosque in Jerusalem
1070–1080	The Seljuks, a Turkish tribe converted to Islam, occupy Syria and Palestine
1099	European Christians (the Crusaders) invade and conquer Palestine, end Arab rule and persecute remaining Jewish community

---

A portrait of Palestine under the Ottomans

The Ottoman empire ruled Palestine from 1517 to 1918. However, most Palestinians were not Turkish but Arab (roughly 90% of whom were Muslim and 10% Christian). The area never constituted a political administrative unit in its own right, but was rather divided into districts (*sanjaks*) – Acre in the north, Balqa in the centre, and Jerusalem (which included Gaza and some of the Negev desert) in the south. Most of *Filastin* (Palestine) fell within the larger Ottoman province (*vilayet*) of Syria, and was ruled by the pasha of Damascus. After 1841, it was further divided, with a northern section going to the *vilayet* of Beirut; and a southern section, the *sanjak* of Jerusalem. Society was organized in terms of recognized religious communities, known as *millets* – one each for Jews, the various Christian denominations, and the Muslim majority. Palestinian Arabs were divided socially, between regional clans (*Yaman* and *Qays*); religiously, between Muslim and Christian and economically, between a majority of peasants (*fellahin*) and smaller numbers of 'notables' (*ayan*). Arab political power, such as it was, resided mainly in sinecure posts and the *Awqaf* (officials who distributed the *waqf*, or Muslim religious endowments). A reformist administration in Turkey allowed land to pass to private ownership after 1858 (the *Tanzimat* laws). Subsistence farming thus gave way to a market economy; but the net effect (contrary to what was intended) was for a few wealthy families to acquire vast properties. Former tenants now became sharecroppers on their own land, and often paid large rentals to absentee landlords. Some Arabs thus welcomed the arrival of European Jews in the late 19th century, believing this would increase employment opportunities. Indeed, Arab immigration to Palestine began to increase. However, by the first decade of the 20th century, more Arabs began to perceive Jewish immigration as a threat. They felt excluded from the Jewish community's more efficient economy (especially after the launch of the *kibbutz* system). A few Palestinians (mainly educated Christians) began organizing nationalist political clubs, ironically using the Zionists as their model; but most Arabs accepted the authority of Ottoman Turks, who were fellow Muslims. Political parties developed during the British Mandate period, but still largely as clients of one or other of the leading notable families. Following a longstanding Ottoman tradition the Higher Muslim Council was the main source of authority. By the 1920s the council had become the main platform from which Palestinians tried to obstruct the Zionists.

1187	Battle of Hattin – Salah al-Din (Saladin), a Kurdish leader of Muslim Arab armies, defeats Crusaders, captures Jerusalem and institutes the Ayubbid dynasty
1247	End of Ayubbid rule in Palestine with invasion of Mamluks (an Egyptian Muslim dynasty)
1260	Mamluks defeat Mongols at 'Ayn Jalut, Palestine
1291	Mamluks capture Acre and defeat a revived Crusaders' Latin Kingdom of Jerusalem. Over the ensuing centuries, some Mamluk rulers encouraged Jewish refugees from Christian persecution in Europe. Generally the province of Palestine fell into decline
1492	*Jews are expelled from Spain after Christians defeat the last Muslim rulers there*
1516	Turkish Muslim dynasty, the Ottomans, defeat Mamluks in Palestine
1517	Ottoman Sultan Selim I incorporates Palestine into Ottoman Empire (1,000 Jewish families live mainly in Jerusalem, Nablus, Hebron, Gaza and Safad)
1566	Death of Suleiman the Magnificent, who improved organization and governance
1634	Ottomans execute Lebanese Christian Prince Fakhr al-Din, who had led a revolt against their rule in Palestine (he had also occupied northern Palestine, including Safad and Nablus)
1749	Prince Daher Omar creates principality in north, encompassing Safad, Galilee and Jaffa coast
1775	Ottoman Sultan backs Ahmad Pasha al-Djazzar in defeating Daher Omar; sets up fiefdom in north
1799	British navy backs al-Djazzar in repulsing Napolean Bonaparte's invasion of Palestine
1808	Ottomans grant Russia the right to protect Christian Holy Places in Palestine
1832	Ibrahim Pasha, son of Egyptian ruler, Muhammad Ali, occupies Palestine and Syria
1834	Palestinian Arabs revolt against the Pasha's drive to conscript their youth
1840	*Treaty of London: Britain and European powers order Egypt to return Palestine to Ottomans*
1841	July: British naval blockade forces Muhammad Ali to return Palestine
1860	Jews build first neighbourhood outside Jerusalem's city walls, Mishkenot Sha'ananim
1863	Creation of municipality of Jerusalem under Ottoman law
1867	Ottomans allow foreigners to buy land in Palestine
1870	Rabbi Zvi Hirsch Kalischer helps set up a Jewish agricultural school in Jaffa
1878	Establishment of Petach Tikvah, first Jewish 'colony' in Palestine
1881	*Assassination of Tzar Alexander II spawns anti-Semitic pogroms in Russian Empire*
1882	Beginning of First Aliyah (Jewish mass immigration to Palestine); *Hibbat Zion* (Lovers of Zion) arrive at Jaffa; Ottomans restrict Jewish immigration. Leon Pinsker writes 'Auto-emancipation'
1891	Arab notables in Jerusalem ask Constantinople to prohibit Jewish immigration and land purchase
1892	Completion of railway line between Jerusalem and Jaffa
1894	*Dreyfus Trial in France convinces Austrian Jewish journalist, Theodor Herzl, that anti-Semitism is endemic even in liberal Western Europe; he sees Zionism as a solution*

Zionism and the creation of Israel

The expression 'Zionism' derives from Mount Zion which adjoins the Old City of Jerusalem. In its simplest version, it acknowledges Jewry's national attachment to the Land of Israel (an area which broadly covers the present State of Israel and the West Bank of the River Jordan). Some draw a distinction between **spiritual Zionism**, which has underpinned the Jewish religion since the Babylonian Exile, if not earlier; and **political Zionism**, which crystallized in Europe in the late 19th century. Political Zionism blended elements of contemporary European nationalism and secular liberalism with the older religious strain. It sought to find a cure to the problem of anti-Semitism (still prevalent in Europe, despite the supposed success of Jews who had tried to assimilate into civil society). Most orthodox Jews opposed its goals as unattainable, or worse, heretical. In their opinion, only the Messiah could bring Diaspora Jewry back to the Land of Israel; any political attempt was premature and doomed to failure. The few orthodox Jews who had settled in Palestine since the 16th century never tried to set up a political entity. However, certain 19th century rabbis, such as Yehuda hai Alkalai of Sarajevo and Zvi Hirsch Kalischer from Poland, began to call on Jews to farm land in their traditional homeland. Secularists like Ahad Ha-Am envisaged a spiritual centre for world Jewry in Palestine ('a truly Jewish state, not merely a state of Jews'); although in 1891 he warned that Jews would not realize their dreams unless they respected the rights and aspirations of Palestinian Arabs. Aharon David Gordon saw Jewish settlement in Palestine as an opportunity to create a 'new Jew' through the dignity of labour. In 1862 the German Jewish socialist and philosopher, Moses Hess, argued that endemic European anti-Semitism demanded a Jewish state, in accordance with the universal dream of autonomy for all peoples. Leon Pinsker foresaw a Jewish state as the only means to win the world's respect and solve the 'Jewish problem'. Ultimately it was Theodor Herzl, a Jewish journalist from Austro-Hungary, who paved the way for the diplomatic success of the Zionist movement by seeking the assistance of the great powers (and not only Jewish philanthropists, as hitherto), and by founding a World Zionist Organization. After Herzl's untimely death in 1904, Chaim Weizmann, a Russian physicist resident in London, continued his diplomatic work and succeeded in winning British support for a 'Jewish homeland' in Palestine (as expressed in the Balfour Declaration of 1917). In the 20th century, David Ben-Gurion espoused the socialist trend in Zionism; this soon became dominant in the guise of the *Histadrut* labour federation and the Labour movement. Revisionists, led by Vladimir Jabotinsky and his successor, Menachem Begin, favoured a more overtly nationalist approach (an 'Iron Wall' against Arab nationalism). Religious Zionism formed a third strain; distinct from the still prevalent anti-Zionism of many orthodox Jews, it was symbolized by Palestine's first Ashkenazi Chief Rabbi, Abraham Isaac Kook. Each of these three strains emerged as political parties after statehood in 1948. After 1967 new elements emerged: a more radical nationalist variant of religious Zionism, which saw divine providence in Israel's acquisition of the biblical Land of Israel after the Six Day War; and ethnic expressions of Zionism, such as various Sephardi political parties which stressed social improvement.

1896	*Herzl publishes* Der Judenstaat, *a blueprint for a Jewish colony in Palestine*
1897	*First Zionist conference in Basel, Switzerland, forms the World Zionist Organization*
1899	Arab–Jewish tension over large Jewish land purchases in the Tiberias region
1901	Establishment of Jewish National Fund (to sponsor Jewish colonies in Palestine)
1902	Beginning of Second Aliyah, which lasts until the start of World War I in 1914
1905	Completion of Jaffa–Deraa railway line; Zionist Conference rejects plans for homelands in Argentina or Uganda in favour of Palestine
1908	Young Turk revolution in Ottoman homeland of Anatolia Ottomans allow first elections in Palestine; Palestinian Arabs publish their first newspaper in Haifa
1909	Sultan Abdul-Hamid II is deposed; establishment of Tel Aviv, first modern all-Jewish city near Jaffa Zionist socialists set up first *kibbutz*, Degania

1914	*Start of First World War. Ottoman Empire supports the German powers.* In Palestine, Arabs number 650,000; Jews number 85,000. Zionists in Palestine support Great Britain with their Jewish Corps
1915	May: Damascus Protocol [*see box below*] July: Hussein–McMahon Correspondence
1916	Sykes Picot Agreement *Arab revolt begins; British troops under T.E. Lawrence help Hashemite Arabs against Turks*
1917	*November 2: UK government issues the Balfour Declaration* December: Allenby captures Jerusalem
1918	Meetings between Chaim Weizmann and the Hasemite Emir, Feisal bin Hussein, 1918–19
1919	Allenby Declaration; Feisal–Weizmann Agreement, Jan. 3 Palestinian Arabs hold first National Conference and register opposition to Balfour Declaration August: US Congressional Commission on Palestine (King–Crane) report, warns against effects of unrestrained Jewish immigration and Zionist plans on Palestinian Arabs Beginning of the Third Aliyah, mainly from Russia and lasting five years
1920	*San Remo conference assigns mandate for Palestine to Britain*; Arabs attack Jewish areas in Jerusalem and Jaffa

---

Contradictory plans for Palestine's future status

In November 1914 the Ottoman Empire joined World War I on the side of Germany. No sooner had this happened than the Allied powers, Britain and France, began planning on how to partition the Middle East after they had defeated the Ottoman rulers of the area. The first idea was the Damascus Protocol. Next came the year-long series of correspondences between the British High Commissioner in Cairo, Sir Henry McMahon, and Hussein, Sharif of Mecca. Britain promised 'independence for the Arabs', but insisted on colonial control over the east Mediterranean litorral (presumably, although not explicitly, including Palestine). Their terms of the correspondence, however, contradicted another (secret) agreement, drafted in May 1916 by Sir Mark Sykes, a British orientalist, and Charles Georges-Picot, formerly French Consul in Beirut. This envisaged two Arab states in the post-Ottoman Middle East, one under British protection and the other under French. Palestine and the West Bank of the Jordan was to come under 'British, French and Russian protection'. (The plan was abandoned at the time of the post-war Paris Peace Conference in 1919.)

However, a Zionist campaign in Britain led by Chaim Weizmann began to win over some leading British politicians, including Sir Herbert Samuel and Lloyd George. Ultimately, it resulted in the so-called Balfour Declaration, which was originally written as a letter from Lord Arthur Balfour, British Foreign Secretary, to Lord Rothschild on Nov. 2, 1917. The letter promised British government assistance to achieve the idea of Palestine as a 'national home for the Jewish people' in Palestine, as long as it did not 'prejudice the civil and religious rights of existing non-Jewish communities [there]'. The declaration fell far short of promising full independent statehood. In January 1919 Emir Feisal, son of Hussein, apparently signed a nine-article agreement with Weizmann at a post-war peace conference, agreeing to a Zionist role in a separate Palestine. (Ten years later he disputed having 'written anything of the kind'). On March 3 he wrote to US Supreme Court Justice Frankfurter, and 'wished the Jews a hearty welcome home', stating: 'There is room in Syria (*sic*) for us both'. Even so, most Palestinian Arab leaders interpreted it as a threat, and sent delegates to the post-war conferences to oppose it. They were partly appeased by a statement from the victorious General Allenby, reaffirming Britain's commitment to Arab independence. The legal authority of his statement, however, was somewhat vague. In the event, the San Remo Conference of 1920 awarded Britain the mandate over Palestine, incorporating the Balfour Declaration as its preamble. However, unlike the case with other Arab mandates, it lacked a definitive plan for, or timetable towards, full independence. So began the British Mandate, which according to interpretation seemed to promise the same or similar things to Arabs and Jews alike.

British mandate Palestine

Year	Event
1920	As Britain assumes effective power in Palestine, the *Yishuv*, or Palestinian Jewish settlement community, sets up various parastatal structures: *Histadrut* – Jewish labour federation; *Va'ad Leumi* – national council to conduct communal affairs; Jewish Agency (*Sochnut*) – to liaise with foreign governments and Mandate authorities First Palestinian National Congress meets in Haifa, and nominates an Arab Executive Committee
1921	March: Palestinian Jews set up the *Haganah* self-defence unit March: Abdullah becomes emir of Transjordan, which is now considered as a separate entity within the Palestine Mandate April: British High Commissioner Sir Herbert Samuel appoints Haj Amin al-Husseini as Grand Mufti
1922	June: British White Paper reaffirms Balfour Declaration, but limits Jewish immigration July: League of Nations ratifies the Palestine Mandate, including provisions of Balfour Declaration September: Transjordan is exempted from Balfour provisions (in effect Jewish settlement east of the Jordan river is banned)
1923	Britain formally acquires Palestine Mandate
1925	Hebrew University opens
1929	August: Riots at Western (Wailing) Wall in Jerusalem and massacres of Jews in Safed, Hebron and Jerusalem
1931	Zionist Revisionists (nationalist and anti-socialist) set up their own underground organization to rival *Haganah*, the *Etzel* (*Irgun Tsevai Leumi*)
1930	March: Shaw Commission Report October: Hope-Simpson Report and Passfield Paper halt Jewish immigration and land sales
1930	February: White Paper is negated by British Prime Minister McDonald
1933	*Adolf Hitler's Nazis take power in Germany*; start of new Jewish influx to Palestine, mainly from Germany, called the Fifth Aliyah Arab Executive Committee demand a strike to protest Jewish immigration and gain independence
1936	Arab Higher Committee is formed; start of a three-year long Arab Revolt against British Mandate and Zionists
1937	Peel Commission Report – first scheme for partition of Palestine into Jewish and Arab areas Arab Higher Committee is outlawed; Hajj Amin al-Husseini flees to Lebanon
1938	*Kristallnacht in Germany intensifies Nazi attack on Jews;* Evian-les-Bains Refugee Conference; British impose martial law on Palestine
1939	London conference on Palestine convened, but ends in failure May: UK White Paper restricts Jewish immigration and land sales; it also drops partition idea in favour of a unitary state, to receive independence within 10 years *Sept. 3: Hitler invades Poland and World War II begins*
1940	*Etzel* and *Haganah* accept the Jewish community's ban on underground activity for the duration of the war; but a renegade *Etzel* element called *Lehi* (or Stern Gang) split off to continue struggle. Land Transfer Regulations restrict Jewish land purchases
1941	*Nazis launch death camps programme; by war's end some six million Jews are killed in Europe*

Figure 1   *Changes in Jewish population distribution, 1939–1994*

These statistics compare the changes in Jewish population distribution per region, between 1939 on the eve of World War II (when the total world Jewish population was estimated at just under 17m) and today. For the purposes of this chart, Europe includes the Soviet Union (where only rough estimates were available). Asia includes Palestine, which after 1948 became the State of Israel. Evidently the figure given for the Americas in 1939 is an over-estimate.

Notice the following changes:

- The Nazi murder of six million Jews severely reduced Europe's population.
- Mass immigration to Israel from Europe and Africa increases the total for Asia (it also altered the distribution within Asia, as most Middle Eastern Jews have moved, mainly to Israel, since 1948).
- Mass emigration from North African countries (notably, Morocco, Egypt and Algeria) reduces the total for Africa; to this must be added further emigrations from Ethiopia and South Africa.
- The population of Jews in Australia and New Zealand has tripled since 1939, but is still small.
- Today Israel accounts for about 25% of the world's total Jewish population, whereas in 1939 the Jewish population of the Palestine *Yishuv* amounted to just 3%.

Area	1939	1994
Europe	10,000,000	3,636,490
N & S America	5,375,000	6,888,757
Asia	830,000	3,692,224
Africa	600,000	146,770
Oceania	33,000	96,320

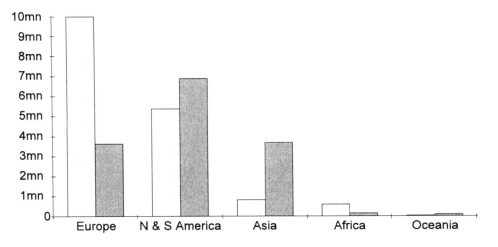

The 1st column represents figures for 1939
The 2nd column represents figures for 1994

Figure 2   *From majority to minority: Arabs in Israel*

The first Arab-Israeli war (known as the War of Independence in Israel) led to a mass exodus of most of the Palestinian Arab population. Those Arabs who remained in the new State of Israel became a minority, whereas before they had constituted a majority. In subsequent years their numbers have grown considerably, but the huge influx of Diaspora Jews to Israel (especially from Arab countries) has ensured that Arabs today make up only a fifth of Israel's population. Unlike their cousins in the occupied territories, Israeli Arabs have the vote and there are a number represented in the Knesset. In the 1992 election they split their support equally between the regular Zionist parties, and a number of left-wing non-Zionist parties.

The diagram below illustrates the dramatic change in Jewish/Arab demography in Israel since the 1948–49 war:

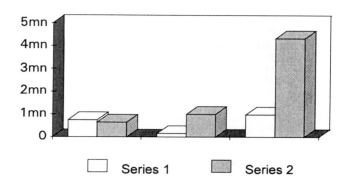

Note:

Series one   =   Arab population
Series two   =   Jewish population

Arab population		Jewish population
1947	750,000 (est.)	650,000
1949	160,000	1,013,900
1993	992,500	4,335,200

[The figure for Arabs in 1993 includes some 200,000 east Jerusalemites, who were offered Israeli citizenship, but unlike Israeli Arabs have refused to take it]

[Sources for figures: Israeli Bureau of Statistics, *Sikkui*, and Encyclopaedia Judaica]

1942	*Biltmore Declaration – first time Zionists openly back the idea of a state of Israel* *Allied victory at Al-Alamein ends threat of Nazi attack on Palestine and the Levant*
1944	*Jewish Brigade formed as part of British forces*
1945	*World War II ends with Allied victory; international shock at discovery of Nazi death camps. Arab states set up an Arab League to show solidarity with Palestinian Arabs*
1946	Jewish underground blows up King David Hotel
1947	Britain decides to surrender mandate over Palestine *UN General Assembly sets up Special Committee on Palestine (UNSCOP), recommends partition Nov. 29: After UNSCOP report is presented, General Assembly votes for partition (Resolution 181)*
1948	January: Arab Liberation Army enters Palestine March: US proposes UN Trusteeship in Palestine (but soon drops the plan) April: Jewish *Irgun* group attacks Arab village of Deir Yassin, sparking Arab refugee crisis and immediate retaliation against bus convoy to Mt Scopus May 14: David Ben-Gurion proclaims State of Israel May 15: UK mandate authorities leave as Arab armies invade – war lasts until July 1949 Underground movements are dissolved and Israeli Defence Force is formed September: Count Bernadotte, UN commissioner, assassinated by Stern Gang *Dec. 11: UN General Assembly passes Resolution 194, concerning Palestinian refugees*

Israel in the Middle East, Palestinians reassert their identity

Year	Event
1949	War ends, Israel signs armistices with Egypt, Jordan, Syria and Lebanon Labour party wins the first Knesset elections in Israel David Ben-Gurion becomes Israel's first prime minister May 11: Israel admitted to UN as its 59th member state Question of Palestinian refugees remains unresolved Dec. 1: Jordan annexes part of Palestine occupied by Arab League and east Jerusalem
1948–52	Period of mass immigration of Jews from post-war Europe and Arab countries
1950	Israel passes the Law of Return Britain and Pakistan recognize Jordanian annexation of West Bank
1954	*Gamal Abdul Nasser becomes Egypt's premier*
1955	*Baghdad Pact established amongst more radical Arab states (Iraq, Egypt)*
1956	Israel fights an eight-day Sinai campaign against Egypt (part of the anti-Nasser Suez Canal War waged by Britain and France); Israel conquers Sinai peninsula
1957	March: Israel agrees to return Sinai to Egypt after UN arbitration UN Emergency Forces (UNEF) stationed in Gaza and Sharm al-Sheikh
1958	Yasser Arafat founds *Fatah* in Kuwait
1961–62	Adolf Eichmann, German Holocaust overseer, is tried and hanged in Israel
1962	First direct sale of US weapons (Hawk missiles) to Israel

1964	National Water Carrier (bringing water from north to semi-arid south) is completed
	May: Cairo summit establishes the PLO and a United Arab Command (four-nation military pact)
1965	Israel lifts martial restrictions on Israeli Arabs

Israel – a nation built on immigration

Jewish immigration to Palestine and later to Israel is the *raison d'être* of Zionist enterprise. Some arrived out of ideological conviction, others as refugees from trouble in Europe or the Middle East. But whatever their motivations, each wave of immigrants (or *Aliyah*) has brought some new element to the country.

First Aliyah	1882–1903	Poorer farming Jews from Russia (*Bilu* and *Hovevei Zion*); orthodox
Second Aliyah	1904–14	Congress Zionists (more ideological and secular in outlook)
Third Aliyah	1919–23	Socialists from Poland
Fourth Aliyah	1924–28	Artisans and middle-class immigrants from central Europe; Yemenites
Fifth Aliyah	1929–39	Refugees from Nazi Germany and neighbouring countries

The British government's White Paper of 1939 severely restricted Jewish immigration to Palestine, largely out of deference to Arab protests. During World War II (1939–45), however, some refugees from Nazi oppression managed to reach Palestine, and Zionists helped to smuggle them in 'illegally'. After the war some 100,000 survivors of Nazi concentration camps entered Palestine.

The new state passed a Law of Return in 1950, which decreed that anyone with at least one Jewish grandparent (and without a criminal record) was eligible to emigrate to the new state. As relations with Arab states deteriorated, Jewish populations throughout the Middle East faced persecution and chose to emigrate to Israel. Where they were blocked, special Israeli intelligence operations (such 'Babylon' for Iraqi Jews and 'Magic Carpet' for Yemenis) used their wartime experience and smuggled in these *olim* (immigrants). Israel set up a Ministry of Absorption to cope with the influx. The Sephardi immigrants (or Oriental Jews from the Middle East and North Africa) gradually altered the character of the country, with attitudes and cultural preferences quite different from those of earlier Ashkenazi Zionists. By the mid-1970s, Sephardi immigrants and their descendants constituted more than half of Israel's population. Many felt that the largely Ashkenazi Labour establishment had neglected or even mistreated them. Their disatisfaction was reflected at the polls, especially in 1977 when their vote helped *Likud* come to power for the first time. Immigration had begun to tail off by the 1980s, when emigrants from Israel (*yordim*) almost equalled in number the *olim* who were arriving.

1948–60	870,000
1961–71	338,000
1972–82	178,000

The collapse of the Soviet Union in 1989, however, speeded up Jewish migration to Israel (many had faced discrimination at home, and were refused the right to immigrate). Over a five-year period more than 500,000 former Soviet Jews entered Israel, in addition to smaller numbers of Ethiopian Jews (Falashas) in 1984 and 1990 and, most recently, Jews from troubled regions like the former Yugoslavia, Azerbaijan and Chechnia.

Since the establishment of Israel, 2.5 million immigrants have arrived in the country, from . . .

Former Soviet Union	795,000 (32%)
Morocco, Algeria and Tunisia	345,000 (14%)
Romania	273,000
Poland	172,000
Iraq	130,000
Iran	76,000
United States	71,000
Turkey	61,000
Yemen	51,000
Ethiopia	48,000
Argentina	43,000
Bulgaria	43,000

The Six Day War – a radical realignment of forces

Year	Event
1967	May: Egyptian President Gamal Abdul Nasser closes Straights of Tiran to Israeli shipping June 5: Israel launches pre-emptive strike, known as the Six Day War Israel defeats the Arab forces (Egypt, Syria and Jordan) and captures following territories: Sinai Peninsula and Gaza Strip from Egypt; West Bank (of the Jordan River) and East Jerusalem from Jordan; Golan Heights from Syria July: Deputy Premier Yigal Allon proposes plan to deal with West Bank (*see next chapter*) Sept. 1: Arab League summit in Khartoum rejects peace with Israel Nov. 22: UN Security Council passes Resolution 242, calling for peace talks between Middle Eastern nations and Israeli withdrawal from occupied territories Egypt, Jordan and Israel in 1970 accept it; PLO and Syria reject it
1968–70	War of Attrition (Palestinian guerrillas launch attacks on Israel from Egypt and Jordan)
1968	First PLO airplane hijacking April: Rabbi Moshe Levinger settles illegally in Hebron, West Bank, site of the Tombs of the Patriarchs (holy to Muslims and Jews), defying policy of Prime Minister Levi Eshkol
1971	Formal foundation of the Land of Israel Movement
1973	Yom Kippur War – surprise Arab attack wounds Israel; Israel Defence Forces recover in final weeks of war Oct. 22: UN Security Council Resolution 338 calls for direct talks based on UN 242
1974	Yitzhak Rabin succeeds Golda Meir as prime minister *Arab summit in Rabat recognize PLO as 'sole legitimate representatives of Palestinians'*
1975	Israel becomes associate member of the European Economic Community Nov 10: UN General Assembly passes resolution equating Zionism with racism
1976	*Israeli rescue hijack hostages in Entebbe, Uganda*
1977	Prime Minister Yitzhak Rabin forced to resign over financial scandal *Likud* Party wins national election for the first time, ending 30 years of Labour rule Menachem Begin is the new prime minister Egyptian President Anwar Sadat visits Jerusalem (first major Arab leader to do so)

Peace with Egypt, war with Lebanon

Year	Event
1978	March–June: Israel invades and then withdraws from Lebanon in Operation Litani Sept. 17: Camp David Accords signed with Egypt; Israel agrees to return Sinai Peninsula (principle of exchanging land for peace and Palestinian autonomy established)
1979	March 26: Israel–Egypt peace treaty signed (but plans for Palestinian autonomy fall by the wayside as PLO rejects stipulations) March 31: *Egypt is expelled from Arab League for signing a 'separate deal' with Israel*

1980	July: *Knesset* declares Jerusalem as the 'indivisible capital' of Israel
1981	Israeli Air Force destroys Iraqi Osirak nuclear reactor *Oct.: Assassination of Anwar Sadat in Egypt* Dec. 14: Israel formally annexes the Golan Heights
1982	Apr. 25: Israel completes withdrawal from the Sinai peninsula June 6: Operation Peace for Galilee – Israel invades Lebanon to flush out PLO bases Israel faces international condemnation for 'allowing' the Sabra and Shatilla massacre Mass protests against Lebanon war in Israel – boost to Peace Now movement
1983	May 17: Agreement signed between Israel and Lebanon (later abrogated) Aug.–Sept.: Begin resigns; Yitzhak Shamir replaces him as *Likud* leader and prime minister Nov. 29: US–Israel memorandum of strategic co-operation
1984	National elections results in hung parliament; *Likud*–Labour coalition ensues, with Labour leader, Shimon Peres, acting as prime minister for first two years
1985	Free Trade Zone Agreement signed with US June 10: Israeli withdrawal from Lebanon completed; smaller units redeployed in southern Lebanese 'security zone', where they periodically battle with Shi'ite *Hizbollah* forces Oct. 1: Israel attacks PLO's Tunis headquarters, retaliating for terror incident in Cyprus Oct. 21: Premier Peres in UN speech calls for Middle East conference, peace with Jordan
1986	*Likud* leader, Yitzhak Shamir, succeeds Peres as prime minister

Intifada – a challenge to the PLO and Israel

Year	Event
1987	Dec. 9: Palestinian *Intifada* (uprising) begins after incident in Gaza Soon spreads to West Bank and lasts for four years (nearly 400 die in first year)
1988	Palestinians set up secret United National Command to steer the *intifada* Defence Minister Yitzhak Rabin responds with 'iron fist' policy; but Israeli left-wingers and security experts call for negotiations with the PLO to end uprising and make peace Creation of *Hamas*, fundamentalist Palestinian rival to PLO King Hussein announces Jordan will withdraw claim to West Bank in favour of PLO Israel rejects PLO's Algiers Declaration (claiming to end terrorism, accepting UN 242 and 338, acknowledging Israel's existence for the first time, and declaring a State of Palestine in Occupied Territories) – USA launches talks with PLO for first time Nov. 1: Israeli general elections – no clear winner Dec. 17: Shamir forms new 'unity government' with Labour as junior partner
1989	Shamir's four-point 'peace initiative' – rejected by PLO and most Arab states Mass immigration of Soviet Jews to Israel begins

Gulf war and the path to peace

| 1990 | March 15: Shamir government falls as Labour withdraws over *Likud's* attitude to peace |

|May: *Intifada* escalates

June 8: Shamir forms right-wing government without Labour

Aug. 2–4: Iraq under Saddam Hussein invades Kuwait, prompting new Middle East crisis

1991

US-led UN Coalition (including Arab states) defeats Iraq in 'high-tech' war

Iraq is forced to surrender Kuwait

During course of war, Iraq fires Scud missiles at Israel; Israel chooses not to retaliate

Oct. 30–31: Middle East peace conference convenes in Madrid

Participants include: Israel, Lebanon, Syria, and joint Jordan-Palestinian delegation

Nov. 10: Repeal of 1975 'Zionism is racism' resolution in the UN

1992

Jan.–Feb.: Israel establishes diplomatic relations with India and China

Jan. 28: Opening of Moscow multilateral summit

June: Labour wins the general election on peace platform; Yitzhak Rabin is new prime minister, Shimon Peres is foreign minister; (*Likud* under leader, Yitzhak Shamir forms the Opposition)

Dec.: Israel deports 413 suspected Islamic fundamentalists from Gaza to south Lebanon

1993

January: Israel lifts the ban on Knesset members talking to the PLO

Feb.–Aug.: secret talks between Israel and PLO in Oslo

Sept. 13: Israel and the PLO sign a Declaration of Principles on Interim Self-Government Arrangements for Palestinian self-rule, initially in Gaza and the Jericho enclave

Sept. 14: Israel and Jordan sign a Common Agenda

1994

Feb. 25: Massacre of Muslim worshippers in Hebron threatens the peace process

May. 4: Israel and PLO sign agreement in Cairo for Palestinian self-government

June 15: Full diplomatic relations with the Holy See (Vatican) for the first time

July 25: King Hussein of Jordan and Rabin declare an end of war between the two states

Aug. 29: Agreement on Preparatory Transfer of Powers in Judaea and Samaria (West Bank area) to Palestinians, concerning education, culture, taxation, welfare, health

Sept. 30: Gulf states agree to end secondary and tertiary boycott of Israel

Sept.–Oct.: Morocco and Tunisia agree to establish interest offices in Israel

Oct. 26: Israel-Jordan Peace Treaty signed

Dec. 10: Rabin, Peres and Arafat awarded Nobel Peace Prize

1995

New wave of Islamic fundamentalist suicide bomb attacks threaten peace process

August: Israeli cabinet approve partial withdrawal from territories, agreed with PLO

Widespread settler protests, sympathetic anti-government demonstrations in cities

Sept. 28: Israel and the PLO sign the Interim Agreement (Oslo 2) in Washington

Oct.: Israel attends the Middle East/North Africa Economic Summit, in Amman, Jordan

Nov. 4: Yitzhak Rabin is assassinated by a right-wing Jewish enemy of the peace process

Foreign Minister Shimon Peres takes over as Prime Minister of Israel, reshuffles cabinet

Nov.: Israeli troops redeploy from Jenin and Ramallah

Dec.: troops redeploy from Tul Karm, Nablus, Qalqilya and Bethlehem

1996

Jan. 20: Palestine Council Elections

Yasser Arafat is elected President, and *Fatah* wins a majority of seats in Council

May 29: Netanyahu defeats Peres; *Likud* coalition government formed

Chapter 2   Palestinian political movements since 1948

The 1948–49 Israeli War of Independence was seen as a miraculous victory for Jews throughout the world, coming only three years after the Nazi genocide had ended in Europe. For the first time in almost 2,000 years there was a Jewish state once more, the fulfillment of long-held dreams and a place of refuge for victims of any future anti-Semitic persecution. To Palestinians, however, it was known as the *nakba* (disaster). Their leaders had rejected the UN partition plan, and then lost the war, in the course of which some 725,000 Palestinians fled the country. Israel now controlled 77% of the area of historic Palestine, 416 villages and towns were allegedly destroyed, and 60% of Palestinian people became refugees.

Palestinian Arabs who chose to remain in Israel now constituted a minority, whereas before the war they had comprised 65% of the population. According to Palestinian estimates made in 1965, they had suffered damage and loss equivalent to $300 billion. The exact causes of the *nakba* remain open to debate. Disunity between Arab forces, the planning and courage of the Israeli military, secret aid from Diaspora Jewry may all explain the course of the war. As for the refugee crisis, the official Israeli position was that Arab propaganda had encouraged Palestinians to leave their homes temporarily, so as to allow Arab armies a free rein in decimating the Jewish state. Palestinians and other Arabs contend that the Israeli Defence Forces (IDF) deliberately drove out Arabs, or exploited fear caused by massacres like that at Deir Yassin, to create a Jewish majority in their new state.

Not surprisingly, Palestinians directed much of their anger at Israel. But there was also anger at the attitudes of Arab states and disillusionment with their own leadership. Such feelings have pervaded Palestinian politics ever since. Nominally, Arab states vowed to support the Palestinians. This led them to refuse to grant Palestinians full citizenship rights (Jordan being the notable exception), pending a final 'liberation' of Palestine. Yet, by and large, Palestinians were neither integrated into their host countries, nor allowed to set up meaningful independent political organizations, until the creation of the PLO in 1964. Even then, the PLO under Ahmed Shukeiri was seen as the product of Gamal Nasser's fancy; Syria duly responded by backing other factions, such as forces loyal to George Habash.

After the 1967 war, Israel gained control of the West Bank and Gaza, the remaining outposts of former Arab Palestine. As Kimmerling and Migdal explain in *Palestinians – the Making of a People*, this profoundly changed the nature of the 'Palestine question'. Between 1948 and 1967 the conflict was largely seen as an international dispute, Israel versus the Arabs. After 1967 it returned to what it had been during the British mandate: two peoples claiming the same soil, in essence an inter-communal dispute. For the first time since 1948, the whole of 'historical Palestine' (including the bulk of the Palestinians) was assembled under a single authority (Israel).

As Jewish settlement of the occupied territories increased, gradually but inexorably, Palestinian refugees now found themselves living cheek by jowl with some of the most nationalistic Israelis, and this increased tensions further. After 1969, the PLO's new leader, Yasser Arafat, succeeded in putting the Palestinian issue back on the international political agenda. An Arab summit in Fez recognized the PLO as the 'sole legitimate representative of the Palestinian people' in 1974, and that same year Arafat addressed the UN General Assembly, and claimed to offer Israel the choice between the gun and the olive branch.

However, many PLO factions resorted to acts of terror against civilians in the 1970s and 1980s. Arafat's leading *Fatah* faction publicly tried to distance itself from this policy, but the PLO as a whole still refused to accept UN Resolution 242 and talk to Israel. Furthermore, it also refused to amend its National Covenant, which vowed to destroy Israel and (in effect) expel all Jews who did not accept an Arab-ruled Palestine. All these factors served to alienate Western opinion, and harden Israel's resolve not to deal with the organization. Throughout the 1970s, Israel sought but failed to find 'moderate' Palestinians outside the PLO as potential negotiating partners.

The PLO's activities also began to antagonize some Arab states. In 1971 most PLO fighters had to decamp from Jordan to Lebanon, after open warfare broke out between them and the Hashemite Kingdom's regular army in 1970. Beirut become the PLO's official headquarters, and such was the PLO's domination of southern Lebanon that it became nicknamed 'Fatah-land'. By 1976 the PLO was embroiled in an even bigger civil war, in Lebanon. Intervention by Syria in 1976 and Israel in 1978 threatened to escalate the conflict into a full-scale regional conflagration.

In 1982 Israel attempted to destroy the PLO in Lebanon, but only partially succeeded. And although the war led in turn to internecine PLO infighting, the PLO emerged relatively intact. In Palestinian eyes, they had taken on the full might of Israel for the first time, which restored some national pride. With the *intifada* of 1987, Palestinians 'inside Palestine' began asserting their case. This put pressure on the PLO to adopt a more realistic and conciliatory position. In 1988 the Palestine National Council (PLO 'parliament in exile') dropped the policy of an armed struggle to liberate 'all of Palestine' (implying the destruction of Israel). It also declared the creation of a State of Palestine. Writing in *Towards the Long-Promised Peace*, the Palestinian academic, Omar Massalha, argued that the declaration was legitimate in international law. Furthermore, he saw it as affirming the essential unity of the Palestinian people; despite divisions of religion and geographical separation caused by the events of 1948, the Palestinians had not only redefined themselves as part of 'the Arab nation', but also as a distinct group whose origins went back to the early Canaanites.

When the USA opened talks with the PLO, another taboo was broken. But the organization still failed to convince Israel of its sincerity, and Arafat's apparent support for Saddam Hussein in 1990 proved to be an almost fatal error of judgement. After the Gulf War, the PLO unequivocally accepted the reality of Israel's existence. It opened negotiations with the state, first by proxy in Madrid in 1991 (through an Israeli-approved Palestinian delegation acting under a Jordanian 'umbrella'), and then directly in 1993. Arafat's supporters hailed his approach as symbolic of a new Palestinian maturity. Opponents derided it as a sign of the PLO's weakness, especially as he was forced to accept terms and conditions which he had rejected out of hand a decade earlier.

No doubt history will judge which side was right. What is clear, however, is that the PLO is changing from a liberation organization to an interim government, responsible for real territory (Gaza and Jericho first, and increasingly other parts of the West Bank). From a Palestinian perspective, 1993 marked the re-unification of the external wing of the PLO (Tunis and the Palestinian diaspora generally) with the internal wing (the United National Command of the *intifada*, and a host of non-governmental organizations that had grown up under Israeli occupation). But as the PNA set about creating new institutions and channelling aid, tensions arose. Later chapters will investigate these areas of dispute.

The years of exile have honed the Palestinians into the best educated group in the Middle East, barring the Israelis themselves. Hence while there are talents aplenty, there is also a natural raising of expectations, which has led to some frustration. Similar frustrations helped nurture a new trend while the PLO was officially absent from the territories – Islamic fundamentalism. It is a trend which could gain the upper hand if the PLO's current approach fails to deliver real benefits.

Palestinians after 1948

1947	Arab Higher Committee rejects UN partition plan as contravening Arab sovereign rights
1948	Palestinians under Abd al-Qadir al-Husseini and Fawzi Qa'ukji participate in Arab attack on new state of Israel; Deir Yassin massacre; Arabs lose war
	Beginning of the Palestinian refugee crisis; most leave their homes
	Sept. 30: Higher Committee sets up 'government-in-exile' in Gaza under Ahmad Helmi Pasha, in the name of the Mufti; in time this becomes Egyptian territory
	Dec. 1: Jordan rejects Gaza Committee; notables meet in Jericho to accept Jordanian rule

1949	Jordan holds elections on both banks of river; poll backs the Kingdom annexing West Bank
	May 12: Lausanne Conference – Arab states accept UN 181 (II) on partition as basis on which to reach political solution to Palestinian problem (having rejected it before the war); Israel not prepared to repatriate refugees under current conditions
1950	May 1: UNRWA (United Nations Relief and Works Administration) is created to deal with the Palestinian refugee problem
1951	George Habash founds Arab Nationalist Movement (with a Palestinian wing)
1953	IDF retaliates against *fedayeen* raids with attack on Kibya, West Bank
1958	Arafat, Abu Jihad and Hassan brothers found *Fatah* in Gaza and Kuwait

Creation of the PLO

1964	Foundation of the Palestine Liberation Organization (PLO) under Ahmed Shukeiri in Cairo. The same forum also established a Palestine Liberation Army (PLA) and Palestine National Council (PNC) and approved the Palestine National Charter (or Covenant). *Fatah* and others see the PLO as Nasser's puppet organization
1965	Israel lifts military restrictions on its Arab population
	Fatah launches 'armed struggle for liberation of Palestine'
1967	Six Day War – Israel gains West Bank, Gaza, Sinai and Golan Heights
	Up to 400,000 Palestinians flee the West Bank, half of them to Jordan; under 'family reunification', Israel allows many to return
	George Habash founds Popular Front for the Liberation of Palestine (PFLP) in Jordan
	PLO chief Shukeiri forced to resign; replaced by Yahyah Hamoudeh
1968	Battle of Karameh (*Fatah* claim to repel Israeli raid); first PLO hijacking
1969	*Fatah* and other 'illegal' groups admitted to PLO
	Naif Hawatmeh leads breakaway from PFLP – the Marxist PDFLP, later known as the DFLP
	Arafat unseats Hamoudeh to become chairman of the PLO Executive Committee
	Arafat signs Cairo Agreement, allowing PLO guerrillas to operate from Lebanon
	Palestine National Charter amended – commitment to 'armed struggle'
1970	'Black September' in Jordan, as Hashemite Kingdom cracks down on radical Palestinians; many recamp in southern Lebanon, which is nick-named 'Fatahland'
1971	Palestinian terrorists assassinate Jordanian Prime Minister Wasfi al-Tal
1972	Black September terrorists attack Israeli athletes at Munich Olympics; 18 die
1973	Communist-controlled Palestine National Front challenges PLO in the West Bank

PLO adopts 'liberation in stages'

1974	June: 12 PNC session adopts 'mini-state' option; also known as 'libera-tion in stages'
	July: PFLP leaves PLO Executive Committee and forms a 'rejectionist front'
	Oct. 28: Rabat Arab leaders' summit acknowledges PLO as 'sole legiti-mate representatives of the Palestinian people'
	Nov. 13: Arafat addresses UN General Assembly, calls for 'united demo-cratic secular state' but refuses to renounce violence as a policy option

	Death of Hajj Amin al-Husseini (effective end of Palestine Higher Council)
1975	PLO becomes embroiled in Lebanese civil war
1976	Elections in territories; victories for pro-PLO candidates; elections annulled; mayors form a National Guidance Committee
1977	March 16: US President Jimmy Carter endorses Palestinian 'homeland' in speech May 17: Israel elects Menachem Begin's Likud to power
1978	PLO bases in south Lebanon bombed by Israel (Operation Litani); new Israeli civilian administrator, Menachem Milson, encourages anti-PLO Village Leagues
1979	Palestinians reject 'autonomy' proposals of Camp David
1982	June 6: Israel invades Lebanon (Operation Peace for Galilee) to root out PLO Sabra and Shatilla massacre in Lebanon; Israel blamed for not controlling Christian militia; Arafat and supporters forced to leave Beirut; PLO sets up new headquarters in Damascus
1983	Palestinian civil war between Arafat loyalists and PLO 'rejectionists' in Lebanon Syria cracks down on Arafat loyalists; PLO headquarters move to Tunis
1985	Oct. 1: Israel bombs PLO headquarters in Tunis after PLO attack on Israelis in Cyprus PLO faction hijacks the *Achille Lauro* ocean liner PLO in Lebanon attacked by Shi'ite *Amal* militia and Syrian troops Amman Agreement – proposal for confederation between Palestinian state and Jordan – lasts a year

The *Intifada* and its effect on Palestinian politics

1987	Dec. 9: Outbreak of the Intifada; creation of pro-PLO 'internal' United National Command (UNC, also known as UNLU) in West Bank and Gaza
1988	Foundation of *Hamas*, fundamentalist opposition to PLO's secular nationalism UNC demands resignation of Palestinian police in occupied territories; most comply Arab states set up a Solidarity Front to aid the *intifada* Assassination of Abu Jihad, PLO second-in-command Jordan announces disengagement from West Bank Nov. 15: The 19th PNC conference issues Algiers Declaration – PLO adopts two-state solution; declares Palestinian 'independence'; tacitly accepts Israeli existence Dec. 13–14: Arafat explicitly recognizes Israel and rejects terrorism, in UN speeches US initiates first official dialogue with PLO
1989	USA suspends dialogue with PLO over Arafat failure to condemn terrorist attack
1990	Arafat attempts to act as broker in Iraq-Kuwait crisis, condemned for 'pro-Saddam' stance Dec.: 17 Palestinians killed on Temple Mount, Jerusalem, after some stoned Jewish worshippers at the adjoining 'Wailing Wall'; international condemnation of Israel

Gulf War and peace talks

1991	Gulf War; Palestinians in territories express joy over Scud attacks; resumption of *intifada*; 350,000 Palestinians leave or are expelled from Kuwait

Pro-Syrian Palestine National Salvation Front demands re-inclusion of dissidents in PLO

Oct.: Madrid conference breakthrough; Palestinians officially in joint 'umbrella' delegation with Jordan; New prominence for '*intifada* generation' internal leaders, Husseini and Ashrawi; meanwhile, Palestinian rejectionists hold alternative conference in Teheran

1992

Talks get bogged down

June–July: Newly elected Labour government promises Palestinian autonomy in a year

Dec.: Rabin expels 413 *Hamas* and Islamic *Jihad* activists after increased terror incidents

1993

Israeli Knesset lifts ban on talks with PLO

Secret Oslo talks yield the Declaration of Principles and Washington agreement

Mutual recognition between PLO and Israel for first time (sidestepping Madrid track); International donors pledge money to PNA at conference in Washington

Palestine National Authority in Gaza and Jericho

1994

Jan.: Anti-PNA Alliance of Palestinian Forces is formed (including eight PLO rejectionist factions, *Hamas* and Islamic *Jihad*)

Feb.: Massacre of Muslim worshippers in Hebron threatens to derail peace talks

April: PLO and Israel sign economic accord in Paris

March: Cairo Agreement – Israel and PLO agree on modalities of PNA

May: Palestine National Authority (PNA) set up in Gaza and Jericho

July: Arafat returns to Gaza

Aug.: Israel and PLO sign 'early empowerment', transferring more powers to PNA; PNA (Palestine National Authority) clamps down on *Hamas*

Sept.: World Bank conference for donors collapses over dispute over funds not arriving; *Israel and Jordan sign peace treaty*

1995

Wave of fundamentalist suicide bombings in Israel, threatens to derail peace talks; Rabin responds by 'sealing the border' with Gaza; Palestinian prisoners go on hunger strike

Talks about Israeli redeployment prior to Palestinian elections repeatedly delayed

Libya expels Palestinians to demonstrate 'emptiness' of PNA claim to independence

Aug.: Progress towards extending PNA remit over other areas in West Bank

Sept. 28: Interim Agreement ('Oslo 2') signed in Washington

Oct.: Release of first batch of Palestinian prisoners

Oct. 26: Assassination of Islamic *Jihad* head, Fathi Shiqaqi, in Malta

Nov. 4: Assassination of Prime Minister Yitzhak Rabin, by a Jew opposed to peace with Palestinians

Nov 13.: Israeli forces pull out of Jenin, first large town vacated acording to Oslo 2

Israel pledges to withdraw forces from Bethlehem before Christmas

1996

Jan.: Yehiya Ayyash, main *Hamas* bomber, killed by Israeli booby-trap bomb

Jan. 20: Yasser Arafat elected President, *Fatah* wins majority in Palestine Council elections

Feb–March: Fundamentalist bus-bombings in Jerusalem, Ashkelon and Tel Aviv; 63 dead; Peres 'seals the territories'

Figure 3   *Palestinian refugee destinations in 1948*

In 1948 Palestinian refugees fled to the following areas and countries – Lebanon, Iraq, Syria, Transjordan, the West Bank (administered by Transjordan), the Gaza Strip (administered by Egypt), and Egypt. Below are the numbers in question, and a graph illustrating the percentage of Palestinians taken in by each area.

Lebanon   100,000
Iraq   4,000
Syria   75,000
Transjordan   70,000
West Bank   280,000
Gaza Strip   190,000
Egypt   7,000

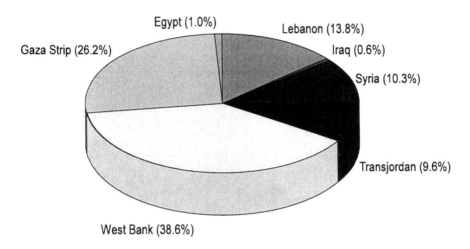

Source: Martin Gilbert, *Atlas of the Arab–Israeli Conflict,* Macmillan 1993

Figure 4   *World Population of Palestinians in 1991*

Jordan	1,357,167
West Bank	1,040,000
Israel	730,664
Gaza Strip	596,464
Lebanon	451,297
Kuwait (before 1991 war)	378,083
USA, Europe, Latin America	368,281
Syria	281,923
Saudi Arabia	169,373
Eqypt	67,749
Other Gulf States	62,285
Iraq	28,410
Libya	22,946
TOTAL	5,554,642

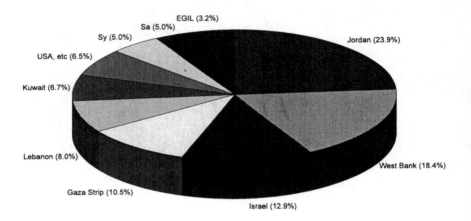

Note:

USA, etc.	= USA, Europe and Latin America
Sy	= Syria
Sa	= Saudi Arabia
EGIL	= (in descending order) Egypt, Gulf States, Iraq and Libya

Source: Palestinian Academic Society for the Study of International Affairs, published in *Los Angeles Times,* July 5, 1991

Figure 5 *World aid to Palestinian refugees, 1950–75*

in millions of dollars

USA	577
UK	133
Canada	32
Germany	27
Sweden	26
Japan	8

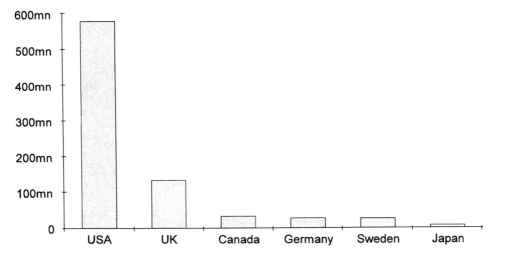

Figure 6   *Regional aid to Palestinian refugees, 1950–75*

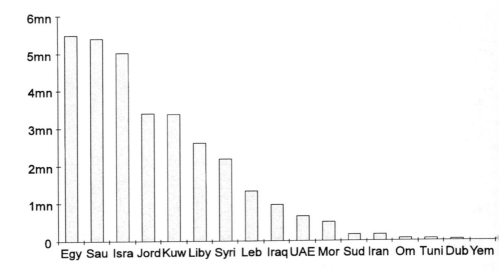

Source: Martin Gilbert, *Atlas of the Arab–Israeli Conflict,* Macmillan 1993

Chapter 3　　Occupied territories – 1967 to the present

An Israeli perspective – Land of Israel, security zone or poisoned chalice?

As soon as Israel took over the West Bank of the Jordan and East Jerusalem, a national debate ensued about their political future. Some in government favoured returning them in exchange for a full and lasting peace in the Middle East. But, faced by increased Arab hostility, and remembering how the return of Sinai to Egypt in 1957 had not guaranteed peace, the proposal grew less attractive. Instead, two main arguments were forwarded for maintaining control over the West Bank: firstly as a security buffer against future Arab attack, and secondly the notion of keeping the land for spiritual reasons. The Chief Sephardi Rabbi and Rector of Bar Ilan University backed the latter cause. Arguing that the West Bank was part and parcel of the biblical Land of Israel, they forbade returning any of it to Arabs. In the end, a plan of the Deputy Premier, Yigal Allon, seemed to govern Labour Party practice over the next decade (although it was never formally adopted). The Allon Plan proposed annexing a 15km-wide strip to the west of the Jordan River and erecting security settlements there; developing urban estates in East Jerusalem; granting Palestinian 'autonomy' in the remaining heavily populated areas; and signing a peace deal on this basis with Jordan [see Chapter 7].

Nonetheless, growing numbers of Jews began settling the territories in defiance of Israeli Defence Force (IDF) restrictions. The first was Rabbi Levinger, who in 1968 illegally set up a *yeshiva* in Hebron, holy to Jews and Muslims; and then built a township in nearby Kiryat Arba. Riding on a wave of post-war euphoria and inspired by a new brand of religious Zionism, many Jews saw God's hand behind Israel's victory in 1967. Their views were voiced by the Land of Israel Movement from 1971, and by the religious settlers' group, *Gush Emunim*, after 1974. Most *Likud* and even some Labour politicians backed the settlers, seeing them as continuing the Zionist pioneering spirit and bolstering Israel's security.

When *Likud* took power in 1977, its policy was more openly pro-settler. In 1978 Begin approved the creation of Ariel, the first large West Bank Jewish town. *Likud* actively subsidized settlements, creating in turn a new breed of often secular settlers who commuted to jobs in Israel proper ('within the green line', or inside pre-1967 borders) from low-cost dormitory towns in the territories. International protests slowed down the growth of settlements somewhat, but only under the 1992 Labour government has Israel agreed to 'freeze' them. Today there are an estimated 130,000 settlers in the West Bank (6.5% of the area's total population; but only 2% of Israel's population). A further 5,000 live in the Gaza Strip. In addition, Palestinians regard as 'settlers' the more than 120,000 Jewish Jersualemites who live in the east of the city (captured in 1967).

Although Prime Minister Rabin promised not to return the entire area to the Palestinians, most settlers feel their future is hanging in the balance. Due to its sensitivity, the issue of settlers has been deferred until 'final status talks' with the PLO; but in 1995 settlers began a series of hilltop protests against Labour's policy. Some feared that open clashes between settlers and IDF troops administering the Knesset's laws were in prospect.

A Palestinian perspective – from occupation to embryonic statehood?

From a Palestinian perspective, the 1967 war was a double disaster. Most West Bank Palestinians were themselves refugees from the first war in 1948; now they were occupied by the enemy. In certain respects, Jordanian law still applied (Jordan surrendered its claim to the West Bank only in 1988). But on the whole Palestinians came under the jurisdiction of an Israeli civil administration. The land was subject to the international 'law of [military] occupation'. Palestinians claimed political and economic discrimination and made allegations of human rights abuses. The area has never been formally annexed. To do so would lead to Palestinians becoming citizens of Israel, thus enabling them to undermine the Jewish state at elections.

Israel banned the PLO from operating in the territories. In 1976 Israel cancelled West Bank municipal elections after pro-PLO candidates threatened to win by a landslide. The PLO for its part wanted all of 'historic Palestine', not just the territories. But after 1974 certain factions approved starting a new Palestine on 'any inch of liberated soil'; in 1988 the PLO limited its (immediate) aim to independence on the West Bank and Gaza, thus in effect recognizing Israeli suzerainty within the pre-1967 lines. The *intifada* (a local Palestinian uprising which began in 1987 and lasted until 1991) brought the issue to international attention. It 'redrew' the green line, after years during which the territories were becoming integrated into Israel (via roadworks and Israeli control of underground water tables). It polarized Israeli opinion and to some extent paved the way for the current peace process.

Under the interim agreements of 1993–94, Palestinians formally enjoyed authority over Gaza and the Jericho enclave. The September 1995 interim agreement significantly increased the area of land coming under Palestinian suzerainty; and also entailed the first free elections for the area. Jerusalem, however, remains a special case for Israel, and since 1967 the town has come more closely under Israeli rule, and is regarded as the national capital. In addition, many Palestinians believe that the security stipulations of the Oslo agreements, especially those concerning Jewish settlers in Gaza and the West Bank, give Israel a pretext for controlling water supplies and 'military land'. The same applies to the West Bank.

In the early years of occupation, Israel gradually drew Palestinians into the Israeli economy. By 1972, 60,000 Arabs were crossing the 'green line' to work in Israel. More than 100,000 Palestinians visited Arab states for work, education and business, a by-product of Israel's 'Open Bridges' policy (set up in 1970) between the West Bank and Jordan. By 1973, 14,500 Palestinians were working in the West Bank local administration, and new universities were built. Alongside these bodies were Jordanian banks and law courts, still operating despite the occupation. However, indigenous Arab institutions began to waste away; compared to Israel proper, Palestinians were badly under-resourced; and the refugee camps were largely left out of the picture. Israel still has the power to 'seal the border' at will, in retaliation for terrorist incidents, thereby depriving Palestinians of the chance to work in Israel. Both Gaza and the West Bank appear to be 'tied in' to the Israeli economy, lending succour to the argument that without massive aid, a PNA-ruled 'Palestine' cannot be economically (and therefore politically) autonomous. The *intifada,* some say, was an attempt by Palestinians to redefine their own identity. It may have led to Israel 'decoupling' from the territories – but the new Palestinian leaders must answer the question, what can they build in its place?

The *intifada* and its consequences

The *intifada* (literally 'shaking off' in Arabic) had a profound effect on the entire Arab–Israeli dispute. It is unlikely that the current peace moves would have occurred without it, although when it began many observers thought it was the harbinger of an inexorable deterioration into all-out war. The *intifada* started with rioting in the Jabalya refugee camp in Gaza on Dec. 9, 1987, after an Israeli taxi had crashed into a group of labourers in Gaza, killing four of them. It soon developed into a general uprising against Israeli rule, and spread to most of the occupied territories. What distinguished the *intifada* from previous Palestinian protests was its ability to generate itself, and involve most sections of the community. Try as they might, Israel's security units in the *Shin Bet* failed to quench it. In fact, many Palestinian *Shin Bet* agents were themselves targetted.

Some Palestinian observers see the *intifada* as making the occupied territories 'ungovernable'. One of its immediate consequences was to force Palestinians in the Israeli-run police force and law courts to resign *en masse.* New non-governmental organizations arose to fulfil many parastatal functions. Thus the *intifada* challenged the legal status of the territories, an area which for 20 years had existed in limbo, neither annexed by the State of Israel nor granted autonomy for its Arab residents.

SIGNIFICANT FEATURES OF THE *INTIFADA*

The intifada began locally at the grassroots. It thus took the Tunis-based PLO by surprise, as much as it did Israel. Yet within a few months the PLO had imposed some control on it, and began cultivating a new internal leadership. Matters were somewhat complicated by the role played by non-*Fatah* forces (PFLP and Islamic groups like *Hamas*) – as yet the Palestine National Authority has failed to reflect many non-*Fatah* views. Because the protagonists were mainly children armed with stones, and not machine-gun-wielding terrorists, it transformed the image of the Palestinian struggle and brought a new measure of international sympathy to both the Palestinians and their putative representatives, the PLO.

The *intifada* also psychologically 're-established' the green line. In other words, whereas before Israelis were becoming used to considering the territories as an integral part of the state, the *intifada* reminded Israelis that they constituted a distinct minority in what they called Judaea and Samaria. Similarly, it forced Jordan to realize the emptiness of its assertion to be the natural mentors of Palestinians in the territories. This led Jordan to abrogate its claims to ruling the West Bank in 1988. The *intifada* also allowed Yasser Arafat to claim that a new Arab State of Palestine was waiting to be born – hence his declaration, also in 1988, of an independent state. While some saw this as merely a publicity stunt, it did return the PLO's focus to the territories; and also offered an implied recognition of the State of Israel, something which the PLO had not sanctioned before. In short, the PLO suggested that it could guarantee peace in the territories in return for Israeli recognition and the granting of autonomy.

In the course of trying to prevent stonings, Israeli troops sometimes resorted to shooting unarmed or lightly armed children; a situation which, like the Lebanon war five years earlier, created a crisis of confidence and brought international condemnation. Yitzhak Rabin was defence minister when the *intifada* erupted, and ordered troops to use 'an iron fist policy', and, if necessary, to 'break bones'. When criticized for this, he responded that Israel's policy was the best in the circumstances; live ammunition was to be used only as a last resort. Within Israel the onerous task of getting young conscripts to quell the *intifada* made many Israelis think anew about the price they had to pay for holding on to the territories. Before, they may have regarded the possessions as useful security buffers against external Arab attack. Now the territories themselves had become a burden and security risk. To Jewish settlers, however, the *intifada* largely had the opposite effect – it galvanized them in their determination to stay. Settlers considered that the IDF was not doing its duty. More radical elements duly took the law into their own hands, thereby separating them from the Israeli mainstream. Some regard this reaction as the beginning of a trend which led to the Rabin assassination of November 1995. The uprising led to widespread resignations from the Israeli-run Palestinian-staffed local police and law courts. A range of non-govenmental organizations tried to fill the breach. Today, many of these have been integrated into the Palestinian Authority, while others prefer to remain in an oppositional role.

Through the Unified National Command – a secret and often ad hoc committee set up to co-ordinate the *intifada* – Palestinians created a new generation of internal leaders. The aims of the *Shabiba* (organized youth) were vocalized by a group known as *al-Shaksiyat al-'aama* (general personalities) – invariably, academics and professionals respected in the community, like Feisal Husseini, Hanan Ashrawi, the editor Hana Siniora, Prof. Sari Nusseibeh, the lawyer Freih Abu Medein, and Sa'eb Erkat, amongst others. In time these 'internal' figures worked with the Tunis-based PLO; although divisions between the two groups sometimes boiled over, as was occassionally seen at Madrid and, later, at the time of the PLO–Israel deal in Oslo and Washington. By 1990, however, the *intifada* had begun to 'turn in on itself'. Groups like the *Fatah* Hawks in Gaza, the Red Eagles of the PFLP, the Black Panthers and some elements of *Hamas* began to punish and occasionally kill 'collaborators', although often these were just disguised acts of gangsterism. There have been fewer mass 'incidents' since the peace accord, but as guns and bombs replace stones, the death count is still high. Nonetheless, a number of the '*intifada* generation' are now active in the post-Oslo Palestine National Authority. Others, amongst the Islamist and Marxist rejectionist camps, in effect form a nascent opposition front to the PLO. By 1993 about 12,000 Palestinians were held in Israeli prisons for *intifada* activities. Half that number remained there by the end of 1995, and the question of their release forms a major section of the Interim agreement.

The *intifada* has proved very costly, in terms of both money and lives. Israel found it had to pay hundreds of millions of dollars to maintain its control. At its height it cost Israel the equivalent of 2% of its GDP to control it. Through imposing curfews and sealing the border, Israel also periodically lost access to the labour pool of the occupied territories. From December 1987 to July 1995, Israeli forces killed 1,418 Palestinians (including 260 under the age of 16). Over the same period, Palestinians killed 297 Israelis. In the period to September 1991, 528 Palestinians were killed by fellow Palestinians (as 'collaborators'), compared to 697 killed by the Israeli Army (the respective wounding rate was 3,000 compared to almost 14,000).

The uprising may have acted as a catalyst for change, but the damage it did to Palestinian and Israeli society is still being counted. Finally, there is another cost which cannot be estimated, but which has certainly exacerbated existing political schisms in Israel – namely, the psychological stress faced by Israeli conscripts who had to patrol the territories.

Chapter 4   The rise of Islam and the Arab nation

Arabic-speaking tribes have lived in the Middle East for many thousands of years. The Old Testament refers to Arabs in the desert hinterland to the east of the Kingdom of Israel. Archaeologists assume that the Nabatean Kingdom (situated in what is today Jordan) was Arab; indeed, the Arabic language shares common Semitic roots with Hebrew and Syriac (now no longer spoken).

However, it was the birth of the Islamic religion which truly galvanized the disparate and largely nomadic Arab peoples into a single nation. Through the Koran, Islam claims to complete the monotheistic message of Judaism and Christianity, and advocates a society based on justice, equality and obedience to Allah (God). Muhammed is regarded as the last prophet after Jesus, the man who was chosen as the messenger of the true faith. However, he is not considered to be the Messiah, nor the 'Son of God'. In the Islamic tradition, Ibrahim (Abraham of the Old Testament) is regarded as the first Muslim; but while Jews trace their descent from Abraham's son, Isaac, Arabs trace theirs through his other son, Ishmael.

With the Koran and the Hadiths (ascribed sayings of the prophet) as its basis, Islam developed a *sunna* (tradition) and a system of laws (*sharia*) to guide the Muslim society. These include the basic five *arkan*, or religious duties – fasting, charity, prayer, pilgrimage to Mecca, and daily testimony of God's greatness. Within a few centuries, Islam had spread from its Arabian heartland to Spain and southern France in the west, and India in the east. Borne by the power of the message of Islam and by their military superiority, the Arabs as a people travelled and settled in new lands. Islam was also adopted by large non-Semitic nations to the north, particularly Turkey and Persia.

In time most Middle Eastern peoples became Muslims. Even those who did not – notably Jewish and Christian minority communities – nonetheless used Arabic as their *lingua franca*. According to the *sharia*, Jews and Christians were regarded as *ahl a-Kitab* (People of the Book, or fellow monotheists). As such they were set above pagans, and were meant to enjoy a 'protected' status (*dhimmi*), as long as they paid a special poll tax. The Caliph Omar set an important precedent through his 'pact' with the indigenous Jews and Christians of Jerusalem. The *dhimmi* were mostly well-treated, but occasionally persecuted, according to the whims of individual rulers. However, those who adopted Islam were generally regarded as Arab, at least in the Middle East, and the initial chauvinism of the conquering 'pure' desert Arabs gradually dissipated. By the time of the Egyptian Mamluks, a military caste who were originally slaves, it was clearly less important to prove descent from the tribes of Muhammed. In short, through intermarriage, conversion and cultural fusion, the concept of 'Arab' had been redefined to include all who spoke Arabic and felt committed to the Arab nation. Early in Arabic history the caliphate moved from Mecca and Medina in the *Hejaz* (central Saudi Arabia) to older centres of civilization, like Syria, Babylon and Egypt, and even to Spain by the 10th century. Islam travelled all the way to the Far East, so that today there are more than 800 million Muslims (of whom Arabs number approximately 150 million).

In theory, Islam would overcome earlier rivalries in the Middle East (all history before Islam was dubbed the *jahiliya*, or period of ignorance). In practice, however, regional rivalries persisted. By the time of the fifth Caliph (successor to Muhammed), Islam had itself divided into two distinct modes of belief, *Sunni* and *Shi'ite*. Soon different dynasties began competing for the Caliphate. These factors led to the eventual fall of the Arab Empire. From 1516 to 1918, Ottoman Turks gained control over most of Arabic Middle East. A resurgent West began eating into the Ottoman domain by the 19th century, and left its impact in Arabic culture and politics. Since then Arab nations have recovered their independence – but their national boundaries were largely set by Europeans, and many an Arab politician has nurtured the dream of reconstituting one great 'Arab Nation'. Exactly what such a nation would be, however, is a matter for debate. Meanwhile, different Arab states have adopted different forms of government – monarchies, revolutionary regimes, military dictatorships, and in some cases, democratic constitutions.

The situation has become even more complicated this century with the introduction of three new elements in the Middle Eastern equation: First was the **discovery of oil**. In the beginning this led to Western commercial exploitation; but by the 1950s newly independent Arab regimes began to nationalize the oilfields. Oil increased their wealth (especially after the price-fixing exercise of 1973), but it also exacerbated national rivalries. Poorer Arab states depend excessively on remittances from expatriate workers in the richer oil-producing nations, primarily Saudi Arabia and the Gulf States. A dispute over oil led to the Iraqi invasion of Kuwait, and that in turn resulted in the Gulf War of 1991.

The second element was the creation of the state of **Israel**. Some Arabs still view Israel as an alien Western import on land which should have stayed Arab and Muslim. The question of Israel and the Palestinians has led to numerous Arab–Israeli wars, although now the parties are attempting a solution.

The third element was **superpower rivalry** in the Middle East. Since the end of World War II, the USA and USSR competed for client states in the region. Broadly, the USA supported conservative oil monarchies and Israel, while the USSR backed 'progressive' forces (like Egypt's Nasser, *Ba'ath* regimes in Syria and Iraq, and the PLO). The end of the Cold War has thus forced a colossal re-alignment of forces in the Middle East. Optimists feel this could herald a new spirit of peace; pessimists fear that a unipolar 'new world order', with a nebulous *pax americana* holding sway in the Middle East, cannot meet ordinary Arabs' aspiritations.

Finally, popular disgruntlement at corrupt government has led to the revival of Islamic fundamentalism, with the non-Arab state of Iran leading the way in 1979. Some in the West see this as the 'next big threat' to liberal democracy after the collapse of Communism. The success or failure of the current Middle East peace process – the subject of this book – thus has a crucial role to play in determining the future shape of the area, and possibly even international security. By the same token, the process is itself subject to the vicissitudes of those older and deep-rooted perceptions, Arab nationhood and Islamic faith.

[Note: Events outside Middle East – defined as Arab lands, Israel, Persia and Turkey – appear in italics. Most events concerning Israel, Palestine, Egypt, Jordan, Syria and Lebanon appear in separate chapters]

Early History

Year	Event
853 BC	First mention of Arabs in inscription of Shalmaneser III
25 BC	Aelius Gallus, Roman explorer, visits southern Arabia
105 AD	Fall of Nabatean Kingdom
273	Romans suppress Kingdom of Palmyra
525	Himyar kingdom of southern Arabia (Arab converts to Judaism) falls to Ethiopians
570	Muhammed is born in Mecca; at 39 he has a divine revelation and writes the Koran
602	Fall of Hira principality in northern Arabia
622	Muhammed and followers migrate to Medina (the *Hijra*); start of Muslim calendar
630	Muhammed conquers Mecca (having defeated pagan and Jewish tribes)
632	Muhammed dies; Abu Bakr, father of his widow, A'isha, becomes first Caliph ('successor')
633	Muslims conquer Syria and Iraq
639	Muslims begin conquest of Egypt
640	Persia comes under Muslim rule
654–655	Naval victory over Byzantines (eastern orthodox Christians in Anatolia)

661	Ali, fifth and last of the *Rashidun* (righteous caliphs) is killed Some followers of Ali form a new Muslim sect, the Shi'ites; but most Muslims remain Sunni Mu'awiya, governor of Syria, establishes new caliphate, the Umayyads, in Damascus
711	*Muslims invade Iberian Peninsula and Indus valley (northern India)*
740	*Muslims establish colony in Kilwa, east Africa*
750	Abbas defeats Marwan II, ends Umayyad rule and sets up Abbasid Caliphate in Hashimiya
760	Mansur moves Abbasid caliphate to Baghdad
788	Morocco (in far west of north Africa) becomes independent under Idrisid dynasty
825	*Aghlabid dynasty start conquest of Sicily*
869	Revolt of black slaves in Iraq
910	Shi'ite Fatimids seize north Africa
929	*Emirate of Cordoba (Spain) becomes third caliphate*
945	Persian Buyids conquer Baghdad and usurp the Arab Empire
969	Fatimids conquer Egypt and build Cairo as capital
970	Seljuk Turks become Muslim and occupy most of Persia
1055	Seljuks seize Baghdad
1099	European Crusaders capture Jerusalem; place restrictions on Muslim and Jewish residents
1171	Saladin overthrows Fatimids and re-establishes orthodox *Sunni* Muslim Ayubbid dynasty
1187	Saladin defeats Crusaders and retakes Jerusalem from Christian rulers
1258	Mongols (pagan tribes from Central Asia) take Baghdad and end Abassid rule
1260	Mamluks sultanate controls Egypt and Syria
1295	Ghazan Khan, Mongol ruler of Persia, is converted to Islam
1453	*Ottoman Turks capture Constantinople – end of eastern Christian Roman Empire (Byzantium)*
1492	*Granada (last outpost of Iberian Muslim rule) falls to Christians; Jews and Muslims expelled*
1502	Safavid dynasty creates Persian empire and imposes Shi'ism as state religion
1517	Ottomans conquer Egypt, Palestine and Syria – they destroy Mamluk dynasty and within two years extend authority to north Africa (later to most of Arabia)
1520	Ottoman Sultan Suleyman the Magnificent begins his 46-year reign
1556	*Akbar becomes emperor in north India, and expands the Mughal Empire there*
1583	*Islam expands to Philippines and New Guinea*
1639	Ottomans conquer Iraq
1683	*Ottoman siege of Vienna fails; start of Ottoman Empire's retreat from zenith*
1798	Napoleon of France occupies Egypt
1805	Mohammed Ali becomes undisputed ruler of Egypt; afterwards Egyptian influence spreads into rest of Middle East, at the expense of the Ottomans
1820	Britain signs pact with Arab Sheikhs in the Gulf – beginning of British supremacy there
1830	France invades Algeria

1869	Suez Canal opens in Egypt
1881	Britain occupies Egypt, France occupies Syria
1906	Revolution in Persia leads to constitutional monarchy
1908	Young Turks revolt and begin to dismantle Ottoman empire

Modern History

Year	Event
1914	Ottomans enter World War I on the side of Austro–Hungary and Germany
1916	Arab Revolt in Hejaz (Arabia) aided by British forces under T.E. Lawrence and Allenby; Hashemite Sharif Hussein assumes title of king
1917	British occupy Baghdad and Damascus
1918	End of Ottoman rule in Arab lands
1919	Yemeni independence
1920	Mandates set up for Syria (French), Palestine and Iraq (British)
1924–25	Ibn Saud (backed by the Wahabi Muslim sect) conquers Hejaz (Arabia); Saudis displace Hashemites as rulers of Mecca and Medina
1932	Ibn Saud proclaims the Kingdom of Saudi Arabia; end of Mandate in Iraq
1936	Anglo–Egyptian treaty formally recognizes Egyptian independence
1939–45	World War II – Allies and Axis powers battle in north Africa, eventual Allied victory
1941	Overthrow of pro-German Rashid Ali in Iraq End of Mandate for Syria and Lebanon, which become republics
1945	Arab League founded
1948–49	Arab–Israeli war (War of Independence); creation of Israel and a Palestinian refugee crisis
1951	Libyan independence
1952	Army coup replaces monarchy with republic in Egypt (Nasser assumes power in two years) Hussein becomes King of Jordan
1955	Egypt leads new Middle Eastern 'anti-imperialist' alliance – Baghdad Pact
1956	Suez Canal War Sudan, Tunisia and Morocco gain independence
1957	Tunisia becomes a republic
1958	Revolution in Iraq overthrows Hashemite monarchy
1960	Mauretanian independence Arab oil-producing states join the new OPEC cartel
1961	Kuwaiti independence
1962	Algerian independence; revolution in Yemen
1963	Revolutions in Syria and Iraq
1967	Arab–Israeli war (Six Day War)
1969	Gadaffi's revolution in Libya
1970	Sadat succeeds Nasser in Egypt
1971	Gulf States gain independence and form United Arab Emirates
1973	Arab–Israeli war (Yom Kippur); Arab states use oil embargo as a political weapon

1975	New civil war breaks out in Lebanon; King Feisal of Saudi Arabia assassinated
1976	Syria intervenes in Lebanon
1979	Egypt and Israel sign peace treaty Ayatollah Khomeini overthrows the Shah, and sets up Islamic Republic in Iran
1980–88	Iran–Iraq war (an estimated 500,000 or more die)
1981	Assassination of President Sadat of Egypt
1982	Israel intervenes in Lebanon
1990	North and South Yemen combine in new united republic Lebanon war ends with Ta'if accord; Syria enhances influence in region
1990–91	Iraq invades Kuwait, leading to the Gulf War
1991	Arab nations and Israel start a new peace process in Madrid
1992	Algeria cancels elections mid-stream after FIS fundamentalists threaten to win

Chapter 5   Arab Nations

Egypt

Egypt is the site of one of the oldest civilizations in the world. Now as then, most of Egypt's vast population (the biggest in the Arab world) lives within a few kilometres of the Nile River. The rest of the country, which occupies Africa's north-eastern corner, remains desert. Early on in Islamic history, Egypt was conquered by Arab invaders. Since then it has prided itself as being a 'natural leader' of the Arab world. Despite lacking natural resources, Egypt has spawned powerful dynasties (Mamluks and Fatimids) and notable leaders (like Mohammed Ali in the 19th century and Gamal Abdel Nasser in the 20th century). They have sought to lead other Arabs against 'outside oppressors' (whether British colonialists, Ottoman imperialists, or a perceived Israel–American axis). Egypt is also the birthplace of contradictory ideologies – Western-style constitutionalism and free trade (the 19th-century *infitah*), Arab nationalism, and Muslim fundamentalism (in its Sunni variation).

In similar vein, President Anwar Sadat saw himself as a pathbreaker when, after years of fighting between Israel and Egypt, the two old enemies made peace in the Camp David Accords. Although Egypt was ostracized at the time by other Arabs, Egypt's current president, Hosni Mubarak, has had the satisfaction of seeing much of the Arab world, including the PLO itself, following in Egypt's footsteps a decade later. This has afforded Egypt a new role as arbiter in general Middle East peace agreements. Even so, it has not stopped Egypt from leading Arab criticism of Israel from time to time (most recently, over Israeli confiscation of land in Jerusalem and its nuclear weapons capacity).

Some have perceived Egypt's relations with Israel as a 'cold peace'. Ultimately, however, the two have enjoyed success inasmuch as neither state has abrogated their ties, despite the impact of outside threats. Nor has there been a hint of the renewed wars which characterized their relations between 1948 and 1973. Both countries are very much in the American camp. Under Mubarak, Egypt has cautiously expanded its level of democracy, but this has often given way to clampdowns as the state battles a host of problems – overpopulation, a poor ecology and ailing economy, and resurgent Islamic fundamentalism. In such circumstances, Egypt continually has to balance the utility of its ties to Israel, the USA and conservative Arab Gulf states (where many of its citizens earn their living), with the dissenting voices from the 'Arab street'.

Early History

Year	Event
2590 BC	The age of the pryamids of Cheops and Giza
1567 BC	Egyptians overthrow Asiatic invaders, the Hyksos
18th cent BC	Dynasty forms empire which includes Palestine and stretches to present-day Iraq
8th cent BC	End of Egyptian empire
525 BC	Persians conquer Egypt
323 BC	Death of Alexander the Great, Macedonian conqueror of Egypt. Hellenistic Ptolemaic rule ensues
14 AD	Egypt becomes a province of the Roman Empire
451	Byzantine Christian rulers 'outlaw' Monophysite Christian beliefs of Egyptian Copts
639	Arab ruler Omar conquers Byzantine rulers of Eypt. New governor is Amr al-Allas
750	Beginning of Abbasid rule (which technically lasted till 1258)
834	Egypt granted in military tenure to a Turkish oligarchy based in Abbasid capital, Baghdad

868	Turkish governor Ahmed Ibn Tulun establishes independent fiefdom in Egypt
969	Fatimid dynasty assumes power after conquering a chaotically divided country
1171	Fatimids overthrown by Saladin. His descendants defend Egypt against Crusaders
1250	Arabs lose power to Mamluks, descendants of Turkish slaves converted to Islam
1260	Egyptian Muslim dynasty, the Mamluks, defeat Mongols at 'Ayn Jalut, Palestine
1291	Mamluks capture Acre and defeat the Crusader Kingdom of Jerusalem
1516	Turkish Muslim dynasty, the Ottomans, defeat Mamluks in Palestine
1517	Ottomans defeat Mamluks in Egypt; under Khair Bey they pacify and subdivide Egypt
1586	Local Egyptians rebel; Ottomans forced to concede effective power to indigenous Mamluk beys
18th cent	Persistant rebellions over access to trade, especially with an expanding Europe; peasant revolts
1798	Napoleon occupies a fractious Egypt for France
1801	Napoleon defeated by Anglo-Ottoman forces
1805	Mohammad Ali, former head of Albanian mercenaries, overthrows Ottomans to become governor
1811	Mohammad Ali assassinates last of his Mamluk foes; launches industrialisation and land reform
1822	Egypt conquers and incorporates Sudan, to the south
1840	Ibrahim Pasha, Mohammad Ali's son and heir, defeats Ottoman revival and 'Egyptianises' the army
1869	Ismail allows French to build Suez Canal, but fails to get Ottomans to grant Egypt independence
1880	Under new Khedivev, Tawfiq, European powers force Egypt to agree to the crippling Law of Liquidation.
1885	Opposition nationalists under Al-Afghani gain ground; ally with Mustafa Kamil's anti-British rebels
1918	British High Commission rebuffs Egyptian '*wafd*' (delegation) plea for independence; riots erupt
1919	*Wafd* leader Saad Zaghlul backed by British consul-general, Lord Cromer; then deported after revolt

Egypt wins independence

Year	Event
1922	Egypt is declared independent as High Commissioner Lord Allenby ends British protectorate, removes martial law (but Britain maintains influence, especially over Suez Canal Zone)
1924	*Wafd* defeats Liberal Constitutionalists at polls and elects Zaghlul prime minister. Fuad is made king
1926	Zaghlul dies and is replaced by the less able Nahhas
1929	Fuad sacks Nahhas and replaces him with Ismail Pasha Sidqi, an autocrat. Depression strikes
1930	Sidqi fails to redraft Egyptian constitution. Hassan al-Banna launches Muslim Brotherhood rebellion
1933–36	A rash of social legislation fails to quell popular unease

1936	King Fuad dies and is replaced by son, Farouk. Nahhas signs a compromise Anglo-Egyptian Treaty
1948	De facto British occupation ends with troops withdrawn from Suez Canal
	Egyptian forces join other Arab states in war against the new state of Israel
1949	Egypt signs armistice with Israel; left in control of Sinai peninsula and Gaza Strip
1951	*Wafd* Parliament abrogates 1936 treaty
1952	July 23: Free Officers' Coup – Muhammad Naguib becomes leader, Farouk abdicates

Egypt becomes a republic

Year	Event
1953	June 18: Republic of Egypt declared
1954	April 18: Gamal Abdul Nasser replaces Naguib as premier
1955	Nasser dominates Bandung non-aligned conference; signs Soviet bloc arms deals
1956	July 26: Nasser nationalizes the Suez Canal Company
	Oct. 29: Israel invades Sinai
	Oct. 31: Britain and France bomb Egyptian airfields
	Nov.: Britain and France invade Egypt but forced to withdraw after UN condemnation
1957	Israel agrees to leave Sinai; Egypt approves UN Emergency Force (UNEF) to keep the peace
1958	Feb 1: Egypt and Syria unite to form United Arab Republic (UAR)
	October: USSR announces financing for Aswan Dam
1961	Syria withdraws from UAR
1962–67	Egypt involved in Yemen civil war
1964	Jan.: Nasser backs founding of the PLO at first Arab summit in Cairo
1966	Egypt signs a defence pact with Syria
1967	Nasser forces UNEF to leave Sinai; blocks Gulf of Aqaba to Israeli shipping
	June 5: Israel launches pre-emptive strike on Egypt – Six Day War begins
	June 10: Ceasefire – Israel has destroyed Egyptian Air Force and captured Sinai and Gaza
1969	March: War of Attrition with Israel across the Suez Canal
1970	June 25: USA launches Rogers peace plan
	August 7: Ceasefire with Israel along the Suez Canal
	Sept. 28: Nasser dies, and is replaced by Col Anwar Sadat
1971	May 27: Egyptian–Soviet Treaty of Friendship signed
1972	July 16: Sadat expels Soviet advisers
1973	Oct. 6: Egypt and Syria launch surprise attack on Israel – Yom Kippur War begins
	Oct. 22: War ends – UN Security Council Resolution 338 calls for direct talks based on UN 242
	Nov. 11: Israel–Egypt ceasefire signed at Kilometre 101
1974	Jan. 18: First Israel–Egypt disengagement acord
	Feb. 28: USA and Egypt restore diplomatic relations
1975	June 5: Suez Canal re-opens after eight years
	Sept. 4: Egypt and Israel sign second disengagement treaty

Egypt makes peace with Israel

Year	Event
1977	Nov. 19: Sadat visits Israel and addresses the Knesset (first external Arab leader to do so)
1978	Sept. 17: Egypt and Israel sign Camp David peace accords; Sadat and Israeli Prime Minister Menachem Begin share Nobel Peace Prize
1979	March 26: Full Egyptian–Israeli Peace Treaty signed in Washington, DC
	Egypt is expelled from Arab League and Islamic Conference for making a 'separate deal' with Israel
	Israel begins withdrawing from Sinai Peninsula
1981	Food riots and Islamic protests sweep country; Coptic minority claims persecution
	Oct. 6: Anwar Sadat assassinated; replaced as president by former deputy, Hosni Mubarak
1982	April 25: Egypt recovers last portion of Sinai from Israel
1983	Dec. 22: Egypt and PLO restore diplomatic relations, severed after Israel–Egypt peace deal
1984	Jan. 19: Egypt re-admitted into Islamic Conference; restores relations with Jordan
1988	Sept. 29: Egypt recovers Taba from Israel after international arbitration
1989	May 22: Egypt re-admitted into the Arab League
1990	Egypt tries but fails to broker peace between Kuwait and Iraq after Saddam's invasion in August
1991	Egyptian troops fight in US-led UN coalition against Iraq in the Gulf War
	Oct. 31: Egyptian delegation attends Madrid peace conference
1992	Former deputy foreign minister, Boutros Boutros-Ghali, becomes UN secretary-general
1994	Cairo hosts signing of Israel–PLO peace accords
	Fundamentalist groups attack tourists, Copts, and political opponents; police clamp down
	The third International Conference on Population and Development is held in Egypt
1995	Mubarak leads Arab campaign against alleged Israeli non-compliance with nuclear ban
	Mubarak hosts 'peace bloc' summit to re-start the stalled peace talks
	Failed attempt to assassinate Mubarak in Ethiopia; Egypt blames Sudanese groups
	Mubarak attends Rabin funeral – his first visit to Israel

Jordan

Jordan has a long history of human habitation, but, unlike Egypt, has only really been established as a distinct area in its own right during this century. Indeed, until the 1920s Jordan was variously regarded as being part of Greater Syria or Palestine. In one view, the Kingdom of Jordan can be seen as the last outpost of the Hashemite Arab dynasty, descendants of the Prophet Muhammed who for centuries had controlled the holy sites in Mecca and Medina (now in Saudi Arabia). For the purposes of this book, however, Jordan's importance lies in its connection to the Palestinian people and the authority of its political voice, which is stronger than its small economy and armed forces may suggest.

After 1948 thousands of Palestinians poured into the country, dramatically altering its demography. Today more than half of the population (even east of the Jordan) is Palestinian. For this reason, many on the Israeli right contended that 'Jordan is Palestine', a charge that the Hashemite Kingdom fiercely opposed. Of all Arab states, only Jordan offered the refugees full citizenship. However, the relationship between King Hussein (the longest-reigning ruler in the Middle East) and the PLO has often been tempestuous. In 1970–71 it erupted into open civil war and resulted in the PLO's expulsion. A crucial factor has been Jordan's claim to the

West Bank (it annexed the area in 1950, rather than allowing Palestinians to set up a state there, then lost it to Israeli occupation after the 1967 war). Yet by abrogating its claim to the land in 1988, King Hussein facilitated the path to 'Palestinian autonomy' of today.

Hussein himself has a reputation for wily leadership (he has survived several assassination attempts). Long before they signed peace with him in 1994, Israelis regarded the king as a vital 'stablizing' influence in the region. Jordan has won praise for accommodating many disparate opinions (Palestinian, fundamentalist, bedouin traditionalist) in its restored democracy. But the true test for the future will be whether the monarchy can survive a transfer of power after King Hussein; and whether it can forge a meaningful and beneficial economic union with Israel and a renascent Palestinian polity.

Early history

Year	Event
6000 BC	Earliest human habitation
1100 BC	Area formerly under control of the Semitic tribes, Edomites, Moabites, Ammonites and Amorites, comes under Solomon's Kingdom of Israel
850 BC	Moabites regain control
500 BC	Arabic-speaking Nabateans rule and build the rock city of Petra
330–323 BC	Rule by Alexander the Great of Macedonia
70 BC	Romans control northern Jordan
105 AD	Romans impose direct rule; Ghassanid Arabs replace Nabateans in the south
330 AD	Ghassanids convert to Christianity with rest of Roman and Byzantine Empire
529–569	Harith ibn Jabal, Ghassanid leader, is named King of the Arabs by Roman Emperor Justinian; but constant fighting with Persians in succeeding years weakens the Ghassanids
629–636	Muslims from Arabia destroy Byzantine Empire, including at key Jordanian battles of Mu'ta and Yarmuk
640–1187	Rule by a succession of Arab dynasties: Ummayads from Damascus, Abbasids from Baghdad, Fatimids from Egypt and Selikuks from present-day Turkey European Christian Crusaders invade south in 12th century, but most locals are now Muslim
1187	Salah al-Din (Saladin) defeats Crusaders and initiates the Ayubid dynasty; a century later they are replaced by Mamluks from Egypt
1518	Ottomans from Asia Minor defeat Mamluks and inherit Arabic homelands, including Jordan. Their rule lasts four centuries but they exercise only limited control. Jordan is treated as a backwater
1893	Ottomans assert direct control of southern region (Karak and environs) after half a century of Egyptian inspired Arabic national self-assertion
1916	Sharif Hussein bin Ali, Emir of Mecca and head of the Hashemite royal family, launches the Great Arab Revolt against Ottoman rule
1918	Ottoman Empire collapses at end of World War I with Hussein's capture of Damascus. Present-day Jordan is included in territories controlled by Arabs

Modern history

Year	Event
1920	League of Nations awards Britain the mandate for Transjordan, Palestine and Iraq, at the San Remo Conference

1921	April 11: Emir Abdullah, son of Hussein, establishes a centralized governmental system in what is now modern Jordan; his brother Faisal becomes King of Iraq
1923	May 15: Britain recognizes the Emirate of Transjordan. The agreement effectively severs Transjordan from Palestine. Abdullah is first head of state
1925	Transjordan gains districts of Aqaba and Ma'an from the Hejaz (since the deposition of Hussein's eldest brother, King Ali, the Hejaz becomes part of the new state of Saudi Arabia)
1928	Jordan's first constitution provides for a Legislative Council
1946	Abdullah negotiates Anglo–Jordanian Treaty, ending British mandate. The Emirate is now known as the Hashemite Kingdom of Jordan, with Abdullah as its first king
1948	Jordan's Arab Legion army joins other Arab League states in invading the newly declared state of Israel. Israel survives the war and adds to its territory; Arab states fail to 'defend the Arabs of Palestine'. However, Jordan holds half of Jerusalem and retains the West Bank
1950	The newly elected Jordanian parliament votes to unite the two banks of the Jordan, thereby constitutionally expanding the Hashemite Kingdom. Some 500,000 or more Palestinian refugees become Jordanian citizens. The Arab League opposes such moves. In the United Nations, only Britain and Pakistan recognize Jordan's effective annexation of the West Bank
1951	July 20: King Abdullah is shot dead by a dissident Palestinian outside the Mosque of Al-Aqsa in Jerusalem. His eldest son, Prince Talal, succeeds him as king
1952	Talal abdicates due to poor health. A regency council ratifies Talal's new constitution which makes government collectively responsible before parliament
1953	May 2: Prince Hussein, Talal's brother, assumes the throne. He is 18
1955	Jordan joins the United Nations
1956	King Hussein dismisses the British commander of the Arab Legion, Glubb 'Pasha'
1957	Hussein ends the Anglo-Jordanian treaty, and imposes martial law in the wake of riots and a coup attempt. Political parties are banned. Jordan loses British subsidy, and turns to USA for aid
1958	Short-lived federal union with Iraq ends after a Nasserist coup there
1964	In Cairo, Jordan and other Arab states vote to reduce water flowing into Israel's Lake Tiberias, after Israel announced it would divert the Jordan's waters for irrigation Jordan joins a United Arab Command (with Egypt, Syria and Lebanon). The same summit establishes the PLO to represent Palestinians
1966	Israeli forces repel Jordanians in Samu, on the West Bank, following Palestinian *fedayeen* raids into Israel
1967	After Egyptian President Nasser closes the Straits of Tiran and evacuates UN forces from Sinai, regional tensions mount. On May 30 Jordan signs a Mutual Defence Treaty with Egypt. On June 5 Israel launches a pre-emptive strike and repulses a Jordanian counter-attack. By June 11 it has gained control of Jerusalem and the entire West Bank. More than 300,000 Palestinian Arabs flee to Jordan. King Hussein backs (and influences the drafting of) UN 242, which calls for Israeli withdrawal from conquered territories
1968	Jordanian and *Fatah* forces defend Karameh against Israeli reprisals
1969	King Hussein discusses peace plan with US President Richard Nixon
1970	Jordan and Egypt accept US Rogers Plan; but Syria, Israel and PLO reject it September: Hussein orders army to crush a revolt by PLO elements, and beats off a purportedly pro-Palestinian Syrian invasion

1971	July: Jordan's final victory over Palestinian *fedayeen*; tension with Syria
1973	Jordan remains neutral in the Yom Kippur War
1974	Jordan accepts PLO as 'sole legitimate representative of Palestinian people' at the Rabat Conference
1977	Co-operation agreement between Jordan and the European Community
1978	In lieu of elections (postponed while Israel occupies the West Bank), King Hussein forms a National Consultative Council to replace parliament
1980	Jordan backs Iraq in its war with Iran
1983	Jordan re-establishes relations with Egypt, broken over Camp David treaty
1984	Hussein dissolves Consultative Council and recalls parliament. 17th Palestine National Council meets in Amman; Hussein tells PLO to make a settlement with Israel based on 'land for peace'
1985	Amman Accord with PLO breaks down; reconciliation with Syria
1988	July 31: Jordan severs all legal and administrative ties with the West Bank (allowing Arafat's 'Algiers Declaration' in November, in which the PLO declared 'statehood' in the area)
1989	May: Tax and price rises cause riots; Hussein dismisses Prime Minister Za'id Rifa'i Nov. 8: Jordanians vote in their first general election in 22 years (non-party). Victory for pro-King factions, although Islamic opposition is the biggest single faction
1991	Gulf War – Jordan chooses not to join anti-Iraqi coalition, causing US displeasure. Jordan gives refuge to an estimated 250,000 Palestinians expelled from Gulf States after war Oct.: Madrid conference – Jordan negotiates with Israel, and provides nominal 'umbrella' to Palestinian delegation.
1993	May: Chief peace negotiator, Salam Abd al-Majali, appointed prime minister Sept. 14: Jordan signs Common Agenda with Israel in Washington, the day after the Declaration of Principles between Israel and the PLO Oct. 1: Jordan joins economic Trilateral Committee with USA and Israel Nov. 8: First multi-party elections in 34 years; opposition Islamic Action Front is largest party, but majority of independents (including tribal representatives) support the king
1994	July 25: Jordan and Israel end state of war, after signing the Washington Declaration Oct. 26: Jordan signs a peace treaty with Israel at Wadi Araba Nov. 2: Lower House approves treaty by 55 votes to 23
1995	Jan.: Cabinet reshuffle after Prime Minister Majali resigns Feb.: Jordan, PLO, Israel and Egypt form 'peace bloc' at Cairo summit meeting Jordan gives refuge to leading Iraqi dissident; seen as sign of changing allegiance PLO and Israel separately try to improve trade links with Jordan Oct.: Amman hosts Middle East/ North Africa Economic Conference; long-awaited trade deal with Israel Nov.: King Hussein delivers eulogy at Yitzhak Rabin's graveside; his first visit to Jerusalem since his grandfather's assassination

Lebanon

In the ancient world Lebanon was famous as the centre of Phoenician culture. Its tradition of trading continues to this day, but its image as a sophisticated 'Arab riviera' was blighted by a bloody civil war which lasted from 1975 to 1990. Uniquely amongst Arab countries, Lebanon has a substantial Christian population (indeed, this factor led to its special status within Greater Syria, and the creation of the modern state under French tutelage in this century). Currently Lebanon is recovering from the ravages of war and is rebuilding its reputation as a financial centre. The state's relations with Israel remain tense, and Lebanon tends to follow Syria's line in matters of foreign policy. Nonetheless, it is committed to making peace with Israel under the Madrid peace process.

Early history

Year	Events
1250–1150 BC	Area of present-day Lebanon invaded by sea peoples, precursors of the Phoenicians Egyptian influence over region
750–550 BC	Phoenicians develop alphabet; colonize Mediterranean rim
550–331 BC	Area absorbed into the Persian Achaemenid Empire
331–185 BC	Area conquered by Hellenic Macedonians and descendants
14–280 AD	A province within the Roman Empire
325	After flirtation with Zoroastrianism, Lebanon becomes strongly Christian. An archbishopric is established in Tyre and bishoprics in Tripolis, Berytus and Sidon. Gradually Lebanon is absorbed into the larger Byzantine Empire
641–936	Lebanon comes under the ambit of Islam, but a large portion of population keeps its Monophysite Christian faith
11th cent.	Crusaders displace Arabs
1289	Crusader city and county of Tripoli falls to Saladin, followed by Sidon two years later
1520	Lebanon comes under Ottoman rule as part of the province of Syria
1860	Civil war breaks out between Maronite Christian peasants and Druze landlords. French army under Napoleon III lands at Beirut; five European powers force the Ottoman Porte to accept Mount Lebanon as a specially privileged district (*sanjak*) detached from the province (*vilayet*) of Damascus (representing Greater Syria). Europeans guarantee a clear Maronite majority in Lebanon
1861–1914	Lebanon is ruled by Christian princes under nominal Ottoman suzerainty. In 1880s educated Christian Arabs in Beirut forment plans for pan-Arab revolt against Ottoman rule, and seek support amongst Muslim fellow-Arabs, but little comes of it
1918	After defeat of the Ottoman Empire in World War I, France occupies Lebanon
1920	France declares a mandate over 'le Grand Liban' at San Remo conference. Remit is expanded to include Tripoli to the north, Sidon and Tyre to the south, and the Beqa'a Valley to the east (at Syria's expense). France harbours desires to control all of Greater Syria
1926	France drafts a Lebanese constitution in 1926, providing for a bicameral assembly, Maronite president and Sunni prime minister
1932	Controversial census deems Christians to be the majority, so their constitutional dominance is reconfirmed. However, the constitution was suspended from 1932 to 1937. Unease grows
1940–42	French forces in the Levant submit to Vichy (pro-German) rule; after heavy fighting in Beirut in 1941, victorious Free French promise 'independence' to Lebanon and Syria

Independence and ethnic rivalry

Year	Events
1943	Lebanese Prime Minister Riyadh Sulh announces the 'Charter of Independence', annulling the French mandate. Muslims and Christians unite in a 'National Pact' to protect state sovereignty

1945	With Britain's connivance, the newly established United Nations compels France to withdraw security forces from Syria and Lebanon
1958	President Camille Chamoun tries to place Lebanon more firmly in the Western camp. His actions spark off civil war with Muslims who feel he is tampering with the guarantees enshrined in the National Pact. They are backed by a Nasserite Syria. A new president, Fuad Shihab, fosters unity with a compromise plan
1967	Lebanon stays out of the Six Day War in 1967, thus avoiding humiliating defeat
1969	Cairo Agreement permits PLO to set up camps in southern Lebanon, under certain restraints
1970	Jordan crushes Palestinian insurrectionists; more PLO guerrillas move to Lebanon. Their armed status upsets the fragile balance of forces and lays the ground for renewed civil war
	Suleyman Franjieh elected president
1975	After sporadic clashes between PLO and Druze with *Kataeb* (Phalange Christian militias) and Lebanese Army, a new civil war breaks out on 13 April with a massacre at Ayn al-Rummaneh. Israeli air raids; Muslims seek Egyptian help

Civil war, Syrian and Israeli invasions, and peace

Year	Events
1976	PLO refugee camp of Tal al-Zatar attacked by Christians; Phalange capture Karantina
	President Franjieh seeks Syrian help, flees Palace after Phalange raid. Maronite Christians condemn Palestinian–Syrian agreement on Lebanon
	Syrian-dominated Arab Deterrent Force (ADF) enters Lebanon, switches allegiance to protecting Christians and fighting Lebanese National Movement (leftist and Muslim coalition)
	Elias Sarkis elected as new president; asks Selim Hoss to be Premier after Riyadh conference
1977	Druze leader Kamal Jumblatt assassinated
1978	Israel launches partial raid on south (Operation Litani)
	Israel helps launch Saad Haddad's South Lebanon Army (SLA militia) in south
	ADF clashes with Christians; Arab Follow-Up Committee tries to end fighting
1981	Follow-up Committee reconvened after new ADF-Christian clashes
	July: US special envoy, Philip Habib, arranges ceasefire after Israeli-Palestinian clashes
1982	June 6: Israel launches Operation Peace for Galilee (invasion of Lebanon) after attempted assassination of its ambassador in London, and repeated rocket attacks from PLO camps in south Lebanon. Besiege Beirut. Anti-Israeli Lebanese Resistance Movement is formed
	Christian President-elect Bashir Gemayel is assassinated
	In revenge *Kataeb* fighters massacre hundreds of Palestinians in Sabra & Shatilla refugee camps, with alleged Israeli connivance
	Sept 23: Amin Gemayel (brother of the late Bashir) becomes president
1983	US, French, British and Italian troops enter Lebanon
	May 13: Israel and Lebanon sign agreement on troop withdrawal; Syria refuses to withdraw
	Sept.: Full-scale war between Christians and Druze in the Shouf mountains
	Saudi peace efforts result in ceasefire
	May: *Fatah* split by rebellion; Syria backs *Fatah* Rebels; PLO troops leave Beirut
	Oct: US & French military compounds destroyed by Shi'ite suicide bombers

1984	March 5: Lebanese government cancels agreement with Israel, after Syrian pressure USA withdraws from Lebanon. Gemayel seeks Syrian help and Rashid Karami becomes prime minister.
1985	Last Israeli soldier leaves Lebanon, apart from a smaller number who redeploy within SLA-controlled 'security enclave' in the south. 'Camps war' erupts between Palestinians and Shi'ite *Amal* militia Syria negotiates 'tripartite accord' with factions, including the Maronite Lebanese Forces (LF)
1986	January: Gemayel opposes accord; anti-Syrian Samir Geagea takes over the LF June: Primer Minister Karami assassinated; replaced by Selim al-Hoss
1988	President Gemayel's term ends; he appoints General Michel Aoun as interim prime minister Selim al-Hoss objects; two governments claim power – Muslim in west Beirut, Christian in east
1989	Aoun attacks LF coastal strongholds, and Muslim forces in west Beirut May: Arab League summit in Casablanca fails to achieve peace Nov. 5: Lebanese parliamentary deputies agree to Charter of National Reconciliation (or Taif Accord), fashioned in Saudi Arabia under Syrian guidance [Taif Accord re-establishes 50/50 Muslim/Christian representation; aims to disband militias] Aoun rejects Accord Nov.: Rene Mouawad elected president; assassinated within two weeks Elias Hrawi becomes the new president
1990	Jan.: Aoun attacks LF in east Beirut Sept.: President Hrawi and PM al-Hoss ratify constitutional amendments in line with Ta'if Accord Oct.: US gives go-ahead to Syrian assault which ends Aoun's challenge
1991	Release of several Western hostages June 3: Lebanon and Syria sign a 'Brotherhood Treaty'; both states 'co-ordinate' their ministries Sept.: Lebanese army and Syrians start disarming militias Consenting militiamen invited to join army, their leaders to enter Parliament; Palestinians resist Oct.: Lebanon attends Madrid conference
1992	Lebanon refuses to accept 413 Gazan Palestinian fundamentalists deported by Israel Israel retaliates in south after *Hezbollah* and *Fatah* rocket attacks Aug.–Sept.: First national elections in almost two decades; Maronites boycott polls Oct.: Rafiq Hariri is prime minister, *Amal* leader Nabih Berri is the speaker
1993	Hariri launches economic reconstruction programme under Syrian patronage Bomb blast at Beirut headquarters of Maronite *Kataeb* party; blamed on renegade LF groups
1994	Syrian pressure and President Elias Hrawi block Hariri's attempt to bring *Kataeb* leaders into cabinet Hariri resigns over alleged financial scandal; agrees to return to power
1995	May–Aug.: Clashes intensify between Israel, the SLA and *Hezbollah* June: Samir Geagea, former leader of the banned LF, is found guilty of murdering his rival, Dany Chamoun, in 1990. Sept.: Renewed *Hezbollah* offensive; Israel blames Syria for using these attacks as bargaining ploy Oct.: President Hrawi's term is extended with Syrian approval
1996	Apr.: Israel launches Operation Grapes of Wrath against Hezbollah

Syria

Syria is one of the most important countries of the Middle East, both as a military power and as a source of pan-Arabist ideology. The modern state has distinct boundaries, but ancient Syria was a more nebulous entity. Situated at the crossroads of ancient empires, Syria assumed substantial power in its own right as the headquarters of the Muslim Umayyad Caliphate after 661. Ever since then it has been a centre of Arabic culture, even when colonized by Seljuks, Mamluks, Mongols, Ottomans and finally the French. Nineteenth-century European Arabists spoke of Greater Syria, a region including Palestine, Lebanon and much of the Arabian hinterland. Some analysts detect the philosophy of 'Greater Syria' in Damascus' claims to hegemony over neighbouring Lebanon and Turkish border lands. The *Ba'ath* (Renaissance) pan-Arabist movement was born in Syria, and after a number of coups and counter-coups, it succeeded in holding on to power in Syria and neighbouring Iraq. During the 1960s *Ba'ath* split into Syrian-backed and Iraqi-backed wings. Since then the two states have been bitter rivals. Unlike Iraq, however, Syria does not enjoy vast reserves of oil, but this has not dented its regional influence. At one stage Syria was the Soviet Union's firmest ally in the Middle East.

Syria under Hafez al-Assad has taken a hard line against Israel. Until 1990 it was regarded as a base for various terrorist groups. For many years Syria backed 'rejectionist' factions in the PLO, and the relationship between the mainstream PLO under Yasser Arafat and Syria is still cool. Internally, Assad's main foes are Sunni Muslim fundamentalists (Sunnis form a majority of the population). Currently Syria has re-entered the Western fold (especially after the Gulf War of 1991) and is engaged in the peace process with Israel. The main issue at stake is control of the Golan Heights (Syria lost this strategic area to Israel in 1967, and refuses to sign a treaty with Israel until the latter returns the area to Syrian rule).

Since the Taif Accord of 1989, Syria has bolstered its ties with (some may say, its control over) Lebanon. This is reflected in Lebanon's apparent caution *vis-à-vis* Israel. Syria remains a dictatorship, although in recent years there has been a distinct liberalization of the economy. Assad belongs to the Alawite minority which dominates the *Ba'ath*, military and government. He has been ill for some years, but has no obvious successor. Many assume that Sunnis will achieve greater prominence once Assad no longer rules Syria.

Early History

Year	Event
*c.*2360–2230 BC	Northern coastal plain ruled by Mesopotamia
*c.*1900 BC	Hurrian and Amorite tribes invade; Syria becomes a major trading thoroughfare
*c.*1500–1200 BC	Hittite Empire rules Syria; then land falls under Egyptian and Assyrian hegemony
*c.*1006–926 BC	Kingdom of Israel conquers and loses Aramean kingdom in Syria
*c.*550–331 BC	Syria falls to Persian Empire
185 BC	Macedonian Empire splits; Seleucids rule vast area from Antioch in Syria
*c.*250 AD	Rise of the Kingdom of Palmyra under Odenathus and later his widow, Zenobia
273	Roman Emperor Aurelian conquers Palmyra
325	Antioch and Damascus become important centres of Nestorian Christianity

Arab conquest

633–37	Muslim Arabs invade Byzantine-ruled Syria and Iraq
635–66	Capture of Damascus by Khalid ibn al-Walid, general of Caliph Abu Bakr

657	Mu'awiya, Governor of Syria, challenges fourth caliph, Ali; indecisive battle at Siffin
661	Mu'awiya becomes Caliph, institutes Umayyad Caliphate from capital in Damascus
705	Caliph Walid begins work on the Great Mosque of Damascus
717	Internal reforms under Umar II
750	Abbas defeats Marwan II, ends Umayyad rule and shifts the new caliphate, the Abbasids, to Iraq
1070–80	Turkish Muslims, the Seljuks, occupy Syria and Palestine
1171	Saladin ends Fatimid Caliphate; establishes Abuyyid dynasty in Syria and Egypt
1250–60	Mamluk Sultanate takes over in Syria and Egypt
1400	Mongols under Timur ravage Syria
1517	Turkish Ottomans take over Syria and Egypt from the Mamluks
1520	Revolt of Janbirdi Ghazali in Syria
1658–59	Revolt of Abaza Kara Hasan Pasha in Aleppo, northern Syria
1831–40	Egyptians occupy Syria
1836	Start of regular British steamship service to Syria
1918	End of Ottoman rule in Arab lands, including Syria
1920	French establish mandate in Syria
1936	Popular Front government negotiates treaty with France for more autonomy

Modern history

1945	Declaration of independence from France; Syria joins the Arab League.
1946	April 17: Formal independence from League of Nations mandate under French administration
1948	Syrians invade newly declared state of Israel in attempt to win Palestine for Arabs. Israel repels their attack, although Syria maintains control over the strategic Golan Heights.
1949	Colonel Husni Zaim stages a putsch, unseating the constitutional government, the first of a series of coups and governments July 20: Syria becomes last frontline Arab state to sign an armistice with Israel
1958	Syria under **Ba'ath** rule joins Egypt and Yemen in United Arab Republic (UAR)
1961	Syria secedes from UAR
1963	**Ba'ath** retakes power.
1966	**Ba'ath** splits; bloody coup brings to power a radical faction including preponderance of minority Druze and Alawites instead of majority Sunni Muslims.
1967	June 5: Syria follows Egypt and Jordan into Six Day War with Israel. In battle, Israel gains the Golan Heights and its prime city, Quneitra. Syria rejects UN 242.
1970	Sept.: Syrian tanks humiliated by Jordan when they intervene on behalf of Palestinian guerrillas. Nov.: Defence Minister Hafez al-Assad overthrows civilian **Ba'ath** leader Salah Jedid.
1971	Hafez al-Assad appointed President of Syrian Arab Republic (confirmed after March elections)
1973	March 12: National referendum declares new and pemanent constitution. Presidential powers increased; Syria is defined as a 'Socialist popular

	democracy'; but no mention of Islam causes widespread disturbances amongst Sunni Muslim majority
	Oct.: Syrian & Egyptian attack on Israel surprises Israel in Yom Kippur War, but despite bloody fighting cannot retake Golan
1976	Syrian forces enter Lebanese war; swap sides from Muslim to Christian
1982	Syria crushes Muslim Brotherhood revolt in Hama, killing tens of thousands
1983	President Assad suffers heart attack; rumours of brother, Rifaat, plotting a coup
1986	EU imposes arms embargo on Syria
1987	Mahmud Zu'bi appointed prime minister
1990	Pro-Syrian forces crush renegade Christian General Michel Aoun in Lebanon
	Taif Accords – Syria formalizes its influence over Lebanon
1991	Syria signs pact with Lebanon
	Syria joins US-led UN anti-Saddam coalition; takes part in war; receives nearly $5 billion from Arab, European and Japanese donors
	Oct. 31: Syria attends Madrid peace conference; first open talks with Israel
	Dec. 2: general election returns Assad to power for a fourth seven-year term
1992	Syria and Lebanon boycott the multilateral peace track negotiations (held initially in Moscow)
1993	Start of a cautious economic liberalization policy, encouragement for private investors
1994	Jan. 16: US President Bill Clinton discusses Syrian–Israeli negotiating impasse with Assad
	Jan. 22: President's son and *heir apparent,* Basil, dies in car crash
	May: Syria opposes creation of Palestinian National Autonomy in Gaza and Jericho
	Aug.: *Ba'ath*-controlled National Progressive Front wins national elections
	Aug.: Assad removes 16 senior military officers to consolidate his power
	Nov.: Prime Minister Zu'bi announces reforms; EU lifts arms embargo
1995	Talks with Israel hit deadlock; restart with security level talks between Israeli and Syrian chiefs of staff (Amnon Shahak and Hikmat Shihabi respectively)
	Signs of willingness to compromise on Golan
	June: Assad and US Secretary of State Warren Christopher hold summit meeting
	July: Talks hit new deadlock after faces *Knesset* opposition
	Nov.: After Rabin assassination, Assad makes new bid for deal with Israel
	Dec. 27: Israel–Syria peace talks resume in USA

PART TWO

THE PEACE PROCESS

Chapter 6   Introducing the Peace Process

General overview – the language of peace

Peace negotiations – whether in Northern Ireland, Bosnia, Chechnia, South Africa or the Middle East – may differ about particulars, but when it comes to their basic structure and psychology, they are remarkably similar. Firstly, all parties concerned have to accept the principle of change – of moving from the present (unsatisfactory) status quo to a new paradigm. Secondly, parties to talks must feel that they are talking as equals. If one party feels that the other is too dominant, talks are liable to fail before they really begin. And thirdly, there is the nature of bargaining itself. If politics is indeed the 'art of the possible', nowhere is this more true than in negotiations. Each side presents a maximalist position, and then moves from there to an agreed compromise. This applies to both overt and covert talks, although arguably in the former there is more pressure to 'play to the gallery'.

But who is the gallery? – or, to put it in other words, 'on whose behalf are the negotiators negotiating?' In short, do negotiators have a mandate to talk; and, if so, what are their agendas? The answer to the first question depends very much on the nature of decision-making in the country concerned. A democracy would entail an electorate authorizing its rulers to follow a particular policy; more authoritarian regimes may enjoy greater leeway to take decisions without consultating the populus, but they still have to consider the opinions of influential vested interests (military, business leaders, clergy, and so on).

Ultimately, the question of a mandate for talks is something of a grey area. For practical reasons, politicians in enemy countries may engage in covert talks if they consider that the full glare of publicity would ruin a fragile peace process. Only when they judge their chances of success to be good will they turn covert talks into overt talks. In addition (as was the case in Oslo) an intermediatory country or organization will play a crucial role, as a facilitator of talks (providing the venue, suggesting compromises when talks become deadlocked, and so on). Once talks become overt, the facilitator may act as a mediator. The ideal role is to be an 'honest broker' – a party perceived to be free of bias.

With respect to the agenda, both parties must first agree on the goals to be attained in their talks. They should also determine at the outset what are fundamental non-negotiable principles, and what can be altered in the course of negotiations. In reality, goals may change with changing outside circumstances. In order to accommodate such changes, both parties must trust each other. Often, however, this becomes a 'chicken and egg' situation – parties will not talk unless they trust each other, but will not trust each other until they start talking. Sometimes trust is the first goal of talks. Here again the role of the mediator is crucial in building up trust between former enemies, and breaking the deadlock. Such negotiations are often called 'talks about talks' or proximity talks. As a damage limitation exercise, proximity talks may initially involve lower grade officials, or trusted academics (as was the case in Oslo). Thus if they collapse, politicians with high public profiles need not suffer. Only when it is 'safe' will politicians themselves become involved.

There are many steps in a process towards full peace. After a war, parties agree to a ceasefire and lines of disengagement, and eventually an armistice. This occurred after each of the Arab–Israeli wars. However, until the Israeli–Egyptian peace treaty of 1979, all Arab states were technically in a 'state of war' with Israel. As a prelude to full peace, countries may change their status to one of 'non-belligerancy' (see the stages of the Israel–Jordan negotiations in Chapter 10).

What distinguishes a full peace treaty from these other stages is the principle of full and mutual recognition – what is called normalization of relations. A full treaty must be ratified by respective parliaments. As such it is binding in law, and (in theory at least) binding on future governments. In practice, there is the risk that one party will abrogate the treaty, on the grounds that the other party has broken the terms of the treaty. As this implies, even the process of implementing a treaty once signed throws up unexpected obstacles. For this reason, the final drafting of a new treaty recquires expert legal advice, and often takes much time to conclude.

Typically, a treaty consists of a preamble and statement of intent, signed by the parties and witnesses; a series of articles, covering the areas under consideration; and annexes, defining modes of implementation, changes to existing legislation, and maps where necessary. To make the drafting and implementation of treaties more consistent, an International Convention on the Laws of Treaties was signed in Vienna on May 23, 1969, and came into force on Jan. 27, 1980.

Despite the potential pitfalls, however, treaties tend to generate a momentum of their own, such that neither party wishes to break it. For one thing, they have vested interests in seeing it work. Further, no party wants to suffer the international opprobrium for causing its failure. Finally, once there is mutual recognition (for instance, between Israel and the PLO), it is virtually impossible to 'de-recognize' the other party (just as it is virtually impossible in a democracy to disenfranchise a voter).

Peace in the Middle East – a legacy of false starts?

The first plans for peace between Israel and Arabs began during the period of the Palestine Mandate, before the state of Israel was declared and full-scale war broke out in 1948. While the largely British-fashioned plans ultimately came to naught, they did establish a few of the themes that still occur today, such as the idea of a binational state, or partition between a Jewish and Arab Palestine. In very broad terms, this was rejected by Palestinians and accepted (albeit somewhat reluctantly) by most Zionists. Today, the PLO endorses the idea of 'two nations in Palestine'; while many in Israel are not prepared to accept another state in the area between Israel and the Kingdom of Jordan.

In the aftermath of the Israeli war of independence, there were a number of attempts to convene a comprehensive peace conference between Israel and her Arab neighbours. The immediate aims were to end the state of war, and to solve the Palestinian refugee problem. For various reasons (see below) both these aims failed, however, a series of disengagement agreements between the warring parties did at least define the internationally accepted borders between Israel and the Arab states. The UNRWA assumed responsibility for refugees, but a political solution was deferred indefinitely. All Arab states maintained a state of war with Israel, and to varying degrees vowed to fight on the Palestinians' behalf to restore their rights. During the 1950s, positions polarized on all sides, with Arabs showing little sign of acknowledging Israel's national existence, Israel maintaining tight security against future Arab attack, and Palestinians feeling that they were denied their homeland by Israel, and denied their political independence by cynical Arab manipulation. In the 1960s, the creation of the PLO (1964), the Six Day War (1967) and a more overt role for the US in the Middle East under the Nixon administration changed the situation considerably.

After the 1967 war (in which Israel gained control of the Sinai Peninsula, Golan Heights, West Bank and Gaza Strip) the UN General Assembly passed Resolution 242 which became the benchmark for planning an eventual peace deal. Egypt, Jordan and Israel all agreed to UN 242 (although their interpretations of it differed in important ways). Both Syria and the PLO, however, refused to back UN 242 at the time.

Catalysts of peace

THE 1967 WAR AND ITS CONSEQUENCES

While the 1967 war was a triumph for Israel, and the possession of new territories was seen as a barrier against future attack, throughout the Arab world it was almost universally regarded as a tragedy. Before 1967, Israel largely saw its conflict as one with the broader Arab world; Palestinians constituted a refugee problem, but little more. As they saw it, Palestinian leaders had rejected the 'half loaf' of a partitioned state in 1947, so they now had no claim on any. Likewise, Palestinians had rejected the very existence of Israel. According to the PLO Charter, they wished to replace the 'Zionist entity' with an Arab-led Palestine 'from the Jordan to the [Mediterranean] sea'.

But the reality of Israeli occupation gradually forced them to recognize the reality of Israeli existence, as well as seeing the chance for a compromise solution. In short, 1967 nudged Palestinians towards shelving their maximalist dreams in favour of a more achievable reality – almost a mirror image of the history of Jews in British Mandate Palestine, before the birth of Israel.

THE ROLE OF PALESTINIANS

Over the succeeding decades (1970s, 1980s and 1990s) the PLO won international recognition as representatives of the Palestinian people. Ironically, the loss of the West Bank and Gaza allowed it to place the issue of Palestinian rights at the centre-stage of Middle East politics. This made a solution to the 'Palestinian problem' a prerequisite for a broader Middle East peace between Israel and the Arabs. As seen in the previous section, Israel rejected the PLO as a terrorist organization, and in 1982 attempted to wipe it out. But all attempts to negotiate with other Palestinians failed, and eventually (as explained below), Israel chose to deal directly with the PLO. Many analysts agree that while the PLO succeeded in putting the Palestinian issue 'on the map', its weakness after the Gulf War forced it to enter into talks with Israel on less than favourable terms. [The PLO's fortunes are examined in greater detail in Part Three, Chapter 14].

CAMP DAVID – PROOF OF THE POSSIBILITY OF AN ISRAELI – ARAB PEACE

In 1973 Egypt and Syria launched a surprise attack on Israel. Although it was largely rebuffed, the cost to Israel and the initial Arab successes led Anwar Sadat of Egypt to consider negotiating from a 'position of strength' (by contrast with Nasser's situation after the 1967 defeat). The resultant peace treaty between Egypt and Israel in 1979 led to Egypt's ostracism from the Arab world at the time. Other Arabs blamed Egypt for making a selfish 'separate peace', and abandoning the Palestinians. However, with hindsight, that treaty broke the 'taboo' about making a peace deal with Israel. It also committed Israel (however vaguely) to accommodating Palestinian aspirations in the territories in some form of autonomy arrangement. To some extent, then, the Israel-Egypt treaty has served as a model for more recent agreements.

OCCUPIED TERRITORIES – FROM CASUS BELLI TO BARGAINING COUNTER

In the absence of a peace conference (envisaged in UN 242), Israel administered the occupied territories. The official government policy was not to annex them (as was done regarding the Golan Heights), but to use them as a 'buffer zone' until some final peace deal was struck. At the same time, possession of the territories (which coincided with the biblical *Eretz Yisrael*) led to a nationalist-religious revival in Israel, and increased Jewish settlements. After 1977 the *Likud* government officially supported settlements; yet they were condemned as illegal by most of the world and by Palestinians, and seen as an impediment to peace. Looking at the situation in a different way, the post-1992 Labour government saw much of the territories as a bargaining chip – peace could be achieved via 'territorial compromise'. (However, the settler issue remains unresolved, and could well test the entire peace process when it comes up for discussion in 1996.)

THE *INTIFADA* – GROWTH OF NEW PALESTINIAN LEADERSHIP

The outbreak of the *intifada* in December 1987 made the territories a crucial issue in Israel. The *intifada* proved very costly (in terms of lives on both sides, and also financially from Israel's perspective). In short, it threatened to make the territories ungovernable. At the same time it fostered a new 'internal' Palestinian leadership which appeared ready (under the right circumstances) to negotiate with Israel in return for ending the uprising. The emergence of a new leadership on the West Bank and Gaza also prompted the PLO to respond by offering its own peace initiative in 1988. Finally, as a 'negative catalyst' for peace, the *intifada* also bred a new group of Islamic fundamentalists – some Israeli strategists reasoned that it would be better to make a deal with the comparitively amenable PLO leaders, before *Hamas* and similar groups achieved the upper hand.

ISRAELI PUBLIC OPINION AND DIASPORA JEWRY'S INFLUENCE

Israel's invasion of Lebanon in 1982 polarized public opinion strongly and led to the birth of a vociferous Peace Now campaign to end the war. This trend soon extended to the issue of the territories, and the outbreak of the *intifada* caused many left-wing Israelis (and several security chiefs) to demand a withdrawal from the territories. The Israeli left enjoyed increased support amongst the influential Diaspora Jewish community. At the same time, the right increased its support for settlers. In electoral terms, this resulted in an almost exact split between Labour and *Likud*, and a succession of awkward coalition governments. Only in 1992 (that is, after *Likud's* Shamir had already agreed to enter the Madrid peace process) did Labour win outright. Rabin's victory probably owed as much to other internal issues (housing, immigrant absorption, economics) as to the peace issue. Nonetheless, without the perception of a 'mandate for peace', it is unlikely that Israel would have made the historic deal with the PLO in 1993.

REGIONAL CONSIDERATIONS

Fear of Iran's influence hastened peace deals by moderate Arab states. Similarly, in military terms, Israel wanted to strike a peace deal before Iran acquired atomic weapons, and thus deprived Israel of its 'nuclear monopoly' in the region. After the invasion of Kuwait, many Arab leaders felt vulnerable, and feared the coming of 'another Saddam'. With US prompting, they saw the value of a comprehensive settlement. (Allied to this is the issue of democracy, to channel the grievances of the Arab street.) Likewise, after the devastation of the Gulf War, an Arab–Israeli peace, it was felt, may lead to a regional economic peace dividend.

THE ROLE OF INTERNATIONAL MEDIATORS

Since 1948, but especially after 1967, the Arab–Israeli dispute became part of the broader Cold War between the USA and USSR, with each supporting their client states in the region. Again, with hindsight it seems that this scenario militated against a Middle East peace solution (witness the failed Geneva talks of the early 1970s as one example). The effective demise of the USSR and the end of the Cold War after 1989 led, in turn, to greater US power throughout the whole Middle East. It was no longer a case of the USA and Israel versus the Arabs. This was particularly so after the Gulf War of 1991. Nonetheless, US support for Israel had grown since the 1970s, which angered Arab states, envious at Israel's 'favoured status'. By the same token, US support for Israel also led to greater US influence over Israeli policy. And in the Camp David accords (controversial as they appeared to non-Egyptian Arabs at the time), the USA proved that it could act as an arbitor in sensitive circumstances. All these factors, plus the enhanced role for the UN in the Gulf War, provided a framework for the USA, Russia and the international community to guarantee a framework for discussing peace in Madrid in 1991. (The international community was represented at Madrid by observers from the UN, EC, Arab League, Japan and Norway.)

The nature of the current peace process

The current peace process began with the Madrid conference which opened on Oct. 30, 1991, and lasted for three days. The conference was held in Spain and co-sponsored by the USA and Russia (then the USSR). The so-called Madrid Framework was described in the Letter of Invitation issued to all particpating parties. In essence, it spoke of two tracks of negotiatons: A bilateral track intended to resolve the conflicts of the past between Israel and her neighbours (Syria, Lebanon, Jordan and the Palestinians). This track, basically four separate sets of negotiations, began on Nov. 3, 1991, immediately after the end of the Madrid plenary session. Most actual negotiations took place in Washington D.C. (hence the 'Madrid track' is also known as the 'Washington peace talks').

A multilateral track was intended to build confidence among the regional parties, and ultimately to build a more harmonious Middle East for the future. These talks opened in Moscow, Russia, in January 1992. They soon divided into five separate forums, each focusing on a key issue – water, environment, arms control, refugees and economic development.

OPPONENTS OF THE PEACE PROCESS

Conventional wisdom states that anyone opposed to the peace process is a radical or extremist. This is an over-simplification. In the Israeli camp, especially in *Likud* but also in Labour, many wish for peace but feel that the Oslo and Madrid tracks cannot deliver a stable structure. There is also wariness of Syria's aims over the Golan Heights, and anger at Lebanon's inability (or unwillingness) to prevent *Hezbollah* attacks on Israelis.

Likewise, in the Palestinian camp many want peace, but feel either that the current deal is a chimera, or that the external wing of the PLO is not capable of delivering it. There are even some Islamic fundamentalists who do not rule out negotiating with Israel, but believe that the current arrangements are unsatisfactory. Meanwhile, many of the early protagonists of peace with Israel (including Hanan Ashrawi, Raja Shehadah and possibly Faisal Husseini) have chosen to stand outside the PLO circle and criticize shortcomings in the implementation of autonomy. They subject Yasser Arafat's human rights record to the same scrutiny as they applied to Israel.

However, it is undeniable that some groups are implacably opposed to peace. Amongst these are the Islamic *Jihad*, militants in *Hamas*, and radical groups within the right-wing Israeli religious settler bloc, the *Gush Emunim* and *Eyal*, one of whose supporters assassinated Prime Minister Yitzhak Rabin in November 1995. Thus part of the challenge of making peace is working out a strategy to cope with those who wish to sabotage it, whether through acts of terror or simple non-compliance.

Chapter 7   Earlier peace plans

A chronological list of all the peace plans in succession inevitably means including a variety of enterprises. Some 'plans' were no more than suggestions; others are complete delimitation agreements signed between nations after wars, but in no way purported to be comprehensive peace plans; and finally, many plans resulted in initial conferences but went no further. Even so, all have in common the desire to achieve peace (but all too often only on one side's terms). Most peace plans were made public, although the initial planning was invariably done secretly. A few remained secret and were aborted before they reached the public arena. Presumably there are others which we may never know about. Ultimately, the test of a successful peace plan is a full peace treaty between states. So far there have been only two: Israel and Egypt in 1979, Israel and Jordan in 1994. The Washington/Oslo accords between Israel and the PLO in 1993 may culminate in a similar treaty in 1999.

Some regional arrangements (like the Israel–Lebanon treaty, signed in 1982 and abrogated in 1983) are included; but others (like the Taif Accords in Lebanon, 1989–90) are not included as they do not involve Israel directly. The declarations of belligerency surrounding, say, the Cairo conference of 1965, cannot be construed as peace proposals, but are listed below because they form part of the metatext of the peace process. As for the various UN resolutions, these merit inclusion inasmuch as they define the goals of peace and suggest a method towards achieving these goals – even though they do not in themselves constitute full peace plans. By the same token, UN resolutions and declarations condemning parties in the Middle East (invariably Israel) are not included as these did not contribute towards resolving the conflict.

UN 242 in particular established three important principles which have since been adopted as benchmarks for successive attempts at finding peace.

These are: that peace would entail mutual recognition by parties in conflict; that territorial compromise could and should lead to peace, and that an ideal peace plan for the Middle East would be comprehensive (in other words, there should be peace on all fronts, rather than just a bilateral deal between two of the parties).

External events often intervene to alter the subject matter of the peace process. Amongst these are economic circumstances, changes in leadership (in Middle East states or in the superpowers which act as arbitrators), but most of all, wars.

Here follows a list of significant wars or conflicts which altered the nature of negotiations:

1939–45	Second World World
1947–49	Israeli War of Independence 1st Arab–Israeli War
1956	Suez Canal Campaign 2nd Arab–Israeli War
1967	Six Day War 3rd Arab–Israeli War
1969–71	War of Attrition 4th Arab–Israeli War
1973	Yom Kippur War 5th Arab–Israeli War
1975–90	Lebanese Civil War
1976	Syrian invasion of Lebanon
1978	Israeli Invasion of Lebanon (Operation Litani) [part of Lebanese civil war]
1982	Israeli Invasion of Lebanon (Operation Peace for Galilee) [part of Lebanese civil war]
1987–90	Palestinian *intifada* in the Occupied Territories
1991	Gulf War (Iraq *v.* a US-led UN coalition)

Finally, it must be noted that even before the State of Israel was created, conflict was already brewing between Arabs and the Jews of the Palestine *Yishuv*. Because of this, a few of the British Mandatory authority's proposals are listed as 'peace plans', even though full-scale war had not yet broken out. Indeed, some of the principles which they cover (such as the notion of a bilateral state, partition, and limits on immigration and settlement) have tended to resurface in subsequent plans.

During the Palestine Mandate

Peel Commission (first British partition plan)

Date   Commission set up in April 1936 and headed by Lord Peel
             July 1937: Report of the Peel Commission issued as Command Paper 5479

Initiators   British Government – after hearing supplications from Zionist and Arab leaders

Context   In the wake of the Arab Revolt in Palestine

Proposals   To divide Palestine into three areas: a Jewish state, an Arab state, and a British-controlled corridor from Jaffa on the coast to Jerusalem, and including Lod, Ramla and Bethlehem. The Jewish state would control most of the coastline and Galilee in the north; the Arab state would cover a much larger area, and include Gaza, the Negev desert in the south, and most of the area now known as the West Bank.

Responses   Jews accepted the plan reluctantly; most Arabs rejected it. In 1938 the Jewish Agency developed its own partition plan which envisaged a larger Jewish state, divided in two sectors. In between these sectors it planned for an Arab enclave in Jaffa, and a larger British-controlled corridor, extended down to the Dead Sea. Jerusalem would be divided between the Jewish state and the British Mandate territory. The Woodhead Commission (see below) reaffirmed the idea of partition but opposed the Jewish Agency plan.

Woodhead Commission (second British partition plan)

Date   Report issued on Oct. 19, 1938 (Command Paper 5854) as a White Paper

Initiators   British Government – after hearing supplications from Zionist and Arab leaders

Context   In response to the debate which followed the Peel Commission Report (see above)

Proposals   Like the earlier Peel Commission Report, Woodhead sought to divide Palestine into three areas: a Jewish state, an Arab state, and a British-controlled corridor. However, this time the corridor would exclude Jaffa (which would become an Arab state enclave on the coast). The corridor would be expanded to include Ramallah. The Jewish state would be reconstituted, losing Galilee and the city of Beit She'an to the Arabs. Under Plan B, the Jewish state would contain 300,400 Jews and 188,400 Arabs; the Jerusalem-Bethlehem-Ramallah area (Mandate corridor) would have 90,000 Arabs and 76,999 Jews.

Responses   Again, Jews accepted the plan reluctantly; most Arabs (apart from the Communist Party) rejected it. A new British Government Command Paper (5893) concluded that partition was impracticable, due to 'administrative, political and financial difficulties'.

White Paper

Date   May 1939

Initiators   Lord Passfield, for the British Government (Command Paper 6019)

Context   An end to the Arab Revolt; fears of a new world war in Europe

Proposals   Palestinian independence within ten years, leading to a single state where power would be shared between Arabs and Jews; more immediately, restrictions on Jewish immigration to Palestine; restrictions on Jewish land purchase in most of Palestine. (The White Paper effectively ended UK support for partition, and claimed to reinstate the promises made to the majority Arab population of Palestine.)

Responses   Zionists opposed it, arguing that it subverted the promise for a 'Jewish National Home' in Palestine, as specified in both the Balfour Declaration in 1917 and the preamble to the Mandate in 1922. Furthermore, they foresaw that it would block Jewish refugees from Nazi persecution in central Europe, from entering Palestine – precisely at a time when the rest of the world was apparently 'shutting its doors' to them. However, they agreed to shelve their paramilitary activities for the duration of the world war, which began in September 1939; but the *Haganah* did help thousands of 'illegal' immigrants enter Palestine, in contravention of Mandatory law. As David Ben-Gurion told his supporters: 'We will fight the White Paper as if there is no war, and fight the war as if there is no White Paper'.

On Feb.28, 1940, Britain, acting on the White Paper's recommendations, passed a law preventing Jewish land purchase in an area of 4.1 million acres. This effectively stopped Jews from extending land holdings in three main areas of settlement – around Beersheva in the south, around (though not in) Jerusalem, and on the coastline north of Acre. (At the time Jews owned about 5% of the land, while constituting almost a third of the population.)

Anglo-American Committee of Inquiry

Dates   Period of examination: Dec. 1945 to April 1946; report: May 1, 1946

Initiators   The governments of Britain and the USA (proposed by UK Foreign Secretary Ernest Bevin and backed by US President Harry Truman) set up a committee of inquiry, headed by Morrison for the UK and Grady for the USA

Context   In the light of the discovery of the horrors of the Nazi concentration camps, the two governments were determined to look anew at the problem of Jewish immigration (then still officially restricted by the terms of the 1939 Passfield White Paper [see above]); and especially at the plight of survivors of the Nazi Holocaust

Proposals   To reject partition as a policy in favour of 'binationalism' – a single state under British rule. Furthermore, it recommended the immediate granting of 100,000 immigration certificates to Jews and ending the land purchase restrictions of 1940.

Responses   Zionists accepted the immigration aspects of the plan, but by now favoured partition (see Jewish Agency Partition Plan below).

Jewish Agency Partition Plan

Date   August 1946

Initiators   The Jewish Agency (chief Zionist body in Palestine)

Proposals   To partition Palestine into separate Jewish and Arab states. The Arab state would control the West Bank area (including Ramallah, Tulkarm, Bethlehem and Hebron); plus an enclave around Jaffa on the Mediterranean coast. The Jewish state would control the rest of Palestine, except for Jerusalem, which would come under international control. By contrast with the British partition plans of the 1930s, the Jewish Agency envisaged a Jewish state expanded to include the Negev, Galilee and the west bank of the Dead Sea. The Jewish state would be substantially bigger than the Arab state and there would be no Mandatory corridor.

Responses   Arabs ignored the plan, which contradicted British policy. However, whether by design or coincidence, the plan almost exactly anticipated the land division of Palestine after the Israeli War of Independence two years later.

United Nations Partition Plan

Date   Aug. 31, 1947 – presentation of UNSCOP report

Initiators   The United Nations Special Committee on Palestine (UNSCOP), was mandated to prepare the report by the UN General Assembly. (Britain had requested the UN Secretary-General to address the issue of Palestine on April 2, 1947.)

Context   On May 22, 1942, the Jewish Agency endorsed the Biltmore Programme, which for the first time committed Zionists to establishing a Jewish Commonwealth (state) in Palestine once it had attained a Jewish majority. On Oct. 7, 1944, Arab states signed the Alexandria Protocol, committing them to 'defence of Palestinian (Arab) national interests'. After the end of World War II, renewed violence broke out between Jews and Arabs in Palestine and the Mandatory authorities. In 1946 King Abdallah of Jordan held secret talks with Zionists to discuss a partition of Palestine between his Kingdom and them. Meanwhile, the Palestinian leader Hajj Amin al-Husseini intensified his campaign against Zionists and now the King. Radical Zionist groups, *Lehi* and *Irgun*, in turn openly attacked British personnel and installations, most spectacularly blowing up the King David Hotel in July 1946, which resulted in 92 deaths. Palestinian groups then attacked and killed Jewish civilians. London hosted a conference on Palestine, and submitted an autonomy plan based on provinces, but Arab delegates demanded a unitary state. Faced with escalating violence, and acknowledging the ungovernability of Palestine, Britain formally decided to end its Mandate over Palestine.

Proposals To partition Palestine into separate Jewish and Arab states and an international zone around Jerusalem and its suburbs. The Jewish state would be divided into three sectors. By contrast with the Jewish Agency plan (see above) the Jewish state would lose northern Galilee and the coastal strip around Gaza to the Arab state. However, by contrast with earlier British partition plans (see above), it did concede the Negev desert to the Jews. There would be an Arab enclave in Jaffa. The plan also envisaged an Economic Union between the two states. Many Jewish settlements would remain within the Arab state, but Arabs would still enjoy a demographic majority. Likewise, the Jewish state would have an Arab minority.

Responses

- UN General Assembly votes to accept partition plan, Nov. 29, 1947 [Resolution 181 (II)] – the vote was 33 in favour, 13 against and 10 abstentions (including Britain)
- Despite the developing Cold War between the USA and USSR, the two states agree to support the new State of Israel, and the UN Partition Plan
- Arab states and Palestinian Arab community leadership reject the plan as contradicting the national rights of Palestine's Arabs, and vow to destroy Jewish state
- On March 19, 1948, the US State Department proposes a Trusteeship Plan as an alternative to partition, but facing Arab and Jewish opposition, it soon reverts to support for 181 (II)
- Britain agrees to end mandate and withdraw, which they do on May 13, 1948
- Zionists accept UN vote as mandate for declaring statehood, which they do on May 14, 1948
- Arab League states invade Israel, thus beginning the Israeli War of Independence
- Israel gains territory in the war; Arabs are defeated; Palestinian refugee crisis ensues
- In 1950 Jordan formally annexes West Bank and East Jerusalem as part of Jordan
- Palestine effectively disappears from the map

Between 1948 war and 1979

Lausanne Conference

Date From April 27, 1949 to Sept. 15, 1949

Initiators A United Nations Conciliation Commission, composed of USA, France and Turkey

Context Conclusion of the first Arab–Israeli War (known in Israel as the War of Independence). In the course of the war, Israel rebuffed invasions from a united Arab force, consisting of the armies of Egypt, Syria and the Arab Legion of Jordan, as well as a force of armed Palestinian Arabs. Israel increased the land mass allocated to her according to the UN Partition Declaration. The war also saw the departure of up to 900,000 Palestinian refugees (the majority of the pre-war Arab population of Palestine). On Nov. 19, 1948 the UN General Assembly passed Resolution 212 (II), which set up a special fund for Palestinian refugees. On Dec. 11 it passed a further Resolution, 194 (III), establishing the refugees' 'right of return'.

Meanwhile, on Nov. 16 the UN Security Council passed Resolution 62 which invited parties to the conflict to seek an agreement through negotiations. On Jan. 19, 1949, the US mediator, Ralph Bunche, presided over a series of Arab–Israeli bilateral negotiations, held on the island of Rhodes. These resulted in armistices between Israel and the various Arab states – with Egypt on Feb. 24; Lebanon on March 23; Jordan on April 3; and Syria on July 20. The still unresolved refugees issue, however, was left for debate at Lausanne. On May 12, 1949, Arab states which had formerly rejected UN 181 (II) – the Partition Resolution – now accepted it as a basis for negotiations.

Proposals Syria and Iraq agreed to receive 300,000 and 350,000 refugees respectively, on condition that Israel implement the Partition Resolution. Israel countered with a proposal to repatriate 45,000 refugees (in addition to the 55,000 who had already returned). It further proposed a Palestinian state in the West Bank under Israeli control, which it argued was necessary because of Israel's legitimate security fears.

Responses

- The Lausanne Conference failed to reach an agreement.
- Palestinians were angered that the UN Conciliation Commission had not involved them.
- In 1950 Jordan formally annexed the West Bank into the Hashemite Kingdom, thereby annulling the terms of the 1948 Partition Plan (which called for a separate Arab Palestinian state).
- The Commission convened another conference in Paris, in Sept. 1951, but this also failed.
- Of all the Arab states hosting Palestinian refugees, only Jordan offered them full citizenship.
- Although armistices had been signed between the warring parties, a state of war existed between Israel and all her Arab neighbours (until the Israel–Egypt peace treaty of 1979).

Cairo Conference proposals

Date	January 1964
Initiators	Egyptian President Gamal Abdel Nasser
Context	The first Arab leaders summit was held in Cairo amidst renewed agitation for an independent Palestinian organization. It also came at a time of tensions arising out of a dispute with Israel regarding exploitation of the River Jordan; a simmering civil war in Yemen, involving Egypt; and a bid by Nasser to lead the Arab world.
Proposals	To set up a joint military pact, and back a PLO (Palestine Liberation Organization) with a PLA (Palestine Liberation Army).
Responses	Escalation of belligerancy, leading to the Six Day War. On May 25, 1967 troops from Egypt, Syria, Jordan, Iraq and Saudi Arabia moved to Israel's borders. Nasser warned of war and ordered the naval blockade of Sharm al-Sheikh, thus closing the Gulf of Aqaba to Israeli shipping. On June 5 Israel launched a pre-emptive strike, and within six days had soundly beaten its foes.

United Nations Security Council Resolution 242

Date	Adopted on Nov. 22, 1967
Initiators	United Nations Security Council, after consultation with parties in the conflict
Context	Response to the Six Day War, and specifically to Israel's capture of lands from her enemies – the Sinai Peninsula and Gaza Strip (from Egypt); East Jerusalem and the West Bank (from Jordan); and the Golan Heights (from Syria). On Sept. 1, eight Arab heads of sate attending a summit conference in Khartoum passed a resolution calling for 'no peace with Israel, no recognition of Israel, no negotiations with Israel'.
Proposals	To reject the 'inadmissibility of gaining territory by war . . .'; to reach peace through negotiations; to ensure secure and defensible borders for all states
Responses	Israel, Egypt and Jordan all accepted UN 242 as the basis for future negotiations. However, UN 242 was interpreted quite differently, depending on whether one read the English or French versions. The Arab states contend that the resolution meant Israel should withdraw from 'all' occupied territories, while Israel said it only meant withdrawal from 'some' territories. The PLO and Syria rejected UN 242, the former on the grounds that it did not address the issue of Palestinian national rights. In the eyes of the US Department of State (and to some extent Israel), acceptance of UN 242 became a litmus test for the PLO's right to participate in future peace negotiations.

Allon Plan

Date	First of many versions tabled in June 1968
Context	Israel's acquisition of new occupied territory in the Six Day War of 1967
Initiators	Israeli Deputy Prime Minister Yigal Allon
Proposals	To return two-thirds of the West Bank to the Kingdom of Jordan, and to annex the remaining one-third to Israel. The Israeli areas would include a Jewish-settled security strip along the Jordan River and territory around Jerusalem. The Jordanian areas were divided into three segments – north, south, and a smaller corridor leading from Jericho to the river. Following the wishes of Prime Minister Eshkol and Defence Minister Dayan, Allon agreed to keep Gaza as part of Israel. However, in later formulations it envisaged Gaza becoming part of a Jordanian-Palestinian state.

Responses   Although not formally adopted by the Israeli cabinet, the Allon Plan informed the ideology of the ruling Labour Party in the decade following the Six Day War. The idea behind the plan was to avoid settling Jews in heavily populated Arab areas, and mainly maintain the West Bank as a buffer against future attack. On taking office in 1977, however, Likud leader Menachem Begin endorsed a vision of the West Bank as part of biblical *Eretz Yisrael*, and consequently approved new settlements beyond the 30% 'Israeli' zone. Jordan refused to accept anything less than the complete return of territory. The PLO rejected it as not taking into account their own 'national rights'. However, aspects of the Allon ethos seem to have re-emerged in the Interim Agreement between Israel and the PLO, signed in September 1995.

Rogers Plan/ Gunnar Initiative

Date   Dec. 9, 1969 [first plan]
        June 19, 1970 [revised plan]

Initiators   US Secretary of State William Rogers

Context   Following UN 242, the UN Secretary-General asked the Swedish Ambassador, Dr Gunnar Jarring, to visit Middle East states and prepare the ground for achieving a 'peaceful and accepted settlement'. His first mission in 1968 proved a failure. Meanwhile, French President Charles de Gaulle proposed a draft settlement based on US, Soviet, British and French commitments to implement UN 242. The 'Big Four' discussed the plan at the UN, but this too failed in the face of US scepticism. In March 1969 a war of attrition broke out between Egypt and Israel; the presence of Soviet SAM missiles to the west of Suez now threatened to drag the superpowers into a new conflict. Meanwhile, *Fatah* leader, Yasser Arafat, gained control of the PLO, and the Palestinian Charter was revised, with a stronger commitment to armed struggle. To revive the flagging peace process (and forestall another war), the USA proposed a new plan.

Proposals   The first plan envisaged a two-track settlement – Israeli–Egyptian peace, to be achieved by Israeli withdrawal from the Sinai and the setting up of demilitarized zones; and an Israeli–Jordanian peace, involving Israeli withdrawal from the West Bank, which would be totally demilitarized. Rogers' second plan called for: a three-month ceasefire, acceptance by all parties of UN 242, and the resumption of the Jarring mission

Responses   Egypt accepted the first plan, but Israel objected to the Israeli–Jordanian element. The revised plan was initially much more successful: Egypt accepted it on 23 July; Jordan on 26 July; and Israel on Aug. 1. As a result Gunnar Jarring resumed his mediation on Sept. 6, 1970. However, Palestinians rejected both Rogers Plans, on the same grounds that they had rejected UN 242 – namely, that it 'denied the national rights' of the Palestinian people, and reduced their status to merely a 'refugee problem'. Somewhat confusingly, Egyptian President Nasser supported the Palestinians, lending succour to the belief that his backing for Rogers was only a tactical ploy to regain territory lost in the 1967 war. Evidently, he had a fall-back military option, known as the 'Granite Plan', if the Rogers Plan proved fruitless. Ultimately, the Rogers Plan foundered because of two events: the Jordan–PLO civil war of Sept. 15 to 27 Sept. ('Black September'); and the death of Nasser on Sept. 28. In 1972 Gunnar Jarring abandoned his mission, and a new US Secretary of State, Henry Kissinger, dropped the Rogers Plan.

Jordanian Federation Proposal

Date   March 15, 1972

Initiators   King Hussein of Jordan

Context   The collapse of the PLO–Jordan partnership in 1970 led to civil war, and Jordanian victory with the expulsion in July 1971 of PLO *fedayeen* from the Kingdom.

Proposals   To set up a United Arab Kingdom, dividing Jordan on federal lines, with autonomous parliaments and administration in the West and East Banks. Central government would deal with foreign affairs and defence matters.

Responses   West Bank Palestinians rejected the plan as not meeting their national aspirations, while the PLO still smarted over its treatment by Jordan. The October 1973 war altered matters considerably, and in 1974 Jordan itself backtracked somewhat by endorsing the Rabat Summit's view of the PLO as the 'sole legitimate representatives of the Palestinian people'.

Figure 7   *War dead in 1967 and 1973*

Country	1967	1973
Israel	983	2,838
Arab total	4,296	8,528
Syria	600	3,100
Egypt	3,000	5,000
Jordan	696	28

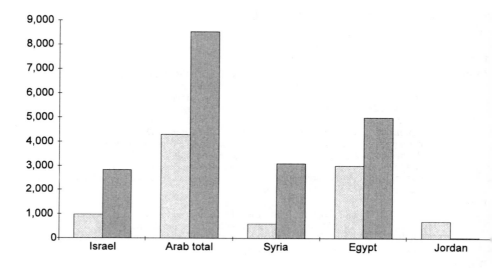

Source: Figures reprinted from Trevor N. Depuy, *Elusive Victory; The Arab–Israeli Wars, 1947–1974,* as found in Ian J. Bickerton and Carla I. Klausner, *A Concise History of the Arab–Israeli conflict*

United Nations Security Council Resolution 338

Date   Adopted on Oct. 22, 1973

Initiators United Nations Security Council (originally a joint US–Soviet text)

Context   In response to the Yom Kippur War, which began on Oct. 6, 1973, and had not yet ended when UN 338 was announced. (The superpower co-operation is significant, as at one stage the Middle East conflict threatened to draw in the USA and USSR.)

Proposals   immediate ceasefire; warring parties to implement in full UN 242 (see above); and the convening of negotiations between those parties to achieve a 'just and durable peace'.

Responses   Accepted by Egypt, Syria and Israel; rejected by the PLO. Considerable pressure and 'shuttle diplomacy' by US Secretary of State Henry Kissinger led to a peace conference in Geneva (see below). One year after UN 338 was passed, Yasser Arafat addressed the General Assembly, which Israel condemned as unjustified approval for a terrorist leader.

Geneva Peace Conference

Date   Dec. 21, 1973

Initiators US Secretary of State Henry Kissinger; participants: Israel, Egypt and Jordan

Context   Pressure to implement UN 338; persistence of the Arab oil boycott

Proposals   No proposal as such emerged from the conference. Instead, during two days of talks each party expressed its position, and then decided to create a 'technical military committee' to discuss disengagement.

Responses   Syria boycotted the first session and the PLO had not been invited to attend. Kissinger and Israel apparently had different agendas from the Arab states. Israel wanted a separate peace with Egypt, and wanted the USSR excluded from the talks. In secret meetings between Egypt and Israel (in the military committee), Israel allegedly proposed dividing the Middle East into 'spheres of influence', with Egypt dominant in Africa, and Israel in Asia. Feeling that it was being sidelined, the Soviet Union tried to end the talks. The only positive results were the various military disengagement agreements which arose in succeeding years (see below).

First Sinai Agreement

Date   Talks open on Nov. 11, 1973; agreement reached on Jan. 18, 1974

Initiators Under US influence, Egyptian and Syrian negotiators meet at Kilometre 101, Sinai

Proposals   To disengage Egyptian and Israeli forces in the Sinai peninsula. Egypt wanted Israel to withdraw from most of peninsula, east of a line from El Arish in north to Sharm el-Sheikh in south; Israel countered with a four-stage planning, culminating in Israeli forces withdrawing to a line 10km west of 1967–73 ceasefire line along the Suez Canal.

Responses   Dispute over extent of withdrawals leads to talks breaking down in December, 1973. Eventually, a compromise agreement was reached and signed in Geneva on Jan. 18, 1974. This was followed by a similar agreement between Israel and Syria, signed in Geneva on May 31, 1974 (Syria regained control of territory east of the Golan which it had lost in the latter stages of the Yom Kippur War).

Second Sinai Agreement

Date   Agreement initialled on Sept. 1, 1975, and signed on Sept. 4

Initiators US Secretary of State Henry Kissinger

Proposals   To disengage Egyptian and Israeli forces in the Sinai peninsula. It was agreed that limited Egyptian forces would occupy a narrow strip to the east of the Suez Canal, and limited Israeli forces would occupy an area behind new redeployment lines. (In effect, Israel keeps most of Sinai but surrenders oil fields and strategic passes in desert.) A buffer zone was established between the two zones with UN observation posts and UN troops in place. (Israel agreed to sign after receiving assurances from the USA consisting of oil, diplomatic support, and military and economic aid.)

Responses   Egypt and Israel agree to forego the use of military force in resolving conflict. Israel withdraws in 14 stages, completed on Feb. 26, 1976. In addition, the US government had agreed with Israel that the Geneva peace process should proceed on a bilateral basis, and that until the PLO accepted UN 242, it should be excluded from peace talks. (This remained US policy until 1989, when it departed from the Israeli view and opened talks with the PLO.)

Joint US–Soviet communiqué

Date   Oct. 1, 1977

Initiators At the instigation of US President Jimmy Carter; communiqué issued jointly by US and Soviet governments

Context   The election of Jimmy Carter as President of the USA in 1976. Earlier, preparing the way for a change in US policy, Senator Fullbright became the first American official to acknowledge the rights of Palestinians *per se*, and Assistant Secretary of State, Joseph Sisco, advocated recognition of a 'Palestinian entity'.

Proposals   Call for 'comprehensive Arab–Israeli agreement' at the Geneva conference (to be convened in December); Israeli withdrawal from occupied territories; superpower guarantees for borders (to be settled in Geneva); and Palestinian participation in the conference.

Responses   Support from Palestinians and Arab states; objections from Israel, US Jewish lobby and US conservatives (wary of a deal struck with the Soviets). Carter retreated somewhat from the communiqué in a US–Israeli 'working paper'. Egyptian President Sadat's visit to Israel in October (see Camp David Accords, below) scuppered plans for a Geneva conference.

Camp David Accords

Date   Talks at Camp David (the US President's country residence) lasted from Sept. 5 to 17, 1978, and the framework accords were signed on Sept. 18

Initiators Egyptian President Sadat, Israeli Prime Minister Begin, US President Jimmy Carter

Context   The election of Menachem Begin and his *Likud* Party; Sadat's historic visit to address the Israeli Knesset, Nov. 19, 1977.

Proposals

- To extend Egyptian control eventually to all of Sinai; phased Israeli withdrawals
- To reach a full peace treaty between Israel and Egypt
- To set up an 'elected self-governing authority' on the West Bank and Gaza Strip
- Ultimate goal: within three years, settling the final status of West Bank and Gaza, and achieving a peace treaty between Israel and Jordan, following negotiations between Egypt, Israel, Jordan and the 'elected representatives of the West Bank and Gaza Strip'.

Responses   Israel and Egypt agree on Sinai return and work towards full peace treaty.
On March 26, 1979, Israel and Egypt sign a full peace treaty and agree on the gradual total return of the Sinai peninsula to Egyptian rule. This entailed the dismantling of the Israeli settlement of Yamit, which *Gush Emunim* (erstwhile allies of Begin) condemned as an act of treachery. Some members of *Likud* (notably Yitzhak Shamir, a future prime minister) refused to ratify the treaty; but the Labour opposition gave it full support. Egypt is ostracized from Arab League; diplomatic relations with Arab states strained and severed; Egypt was criticized for signing a 'separate peace' with Israel in exchange for recovered land. Negotiations on Palestinian autonomy began on 25 May, 1979, but became deadlocked as the PLO and then Jordan rejected terms (Jordan still had a legal claim over the area, so its co-operation was crucial). Israel for its part based its approach on Menachem Begin's autonomy plan for the Occupied Territories as presented to the Knesset on Dec. 28, 1977. It envisaged continuing Israeli control of security, and land and water resources; a Palestinian 'administrative council' would deal with other, local matters. The settlement policy would continue. Israel refused to negotiate with the PLO, but found no alternative Palestinian representatives. Egypt, by contrast, favoured autonomy as a step towards full Palestinian sovereign independence. After eight fruitless sessions, and Israel's formal annexation of east Jerusalem on July 30, 1980, Egyptian–Israeli talks on autonomy collapsed.
Egyptian President Anwar Sadat was assassinated in October 1981. His successor, Hosni Mubarak, carried out the terms of the Camp David Accords and the peace treaty.

The last parts of Sinai were handed over to Egypt on April 25, 1982. On June 6, 1982, Israel invaded Lebanon (following the attempted assassination of its ambassador to London). It aimed to dislodge the PLO from bases in southern Lebanon, which threatened northern Israel. Begin's critics claimed that he had used Camp David to 'neutralize' Egypt in the south, so as to get a free reign in the north.

Between 1980 and 1991

Venice Declaration

Date   June 1980

Initiators   European Community (EC) heads of government, meeting in Venice, Italy

Proposals   Mutual recognition of the right to existence of all peoples in the Middle East; inclusion of PLO in talks with Israel; praise for Israeli withdrawal from Sinai coupled with calls for Israeli withdrawal from all areas taken in 1967.

Responses   Israel rejects PLO participation; Foreign Minister Abba Eban chides the EC for favouring the PLO and thereby 'giving no incentive for moderate Palestinians'.

Fahd Plan

Date   Aug. 8, 1981

Initiators   Saudi Arabian Crown Prince (later King) Fahd ibn Saud

Context   Following the Venice Declaration (see above), Soviet President Leonid Brezhnev proposed in February 1981, a new formulation – the right of Palestinians to set up their own state, combined with guaranteed security and sovereignty for all states in the region, including Israel. The PNC unanimously endorsed this proposal at their April 1981 session, and Arab leaders interpreted this as a sign of PLO willingness to compromise.

Proposals   Support for a Palestinian state on the West Bank with East Jerusalem as its capital; and the right of all states in the region to live in peace and security. Some regard it as the first non-Egyptian Arab plan to recognize Israel's legitimacy and existence.

Responses   The Fahd Plan threatened to split the Arab League, which aborted its planned summit in Fez on Nov. 25, 1981. On Jan. 4, 1982, the League denied that it had recognized Israel, and Jordan reaffirmed the PLO as 'sole legitimate representative of the Palestinian people'. Nonetheless, the Fahd Plan planted the seeds for a new approach in Arab relations with Israel, and led to the Reagan and Fez Plans (see below).

Reagan Plan

Date   Sept. 1, 1982

Initiator   US President Ronald Reagan, in a speech to the nation, Burbank, California

Context   Arab condemnation of Israel grew after its invasion of Lebanon on June 5 escalated into a fullscale operation, and its forces entered Beirut. Despite this, a month later the PNC moderate Issam Sartawi reiterated the PLO's acceptance of the Brezhnev plan; and called for reciprocal talks between the PLO, Israel and USA. President Reagan saw an opportunity for the US to act as an 'international policeman', and at the same time reach a final peace accord in the region.

Proposals   Reagan called on Israel to make clear that security only comes from peace; he called on Palestinians to acknowledge that 'their own aspirations are inextricably bound to recognition of Israel's right to a secure future' and called on Arab states to 'accept the reality of Israel' and begin negotiations for peace. Specifically, the plan demanded that Israel freeze new settlements, and begin to withdraw from the West Bank and Gaza. After a five-year transitional period, Palestinians would enjoy 'self-government' in the territories 'in association with Jordan'. The USA promised to 'guarantee Israel's security . . . behind defensible borders'. (In short, the Reagan Plan resuscitated elements of the Camp David autonomy proposals, and echoed the Fahd Plan, but stopped short of recognizing the PLO.)

Responses   On Sept. 2, the Israeli cabinet rejected the plan as a 'deviation from Camp David', and three days later announced a grant for building three new settlements. Jordan, Egypt and the PLO's 'foreign minister', Farouk Qaddumi, thought the plan had 'positive aspects'; but Syria and Damascus-based PLO factions rejected it outright. The Arab League, meeting in Fez barely a week later, announced a counter-proposal (see below). In October 1983 Issam Sartawi was assassinated by radical Palestinians. As for US policy, they were to spearhead a multinational peace-keeping force in Lebanon. Faced with a string of suicide bomb attacks, US and allied forces withdrew in 1984.

Fez Plan

Date Sept. 9, 1982 (final conference statement).

Initiators Delegates to the 12th Arab League Summit Conference, in Fez, Morocco.

Context In response to the Reagan Plan (see above)

Proposals Resuscitating the earlier Fahd/Saudi plan, the Fez delegates demanded Israeli withdrawal from occupied territories. But this time it overtly recognized the 'guiding role' of the PLO; proposed putting UN (and not Arab) peace-keeping forces in the territories; and back-tracked somewhat on explicitly recognizing Israel.

Responses On Sept. 10, 1982, Israel rejected the call for a Palestinian 'mini-state', but US Secretary of State George Schultz said it contained the seeds of a 'possible breakthrough'. The Sabra and Shatilla massacre the following week cast a pall upon such optimism. Nonetheless, Reagan met a League delegation in October to evaluate the two plans; and in December King Hussein discussed the possibility of Jordan's pivotal role in Palestinian autonomy with top US and Soviet leaders. (As late as 1986, King Hassan of Morocco invited Shimon Peres to Ifran, to discuss the Fez Plan, but little progress was made.)

Framework for Peace (Hussein–Arafat Plan)

Date Feb. 11, 1985

Initiators Jordanian King Hussein of Jordan; PLO Chairman Yasser Arafat; and backed by Egyptian President Hosni Mubarak.

Context Throughout 1983 the PLO was split between *Fatah* and two opposition groups, the Syrian-backed National Alliance and the Democratic Alliance. Some PLO moderates began talking secretly to Israel's Labour opposition (PLO adviser Issam Sartawi was assassinated for doing so, presumably by the Abu Nidal group). Begin had resigned in 1983, and his successor, Yitzhak Shamir, failed to win an outright *Likud* victory in 1984. As a result Labour's Shimon Peres became Israel's new prime minister (presiding over a *Likud*-Labour coalition government). In September 1984 Jordan announced it would restore diplomatic relations with Egypt, which in turn paved the way for a partial PLO rapprochement with Egypt. All these factors renewed hopes for peace based on a new plan issued by King Hussein of Jordan.

Proposals Confederation between Jordan and an independent Palestinian state on the West Bank. This was based on Hussein's 'territory for peace' plan according to UN 242, as presented to the 17th PNC session in November 1984. Arafat denied, however, that the PLO had accepted UN 242.

Responses May 1985: US Secretary of State George Schultz proposes PNC members within a joint Palestinian-Jordanian negotiating team, but Israel rejects this on the grounds that the PNC was an extension of the PLO. Hussein responds with a two-stage plan: a joint PNC–Jordanian negotiating team to hold an international conference with the USA, followed by direct talks with Israel. In June Peres proposes a five-stage timetable leading to a conference. The PLO list of candidates is whittled down from 22 to seven.
The Israeli cabinet rejects them, although Peres approves of two members.
In August Arab League summit backs PLO–Jordan accord.
In October Israeli bombers destroy PLO headquarters in Tunis, retaliating for an earlier terrorist attack. Two weeks later Israeli Prime Minister Shimon Peres speaks at the UN and calls for a Middle East conference based on the principle of 'territorial compromises', and peace with Jordan.
Feb. 19, 1986: Frustrated by Arafat's inconsistencies, failure to endorse UN 242 and inability to prevent terrorism, King Hussein abrogates the PLO–Jordan accord. The re-appointment of Yitzhak Shamir as Israel's prime minister further stymies hopes of progress.

London Plan

Date April 11, 1987

Initiators King Hussein of Jordan and Israeli Foreign Minister Shimon Peres, in London

Context Following the 'Jordanian option' role hinted at in Fahd, Reagan and Fez Plans; as an attempt to revive aspects of the Framework for Peace plan of Hussein and Araft (see above); and as a bid by Peres to pre-empt Shamir's more right-wing plans.

Proposals The two leaders endorsed a UN-sponsored peace conference, using UN 242 and 338 as guidelines; Palestinian delegates would form part of the Jordanian delegation.

Responses When details of the initially secret plan emerged, it was soon sabotaged by more conservative figures in Israel and Jordan. Attempts to revive it flagged after the outbreak of the *intifada* in the territories, in Dec. 9, 1987. (However, the modalities suggested in the London Plan were later adopted at the Madrid conference of 1991.)

Algiers Declaration

Date Nov. 12–15, 1988

Initiators Yasser Arafat at 19th session of the Palestine National Council, called by the Palestine Central Council of the PLO and held in Algiers.

Context On Dec. 12, 1987, an *intifada* (uprising) began amongst Palestinians in the occupied territories. It soon spread and, despite strenuous Israeli efforts to quell it, showed no sign of dying down. The *intifada* came to be directed by two organizations: a Unified National Command (which espoused the views of various PLO factions, but did not initially take orders from Tunis); and *Hamas*, a newly established Islamic fundamentalist grouping. Although at first the PLO was taken by surprise at this 'internal' development, it soon came up with a policy reflecting the new realities in the region. Another cause (indeed, prerequisite) for the Algiers Declaration was the announcement by King Hussein that Jordan would sever all of its legal and administrative ties with the West Bank (made on July 31, 1988). Bassam Abu Sharif, senior PLO advisor to Yasser Arafat, had laid the groundwork for a 'two-state' formula at a meeting of the Arab League in June 1988. Arafat himself then informed the Socialist Group of the European Parliament in September 1988 that the PLO was prepared to attend an international peace conference with Israel on the basis of UN Resolutions 242 and 338.

Proposals To declare Palestinian statehood on the basis of UN 181 (see UN Partition Plan, above); to make Jerusalem its capital; and also, to attend an international Middle East conference under UN auspices, on the basis of UN Resolutions 242 and 338. In effect, Arafat was recognising the state of Israel. He also claimed to be putting an end to the PLO's earlier endorsement of terrorism as a political weapon.

Responses Immediately after the conference, Arafat set about forming a provisional 'government-in-exile', with himself as President and Farouk Qaddumi as Foreign Minister. The PLO Executive Committee endorsed this in April 1989; but rejectionists (notably the PFLP-GC and *Fatah* Rebels) refused to go along with the new policy, and vowed to set up an 'alternative PLO'. All Arab states apart from Syria recognized the 'new state'. The Soviet Union recognized the declaration but not the state. By mid-1990 more than 90 countries had either recognized the state or the declaration.

On Dec. 13 and 14 Arafat addressed the UN General Assembly and explicitly recognized Israel and renounced terrorism. This satisfied US conditions set by US Secretary of State George Schultz, and on Dec. 16 the USA and PLO began their first open talks in Tunisia. After Arafat failed to condemn a beachfront attack in Israel by the Palestine Liberation Front in May 1990, US President George Bush suspended the US–PLO dialogue.

The Israeli government (under Prime Minister Yitzhak Shamir) questioned Arafat's sincerity, and thus refused to either talk to the PLO or to participate in the US peace initiative. Shamir pointed out that the PLO National Covenant (which called for the destruction of Israel) had still not been revoked. As Palestinian terrorist incidents continued, Shamir argued that either the PLO had not truly given up terrorism as a policy, or at best the PLO could not control renegade Palestinian groups, and thus could not be considered to be a suitable partner for negotiation. Nonetheless, Shamir presented his own peace plan in April 1990 [see below].

After the PLO Executive Committee failed to condemn a Palestine Liberation Front terrorist attack at Tel Aviv beach in May 1990, the US suspended its talks with the PLO.

Shamir Plan 1

Date	Presented on April 6, 1989; approved by Israeli government on May 14, 1989
Initiators	Israeli Prime Minister Yitzhak Shamir; based on draft proposals by Defence Minister Rabin
Context	A counter-proposal to the PLO's Algiers Declaration [see above]
Proposals	Elections in ten constituencies for a Palestinian autonomous council; the council would negotiate 'interim autonomy status' for a five-year period; after three years, talks would start on a 'final status'; East Jerusalem Arabs and Palestinians living outside Gaza and the West Bank (ie the Palestinian Diaspora) would be excluded from talks; Jewish settlements would continue, and Israel would maintain its occupation until autonomy status entered into force. No negotiations would begin until the *intifada* ended.
Responses	US Secretary of State James Baker accepted the plan in May, but restated his equal opposition to both permanent Israeli occupation of the territories, and the creation of a Palestinian state. In March Egypt was re-admitted to the Arab League. Armed with renewed regional authority, in August Egyptian President Hosni Mubarak submitted a ten-point plan in the form of questions and clarifications on the Shamir Plan. Israel rejected this plan.

Baker Plan 1

Dates	December 1989
Initiators	US Secretary of State James Baker (under President George Bush)
Context	In response to the Shamir and Mubarak plans [see above]
Proposals	In synthesizing the two above-mentioned plans, Baker called for: a dialogue between an Israeli and a Palestinian delegation in Cairo; a consultative role for Egypt; a Palestinian delegation list which would meet Israeli demands; Israeli participation on the basis of the Shamir Plan, and freedom for Palestinians to express their views on this plan; a tripartite meeting before the negotiating process started, between US, Israeli and Egyptian foreign ministers.
Responses	On March 9, 1990, Shamir accepted part of the plan, but wished to exclude the PLO and East Jerusalemites from the proposed talks. The Labour leader, Shimon Peres, accepted the plan in its entirety, however, and led a successful vote of no-confidence in the Shamir government on March 15. As a result the Likud-Labour government of national unity collapsed, and on June 11, 1990, Shamir managed to form a new government (without Labour), including new religous and right-wing nationalist allies. [See below for Shamir Plan 2.]

Shamir Plan 2

Date	June 11, 1990
Initiators	Israeli Prime Minister Yitzhak Shamir
Context	The dissolution of the *Likud*-Labour coalition, and the formation of a more right-wing *Likud*-led government in Israel. In May, Iraqi leader Saddam Hussein had addressed the Baghdad Arab summit and called on Arab countries to 'liberate the Holy City of Jerusalem'. In this threatening atmosphere, Shamir added new, tougher conditions to his earlier plan:
Proposals	Palestinians could only discuss the Camp David Accords autonomy proposal; Arab states should 'make a gesture' to Israel before it talked to Palestinians; the question of Arab–Israeli relations should be addressed before discussion on the Palestinian question.
Responses	On June 13, 1990, James Baker denounced the Shamir government as 'not being serious about peace'. Shamir responded by hardening his settlements policy. Palestinians began denouncing the futility of the peace process, pointing to the continuing 'repression' of the *intifada*, and the mass influx of Soviet Jews to Israel. On Aug. 2, Saddam Hussein invaded Kuwait. Arafat proposed an Arab-led Good Offices Council to resolve the Kuwait crisis, but most Arab states rejected this in favour of UN-led military intervention to force Iraqi withdrawal from Kuwait. The PLO found itself ostracized from most Arab leaders. In January 1991, a US-led UN coalition began air raids on Iraq, in a campaign known as Operation Desert Storm.

Baker Plan 2

Date   Initiated on March 6, 1991; and evolved through US Secretary of State James Baker's meetings with Israeli and Arab leaders in eight trips to the Middle East

Initiators Announced by President George Bush, and later amplified by James Baker

Context   After the success of Operation Desert Storm, the US government saw an opportunity to 'break the logjam' of Middle East peace. James Baker was mandated by President Bush to canvas opinion in the Middle East to that end.

Proposals   Bush and Baker regarded Arab–Israeli peace as a prerequisite to regional security. They proposed a regional conference, held under the auspices of the USA and USSR, and based on the earlier Baker Plan, and on UN 242 and UN 338. It would aim to provide for Israel's security and recognition and also provide for 'legitimate Palestinian rights'. Baker stressed the notion of 'territory for peace' and 'confidence-building measures'.

Responses   Baker's peregrinations eventually resulted in the Madrid peace conference of October 1991. [*This is the subject matter of the following chapter.*]

Chapter 8   Madrid and Oslo

The Madrid Channel

THE PATH TO MADRID

The Gulf War as a catalyst

The Madrid Peace conference was a direct result of the Gulf War of 1991 (sometimes known as the Second Gulf War to distinguish it from the war fought between Iran and Iraq between 1979 and 1988). The Gulf War aimed to ensure that Iraq withdrew from Kuwait, which it had invaded and 'annexed' in a lightning campaign in August 1990. The ostensible cause for Saddam Hussein's invasion was a dispute between the two oil-producing nations concerning the price of oil. For the purposes of this book, the actual details of the war and the crisis which led to it are not vitally important. However, the following facts should be noted:

- The war was fought between a 13-nation coalition and Iraq.
- This coalition was nominally under the UN flag, but was in fact masterminded by the USA.
- The coalition included several Arab countries (including Egypt, Saudi Arabia and Syria).
- The coalition did not include Israel, but for obvious reasons Israel supported its activities.
- Several attempts at brokering a regional (that is, intra-Arab) peace with Iraq failed.
- The PLO and Jordan did not join the coalition (whose members criticized them for this).
- Iran also maintained its neutrality during the war.
- The war was sanctioned by UN Resolution 790 after Iraq failed to leave Kuwait.
- Air strikes were launched by the Allies from bases in Saudi Arabia until the end of the conflict.
- Using high technology weapons, the Allies 'softened up' Iraq for the final ground offensive.
- During the course of the war, Iraq fired Scud missiles at Israel and Saudi Arabia.
- Despite such provocations, Israel did not retaliate, nor attempt to join the coalition forces.
- Thus Saddam Hussein failed in his attempt to involve Israel and so shatter Arab unity.
- Likewise, Saddam's attempts to 'link' the Kuwaiti issue with Palestine also backfired.

On Feb. 28, 1991, US President George Bush suspended the final 100-hour stage of the war, a ground offensive codenamed Operation Hail Mary, pending a ceasefire agreement. All in all, the war claimed the lives of between 30,000 and 60,000 Iraqi soldiers and 22,000 civilians. Coalition casualties were miniscule by comparison. It achieved its prime aims: Saddam was forced to pull out of Kuwait and, in effect, admitted defeat. However, some criticized the US for not overthrowing Saddam Hussein and his government. Bush retorted that this was beyond the UN's remit. Instead, he called on Iraqi people to 'finish the job'.

In March and April, Kurds in the north and Shi'ites in the south launched simultaneous uprisings. After initial successes, however, both uprisings failed and following British proposals, the UN established 'safe havens' for the many thousands of Kurds who were forced to flee from retaliating Iraqi forces. Meanwhile, inspectors acting under the authority of UN Resolution 687 entered Iraq between May and July to ensure that Iraq had no nuclear and biological weapons. Furthermore, the UN imposed sanctions on Iraq to compensate for the damage done to Kuwait. With the notable exception of humanitarian supplies (essential foods and medicines) for Iraqi civilians, these sanctions still apply.

President Bush outlines his 'New World Order'

In his speech after the conclusion of the Gulf War, delivered on March 6, 1991, US President Bush developed his ideas of a 'New World Order', in which the USA would guard against future acts of aggression. In the Middle East context, the USA called for progress on three fronts: Increased democracy in the Middle East; arms reductions (as a means to limit the threat of future conflict); and a solution to the Israeli–Palestinian problem.

It soon became clear that it would take longer than anticipated to establish democratic systems in some countries, including Arab coalition partners (such as Syria, the Gulf States, and, not least, in Kuwait itself). Furthermore, lack of democracy did not appear to prevent those countries from enjoying the benefits of American largesse. Similarly, a huge $2.5 billion arms bazaar held at Al-Yamameh in Saudi Arabia after the war also illustrated quite graphically how unlikely a Middle East arms freeze was to be. Indeed, fear of future wars, and the impressive record of 'smart bombs' and the like in the Gulf War, only served to increase the demand for weapons.

Ultimately, the third strand of Bush's plan (namely, progress on the Israeli–Palestinian problem) was to bear the most fruit. Between March and October of 1991, US Secretary of State James Baker made eight tours of Middle East capitals. His purpose was primarily to persuade or cajole Arab and Israeli leaders to agree to attend an international peace conference. On March 12 he met ten leading Palestinians from the territories – the first such meeting between a Palestinian delegation and a US Secretary of State.

In April Baker secured Israeli agreement to the holding of a regional conference. However, Israel's Prime Minister Yitzhak Shamir in turn set nine conditions for talks, which the USA apparently accepted. These included an Israeli right to 'vet' the Palestinian delegation; rejection of a Palestinian state as a goal of the talks; and a demand that the USSR should re-establish diplomatic relations with Israel (which it had severed in 1967). Nonetheless, Shamir was prepared to accept negotiations towards Palestinian self-government in the West Bank and Gaza. Yasser Arafat, meanwhile, favoured an international conference instead of a regional one, fearing that the latter would ignore the Palestinian question.

In May President Bush condemned Israeli settlements in the occupied territories as 'an impediment to peace' (a point reiterated by Baker when he visited Israel). These statements began to convince previously sceptical Arab states that the US was sincere about peace, and was even prepared to pressurize its long-time ally, Israel, into considering a profound change in policy.

Nonetheless, the war had also cast up a host of new factors, some of which favoured peace, while others appeared to counter it. Amongst these were: the PLO's decrease in prestige after Arafat had appeared to 'appease' Saddam Hussein; the expulsion (or departure) of hundreds of thousands of Palestinians from post-war Kuwait; anger in 'the Arab street' at Arab governments' perceived dependence on US protection; Israeli anger at the jubilation shown by some Palestinians when Scuds fell on Tel Aviv; and most ironically, Saddam Hussein's 'linkage' statement which had put Palestine back on the agenda.

Baker's powers of persuasion

If peace was to work, Jordanian participation was essential. But here, too, the USA faced a problem. In the lead-up to the Gulf War, King Hussein (usually considered to be among the most 'moderate' and pro-Western of Arab leaders) was suspected of courting Saddam Hussein. (Jordan argued that it was merely seeking a peaceful and regional Arab settlement, so as to avoid war.) This antagonized US opinion, as well as the conservative Arab Gulf States, without whose backing a peace conference was impossible. Post-war sanctions on Iraq damaged Jordan's economy, which had traditionally benefited from trade passing through the Gulf of Aqaba and on to Baghdad. Furthermore, many of the Palestinians expelled from Kuwait and neighbouring countries returned in droves to Jordan, thus placing another huge strain on its already fragile economy.

Baker's challenge, then, was to re-establish relations with Jordan, and win the approval of the PLO for talks, without offending Saudi Arabia and Kuwait. The USA found it could wield some economic leverage, by hinting that it might increase aid to Jordan, and also forgive (or at least reduce) earlier debts. Significantly, a Jordanian think-tank headed by Crown Prince Hassan warned against the policy of despair amongst Arabs, and in some small measure began restoring relations between Jordan, the USA and other Arab states.

With regard to Israel, Yitzhak Shamir was proving to be intransigent. Some observers ascribed this defiance to a realization that Israel was no longer the USA's only ally in the

Middle East. A crisis blew up over a US loan guarantee to Israel of $10 billion, which had been earmarked to help the Jewish state absorb 500,000 new immigrants from the Soviet Union. When Shamir insisted on expanding new settlements, Bush threatened to veto Congress if it accepted Israel's application for the loan. Luckily, last minute compromises managed to avert the crisis, but ill-feelings lingered on.

No peace deal would 'hold' unless Syria was involved. But US public opinion found it hard to accept Syria as a genuine ally of the West after so many years when it had been depicted as a 'terrorist state' (to borrow former President Reagan's terminology). As a result, the State Department had to wage an internal public relations offensive, while at the same time encouraging Arab states to participate. For its part, Syria was unwilling to deal openly with Israel in any forum. Only when Baker persuaded President Assad that Syria might find itself 'left out', did Syria join the process. As an indication of Arab wariness, Libya's leader, Muammar Ghaddafi, won support when he argued strongly against any deal with the 'Zionist enemy' at a Maghrebi (North African) Arab states summit, held on Sept. 15.

Inasmuch as the PLO was still officially seen as a the 'sole representative of the Palestinian people', it realized it had much to gain from a peace conference. However, Arafat's strategy during the Gulf War, his consequent loss of funds from oil-rich Arab states, and the exacerbated divisions within the PLO, all served to undermine his bargaining position. As a result, when the Madrid conference eventually convened, the PLO had to accept (albeit reluctantly) a lower profile. To accommodate Shamir's objections, the PLO was not officially represented. Instead, Jordan agreed to preside over a joint Jordanian-Palestinian 'umbrella' delegation. (Although as the conference got underway, it soon became obvious that not only were Palestinians able to speak for themselves, but the PLO could pass on commands to the official 'non-PLO' delegates from outside.)

Superpower co-operation

Throughout the run-up to Madrid, Baker skilfully avoided matters of substance and concentrated on procedural issues. Arab leaders generally would have preferred a UN initiative, but accepted American steerage as a *fait accompli*. To make its initiative more acceptable, the US co-ordinated with Western allies (notably Britain and France), and, most importantly, with the Soviet Union. Indeed, the real breakthrough came after a US–Soviet summit in Moscow. On July 31, Presidents Bush and Gorbachev issued a joint communiqué announcing that a Middle East conference would be held in October 'to promote peace and genuine reconciliation among the Arab states, Israel and the Palestinians'.

In August 1991, however, a coup in the Soviet Union threatened to undermine all Baker's best-laid plans. Fortunately for the USA, President Gorbachev was restored to power – although by the time the Madrid conference convened, the former Soviet Union had crumbled. Even so, Russia (the leading state within the newly established Confederation of Independent States) was the official co-sponsor. On his seventh tour (in September) Baker issued 'letters of assurance' to each of the potential negotiating groups. Later that month the Palestine National Council voted by 256 to 68 (with 12 abstentions) to mandate the PLO Executive Committee to 'negotiate the terms of Palestinian participation at the peace conference'.

Russia's new foreign minister, Boris Pankin, soon struck up a rapport with Baker. On Oct. 18 the two met in Israel to conclude preparatory negotiations. In the event, it was Pankin who managed to persuade a still recalcitrant Shamir to agree to a conference, by threatening not to restore relations with Israel unless Israel attended. That same day relations between the two states were officially resumed.

Pankin and Baker then issued invitiations on behalf of their presidents, and the long promised Middle East peace conference opened on Oct. 30 in Madrid. (The choice of the Spanish capital as a venue proved to be an inspired one. Spain was perceived to be politically neutral; as a kingdom it provided the right measure of regality for what both superpowers described as a 'historic opportunity for peace'; and, as some observers noted, it conjured up memories of the 'golden age' of Moorish Spain, a period of unparallelled co-operation and creativity between Jews and Muslims in the Middle Ages.)

The format for the conference was broadly as follows:

- After opening statements by the co-sponsors, each delegation would put its case.
- Following two day-long plenary session, delegates would reconvene in Moscow for multilateral talks (see Chapter 11).
- Bilateral talks would commence in Washington DC.
- The USA favoured an interim solution of a five-year transition period.
- As a concession to Israel, a Palestinian delegation would come under a Jordanian 'umbrella'.

DELEGATIONS AT MADRID

Israeli delegation

Yitzhak Shamir (b. 1915)	Prime Minister and delegation head
As'ad As'ad (b. 1944)	Prime Minister's adviser on Druze affairs
Yossi Ben-Aharon (b. 1932)	Head of the Prime Minister's office
Shlomo Ben-Ami (b. 1943)	Ambassador to Spain
Eliahu Ben-Elissar (b. 1942)	MK and head of Knesset foreign affairs and defence committee
Eitan Ben-Tsur (b. 1948)	Deputy Director-General, Foreign Ministry (a 1973 Geneva delegate)
Sarah Doron (b. 1922)	MK and head of *Likud* faction in Knesset
Yosef Hadas (b. 1928)	Acting director-general, Foreign Ministry
Uzi Landau (b. 1943)	*Likud* MK
Salai Meridor (b. 1955)	Adviser to Defence Minister Moshe Arens
Yekutiel Mor (b. 1946)	Brigadier-general and head of analysis at military intelligence
Benjamin Netanyahu (b. 1950)	Deputy Foreign Minister and interface with media in Madrid
Elyakim Rubinstein (b. 1947)	Cabinet Secretary, delegate to Egyptian talks, 1978–79
Zalman Shoval (b. 1930)	Ambassador to USA

Jordanian delegation

Kamal Abu Jabber (b. 1932)	Foreign Minister of Jordan; head of the umbrella 'joint delegation' with Palestinians
Abd al-Salam Majali (b. 1925)	Head of Jordanian national delegation; former foreign minister
Muhammad 'Adwan	Ambassador to Moscow
Fu'ad Ayyad (b. 1944)	Ambassador to UK, ex-secretary to King Hussein
'Adnan Bakhit (b. 1941)	Vice-president of Jordan University, history professor
Muhammad Bani-Hani	Head of Jordan Water Authority
Mussa Breizat	Palace official
Talal Hassan	Ambassador to Belgium
Ghassan Jundi	Lecturer in international law
'Awad Khalidi	General and Ambassador to France
Walid Khalidi	Professor in international law at Harvard University
'Awa Khasawna	Expert in international law
Abd al-Hafez Mar'i	General, deputy chief of staff, head of military intelligence
Marwan Muashsher (b. 1954)	Head of Jordan's information office in Washington, adviser

Palestinian delegation

Haidar Abd al-Shafi (b. 1919)	Head of delegation, doctor
Samir Abdullah (b. 1950)	Chair of economic department, an-Najah University

Freih Abu Medein (b. 1944)	Lawyer
Zakaria al-Agha (b. 1942)	Chair, Gaza Medical Society; diplomat
Mahmoud al-Aker (b. 1943)	Urologist
Sa'eb Erekat (b. 1955)	Associate professor in political science, an-Najah University
Elias Freij (b. 1920)	Mayor of Bethlehem since 1972
'Abd al-Rahman Hammad (b. 1946)	Head, Palestine Academic Society
Nabil Ja'abari	Dentist, chair of Hebron University board of trustees
Samah Kan'an (b. 1954)	Nablus Chamber of Commerce employee; ex-political prisoner
Ghassan al-Khatib (b. 1954)	Head, Jerusalem Media and Communications Centre
Sami Kilani (b. 1952)	Writer, poet and physics lecturer
Mustafa al-Natsheh (b. 1930)	Former acting mayor of Hebron until deposed by Israel
Nabil Qassis (b. 1947)	Physicist, vice-president of Bir Zeit University

Palestinian advisory committee

Faisal Husseini	Effective head of committee
Radwan Abu Ayyash (b. 1950)	Journalist and veteran of contacts with Israelis and US officials
Ziyyad Abu Zayyad (b. 1940)	Journalist and lawyer
Hanan Ashrawi	Literature lecturer, *intifada* activist
Radi Jara'i (b. 1941)	Journalist, ex-political prisoner
Zuheira Kamal (b. 1945)	Head of Palestinian womens' organizations, allied to DFLP
Rashid Khalidi (b. 1948)	Professor at University of Chicago
Kamal Mansur	
Sari Nusseibeh (b. 1946)	Philosopher, lecturer
Anis Qassem (b. 1925)	Jurist, adviser to Libyan Ministry of Justice in 1959
Jamil Tarifi (b. 1947)	Ramallah businessman

Egyptian delegation

Moussa 'Amr	Foreign Minister and head of delegation
Ahmad Abu al-Gheit	Head of the Foreign Ministry
Mahmud Abu Nasr	Former deputy foreign minister, ex-ambassador to Spain
Salah 'Amer	Professor of international law, Cairo University
'Ala Barakat	Ambassador to Spain, former Air Force chief of staff
Nabil Fahmi	Diplomat and son of former foreign minister, Ismail Fahmi
Ahmed Fakhr	Retired major-general, foreign adviser to PM, heads independent think tank
Wagih Hamdi	Diplomat and director of Foreign Ministry's Arab department
Qadri Hifni	Pyschology professor, 'Ain Shams University
Lotfi al-Kholi	Leftist writer for *Al-Ahram* newspaper
Yunan Labib Rizki	Modern history professor, 'Ain Shams University; negotiator at Taba
Ramzi al-Sha'er	President, Zagazig University; expert in international law
Rida Shihata	Director of Foreign Ministry's department for international organizations

Syrian delegation

Faruk Shar'a	Foreign Minister and head of delegation
Muwaffaq al-'Allaf	Former ambassador to UN offices in Geneva

Ahmad 'Arnawas	Diplomat
Zuheir 'Aqqad	Ambassador to Spain
Dia'ullah Fattal	Ambassador to UN
Sabr Falhut	Chairman of Syrian Journalists' Association
Nasrat'ullah Haidar (b. 1931)	Legal adviser
Zakariya Isma'il (b. 1924)	Former ambassador to Czechoslovakia
Majdi Jazzar (b. 1936)	Director of Foreign Ministry's department for international organizations
Muhammad Khadr	Ambassador to UK
Ahmad Fathi al-Masri	Foreign Ministry diplomat
Walid al-Mu'allem	Ambassador to USA
Elias Rizqallah	History professor, University of Damascus
'Adnan Tayara	General

Lebanese delegation

Fares Buweiz	Foreign Minister and head of delegation
Naji Abu 'Assi	Ambassador to Senegal
Yusuf Arsnius	
Isabelle Edde'	
'Abbas Hamiyah	Ambassador to Spain
Mahmud Hamud	Ambassador to UK
Zafer Hassan	Secretary-General, Foreign Ministry
Antoine Kheir	Expert in international law
Shafiq Mahren	
Ja'far Mu'awiya	Deputy head of economics, Foreign Ministry
Samir Mubarak	Foreign Ministry official
Jihad Mustada	Foreign Ministry official
Ghassan Salama	Expert in international law
Maher Tufaili	

Jordan agreed to provide an 'umbrella' for the Palestinian delegation, in order to meet Israeli requirements. In practice, however, the two sub-delegations negotiated independently.

In addition to the official Palestinian delegation, there was also an advisory committee. Many of its members were barred from the official delegation because they came from East Jerusalem, or had strong connections to the PLO (Yitzhak Shamir and his Israeli delegation objected to dealing directly with such people). In the event, not all of those listed as committee members actually chose to join it. In time, however, this 'unofficial' delegation grew into a steering committee which to a large extent directed the official delegation with orders relayed from PLO headquarters in Tunis. By 1992 Faisal Husseini was acknowledged as its leader, and Hanan Ashrawi as its spokesperson.

Only the Israeli delegation was headed by a prime minister (Yitzhak Shamir). All other national delegations were headed by foreign ministers. The Palestinians were represented by Dr Haidar Abd al-Shafi, a respected doctor from Gaza and founding member of the PNC in 1964. However, none of the official delegation was an actual member of the PLO.

As the negotiations progressed, different personalities within the teams assumed responsibilities for leading in the negotiations. Amongst the Israelis, Uri Lubrani and Yossi Hadas dealt with Lebanon; Elyakim Rubinstein headed talks with the Jordanian-Palestinian delegation; and Yossi Ben Aharon led talks with Syria. Muwaffaq al-Allaf became the operative head of the Syrian delegation, and Souhail Shammas headed the Lebanese delegation. At the 10th round, Fayez Tarawneh, Jordan's ambassador to the USA, replaced Abdul Salam al-Majali as head of his nation's delegation (Majali left the post on becoming Prime Minister of Jordan.)

TIMETABLE OF BILATERAL TALKS AFTER MADRID

[For information on the multilateral talks, see Chapter 11]

Round 1	Nov. 3, 1991	Madrid, Spain (Plenary Session)
Round 2	Dec. 10–18, 1991	Washington, DC, USA
Round 3	Jan. 7–16,1992	Washington, DC, USA
Round 4	Feb. 24 – March 4, 1992	Washington, DC, USA
Round 5	April 27–30, 1992	Washington, DC, USA
Round 6		
Session I	August 24 – Sept. 3, 1992	Washington DC, USA
Session II	Sept. 14–24, 1992	Washington, DC, USA
Round 7		
Session I	Oct. 21–29, 1992	Washington, DC, USA
Session II	Nov. 9–19, 1992	Washington, DC, USA
Round 8	Dec. 7–17, 1992	
Round 9	April 27 – May 13, 1993	
Round 10	June 15 – July 1, 1993	

SUCCESS AND FAILURE ON THE 'MADRID TRACK'

What was new about Madrid?

The Madrid peace track certainly bears the hallmark of earlier peace proposals (see previous chapter).

• The idea of trading land for peace	UN 242 and Camp David peace accord
• The suggestion of limited withdrawal	Allon Plan of 1967
• The idea of dividing historic Palestine	Partition Plans (UK in 1938 and UN in 1947)
• Demilitarized zones	After 1973 war; and in southern Lebanon

However, Madrid also had some new elements, which arguably forced the process onto a new quantum level, and would lead to something irreversable:

• Confidence-building measures	Building trust through constructive acts of good faith
• Two track negotiations	Simultaneous multilateral and bilateral talks
• Direct talks between Israel and the Palestinians	Avoiding need for intercession

Plenary session statements

The first day consisted of opening statements by the host, Spanish Prime Minister Felipe González, US President George Bush, USSR President Mikhail Gorbachev, Dutch Foreign Minister Hans van den Broek (speaking on behalf of the EC), and Egyptian Foreign Minister Amr Moussa. On the second day the parties to the conflict spoke. Each in turn referred to earlier peace plans, and stated what their peoples wished for. Shamir wanted 'peace for peace' (mutual recognition as a prerequisite to further talks) and spoke of the Jewish people's desire to live in harmony with the Arab world.

The Palestinians' Haidar al-Shafi demanded an end to settlements, but an acceptance of interim plans. His speech (largely scripted by Hanan Ashrawi) was noted for its moving depiction of the course of Palestinian history. Other speakers included Fares Boueiz (Lebanon), Farouk al-Shara (Syria) and Kamal Abu Jaber (Jordan). On day three the parties exercised the right to reply, and harsh words were exchanged. James Baker insisted that 'Land, peace and security are inseparable elements in the search for a comprehensive peace', and that each party should listen to the others.

Rounds one, two and three

The opening talks (first round) were held in Madrid in November 1991; the second round was held in Washington in December. They soon became deadlocked over procedural issues. Palestinians demanded to negotiate as a separate body, to which Jordan concurred. When

Israel refused to accept this, Jordanian and Palestinian negotiators remained literally in the corridors, talking to US officials. Back in Israel, the government authorized new settlements and resolved that the Golan was not negotiable. Arafat in turn sent out his own mixed messages – calling for political committees to 'support' the negotiators on the one hand, and backing the *intifada* on the other.

In the third round talks, held in January 1992, the Palestinians presented their first concrete proposal – a 180-strong elected Palestine Interim Self-Government Authority (PISGA), with a 20-member executive council and judiciary. In five years this would lead to sovereign independence. But Israel stuck to the old Camp David formulation of Begin's, namely, autonomy of persons, not territory. (Even so, the perception of Israel accepting even limited Palestinian autonomy was bad enough for two right-wing parties in the *Likud*-led coalition, *Moledet* and *Tehiya*; they promptly left the government, thus depriving Shamir of a workable majority.)

Rounds four, five and six

The long-delayed fourth round opened with an Israeli counter-proposal to the Palestinians – an interim arrangement delegating authority over 13 areas to Palestinian Executive. Israel would continue to control security, and would continue developing settlements. The Palestinians responded with PISGA in three stages; but the USA accused them of being 'unrealistic', and stalemate ensued. The fifth round, held in April, witnessed more deadlock, as Israel proposed municipal elections, while Palestinians insisted on legislative elections. Talks with Jordan proved more fruitful. In May 1992, the Palestinian Central Council (PCC, or acting PLO legislature) told the Palestinian delegation to demand that settlements should be halted, before anything else.

On 23 June, Labour won the elections in Israel, which changed the political climate markedly. (In a post-election interview, the outgoing Premier Shamir admitted that he had intended to drag out the talks for as long as possible, and had no wish to grant Palestinians real autonomy.) After Israel's new Prime Minister Rabin promised to freeze 'political settlements', the USA unblocked the $10bn loan guarantee. Bush and Mubarak called on Rabin to make a deal with Syria. After a series of confidence-building measures, such as acknowledging Faisal Husseini's status as an East Jerusalemite, Rabin spoke of a Palestine Administrative Council and a greater role for Husseini's adjoint committee. He stopped short, however, of endorsing his *Meretz* colleagues' appeal for open talks with the PLO.

Prior to the sixth round, Rabin released 800 Palestinian prisoners and allowed Palestinians aged over 50 to enter Israel without authorization. In August he replaced the hardline negotiator with Syria, Yossi Ben Aharon, with the more amenable academic, Itamar Rabinovich. Consequently, in September Syria offered the possibility of a 'full peace treaty' with Israel for the first time, in exchange for the Golan Heights. Jordan too hailed the round as a 'new beginning'. But the Lebanese delegation was upset that Israel refused to leave their 850km southern security zone; and Palestinians were disillusioned with the limited size of the assembly proposed by Israel (15 members).

Rounds seven, eight, nine and ten

The seventh round hardly progressed, and the PCC called for a greater European Community role in the talks, and a high priority to the question of Jerusalem. While Jordan and Israel set out a proper working agenda – on security, water, territory, refugees – there was stalemate in the other talks. The pending US presidential elections also distracted attention from the Madrid peace process.

By the eighth round the Palestinian delegation had been whittled down to five members, as they felt increasingly disgruntled with the lack of progress. All talks ceased after the announcement of Israel's deportation of 413 fundamentalists to Lebanon in December. The UN passed Resolution 799 to demand an Israeli climb-down, but Israel rejected the resultant UN report, and the Israeli Supreme Court broadly upheld Rabin's policy. In February 1993 the new US Secretary of State, Warren Christopher, toured the Middle East. But the atmosphere was tense. In March, Palestinians relaunched the *intifada* in frustration at what they saw as broken promises at Madrid, and a false dawn with Labour's victory. In response, Israel sealed off the West Bank and Gaza Strip.

A flurry of diplomatic activity followed Christopher's visit, including a meeting between him and Husseini in Washington. On April 8, Israel accepted Husseini moving from the steering committee to head the main delegation (under *Likud*, his PLO ties and Jerusalemite status had blocked such participation). Meanwhile, Egyptian President Mubarak acted as a go-between for Rabin and Arafat. Rabin admitted that the deportations had been 'an exceptional measure'. Arab foreign ministers convened in Damascus, and, with some more finessing from Christopher, they managed to relaunch the talks in late April. Even so, the resultant ninth round did not move very far, as the Palestinian delegation failed to satisfy demands from *intifada* activists in the territories, and from PLO headquarters in Tunis.

The tenth round also ended in deadlock. Israel and the Palestinians failed to agree on a 'declaration of principles', and the issue of Jerusalem became a key obstacle to further progress. There was similar deadlock regarding talks between Israel and Syria, and Israel and Jordan. Halfway through the session, the US State Department expressed its dissatisfaction with the talks' failure. On June 28, Dennis Ross, an advisor to Warren Christopher, became a 'special co-ordinator' for the peace talks.

[*For more on talks between Israel, Syria and Lebanon beyond this point, see Chapter* 12.]

The Oslo channel

Israel realized that the official PLO delegation in Washington was taking orders from Tunis, but it maintained the fiction that the PLO was not involved. However, as the Madrid track was clearly not yielding dividends, both PLO and Israeli officials began thinking about opening direct talks. *Likud* was adamantly opposed to any overt role for the PLO, and indeed, talks between Israeli citizens and the PLO were still banned by Israeli law. With the election of a new Labour Party government in Israel in June 1992, momentum grew for secret preliminary talks with the banned organization.

Yitzhak Rabin, the new prime minister, was more clearly committed to making peace with Palestinians and had campaigned partly on a 'peace ticket'. (However, analysts suggest that national anger at *Likud*'s in-fighting and its poor economic record, plus an unexpectedly large 'protest vote' from new Soviet immigrants, contributed at least as much to Labour's victory.) On taking office, Rabin promised Palestinian autonomy within a year, a stance welcomed by the left-wing *Meretz* coalition, which formed part of his government. But this did not materialize. Instead, Rabin continued with the Madrid formula, changing the negotiating team only slightly. Israel was still officially committed to reaching an agreement only with 'internal' Palestinians. Despite a range of 'confidence-measures', Rabin's call to freeze 'political settlements' failed to assuage Palestinians hoping for a change.

Following a spate of Palestinian terror incidents in December, the Rabin government deported 413 suspected members of *Hamas* and Islamic *Jihad*. The net effect was to enrage international opinion, embarrass the United States, divide the Israeli left and re-unite most wings of Palestinian opinion against the Labour government. The first signs of a change came when the Knesset voted (by 39 votes to 20) to rescind the ban on talks with the PLO, on Jan. 19, 1993. But the government needed to come up with something tangible and obviously beneficial to Israel – something which could negate the antipathetic psychology engendered by years of conflict. Until that stage was reached, talks could only be held in secret.

Failed initiatives

Labour endorsed a number of clandestine initiatives, but ultimately only one paid off. As Abu Mazen wrote in his book, *Through Secret Channels*, the PLO had over the years furtively approached both Labour and Likud politicians. Often intermediate groups (like Peace Now, or the *Sephardi* group, Orient for Peace) were used to facilitate meetings. Two *Likud* MKs had been censured for secret talks with PLO officials. In the new post-Madrid phase, there were other channels, involving Israeli minister Yossi Sarid and the PLO's Nabil Sha'ath, Haim

Ramon and Ahmed Tibi (an Israeli Arab with close connections to Arafat), and others, including Hanan Ashrawi and Bassam Abu Sharif. An Egyptian 'intermediary channel' was opened too, involving Foreign Minister Amr Moussa and adviser Osama al-Baz, which in time would prove particularly significant.

The Oslo connection

In the end, it was a confluence of events and personalities which led to the success of the Oslo channel. The key go-between was Terje Larsen, a social scientist who had set up the Norwegian FAFO research institute in 1981, and was currently conducting a survey of living conditions in Gaza. His wife, Mona Juul, was a diplomat in the Norwegian Foreign Office. This afforded Larsen an entree to Jan Egeland, deputy foreign minister, and Thorvald Stoltenberg, a former foreign minister. Both men took a keen interest in the Middle East, and indeed had been approached separately by the PLO and Israel as possible intermediatories. In 1989, the Larsens met Fathi Arafat (Yasser Arafat's brother and head of the Palestinian Red Crescent Society), and this later proved to be an invaluable link to the PLO leader. Larsen was a member of the Norwegian delegation at the multilateral talks, so he had first-hand experience of the realities of Middle Eastern negotiations. In May 1992, Larsen met Yossi Beilin, a rising Labour MK who was close to Shimon Peres.

Together, the Norwegian researcher and Israeli opposition politician began a 'secret track' to open the way for direct talks between Israel and the PLO. Working under the guise of his social research unit in Gaza, Larsen acted as middle-man between his PLO contacts (notably Abu Mazen, an Arafat adviser on Israeli affairs, and Abu 'Ala, a senior manager of PLO finances) and two Israeli academics. While other secret channels were blown by leaks, Larsen succeeded in keeping his quiet and won the backing of the Norwegian government. When Labour took power in 1992, and Beilin became deputy foreign minister, the negotiations gained a fresh impetus. In December Abu 'Ala and the PLO representative in Britain, Afif Safieh, met in London with the Israeli academics, Yair Hirschfeld and Ron Pundak. Both men were friends of Yossi Beilin. Abu 'Ala reported back to Abu Mazen (Mahmoud Abbas), who was responsible for PLO contacts with Israel, and the latter approved.

First stage – testing the waters

In January 1993 official talks officially began, in Sarpsborg outside Olso. The initial participants were, for Israel, Hirschfeld and Pundak; for the PLO, Abu 'Ala (Ahmed Qurei), Hassan Asfour and Maher al-Kurd, an economist. When Johan Joergen Holst became the new Norwegian foreign minister in April, he steered the ministry into taking a more direct role (in the person of Geir Pedersen). Arafat, Peres and then Rabin were all informed, and gradually passed their wishes on to their representatives as talks moved from exploratory conversations to serious negotiations. The US State Department (notably Dennis Ross and Dan Kurtzer) was informed at the beginning, but not directly involved until the final stages. King Hussein was conspicuously not involved, which was to cause something of a rift in the normally cordial (albeit unofficial) relations between Israel and the Hashemite Kingdom.

Learning from the mistakes at Madrid, the negotiators agreed to produce a 'declaration of principles' for the future, and not dwell on past recriminations. As an opening gambit, Abu 'Ala proposed that Israel withdraw from the Gaza Strip, to make way for an interim Palestinian administration. It was an astute move, as many Israelis, not least Rabin himself, had lately been suggesting jettisoning the troubled Gaza Strip. From the Israeli perspective, a Gaza option had several advantages. These included: far fewer Jewish settlers compared to the West Bank (5,000 versus 130,000 or so); unlike the West Bank, it was not a central part of *Eretz Yisrael*; and arguments to hold on to the territory for security would not hold water, as Gaza's only borders to the south are with Egypt, a friendly state since the peace treaty of 1979.

However, 'Gaza Only' would not be enough to satisfy Palestinian aspirations. There had to be some sign of power for Palestinians in the West Bank. Yasser Arafat then suggested Jericho, and Abu 'Ala duly raised this at Oslo. By March the teams agreed on 'Gaza first', stage-by-stage withdrawals, and economic co-operation.

Second stage – concrete proposals

As the talks progressed, and obstacles were ironed out, Israeli diplomatic officials and in time high-ranking politicians joined the process. The entry of Uri Savir in round six (May 15), and Joel Singer in round seven (June 11), raised the stakes. Savir was the director of the Israeli Foreign Ministry, and answerable directly to Peres, so his presence convinced Palestinian negotiators that Israel was serious about the talks. Singer, a legal expert and friend of Yitzhak Rabin, reinforced this impression – even though his tough negotiating stance at times threatened to put the talks in jeopardy. Abu Mazen (Mahmoud Abbas) and Mohammed Abu Koush, a lawyer, joined the Palestinian side. Deadlock was broken when the PLO team agreed to defer the issue of Jerusalem to a 'final stage solution'. (By now, Israel had accepted the principle of 'Jericho too'.)

On June 23 Arafat's aide, Bassam Abu Sharif, sent Peres a letter affirming Tunis's commitment to the talks. By July, Israeli concerns about security and Palestinian concerns about refugees threatened to end the progress. However, Holst's personal intervention helped overcome these obstacles in a conference phone session with Arafat and another aide, Yasser Abed Rabbo. Both sides made important concessions – the PLO accepting Israeli settlements and Israeli security control, and Israel accepting a timetable for Palestinian autonomy and transferance of five areas of administration to the PLO. Israel also softened its stance on demanding that the PLO disown the *intifada*, as this might make it lose face in the territories. In August, Shimon Peres personally entered the talks, and finalized the draft peace agreement.

Oslo goes public

On Aug. 19, 1993, Israel and the PLO agreed on a draft peace agreement, on interim self-rule for Palestinians in the occupied territories. The US State Department was informed on Aug. 27, and the announcement was made public on Aug. 30. The initial Arab reaction was mixed – relief from Arafat and most of the the PLO executive, but anger from the rejectionist PLO and *Hamas*. As for the official Palestinian delegation at Madrid, they were peeved by being excluded from the talks, and especially for having (in effect) wasted their time while the real talks were going on elsewhere. Norway was glad to have played a historic role, something they continued after the official signing in Washington, via the Holst fund. Terje Larsen was later rewarded with a post as aid fund co-ordinator in Gaza. There was still a lot of last-minute bargaining before the September signing (see Chapter 9), involving Nabil Sha'ath, Hanan Ashrawi and Joel Singer.

All of this coincided with the 11th round in the Madrid talks, but, understandably, completely overshadowed them. Beyond all the euphoria, however, no-one was in any doubt that a historic *volte-face* on the part of Israel and the PLO had taken place – for the first time Israel sanctioned a PLO autonomous presence in the occupied territories.

[For details on further talks between Israel and the Palestinians, see Chapter 9.]

Chapter 9   Agreements between Israel and the Palestinians

A new phase of Israeli–Palestinian relations began on Sept. 13, 1993 with the signing in Washington, D.C. of the Declaration of Principles (DOP) between Israel and the PLO. Although technically this was an independent venture, it actually grew out of the Madrid peace process which began in October 1991. However, the talks between Israel and a Palestinian team became seriously bogged down throughout 1992 and 1993. The DOP marked a distinct change in approach by both sides – an Israeli willingness to speak directly to the PLO, and a willingness by the PLO to both recognize and strike a deal with Israel.

The DOP emerged from the secret negotiations in Oslo. (For details of the negotiating process, see Chapter 8 in this section. Details of the main negotiators can be found in Part 4, Biographies.) Together, the secret negotiations and the change in Israeli law set the stage for a dramatic and open signed deal between Israel and the PLO. This came about after PLO Chairman Yasser Arafat sent a letter to Israeli Prime Minister Yitzhak Rabin on Sept. 9, 1993, in which he stated that the PLO would recognize the right of Israel to exist in peace; accept UN Security Council Resolutions 242 and 338; commit the PLO to a peaceful resolution of the conflict and renounce the use of terrorism; ensure that all PLO factions would comply and 'discipline' any violaters. Furthermore, he promised to regard as 'invalid' articles in the PLO Covenant which deny Israel's right to exist and submit proposed changes in the Covenant to the Palestinian National Council.

In his reply Yitzhak Rabin recognized the PLO as the representative of the Palestinians in the peace negotiations. It was a stance which the Arab League had accepted since the Rabat conference of 1974, but one which had Israel shunned because of its profound mistrust of the PLO as an organization that still harboured terrorist and maximalist factions. In short, Yasser Arafat had met all the requirements which Israel had for so long demanded of the PLO.

Two other aspects of the DOP marked a breach with the past. For the first time Israelis and Palestinians agreed on a definite timetable for effecting changes; and both parties accepted the principle of immediate territorial authority for Palestinians. The territory in question was Gaza and the Jericho district.

The DOP (or so-called Oslo Accords, named after the secret preparatory talks in Norway which preceded the signing) envisaged a two stage process:

- Stage 1 Interim Self-Goverment Arrangements
- Stage 2 Permanent Status

The official timetable of the Washington agreement was as follows:

Oct. 13, 1993	Entry into force of Washington Accords
Dec. 13, 1993	Agreement on Israeli army withdrawal from Gaza and Jericho *Beginning of first phase of five-year transitional plan*
April 13, 1994	Completion of Israeli withdrawal *Beginning of second phase of transitional plan*
July 13, 1994	Deadline for elections to self-governing authority
Dec. 13, 1995	Start of final status negotiations
April 13, 1996	End of final status negotiations
Dec.13, 1998	Entry into force of permanent status in West Bank and Gaza *Beginning of third phase of transitional plan*
April 13, 1999	Final date for implementing permanent status

In practice, almost all the deadlines set above have had to be postponed, in some cases for up to a year. The true picture of major achievements in setting up Palestinian Interim Self-government is as follows:

- Declaration of Principles Signed: Sept. 13, 1994
- Donors' Conference Met: Oct. 1, 1993

- Paris Economic Protocol Agreement Signed: May 1, 1994
- Gaza-Jericho Agreement Signed: May 4, 1994
- Preparatory Transfer of Powers Signed: Aug. 29, 1994
- Interim Agreement (redeployment and elections) Signed: Sept. 28, 1995

Talks about the permanent status officially opened on 4, May 1996; the resultant Permanent Status Agreement will enter into force after the fifth year of self-government, namely May 1999. (Although considering that all other deadlines have been delayed, perhaps these should not be considered as absolute dates.) At the time of going to press all progress has concerned the Interim Self-Government stage. Following *Likud's* election victory some observers now doubt whether 'permanent' talks will proceed as planned.

A summary of the agreements

THE DECLARATION OF PRINCIPLES (DOP)

The DOP outlined the proposed interim five-year self-governing arrangements for the Palestinians, as agreed by both parties. This would be a three-phase process:

- Immediate Palestinian self-rule in Jericho and Gaza; followed by
- 'Early empowerment' for Palestinians in rest of the West Bank; and an
- Interim Agreement, preparing for the election of a Palestinian council.

[Note: the first two phases were accomplished in the Gaza-Jericho agreement in May 1994 and the Transfer of Powers in August 1994; talks on the third phase, for an interim agreement, were scheduled to conclude on July 1, 1995, but were twice delayed until September 1995.]

The DOP agreed to the principle of transferring power to Palestinians in the West Bank and Gaza. It does not prejudge the permanent status; talks about this are deferred until the third year of the interim stage. So at this stage it precludes discussion of such issues as Jerusalem, settlements, security arrangements and final borders.

The Israeli government retains sole responsibility for foreign affairs, defence and borders during the interim phase, and security remains an Israeli responsibility along international borders and at crossing points to Egypt and Jordan. Israel is also responsible for the security of Israelis in the West Bank and Gaza.

The DOP did, however, agree to an Israeli troop withdrawal from Gaza and Jericho (in phase one). More specifically, 'early empowerment' (in phase 2) concerned five areas: education and culture, health, social welfare, direct taxation and tourism. To facilitate the Interim Agreement elections (phase three), Israeli forces would be 'redeployed outside populated areas'. The Palestinian Council will guarantee public order with its own police force.

Ratification:

By United Nations

Dec. 14, 1993 UN General Assembly Resolution 48/58: The eight-point resolution, passed at the 79th plenary session of the General Assembly, expressed full support for the Israeli–Palestinian Declaration of Principles, and the Common Agenda between Israel and Jordan. It also backed the international donors' Conference to Support Middle East Peace (of Oct. 1, 1993); the establishment of a high-level UN task force to 'support the economic and social development of the Palestinian people'; and the continuance of multilateral track talks (under the auspices of UNSC Resolutions 242 and 338).

By Israel

The *Knesset* endorsed the DOP by 61 votes to 50 on Sept. 23, 1995. The *Likud* opposition voted against it, while eight MKs abstained (including five *Shas* MKs). During the stormy three-day debate which preceded the vote, *Shas* had called for a referendum on the issue, while *Likud* demanded a new general election.

By the Palestinians

Yasser Arafat won approval for the DOP deal from the *Fatah* Central Committee and the PLO Executive Committee (although some former allies, notably Faruq Qaddumi, Secretary-General of *Fatah* and PLO 'foreign minister', disassociated himself from the decision). More predictably, *Hamas* and the Damascus-based ten-party 'rejectionist front' (including the PFLP and DFLP) rejected the deal; but failed to agree on common strategy to oppose it. On Oct. 11 the PLO Central Council, meeting in Tunis, approved the peace agreement by 63 votes to eight, with nine abstentions. About a fifth of the Council's 107 members boycotted the meeting.

Other Arab reactions

Egypt had played a major role in facilitating the DOP deal, and not surprisingly endorsed it enthusiastically. So too did the GCC (Gulf Co-operation Council). **Jordan's** reaction was more equivocal; King Hussein expressed concern over the Kingdom's exclusion from the peace process, and the impact the deal may have on his own Palestinian citizens. These fears were partly assuaged by the 'Common Agenda' which Israel soon signed with Jordan (see Chapter 10). **Syria** denounced the principle of Arab parties reaching 'separate and incomplete deals with Israel'. After meeting Arafat, President Assad stated that the 'the PLO has lost, as have the Arabs'; but he stopped short of opposing the deal outright.

During September, the government of **Lebanon**, President Rafsanjani of **Iran**, and Col. Ghaddafi of **Libya** all rejected the deal. However, there was a better reception in **Morocco**, where Shimon Peres visited King Hassan II on Sept. 14; and **Tunisia**, which hosted the first official Israeli delegation on Sept. 21. The DOP received firm support from the USA, Russia, China, India and the European Commission.

New negotiating mechanisms

The signing of the DOP led to an intense period of negotiations on all fronts. While the main bilateral talks continued in Washington, DC, involving Arafat and Rabin, a Liaison Committee met for the first time in Cairo on Oct. 13 to implement the DOP and deal with questions raised by other committees (as stipulated by DOP Article X). Israeli Foreign Minister Shimon Peres headed his nation's delegation. His Palestinian counterpart was Abu Mazen (Mahmoud Abbas), one of the key Oslo negotiators.

Another body, the Co-ordinating Committee, (also known as the Technical Committee) was mandated to deal with the practical problems involved with finalizing the full Gaza-Jericho agreement. It too met on Oct. 13, and held regular sessions at Taba (an Egyptian Sinai port), Cairo and El-Arish. Deputy Chief of Staff Maj.-Gen. Amnon Shahak headed the Israeli delegation, while Nabil Sha'ath headed the Palestinian delegation. Economic matters (DOP Article XI) were the concern of an Economic Co-operation Committee which met in Paris. Finally, an Israel–PLO–Jordan–Egypt Continuing Committee discussed the admission of Palestinians displaced from the West Bank and Gaza in 1967 and related issues (DOP Article XII).

DONORS' CONFERENCE

Washington hosted an aid donors conference of 47 governments and organizations on Oct. 1, 1993. Its aim was to finance the five-year interim period of Palestinian self-rule. The USA pledged $600m (mostly in the form of grants) for 1994; the EC agreed to provide $577m through the EC Commission and European Investment Bank. Japan promised $200m (for 1994–95), Saudi Arabia $100m (for 1994) and Scandinavian countries $150m (over an unspecified period). In addition, Israel offered $75m in grants and credits; the World Bank pledged $50m in a concessionary credit and $35m in a Trust Fund loan. The UN Development Programme proposed projects worth $250m for 1994.

While US Secretary of State Warren Christopher hailed the conference as a 'striking success', Yasser Arafat warned that the Palestinians needed at least $5 billion in aid to make a success of their new autonomy. As it turned out, there were to be numerous clashes between the Palestinian Authority and the donor countries in the following months and years, with the former alleging 'broken promises', and the latter complaining of inefficiency and a 'lack of financial transparency' on the part of the self-governing authority.

Nonetheless, the Washington conference did at least set in motion the framework for a colossal aid engine to support Palestinians. It also created the impetus for a PLO–Jordan economic co-operation pact to create a joint free-trade regime; and plans for a joint invest-ment company in the West Bank and Gaza Strip, agreed between Israel's giant Koor Industries and Palestinian investors led by Jawid Ghussein, head of the Palestinian National Fund (both agreements were concluded in October). Most importantly, the conference saw the creation of two new structures to oversee the flow of money to worthy aid projects: an ad hoc liaison committee, consisting of the USA, Canada, the EC, Japan, Russia, Norway and Saudi Arabia (with Israel, the PLO, Egypt and Jordan enjoying 'associate membership'); and a corresponding Palestinian body to administer the aid, the Palestine Economic Co-operation Development and Reconstruction Authority (PECDAR).

PARIS PROTOCOL ON ECONOMIC RELATIONS

Although somewhat overshadowed by talks about the Gaza-Jericho Agreement, the joint Israeli–Palestinian Economic Co-operation Committee made significant progress in Paris towards defining the future economic relationship between Israel and a self-governing Pales-tinian authority. Finance Minister Avraham Shochat headed the Israeli delegation; his Palestinian counterpart was Ahmed Qurei (Abu 'Ala), the PLO's expert on economics and a veteran of the Oslo talks.

The economic talks got off to a shaky start, when in November 1993 Qurei revealed that the PLO was virtually bankrupt, and that international donors had not met their obligations. (In fact the PLO, once said to be the wealthiest liberation movement in the world, had suffered financially when Gulf States cut off their funding in protest at Arafat's stance during the Gulf crisis of 1990–91). However, after Qurei gained greater powers as executive director of PECDAR (which was set up to handle aid donations), this had a positive knock-on effect in Paris. Likewise, in 1994 Israeli Foreign Minister Shimon Peres entered the talks, and thus played a key role in lending weight to them.

Two large bones of contention troubled negotiators until the final accord. Firstly, Palestin-ians wanted their own central bank to direct monetary policy, which Israel opposed. Secondly, Israel wanted a full customs union with the Palestinians, while the latter preferred an independent customs authority. In the end they reached a compromise. On April 29, 1994, the two parties signed the Paris Economic Relations Pact, also known as the Protocol on Economic Relations. Its main points are:

Import policy

Israel and the Palestinian Authority (PA) [also called Palestine National Authority, PNA] will have a similar policy regarding imports and customs. Additionally, the PA will be able to import mutually agreed goods at customs rates different from those in Israel and can import goods from Arab countries in agreed limited quantities. The protocol arranged for the two customs authorities to jointly operate the border crossing in Jericho and Gaza.

Monetary policy

A PA monetary authority will regulate and supervise the banks operating in the area. It will also determine (within limits) the liquidity ratios on deposits; management of foreign exchange reserves; and the supervision of foreign exchange transactions. Until the issue of a Palestinian currency is resolved, the NIS (Israeli currency) will remain legal tender in the PA area, alongside other currencies. To encourage trade, Israel and the PA will allow the mutual opening of bank branches.

Taxation

The Palestinian Tax Administration will conduct its own direct tax policy, including income tax on individuals and corporations, property taxes, municipal rates and fees, according to the policy and the rates determined by the PA. The two parties will collect income taxes on economic activities conducted in their respective areas. Israel will transfer to the PA 75% of revenues from income tax collected from Palestinians employed in Israel. Regarding **indirect** taxation, the PA will operate a similar VAT system to that used in Israel, at rates of between 15% and 16%.

Labour

The Protocol acknowledged that many Palestinians worked in Israel to 'expand their employ- ment opportunities'. It thus committed both parties to ensuring 'mutual movement of labour', and preserving the rights of Palestinian workers in Israel according to existing Israeli arrangements. Meanwhile, the PA would establish a social security system.

Agriculture

Agricultural produce from the PA area will enter Israel freely, except for five goods on which agreed import quotas have been imposed for five years: tomatoes, cucumbers, potatoes, eggs and broilers.

Manufacturing and tourism

There will be free movement of goods manufactured in the area. A Palestinian tourist administration will be set up to manage subjects related to tourism in the areas of the PA. Tourists will move freely between Israel and the PA area. Tourist agencies, companies and guides will be able to operate 'on the other side' provided they satisfy the relevant professional criteria.

Fuel

The price of petrol in the PA area will be determined according to the cost of purchase and the taxes levied on petrol in the area. The agreement stipulates that the prices of petrol will not fall short by more than 15% of the maximum petrol price in Israel.

Insurance

The would be a full transfer of the licensing and supervision authority over the insurance business in the areas of the PA. In addition, the two sides agreed on compulsory insurance of motor vehicles, and the compensation of the victims of road accidents. Policies issued by the PA were to be valid also in Israel, and vice versa.

GAZA-JERICHO AGREEMENT
CAIRO AGREEMENT
'OSLO 1'

Progress towards finalizing the Gaza-Jericho Accord, initially scheduled for April 13, 1994, was delayed by serious threats to the negotiating process. Amongst these were Palestinian anger at the lack of promised international funds for Gaza, and the slowness of Israeli military withdrawal. A massacre of Muslim worshippers in Hebron on Feb. 25 threatened to sabotage the peace process, but Egyptian and US pressure managed to pull it back on track. UN Security Council Resolution 904 (March 18) condemned the massacre and called for more Israeli clampdowns on extremists (Israel had outlawed two such groups, *Kach* and *Kahane Chai*, five days earlier). This went some way towards assuaging Palestinian qualms about negotiations. Even so, in response to the Hebron massacre, *Hamas* launched suicide bomb attacks in April on Israeli buses in Afula and Hadera. This in turn enraged Israelis, who felt that the peace process should have put an end to such acts of terror.

Nonetheless, feverish talking resumed in April, after an agreement in Cairo (March 31), under which Israel agreed to a 160-strong international observer force in Hebron. Arafat and Peres met in Bucharest and made further progress. Buoyed by its reception at multilateral water talks in Oman, Israel renewed talks with Palestinians in Cairo. This led to several breakthroughs: Israel agreed to the deployment of Palestinian police in Gaza and Jericho, and furthermore set a timetable for releasing some 5,000 Palestinian prisoners. By April 28, only three issues remained unresolved: the size of the Jericho enclave, the question of a Palestinian armed presence at crossing points between the West Bank and Jordan, and control of the Gaza sea area. The next day Israeli finance minister, Avraham Shochat, and the PLO's economics expert, Abu 'Ala (Ahmed Qurei) signed the Paris Economic Protocol (see above).

Eventually, a full agreement was signed on May 4, 1994, in Cairo (notwithstanding a last minute refusal by Arafat to sign a map of Jericho, subsequently ironed out in a compromise deal). The Gaza-Jericho accord was a complicated document, but essentially it dealt with four categories:

- Security arrangements and withdrawal of Israeli forces
- Transfer of civil affairs
- Legal matters
- Economic relations (essentially an annex reiterating the Paris Protocol)

Security

Withdrawal of Israeli forces

Under the aegis of a newly established Joint Israeli–Palestinian Security and Co-ordination and Co-operation Committee, Israeli forces withdrew from most of Gaza and the Jericho enclave (defined as an area of 65 sq km). They redeployed to agreed areas – the Military Installation Area along the Egyptian border, and Israeli settlements in Gaza. Gaza and Jericho were still within an Israeli 'security envelope' – but Palestinians were now responsible for their own internal security.

Security guarantees for Israelis

The IDF agreed to patrol and protect Israeli settlements in the Gaza Strip, including Gush Katif, Netzarim and Erez, as well as some Palestinian land surrounding the settlements. Officially, this covered an area of 11% of Gaza.

Security on the roads

Israel took full responsibility for the security of Israelis on main routes leading to the settlements. Joint Israeli-Palestinian patrols would be set up to ensure free movement on the roads.

Israel to control movements in and out of Gaza-Jericho

Israel would supervise persons, vehicles and weapons at all points of entry; and retain 'security control' over the sea and air space. Israel would further guarantee 'safe passage' for Palestinians travelling between Gaza and Jericho (i.e. over Israeli territory) during daylight hours.

Israeli forces to be replaced by Palestine police

Some 9,000 Palestinian police (including 7,000 from abroad) would replace the vacating Israeli forces. The new police force would control 'internal security and public order', and would 'act to prevent terror' against Israelis in their areas.

Release of Palestinian prisoners

Israel agreed to release 5,000 Palestinian prisoners. This number would exclude – prisoners involved in fatal terror incidents, or who had been arrested for terrorist activities after the DOP signing, or members of 'anti-peace' movements (such as *Hamas* and Islamic *Jihad*).

Transfer of civil affairs

A Palestinian Authority (PA or PNA) would manage Palestinian affairs. The Israeli Civil Administration in Gaza and Jericho was dissolved. Its powers and responsibilities were passed to the PA in the following 25 civilian spheres: education, public works, tourism, telecommunications, commerce and industry, planning and zoning, agriculture, population registry and documentation, nature reserves, housing, parks, archaelogy, water and sewage, transportation, electricity, environmental protection, insurance, social welfare, postal services, religious affairs, employee pensions, health, direct taxation, employment, and treasury.

Elections for a Palestine Council, which would eventually succeed the interim PA in in Gaza and the West Bank, were set for October, 1994.

Joint Committee established

The PA and Israel set up a Joint Civil Affairs Co-ordination and Co-operation Committee (CAC). In addition to questions of civil matters, the committee would co-ordinate on issues regarding infrastructure, passage and 'general contacts'.

Legal matters

Palestinian courts and judicial authorities were to have jurisdiction in all civil matters, including criminal offences in areas under their territorial control.

However, this does not extend to Israeli citizens, Israeli settlements, or foreign affairs, all of which would remain areas of Israeli responsibility. Palestinians thus had no autonomous jurisdiction over civil actions in which an Israeli was a party, unless related to a property or business located in the autonomous area.

Israel maintains jurisdiction over offences committed by Israelis, or in settlements or in the Military Installation Area. Palestinians arrested in Israeli-controlled areas would first be questioned by Israeli officials. Israel and the PA may request the transfer of suspects that fall under their jurisdiction.

Progress and opposition after the signing

In practice, certain issues were deferred till later, notably the release of a further 5,000 Palestinian prisoners; and the status of settlers (to be decided at 'final status talks').

On May 18, Arafat and Peres met in Oslo and agreed on an agenda for talks about widening the authority of Palestinian self-rule in the whole West Bank. The Gaza-Jericho Accord invoked fierce opposition from Syria, and *Hamas*, which vowed to resist attempts by Palestinian police to arrest its fighters. *Hamas* belonged to an anti-Oslo Alliance of Palestinian Forces or National Alliance, which also included: PFLP, DFLP, PLF, PFLP-GC, PPSF, PRCP, *Fatah* Uprising, *Saiqa*, and Islamic *Jihad* (see Chapter 14). In addition, many 'moderate' Palestinians, like Haider Abd al-Shafi, Hani al-Hassan, Muhammed Ghneim, and later Hanan Ashrawi, also opposed the accord.

Meanwhile, the PNA cabinet (appointed by Arafat in May), met for the first time on June 26, 1994. Nabil Sha'ath was the convenor of the PNA's first session, and he was also involved in talks for 'further empowerment' (extending PNA authority beyond Gaza and Jericho) with his Israeli counterpart, Maj.-Gen. Danny Rothschild. An initial decrease in violence pleased Israeli Chief of Staff Ehud Barak. By the end of June, Israel had released 4,000 Palestinian prisoners.

On the economic front, PECDAR (the Palestinian Economic Council for Development and Reconstruction) seemed to be overcoming earlier problems with acquiring funds promised to Gaza-Jericho (the World Bank had promised $1.2 billion in emergency assistance over three years). At the same time, Israel and the PLO opened new talks (separately) with Jordan.

PREPARATORY TRANSFER OF POWERS

Taking the original Gaza-Jericho agreement one stage further, on Aug. 29, 1994, Israel and the PLO agreed to a 'preparatory transfer of powers' from the Israeli Civil Administration in the West Bank to the Palestinian Authority (PNA). This was an important step towards the ultimate goal of extending the PNA's remit beyond the confines of the Jericho enclave to the rest of the West Bank. It thus prepared the way for Israeli troop redeployment and elections to a Palestinian Council, as agreed in September 1995.

The Transfer Agreement consisted of the following elements:

PREAMBLE
ARTICLE 1   Definitions
ARTICLE 2   Preparatory Transfer of Powers and Responsibilities

ARTICLE 3   Scope of the Transferred Powers
ARTICLE 4   Modalities of the Transfer
ARTICLE 5   Administration of the Transferred Offices
ARTICLE 6   Relations Between the Two Sides
ARTICLE 7   Legislative Powers of the Palestinian Authority
ARTICLE 8   Law Enforcement
ARTICLE 9   Rights, Liabilities and Obligations
ARTICLE 10   Liaison and Co-ordination
ARTICLE 11   Budgetary Issues
ARTICLE 12   Mutual Contribution to Peace and Reconciliation
ARTICLE 13   Final Clauses

There then followed six annexes, each listing the protocol concerning preparatory transfer of powers and responsibilies in a particular 'sphere'. An appendix listing relevant existing legislation was attached to each one. The annexes are as follows:

ANNEX 1   Education and culture
ANNEX 2   Health
ANNEX 3   Social Welfare
ANNEX 4   Tourism
ANNEX 5   Direct Taxation
ANNEX 6   VAT on Local Population

On Aug. 21, 1995, just under a year since the above agreement was signed, Israel agreed to transfer to the PNA eight more 'civilian powers'. These were – fuel, transport, postal services, statistics and census, insurance, agriculture, local government and tourism. This was widely interpreted as satisfaction with the success of the original transfer agreement. Jamil Tarifi for the PLO and Oren Shahor for Israel signed a new protocol to this effect on Aug. 27 in Cairo.

INTERIM AGREEMENT (EXTENSION OF PNA RULE TO WEST BANK) 'OSLO 2'

The long road to Oslo 2

As seen above, under the DOP, Gaza and Jericho First was meant to be only the first stage of Palestinian self-rule – in the vernacular, Oslo 1. Israel had already begun transferring powers to the PNA (according to the Preparatory Transfer Agreements of August 1994). Oslo 2 would take this a stage further, by setting a timetable for the extension of Palestinian rule to most of the rest of the West Bank, as Israeli forces withdrew from determined areas in preparation for the Palestinian Council elections.

In some respects the regional portents were good: Israel signed a peace treaty with Jordan in October 1994, and Morocco and Tunisia showed signs of establishing offices in Israel; in December, Arafat, Peres and Rabin shared the Nobel Peace Prize. However, realities on the ground were threatening to sabotage the process. A wave of *Hamas* bomb attacks in Israel enraged most civilians and gave succour to the right. Then Israel was blamed for not preventing settlers from extending their building in the Bethlehem area. Furthermore, Israel's refusal to sign the Nuclear Non-Proliferation Treaty angered the Arab world, led by Israel's oldest regional ally, Egypt.

To unblock the process, President Hosni Mubarak hosted a Cairo summit on Feb. 2 1995, between Israel, the PNA, Jordan and Egypt. The four parties agreed to redouble their efforts to achieve results and formed an unofficial 'peace bloc'. On Feb. 12, the four met again in Washington, this time joining forces with the USA in issuing the Blair House Joint Communiqué. The five parties committed themselves to a concerted and wide-ranging regional strategy for achieving peace. It would encompass security (hastening disarmament and preventing terrorism); freer trade; investment in the PNA's new industrial zones; promotion of private sector projects; and educational and cultural co-operation to 'overcome barriers to understanding and share expertise to deal with common problems'. For its part, the USA offered the PNA and Jordan the incentive of duty-free trade. It also agreed to consult with Russia, Japan, Norway and the EU on creative ventures for the region. But above all, the communiqué insisted on 'no turning back' in the Arab–Israeli peace process.

Between January and March 1995, Israeli officials (notably Uri Savir, Director-General of the Foreign Ministry) and Palestinians had met in secret to analyse – and learn from – the mistakes that had been made in implementing the Gaza-Jericho Agreement. They decided to co-operate more openly at every stage, and introduce a principle of 'graduality' and stricter mutual monitoring of implementation.

Identifying problem areas

On June 19, Joel Singer and Sa'eb Erakat, the heads of the committee negotiating the issue of elections for the Palestinians Council, met a European Union delegation. Headed by the French diplomat, Jean-Luc Sibiud, the EU team was preparing for its observation role in the planned Palestinian Council elections, and together with the Palestinians and Israelis, they ironed out logistical difficulties. Meanwhile, Savir and Abu'Ala had begun formal negotiations, but pressing issues again threatened to derail their efforts. Some 4,500 Palestinians held in Israeli prisons, jails and detainment camps, out of a total of 6,300, started a hunger strike on June 18. On June 23 most of the West Bank responded to a call by the PLO, PNA and *Hamas* for a general strike in solidarity with the hunger strikers. On July 4, Peres and Arafat announced that, after months of public and discreet meetings, they had 'reached an understanding' about an interim agreement. They mandated negotiating teams, under Uri Savir and Abu 'Ala respectively, to finalize the Interim Agreement by July 25.

In the event it was delayed again. Settler civil disobedience increased, and in July a Palestinian suicide bomber killed six and wounded 30 in Tel Aviv. There were other problems, caused by Israel's expropriation of land in East Jerusalem (jettisoned after Palestinian, Israeli Arab and left-wing protest) and settlement encroachment on Arab villages. Palestinians accused Israel of negotiating in bad faith; Israel in turn accused the PNA of harbouring bus-bombing terrorists, and breaking the terms of Oslo 1 by maintaining PLO offices in Orient House, Jerusalem.

Nonetheless, in August there was talk of a breakthrough at the high level Taba summit between Arafat and Peres. On Aug.11 the two leaders initialled the draft agreement. Two days later, the Israeli cabinet accepted it (with one objection and one abstention). Arafat on Aug. 14 presented the draft to the PLO executive committee in Tunis.

The agreement is signed

By Sept. 22, 1995, on the eve of the Jewish festival of *Rosh Hashana* (New Year), the long and often gruelling negotiations eventually bore fruit in the shape of a 350-page document. On Sept. 28, 1995, the agreement was signed in Washington, but not before last-minute wranglings about outstanding contentious issues. Some issues remained, however, especially Hebron and the modalities of releasing prisoners. Nonetheless, the officer of Central Command, Maj.-Gen. Ilan Biran, managed to strike a security deal acceptable to some settlers. One other impediment, the question of water, was deferred to 'final status talks' by mutual agreement.

In its final stages, the Interim Agremeent negotiations involved primarily Shimon Peres, Israel's foreign minister, and Abu 'Ala, PLO chief negotiator. However, Arafat and Rabin were intimately involved, often meeting in person to iron out differences. And unlike the earlier Oslo accords, and preparation for the Gaza-Jericho handover, this agreement (known colloquially as 'Oslo 2') at one stage involved as many as a hundred personnel on each side. Thus it spred responsibility wider, and covered more issues in more detail, than any previous Arab–Israeli negotiations.

The eventual agreement included **seven annexes**, dealing with

- Security arrangements;
- Elections;
- Civil affairs (transfer of powers);

- Legal matters;
- Economic relations;
- Israeli–Palestinian co-operation; and
- The release of Palestinian prisoners.

The agreement states that a Palestinian Council will be elected for an interim period not exceeding five years from the signing of the Gaza-Jericho Agreement (in other words, no later than May 1999). Permanent status talks must begin no later than May 1996.

Summary of Interim Agreement

Israeli troop withdrawal

Israel agreed to withdraw (over a specified time-period) from 70% of the West Bank area. This would take place in three stages, the first being in order to allow for Palestinian Council elections on Jan. 20, 1996. At the end of this stage, there would be no Israeli presence in major Palestinian population centres (defined as the six cities of Area A, and the 450 towns and villages of Area B). However, Israel will would retain control of Jewish settlements, where its troops would be deployed (that is, until the Interim Agreement has run its course, and the subject of settlements is discussed at final status talks).

After the inauguration of the Palestinian Council, Israeli redeployments would take place at six-monthly intervals. During this period, additional parts of Area C would come under Palestinian jurisdiction (*see three-stage timetable below*). Arguing his case before the cabinet, Peres had said that the deal allows Israel to keep '73% of the lands, 97% of the security and 80% of the water'.

Elections to a Palestinian Council

Elections to a Palestinian Council must be held 22 days after the first stage of redeployment is concluded. All Palestinians aged 18 or over and living in the West Bank and Gaza may vote. There will also be a separate election for the Head of the Executive Authority of the Council. (The agreement thus grants all Palestinians the the West Bank and Gaza *autonomy* to chose their own representatives at the interim stage; but actual *control* of territory is limited to certain areas and granted in stages, as explained below.)

Candidates who profess racist views, or act in an 'illegal or undemocratic manner', will not be allowed to stand for election. The agreement makes special arrangements for East Jerusalem Palestinians to participate in the election. Only Jerusalemites with additional addresses in the West Bank or Gaza may stand for election. The European Union (EU) will co-ordinate teams of election observers (consisting of representatives from the EU, UN, USA, Russian Federation, Canada, Egypt, Jordan, Norway, South Africa, Non-Aligned Nations, OAU and Islamic Conference Organization).

The Palestinian Council – powers and jurisdiction

The council will have 82 members. (This was later expanded to 88, after further Palestinian talks with Israel.) The council as a whole will exercise legislative powers; a committee of the Council, the Executive Authority, will exercise executive powers. The Israeli Civil Administration will be dissolved once the Council is established. According to a special annex, Civil Administration powers will be transferred to the Council in Areas A and B. In Area C, a similar process would take place, but it would not immediately deal with powers over territory. Such transfers are subject to detailed provisions to ensure Israeli land rights, and provision of water, electricity and communications to the settlements. In effect, Palestinians would then enjoy self-government over most of the West Bank, in all major areas other than foreign relations. However, the agreement provides for the PLO to conduct negotiations (with donor countries and concerning regional development), on behalf of the Council.

Division of land

For logistic purposes, the West Bank was divided into three areas. Together, these areas are home to more than 1.3 million Palestinians, and include all Arab cities, villages and rural districts.

Area A	Major cities – Jenin, Nablus, Tulkarem, Qalqilya, Ramallah, Bethlehem
Area B	Towns and villages of the West Bank (containing 68% of Palestinians)
Area C	Unpopulated areas of 'strategic importance' and Jewish settlements

Three-stage timetable for implementation

The agreement specifies a three-stage timetable for IDF redeployment, corresponding in each stage to the three areas listed above.

First stage

Israeli withdrawal from six cities in Area A, within 100 days of the signing of the agreement in Washington, DC. The Palestinian Authority (PA) will then hold its first elections for a Palestinian Council, by late January 1996, in time for the beginning of the Muslim fasting month of Ramadan. Special arrangements were made for the city of Hebron (see below).

Second stage

Starting in March or April 1996, the PA will acquire control of some 400 Palestinian villages. In some cases, Israeli troops would remain until 'bypass roads' are completed (the idea being that Jewish settlers need not pass through heavily populated Palestinian areas). This stage is scheduled to take over a year to implement.

Third stage

Final status negotiations, which will deal with the issues of Jewish settlements, Jerusalem, permanent borders, refugees, and quite possibly the nature of Palestinian autonomy (Israel still favours self-government, whereas the PLO favours full sovereign statehood in the West Bank and Gaza).

Changes to the Palestinian covenant

After much horse-trading between the PLO and Israel, PLO leader Yasser Arafat pledged to amend the Palestinian Covenant, two months after the Palestinian Council is elected. The Covenant at present still calls for the destruction of the state of Israel. (Israeli Prime Minister Yitzhak Rabin had warned that if the PLO reneged on this, redeployment of troops would cease immediately.)

Release of prisoners

Palestinian prisoners will be released in three stages:

- On signing of the agreement
- On the eve of the Council elections
- and according to other principles.

A joint committee was set up to discuss who was eligible for release, on what grounds, and how this would be done. (After the signing, this became a sensitive issue because of differences of interpretation; Israel initially refused to release prisoners who had been involved in terrorist incidents, or acts of violence. Likewise, there was confusion over special stipulations regarding women prisoners.)

Security policy for preventing terrorism and violence

Israel will retain control of security in the Jordan Valley, and most of the Judean Desert between the settlement of Ma'aleh Adumim (east of Jerusalem) and the Dead Sea. Other than that, a strong Palestinian police force, consisting of 12,000 members, will be regarded as the sole legitimate security force in the area under the Council's authority in the West Bank. These police will operate freely in Area A; in addition, a further 25 police stations would be built for them in Area B. The Gaza police contingent will be increased to 18,000.

The Security Annex stipulates the exact number of weapons to be deployed in Palestinian areas, and gives Israel the right to veto appointees to the new force. It also specifies how and where they will be deployed, and defines the force's duty to combat terrrorism, whether by Palestinians or Israelis. To this end, joint security committees will co-ordinate between the IDF and the Palestinian police. The annex envisages joint patrols on roads (such as those already operative in Jericho and Gaza), and joint mobile units to respond to emergency incidents. Officials have distinguished between Area A, where Palestinians fully control security, and Area B, where Israel controls security and Palestinians control 'civil order'.

Water

Israel will allocate a further 28 million cubic metres of water to Palestinians. A tripartite US-Israeli-Palestinian forum will meet after this agreement, and deal with extra funding. A joint water committee will manage water resources between both parties, and to steps to prevent uncontrolled drilling. Other water issues are deferred until final status talks.

Economic co-operation

Applying the principles established in the Gaza-Jericho Agreement's Economic Annex, the new agreement extends the idea of a 'single economic unit' between Israelis and Palestinians to the entire West Bank and Gaza Strip. An additional annex commits both parties to co-operation in matters of environment, economics, science and technology, agriculture, tourism, investments in infrastructure, society and education. It gives the private sector a role, alongside the Israeli government and Palestinian Council; and furthermore established a standing committee to oversee developments here. The annex also laid great stress on protecting the environment and advancing tourism, education and support for young people.

Education and human rights

The Agreement commits both Israel and the Council to 'strengthen understanding and tolerance' between the two peoples. To this end, both sides pledged to curb hostile propaganda, and, through their educational systems, to encourage a spirit of peace. Overall, Israel and the Council promised to 'adhere to the international norms of human rights and the rule of law'.

Religious sites

Palestinians will be responsible for the upkeep of, and safety at, religious sites in the West Bank and Gaza. They will guarantee access to them, and allow worshippers (whether Muslim, Christian, Jewish or Samaritan) freedom of to pray at these sites. Of particular importance to Jews are the Tombs of the Patriarchs in Hebron (see below), Joseph's Tomb in Nablus, and Rachel's Tomb in Bethlehem.

Special status for Hebron

The question of security arrangements in Hebron was one of the main sticking points in the negotiations. In order to protect the 450 Jewish settlers in the city, the negotiators agreed on an exception to the general rule of total Israeli troop withdrawal from West Bank cities. Instead, forces would redeploy within six months, in March 1996, but would continue to safeguard Israelis there. Palestinian police would look after Palestinian residents, and there would be a 'temporary international presence' in Hebron. The status quo at the Tomb of the Patriarchs will remain initially unchanged; although in time Israel may be willing to accept a symbolic unarmed Palestinian presence at the entrance to the Muslim side of the Cave of the Patriachs (the Ibrahimi Mosque). *(see box for more details.)*

Timetable for implementing the Interim Agreement

Sept. 28, 1995	Signing in Washington
Oct. 6, 1995	Knesset approval achieved
Oct. 10, 1995	Start of three-phase programme of releasing Palestinian prisoners
Nov. 19, 1995	Planned start of major IDF pullout (Starting in Jenin, and scheduled completion for end of the year)
Jan. 20, 1996	Date for Palestinian Council elections [After the Council is inaugurated, Israel will carry out three further redeployments at six-monthly intervals; and more of the West Bank will be handed over to Palestinian jurisdiction]

Hebron – source of faith and friction

Hebron is the only city in the West Bank with a Jewish population (450 settlers living amidst some 120,000 mainly Muslim Palestinians). Small though their numbers may be, the Jews of Hebron tend to be amongst the most radical of the Israeli religious nationalist right-wing. Likewise, Hebron is the main West Bank centre for the Islamic fundamentalist *Hamas* movement. Not surprisingly, many Israelis and Palestinians fear that Hebron is a powder keg which could explode and destroy the fragile peace process. The city (35 km south of Jerusalem and 1,000 m up in the Judean Hills) can be seen as a microcosm of the Arab–Israeli dispute. Ironically, the antagonism between Jew and Muslim in Hebron stems from the common origins of their two faiths. According to the Bible, Hebron is where Abraham, the progenitor of the Jewish people, first bought land in *Eretz Yisrael,* 4000 years ago. He chose the Cave of Machpelah as a burial place for his wife, Sarah. Tradition says that Abraham and Sarah, Isaac and Rebecca, Jacob and Leah, and Joseph, are all buried in or around the cave. This makes Hebron one of the four holy cities in Judaism (the others being Jerusalem, Safad and Shechem). By the same token, Hebron is holy to Muslims, as Abraham (or Ibrahim) is regarded in the Koran as 'the first Muslim'. In Arabic, Hebron is called 'Al-Khalil' (the friend), in honour of Ibrahim's closeness to God. Jews continued to live and pray in Hebron until they were expelled after the fall of Jerusalem in 70 AD; but they returned under the Arabs. Saladin added to the existing Hebrew shrine and Byzantine Christian basilica, and in time Muslims built the Ibrahimi Mosque at the same site. In 1266 Jews were forbidden to enter the Cave to pray; in 1588 they suffered a massacre at the hands of Ottoman Turks. The community's tenuous history there appeared to end with the Arab massacres of 1929 and 1936 (the first of which claimed 69 Jewish lives). However, after the Six Day War of 1967, Israel controlled the area. The Israeli army was under strict orders not to allow Jewish settlement there, out of sensitivity to Muslim wishes; but in 1968 Rabbi Moshe Levinger established an illegal Jewish presence in the city centre, made permanent in 1974. Most of his followers (generally right-wing, messianic *Gush Emunim* followers) settled in nearby Kiryat Arba, to the east, where today they number 6,000. In February 1994, one Kiryat Arba resident, Dr Baruch Goldstein, entered the mosque and shot dead 29 Muslim worshippers, before being overwhelmed and himself killed. Most Israelis deplored his action, but a radical minority hailed him as a martyr. The massacre temporarily derailed the peace process; to prevent further incidents, security was tightened. However, to Palestinians living in the Tel Rumeida suburb, near the Jewish enclave, Israeli forces severely restrict their daily lives and turn a blind eye to Jewish acts of vandalism. The Israeli authorities are still wrestling with a dilemma – to evict the settlers would outrage the right-wing in Israel, and appear to cast scorn on the Jewish attachment to Hebron; but to allow them to stay requires a heavy military presence, which flies in the face of the letter and spirit of the deal with the PLO. Of all West Bank settlers, Jewish Hebronites are the least likely to move, no matter how much compensation they are offered. Arafat, too, faces a dilemma – to allow Israel to dominate security in Hebron makes him appear weak, and certainly bolsters his foes in *Hamas*; but to risk the entire self-government deal on this issue is equally unconscionable. According to the Interim Agreement, Israeli troops will redeploy from Hebron, over six months except from places and roads where they can protect the security of Israelis. Palestinian police would control the rest of the town, and a temporary international presence will secure a smooth transition. Whether Hebronites, Jewish and Muslim, will accept this remains an open question.

March 28, 1996	Scheduled completion of redeployment from Hebron
May 4, 1996	Latest starting date for talks on permanent status of territories
May 4, 1999	Latest completion date for talks on permanent status

Co-ordinating mechanisms

Oslo 2 differs from Oslo 1 in the extent to which Israel and the PLO will co-operate in a range of fields. This led to the creation of a plethora of co-ordinating bodies, and special committees. Annex VI of the Agreement established a Standing Co-operation Committee (SCC) composed of equal numbers from each side. The SCC has a broad remit to improvise new working groups, but its main function is to define for both peoples aspects of co-operation in agriculture, industry, environmental concerns, energy, transport, tourism, scientific research ventures, cultural and educational ties, youth and sports, and anti-drug abuse projects. In addition, the Kingdom of Norway will oversee a 'People-to-People

Programme', designed to 'enhance dialogue and remove barriers to interaction' between ordinary Israelis and Palestinians.

A Joint Civil Affairs Co-ordination and Co-operation Committee (CAC) handled all election-related issues. In addition, Yasser Arafat nominated members of a Central Elections Committee (CEC), to monitor the election campaign, and ensure that elections themselves were not rigged. (These provisions assumed greater importance closer to election day, especially regarding the complicated arrangements for voting in East Jerusalem).

A Joint Security Co-ordination and Co-operation Committee (JSC) was set up to monitor security aspects of the treaty. Senior officers from the PLO and the IDF comprise its members.

Under the JSC are localized District Co-ordination Offices (DCOs), which in turn run joint patrols and quick response Joint Mobile Units (JMUs).

EVENTS AFTER SIGNING OF AGREEMENT

Ratification

The Labour government narrowly won a vote in the Knesset (by 61 to 59) in support of the agreement. The Leader of the Opposition, Benjamin Netanyahu, virulently opposed it, saying that Israeli redeployment would create a base for Islamic fundamentalist terrorists second only to Iran. Benjamin Begin, a leading younger *Likud* politician and son of the late Menachem Begin, warned that the agreement would inevitably lead to another war. However, in an interview with the British *Daily Telegraph* in New York, Netanyahu said Israel would honour the agreement; but warned that any sign of Palestinian non-compliance would render it null and void. He preferred a more limited version of Palestinian autonomy, without conceding control over actual territory or security matters. 'Palestinians will have to limit their expectations', he proclaimed, although was loath to elaborate on his plans before the Israeli general elections, scheduled for 1996.

Yasser Arafat presented the agreement to the Executive Committee of the PLO in Tunis, and managed to see it passed (albeit with a number of abstentions and objections by sceptical committee members). Predictably, Marxist factions of the PLO and *Hamas* condemned the deal.

US role via Trilateral Committee

The day after the signing of Oslo 2, US Secretary Warren Christopher, Israeli Foreign Minister Shimon Peres, and Chairman Arafat met to convene the first meeting of the US-Israel-Palestinian Trilateral Committee (intended to emulate the success of the Trilateral with Jordan — see p 97). The parties agreed: to promote co-operative efforts to foster economic development in the West Bank and Gaza; to explore ways to increase the availability and more efficient use of water resources; to consult on matters of mutual interest; and to promote cooperation on regional issues.

Implementing the agreement

In many respects, Gaza and Jericho First (the essence of Oslo 1) was a testing ground for Oslo 2. Oslo 2 in turn is the 'interim phase', in a process that will culminate in a final settlement. By August 1995, however, Israeli and Palestinian negotiators had reached a new *modus operandi*, and were willing to compromise. Where necessary, they had postponed difficult decisions until the final status talks. Uri Savir, Director-General of the Israeli Foreign Ministry, told Israeli and Jewish audiences that both sides had learnt from the mistakes of Oslo 1. He also praised the growing maturity of the PNA as it acquired more powers over areas of authority beyond Jericho. Rather than the strict separation between Israel and the PNA which typified the Gaza and Jericho Agreements, Oslo 2 would emphasize closer co-operation, he said, while at the same time giving the new Council real authority.

In order to meet the deadline for redeployment and also appease the settlers, the Israeli government poured almost $300 million into a massive project to build 'bypass roads'. These highways connect settlements but avoid major Palestinian population centres. Even so, right-wing protests mounted, with some rallies depicting Yitzhak Rabin in SS uniform. *Tsomet* party leader, Rafael Eitan, spoke for many right-wing Israelis when he rued the idea that 'In Taba, Shimon Peres established the Palestinian state'. Many analysts draw a direct link between Oslo 2 and the assassination of Yitzhak Rabin just over a month later.

A crisis developed when Israel seemed to baulk on releasing women prisoners who were guilty of acts of violence (in apparent contradiction to the terms of the treaty). Only some women prisoners were willing to renounce further violence. This situation was exacerbated by remarks made by Israel's President Ezer Weizman, but later defused by a compromise arrangement. Shimon Peres said in October that he hoped Israel could redeploy from the city of Jenin ahead of schedule. Meanwhile, there were frantic efforts to complete bypass roads for settlers before redeployment.

Murder of Yitzhak Rabin

Despite this concession, West Bank Jewish settlers stepped up their protests. In a bid to demonstrate the groundswell of opinion for peace, Rabin and Peres addressed a 150,000-strong peace rally in Tel Aviv on Nov. 4. In his speech Rabin said there had to be an end to violence, and people should take a chance for peace. Immediately after the rally he was gunned down by a right-wing Jewish extremist, from the *Eyal* movement; he died hours later in hospital.

Foreign Minister Shimon Peres became acting Prime Minister, a position later confirmed as permanent. He re-committed Israel for peace, saying that the nation was not going to cow to violence. Peres appointed Foreign Ministry Director-General Uri Savir, chief architect of the Interim Agreement, as the government's special peace process co-ordinator. He also formed a 'peace team' within the cabinet, consisting of the newly appointed Foreign Minister Ehud Barak, Internal Security Minister Moshe Shahal, Interior Minister Haim Ramon, Environment Minister Yossi Sarid, and Minister Without Portfolio (within the Prime Minister's Office) Yossi Beilin.

Sceptics who felt the murder had 'killed the peace process' were proved wrong. At Rabin's funeral, speaker after speaker (including powerful addresses from US President Bill Clinton and Jordan's King Hussein) stressed the need to continue with Rabin's plan for peace. In a highly symbolic gesture, Yasser Arafat made his first legal trip to Israel, when he travelled incognito to pay his condolences to Rabin's widow, Leah, in Tel Aviv.

Elections in the West Bank and Gaza

Arafat also surprised many pundits by promising to hold Council elections by the earlier suggested date, Jan. 20, 1996. This led to a telescoping of the election timetable, and a flurry of activity to get people registered. Again, observers were surprised at popular enthusiasm, as more than 500,000 voters rushed to register in just 10 days, and about a million over a full month.

Israel responded in kind, by leaving Jenin (first of the six West Bank cities to be vacated by the end of December) earlier than scheduled. On Nov. 13. Palestinian security forces based in Jericho, and under the command of Col Jibril Rajoub, instantly replaced the departing Israeli troops. Peres promised Arafat that Israeli forces would leave Bethlehem by Christmas, which they did. In the jargon of the peace process, it was a significant 'confidence-building measure'. By the year's end, Israeli forces had left not only these two towns, but also Qalqilyah, Ramallah, Tul Karm and other places. The Palestine National Authority officially dissolved itself for the election campaign, and polls were held on schedule, on Jan. 20, 1996. Yasser Arafat was (as expected) elected President, or Chairman of the Council. Hundreds of candidates participated, including a few independents who had *Hamas* affiliations. By and large, it was a victory for *Fatah*, but the seeds of an opposition force was planted at the same time.

Chapter 10 Peace treaty between Israel and Jordan

The peace treaty between Israel and Jordan, signed at the Arava border crossing on Oct. 26, 1994, was the culmination of years of secret talks between the two countries. Nominally enemies, they had clashed in 1967, when Jordan lost control of the West Bank to Israel; but had in fact maintained close ties on strategic issues since then (Jordan remained neutral in the Yom Kippur War of 1973).

On April 11, 1987, the then Israeli Foreign Minister, Shimon Peres, and King Hussein reached a secret agreement in London to achieve regional peace, but this soon fell apart because of opposition in the home countries. The Israel–Jordan peace treaty was the first one signed between Israel and another Arab country since Israel's Menachem Begin and Egypt's Anwar Sadat had concluded their treaty in 1979. Indeed, the Camp David Accords, which led to the Israel–Egypt peace treaty, also envisaged a Jordanian role in achieving 'Palestinian autonomy' in the Israeli-occupied territories. But Jordan boycotted the talks when it became clear that the PLO was to be excluded, and when it seemed that the autonomy in question was limited to personal as opposed to territorial affairs [see Chapter 7].

Background to the signing

Jordan participated in the Madrid conference in October 1991, and the subsequent bilateral track of talks with Israel [see Chapter 8]. Initially, some politicians suggested a joint Jordanian-Palestinian delegation, which would culminate in a peace treaty between Israel and a Jordanian-Palestinian confederation. Former Israeli Foreign Minister, Abba Eban, even spoke of a 'Benelux' option, joining the three lands in a loose economic union.

Behind such a 'Jordan option' lay a host of different ideas. More than half of Jordan's population is Palestinian; thus several right-wing Israelis have contended that 'Jordan is Palestine', that the Hashemite Kingdom effectively spoke for the Palestinians, and that there was no room for a third state in the Jordan valley. In an extreme version of this argument, *Likud* right-winger Ariel Sharon had once suggested that Palestinians depose King Hussein and set up their own state in Jordan; then Israel could 'transfer' Palestinians from the territories to the new state. Shimon Peres, speaking for the Israeli left, developed his own 'Jordan option'. He felt that Israel should address the Palestinian issue, but that only King Hussein could deliver a solution. Some form of confederation, perhaps ultimately joined economically with Israel in a Benelux configuration, was mooted. Similarly, some Israelis felt that as long as the PLO was illegal, the Hashemite Kingdom was the only alternative voice.

Several Palestinians themselves doubted whether any Palestinian entity could be economically self-sufficient, and that it was therefore better then to co-operate with Jordan, which was stable and had long experience of governing the West Bank area. Within Jordan, many officials recalled the violent rift between the PLO and the state, culminating in 'Black September' of 1971. To them, a confederation was a chance to stamp their authority on a potentially rebellious Palestinian populus.

But as the Madrid track unfolded, most Jordanians close to the Royal Court realized that the Palestinians had begun asserting themselves as an independent entity. Indeed, Jordanian negotiators refused to speak to Israel until it accepted the Palestinian delegation's wish to negotiate separately (their protest was known as the 'corridor negotiations').

This Jordanian stance was consistent with a joint understanding between the PLO and Jordan which originated in 1988. On July 31 of that year, King Hussein of Jordan had voluntarily abrogated his nation's longstanding claim to rule the West Bank. The 19th Palestinian National Council (PNC), meeting in Algiers in November, 1988, responded by supporting (even 'declaring') Palestinian independence in the occupied territories. In a philosophical sense, the Hashemite Kingdom was acknowledging that Palestinians had 'come of age', and no longer needed the guardianship of Jordanian or any other external Arab rule.

The decision to disengage from the West Bank had two important consequences in that it served to end the 'Jordan is Palestine' argument in Israel, and it abolished those seats of the Jordanian parliament which were located on the West Bank (half of the total number), thus allowing for elections in Jordan (East Bank only) in 1989, for the first time since 1967.

The benefits of peace

Peace between Israel and Jordan would bring obvious benefits to both countries, for long-term strategic reasons, and for short-term political advantage. According to the International Institute of Strategic Studies, Jordan wanted to maintain some influence over the West Bank, but feared being left behind by a possible Israeli deal with Syria. The peace treaty thus relieved this pressure, and allowed Jordan greater freedom from Syrian influence. Economically, peace would bring direct and indirect advantages – directly, in terms of trade with Israel, and access to Mediterranean ports; indirectly, through the promise of the USA to forgive Jordan its large debt (in 1994 estimated at three times the country's gross national product). Peace with Israel would also involve Jordan in attempts to solve the Palestinian refugee problem (many hundreds of thousands of whom still lived in Jordan). It would restore land lost in war, and improve Jordan's water supply. For Israel, peace with Jordan would open up new tourist destinations, but more importantly, it would seal a potentially vulnerable eastern front from attack (probably not from Jordan, but from a hostile third party; the treaty expressly prevents such an eventuality). Jordan's co-operation was vital for Israel's economic plans in the region. Finally, Israel trusted King Hussein as a genuine ally, and a Muslim leader of world standing.

From Common Agenda to full peace

The announcement of an Israel–PLO deal (on Aug. 24, 1993, in Oslo) took King Hussein by surprise and he was angry to have been excluded from such an important development. Ultimately, however, the resulting Israel–PLO Declaration of Principles (the DOP, signed on Sept. 13, 1993), which was fashioned *outside* the official Madrid framework, broke the log-jam between Jordan and Israel. What followed was a three-stage process (a Common Agenda, Trilateral Economic Committee and the Washington Declaration of non-belligerency), culminating in a full peace treaty in October 1994.

The Common Agenda between Israel and Jordan was signed on Sept. 14, 1993, just a day after the signing of the DOP between Israel and the PLO. It formally separated the Palestinian from the Jordanian negotiating team (although in reality they had really been negotiating separately since 1992), and helped to assuage Jordanians who feared that Jordan had been 'left behind' by the sudden Israeli–PLO rapprochement.

The agenda defined four areas for future negotiations: security, water, borders and territorial matters, and a 'just solution to the bilateral aspects of the problem of refugees and displaced persons in accordance with international law'. Both parties agreed to base their talks on UN Resolutions 242 and 338, and sought to find ways of co-operating on human and natural resources, infrastructure and economic areas.

The USA has played an important guiding role in determining Israeli–Jordanian relations. Successive US Secretaries of State, George Schultz, James Baker and Warren Christopher, all consulted King Hussein closely about events in the Middle East. Apart from a temporary fallout with Jordan over how to treat Saddam Hussein in the run-up to the Gulf War, the USA has generally regarded Jordan as one of its most trusted 'moderate' allies in the Middle East.

This close US interest has been reflected most clearly in the economic arena. President Bill Clinton of the US, Crown Prince Hassan of Jordan and Foreign Minister Shimon Peres of Israel set up a Trilateral Economic Committee on Oct.1,1993 to discuss economic co-operation and development between the three countries. The committee held its first meeting on Nov. 30, 1993. Committee sub-groups set about discussing issues such as trade, finance, banking, the Jordan Valley Co-operative Projects, and civil aviation.

In December 1993 Jordan signed its first economic agreement with the PLO. This allowed for a substantial Central Bank of Jordan role in the monetary affairs of the new Palestinian entity (where the Jordanian dinar was legal tender, alongside the Israeli shekel and US dollar). It was followed by a more official signing on Jan. 7, 1994. In April 1994 Israel and the PLO signed their own economic agreement in Paris, which gave Palestinians the right to import commodities (like oil, cement and fertilisers) from or through Jordan.

However, another aspect of trade through Jordan threatened to kill the developing peace process with Israel. Under the terms of UN sanctions against Iraq, US naval patrols often impounded and searched vessels arriving at the Jordanian port of Aqaba. Jordan protested that these measures were crippling its economy. Behind the dispute lay deeper antagonisms, especially a feeling that the USA still did not trust Jordan after its apparent show of sympathy for Iraq (its natural trading partner) during the Gulf Crisis. On March 28 King Hussein threatened to pull out of talks unless this matter was resolved. On April 25, the US Secretary of State met the king in London, and assured him that the USA approved of a less debilitating land-based inspection system. Talks between Israel and Jordan resumed in June.

July 1994 saw a sudden quickening of pace in Jordanian–Israeli relations. On July 18, 1994, the Bilateral negotiators met at Wadi Araba'Arava and agreed to set up a Co-operation Initiative on the Jordan Rift Valley and Jordan River Basin. The main issues discussed were the relationship between population and water resources, and proposals to share water more equitably (Jordan alleged that Israel had effectively deprived Jordan of water usage from the Rivers Jordan and Yarmouk).

The fifth meeting of the Trilateral Committee met at the Dead Sea on July 20–21, 1994, and marked a significant breakthrough in the peace talks. Dr Fayez Tarawneh led the Jordanian delegation, and Elyakim Rubinstein led the Israeli delegation. The main issues discussed were:

ENVIRONMENT

Areas of agreed co-operation included: sharing water resources, protecting the ecology of the Gulf of Aqaba, preserving soil from contamination and over-exploitation, controlling air quality, setting up nature reserves, combating desertification, and improving environmental education. The Trilateral Committee also agreed on joint mechanisms for Israel and Jordan to pool their resources when dealing with emergencies, whether natural disasters or pollution-related disasters.

JORDAN'S ENERGY

The Trilateral meeting considered in detail how to exploit Jordan's potential energy resources. These included: renewable energy (wind and solar power), oil shale, geothermal energy, and oil and gas exploration.

PALESTINIAN REFUGEES

Jordan raised the issue of Palestinian refugees in Jordan (defined as those who left Palestine in 1948), and 'displaced persons' (those who left the West Bank and Gaza in 1967). Jordan hosts the largest single community of Palestinian refugees, totalling 1.7 million people, which makes up one-third of the Kingdom's total population. King Hussein reiterated that before Israel and Jordan signed a full peace treaty, both states should commit themselves to solving the 'bilateral aspects' of the refugee problem, according to UN General Assembly Resolution 194 (1948), UN Security Council Resolution 237 (1967) and the Common Agenda (1993). Jordan stressed in particular the Palestinian 'right of return'. As to an overall solution to the problem, this could only be solved through the permanent stage talks between Israel and the PLO, and the multilateral working group on refugees.

TOURISM

Israel and Jordan discussed potential avenues of co-operation, including archaeological studies, tourist packages, encouraging religious travel, protecting wildlife, improving border crossings and transport, better education and information, and promoting a region-wide tourism initiative.

These talks were also the first occasion for the respective national leaders to meet publicly in the region – Jordan's Prime Minister Majali and Israel's Foreign Minister Peres. They were followed by the Washington Declaration of July 25, 1994, the first public meeting between

King Hussein and Prime Minister Rabin. US President Bill Clinton was the witness. Jordan and Israel agreed to three immediate steps:

- Ending the state of belligerancy between the two countries
- Acceptance of a lasting peace based on UN Resolutions 242 and 338
- Respect for Jordan's special role concerning Muslim holy sites in Jerusalem.

The Washington Declaration also proposed setting up direct telephone links, joint electricity grids, new border crossings, free access to third country tourists, police co-operation and anti-drug smuggling measures. The day after the declaration, King Hussein and Yitzhak Rabin made history by becoming the first foreign leaders to jointly address the House of Representatives. Meanwhile, bilateral talks continued, dealing with: economic co-operation; moves towards abolishing economic boycotts; and preparation of a full peace treaty.

On Oct. 17, Israeli Prime Minister Rabin and Jordanian Prime Minister Majali initialled the text of the treaty. On Oct. 26, 1994, Israel and Jordan signed a full peace treaty at the Araba crossing, in the presence of US President Bill Clinton. The treaty itself included, but also amplified, many of the issues agreed to at the Wadi Araba Bilaterals, Dead Sea Trilaterals, and in Washington.

Overview of the treaty

The Peace Treaty consists of 30 articles, five annexes and six maps.

SUMMARY OF MAIN POINTS OF THE TREATY

International boundary

This broadly follows the old British Mandate boundary, including territorial waters and airspace. In essence the boundary (as stipulated in article 3 and annex 1[a] of the treaty) consists of four sectors:

- The Jordan and Yarmouk Rivers
- The Dead Sea
- The Emek Ha'arava, or Wadi Araba
- The Gulf of Aqaba.

The agreement did, however, provide for some minor alterations: Israeli farmers in the Arava were allowed to continue to cultivate their land, which they had started to occupy between 1968 and 1970, although technically these 344 sq km returned to Jordanian rule. The Naharayim/Baqura and Zofar areas fell under Jordanian sovereignty, with Israeli rights for private land use affirmed (enforceable for 25 years, pending re-consultation).

Security

Both parties agreed to 'refrain from acts of belligerancy or hostility'. They also agreed to prevent acts of terrorism on the other party from their territory, and to repeal all discriminatory references in their respective legislation. Jordan and Israel planned to set up a Conference on Security and Co-operation in the Middle East.

Water

Israel and Jordan agreed to divide the water from the Yarmouk and Jordan Rivers, and from the Arava/Araba groundwaters. Jordan would receive an additional 215 mn cu m from these sources (equivalent to 30% of its renewable water resources before the treaty). In addition, Israel agreed to transfer 50 mn cu m of water annually to Jordan, from its northern regions. Both parties agreed to co-operate in fighting water shortages and water contamination.

Freedom of passage

Nationals and their vehicles are permitted free passage through open roads and border crossings; the same applied to vessels of either country in territorial waters. The Straits of Tiran and Gulf of Aqaba are considered to be open and international waterways.

Crime and drugs

Annex III outlined plans for Jordan and Israel to co-operate in fighting crime, especially drug smuggling. Both states would share information, and participate in joint research, training and anti-drug education programmes.

Environment

Annex IV reaffirmed the July Trilateral's plans to develop and protect the Eilat-Aqaba region, and also aimed to rehabilitate the Jordan Rift Valley (including the Dead Sea). The annex provided for mechanisms to share information, fight pollution and protect water resources, while developing ecologically sound tourist attractions and encouraging non-polluting industries.

Places of historical and religious significance

The treaty guaranteed free access to such places (Petra and Wadi Rum, Jerusalem and Caeserea). Furthermore, Israel re-affirmed its recognition of Jordan's special interest in the Muslim shrines of Jerusalem. When the issue of Jerusalem comes onto the agenda (as part of the 'permanent status' negotiations between Israel and the PLO), Israel has promised to 'give high priority to the Jordanian historical role in these shrines'.

Refugees and displaced persons

Recognizing the human cost of conflict in the Middle East, Jordan and Israel agreed to try to resolve them through three channels: a four-member committee (with Egypt and Palestinians) on displaced persons; the multilateral working group on refugees; and the permanent status talks between Israel and the Palestinians (see above).

Article 2, clause 6, forbids either party from moving a population against its will, to the detriment of the other party – Jordan took this as a guarantee against any future forced influx of Palestinians from the occupied territories.

Normalization of relations

The two parties agreed to exchange ambassadors and establish embassies. In addition, various articles of the treaty covered normalization through co-operation in energy, tourism, trade, policing, culture, science, transport, communications, environment, agriculture and economic development (including a free trade area).

Border crossings

The treaty provided for the first ever direct border crossings with Israel – one in southern Araba (opened after the Washington Declaration); the other near Jordan's northern city of Irbid.

Forgiveness of debt

The USA agreed to forgive Jordan its public debt of $700m.

Major developments since the treaty

RATIFICATION

The Israeli Knesset approved the peace treaty on Oct. 25, 1994, by 105 votes to three. Six members were not present to vote. The Jordanian Lower House approved the treaty on Nov. 6, 1994, by 55 votes to 23. Two MPs did not vote (one was absent and the other was the Speaker). Seventeen of the 23 'no' votes came from the Islamic Action Front, the largest single party in Jordan, and in effect the chief opposition. On Nov. 9, 1994, Israel and Jordan exchanged documents of ratification. They also established the supervision committee and the joint border committee, to meet again in three months' time. In his address to the nation on Nov. 15, King Hussein thanked God for 'making us the builders of a . . . comprehensive and total peace between God's faithful creatures, the sons of Abraham . . . in the land of prophets and divine messages'.

OTHER REACTIONS

There was widespread support for the treaty across the Israeli political spectrum, notably from the Leader of the Opposition, *Likud* Chairman Benjamin Netanyahu. But Islamic activists within Jordan started a campaign against it, and joint PLO-*Hamas* demonstrations against the treaty erupted throughout the West Bank and Gaza in late October. Syrian President Hafez al-Assad said it was 'blasphemy for any country to speak of renting its land to any other leadership' (a reference to the lease-back clauses dealing with Araba, Zohar and Baqura).

Palestinian leaders objected to clauses which apparently entrenched King Hussein's role in administering Jerusalem's Muslim sites. They feared that this would pre-empt discussions on Jerusalem at the 'final status talks' with Israel. Jordanian officials swiftly moved to clarify their position, by stressing that Jordan will transfer its 'temporary custodianship' of the sites to Palestinians, but only after the area (that is, East Jerusalem and the Old City) is 'returned to the Palestinian people'. Meanwhile, Jordan saw its custodianship as 'a sacred duty', and reminded Palestinians that fully half of the *Awqaf* (religious trusts) Ministry budget had been spent on Jerusalem – amounting to more than $500 million over four decades. The problem of the holy city was thrown into graphic relief on Oct. 16, 1994, when the Mufti of Jerusalem, Sheikh Sulaiman al-Jabari, suddenly died. Immediately, Jordan appointed Sheikh Abdel-Qadir Abideen to replace him; within hours the PNA announced its own appointment, Sheikh Akram Said Sabri.

CHANGE OF PERSONNEL

Jordan and Israel established diplomatic relations on Nov. 27, with an exchange of ambassadors. Shimon Shamir was appointed Israel's ambassador to Jordan; Marwan Muasher, who had been one of Jordan's key negotiators, now became Jordan's Ambassador to Israel. (Jordan had rejected Israel's original nominee as Israeli Ambassador, the negotiator Efraim Halevy, because his connections with Mossad were regarded as too sensitive.)

On Jan. 8,1995, King Hussein reshuffled his cabinet, replacing Prime Minister Salam al-Majali with the then head of the Royal Court, Field Marshal Sharif Zaid ibn Shaker. Al-Majali had held the position since May 1993 and was a prime mover behind the peace treaty negotiations. Shaker had been prime minister twice before, in 1989 and 1991. Suggestions that Al-Majali's replacement marked a sign of unease about the peace deal were largely dispelled on Jan. 29, 1995, when the new government won a vote of confidence, and pledged to press ahead with implementing the new laws required under the treaty with Israel.

FORMING THE 'PEACE BLOC'

President Mubarak of Egypt hosted a historic meeting in Cairo on Feb. 2, 1995, bringing together for the first time parties who had concluded peace agreements, including Israel and Jordan. This 'peace bloc' set itself the task of putting flesh on the bones of the signed agreements, by encouraging the spirit of peace through practical co-operation. It also determined to fight against enemies of the peace process. US Commerce Secretary Ron Brown met senior Egyptian, Israeli, Jordanian, and Palestinian trade officials in Taba (Egyptian Sinai) on Feb. 7 and 8, and they released a statement reaffirming their commitment to economic co-operation and ending the boycott of Israel.

Finally, Jordan's rulers met with those of Israel, Egypt, and the Palestinians, as well as President Clinton and Secretary of State Christopher, in the Blair House ministerial meeting in Washington on Feb. 12. At this meeting the US administration pledged itself to helping the peace process as defined at the Cairo Summit.

IMPLEMENTING THE PEACE IN 1995

The peace treaty between Israel and Jordan defined the goals of real peace between the two countries, but its implementation was an involved affair.

On Feb. 6 the implementation supervision committee met in Dir Ala, Jordan, and heard reports on the progress in negotiations towards agreements on trade, transportation and military liaison. It finalized a tourism agreement, and defined the parameters of co-ordination arrangements between the IDF and the Jordanian Army. The two sides also began talks on establishing an air corridor between Israel and Jordan.

On Feb. 9 Israel completed its full withdrawal from Jordanian territories, as agreed in the treaty. The supervision and joint border committees met in the Zofar and Naharayim areas. These areas were placed under Jordanian authority, although a special regime was enforced, to guarantee the agricultural rights of Israelis working there. The two armies deployed along the newly defined borders, and the committees set about establishing border crossings.

On May 8 the Israeli Environment Ministry Director-General Dr Yisrael Peleg and his Jordanian counterpart, Dr Duryad Hahshana, signed an environmental co-operation agreement at the Moriah Hotel, Tiberias, in Israel. The still brewing conflict between Israel and Jordan over sharing water resources was to some extent resolved on June 5 at a meeting held in Baqoura, Jordan.

In late July, the Jordanian National Assembly repealed three laws directed against Israel – the 1953 ban on trade, the 1958 economic boycott, and the1973 law prohibiting the sale of land to Israel or Israeli citizens (the repeal of the laws was stipulated in the 1994 treaty).

On Oct. 24 the Jordanian Interior Minister Salameh Hammad and Israeli Police Minister Moshe Shahal met in Beit Gavriel, on Lake Kinneret (Tiberias), and signed a police co-operation agreement on fighting crime and the drugs trade. The agreement added to the terms of the peace treaty, and established a framework for exchanging information and setting up a hotline between the two forces; co-operation on forensic and identification matters (including DNA tests); and provisions for coping with disasters.

FINAL AGREEMENT ON TRADE

On Oct. 25, the Israeli Industry and Trade Minister, Micha Harish, and the Jordanian Trade Minister, Ali Abu al-Ragheb, signed a long awaited bilateral trade agreement at the Moriah Hotel. Negotiations had taken nearly a year to complete. They became deadlocked in June when Jordan objected to the unfair advantages Israeli industries enjoyed in terms of subsidies. Jordanian negotatiors also feared that Israel would 'dump' cheaper goods on Jordan, and thus swamp the weaker Jordanian economy. Finally, Jordan was wary of an Israeli timetable to eliminate all duties within 12 years.

Without an agreement, however, all the ambitious joint projects envisaged in the original peace treaty would be stymied. With the anniversary of the peace treaty signing loomed, and as delegates began arriving for the showpiece Amman regional economic summit, pressure built up for a final accord. So Harish and Abu al-Ragheb reconvened and worked out a new agreement, altogether more complicated but also more cautious than the original draft plan. The final agreement set up a three-level structure of preferences – Israel would grant Jordan tariff reductions of up to 50% on most industrial products; a limited range of Israeli imports would get reductions of 15%; and 5% would apply two years after the start of the agreement. The preferences regime would apply for three years, and then be reviewed. Israel furthermore promised not to compete unfairly with certain Jordanian goods, such as plywood and tyres. For its part, Jordan passed a bill lifting the boycott of Israeli goods. The agreement set up a joint economic committee to encourage economic co-operation and share information. An annex to the agreement listed conditions for 'rules of origin' of goods, which had been a source of some dispute during negotiations.

OPPOSITION IN JORDAN

Israelis had hoped for an immediate 'warm peace' with Jordan (by contrast with the 'cold peace' that had prevailed with Egypt). Israeli tourists began flocking to formerly forbidden sites like Petra and the Wadi Rum Desert, and one enterprising Palestinian Jordanian opened Amman's first ever kosher restaurant to cater for the new visitors. But initial hopes of fostering lucrative economic joint ventures between the two states failed to materialize. This was partly due to difficulties in finalizing a free trade agreement (see above).

Meanwhile, popular opposition to the Jordan–Israel treaty in the Hashemite Kingdom did not go away. On May 29 the government banned an anti-peace conference sponsored by 11 Islamic and left-wing opposition parties, on the grounds that its conveners had made 'provocative statements against the homeland'. The anti-peace lobby particularly objected to suggestions of a Middle East common economic community, which they felt Israel would naturally dominate. Doubts about the lobby's real strength arose after the Islamic Action Front (Jordan's largest party and a fierce opponent of the peace treaty) was heavily defeated in municipal elections held on July 11 and 12.

Even so, opponents of peace did manage to hold a conference on Sept. 29. Salem Nahhas, the event's main convener, issued a call on all Jordanians to boycott Israeli businessmen and tourists, and stop all forms of 'normalization' between the two states. In October King Hussein condemned the 11 professional associations that had called on their members to boycott Israel. Many individual Jordanians complained that intimidation by anti-peace activists prevented them from pursuing opportunities with potential Israeli colleagues.

US ROLE AS GUARANTOR OF PEACE

On July 21 the US Congress passed a bill which financed the writing off of Jordan's remaining US$480mn debt to the USA. President Clinton repeatedly assured Israel and Jordan that the USA would be an active partner in their mutual peace process.

One year after the signing of the peace treaty, Israeli and Jordanian politicians, notably Foreign Minister Shimon Peres and Crown Prince Hassan, announced a string of new initiatives to define maritime boundaries, co-operate on trade and transportation links, develop tourism around the Dead Sea (shared between the two nations) and build a new international airport to serve Eilat and Aqaba jointly. Many of the ventures centre around the latter area. These include – a Red Sea Marine Peace Park (with aid from the US government) and schemes to establish a free-trade zone in Aqaba-Eilat. The long-term goal is to make the region an economic hub for the northern peninsula of the Red Sea. The anniversary was marked by a joint military fly-past over both nations. By this time, the US-Jordan-Israel Trilateral Economic Committee had completed the first phase of the Jordan Rift Valley (JRV) Joint Master Plan. The second phase, an 18-month Integrated Development Study of the JRV, began in Oct. 1995.

AMMAN CONFERENCE AND RABIN'S ASSASSINATION

These developments preceded a major regional economic conference in Amman, held in October 1995. At the conference, Israel presented 218 possible projects in a paper called 'Development Options for Middle East Co-operation'. The ambitious proposal anticipated expenditure of $25 billion. Many projects involved Jordan, including schemes to develop advanced optic fibre telecommunications throughout the Jordan Rift Valley. The conference concluded with an announcement that Jordan was chosen to be the permanent site of the Regional Economic Development Working Group of the multilateral talks.

The shocking assassination of Israeli Prime Minister Yitzhak Rabin on Nov. 4 seemed to throw the future of the peace process into doubt. Yet King Hussein's moving eulogy at Rabin's graveside reminded all parties of the importance of keeping peace alive, all the more striking as this was the first time he had visited Jerusalem since the day his grandfather was assassinated outside the Al-Aqsa Mosque in 1951.

LAST REMAINING TREATIES SIGNED

King Hussein paid his first official visit to Israel in January 1996, and was greeted by thousands of cheering Israelis. It was also the occasion for honouring the peace negotiators, Fayez Tarawneh and Elyakim Rubinstein. But most importantly, it coincided with the signing of the last remaining enabling treaties between Israel and Jordan on Jan. 16 and Jan. 18. These were

- Transportation and Civil Aviation
- Science and Culture
- Communications
- Aqaba-Eilat Agreement
- Maritime Borders Agreement

With the long-awaited signing of these agreements, politicians on both sides of the border expected a boom in bilateral trade and cultural contacts. In addition, Israel and Jordan held high level talks, about Israeli assistance to the Jordanian Armed Forces.

[Details of the enabling agreements are found at the end of Chapter 15.]

Chapter 11   Multilateral Talks

The principle of multilateral talks on region-wide issues was established at the Madrid Peace Conference of October 1991. As many see it, where the bilaterals try to sort out the problems of the past, the multilaterals address themselves to the challenges of the future. In theory, multilateral talks were to proceed simultaneously with (but separately from) bilateral talks. In practice, success or failure in one track inevitably effected progress in the other. Nonetheless, speaking in Jerusalem in July 1994, US Deputy Assistant Secretary of Near East Affairs, Dan Kurtzer, described them as the 'stealth peace process' – not often reported in the headlines, generally less 'glamorous' than head-on bilateral talks, yet in many ways more successful. In his view the multilaterals had not only quietly transformed themselves, but had also begun transforming the region. They have even laid the groundwork for Israel and Arab states to co-operate on tangible projects, long before they officially recognized each other.

It is an assessment shared by Israel's Foreign Ministry, which sees multilaterals as a means towards the long-term (but hitherto elusive) goal of regional 'normalization'. The ministry now has a distinct section to deal with 'the multilateral track' (alongside existing sections for relations with Egypt, Jordan, the PNA and the Maghreb). After the dramatic events of September 1993 (Israel's new understanding with the PLO and Jordan), the co-inciding 'fourth round' of multilateral talks displayed less posturing, and more concentration on actual projects to better the region. There was also a trend to base the talks in the Middle East itself. Most significantly, the multilaterals have extended the peace process beyond the confines of Israel and the 'frontline states', to the entire region. At present some 40 countries are involved.

NATURE OF THE TALKS

The talks tend to be looser in structure and more informal than bilateral negotiations. Because they are conducted less publicly, the various parties can try out new ideas without feeling they will 'lose out' politically. Quieter bargaining has superceded adversorial confrontation. While some may criticize the multilateral track for not delivering immediate practical results, it has opened new channels for former enemies. Equally, in early 1992 it provided the first forum for Palestinians from outside the territories to take part in talks. On all sides the track has served to 'de-demonize' the other; to identify common problems; and to create 'confidence-building measures' for a post-settlement Middle East. To sum up, the 'multilaterals' have two main purposes: to solve regional problems in a pragmatic manner; and to thereby promote normalized relations among the nations of the Middle East.

NEW MECHANISMS

The multilateral track has developed its own unique mechanisms – and occasionally bewildering organizational jargon (*see below*). Specialized *working groups*, consisting of delegations from the countries involved, consider particular issues of regional concern, and prepare reports and proposals. Over time these have led to practical infrastructure projects (such as highways and water pipelines) and codes of conduct on the environment, arms control, trade and so on. Ultimately, it was hoped, success on the ground would lead to open borders and economic partnership. Such developments would in turn give each of the Middle East countries a vested interest in achieving a peace that was much more than merely an 'absence of war'.

To lend prestige to the proceedings (and facilitate financial backing), important countries outside the Middle East (like the European Union, USA, Russia and Japan) act as *co-sponsors*, or guarantors, of the talks. Moscow was chosen as the setting for the initial talks, which opened on Jan. 28–29, 1992. (Thus analysts sometimes call multilaterals the 'Moscow track'.) Following the opening presentations by the co-sponsors and the participants – 36 parties in all – the delegations broke up into six specific *working groups*.

Each group is run by a *gavel-holder* (sometimes called a *lead organizer*), who is assisted by two or three *co-organizers*. The group also has a *bureau*, an ad hoc body consisting of US and Russian representatives, the gavel-holder, and representatives from the country hosting the next *plenary* session. In practice, much of the multilaterals' busiest work has taken place, not at plenaries, but at *inter-sessional* meetings. These can take the form of workshops, or visits (for instance, to schools, military sites or engineering works outside the Middle East, depending on the interest of the working group). In most cases, extra-regional countries have acted as *shepherds* to guide, promote and chivvy along projects which are considered during the intersessionals.

The five working groups deal with:

- Arms control and regional security
- Water resources
- Environment
- Economic development
- Refugees

THE KEY ROLE OF THE STEERING COMMITTEE

A multilateral steering committee constitutes the sixth working group, and is meant to be the cement which binds together the other five groups. Comprised of representatives from the key delegations, and co-chaired by the Madrid Conference sponsors, USA and Russia, it co-ordinates the multilateral talks and sets dates and venues for the various working groups. The committee meets at the end of each round of multilateral talks. It hears their reports, confirms their decisions and sets priorities for the allocation of resources. Ultimately, the committee aims to integrate the work of the individual working groups.

As with all groups, the committee uses consensus to reach its decisions, not majority voting. Joel Peters (an expert from the UK's Royal Institute of International Affairs) notes that this has introduced a 'formal egalitarianism' between parties. The advantage of such a format is especially valid in the light of certain Arab fears that Israel, backed by its US ally, would use its economic sophistication to mould the future shape of the Middle East. At the same time, though, 'egalitarianism' has led to committee members agreeing only on the 'lowest common denominator' – thus deferring more contentious decisions till later sessions.

The steering committee discusses broader issues as well, such as an overall vision of the future of the Middle East. There have been calls to extend its remit and make it more proactive, but so far the committee has blocked attempts to introduce extra working groups on vexing problems, like the question of Jerusalem. Nonetheless, on May 17 and 18, 1995, the steering group mandated Switzerland to 'shepherd' activities across a broad range of topics – civil, political, social and economic spheres, and cultural rights. Switzerland also advises co-sponsors on the 'human dimension' of the multilateral process, and strives to improve 'inter-cultural understanding' within the working groups.

THE PSYCHOLOGICAL DIMENSION

Alongside the nuts and bolts of the process is another consideration – the psychology of co-operating to achieve results. As one senior Israeli official explained: 'Each party has its own agenda. The challenge is not to let any one party dominate, but rather to find the common denominator. Often if there is a problem with one group, the solution may be found by the example of another. In fact, the very nature of the subject matter (water, for instance) is such that it does not make sense to 'solve' a problem within the borders of one country alone. If we all learn these lessons, the possibilities are enormous'.

Following that argument, the track appeared to reach a new level in mid-1995, with formal joint meetings between groups working in overlapping areas (for instance, water and the environment, which met in Amman). In addition, the spirit of the multilateral talks has increasingly seeped into events which occur outside it particular framework – most notably, the Middle East/ North Africa economic summits which took place in Casablanca in October 1994, and Amman in October 1995, and the Barcelona economic conference of Mediterranean rim countries, in November 1995. The talks have changed attitudes quite profoundly, one of the spin-offs being the Gulf Co-operation Council's decision to suspend secondary and tertiary boycotts of Israel.

IMPEDIMENTS TO PEACE

Finally, though, a word of caution – Syria and Lebanon have refused to participate in the multilateral process until they conclude their bilateral negotiations with Israel. Until that happens, many of the intra-regional projects involving other countries (including water, refugees, tourism and transport schemes) will remain effectively stymied. Conversely, some predict that as the multilateral talks achieve practical benefits, Lebanon and Syria may not wish to be 'left out', and will hasten their bilateral track talks so as to join in the multilateral track.

Aside from Israel's two northern neighbours, however, other countries also represent impediments to the process. Saudi Arabia is formally involved in talks, but in practice has been less active than other Gulf states (like Oman and Kuwait). As the home of Mecca and Medina, the holiest sites in Islam, and as the largest regional oil-producer and arms-purchaser, Saudi Arabia could herald a breakthrough if it participated more fully in the economics and arms control working groups. Iran still opposes deals with Israel, and consequently rejects the multilateral track. Its role cannot be ignored, considering its influence over Syria, its symbolic importance for Muslim fundamentalists, and its probable nuclear status. As long as it is excluded, Iran acts as a nexus for anti-peace agitation. Finally, Iraq is excluded from the talks, for legal reasons (UN sanctions) and political reasons (enmity of Gulf States and the USA against Saddam Hussein after the Gulf War). Yet in the long term, Iraq's participation (probably after Saddam's departure) could well open up huge possibilities for a revival of the Fertile Crescent.

For the present, these remain distant dreams – proof, perhaps, of the ultimate failure of 'rationality' and market forces to overcome political strife. If anything, they remind one of the realities in the Middle East, and make the multilaterals' achievements so far seem all the more remarkable.

Below is a summary of the dates and venues of multilateral sessions held to date.

Timetable

MADRID PEACE CONFERENCE – LAUNCHING THE PROCESS

Oct. 30 – Nov. 1, 1991

Co-sponsors
United States and Russia

Regional participants
Israel, Jordan, Palestinians, Egypt, Syria and Lebanon

MOSCOW PEACE CONFERENCE – MULTILATERAL OPENING SESSION

Jan. 28–29, 1992

Co-sponsors
United States and Russia

Regional participants
Israel, Jordan, Palestinians and Egypt
(Syria and Lebanon are boycotting the multilateral talks until more progress is made at the bilateral track)

Arab states
Saudi Arabia, United Arab Emirates, Oman, Kuwait, Bahrain, Qatar, Yemen, Morocco, Algeria, Tunisia and Mauretania

Other participating states
Japan, Italy, France, Germany, Great Britain, Canada, Netherlands, Belgium, Luxembourg, Finland,

Sweden, Norway, Denmark, India, China, Greece, Turkey, Spain, Portugal, Switzerland and Austria (Hungary, Romania and South Korea joined in July 1994)

Other bodies
United Nations and UN Development Programme, World Bank, and the European Union

MULTILATERAL WORKING GROUPS

Multilateral steering group
(US/Russia: co-chair)

Members
USA, Russia, EC, Saudi Arabia (on behalf of the GCC), Tunisia (on behalf of the Arab Maghreb Union), Egypt; and the parties to the conflict.
(Norway, as chair of the Ad Hoc Liaison Committee to the October 1993 donors' conference on aid to the Palestinians, was invited to join the group in December 1993).

Round 1	Jan. 28–29, 1992	Moscow, Russia
Round 2	May 27, 1992	Lisbon, Portugal
Round 3	Dec. 3–4, 1992	London, UK
Round 4	July 7, 1993	Moscow, Russia
Round 5	Dec. 15, 1993	Tokyo, Japan
Round 6	July 12–13, 1994	Tabarka, Tunisia
Round 7	Feb. 1995	Montebello, Canada

Arms control and regional security
(US/Russia: co-lead organizer)

Round 1	Jan. 28–29, 1992	Moscow, Russia
Round 2	May 11–14, 1992	Washington DC, USA
Round 3	Sept. 15–17, 1992	Moscow, Russia
Round 4	May 18–20, 1993	Washington DC, USA
Round 5	Nov. 2–4, 1993	Moscow, Russia
Round 6	May 3–5, 1994	Doha, Qatar
Intersessional	October	Paris, France
Round 7	Dec. 13–15 1994	Tunis, Tunisia
Intersessional	April 4–6 1995	Analya, Turkey
Intersessional	May 29 – June 1, 1995	Helsinki, Finland
Intersessional	Sept. 20–21 1995	Amman, Jordan

Water resources
(US: lead organizer; Japan and EU: co-lead)

Round 1	Jan. 28–29, 1992	Moscow, Russia
Round 2	May 14–15, 1992	Vienna, Austria
Round 3	Sept. 16–17, 1992	Washington, DC, USA
Round 4	April 27–29, 1993	Geneva, Switzerland
Round 5	Oct. 26–28, 1993	Beijing, China
Round 6	April 17–19, 1994	Muscat, Oman
Round 7	Nov. 7–9, 1994	Athens, Greece
Round 8	June 21,1995	Amman, Jordan [combined with environment group]

Environment
(Japan: permanent gavel holder; EU: co-organizer)

Round 1	Jan. 28–29, 1992	Moscow, Russia
Round 2	May 18–19, 1992	Tokyo, Japan
Round 3	Sept. 26–27, 1992	The Hague, Netherlands
Round 4	April 24–25, 1993	Tokyo, Japan

Round 5	Nov. 15–16, 1993	Cairo, Egypt
Round 6	April 6–7, 1994	The Hague, Netherlands
Round 7	Oct. 25–26, 1994	Manama, Bahrain
Round 8	June 21, 1995	Amman, Jordan [combined with water group]

Economic development
(EU: lead organizer; US and Japan: co-lead)

Round 1	Jan. 28–29, 1992	Moscow, Russia
Round 2	May 11–12, 1992	Brussels, Belgium
Round 3	Oct. 29–30, 1992	Paris, France
Round 4	May 4–5, 1993	Rome, Italy
Round 5	Nov. 8–9, 1993	Copenhagen, Denmark
Round 6	June 15–16, 1994	Rabat, Morocco
Round 7		Germany

Refugees
(Canada: lead organizer)

Round 1	Jan. 28–29, 1992	Moscow, Russia
Round 2	May 13–15, 1992	Ottawa, Canada
Round 3	Nov. 11–12, 1992	Ottawa, Canada
Round 4	May 11–13, 1993	Oslo, Norway
Round 5	Oct. 12–14, 1993	Tunis, Tunisia
Round 6	May 10–12, 1994	Cairo, Egypt
Round 7	[date to be announced]	Turkey

Achievements to date

ARMS CONTROL AND REGIONAL SECURITY

Key projects

- Crisis Prevention Centre
- Regional Security Centre
- Arms Control data-bank
- Naval exercise and conference of regional naval officers
- Communications Centre

Progress to date

In the wake of the Gulf War, most parties in the Middle East appreciate the value of knowing where and how conflicts may arise. Equally, they want to have mechanisms available to prevent them occurring where possible. Thus transparency and mutual assurance have been key elements of all sessions run by this particular working group. Since the Qatar plenary meeting, the group dealt with pressing issues at intersessional meetings, in Paris, Jordan, Canada, Germany and Switzerland. These basically divide into two sorts – operative and conceptual.

'Operative' issues included: papers on search and rescue at sea; plans for a senior naval officers' conference; an agreement on prenotification of military exercises; an agreement to exchange information on military matters; plans for a regional regional military communications centre, with several sub-stations ordered; plans to set up a Regional Security Centre (RSC) to prevent, manage and resolve crises as they occur.

'Conceptual' issues included: a statement on arms control and regional security, including definitions of long-term goals in this field; a seminar on 'threat perception in the Middle East'; a geographical 'delineation' of the Middle East for purposes of regional security; groundwork towards a discussion on controlling nuclear, conventional, chemical and biological arms, and ballistic missiles.

In October 1994, delegates from Saudia Arabia, Israel, the Gulf States, Tunisia and Algeria met at an intersessional meeting in Paris and formulated a document describing the security and peace relations of the whole region. Forty-three participants (15 of them from the region) attended the last plenary session, held in Tunis in December. Delegates decided to establish the RSC in Amman, with secondary centres in Tunisia and Oman. Since then, there were three intersessionals – operational issues were discussed in Turkey in April 1995, conceptual issues in Finland in May, and an experts' meeting was held in Amman in September.

The Turkish meeting considered three confidence-building measures:

- a temporary working group communications network, which started operating in March 1995;
- a draft agreement on prevention of incidents at sea; and
- methods of exchanging information (including unclassified military publications) between military officers, and prenotifying each other about military exercises.

The Helsinki meeting discussed the aims, methods and parameters which were needed to begin negotiations on arms control. Experts from Australia, France, India and the UN attended this meeting. The French elected to hold a seminar on military doctrines in Amman at the end of 1995. Finally, the experts' meeting in Amman thrashed out details of how the proposed RSC would operate, and what should be covered by its seminars.

ENVIRONMENT

Key projects

- Gulf of Aqaba/Eilat: Regional oil spill emergency centres
- Environment management: Workshops, databanks, studies
- Desertification: Projects to address the degradation of natural resources
- Bahrain Code of Conduct: Blueprint for environmental action in the Middle East

Progress to date

The Bahrain round of the working group, which consisted of 41 delegations, was considered a particular success. Held in October 1994, it endorsed an Environmental Code of Conduct for the Middle East, which delegates claimed could serve as a model by other working groups. The code stressed that regional peace and environmental protection were interdependent. To that end, it committed delegates to co-operate in encouraging public awareness and to join forces in protecting water, marine and coastal environments, air, and waste management.

In June 1994, delegates issued a joint statement on sewage treatment in small communities, (and Bahrain took this a stage further). The Gulf of Eilat/Aqaba Pollution Project was reported to be ahead of schedule, and had firm promises of EU funding. There were also discussions on setting up a Palestinian Environmental Management Structure.

Furthermore, in November 1994, a plan originally mooted by Canada at the May 1993 Tokyo meeting came to fruition, when Cairo hosted an advanced 'environmental impact assessment' (EIA) training course for water and environment working group delegates. In time, it is hoped, the whole Middle East will become part of an EIA network, using the latest satellite technology to communicate possible sources of ecological danger. In December 1994, Cairo also convened a US-sponsored workshop to define threats to public health in the region. It particularly concentrated on the safe use of pesticides, and entailed setting up a thorough training, communications and research programme.

At the working group's meeting in Amman on June 21, 1995, the World Bank reported on how to fund a joint Tunisian-Egyptian-Jordanian-Israeli project to combat desertification. (The project was first proposed at the Cairo session in November 1993, and included plans to establish grazing lands, wildlife and even orchards in arid areas.) Five regional stations would be set up, each looking into a specific aspect of the problem.

The Amman talks also revealed that three stations had been set up (in Aqaba, Eilat and

Nuweiba), to help co-ordinate the fight against pollution in the Gulf of Aqaba. The Gulf project is funded by the EU and Japan, and Norway will run training programmes for participating countries. Regional environment centres were planned for Jordan and Bahrain. Crown Prince Hassan opened a joint meeting of the environmental and water working groups. Participants there unanimously adopted the Code of Conduct.

WATER RESOURCES

Key projects

- Desalination research and technology centre in Muscat
- Waste water treatment facilities (at several Middle Eastern sites)
- Regional training programme for water personnel

Progress to date

At the fourth round, the working party met in Muscat, Oman in April 1994, and raised the possibility of a desalination research and technology centre there. It was a significant meeting – the first held in the Gulf region, and the first attended by a senior Israeli politician (Deputy Foreign Minister, Yossi Beilin).

In Athens, November 1994, delegates explored an Israeli proposal to overhaul water systems in small-sized communities (primarily by repairing leaking pipes), and agreed to set up a project committee to identify sites. New plans were raised, including collecting water in Gaza, desalinating brackish water in Jordan, and training people in how to use geothermal water in hothouses. The group endorsed a US/EU plan for regional water data banks. This tallied with an investigation into how to manage Middle Eastern water resources in a strategic way.

Much of the group's work complemented bilateral projects – for instance, the Israel–Jordan agreement on sharing the waters of the Yarmuk and Jordan Rivers, and the Israel–Palestinian Interim Agreement (September 1995) regarding access to the water table in the West Bank area.

In June 1995, the water resources group met jointly with the environmental group in Amman, Jordan, to plan common strategies in related fields. For the first time Palestinians were represented (by their Water Commissioner, Nabil Sharif). The head of the Israeli delegation, Avraham Katz-Oz, estimated that some $200m would be needed each year to set up projects and supply water to the Middle East states. A number of new plans were added to older ones, including a Dutch proposal to build a dam in Nahal Besor/ Wadi Aza, to enrich the Gaza Strip's aquifer. The USA, EU, Japan, Austria, Israel and the Netherlands all promised funding for joint projects.

ECONOMIC DEVELOPMENT

Key projects

- Aqaba-Eilat-Sinai highway
- Hydro-electric project study of Dead Sea–Red Sea and Dead Sea–Mediterranean canals
- Linking regional electricity grids (Israel, Egypt, Jordan and the Palestinian autonomous area)
- Regional veterinary services
- Regional tourist centre

Progress to date

A Copenhagen Action Plan (consisting of 35 projects) was adopted at the fifth round of the economic development working group, on Nov. 9, 1993. At the next round, held in Rabat on June 15 and 16, 1994, the group discussed how to implement the Action Plan. It also set up a monitoring committee to set priorities for the working group, with the following aims:

- to encourage free movement of people, goods, capital and services
- to stimulate economic development and reduce regional disparities

- to integrate the region into global markets, and
- to promote regional trade and investment.

The working group heard reports on the major projects. An EU-Austrian initiative examined the possibility of integrating the region's electricity grids and harnessing hydro-electric power in the Dead Sea. Italy offered a pre-feasability study of an Egypt–Gaza pipeline. Spain presented plans for developing agriculture in the region, and sent two teams of experts to investigate the potential. The UK concentrated on finding ways to improve co-operation between Middle Eastern stock markets. The USA ran a public administration training course for Palestinians and a regional seminar on agriculture.

The EU is committed to creating networks between cities, universities and the media in Israel, Jordan, Egypt and the territories. Germany produced one study on regional trade co-operation, and another on vocational training; while Switzerland offered training in hotel management. Japan assumed responsibility for promoting tourism in the region, and ran a workshop to this effect in Cairo. Plans were afoot to set up a regional tourist centre in Egypt; and convene meetings of tourist agents in Cairo and Amman in 1994. Egypt also suggested better ways to exchange economic data in the region; while Canada started producing literature on economic co-operation in the Middle East. The World Bank planned a regional workshop to help integrate the private sector into infrastructure projects. Other projects dealt with developing civil aviation and ports.

Partially as a consequence of this success, the Gulf Co-operation Council (GCC) lifted its secondary and tertiary boycott of Israel on Sept. 30, 1994. This in turn set the scene for an important Middle East/North Africa Economic Summit, which was held in Casablanca, Morocco, from Oct. 30 to Nov. 1, 1994. Representatives from 61 countries and 1,114 international business leaders met there to discuss further projects in the region. The Casablanca Summit endorsed the GCC ban on the boycott. It also agreed to set up four regional centres:

- A Middle East and North Africa bank
- A Tourist Board
- A regional Chamber of Commerce and Business Council
- A Steering Committee (to follow up issues raised at the conference)

In January 1995, the working group endorsed ambitious plans to build trans-national highways in the Middle East. Based on French proposals at the Copenhagen meeting, it includes 13 cross-border highways, six running north–south, and seven east–west. In October 1994 representatives from Egypt, Israel, the PNA and Jordan decided to set up a task force to investigate the possiblity of a regional Middle Eastern/North African bank to further economic development in the region. As a result, some 30 parties met in Washington in March 1995, under the guidance of US Under Secretary of State Janet Spero (economics chief of the Department of State). They later reconvened in Amman.

An important regional economic summit in Amman, Jordan, held between Oct. 29 and 31, 1995, patroned by King Hussein, co-sponsored by the Presidents of the USA and Russia, and convened by the World Economic Forum (based in Geneva, Switzerland). Israel sent 40 government officials and 60 representatives from the private sector. The summit concentrated on plans to integrate the private sector into government schemes. To this end, participants focused on trade liberalization, privatization, exchange controls and capital markets. Apart from providing a forum for all parties to present projects for the private sector, there were also many 'industry workshops', where participants met government officials and business counterparts to explore opportunities for partnerships. Business executives and cabinet ministers examined the most suitable economic policies essential for decreasing commercial barriers while also providing a 'hands on' approach to doing business in the region. Each participating country hosted a luncheon to encourage 'networking' with key decision makers.

At the end of the conference, delegates endorsed a decision to set up the Middle East bank (see above). It would be built in Cairo over a period of three years.

REFUGEES

Key projects

- Human resources: Training courses for refugees
- Child welfare: Programmes to assist refugee children
- Social and economic infrastructure:Rehabilitation and housing for refugees
- Public health: Regional laboratory for medical care of refugees
- Database: Surveys and statistics as bedrock of future policy
- Family reunification: Proposals for a framework

Progress to date

Of all the working groups, this one seems to be most dependent on progress at bilateral talks. The question of refugees and displaced persons was a key issue in the Israel–Jordan peace treaty. (Technically, *refugees* refers to Palestinians who left Palestine in 1948; *displaced persons* refers to Palestinians who left the West Bank and Gaza in 1967.) The issue of refugees will also be one of the main points of contention in the 'final status' bilateral talks between Israel and the Palestinians (scheduled to begin in 1996).

In October 1992, Egyptian Foreign Minister Amr Moussa persuaded Israel to accept a delegation of diaspora Palestinians, headed by Dr Muhammad Hallaj, at the November talks in Ottawa. This was regarded as a major procedural breakthrough, and indicated that Israel's new Labour government was willing to address the broader ramifications of Palestinian rights. Meanwhile, the Norwegian Institute for Social Sciences (FAFO) was busy preparing a survey on real living conditions in refugee camps. FAFO issued reports in July 1992 and November 1993. (Incidentally, FAFO was also used as the cover for initiatives by its head, Terje Larsen, which led to the secret Oslo talks between Israel and the PLO, and ultimately to the Declaration of Principles of Sept. 13, 1993.)

Just before the official Oslo talks (round four of the working group), the French diplomat, Bernard Bajolet, visited the region in April 1993, and met experts in family re-unification from Egypt, Jordan, Israel and the Palestinians. Bajolet's recommendations were largely adopted. These included widening the net of beneficiaries, but slowing down the number of new applications, and making Israeli policy more 'transparent'. The Tunis talks (October 1993) concentrated on the immediate humanitarian aspects of the refugee issue. Israel agreed to approve 2,000 family re-unification certificates annually, and permitted several deportees of the early 1970s to return to the territories, together with their families.

At Cairo (May 1994) it was agreed to harness much of the World Bank's Emergency Assistance Programme to a number of projects. These included: human resources training for refugees, in agriculture, job creation, paramedics and public health, and education (run by Israel, USA, the Netherlands, Germany, Turkey and China, amongst others); child welfare programmes (Sweden to provide $2m); rehabilitation and housing projects for refugees in Syria and Lebanon (with aid from USA); and a regional laboratory for the medical needs of West Bank refugees.

On March 7, 1995, ministers from Israel, PLO, Jordan and Egypt met in Amman, Jordan, and set up a Continuing Committee to decide on the practicalities of absorbing back into Gaza and the West Bank the displaced persons of 1967. They agreed to establish two levels of investigation – interministerial, meeting every three months; and technical, meeting every three weeks.

Chapter 12   Other Bilateral Talks

A comprehensive Middle East peace will never become a reality until Israel reaches an accord with Syria and Lebanon. To date, both countries have boycotted the multilateral track talks, pending progress on the bilateral front. So Israel–Syria and Israel–Lebanon peace treaties would therefore not only be good in themselves, but would also greatly boost the multilateral regional peace track.

So far no deal has been struck between Israel and her two neighbours, despite frenetic negotiations, and many raised hopes. Below is a summary of the progress on these two tracks, and an introduction to the issues concerned. This chapter also gives an overview of the talks which led to a treaty between the Israel and the Holy See. Although not part of the Madrid process, these talks were certainly one successful by-product of the new negotiating process taking place in the Middle East, and could well have positive repercussions for the cause of peace. Finally, there is a record of Israel's restored diplomatic relations with other non-Middle Eastern nations – an indirect 'peace dividend'.

Israel and Syria

Ever since the mid-1970s, when Egypt began its slow rapprochement with Israel, Syria has regarded itself as the natural leader of the Arab campaign against Israel. From time to time President Assad has presumed to dictate terms to the PLO. When the mainstream PLO under Arafat rejected such terms, especially after 1982, Syria openly backed anti-Arafat factions in the refugee camps of Lebanon. Although subsequently Arafat and Assad patched up relations, Syria still hosts many PLO 'rejectionist' movements, as well as *Hamas* and Islamic *Jihad* leaders.

The collapse of the Soviet Union (Syria's superpower ally), and the circumstances of the Gulf War, both forced Syria into the broadly 'Western camp'. In November 1990 US President George Bush spoke with President Assad and permitted Syria to enter Lebanon, crush the renegade General Michel Aoun, and thereby 'restore order'. Some saw this as the price to pay for getting Syria to join the anti-Saddam coalition. The USA also dropped its naming of Syria as a 'terrorist state', lifted existing trade sanctions, and in 1991 managed to persuade Damascus to do what just a year earlier would have been unthinkable – join in talks with an Israeli delegation at the Madrid peace conference.

From the American perspective, Syria was now seen as a vital counterweight to neighbouring Iraq. For its part, Israel regarded a peace treaty with Syria as the final piece in a puzzle – attaining real security in its vulnerable north-east corner, and neutralizing the threat posed by Israel's strongest military foe in the region. Israel also calculated that a deal with Syria would immediately open the door to a similar deal with Lebanon (seeing as Lebanese foreign policy has been largely determined by Syria ever since the 1989 Taif Accord). However, day three of the Madrid summit, in November 1991, where the delegation heads exchanged insults, revealed the enormous gulf that existed between Israel and Syria. In successive months of negotiations, talks scarcely moved beyond the procedural stage.

THE PROBLEM OF THE GOLAN HEIGHTS

Ostensibly, control of the Golan Heights is the main impediment to peace between Syria and Israel. Israel gained the Golan Heights in 1967, and beat off a concerted Syrian attack to regain them in 1973. On Dec. 14, 1981, Israel formally annexed the Heights. Since 1973, the two states have maintained their state of war, but apart from peripheral clashes in Lebanon there has been no open conflict. Indeed, in the Gulf War of 1991, Israel and Syria found themselves on the same side for the first time (against Saddam Hussein), although Israel was technically neutral.

To explain the negotiating stances of each nation, one has to investigate their perceptions of each other. Israel considers Syria to be its biggest single military threat, and thus wants to keep the Golan Heights for security reasons. It fears that if Syria re-possessed the Golan, its heavy guns would be continually aimed at vulnerable Israeli settlements in the valley below, as was the case before 1967. Israel also fears that Syria has not abandoned its dream of a Greater Syria, encompassing Lebanon and all of 'historic Palestine' (ironically, a fear also shared by the PLO). As a 'confidence-building measure', Israel called on Syria to allow its small Jewish community the right to emigrate. The presence of 14,000 Jewish inhabitants in the Golan is another factor. Only a full peace deal with Syria will suffice for Israel to return the territory.

Syria, however, demands the full return of the Golan in exchange for peace. For its part, Syria perceives Israel as its greatest threat. For that reason it also wants the security of the Golan, which it regards as a symbol of Syrian territorial integrity. Syria furthermore called for a 'comprehensive peace', implying that it will not move on the Golan issue until the Palestinians and Lebanese strike satisfactory peace deals with Israel. What has ensued ever since is a waiting game, with possible agreements continually thwarted by a profound lack of trust between the two states.

FAINT SIGNS OF PROGRESS

The first signs of a Syrian overture came in April 1992 with the lifting of travel restrictions for Syria's Jewish community. After the election of Labour in Israel in June 1992, the new Rabin government renewed efforts to reach a deal with Syria. Yossi Ben Aharon, Israel's hardline chief negotiator with Syria, was replaced by Prof. Itamar Rabinovitch, and in September 1992 Israel intimated that it could return part of the Golan in exchange for peace. Israel's deportation of alleged *Hamas* militants in December threw the entire peace process in jeopardy. Notwithstanding rumours of secret Israeli–Syrian talks in a European capital, the official Syrian line was best expresed when Vice-President Khaddam and Foreign Minister ash-Shar'a visited Iran, and seemed to reaffirm an anti-Israel alliance.

Hopes rose at the ninth round of bilateral talks, held in April and May, but these too came to nothing. If anything, matters worsened at the 10th round (June–July 1993) when the Syrian delegation head, Muwaffaq al-Alaf, criticized Rabin's early alleged remarks about never returning all of the Golan to Syria. US Secretary Warren Christopher then promised Israel 'security guarantees' on the Golan if it made significant progress in talks with Syria.

The 11th round in September was eclipsed by the news of the Israeli–Palestinian break-through (the result of the Oslo negotiations). Syria objected to the deal, but Warren Christopher met Assad and ash-Shar'a in Damascus in December, and President Clinton himself followed this up with a five-hour meeting in Geneva on Jan. 16, 1994. The result was Syria's first affirmation that it was prepared to establish 'normal, peaceful relations' with Israel. Two days later, Yitzhak Rabin responded by saying Israel was willing to pay 'a painful price' for peace. However, he also said that Israel should hold a referendum prior to any withdrawal – a view criticized by ash-Shar'a as being 'against international law'.

Nonetheless, in March Assad personally met a 57-strong delegation of Israeli Arabs, who came to pay their condolences over the death of Assad's son, Basil. This was seen as a new advance for Israel–Syria relations, all the more so when Assad suggested he would meet Rabin in person if that might further the peace process. Political analysts began to suggest that Syria feared being 'left out' of the peace process, as the PLO, Morocco, Jordan, and even Oman and Qatar were improving relations with the Jewish state.

TALKING ABOUT PRACTICALITIES

On April 30, 1994, Warren Christopher visited Assad in Damascus, and presented the first practical proposals for a staged Israeli withdrawal. Known as 'Majdal Shams First', it envisaged an eight-year process, including

- Stage One: Syrian control of four Druze settlements on the Golan Heights
- Stage Two: Israeli closure of Jewish settlements
- Stage Three: A final and full withdrawal.

While officially rejecting these terms, Syria kept the door open. Quietly, talks began between Israel's chief of staff, Ehud Barak, and his Syrian opposite number, Hikmat Shihabi (re-garded by some observers as number two to Assad himself). These security talks paralleled the more overtly political talks in Washington. In September Rabin presented new plans for a partial Israeli withdrawal, to be followed by a three-year trial period of Israeli–Syrian 'normalization'. While rejecting the plan, Assad did say Syria would meet the 'objective requirements of peace'. While a clutch of politicians welcomed the new signals from Damascus (including Shimon Peres, Itamar Rabinovich and Denis Ross, US special co-ordinator for the peace talks), many Israeli Golan settlers began an 'anti-withdrawal' hunger strike. Prospects of a Golan withdrawal also threatened to split the ruling Labour party. Seven Labour 'Golan rebels' tabling a motion demanding that withdrawal was only acceptable if approved by 70 out of 120 MKs, or 65% of voters in a referendum.

On Oct. 27 saw Clinton visited Assad for talks in Damascus, the first such visit by a US president in 20 years. He reported to the Israeli *Knesset* that Syria had made 'a strategic choice for peace with Israel'. In late 1994 Israel suggested that there might be mutual cutbacks in the standing armies of each country. (Syria had five divisions posted near the Golan, while Israel had two, augmented by reserves.) But Hafez al-Assad interpreted this as unjustified interference in Syrian internal affairs, and promptly suspended negotiations. Evidently he was also angry that Jordan had signed a separate peace deal with Israel, without properly consulting Damascus.

BREAKING THE DEADLOCK

On Jan. 5, 1995, the prominent Syrian Sunni cleric, Sheikh Muhammad Said Albouti, issued an unprecedented *fatwa* (religious ruling) in support of a peace treaty between Syria and Israel. However, talks only resumed in March 1995. The breakthrough came on May 24, 1995, with the announcement of a 'framework understanding on security arrangements'. It was mainly brokered by the hard-working US State Department team, and provided for clearly established goals for military talks in Washington.

This time they focused on four 'legs' – security, normalization, withdrawal and a time framework for implementation. The military chiefs of staff of each country are discussing security issues – Amnon Shahak for Israel, formerly deputy to his predecessor, Ehud Barak; and Hikmat Shihabi for Syria. The remaining three legs are the domain of each country's ambassador to Washington (Itamar Rabinovich for Israel and Walid Mualem for Syria).

The teams remained deeply divided over ultimate goals and timetables – Syrians wanted a full return, at the latest within 18 months; while the Israelis preferred a staged and partial withdrawal over four years (not eight, as earlier). Rabin's plan (announced to the cabinet in January, but only made public now) aimed to minimize the risk of a surprise attack from Syria. It consists of a two-stage withdrawal of Israeli forces and stressed four key elements:

● Early warning: Israel to get an early warning station on Mt Hermon near the Syrian border; Syria to get a similar facility near Safad in Israel
● Demilitarized zones: The entire Golan Heights area would be demilitarized, and there would be a limited forces zone some 40km into Syria
● International forces: A US-led force would monitor movements of forces and act as a tripwire in the event of a Syrian attack
● Confidence measures: Joint Syrian–Israeli military patrols, exchanges of military observers, a hotline between high commands of both armies.

Arye Shalev of the Jaffee Centre for Strategic Studies, a strategic analyst close to *Likud* leader Benjamin Netanyahu, argued that this conceded too much to Syria. In his view, a 'peace between peoples' should precede any border changes. Countering this argument, Labour supporters, like Ori Orr, chairman of the Knesset's Foreign Affairs and Defence Committee, believed excessive Israeli caution would only undermine the pro-peace lobby in Syria. Yet despite differences of emphasis, both Labour and *Likud* seem to have accepted the principle that some, if not all, of the Golan could be returned in exchange for a lasting peace with Syria.

In June 1995, Syrian and Iranian officials met in Teheran and issued a joint statement, reaffirming their strategic alliance, and committing Syria to deny Israel a peace deal until it completely withdrew from the Golan and its 'security zone' in south Lebanon. Syrian Vice-President Khaddam described the gap between Israel and his country as 'vast'.

On July 4 Syria seemed to display a new mood of pragmatism. Amnon Shahak revealed to the Israeli cabinet a new proposal, reportedly given to him by his opposite number, General Hikmat Shihabi. In it, Syria would withdraw 1,000m for every 600m withdrawn by Israel. This was the first time Syria had accepted the principle of 'assymetrical withdrawal' which Israel had insisted on (to compensate Israel for its lack of strategic depth, and the comparitive smallness of its standing defence forces). As ever, the optimism was shortlived, with Syria regarding the early warning stations as 'unpalatable'. Rabin stated publicly, 'the degree of the Israeli withdrawal is related to the degree of peace achieved'.

ISRAELI BACKLASH, SYRIAN INTRANSIGENCE

In late July, the Israeli Knesset narrowly voted down a bill to delay talks until a referendum was held. Although the mainstream Labour Party had technically won, it was a tied ballot (59–59) with the Speaker voting with the government. With such a small margin, the talks were downgraded. The bill's main proposer was a former general and now leading Labour MK, Avigdor Kahalani, who had led Israel's counter-attack against a Syrian thrust in the Golan area in 1973. Together with other Labour colleagues, Kahalani belongs to The Third Way, a group which in October 1995 announced that it might stand as an independent party.

Such are the sort of questions which Prime Minister Yitzhak Rabin faced as he viewed the prospect of elections in 1996. In his bid to win national popularity, he had to balance the benefits of the longed-for peace with Syria, against the deficit of 'sacrificing' the Golan (the expected price of a lasting peace deal). In the process, he risked a Labour revolt which prompted early elections. Some analysts believed the timescale was too tight, and emotions too fraught, for Rabin to grasp the Golan nettle. Achieving a treaty would be the ultimate Labour electoral 'trump card'; but trying and failing would be seen as a bitter defeat.

From Assad's point of view, time is the essential ingredient. He knows how keen the Israeli government is to achieve a treaty, and so believes he can afford to hold out as long as possible for the best terms. On the other hand, if he waited until after a possible *Likud* victory in 1996, the window of opportunity may have closed. The final imponderable is Syria's sincerity. Certainly, Syria appears to speak in two voices – ameliatory when talking to the USA, but belligerently anti-Israeli when in the company of its Iranian allies. And as *Likud* politicians repeatedly point out, who can say whether Syria will be satisfied with just the Golan? Assad's past record suggests that he is quite likely to 'move the goalposts' whenever it suits Syrian interests. By late August, Rabin seemed to be moving towards temporarily shelving the Syrian/Golan Heights issue. Israel openly voiced anger at *Hezbollah* attacks in southern Lebanon, which it saw as a Syrian venture by proxy.

Rabin chose to concentrate instead on the Palestinian front, the result being the Interim Agreement, or 'Oslo 2', of Sept. 28, 1995. His assassination, on Nov. 4, appeared to force a Syrian reappraisal of affairs. Although Syria did not send a delegation to the funeral (as Egypt, Oman, Qatar and Jordan all did), President Assad did tell US Secretary of State Warren Christopher that he was keen for a 'quick peace treaty' with Israel. He also contacted Israel's new prime minister, Shimon Peres, directly, and said only a comprehensive peace would prevent further tragedies in the region.

Peres's advisers have responded in kind. However, Peres's first priority was to restore unity to a shocked Israeli populus, and this might displace considerations about a Syrian peace treaty. Furthermore, in the public eye Peres lacks the military reputation which Rabin drew on, when persuading sceptics to risk a Golan withdrawal. Even so, Peres is a wily politician, who felt that he had a full year to complete Rabin's programme before election-time. Israeli commentator, Chemi Shalev, noted that Peres's style may suit the Syrians better than Rabin's did. Where Rabin favoured security as the main feature, Peres sees it as part of a total 'package'. And where Rabin encouraged piece by piece negotiations, Peres is known for his simultaneous 'multipolar' negotiating stance. Unlike Rabin, Peres is on record as saying that Israel may return the entire Golan to Syria, if the conditions are right. Israeli right-wingers feared Assad may call Peres's bluff. But few Israelis have better diplomatic experience than Peres who hoped to attain the goal of peace with Syria – if Assad willed it.

[For an update on Israel-Syria talks during the Peres Prime Ministership see Chapter 20.]

Israel and Lebanon

Relations between Israel and Lebanon have been blighted by open warfare in the past, and a smouldering conflict today. The Madrid track talks of late 1991 seemed to offer a chance for peace; but these talks stalled in February 1994, and at present there is no official contact between the two sides. Israel's interest in Lebanon stemmed from two factors – a desire to counter the PLO, which was based in Lebanon; and a belief that Lebanese Christians were natural allies of Israel. Israel currently holds a piece of Lebanese territory, the southern 'security zone'. But as Lebanon is not considered part of *Eretz Yisrael*, there should be no theological objections to returning it to Lebanese authority, if peace were to bring real security.

In 1978 Israel launched Operation Litani, a limited campaign to retaliate against PLO attacks across the border. In June 1982, Israel invaded on a much larger scale, after the attempted assassination of its ambassador in London. Israel's initial aim was to drive the PLO out of their southern Lebanese camps, from which they had often attacked civilian sites in Israel. Once in motion, however, Operation 'Peace for Galilee' carried the Israel Defence Forces on towards the outskirts of Beirut, where the PLO was headquartered. Urged forward by an inner cabinet clique led by Ariel Sharon, they were now following a more ambitious two-pronged strategy – to eradicate the PLO as an organization, and to forge an alliance with right-wing Christian Arabs in Lebanon, the Maronite *Phalange*. The latter policy conforms to a long-standing Israeli tradition, of finding allies amongst fellow minorities in the Middle East. (By the same logic Israel used to support the Iranians under the Shah, and the Kurds, groups which were Muslim but not Arab.)

LEGACY OF WAR

Ultimately, Israel hoped to sign a peace treaty with a friendly Lebanon. Following hard upon the implementation of the Egyptian peace treaty, this would mean Israel could enjoy secure relations with two of the four neighbouring 'confrontation states' (the other two being Jordan and Syria). In military terms, the operation began successfully and Israeli forces overran PLO positions. However, Israel soon became embroiled in the internecine conflicts of Lebanon's remarkably complicated ethnic civil war. Worse still for public morale, and for Israel's international reputation, the IDF's vigorous attack led to increased civilian casualties. Israel pinned its hopes on a deal with president-elect Bashir Gemayel, a determined enemy of the PLO. However, he was assassinated in September before taking office.

When Christian militias took revenge by massacring inhabitants in two Palestinian refugee camps under Israel's temporary suzerainty, Sabra and Chatilla, Israel was condemned internationally. The tragedy also launched an anti-war mass movement within Israel, led by a revived Peace Now. Ultimately, it may explain Begin's surprise resignation in 1983. In May of that year Israel did sign an agreement with Amin Gemayel, Bashir's brother and successor as president. However, it fell far short of a full peace treaty, and Lebanon abrogated it within less than a year, after bowing to Syrian pressure. The net result was that Israel withdrew to its previous 'security zone' in the south, while Israel's arch-enemy, Syria, remained ensconced in the north, around the Beka'a Valley, as it had been since 1976.

After Israel's 1978 invasion, and even after 1982, some Shi'ites living in the south welcomed Israeli intervention, as they felt the armed PLO was becoming a law unto itself. But by the mid-1980s, a new militant Shi'ite group, *Hezbollah*, began harrying Israeli forces, often resorting to suicide car bombings. They have proved to be a worse enemy than the PLO factions ever were. *Hezbollah* was also responsible for driving out US and French peace-keeping forces. Splinter factions, like the Lebanese Islamic *Jihad*, started taking Westerners hostage. To this day, *Hezbollah* continues to attack civilians in northern Israel, and Israel continues to retaliate with military strikes against guerrillas (and civilians based in or near to suspected armed bases) from their 'security zone'. The Lebanese government is loath to discipline *Hezbollah,* which is now a constituent party in the Lebanese Assembly. As for Israel's initial aim to punish the PLO, it only partly successful. The organization was forced to vacate Beirut for Damascus, and soon afterwards Tunis. But many PLO factions remained, and over the years the *fedayeen* have returned.

Security – at a cost

According to Israeli sources, between 1982 and 1995 about 940 Israelis have been killed in Lebanon. Of that total, 136 were killed and about 400 wounded since Israel's pullback in June 1985. Israel opted for a more limited role in southern Lebanon, in control of a security zone of some 1,550 sq km, 7 to 11 km wide and 120 km long. The strip contains about 180,000 Lebanese, most of them Shi'ite Muslims, but also including a significant Christian minority. To date Israel has shunned repeated UN calls for withdrawal from the security zone, arguing that to do so would imperil her northern towns and *kibbutzim*. Israel has spent millions of dollars on maintaining its troops and arming a proxy force of 2,500 known as the South Lebanon Army (SLA), which it helped establish in 1978 after Operation Litani. The SLA has lost about 400 killed and 1,000 wounded since 1985, and is reportedly suffering from serious problems of morale. Israel has tried to improve matters by raising SLA front-line pay and offering medical services and jobs in Israel. But many SLA soldiers fear that Israel will eventually strike a deal with Syria and abandon them. In addition, 680 Lebanese have died as a result of Israeli military action since 1988. The United Nations estimates that 302 Palestinian and Lebanese guerrillas were also killed in this period. UN peace-keeping forces have lost 206 soldiers since they were deployed in south Lebanon in 1978.

LEBANON IN THE MADRID PEACE TALKS

Lebanon is believed to be very much under the influence of Syria, a relationship formally enshrined in the Taif Accord of 1989 and the Brotherhood Treaty of 1991. As a result, until Syria signs a peace deal with Israel, Lebanon is unlikely to take the initiative and make a separate deal. Lebanon joined in the Madrid peace talks in October 1991, but from the outset it was determined to strike a hard bargain with Israel. Fares Boueiz, Lebanon's Foreign Minister and chief spokesman at the opening sessions, insisted that Israel obey UN 425, a resolution dating back to 1978, and withdraw totally from Lebanon. Israel retorted that it would leave only when Syria did. In fact, Syria promised to begin pulling its 35,000 troops out in September 1992, but when it did not, Israel joined in the international protests against Damascus' stance. Furthermore, it accused Beirut of being unable (or unwilling) to carry out its policy of disarming militias. Amidst such acrimony, Lebanon followed Syria in boycotting the multilateral talks which arose out of the Madrid summit.

Israeli–Lebanese relations worsened when Israel deported 413 suspected Islamic fundamentalists to a hilltop camp just outside its security zone, in December. A new government in Lebanon, under Prime Minister Rafiq Hariri refused to accept them, and called for international measures against Israel. This effectively paralysed talks with Israel for months to come.

In what became a mirror image of Syria's stance *vis-à-vis* the Golan Heights, the new head of Lebanon's delegation, Suhayl Shammas, demanded an unconditional Israeli withdrawal from the security zone in May 1993. For its part, Israel proposed a conditional withdrawal, tied to a 'comprehensive peace settlement'. Israel's delegation, led by Uri Lubrani, insisted that the SLA should be integrated into the Lebanese army. Throughout that year, the SLA and *Hezbollah* fought a running battle in the south, while their sponsors (Syria and Israel) tried to avoid getting sucked into a larger war on their account.

On July 25, 1993, Israel adopted a high risk strategy, in the shape of Operation Accountability – an aerial and land assault calculated to dislodge *Hezbollah* from its hiding places amidst ordinary villages. It was the largest Israeli action since its invasion in 1982. In the event, some 200,000 civilians fled their homes. Apparently this was a deliberate Israeli aim, intended to force Damascus and Beirut to discipline *Hezbollah*. In practice, it led to fierce international criticism of the year-old Rabin government. US President Clinton openly praised Syria for its restraint. Israel drew two important conclusions from the exercise. *Hezbollah* knew how to survive (*katyusha* attacks into Israel actually increased), so conventional military force was not the answer. But equally, Syria did little to come to its aid.

In February 1994 *Hezbollah* targeted Israeli troops directly. This led to a number of Israeli reprisals – the abduction in May of Mustapha al-Dirani, a Shi'ite leader, from his home in the Beqa'a valley (far outside the security zone); and Israeli bombardments near Sidon in August and Nabatiyeh in October. In December, a senior *Hezbollah* official and mastermind of the hostage-taking campaign of the 1980s, Fuad Mughniya, was killed by a bomb in south Beirut. Lebanese leftists claimed this was proof of an extensive Israeli spy network in operation.

While Israel accused Lebanese officials (and by extension, Syria) for not controlling *Hezbollah*, the Lebanese responded that Israel had no right to intervene in Lebanon's internal affairs.

SIGNS OF CHANGE?

In early 1995 Israel began a policy of 'hot pursuit', targeting *Hezbollah* forces beyond the security zone. Israel claimed that *Hezbollah* was providing cover for the rejectionist Palestinian PFLP-GC (a radical group led by Ahmed Jibril, thought to be behind the Lockerbie airplane bombing). In February Israel blockaded Lebanon's coastline off Tyre, in retaliation for a tightening of Lebanese army controls at crossing points with the security zone. That same month, however, Israel released 32 prisoners from the zone's notorious Khiyam jail, which some observers interpreted as a possible olive branch to the Shi'ite community. Fighting resumed with *Hezbollah* in May, however, and Israel was embarassed by the guerrillas' ability to fire *katyusha* rockets across the border and into Israel (something they managed to do with more lethal effect in June).

As fighting escalated into August and September, Israeli officials increasingly held Syria directly responsible, and saw *Hezbollah* action as a cynical ploy by Damascus to wield influence at the negotiating table. Others, like the Israeli academic Eyal Zisser, argue that as *Hezbollah* gets parliamentary experience, it may become more amenable to striking a deal on its own with Israel. In the battle of wits surrounding Israel and Lebanon, the Lebanese government appears either too preoccupied with reviving its shattered economy, too dependant on Syria, or too distrustful of Israel, to risk taking the initiative.

Israel's official position consists of three demands:

- That 'terrorist' groups from Lebanon must be disbanded;
- That the Lebanese army deploys north of the security zone, holds a six-month ceasefire and stop terrors attacks on Israel;
- That Lebanon guarantee the safety of the SLA and Lebanese citizens living in the security zone, and that they be 'absorbed in [Lebanon's] governmental fabric'.

Within three months of these conditions being met, Israel will sign a peace treaty with Lebanon and withdraw fully from the zone.

By the end of 1995, two contrasting scenarios emerged as a way to break the stalemate. First, a unilateral Israeli withdrawal. This would call Beirut's bluff, and deprive it of a vital bargaining counter. The drawback is that it may be seen as a sign of Israeli weakness, by both the Israeli right wing and strategists in Damascus. The second plan is to take the battle to *Hezbollah* bases in the Beqa'a Valley, and thereby make the group Syria's problem rather than Israel's. Eyal Baili, advisor to the Israeli military on Shi'ite affairs, backs this view, and believes that the Shi'ite community's attachment to *Hezbollah* is only skindeep. As soon as it becomes inconvenient to shield *Hezbollah*, they will jettison the organization and return to the more moderate *Amal*, he argues.

But the final piece in the jigsaw is surely Iran, the country which originally founded *Hezbollah* in 1982. Syria's favoured party is *Amal*; in the past, it has backed *Amal* as a proxy army against Arafat's wing of the PLO, and *Amal* and *Hezbollah* have clashed in the past. Syria and Iran are currently close allies, and presumably Syria would need Teheran's consent if it decided to clamp down on *Hezbollah*. Or might Iran force *Hezbollah* to cease activities unilaterally, as a favour to Syria? These remain imponderables; yet events could move quickly at any moment.

[See Chapter 20 for coverage of Operation Grapes of Wrath, April, 1996]

Israel and the Vatican

Although technically operating outside the framework of the Madrid process, bilateral talks between the Holy See and the State of Israel proceeded in parallel with the other negotiations. These ultimately resulted in the first ever treaty between the Jewish state and the Roman Catholic Church.

To call Catholic–Jewish relations tempestuous would be something of an understatement. The conflict originates in a theological dispute which is really beyond the realm of this book.

Suffice to say that Christianity – and, by extension, Roman Catholicism – grew out of Judaism. By the end of the 1st century AD, it had developed into a distinct religion, and quickly gained new converts. Most Jews, however, rejected the doctrine which decreed Jesus Christ to be the Messiah. Christians saw this as 'obstinate' and heretical; in their view, the New Covenant of Christianity had surplanted the Old Covenant of the Jews. Hence the continued existence of the Jewish people represented a challenge to the Christian faith.

In the early centuries AD, Christians were a persecuted minority in the Roman Empire. However, after Emperor Constantine converted to Christianity in AD313, Roman Catholicism became the official state religion of the Western Roman Empire. (A separate Eastern Roman Empire, also called Byzantium, followed the Greek Orthodox rites.) Paradoxically, the religion which preached universal love and Christ's spiritual majesty now became associated with state power in Europe and parts of the Middle East. A few less scrupulous Catholic rulers encouraged persecution of the Jewish minority. In time, this developed into a virulent strain of anti-Semitism. At its worst, it resulted in massacres of European Jewish communities by Catholic crusaders *en route* to Palestine. By contrast, the Jews of Byzantium generally lived in harmony with the Christian majority.

Since that period, Catholicism has spread throughout the world, its dominance in Europe only challenged by the Protestant Reformation. Jewish–Catholic relations reached a new nadir with the expulsion of Jews and Muslims from Spain in 1492. However, relations slowly began to improve, especially after the Enlightenment. Jews and Catholics learnt to live together in civil society, as matters of confession became less important. Even so, from time to time the old dispute has re-emerged (the Damascus blood libel in 1860, and Jewish bitterness at the Concordat which the Vatican signed with Hitler in July 1933). Today there are estimated to be approximately 700 million Catholics worldwide. The religion is very strong in South America and parts of Africa, as well as most of southern and much of eastern and northern Europe. Fully 59 million US citizens are Catholic, making it the largest single Christian denomination in the country which is Israel's closest ally.

CATHOLICISM AND ZIONISM

In the 19th century Jerusalem became once again a place for Christian pilgrimage, and on the whole there was tolerance between Catholics, Jews and Muslims in the holy city. By the end of the century, some Protestant and Anglican theologians saw the first Zionist colonists in Palestine as fulfilling the biblical promise of 'a return to Zion', which, in their view, was a harbinger for Christ's Second Coming. The Holy See, however, did not share these views, and felt that the Jewish people had forfeited their claims to Palestine through their participation in the crucifixion of Jesus Christ. It also objected to a secular state incorporating the holy city of Jerusalem, and was concerned about the position of Roman Catholic Palestinian Arabs. Consequently, the Vatican refused to recognize the State of Israel after its establishment in 1948. In 1949 Pope Pius XII stated that Jerusalem should become an international *Corpus Separatum*, with parity for its three religious communities.

The current phase in Jewish–Catholic relations began in 1965, with the Second Vatican Council (often referred to as Vatican II), in which Pope Paul VI issued *Nostra Aetate* which formally dropped the charge of deicide against the Jewish people. On the theological level, Vatican II marked a belated acceptance of the legitimacy of the Jewish faith, and indeed the Jewish inheritance within Christianity. But for largely political reasons, and a sympathy for the plight of Palestinians, the Vatican withheld recognition of Israel. Nonetheless, in succeeding years two Israeli prime ministers and two foreign ministers held private audiences with the Pope. In 1973 Pope Paul VI offered the Vatican's co-operation towards attaining an Arab–Israeli agreement. In 1977 the Pope approached Israeli President Ephraim Katzir, and succeeded in getting him to commute the sentence passed on Hilarion Capucci, the Greek Catholic Archbishop of Jerusalem, who had been jailed for smuggling arms from Lebanon into Israel.

Relations began to visibly thaw under the papacy of John Paul II. Initially, the Israeli government was offended by the Pope's private audience with Yasser Arafat in 1982. However, in September 1987 the Pope told visiting Jewish leaders that there was no theological objections to full diplomatic relations. He amplified these remarks in January 1991, stating

Figure 8 *The Israeli Army in regional comparison*

Country	Regular Force	Reserve Force
Israel	136,000	363,000
Egypt	1,100,000	
Syria	532,500	
Iraq	500,000	
Jordan	150,000	
Saudi Arabia	130,000	

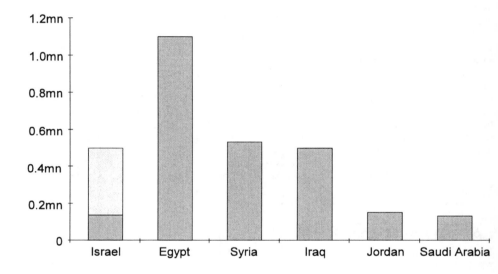

[Note: top part of Israeli column represents reservists, bottom part represents permanent force]

The Israeli Defence Forces

Army	36,000 regulars
	363,000 reservists
	16 divisions
	13 independent brigades
	3,850 tanks

Air Force   32,500 regulars
54,000 reservists
742 combat aircraft

Navy   9,000 regulars
10,000 reservists
62 combat vessels

Source: Jewish Chronicle, July 14, 1995

that the only impediments to relations were legal ones, including the annexation of Jerusalem and Israel's occupation of the territories. Ultimately, it was the Madrid Conference of October 1991 which broke the deadlock.

FUNDAMENTAL AGREEMENT AND DIPLOMATIC RELATIONS

In July 1992 Israel and the Holy See set up a Bilateral Working Commission to investigate ways of improving relations. On Dec. 30, 1993, three months after Israel and the PLO signed the Declaration of Principles in Washington, the Vatican and Israel signed a Fundamental Agreement, which provided for mutual recognition. The Vatican agreed to refrain from intervening in 'temporal conflicts', and Israel agreed to recognize the Catholic Church in Israel, and its right to promote its institutions. The agreement stipulates that both sides are 'committed to appropriate co-operation in combating all kinds of racism and of religious intolerance . . . and recognize that both [parties] are free in the exercise of their respective rights and powers . . .' The Holy See condemned 'hatred, persecution and all other manifestations of anti-Semitism'. Israel reconfirmed its pledge to protect the rights of all religious groups in the state, including free access to their holy sites and shrines.

On March 3, 1994, the Vatican established full diplomatic relations with Jordan. This paved the way for the establishment of full diplomatic relations with Israel, on June 15, 1994. Israel and the Holy See exchanged diplomatic representatives. Shmuel Hadas became Israel's ambassador to the Holy See; Monsignor Claudio Maria Celli became the Apostolic Nuncio to Israel. To keep lines of communication open, an Israel–Vatican Committee was set up, which is currently headed by Israel's Deputy Foreign Minister Eli Dayan and Vatican Under-Secretary for Foreign Affairs Mgr Celli.

After the assassination of Israeli Prime Minister Yitzhak Rabin in November, 1995, the committee met in special session. Mgr Celli expressed condolences to Israel on the murder of the Prime Minister, and stated that the diplomatic relationship between the Vatican and Israel was a means of safeguarding Catholic interests in the Middle East. Dayan stressed the need to broaden inter-faith activities, and noted that 'in these difficult times' there should be real understanding and tolerance between all religions. The two figures also discussed deepening cultural ties, and guaranteed the status of Catholic churches and seminaries in Israel. In addition, they sought to clarify the ramifications of Oslo 2 on Catholic institutions in the West Bank.

IMPLICATIONS FOR THE PEACE PROCESS

The Israel–Vatican agreement is significant for a number of reasons. On the local level, it alleviates some of the tensions between Israel and Roman Catholic Palestinians (even though the latter represent only a minority within a minority). With papal sanction, Roman Catholic pilgrims may be more willing to visit Jerusalem and Israel, thus boosting the local tourism industry. Some argue that the agreement removes one obstacle on the road towards determining Jerusalem's final status. It may also have helped to resolve the status of Bethlehem, which became one of the six Arab towns to gain autonomy under the September 1995 Interim Agreement.

On a more global level, the benefits are both spiritual and political. Spiritually, the agreement should have laid to rest remaining suspicions between Jews and Roman Catholics (and, by extension, other Christians). Politically, the fact that the Pope has recognized the Jewish state potentially opens the way for a range of Catholic countries to open relations with Israel. Pope John Paul II's planned visit to Jerusalem in 1996 is sure to reinforce this trend, while at the same time it will remind both Israelis and Palestinians of the Church's special interests in the Holy City.

Israel's improved diplomatic relations

The Middle East peace process has benefited Israel in terms of new relations with her Arab neighbours. Apart from the treaties with the Palestinians and Jordan, dealt with in this section, in recent years, Israel has branched out in the Maghreb, with a consulate in Morocco, and Tunisia opened a special interests office in 1996. In time, Israel hopes that these will blossom into full diplomatic relations. The presence of the Omani and Qatari foreign ministers at Yitzhak Rabin's funeral in November, 1995, was interpreted as a tangible sign of Israel's new understanding with the Gulf States.

However, the peace dividend also seems to have brought improved diplomatic relations with the rest of the world. After the 1967 war, and particularly after the 1973 war, Israel lost its close ties with many former allies, including most African nations (the Organization of African Unity followed a North African anti-Israeli policy). At one stage the PLO enjoyed more diplomatic contacts than Israel did. The 'Zionism is racism' UN resolution of 1975 made Israel feel like a pariah. That motion was repealed on Dec. 15, 1991, and today, Israel enjoys diplomatic relations with 153 nations. Of these, 59 renewed or established relations after the Madrid Conference in October 1991, and a further 26 renewed or established relations after the signing of the Israel–PLO Declaration of Principles in September 1993.

At the beginning of 1991, there were only two Israeli embassies (in Romania and Nepal) and one consulate (in Bombay, India) in the territory extending from former East Germany in the west to Vladivostok in the east and India in the south. Today, Israel has embassies in all but five countries in this swathe of land – North Korea, Pakistan, Afghanistan, Bangladesh and Bhutan.

Israel has recently made huge progress in relations with non-Arab Muslim countries across Asia and Africa. Diplomatic ties have been established with nine states: Albania, Gambia, Nigeria, Azerbaijan, Kazakhstan, Kyrgystan, Turkmenistan, Tajikistan and Uzbekistan. There has also been a marked improvement in relations with Turkey, which has a consul-general in Tel Aviv.

In Africa, Israel today has ties with 32 of the 43 states south of the Sahara which are not members of the Arab League. Twenty-three of these relations were renewed since 1991. Israel maintains contacts with 11 other states who have not yet renewed diplomatic relations.

Perhaps most significantly, Israel restored relations with the two great Asian powers, India and China, both in January 1992. This followed months of careful negotiations, but ultimately came in the wake of the Madrid Conference. As an Israeli Foreign Ministry official explained: 'The establishment of relations with these powers holds the promise of tremendous strategic and economic potential, which we have begun to fill with real substance'.

PART THREE

THE NATIONS INVOLVED – CONTEMPORARY STATUS

Chapter 13   Israel

National statistics

Capital	Jerusalem (not recognized as such by UN; most embassies in Tel Aviv)
Official languages	Hebrew; Arabic (spoken by 15%), other European languages
Religion	Judaism (about 82%), Islam (about 15%), Christian minorities
Ethnic divisions	Jews 82% (50% born in Israel, 20% in Europe, Americas or Oceania, 7% born in Africa and 5% born in Asia) Non-Jews (mainly Arab) 18%
Currency	New Israeli Shekel (NIS) = 100 agorot
Exchange Rate	US$1.00 = NIS 3.0174 as at Dec. 31, 1994
Land Area	20,770 sq km (excluding occupied territories)
Population	5.4m (1994 UN Fund for Population Activities est.)
Settler population	West Bank 122,000 in 199 settlements (Aug. 1994 est.) Golan Heights 14,500 in 42 settlements Gaza Strip 4,800 in 24 settlements East Jerusalem 149,000 in 25 settlements and suburbs
Armed forces	172,300 (1993)
GDP	$69.762 billion (1992) $70.1 billion (1994 est.)
GDP per capita	$13,880 (1994 est.)
GDP real growth	6.8% (1994 est.)
GNP per capita	$13,760 (1993)
GNP real growth	4% (1993 est.)
Industrial growth	8% (1994 est.)
Unemployment	11.2% of workforce (1992) 7.5% of workforce (1994 est.)
Inflation	10.9% (1993) 14.5% (1994 est.)
Balance of payments	$1.373 billion (1992)
Foreign debt	$10 billion (1990) $25.9 billion (Nov. 1994 est.)
Economic aid	USA $18.2 billion Other Western sources $2.8 billion
Defence expenditure	$6.5 billion (approx 10% of GDP, 1995) [Figures from *Keesing's Record of World Events*, Reference Section, 1995; and CIA *World Factbook* 1995]

Depiction of the state

Israel is barely half a century old, yet it has witnessed changes which most nations do not see in centuries. With remarkable prescience, Theodore Hertzl, the founder of modern political Zionism, titled his novel about a future Jewish state in the Middle East, *Der Altneuland* (The Old-New Land). In one sense Israel is a contemporary and necessarily artificial invention, a triumph of political will over the 'facts of history'. Yet, in another sense, Israel and Zionism claim to pick up the thread of a much older story, one which was interrupted some 2,000 years ago. Of course, the intensity of the present tale owes much to the nature of the state's creation – the miracle, for Israeli Jews, that their statehood came so soon after the Nazis had nearly destroyed all of European Jewry; the sadness, for Palestinian Arabs, that the creation of Israel led to a war which eliminated Palestine.

Scholars have written at length about the rights and wrongs of history, and the ideological intention of the Israel's founders. The purpose of this chapter, however, (and the other chapters in this section) is rather to describe in outline the political make-up of the country today. It also considers many of the issues which inevitably impinge on the peace process, and may well determine the nature of the country and its relations with its neighbours.

THE EFFECT OF IMMIGRATION

Today Israel has a population of over five million people – broadly 4/5th Jewish and 1/5th Arab. It is the world's only Jewish state, although technically Judaism is not the state religion. While the majority of its population is native-born, Israel is unusual in relying on huge immigration to increase its numbers. Since its inception 48 years ago, Israel has absorbed about 2.4 million immigrants, well over three times the size of the population at independence.

Reliance on mass immigration is one of the *raisons d'êtres* of the state. According to its Zionist founding philosophy, enshrined in the Law of Return (1950), Israel should serve as a national home and refuge for Jews throughout the world. From 1948 to 1957, 567,000 Jews left Muslim countries in the Middle East and North Africa. Most of these people (called Sephardim, or, more accurately, *Mizrachim*) emigrated to Israel. Thus just one generation after independence, more than half of the Jewish citizens of Israel were of Sephardi Oriental stock.

Not surprisingly, this has profoundly affected the character of Israel, for a number of reasons. Before 1948, the Zionist movement which built up the *Yishuv* (Jewish community of Palestine) were mainly Ashkenazi Jews from eastern and central Europe. Perhaps inevitably, their customs and tastes reflected their European origins, and coloured the institutions of the state-in-waiting. Many of the ideas which earlier immigrants took for granted – belief in the benefits of scientific rationalism, secularism, socialist notions, democratic assemblies – were alien to the newcomers. The confluence of these two groups severely tested the original ethos of the common Jewish peoplehood. In time, many Sephardim resented what they saw as pressure to conform to a notion of the 'ideal Israeli', and gave vent to their feelings at the ballot box. Yet simultaneously, almost impercetively at first, Sephardim have begun to redefine 'Israeli-ness', by influencing the national cuisine, arts, literature, social customs, political style and the nature of religious expression. Today, intermarriage between the various communities, and the phenomenom of second generation Israelis being raised in the same environment, has blunted what was once called the schism between the Ashkenazi Establishment and the Second Israel.

TOWARDS A PLURALISTIC SOCIETY

In truth, this simplistic division papered over other existing divisions – within Sephardim, between the Jews of Morocco and those from Iraq, for instance; and within Ashkenazim, between Polish, Lithuanian, Russian and German Jews, all of whom had different outlooks. Most importantly, the so-called 'ethnic division' added to and transformed those political divisions (between socialist versus capitalist, religious versus secular, nationalist versus universalist) which already existed in the Israeli body politic.

Two other features of the Sephardi influx are significant to the question of Israel's relations with the Arab Middle East. Their mass immigration also coincided with (some might argue, indirectly led to) the virtual depletion of the millenia-old Jewish community in the rest of the Middle East. And, while some argue that Sephardim have made Israel a more truly 'Middle Eastern country', it is equally true that many Sephardim still feel resentment at the manner in which they were forced out of their countries of origin, and reflect this in their political views. There is evidence for both scenarios. Those who see Sephardim as a 'bridge' to the Middle East can point to the Black Panther movement of disgruntled Moroccan Jewish youth in Tel Aviv, who found common cause with the Palestinians; or there is the example of two current Iraqi-born government ministers who favour closer ties with Iraq. On the other hand, there are instances of Sephardi support for politicians who are 'tough on the Arabs', or who are aggressive towards their fellow Israeli Arab citizens.

In addition to the Sephardim, Israel has absorbed many thousands of Holocaust survivors and Jewish refugees from Nazi Europe, as well as other Jews from South America, eastern Europe, and the English-speaking world (USA, Canada, South Africa, Britain, India and

Australia). Over the last six years there has been an enormous influx of some 600,000 people from the former Soviet Union. Indeed, their situation has provided a new twist to the old ethnic argument. Now many Sephardi Jews are prominent in politics and the military, while the newcomers, albeit Ashkenazi, have sometimes felt 'inferior', because they know little Hebrew, are unused to Israeli social norms, and many are ignorant about Judaism – in short, they are not yet 'acculturated' as Israelis.

Absorbing so many people from such a pot-pourri of backgrounds has proven to be almost as great a challenge to Israelis as the security issue. The recent debate about the treatment of Israel's 60,000 Ethiopian Jews has re-awakened older arguments about alleged racism and patronizing behaviour by the majority. It has also called into question whether Israel as a state has attained the maturity to cope with its inevitably pluralist nature. But, by and large, despite a number of wrong turnings, and given the enormity of the challenge, Israel's immigration policy has been a remarkable success.

MUSLIMS AND CHRISTIANS IN A JEWISH STATE

The ultimate test of Israel's pluralism, however, concerns Israeli Muslim, Christian and Druze Arabs. These are the descendants of the minority of Arabs who remained in Israel after the state's creation. Indeed, this issue tests the fundamental question of whether one can have a state which is truly democratic (i.e. for all its citizens), and which is, at the same time, a Jewish state (that is, of special importance for some of its citizens).

Since independence, the minority non-Jewish population of Israel has risen more than sixfold, from 160,000 in 1949 to 992,500 in 1993. This means that, despite Jewish immigration, the non-Jewish (mainly Arab) proportion of the population has risen from 13.6% of the total to 18.6% over the same period. Several factors account for this tremendous growth in numbers. In the first decades of the state, Israeli Arabs had one of the highest birth rates in the world, averaging 4% annually in 1950–67 and peaking at 4.5% in the 1960s. The birth rate dipped perceptibly after the Six Day War, and even more so after 1977, as living standards rose and labour-intensive family-based agriculture became a less vital sector in the Arab community. In addition, several thousand Arabs who had left Israel, when it was Palestine, returned under the 'family reunification' programme.

As for Arabs' legal status, they are fully Israeli citizens – they can vote in elections, and several stand as Members of the Knesset (MKs), both for 'Arab parties' and in the 'mainstream Zionist parties'. Almost all speak Hebrew in addition to Arabic, and many are educated in the state system. Yet even the current government does not deny that there has been discrimination. Now that Palestinians in the territories (the neighbours and often literal cousins of Israeli Arabs) gain autonomy, the issue of Arab identity within Israel is sure to grow in years to come.

UNIFYING FACTORS

Israel has many anomalies: a vibrant multi-party democracy, but also a strong military establishment; a socialistic state structure, married to a highly entrepreneurial industrial sector; strongly secular political mores, but a solid religious political grouping always in the wings. So what does unite the country?

For its first half a century, security concerns have taken up much of the nation's energy, and accounted for huge chunks of its budget. National military conscription is a familiar (arguably essential) rite of passage, with males doing three years of military service, and females, two years. As such, it is seen as a national unifying factor for most Israelis (although ultra-orthodox Jews and Israeli Arabs, other than Druze and bedouin, are exempted from military service). Unusually for a democracy, Israel has a tradition of army officers entering politics, and rising to the top (the late Prime Minister Yitzhak Rabin being just one example). Yet the military itself is strictly unanswerable to the national will. In addition, the military élite quite often advocates the pragmatic need to make peace, where 'civilian' politicians advocate more toughness.

Some sceptics maintain that without the need to respond to a common external enemy, Israel would divide against itself. A different viewpoint, akin to earlier Zionist notions and often repeated by the *Likud* Leader , Benjamin Netanyahu, states that Israeli armed might has negated 2,000 years of 'historically unnatural' Jewish powerlessness. Israel likes to claim that its armed forces (the IDF) tempers its strength with a strict moral code. However, the 1982 Lebanon War and the 'iron fist' reaction to the *intifada* severely tested this belief, undermined the formerly unanimous unity behind Israel's militgary policy, and sparked a national debate which still rages today. Indeed, the issue has played a large role in shaping the timing and the nature of the current peace process.

The other main unifying factor is the Hebrew language. For thousands of years, Hebrew was a mainly liturgical language. Although most Jews could read it in prayerbooks, or used Hebrew characters to write their own native languages, few actually spoke Hebrew as their daily tongue. But a century or so ago, Eliezer Ben-Yehudah began to revive it for modern usage. In time, the modern Hebrew movement became appended to the Zionist movement, and Hebrew (rather than the suggested alternatives: German, Yiddish, French or English) was chosen as the appropriate language to be adopted in its place of origin, Palestine/Israel. In fact, it can be argued that the very pronunciation of modern Israeli Hebrew (a compromise between Sephardi and Ashkenazi elements) symbolizes its unifying influence.

RELIGIOUS AND SECULAR CAMPS

But aside from this, modern Israel is still trying to solve the existential problems raised by the early Zionists – what does it mean to have a 'Jewish state', and how can this state help Diaspora Jews? In this regard, the issue of religion, which ought to have been a unifying factor, in many respects has divided the nation. Many books have been written about the ambiguous yet crucial role of religion in Israeli politics. It is a complicated issue, and goes back to the roots of the Zionist movement. Suffice to say that early political Zionism tended to be secular in orientation; many orthodox Jews rejected what they saw as its atheistic and socialist tenets, and felt that Zionism did not answer the requirements of the *Torah*. Nonetheless, a new strain of religious Zionism did develop in this century, and since the beginning of Israeli statehood, religious parties, while always in the minority, have wielded a lot of influence in successive coalition governments. The changes wrought by the 1967 war – in particular, the acquisition of territories known as *Eretz Yisrael* – reinvigorated the so-called National Religious Camp. Many religious Zionists now found common cause with right-wing secular Zionist parties, and together they have fought for the retention of the 'occupied territories'.

Not all religious Jews in Israel support this view, however. The *haredim* (ultra-Orthodox Jews), recognizable through their men's bearded and black-garbardined appearance, believe Jewish sovereignty in the Land of Israel can only be re-established after the coming of the Messiah. The most extreme example is the anti-Zionist *Neturei Karta* movement. Many other *dati'im* (including the modern, or neo-orthodox Jews) believe that their religious and political identities should be separate, and that religious parties *per se* are anathema (Labour MK Avraham Burg is one example). However, between 10% and 15% of *dati'im* regularly vote for religious parties.

Once again, it is difficult to say with certainty how many of today's Israelis are 'religious or secular'. Recent figures suggest that 20% follow all religious obligations, another 20% (sometimes called *chilonim*) are totally non-observant, and the 60% in between subscribe to a mixture of both. Finally, there is the complicating factor of ethnicity, where most Sephardim are described as coming from 'traditional' backgrounds, but only a minority could be called ultra-orthodox.

The religious issue does not only concern the issue of the territories. It also informs the whole debate about the authority of a secular state to pass laws, in areas where religious law has other views. If anything, the debate has grown more intense. At the end of 1995, the perennial question, 'Who is a Jew?' (as defined by ethnic identification, or religious law) was once again threatening the coherence of a national governing coalition. The Rabin assassination certainly had a religious dimension, and this too drew attention to a potential national schism.

ECONOMIC CHANGE AND ISRAELI SOCIETY

The early *Yishuv* stressed the importance of returning Jews to the soil, and the socialist *kibbutz* and *moshav* movements symbolized the new pioneering Palestine Jew. One of the early slogans was to 'make the desert bloom'. The *kibbutzim* became world famous for their productivity and collectivist ethic; they also contributed disproportionately to the armed forces and the world of politics. However, in absolute terms *kibbutzniks* always formed a minority, and are now a dwindling minority. Since independence, many have turned to industry, and in fact this is true of the economy in general. The share of agricultural production has fallen from 11% to 3.5% of Israel's GNP, between 1950 and 1993, even though the amount of cultivated land has increased by a factor of 2.6 over the same period.

In the half-century since independence, the Israeli economy has transformed itself from a somewhat fragile state, still building its infrastructure, to a modern Western style exporter of high technology, services and industrial goods. It has the fastest growth rate among Western (OECD) economies (averaging 5.6% in 1990–93, and reaching 7% in 1994); Israel's per capita income places it 21st among 200 countries in the world. Israel's economy specializes in certain fields. Some reflect Jewish expertise from family crafts – for instance, it produces 80% of the world output of small polished diamonds. Other sectors reflect the result of Israel's heavy investment in research and development – it is now one of the largest producers of CD-ROMs.

The socialist institutions of the early days begun to give way to a more free enterprise culture. The *Likud*-led governments after 1977 stressed the market, but Labour too now believes that a mixed economy will best suit Israel's needs. Indeed, Israel under Labour has been preaching a free enterprise message to her Arab neighbours, at regional economic summits at Casablanca in 1994, and Amman in 1995. At the same time, Labour is loath to cut back on funding for education and health insurance, two areas where Israel is world-renowned.

Another vital area of expenditure is defence. This currently stands at 10–15% of GDP, which is less than the 25% spent during the 1970s, but significantly higher than the Western average of 3–5%. Clearly, one strong argument for pursuing a vigorous peace policy is the expected peace dividend, and lower military budgets are a very tangible sign of that. Till now, defence and the need to absorb so many immigrants necessitated a high growth rate. The inevitable drawback was high inflation, which reached a crippling 445% in 1984, but which ten years later stood at the much more acceptable level of 14.5%.

With inflation under control, growth returned in the late 1980s, leading to a still spiralling balance of payments deficit, where imports are outstripping exports. Growth nonetheless did help to reduce unemployment from 11.2% in 1992, to 7.5% in 1994. Over the years, Israel has relied on enormous transfers from the USA (Israel is the USA's largest aid recipient) to meet its special needs. It also received smaller but still substantial donations from Diaspora Jewry, a tradition that goes back to the earliest days of the Zionist enterprise. In the long term, Israel wants more economic independence from the USA. Several prominent Israelis have told Zionist conferences in the Diaspora that Israel is no longer a 'charity case', and have invited Diaspora Jews to join the economic boom. It is probably true, however, that while Diaspora contributions are not essential to maintain Israel's economic momentum, US aid still is. This will probably remain the case for the duration of the peace process, where Israel will be hard-pressed to make the initial outlays (on troop redeployment, aid and advice to Palestinian industries, and the costs of monitoring and policing the accords). In the longer term, though, the ending of the Arab economic boycott (one by-product of peace) should lead to a boom in trade with the Arab and Muslim world.

GEOGRAPHICAL FEATURES

The state of Israel is defined by the armistice agreements signed between Israel and her neighours in 1949, after the War of Independence (1947–49). In 1967 Israel acquired the following territories:

- Sinai Peninsula
- Gaza Strip
- West Bank and East Jerusalem
- Golan Heights

Figure 9   *Israel and world Jewry*

The total world Jewish population was reported to stand at 14,343,910, according to the *Jewish Year Book 1994* (figures collated in 1993). This included an estimated 2.2m in the former Soviet Union.

The figures break down as follows:

Israel	3,653,100
USA	5,828,000
Europe	3,636,490
S America & Canada	1,060,757
Africa	146,770
Oceania	96,320
Asia	39,124

Interpreting the figures, we see that the USA has the largest Jewish population in the world, followed by Israel, and probably the former Soviet Union. (In fact, the inclusion of the former Soviet Union largely explains the large figure for Europe.) According to the *CIA World Factbook*, Israel's total estimated population was 5,050,850 in July 1994. Israel today has approximately one-quarter of the world's total Jewish population.

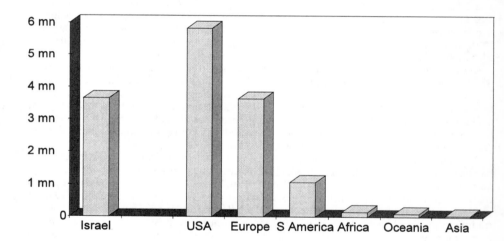

On April 25, 1982, Israel withdrew from the Sinai in accordance with the 1979 Israel–Egypt Peace treaty. The area was returned to Egypt in its entirety. (The Sinai constituted approximately 2/3rds of the total land mass controlled by Israel.) In keeping with the framework established at the Madrid Conference in October 1991, bilateral negotiations are being conducted between Israel and Palestinian representatives, Syria, and Jordan to determine the final status of the occupied territories. Gaza and Jericho were handed over to a Palestine National Authority (PNA) (see next chapter), according to the Cairo Accords of 1994 (Oslo 1). Under the Interim Agreement of September 1995, other areas of the West Bank (primarily heavily populated cities at first) have since come under the PNA's control.

Small areas of disputed land were returned to Jordan under the 1994 peace treaty. Israel and Syria are debating the future of the Golan Heights, which Syria wants returned before a full peace treaty is signed. Since June 1982, Israel has controlled a strip of southern Lebanese territory as a 'buffer zone' against attacks on northern Israel. Lebanon wants Israeli forces to leave this area before it signs a peace treaty with Israel. Israel, for its part, has no long term desire to hold on to any Lebanese territory. Under Israeli law, only the Golan Heights and East Jerusalem have been officially annexed.

SIZE AND LOCATION

Israel is bordered to the south by Egypt, to the east by Jordan and Syria, and to the north by Lebanon. Its total area is 20,770 sq km (land area 20,330 sq km) which is slightly larger than the state of New Jersey. Israel's coastline is 273km in length.

Land boundaries:

Total	1,006 km
Egypt	255 km
Gaza Strip	51 km
Jordan	238 km
Lebanon	79 km
Syria	76 km
West Bank	307 km

Israeli politics and parties

POLITICAL LEADERSHIP

President	Ezer Weizmann (elected in 1993)
Prime Minister	Yitzhak Rabin (elected in 1992; assassinated on Nov. 4, 1995)

• On Nov. 4, Deputy Prime Minister Shimon Peres took over from the late Yitzhak Rabin as acting Prime Minister. In February, Shimon Peres announced that elections would be held earlier than scheduled, on May 28, 1996.

• Benjamin Netanyahu defeated Shimon Peres to become Prime Minister. As of June 18, he heads a new *Likud*-led cabinet (details of which are at the end of Chapter 20).

Cabinet
(as of August 1995)

Foreign Affairs	Shimon Peres (Labour)
Foreign Affairs (Deputy)	Eli Dayan (Labour)
Defence	Yitzhak Rabin (Labour)
Interior	Ehud Barak (Labour) *
Finance	Avraham Shochat (Labour)
Communications and Science	Shulamit Aloni (*Meretz*)
Environment	Yossi Sarid (*Meretz*)
Trade and Industry	Michael Harish (Labour)
Energy and Infrastructure	Dr Gonen Segev (*Ye'ud*)

Police	Moshe Shahal (Labour)
Labour/ Social Development	Ora Namir (Labour)
Immigration and Absorption	Ya'akov Tsaban (*Meretz*)
Justice	David Libai (Labour)
Economics and Planning	Yossi Beilin (Labour) *
Religious Affairs, Science and Technology	Shimon Shetreet (Labour)
Agriculture	Ya'akov Tzur (Labour)
Education and Culture	Prof. Amnon Rubinstein (*Meretz*)
Health	Ephraim Sneh (Labour)
Tourism	Uzi Baram (Labour)

Changes in July

Ehud Barak and Yossi Beilin entered the cabinet on July 17, 1995. Barak had previously been Chief of Staff of the IDF. Beilin had been Deputy Foreign Affairs Minister to Shimon Peres.

Changes in November

Since the assassination of Yitzhak Rabin, Shimon Peres became Prime Minister, and also retained Rabin's other portfolio of Defence Minister. Ehud Barak was appointed as Foreign Minister, and Haim Ramon (a former Health Minister who had left the government in 1994) was named as Interior Minister. In addition, Moshe Shahal was appointed as Internal Security Minister and the authority of the Police Ministry was expanded. Rabbi Yehuda Amital, head of the Mount Etzion Hesder Yeshiva, joined the government as a non-party Minister Without Portfolio.

Shimon Peres also announced that the Director-General of the Foreign Ministry, Uri Savir, would be the government's 'special peace process co-ordinator'. His prime tasks would be to oversee the implementation of the Interim Agreement with the Palestinians. In addition, Savir would liaise with an inner cabinet 'peace process team', consisting of the following ministers: Ehud Barak, Moshe Shahal, Haim Ramon, Yossi Sarid and Yossi Beilin.

New Deputy Ministers appointed in 1995

Construction and Housing	Eli Ben-Menachem and Alex Goldfarb
Education, Culture and Sport	Micha Goldman
Foreign Affairs	Eli Dayan
Industry and Trade	Masha Lubelsky
Health	Nawaf Massalha*
Agriculture and Rural Development	Walid Sadeq*
Defence	Ori Orr
Interior	Salah Tarif*

*Nawaf Massalha, Walid Sadeq and Salah Tarif are Israeli Arabs

Members of the Knesset Foreign Affairs and Defence Committee

(as of July 1994)

Ori Orr	(Labour) – Chairman
Ze'ev Benjamin Begin	(*Likud*)
Eliahu Ben-Elissar	(*Likud*)
Ran Cohen	(*Meretz*)
Raanan Cohen	(Labour)
Yael Dayan	(Labour)
Arieh Deri	(Shas)
Zevulun Hammer	(NRP)

Naomi Hazan	(*Meretz*)
Avigdor Kahalani	(Labour)
Hagai Merom	(Labour)
Benjamin Netanyahu	(*Likud*)
Moshe Nissim	(*Likud*)
Moshe Peled	(*Tzomet*)
Ariel Sharon	(*Likud*)
Emanuel Zissman	(Labour)
Nissim Zvili	(Labour) [also secretary-general of the Labour Party]

Chairs of other Knesset Committees
(as of July 1994)

House Committee	Hagai Merom (Labour)
Finance	Gedalya Gal (Labour)
Constitution, Law and Justice	David Zucker (*Meretz*)
Labour and Welfare	Amir Peretz (Labour)
Education and Culture	Avraham Burg (Labour)
Immigration and Absorption	Emanuel Zismann (Labour)
Interior and Environment	Joshua Matza (*Likud*)
Economy	Tzachi Hanegbi (*Likud*)
Public Audit	David Magen (*Likud*)
Anti-Drug Abuse	Rafael Eitan (*Tsomet*)
Advancement of Women	Limor Livnat (*Likud*)

Party in government

A coalition formed of the Labour Party, *Meretz*, and (since 1994) *Ye'ud*, with the passive support of five MKs from two mainly Arab parties, *Hadash* and the Arab Democratic Party.
[*Shas* had belonged to the government since June 1992, but withdrew in September 1993. Despite talk of rejoining the coalition, it formally entered the opposition in February 1995.]

Opposition political parties

Likud
Shas (Torah Guardians Party)
Tsomet
Moledet
National Religious Party
United Torah Judaism

Banned groupings

Kach
Kahane Chai
Eyal

Influential pressure groups

Gush Emunim
Yesha Council
Peace Now
B'Tselem
Zo Artzeinu

BACKGROUND TO ISRAELI PARTY POLITICS

Israel's multi-party political system, the most democratic in the Middle East, is actually a blend of many different elements. As such it presents a fascinating insight into the nation's origins. Many of its structures reflect the influence of the British Mandate. Functionally, the

Israeli Knesset resembles the Palace of Westminster in Britain – the prime minister enjoys real executive authority at the head of a Cabinet of his or her choice, and is the leader of the ruling party. Like the British monarch, a state president acts as a largely titular head of state (although is elected every five years by popular mandate). The Knesset Speaker acts much like the Commons Speaker. However, the Knesset is a unicameral assembly – there is no nominated or hereditary second chamber, like the House of Lords. Israel, like Britain, lacks a formal written constitution. The closest it comes to this is a series of Basic Laws. Again, as in Britain, Israel has enjoyed a basically two-party structure, with Labour and *Likud* occupying the broad centre-left and centre-right respectively.

Israel's democracy also has many checks and balances – like the USA it has a strong independent Judiciary, and an Attorney-General who, although appointed by government, is deemed to be politically independent (he or she has the last word on constitutional legal matters). The State Comptroller and Ombudsman scrutinizes the public services, and is answerable to the Knesset. Again, like the USA, Israel has a powerful Committee system, where many politicians make their reputations. Due to the constant security concerns, there is traditionally a close bond between the military establishment (headed by a chief of staff) and the Defence Ministry. It is a peculiarity of Israeli politics (especially Labour politics) that military personnel often enter politics, and are often pragmatic about the need for making concessions to achieve peace.

However, other elements are important too, not least the Jewish roots of Israel. The Knesset is named after the *Knesset Ha-Gedolah*, the Great Assembly of Jewish Commonwealth in ancient Israel. Unlike its biblical antecedents, modern Israel follows the Western liberal model of separating Church (or in this case, Synagogue) and State. The Knesset enjoys sovereign power over most areas. In a historical compromise, though, known as the 'status quo', Israel did delegate jurisdiction over a few civil matters (including marriage, Jewish education and questions of Jewish identity) to the *Bet Din* (religious law courts). Similar religious courts exist for Muslim and Christian minority communities. Israel also set up the office of Chief Rabbi (one each for the Ashkenazi and Sephardi communities) to rule on specifically religious matters and offer spiritual guidance.

As to the origin of political parties, many stem from political groupings that originated in Zionist circles in central and eastern Europe in the early years of this century. Broadly, by the mid-1930s political Zionism had divided into three trends – Labour Zionism, essentially nationalist but with a strong socialist component; Revisionist Zionism, which originated as a revolt against the former, and which stressed free market values and strong defence; and finally Religious Zionism, which combined Jewish faith with acceptance of the renaissance of a Jewish secular state. (Another trend, General Zionism, was gradually subsumed into the other groupings.)

Each of the three trends exists today, but there are new elements too. A Marxist strain, which took its line from the Soviet Union, still exists, at times allying itself with the broad Zionist consensus, on other occasions providing a home for Israeli Arab grievances. Indeed, a number of parties have always existed outside the Zionist consensus. These include ultra-orthodox Jewish parties, which reject the secular State of Israel, yet participate politically to win benefits for its constituents; and Israeli Arab parties, which also represent their constituents (the Israeli Arab minority).

Since the 1970s Israel witnessed a growth in ethnic parties, initially set up by groups of Sephardi Jews who felt that major parties were ignoring their interests. Examples include the secular (*Tami*, now defunct); and religious (*Shas*, which from 1992 to early 1995 was part of the Labour-led governing coalition). In June 1995, two new ethnic parties emerged: a Moroccan Jewish breakaway from *Likud* led by ex-deputy prime minister David Levy, and a Russian Jewish immigrants' forum led by Natan Sharansky.

STRUCTURE OF POLITICS

The most distinctive feature of Israeli politics is its very pure system of proportional representation (PR). Israeli parties submit lists of candidates, with their most important potential MKs placed higher, and lesser lights placed lower. Parties win seats in direct proportion to the number of votes cast nationally. What results at election time is typical of

PR – an accurate depiction of the national will, but a proliferation of parties, with no one party enjoying an outright majority. That often leads to unwieldy coalition governments, led by either *Likud* or Labour (and on occasion, by both).

A series of electoral reforms, however, is changing the system, and with it, the nature of politics in Israel. Firstly, the Knesset voted for a threshold to exclude extremely small parties (the initial idea behind this move was to prevent extremist groups, like the neo-fascist *Kach*, from enjoying access to power). Next, internal party reforms led to primary systems of voting for candidates. This removed much of the influence which party committees had previously enjoyed, and was thus considered to be more 'democratic'. More recently, the Knesset voted to have separate and direct election of the prime minister (making its system more akin to the USA or France). This raises the possibility of having a premier of one party presiding over a government of another. Some still advocate constituency elections (as opposed to PR list elections), to make MKs more directly accountable, but this lies in the future.

On a more abstract level, the assassination of Prime Minister Yitzhak Rabin has caused many Israelis to question what was once seen as a positive aspect of their democracy – namely, the extreme openness and vigour of political debate. Violent words, it appears, can lead to violent actions, and there is talk of tighter controls on potential libel, defamation and incitement to hatred.

ISSUES

The peace process is just one of many issues which exercise the minds of Israeli voters. Parties take widely differing views on the economy (privatization versus retaining the state sector). Related to this is the vexed question of how best to absorb new Israeli immigrants (an issue which has led to a new party, *Yisrael Ba'Aliyah*, to contest the 1996 elections). This in turn has thrown the spotlight on education, an issue with many dimensions. On the economic side, teachers and university lecturers went on strike during the early years of the Rabin administration, as Rabin strove to reduce the mounting state deficit. But educationalists say they need more funds to cope with the special needs of immigrants (including instruction in Hebrew, and classes for those who come from largely non-industrialized countries, like the Ethiopian or Chechen Jews). Shulamit Aloni, the militantly secular Education Minister, revealed another aspect, when she tried to amend the national curriculum, and curb the influence of religious authorities (in Israel, the state runs essentially three streams of schooling – secular Israeli, religious Israeli, and Israeli Arab – a delicate balance).

Environmental issues are another new concern, as Israeli roads and towns expand (a problem liable to be exacerbated by the expected return of settlers from the West Bank). Through the influence of the *Meretz* party, issues surrounding women's rights, and civil rights in general, are back on the agenda. There are also parties which serve narrow constituencies – such as the various religious parties. Although strictly religious Jews make up only about 20% of the Jewish electorate in Israel, the PR system means that they often enjoy powers beyond their numbers.

As seen below, some stress the relation between religion and the question of keeping the territories, which is inextricably bound with the debate on the peace process. Others stress the importance of Sabbath observance, and blocks on desecrating graves (Israel's enthusiasm for archaeology, heightened since territories are to be given to the Palestinians, has led to digs which occasionally uncover old graves; but this is forbidden by strict Jewish law). On a more abstract level, some have condemned the 'Americanization' of Israeli society (a concern shared by secular parties of traditional Zionist cast). There was also concern over a decline in public morals; although right-wing religious politicians were embarrassed when Rabin's assassin backed this camp. Most profoundly for Israel's future, the old debate about 'Who is a Jew?' has resurfaced in several guises: a recent debate erupted over whether to accept the converted formerly Gentile partners of American Reform Jews, as people who could enter Israel under the Law of Return. Currently, the law is determined by national law (someone is Jewish if they have at least one Jewish grandparent); rather than *Halakha* (where one is Jewish through the mother's line). In this regard, the large number of non-Jewish spouses of former Soviet immigrants is a relevant issue; likewise, the Ethiopian Jewish community still resents doubts cast on their 'Jewishness' (for historical reasons, their faith does not incorporate the

Talmudic tradition, which is meant to underpin normative Jewish orthodoxy). Finally, questions regarding the Law of Return will no doubt be influenced by the forthcoming debate amongst Palestinians on their own Law of Return. Whatever compromises emerge, will certainly have repurcussions in Israel.

Religious parties can be divided into three main blocs

- Religious Zionists: in particular, the National Religious Party (*Mafdal*) which represents 'modern orthodox' Jews, promotes higher religious content in education and backs the settler movement.
- Ultra-orthodox Jews: largely Ashkenazi, often anti-Zionist (as in *Neturei Karta*) or non-Zionist (*Agudath Yisrael*). Some choose to accept the reality of the Zionist secular state and through parties like *Agudath* and the umbrella group, United Torah Judaism, lobby for their community concerns.
- Sephardi orthodox Jews: many Sephardim (a misnomer for Oriental Jews) broke away from *Agudath* and *Mafdal* to form their own distinctive party, *Shas*. It tends to be conservative on religious and social matters, but accommodating on peace.

Within the Arab electorate, the 1990s saw a partial desertion of their vote from Arab parties to Zionist parties. However, with the prospect of a renascent Arab Palestine on Israel's border, it remains to be seen how this will effect the Israeli Arab vote in the future. For the present, the government is committed to improving the 'Arab sector', by giving more grants to Arab neighbourhoods (having admitted that they were ill-served by previous administrations).

Finally, there are several other topics, each small in itself, but which may flare up into bigger issues, given the highly-charged nature of Israeli politics. One is political corruption and embezzlement, charges laid against individual politicians in all parties. Another is the future of the monolithic *Histadrut* Labour Federation, and, allied with it, the *Kupat Cholim* medical insurance scheme. And as Israel approached its next election in 1996, the persistance of Palestinian terror attacks, not to mention Jewish terrorism as seen in the Rabin assassination, had made the issue of security once again of prime importance to Israeli voters.

Prime Ministers since 1948		Foreign Ministers since 1948	
1948–53	David Ben-Gurion	1948–49	David Ben-Gurion
1953–55	Moshe Sharett	1949–56	Moshe Sharett
1955–63	David Ben-Gurion	1956–66	Golda Meir
1963–69	Levi Eshkol	1966–74	Abba Eban
1969	Yigal Allon (acting)	1974–77	Yigal Allon
1969–74	Golda Meir	1977–79	Moshe Dayan
1974–77	Yitzhak Rabin	1979–80	Menachem Begin
1977	Shimon Peres (acting)	1980–86	Yitzhak Shamir
1977–83	Menachem Begin	1986–88	Shimon Peres
1983–84	Yitzhak Shamir	1988–90	Moshe Arens
1984–86	Shimon Peres	1990–92	David Levy
1986–92	Yitzhak Shamir	1992–95	Shimon Peres
1992–95	Yitzhak Rabin	1995–	Ehud Barak
1995–	Shimon Peres		

Changes since 1992

In 1994, three new parties were formed out of existing parties, which altered the tally of seats in the Knesset.

- *Tsomet* lost three MKs to the new *Ye'ud* Party. Its total declined from 8 to 5
- *Moledet* lost one MK to the new Peace Guard. Its total declined from 3 to 2
- Labour lost three MKs to the new *Histadrut* List. Its total declined from 44 to 41.

In June 1995 David Levy led a breakaway faction from *Likud* (see *Derech ha-Hadash* under Parties, below).

The Rabin Assassination and Israeli politics

On Nov. 4, 1995, Yitzhak Rabin was assassinated by a lone gunman after attending a peace rally in Kikar Malchei Yisrael (Kings of Israel Square) in Tel Aviv. Rabin was rushed to the Ichilov Clinic, but died of two gunshot wounds shortly after arriving. The assassin, Yigal Amir, said he had intended to kill Shimon Peres too. He claimed to be acting alone, 'perhaps with the help of God'. It since emerged that he was affiliated to the extremist *Eyal* group, and may have been following rulings from certain rabbis. The murder evoked outrage and mourning throughout Israel, and most of the world. It also unleashed a welter of charges, with members of the Labour Party accusing the opposition *Likud* of formenting an 'atmosphere of violent rhetoric' which had encouraged such an atrocity. In fact, posters of Rabin in SS uniform, and calling him a traitor and murderer for signing the Oslo Accords, had appeared at anti-peace rallies in the months leading up to the assassination. Benjamin Netanyahu and virtually all leaders of the right condemned the murder; but a few extremists on the religious right said that Labour's policy of surrendering parts of *Eretz Yisrael* was against Jewish law, and deserved execution (a charge refuted by both of Israel's Chief Rabbis). The immediate effect of the assassination was an investigation into the profound lapse in security which enabled Amir to kill Rabin so easily. By January 1996, the head of Israel's General Security Services, Karmi Gillon, tendered his resignation. A commission headed by Justice Meir Shamgar continued with its inquiries, while Amir appeared on remand, charged with murder. As yet, talk of a conspiracy has yet to be proven. The funeral of Yitzhak Rabin, held on Nov. 5, was attended by an unprecedented array of world leaders, including President Bill Clinton, Jordanian King Hussein, Russian Prime Minister Viktor Chernomyrdin, British Prime Minister John Major, Egyptian President Hosni Mubarak and Britain's heir apparent Prince Charles, along with some other 80 leaders from Europe, the Middle East, Africa and America. PLO Chairman Yasser Arafat paid his first official visit to Israel, when he travelled to Tel Aviv and personally offered his condolences to Yitzhak Rabin's widow, Leah. Nine days later, 250,000 Israelis attended a memorial rally for the slain prime minister. Netanyahu pledged his support for a new and less incendiary style of politics, and refused to force a general election. Shimon Peres took over as acting Prime Minister, and was sworn in by President Ezer Weizman in late November, with new cabinet members. Most significantly, far from 'killing the peace process', Yigal Amir seemed to restore its flagging popularity. Opinion polls showed huge support for Peres and the Labour Party, and Rabin's grave became a place of pilgrimage for many Israelis, who still suffered from the national trauma – the first Israeli Prime Minister to be killed. Shimon Peres pledged to continue with the peace proces, and indeed, Oslo 2 was enacted ahead of schedule. The assassination brought shockwaves to every part of the Middle East; some analysts say it led Syrian President Hafez al-Assad to abandon his customary caution, and call for an accelerated peace with Israel. In the months succeeding the murder, Shimon Peres initially chose not to call a general election, to capitalize on national sympathy, but rather preferred to press ashead with the peace agenda laid out by his slain predecessor. However, with the Syrian talks still delivering less than was hoped for, he decided to contest elections in late May, 1996. In the longer term, Rabin's assassination will remain a benchmark for those who warned against undemocratic opposition. Many are still shocked that a Jew could have killed the leader of the Jewish state. Yet Israel's democratic institutions have remained intact, a tribute in part to respect for Rabin's legacy.

OFFICIAL PARTIES AND PARTY GROUPINGS

Main blocs

Labour (Israel Labour Party)

Chairman	Shimon Peres [and also Prime Minister since the assassination of Yitzhak Rabin on Nov. 4, 1995]
Secretary General	Nissim Zvili
Knesset faction leader	Ra'anan Cohen

From the founding of the State of Israel in 1948 until the election of 1977, the Labour Party (in its various guises) not only ruled Israel continuously, but effectively shaped the reality of Israeli politics. It lost power in 1977 to *Likud*, its traditional enemy. After a hung election in 1984, Labour and *Likud* formed a government of national unity. This eventually ended in

Figure 10   *Israeli election results, 1992 and 1988*

The election of June 23, 1992, saw a Labour-led coalition defeat the incumbent Likud-led government. Here is a tally of the seats won by each party, comparing 1992 with 1988:

Party	Seats 1992	Seats 1988
Hadash	3	4
PLP	0	1
ADP	2	1
Meretz	12	10
Labour	44	39
Likud	32	40
Shas	6	5
NRP	6	5
UTJ	4	8
Tsomet	8	2
Moledet	3	2
Tehiya	0	3

Hadash is an acronym in Hebrew for the Democratic Front for Peace and Equality
PLP stands for Progressive List for Peace
ADP stands for Arab Democratic List
NRP stands for National Religious Party
UTJ stands for United Torah Judaism

Percentage breakdown of parties' share of seats in the Israeli *Knesset*, comparing results for 1992 (series 1) with results for 1988 (series 2).

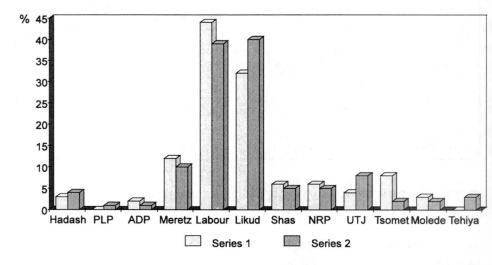

Figure 11   *Israeli election results, 1992 – voter breakdown*

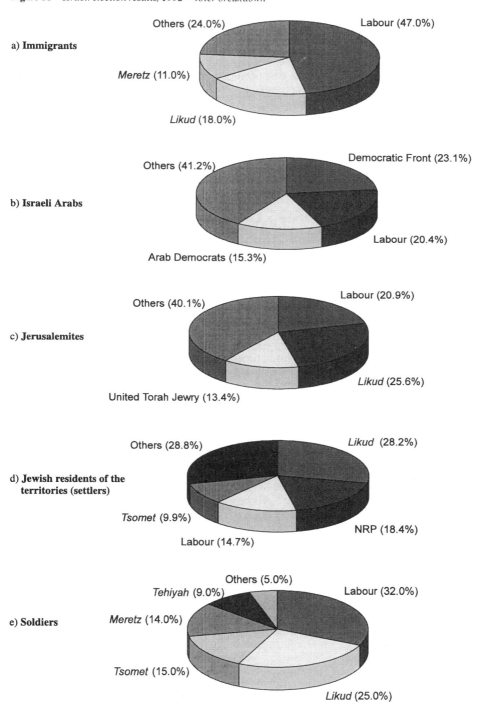

a) **Immigrants**

Others (24.0%)   Labour (47.0%)

Meretz (11.0%)

Likud (18.0%)

b) **Israeli Arabs**

Others (41.2%)   Democratic Front (23.1%)

Labour (20.4%)

Arab Democrats (15.3%)

c) **Jerusalemites**

Others (40.1%)   Labour (20.9%)

Likud (25.6%)

United Torah Jewry (13.4%)

d) **Jewish residents of the territories (settlers)**

Others (28.8%)   Likud (28.2%)

Tsomet (9.9%)

NRP (18.4%)

Labour (14.7%)

e) **Soldiers**

Others (5.0%)

Tehiyah (9.0%)   Labour (32.0%)

Meretz (14.0%)

Tsomet (15.0%)

Likud (25.0%)

Source: Jerusalem Report magazine

1990. After two years in opposition, Labour won the 1992 election under the new Prime Minister, Yitzhak Rabin.

However, because of the nature of Israel's PR electoral system, Labour has never enjoyed outright majority power. Instead, it was (and still is) forced to form partnerships of convenience with smaller special interest parties (notably the National Religious Party). The dominant faction within Labour is *Mapai*, the old party of David Ben-Gurion, Israel's first prime minister. The current Labour Party was formed in 1968 from a merger between *Mapai*, a Labour breakaway group called *Rafi*, and *Achdut Ha'Avodah* (the coalition was known as *Ma'arakh*, or the Labour Alignment).

Strictly speaking, Labour is not so much a single party as an alignment of factions, these days centred on members of the up and coming new generation of Labour leaders. The strongest element has always been *Mapai*, but in the earlier days the more left-wing *Mapam* (now a member of the *Meretz* grouping) was part of Labour too. In the *Yishuv* period (that is, before the declaration of independence on May 14, 1948), David Ben-Gurion created the party from a myriad of Socialist Zionist groups. The *kibbutz* movement provided much of its early leadership. Another source of power was the *Histadrut* labour federation, which Labour dominated until the 1980s.

In power, Labour tended to dilute its socialist ideology and devoted more attention to building up the fledgling nation, keeping its defences intact, and trying to absorb the hundreds of thousands of Jews who emigrated to Israel. Labour's durability was proven in the mid-1960s, when the venerable former leader, Ben-Gurion, led a breakaway group, *Rafi*; but this did not weaken Labour's grip on power (*Rafi* and its young scion, Shimon Peres, ultimately rejoined the Alignment). Labour opposed ideologically motivated settlers in the territories after 1967, but on numerous occasions chose to accept them as a fait accompli, rather than risk confrontation. The 1973 Yom Kippur War was a body blow to the Labour élite, and led to the resignation of Defence Minister Moshe Dayan and Prime Minister Golda Meir. Yitzhak Rabin succeeded Meir as party leader and prime minister in 1974, with the backing of the *Mapai* faction (Shimon Peres was his opponent in internal party elections, and their clash then was to repeat itself several times over the next two decades).

In 1984, after seven years in opposition, Labour entered a government of national unity with the *Likud*. Many on the party's left feared it was an alliance of opposites. In a complicated arrangement, Shimon Peres ruled as prime minister for the first two years of the four-year term, and Likud's Yitzhak Shamir was foreign minister. After two years, the leaders swopped places. Another inconclusive election in 1988 resulted in a new Labour-*Likud* coalition, but this time with *Likud* in a stronger position. In the interim, the *intifada* had broken out in the territories. While Labour Defence Minister Yitzhak Rabin imposed an 'iron fist' policy on the uprising, thus winning plaudits on the right, Shimon Peres, the party leader, despaired as his hopes for striking a peace deal with the Arabs receded.

As predicted, incompatible political outlooks (especially on the peace issue) led to the union crumbling in 1990. *Likud*, now unrestrained by Labour's moderating influence, launched a more right-wing policy. In 1992, however, Labour (under its newly elected leader, Yitzhak Rabin) won a working majority in the general election. Almost miraculously, the old foes, Rabin and Peres, emerged as a compelling duo (prime minister and foreign minister respectively) committed to restoring the Israeli economy and pursuing an enthusiastic peace initiative. After the 1992 victory, horse-trading resulted in a sometimes strained coalition between Labour, *Meretz, Shas*, with passive support from Arab political parties. *Likud* has been confined to its traditional role of opposition to the Labour 'establishment'.

Internal party reforms in 1991 had clearly helped revive the Labour party's fortunes. A vigorous membership drive brought in new types of members – Sephardim disillusioned with *Likud*'s broken promises, new Russian immigrants, youth, and growing numbers of Israeli Arabs. Furthermore, a system of chosing leaders and electoral candidates through primary elections took away much of the power which had formerly resided with the party's central committee. There were new openings for non-*Histadrut* members. However, commentators noted that the perennial Rabin–Peres feud had created a missing 'middle generation' of potential leaders. In similar vein, few women (Ora Namir and Yael Dayan being notable exceptions) were in positions of prominence.

Labour optimists retorted that there was a new generation of MKs whose talents would not be similarly wasted. At its head was the so-called 'Group of Seven'. Stereotyped by foes as 'the blazers', or 'North Tel Aviv yuppies', this group was dovish in foreign affairs, yet non-doctrinaire as socialists. Some even called for more privatization – an unusual stance for the party of 'big government'. Yossi Beilin, Haim Ramon and Avraham Burg were the most-quoted names. However, after the 1992 victory, Ramon and Burg seem to have been frustrated by not finding high office more quickly, and chose to pursue their careers in other spheres (as head of the *Histadrut* and Jewish Agency respectively). Only Beilin entered the inner cabinet in 1995, after serving successfully as deputy to his mentor, Foreign Minister Shimon Peres.

By contrast with Rabin's previous government (1974 to 1977), the current coalition includes several Labour ministers of Sephardi descent – Police Minister Moshe Shahal and Housing Minister Binyamin Ben-Eliezer, both born in Iraq; Religious Affairs Minister Shimon Shitreet and Deputy Foreign Minister Eli Dayan, both born in Morocco; and Transport Minister Yisrael Kessar, born in Yemen.

The strains within the coalition eventually led to *Shas* leaving the cabinet and government, ironically at just the time when Israel was signing its historic peace accords with the PLO in Washington (September 1993). In 1994 Haim Ramon and two MK allies broke away to form a *Histadrut* List Party. Labour was thus compelled to rely even more on the passive support of two Arab parties to stay in power, which in turn prompted racist elements in the right-wing opposition to call into question Rabin's mandate to govern.

After Rabin's assassination on Nov. 4, 1995, Foreign Minister Shimon Peres became Israel's prime minister. Some Labour politicians openly accused *Likud* of encouraging the vitriol that led to Rabin's death. Haim Ramon and his *Histadrut* List announced it was returning to the Labour fold, and Ramon was rewarded with the Interior portfolio. Peres recommitted his party and government to pursuing the peace process, and he ensured that the Oslo 2 accords with the Palestinians, which was Rabin's last major achievement, were implemented on schedule and with little right-wing opposition. Presumably to ward off further right-wing taunts, Peres appointed the tough former military Chief of Staff, Ehud Barak (Interior Minister since July 1995) as Foreign Minister. Although opinion polls suggested that Labour would win a flash election, Peres initially chose instead to see Rabin's policies through until late 1996. In February 1996, Peres announced that elections would be held earlier after all, in May. Political observers noted that the hoped-for breakthrough with Syria would not material-ize, so while Peres still enjoyed a 'mandate for peace', he should hold elections sooner rather than later. However, it transpired that Peres lost and Labour went into opposition in June 1996.

Likud

Chairman   Binyamin (Benjamin) Netanyahu Prime Minister

The Likud coalition was created when Menachem Begin fused his *Herut* (Freedom) party with four smaller right-wing parties in 1973 (Liberal Party, *La'am, Ahdut* and *Tami*). It is the successor to the Revisionist Zionist movement founded by Vladimir Ze'ev Jabotinsky in 1925, and it was in government continuously from 1977 to 1992. (From 1984 to 1990 Likud joined with its traditional enemy, the Labour alignment, to form a 'government of national unity'.) *Herut* itself was founded in 1948 by Menachem Begin. Until 1996, *Likud*, under the leader-ship of Binyamin Netanyahu, was the chief opposition to the Labour government.

The Revisionist movement was initially formed by Zionists who resented the socialist orientation of the majority Labour Zionists in the early days of the Palestine *Yishuv*. It also favoured a harder line on resisting the British Mandate, and in fighting Arab nationalism, a stance which *Herut* and *Likud* have backed ever since. In the 1930s Revisionists spawned a militant youth group, *Betar*, as well as the *Irgun Zvei Leumi (Etzel)* 'self-defence' force. In the 1940s *Irgun* and its more militant offshoot, *Lehi* (colloquially known as the Stern Gang after its founder, Avraham Stern) pursued a policy of anti-Arab and anti-British attacks. The rival *Haganah*, which represented the Labour trend, followed a policy of *havlagah* (restraint). Revisionist elements played a key role in the Deir Yassin massacre, the King David Hotel bombing, and the murders of the British High Commissioner, Lord Moyne, and the UN mediator, Count Folke Bernadotte. Future prime ministers Menachem Begin and Yitzhak Shamir cut their political teeth in these movements (having at times led *Etzel* and *Lehi* respectively).

At one stage it appeared that civil war might erupt between the Revisionists and Labour Zionists (the *Altalena* Incident); but the War of Independence created a new sense of unity. With the creation of the new state, Menachem Begin led *Herut* (Freedom Party) as a small right-wing opposition to the dominant Labourites. Begin fiercely opposed the idea of Israel accepting reparations from Germany, but failed to win an election. His first taste of office was only in 1967, when he was invited to join a government of national unity (in the face of the Egyptian threats of war, prior to June). The coalition lasted until 1970. *Herut* joined smaller centrist parties to form *Gahal,* and then absorbed the Liberal Party to become the *Likud.*

In the late 1960s and early 1970s *Herut/Likud* began winning support from Israel's growing Sephardi community. Consisting of immigrants from Arab lands and their descendants, the community felt stymied by the Labour-dominated and largely European-born Ashkenazi establishment. *Likud* offered them a new political home. In sociological terms the result was somewhat ironic – a perceived under-class voting in droves for an anti-socialist party. *Likud* owed much of its 1977 electoral success to the promise of Sephardi advancement; likewise it probably owed its 1992 electoral failure to the fact that it had broken that promise several times over. The latest chapter in this saga occurred in June 1995, when David Levy, *Likud*'s leading Sephardi politician, broke away from *Likud* after a lifetime's service, to form his own party.

Toughness in international affairs was another great attraction to the electorate, after years of perceived Labour dithering. Menachem Begin epitomized this stance. He was probably the only opposition party leader in the democratic world to lose eight elections in a row and still remain leader. However, when he eventually did win in 1977, he and his *Likud* party did change things considerably. They had a three-prong platform: liberalization of the economy, encouragement of Jewish settlers in the occupied territories, and succour for Sephardi Israelis (who constituted about half the population).

Confounding the analysts, the apparently belligerent Begin responded to an approach from Egypt's President Sadat, and in 1977 Sadat became the first Arab leader to officially visit Israel. Together, the two leaders signed the Camp David Accords, which led to a full peace treaty between the two countries in 1979. According to the treaty, Israel agreed to return all of the Sinai to Egypt. This was completed in 1982. That same year a *Likud* inner cabinet, strongly influenced by Yitzhak Shamir and Ariel Sharon, decided to invade Lebanon in a bid to destroy the PLO forces based there. Although the PLO and Arafat were dislodged, the war proved very costly to Israel. In 1983 Begin resigned, citing health reasons, and Shamir took over as party leader and prime minister. He inherited galloping inflation and national unease over the war. Opponents both inside and outside *Likud* felt he could not last long, given his rejectionist views and his lacklustre reputation (at least compared to Begin); but in the event, he remained at the top for nearly a decade.

The 1984 elections delivered a hung parliament, and *Likud* was forced to share power with Labour (then under Shimon Peres). It was an uncomfortable partnership, but one both sides were forced to repeat after another inconclusive election in 1988. In 1990 Labour left the coalition over disagreement with Shamir's 'peace plan'. Shamir (who managed to fend off several threats to his leadership) was now at liberty to include right-wing nationalist and religious parties in the governing coalition. Shamir was praised for his mature restraint in the face of Scud attacks from Iraq in the 1991 Gulf War. However, internal party squabbles, and a general resistance by the old guard to make way for younger faces, eroded *Likud's* support. Despite the initial high hopes of the Madrid peace conference, the electorate complained when talks became deadlocked. Many traditional *Likud* supporters feared that Shamir and his colleagues were concentrating too much on the rights of settlers, at the expense of the majority of Israelis who lived 'within the green line'. An impression of domestic stagnation particularly galled Sephardi voters, who felt let down by their party, and voted instead for a resurgent Labour in 1992.

Back in opposition, *Likud* replaced Shamir with the younger Benjamin Netanyahu, who beat off challenges for the job from David Levy, Ariel Sharon and Binyamin Begin. He reaffirmed his party's promise to keep *Eretz Yisrael*, and defend the settlers. However, Netanyahu's new-look *Likud* also emphasized the need to restore Israel's ties with the West (through better publicity), and embrace privatization more decisively. *Likud* opposed Labour's deal with the PLO in 1993, but vowed to honour signed agreements if it came to power.

Netanyahu prides himself on his expertise in fighting terrorism, and in fact his support rises after every terror incident. Detractors say he has no alternative blueprint to the current peace process, and they deem as unrealistic his notion of Arabs being forced to accept a strong Israeli 'Iron Wall'. Officially, *Likud* has welcomed the peace treaty with Jordan and says it will not re-occupy the Gaza Strip; however, it opposes many aspects of Oslo 2 and favours retaining the Golan Heights.

David Levy's desertion from *Likud* in 1995 threatened to erode a vital base of the party's support (the urban Sephardim). Yet Netanyahu appears quite secure in his leadership role, with the populist hardliner, Tzachi Hanegbi as his close aide, and a truce with potential rivals, Benny Begin and the more moderate Dan Meridor. After the Rabin assassination, leading figures in the Labour movement (notably Leah Rabin, the late prime minister's widow, and Health Minister Ephraim Sneh) accused Netanyahu and *Likud* of aiding and abetting the culture of verbal violence which, they said, led to Rabin's death. Opinion polls registered a temporary collapse in *Likud's* support, and unprecedented backing for Labour's peace initiative. In response, certain *Likud* MKs advocated tough legal restrictions on incendiary political language. Nonetheless, with direct elections for prime minister planned for 1996, Netanyahu's charisma and flair for publicity seemed to boost his chances – and *Likud's* with him. In February 1996, Netanyahu announced an electoral pact between *Likud* and the smaller right-wing *Tsomet* Party. While it guaranteed him a clear run for the prime ministerial elections, many *Likud* supporters felt it indicated an unwise lurch towards the right, just when *Likud* needed to shed the taint of extremism. In the event Netanyahu won, although *Likud* itself lost seats to smaller parties.

Smaller parties

Agudat Yisrael

Leader: Rabbi Menachem Porush

Agudat Yisrael is strong amongst mainly Ashkenazi ultra-Orthodox Jews. It joined a coalition of ultra-orthodox parties, known as the United Torah Judaism Front [q.v]. The party was originally founded in 1912 as the Palestine branch of the *Agudat Yisrael* World Organization. It stands for strict observance of Jewish religious law, to be backed by state legislation. Unlike the National Religious Party, it is not strictly speaking Zionist, although it is prepared to co-operate with major parties in order to achieve its own ends. During the 1980s *Agudat* aligned itself with the *Likud*. It is currently in opposition.

Aliyah Leumi

Leader: Natan Sharansky

Founded in 1995, *Aliyah Leumi* (Ascent to the People; also a pun on 'immigration') intends to compete in the 1996 elections as a party representing the interests of new immigrants, especially those from the former Soviet Union. Its leader is Natan Sharansky, a renowned former 'refusenik'. Its platform calls for a referendum on the future of the peace process and rejection of a Palestinian state; but it favours territorial compromise on the Golan. In early 1996, the party (which now seemed to go under the name *Yisrael Ba-Aliyah*) announced that it would stand in the forthcoming elections. It also added a new free enterprise strand to its political platform.

Arab Democratic Party

Leader: Abd al-Wahab Darawshe

The Arab Democratic Party (*Mada*) is one of two Arab-dominated non-Zionist parties in the Knesset (the other being the Communist-led *Hadash*). The party supports equal rights for Israel's Arab citizens, and a greater role for Arab politicians at cabinet level. It also backs the peace process, and favours the creation of a Palestinian state. Although not a member of the Labour-led coalition government, it tends to vote with the government, in opposition to *Likud*. In March 1994, Darawshe led a group of 57 Israeli Arabs to meet Syrian President Assad. This action was variously interpreted as a breakthrough in Israeli–Syrian relations; or a symbol of the Israeli Arab minority's desire to affiliate with the broader Arab world. In May 1995 *Mada* and *Hadash* tabled a motion of no-confidence over Labour's plan to expropriate 54 acres of Arab land in East Jerusalem. *Mada* (unlike *Hadash*) persisted with the vote, even after Labour agreed to suspend the expropriation, but lost. The party protested against suggestions from right-wing parties that 'Arab votes' in the *Knesset* are somehow less valid than 'Jewish votes'. *Mada* and *Hadash* currently face the threat of a new rival Israeli Arab grouping, based around a reputed alliance between the Islamic Movement and Arafat's adviser, Dr Ahmed Tibi.

Degel ha-Torah

Secretary General: Haim Epstein

Established in 1988 as a breakaway from *Agudat Yisrael* (q.v.), *Degel ha-Torah* (or 'Flag of the Torah') was very much the institution of Rabbi Eliezer Shach, the revered head of the ultra-orthodox Ponevezh Yeshiva in Benei Brak. Some regarded it as the Ashkenazi sister party to the Sephardi *Shas*. But unlike the latter party, *Degel ha-Torah* did not prosper. Since 1992 it rejoined *Agudat* in the United Torah Judaism electoral front, which all told holds four seats in the current Knesset.

Democratic Front for Peace and Equality

[see Hadash]

Derech ha-Hadash

Leader: David Levy

David Levy, Foreign Minister in Yizhak Shamir's *Likud* administration, led a small and mainly Sephardi-based faction out of the *Likud* in June 1995. Some observers ascribed his move to recurrent clashes with *Likud* leader, Benjamin Netanyahu, and his stymied ambitions to be *Likud* leader himself. Others have suggested that the new movement reflects widespread Sephardi dissatisfaction with the *Likud* party. Whatever the case, *Derech ha-Hadash* (The New Path) seems to take a more amelioratory line on the peace process, but above all emphasizes the need to improve living conditions for economically disadvantaged Israelis. At first, the movement appeared not to have totally untethered itself from *Likud* and formed a distinct new party. In 1996, Levy's party was renamed *Gesher* (Bridge). After bargaining, he withdrew from the prime ministerial race to back Netanyahu, and win Knesset seats on a joint list with *Likud* and *Tsomet*.

Hadash

Leader: Hashim Mahamid

The Democratic Front for Peace and Equality (DFPE, also known as *Hadash*, or New, in its Hebrew acronym) was set up in 1977 as an alliance between the New Communist Party (*Rakah*) and the (Sephardi Jewish) Black Panthers. It enjoys strong support from Israeli Arabs, although it prides itself on a joint Arab–Jewish list of Knesset candidates and MKs. Throughout the 1980s, *Hadash* openly supported the creation of a Palestinian state in the West Bank and Gaza. The party enjoyed strong unofficial ties with the PLO (which was effectively banned in Israel and the territories until the Oslo deal in 1993). As such it was the target of much right-wing ire in the Israeli Knesset. At one stage it was banned (along with the Jewish extremist group, *Kach*), but this was later rescinded. Nonetheless, *Hadash* offered tacit support to Yitzhak Rabin's government, even though it is not formally a member of the ruling coalition. *Hadash* lost ground to the Arab Democratic Party in the 1992 elections.

Histadrut List

Leader: Haim Ramon

Three MKs broke from Labour to form this party after Haim Ramon (its leading light) was expelled from Labour in April, 1994. Ramon, tipped as one of the brightest of Labour's 'new generation', had resigned as Health Minister the previous month, when the government dropped his proposal for a radical new health insurance bill. In May, Ramon led a 'Ram' or 'New Life' list to a surprise victory against a Labour old guard, to take control of the *Histadrut* labour federation. The *Histadrut* List had three MKs in the *Knesset*; but after Yitzhak Rabin's assassination in November 1995, the party decided to rejoin the main Labour caucus.

Islamic Movement

Leader: Sheikh Abdullah Nimr Darwish

The Islamic Movement has never contested a general election in Israel, although recently its central executive only narrowly voted against doing so. Thought to enjoy the support of about 20% of Israeli Arabs, the Movement follows a strictly Islamic political line, and ultimately favours Muslim rule over all of 'Palestine'. However, while it is anti-Zionist and ideologically affiliated with *Hamas* and similar groups, the Movement eschews violence. In practice, the Islamic Movement co-operates with Israeli civic authorities, and from time to time holds discussions with Jewish Israelis, especially rabbis, on issues of mutual interest. It has been suggested that the Movement has acted as a 'go-between' with *Hamas,* the PLO and Israel, when ordinarily the latter two could not be seen to be talking openly with the former. Sheikh Darwish is thought to represent the moderate, centrist wing of the Movement. His main opponent within the movement is Kamal Khatib. The Movement enjoys strongest support in Umm al-Fahm, a largely Arab town of 30,000 inside Israel. In 1995 there were rumours that Sheikh Darwish was about to form an electoral pact with Dr Ahmed Tibi; instead, the IM joined forces with the ADP to run as a United Arab List in 1996 .

Mafdal

[see National Religious Party]

Mapam

Chairman: Erez Chanan

Founded in 1948, the United Workers' Party (better known as *Mapam* in its Hebrew acronym) has traditionally taken a more left-wing stance on domestic policy and relations with the Palestinians than the more mainstream Labour Party. Between 1969 and 1984 *Mapam* was part of the Labour Alignment, but broke away over Labour's coalition agreement with Likud in 1984. Together with *Ratz* and *Shinui, Mapam* is currently one of the three constituent parties in the *Meretz* bloc (q.v.), which after the 1992 elections became the third biggest grouping after Labour and *Likud.* Since 1992 *Meretz* has been part of the Rabin government, and *Mapam* MKs hold cabinet posts (notably Immigrant Absorbtion Minister Ya'ir Tsaban, a former *Mapam* chairman) . While in the 1950s *Mapam's* challenge was to blend its Marxist tendencies with a commitment to Zionism, in the 1990s it sought to adapt socialism to new 'global realities'. Also, through a series of Congresses (chaired by an Arab member, Asaf Nahir, and prepared by a Jewish member, Aryeh Yaffe) it devised a new formulation, the land of Israel as a 'common homeland' for Palestinians and Jews.

Meretz

Leader: Shulamit Aloni (until January 1996)
Current leader: Yossi Sarid

A left-wing coalition group which was formed just before the 1992 elections, consisting of *Ratz* (q.v.), *Mapam* (q.v.) and *Shinui* (Change). While individual parties maintain a measure of independence, they presented a broadly common front (typically pro-peace and for a deal with the PLO), and a common list. The idea for the common list arose after the 1988 elections, and soon galvanized around the dynamic personality of *Ratz* leader, Shulamit Aloni. *Meretz* gained 12 seats in all, making it the third biggest bloc after Labour and *Likud.* The bloc gained three major cabinet posts (Shulamit Aloni, Yair Tsaban and Amnon Rubinstein) and a fourth (Yossi Sarid) in December 1992.

Its first year in office was characterized by infighting with *Shas,* who, although being their colleagues in the governing coalition, strongly opposed its secularist approach in the education department. Ultimately, Shulamit Aloni was forced from her Education portfolio, and became Minister for Science and Communications. The party was also embarrassed into supporting the December 1993 deportation of Islamic fundamentalists to South Lebanon. Although the *Meretz* rank-and-file opposed the policy, its leaders backed it as a price to pay for keeping the peace process on track.

By 1995, a clear split emerged within *Meretz*, with the dovish ex-Labourite, Yossi Sarid, now Environment Minister, veering more towards the centre, and away from the more ideologically pure Aloni and others. Matters came to a head in early 1996, when Aloni announced her resignation as party leader, and reluctantly handed over power to Sarid. There were rumours that she intended to form her own party. Within *Meretz*, many former supporters blamed Aloni for squandering opportunities by adopting an inappropriately 'oppositionist' stance while in government. On paper, *Meretz* has achieved a number of successes in office (help for new immigrants, curbs on religious priviledges, and women on rabbinical councils). However, opinion polls show that Labour has largely usurped *Meretz's* peace platform. The assassination of Yitzhak Rabin jolted many younger Israelis out of their political apathy, and many have responded by flocking to support the Peres government, rather than *Meretz*.

Moledet

Leader: Gen. Rechavam Ze'evi

Moledet (which means 'homeland') is a far-right party which demands the 'transfer' (expulsion) of Palestinians from the West Bank and Gaza. Founded in 1988, it joined a coalition with the *Likud* govenment in 1990, but after the 1992 election went into opposition. Much of its support comes from settlers. In 1994, one of its three MKs (Shoul Gutman) defected to form a one-man Peace Guard Party.

National Religious Party

Leader: Zevulun Hammer

Also known by its acronym, *Mafdal* (for *Mifleget Datit Leumi*), the National Religious Party succeeded the old *Mizrachi* Party in 1956. Like its predecessor, the NRP represents the nationalist religious trend (some other orthodox Jews remain lukewarm or positively antagonistic to the idea of a secular State of Israel). Party supporters like to portray themselves as 'modern orthodox', in contrast to the black-gaberdined ultra-orthodox or *haredim*. The small religious *kibbutz* movement has close ties to the NRP (with Avraham Stern as its current representative). Since the 1967 war, the party gained a new lease of life when it harnessed its fortunes to the growing Land of Israel Movement, a pressure group which favoured Jewish settlement on the territories conquered by Israel (which it considered to be part of *Eretz Yisrael*, the land promised to Jews in the Bible). Following this trend, the NRP became closely associated with the *Gush Emunim* religious settlers' movement in the 1980s. However, recently the centre of the party has tried to loosen its ties with *Gush*, as that organization became tainted by militancy.

Zevulun Hammer replaced Yosef Burg as party leader in the 1980s, at a time when strains started emerging between Sephardi and Ashkenazi supporters. Many of the former split away to form the *Shas* party (see separate heading). The NRP also became divided between centrists and those who called for active support for settlers, and it began to lose votes to rival right-wing groupings, not least *Moledet*. Some supporters favoured extra-parliamentary action, either through the pressure group, *Gush Emunim*, or through more radical and militant groups, like the outlawed *Kach* party. In 1986 the NRP absorbed the more radical religious Zionist *Morasha* (Heritage) Party. Two years later, a group of disillusioned pro-peace NRP supporters split away to form *Meimad* (see separate heading in 'Pressure Groups' section). Apparently there is still a schism within the party, with a moderate faction led by party leader Hammer, and a right-wing pro-settler faction led by Yigal Bibi.

In 1992 the NRP's number of seats dropped to six. After tempestuous inner party debates, the party chose not to join Rabin's new government, thus marking the first time that the NRP found itself outside Israel's ruling coalition. A few members remain disgruntled that *Shas* (which did join the government), and not the NRP, gained influence over religious councils which disburse funds for religious activities). Most, however, seemed pleased not to be associated with a government which was daily losing support amongst religious right-wingers as the peace process with the PLO unfolded. However, after the assassination of Yitzhak Rabin by a supporter of the 'national religious trend', the NRP went through a period of soul-searching, and vowed to uproot radical elements. The party responded to Peres's calls for national reconciliation, and most party members now accept the Oslo 2 deal as a fait accompli. The NRP now regards the 'unity' of Jerusalem under Israeli rule as the top priority, and vowed not to split the right-wing vote in the forthcoming direct elections for prime minister, in May 1996.

Ratz

Leader: Shulamit Aloni

An acronym for the Citizens' Rights Party (*Reshimot Zechoyot ha-Ezrach*), *Ratz* was founded by a former Labour MK, Shulamit Aloni, in 1973. It campaigns for human rights and women's rights, opposes religious 'interference' in politics and has long advocated a peace settlement with Palestinians. While its stance is left-wing, it opposes the more doctrinaire socialist aspects of the older Labour Party, from which most of its earlier members came. The party has close ties with the extra-parliamentary Peace Now movement. Today *Ratz* is a central player in the *Meretz* bloc, and as such it controls several cabinet portfolios.

Shas

Leader: Rabbi Aryeh Deri

Founded in 1984 as a breakaway Sephardi faction of *Agudat Yisrael* (q.v.), *Shas* (which stands for Sephardi Torah Guardians) has largely overtaken its parent party as a national political force. It has also drawn support away from the National Religious Party, and some see it as a successor to the earlier Sephardi-based party, *Tami*. Initially, *Shas* was dominated by the Ashkenazi nonagenerian, Rabbi Menachem Eliezer Shach, who backed it as a Sephardi sister-party to *Degel ha-Torah*. However, after Shach antagonized *Shas* members with his unbidden interference and allegedly demeaning attitude, former Sephardi Chief Rabbi, Ovadiah Yosef, wrested it away from his grasp. *Shas* is 'guided and directed' by the Council of Torah Sages.

Under its dynamic leader, the Moroccan-born Aryeh Deri, a protege of Yosef's, it prospered for a while, but then suffered from the taint of financial and vote-buying scandals (still not resolved). It joined the Labour government in 1992, but soon clashed with its left-wing coalition partners, the secular *Meretz* movement, particularly over education policy. In September 1993 (exactly when Israel was signing the historic agreement with the PLO in Washington), *Shas* withdrew from the coalition. This was prompted by Deri's forced resignation as Interior Minister over corruption allegations. Deri and Rabin initialled a new coalition agreement in March 1994. However, in February 1995, *Shas* announced that it was formally joining the opposition. The party's position on peace is ambiguous; it tends to be more conciliatory than of the National Religious Party, although in 1995 it expressed concern over the fate of West Bank settlers in the light of the peace accords. While in government, *Shas* ran the Religious Affairs ministry. Curiously, perhaps, as the party entrusted with bestowing religious endowments, it enjoyed good ties with Israeli Arabs.

Tehiyah

Tehiyah was founded in 1979 to oppose the Camp David accords, and demand Israeli sovereignty over the occupied territories. Along with *Tsomet* and *Moledet*, it became one of the leading radical parties of the far right in Israel in the 1980s. Its doyen was the Elyakim Haetzni, a fiery Kiryat Arba veteran and opponent of compromise with Palestinians. In its latter years, *Tehiyah* advocated partial 'transfer' of Palestinians from the occupied territories, a policy first advocated by *Kach*. In 1992, however, the party's three MKs all lost their seats. Since then the party has disintegrated, with former members drifting into radical pressure groups, like *Zo Artzeinu* and *Eyal*, or other right-wing parties. Part of its election failure is ascribed to confusion caused by Moshe Levinger purporting to stand for a united radical right.

Third Way

Leader: Avigdor Kahalani

The Third Way started life in 1994 as an extra-parliamentary grouping, but by December 1995, a faction led by Labour MPs Avigdor Kahalani and Emanuel Zissman decided to turn the movement into a separate political party. As its name implies, the Third Way intended to draw cross-party support for a policy which sought a middle path to the peace process, between *Likud* on the right and Labour on the left. It stands for 'peace with security', and while supporting territorial compromise, opposes withdrawal to pre-1967 borders. Its executive included the *Meimad* leader, Rabbi Yehuda Amital, although since he joined the cabinet in November 1995, it appears he no longer endorses the party's increasingly right-wing stance. Brig.-Gen. Avigdor Kahalani, a former military hero, led the parliamentary campaign against Rabin making concessions on the Golan Heights issue. After the assassination of Yitzhak Rabin in November 1995, the Third Way appeared to waver about striking out as a distinct party. In the event, it chose to do so; prospective leader Dan Shomron decided not to stand, which left the way clear for Kahalani. Its prospects in the forthcoming election appeared uncertain, as its central stance (defence of the Golan) is almost indistinguishable from the *Likud* platform; while its policies on more domestic issues have hardly been thrashed out. Nonetheless, Kahalani's personal popularity amongst urban Sephardi voters, and the party's freedom from the taint of religiosity or violent extremism, may win it enough seats to hold the balance of power in the future.

Tsomet

Leader: Rafael Eitan

Founded in 1988 and led by former a chief of staff, Rafael Eitan, *Tsomet* surprised political analysts with its good showing in the 1992 election. While *Likud* dropped from 40 to 32 seats in the Knesset, *Tsomet*, hitherto regarded as a distinctly minority conservative grouping, seemed to buck the prevailing trend towards peace by raising its total of seats from two to eight. Indeed, *Tsomet* was at least partly responsible for the election being held when it was: when in early 1992 *Tsomet* and *Moledet* left the *Likud* coalition, in protest at perceived concessions to Palestinians, this deprived Shamir of a working majority, and hastened the new elections.

In the immediate post-election horse-trading, the new prime minister, Labour's Yitzhak Rabin, strove to woo *Tsomet* into joining his coalition cabinet. It was thought that he intended to counter-balance the leftist bias represented by his coalition partners in *Meretz*. In the event *Tsomet* stayed out of government, much to the relief of left-leaning Labourites like Peres and Beilin, thus forcing Rabin to rely instead on *Meretz, Shas*, and passive support from Arab political parties.

The *Tsomet* political agenda is dominated by one issue – the preservation of *Eretz Yisrael* (Greater Israel, or the occupied territories). However, unlike *Gush Emunim, Tsomet* is distinctly secular in outlook, and on occasion has lambasted the ultra-orthodox for 'sponging off the state' while not contributing to the nation's defence. Its arguments for retaining territory are exclusively strategic. Indeed, *Tsomet* was formed by the desertion of key 'securocrats' from the Labour movement. On certain issues (such as the question of the Golan Heights), *Tsomet* has the authority to attract support from fellow right-wingers still in Labour, although Avigdor Kahalani's Third Way (q.v.) seems to be fishing in the same pond. The party is dominated by the personality of Rafael 'Raful' Eitan, a controversial but popular figure. (Eitan was Chief of Staff in 1982 and together with Ariel Sharon masterminded Israel's invasion of Lebanon in that year.) In February 1994, three *Tsomet* MKs, led by Gonen Segev, deserted to form the *Ye'ud* Party (q.v.).

In February 1996, Eitan and *Likud* leader, Benjamin Netanyahu, announced a pact between their two parties. Under the terms of the agreement, *Tsomet* would be guaranteed eight seats in a joint list; while Eitan would get a leading cabinet post (presumably defence) if

Likud-Tsomet won the election. In return, Eitan agreed not to stand in the first direct elections for the prime ministership; instead he would throw his weight behind Netanyahu's candidacy.

United Torah Judaism

Leader: Avraham Shapira

United Torah Judaism established itself as an influential umbrella group for ultra-orthodox parties (*Degel Ha-Torah, Agudath Yisrael*, and, at one stage, *Shas*). Its main role was to fight for 'Torah-true Judaism', at the expense of the secular state. This includes a narrower definition of 'who is a Jew', as well as strictures on public transport on the Sabbath and the sale of pork and other non-kosher products. While the UTJ believes in an ultimate messianic redemption for *Eretz Yisrael*, it has left more militant campaigning for West Bank settlers to other parties (NRP, *Tsomet, Moledet* and such groups). At the 1988 elections it won eight seats and thus held the balance of power in the country. However, internal splits, and wrangling between its various aspirant rabbinical mentors (Eliezer Shach, Ovadiah Yosef and at times the New York-based Lubavitcher Rebbe, Menachem Mendel Schneerson) led to a halving of its vote in 1992. The party enjoyed local success in galvanizing orthodox support for Ehud Olmert, the ex-*Likud* minister, who in late 1993 defeated Labour's Teddy Kollek to become Mayor of Jerusalem.

Ye'ud

Leader: Gonen Segev

In 1994 three *Tsomet* MKs broke away to form a new party, *Ye'ud*. Members of the party are now in the government. Party leader, Gonen Segev, is currently Minister of Energy and Infrastructure, and is also a member of the inner 'security' cabinet. Segev was one of the founders of *Tsomet*, but grew increasingly uneasy with its extreme right-wing stance.

Banned Parties:

Kach

Leader: Baruch Merzel

Founded by the militant right-wing US-born rabbi, Meir Kahane, *Kach* initially developed as an offshoot of Kahane's Jewish Defence League (JDL). It contested two elections, then was banned from competing in future polls for being a fascist party. *Kach* enjoyed a young membership, consisting of disgruntled Sephardim, and US immigrants (typically, *ba'alei teshuvah,* or newly orthodox Jews). It soon won a reputation for defining the outer limits of right-wing extremism (even overt racism) in Israel. *Kach* had connections with *Gush Emunim* (q.v.), and other more right-wing groups, such as the avowedly terrorist Jewish Underground and *Ateret Ha-Cohanim* (a movement to rebuild the Jewish Temple on the ruins of the mosques on the *Haram al-Sharif*, Jerusalem).

After Rabbi Kahane was assassinated in the USA in 1990, Rabbi Avraham Toledano became the group's leader, but he was later replaced by younger men, such as Baruch Merzel. Kahane's son, Binyamin, founded another right-wing group, *Kahane Chai*, when thwarted from gaining the *Kach* leadership. Many *Kach* supporters live amongst Jewish settlers in Hebron and Kiryat Arba, on the West Bank. One of these was Baruch Goldstein, who instigated the Hebron massacre of Muslim worshippers in 1994. After that event, both *Kach* and *Kahane Chai* were banned outright. Membership of either group was henceforth a criminal offence; and Israeli security forces actively disarmed former members. Nonetheless, *Kach* continued to receive funds from supporters in the USA, and Israel took extraordinary measures to try and block such transfers.

Prominent figures in *Kach* have resurfaced in other groups, such as *Eyal*. Noam Federman, an operations expert for *Kach*, is currently active in the Committee for Safety on the Roads (q.v.). Meanwhile, several *Kach* policies (notably 'transfer' of Palestinians from the occupied territories) were openly adopted by still-legal right-wing parties (like *Tehiyah* and *Tsomet*). When these parties entered Shamir's post-1990 *Likud*-led coalition government, it seemed that sections in Israel were sanctioning what only months earlier would have seemed outrageous. Within a fortnight of the assassination of Prime Minister Rabin by a right-wing Jewish fanatic in November 1995, Interior Minister Ehud Barak applied an amendment to the Law of Return, and barred a US *Kach* supporter from entering Israel.

Kahane Chai

Leader: **Binyamin Kahane**

Kahane Chai (Kahane Lives) broke away from the parent *Kach* Party (see separate entry) after the assassination of *Kach* founder and leader, Rabbi Meir Kahane, in November 1990. Ideologically, it is little different from *Kach*, and is seen as a platform for Binyamin Kahane, son of the late rabbi, whose dreams to lead *Kach* were thwarted after his father's death. Like *Kach, Kahane Chai* was banned in the aftermath of the Hebron massacre of 1994. Supporters of both groups remain active in West Bank settlements, notably Kiryat Arba and Tapuach.

Pressure groups

Bat Shalom

Leader: **Daphna Golan**

This women's peace group campaigns for women's rights, both Jewish and Palestinian, within the framework of the peace accord. Its leader, Daphna Golan, was a founder member of *Betselem*. *Bat Shalom* (which means 'daughter of peace') is affiliated to the Jerusalem Link, a joint Palestinian–Israeli womens' peace group.

Betselem

Betselem is the best-known and arguably most active practical human rights group in Israel. While not formally attached to any political party, it highlights alleged human rights abuses by Israel in the occupied territories, and is often quoted in the international media. It is mainly staffed by Israelis, including legal experts, and also has a network of Arab contacts in the West Bank and Gaza. Since the establishment of the PNA, *Betselem* has criticized its human rights record too.

Black Panthers

This group was founded in the Musrara slum of Jerusalem in 1971 to represent the grievances of Sephardim and *mizrachim* (Oriental Jews). Loosely modelled on the African-American movement of the same name, the Panthers attacked what they saw as discrimination by the *Ashkenazi* establishment against them and Arabs. Since officially disbanding in 1977, its main leaders – Charlie Biton, Kokhavi Shemesh and Sa'adya Marciano – have resurfaced in a range of political parties (including *Likud* and *Shas*), as well as a number of pro-peace pressure groups, notably the Committee for Israeli-Palestinian Dialogue and *Dai La-Kibbush*.

Committee for Safety on the Roads

Despite its innocuous title, the Committee is actually one of the most active pressure groups opposed to the peace process. Its ostensible *raison d'être* is to keep the West Bank tributary roads safe for passage by Jewish settlers. In 1995 the Committee stepped up its programme of civil disobedience. Individual members have been accused of acts of violence against Palestinians. Other associated groups include Struggle Command Against Autonomy (leader: former *Tehiya* Party chief, Elyakim Ha'etzni), Women in Green (leader: Nadia Mattar), *Eyal* (q.v.), and Zo Artzenu (q.v.).

Constitution for Israel

A lobbying group directed by Eyal Arad, which supports radical constitutional reform in Israel (including direct election of the prime minister).

Dai La-Kibbush

Meaning 'Stop the Occupation', this group arose as an Israeli solidarity front with Palestinian demonstrators involved in the *intifada*. Smaller and less well organized than Peace Now, the group was possibly more radical.

Eyal

Leader: Avishai Raviv

Eyal first emerged in 1995 as a shadowy right-wing group centred around Hebron and Kiryat Arba. After Nov. 4, 1995, it gained international notoriety as the organization which spawned Yigal Amir, the law student who assassinated Prime Minister Yitzhak Rabin on that day. *Eyal's* chief plank was implacable opposition to the 'Oslo 2' agreement, whereby the Palestinian Authority would extend its controls over West Bank cities (other than Jericho, which it already ruled). Most of its members are very young, including its leader, a history student, Avishai Raviv. Television footage showed hooded *Eyal* cadres posing with guns and swearing allegiance to future violence against opponents, at the graveside of Baruch Goldstein (the Hebron massacrer whom a few radicals regard as a martyr for *Eretz Yisrael*). *Eyal* and like-minded groups may be the visible signs of a resurgent 'Jewish Underground' (which through *Kach*-affiliated cells, named variously Sicarites and TNT, used violence against Palestinians in the 1980s).

Some *Eyal* members in Hebron pledged to kill any Palestinian soldier who entered the city (which is planned under the terms of the September 1995 Interim Agreement, or Oslo 2). Mainstream settler organizations like *Yesha* officially disown such policies. Following the Rabin assassination, several of the *Eyal* leadership (including Raviv) were arrested. Initially Israelis believed that the murder was the action of a crazed individual; but increasingly, there appeared to be evidence of a conspiracy at work (an enormous arms cache was found at Amir's home, and it seems that Raviv and others may have known of Amir's plans). By late November the Israeli media was accusing Raviv of being a *Shin Bet* (internal security) mole, code-named 'Champagne'. Allegedly, he was planted in Kiryat Arba to bring the extreme right into disrepute – a charge both he and the government denies.

Gush Emunim

Leader: Rabbi Benny Elon

The pre-eminent religious settlers' group, *Gush Emunim* (Bloc of the Faithful) wielded tremendous influence over the *Likud* administrations of Menachem Begin and Yitzhak Shamir. *Gush Emunim* regards the West Bank as Biblical *Eretz Yisrael* (also called Judea and Samaria), and sees Jewish settlement there as a *mitzvah* (religiously ordained duty). The *Gush* was founded in February 1974, by activists in the National Religious Party (q.v.). Seen as a successor to the Land of Israel Movement, it claimed to enjoy support from secular settlers (who make up approximately 60% of the total settler population), and through dynamic figures like Daniella Weiss it ran an effective public relations machine in the territories. Initially its spiritual leader was Rabbi Zvi Kook, son of the revered first Ashkenazi Chief Rabbi of Palestine, the moderate Rabbi Abraham Isaac Kook. Followers thus believed that the torch of religious Zionism (the 'national religious trend') had been passed to them. Rabbi Moshe Levinger, the militant founder of Jewish settlement in Hebron and the adjoining Kiryat Arba, was an early leader.

However, by the 1980s, the group's reputation became tarnished when it was accused of harbouring members of the Jewish Underground, Terror Against Terror (TNT) and the Sicarites, a group which vowed to avenge tit-for-tat the fatal stabbing of Jews by fundamentalist Palestinians. The Underground was led by Menachem Livni, who in 1984 was found guilty of murdering Arabs, but was released from jail seven years later under a presidential pardon. In addition, the *Gush* had ties with *Kach* (q.v.) and the *Ateret Ha-Cohanim* (Priests on the Heights, better know as the Temple Mount Faithful). On various occasions the latter group (led by Gershom Salomon) has tried to blow up the Mosques on the *Haram al-Sharif*, so as to herald the rebuilding of the Jewish Temple and the advent of the Messiah. Since the 1990s, the *Yesha* Council (q.v.) has largely superceded the somewhat marginalized *Gush* as the voice of settlers. Rabbi Benny Elon was said to be the new leader of *Gush Emunim* in 1992. More militant *Gush* supporters now lend support to protest groups like *Zo Artzeinu* and *Eyal*.

Gush Shalom

An offshoot of Peace Now, *Gush Shalom* (Peace Bloc) deliberately casts itself as the antithesis of *Gush Emunim*. *Shalom* activists often join Palestinians in protesting against settlers and their attempts to build new sites.

Harish

Leader: Rabbi Yitzhak Bar-Da

The Israeli Rabbi's Group (or *Harish* in its Hebrew acronym) was formed in 1994 in a bid to counter the influence of right-wing rabbis opposed to the peace process (see Rabbinical Authority). It claimed to have the backing of Rabbi Ovadiah Yosef, former Sephardi Chief Rabbi of Israel and the spiritual mentor of the orthodox *Shas* Party. One of the group's leaders, Yitzhak Bar-Da, Sephardi Chief Rabbi of Ramat Gan, sought meetings with moderate Islamic leaders. Explaining the rational for *Harish*, he said: 'Making peace is far more in harmony with Jewish tradition than making war'.

Meimad

Leader: Rabbi Yehuda Amital

A group of members from the National Religious Party (q.v.) found they could not go along with its hardline approach on the peace process, so in 1988 they split away to form *Meimad*. The party won no seats in the election of that year, and has since constituted itself as a religious Zionist pressure group which favoured territorial compromise for peace in the territories. More recently Rabbi Amital joined the executive of the Third Way (q.v.), marking a drift rightward. They fear for the safety of settlers' lives. In November 1995, after the Rabin assassination prompted a cabinet reshuffle, acting Prime Minister Shimon Peres invited Rabbi Amital into the cabinet as a minister without portfolio. This was widely seen as an attempt to bridge the gap between religious and secular Jews in Israel (a schism which in part led to the atrocity), while at the same time keeping alive the peace process.

Neturei Karta

Leader: Rabbi Moshe Hirsch

Although strictly speaking a purely religious Jewish group, *Neturei Karta* (Aramaic for 'Guardians of the City Gates') is well known as a leading ultra-orthodox (*haredi*) and militantly anti-Zionist group. The group broke away from the orthodox *Agudath Yisrael* in 1935. On occasion *Neturei Karta* has disrupted archaeological digs (which it regards as desecration of the dead), and blocked off roads on the Sabbath to prevent traffic from 'violating the holy day of rest'. Group members refuse to either pay taxes to, or receive funds from, the state of Israel. In 1981 they asked the United Nations to protect Jewish holy places in Jerusalem from 'Zionist oppression'. Quoting from rabbinical sources, the group rejects as heretical the establishment of a Jewish state in Palestine/*Eretz Yisrael* until the advent of the Messiah. This view is shared by certain *Hassidic* sects, notably the Satmar. Consequently it prefers to live under Arab rule. Rabbi Hirsch serves on the PLO-led Palestinian Authority as the representative of the 'Palestinian Jewish community'.

Oz Ve-shalom/ Netivot Shalom

Meaning Strength with Peace, and Paths of Peace, respectively, these affiliated groups act as lobbies for a small pro-peace grouping amongst religious Zionists in Israel. Generally, *Oz Ve-shalom* stands to the left of *Meimad* (see entry) and is close to Peace Now, but favours a stronger religious spirit in Israel.

Peace Now

Also known in Hebrew as *Shalom Achshav*, Peace Now is the largest and best-known extra-parliamentary peace lobby in Israel. As such it has taken some of the credit for the deal with the PLO, but by the same token has criticized the Labour government for not sticking to the peace process. Peace Now has long had strong affiliations to the Citizens' Rights Party (*Ratz* – see separate entry), and to some extent *Ratz* leader Shulamit Aloni made her name in its cause. Similarly, Yossi Sarid, now environment minister and a leader in the *Meretz* coalition, was active in the more centrist wing of Peace Now.

The organization was founded as a group of army officers who wanted to ensure that Menachem Begin did not waver on his promise for peace with Egypt, in 1978. Its national prominence grew as a focus for opposition to the Israeli invasion of Lebanon in 1982. In that year it succeeded in bringing between 200,000 and 400,000 people out in a demonstration in Tel Aviv (the largest protest to date in Israel). In succeeding years it has turned its attention to campaigning for withdrawal (partial or full, depending on members' views) from the occupied territories. This campaign increased in vigour with the advent of the *intifada* in December 1987.

Peace Now members often breached the 'Counter-Terrorism Act' (passed by the Knesset on Aug. 6, 1986), which forbade contacts between Israeli citizens and PLO officials. (The act was overturned in 1993.) Peace Now has no one clear leader, but retired general, Mattityahu 'Matti' Peled, was perhaps its most authoritative figure outside the Knesset. The novelist Amos Oz is another well-known and vocal member. Others include the veteran peace campaigner and civil disobedient, Abie Nathan; women's rights doyen, Alice Shalvi; and former *Likud* mayor of Tel Aviv turned peace activist, Shlomo 'Chich' Lahat. There are strong branches of Friends of Peace Now in the US and UK. Peace Now members have links with research bodies *cum* pressure groups, such as the International Center for Peace in the Middle East (Director: Ofer Bronstein) and the Israeli Council for Israeli–Palestinian Peace (led by Mattityahu Peled before his death).

During the Gulf War, Peace Now suffered from some strain as certain members objected to Palestinian policy *vis á vis* Saddam Hussein. The group is generally secular in orientation and draws much support from the *kibbutz* movement. It thus opposes religious 'fundamentalism', whether Jewish (like *Gush Emunim*) or Muslim (like *Hamas*). Some Sephardi Jews have not felt comfortable supporting Peace Now, and so have formed their own pressure groups. Likewise, religious Jewish peace activists tend to prefer voicing their feelings in forums like *Meimad* or *Oz ve-Shalom*. Even so, Peace Now has acted as an umbrella for a wide variety of groups, including Women in Black, a protest organization consisting of Israeli Jewish and Palestinian Arab women opposed to the occupation. In 1995 Peace Now activists protested in solidarity with Palestinians, against the 'hilltop protests' of Jewish settlers. On Nov. 4, 1995, Peace Now organized a rally in central Tel Aviv, in support of the government's peace initiative with the Palestinians. It was the biggest pro-peace demonstration in years, with up to 150,000 in attendance; but as it ended, it was blighted by the shocking assassination of Prime Minister Yitzhak Rabin by a right-wing extremist.

Peace Watch

Spokesman: Bob Lang

This group acts as a monitor of the peace process. Since the Declaration of Principles in September 1993, it has highlighted shortcomings in the Palestine Authority, and persistant acts of Palestinian terrorism. Although its members are generally right-wing, and include former settler leaders, Peace Watch claims to be objective.

Rabbinical Authority

Leader: Rabbi Avraham Shapira

In 1995 this 1,500-strong organization of Israeli rabbis issued a *halachic* ruling for religious military conscripts to defy any orders to withdraw from the occupied territories. It also forbade the 'evacuation of bases and the handing over of land to non-Jews'. Rabbi Nahum Rabinovich, spiritual head of the large Ma'ale Adumim settlement outside Jerusalem, allegedly told his students to place landmines in the path of defence forces if they tried to make settlers evacuate their homes. The original edict came from the Authority's leader, former Ashkenazi Chief Rabbi Avraham Shapira. However, the current Chief Rabbi, Yisrael Lau, while urging the government to take cognisance of strong religious feeling, spoke out against soldiers disobeying orders (which would be the logical result of the Authority's ruling). He denied the 'ruling' had any religious veracity. The ruling came in the wake of similar edicts from right-wing orthodox rabbis in the USA. The Authority's action was condemned by *Likud* leader Binyamin Netanyahu and right-wing *Tsomet* party leader, Rafael Eitan. To date, there have been no recorded instances of any conscripts heeding the Authority's ruling. In the light of the Rabin assassination, the General Security Services are investigating whether militant rabbis in the Authority, in particular Haim Druckman, leader of *Matzad*, might have fomented the atmosphere of violence which led to the tragedy.

Yesh Gvul

Yesh Gvul (or 'There is a limit') began as a lobby for soldiers who refused to fight in the 1982 Lebanon war. Soon it expanded its remit to cover conscientious objection amongst soldiers conscripted to patrol the occupied territories, especially during the *intifada* (Palestinian uprising after 1987).

Yesha Council

Chair	**Yisrael Harel; Yehiel Leiter**
Executive Director	**Uri Ariel**
Spokesman	**Aharon Domb**

Since the heyday of *Gush Emunim* (q.v.) in the 1980s, the *Yesha* Council has taken over as the foremost representatives of Jewish settlers in the territories. Its name, *Yesha,* derives from an acronym of *Yehuda, Shomron,* and '*Azza* (Judea, Samaria and Gaza – the constituent parts of *Eretz Yisrael,* the biblical Land of Israel). Yisrael Harel founded the Council in 1979. In 1985, *Yesha* warned that its members would not pay taxes or serve in the Israeli army if the government ever negotiated away settlers' land. It was closely affiliated to *Amana* (*Yesha* works for existing settlements, while *Amana* sets up new ones).

In 1995 *Yesha* took the side of settlers who protested against alleged Israeli plans to dismantle their settlements. They opposed any attempt to increase the PLO's authority over most of the West Bank. *Yesha* has an active information machine, and details shortcomings in the peace process to Diaspora Jewry. It often draws on the testimony of security experts to refute Labour's view that a smaller Israel could be easier to defend. Unlike *Gush Emunim,* the Council enjoyed broad support amongst more moderate and secular settlers. However, in late 1995 the leaders of five prominent settlement cities, including the biggest, Ariel, resigned from Yesha and seem to be setting up their own less ideologically driven group. *Yesha* condemned the assassination of Yitzhak Rabin in November 1995, but appears unwilling to accept the compromises which Shimon Peres and the new minister without portfolio, Rabbi Yehuda Amital, wish it to consider. At the same time, certain *Yesha* leaders, notably Rabbi Yoel Bin-Nun, and settlement mayors, like Shlomo Kattan of Alfei Menashe, are working towards accepting Oslo 2 as a fait accompli.

Zo Artzeinu

Leader: Moshe Feiglin

Zo Artzeinu ('This is Our Land') came to prominence in 1995 by organizing 15 'hill-top protests' by settlers who opposed the policies of the Rabin government. Some even blocked traffic in Israel itself, thereby seeking to spread their message to the general Israeli public. In their opinion, Israel threatens to evict them from their homes in exchange for a nebulous peace with the PLO. Rabbi Shlomo Riskin, head of the Efrat settlement and hitherto regarded as a moderate force amongst settlers, appears to be a leading figure in *Zo Artzeinu* (he is also involved with the Third Way, q.v.). In September 1995, Moshe Feiglin said his group held the government responsible for 'its crime against security and Judaism'. The group strongly condemned the Rabin assassination in November.

Chapter 14   Palestine National Authority

Whereas other chapters in this book deal with established states, this one necessarily differs, in that it describes a Palestine National Authority (PNA), a link in a process, a legislative authority over areas of land. Initially under Oslo 1 it consisted of Gaza and Jericho (since May 1994); by increments other areas in the West Bank have been added (according to Oslo 2, the Interim Agreement of September 1995). Thus the final status of the PNA's geographical remit (that is, exactly how much of the West Bank will be Palestinian-run) has yet to be decided. Likewise, the ultimate nature of this entity – autonomy, full statehood, confederation with another state, or something else – is also open to speculation.

According to the Washington Agreement and Declaration of Principles (DOP) of 1993, all such questions will be decided at 'final status talks', to begin in 1996. There are other issues to be resolved apart from borders and constitutional status – most crucially, the question of Palestinian refugees and the future of Jewish settlers in the (formerly) occupied territories. Whatever is agreed on ought to be fully implemented by 1999.

THE CENTRAL ROLE OF THE PLO

Five years ago, this chapter would have been primarily about the PLO as a liberation organization, with addenda on Palestinian life under Israeli occupation, and the progress of the *intifada*. Today, however, the PLO has begun to transform itself. Its officers enjoy real authority in the areas under the PNA. The very process of empowerment has rendered the PLO both more important, as a source of PNA personnel; and less important as an organization in its own right. For this reason, this chapter includes a section on the PLO, but the main stress is on the PNA as a developing entity.

WHAT OF PALESTINIANS OUTSIDE 'HISTORIC PALESTINE'?

The aim of most early Zionists was a home for all Jews, and, as a corollary, the end of Diaspora. The reality has been a remarkable birth of a Jewish state in 1948, which today has almost four million Jewish inhabitants. But the Jewish Diaspora persists, and today's Zionists realize that this status is probably permanent. In similar vein, the Palestinian *nakba* of 1948 created its own Palestinian diaspora. Most fled to the West Bank and Gaza; others to Arab countries; a few to Europe and North and South America. The 1967 war placed all of 'historic Palestine' – including the Palestinians of the West Bank and Gaza – under Israeli rule. But this still left many in the diaspora. Like the early Zionists, PLO ideologues spoke of their own people's 'Right of Return' to 'Palestine'.

However, just as the Zionists discovered, the chances are that a Palestinian diaspora, too, is destined to be a permanent feature. Whether all Palestinians will get the right of return, is again a question for the final status talks. As to whether they will exercise this right, if they get it – this is a matter of personal choice. In all events, the Palestinian diaspora plays, and will continue to play, a central part in the future of the newly autonomous Palestine, and so merits inclusion in this chapter.

Palestine National Authority

POLITICAL DETAILS

The Palestine National Authority (PNA) arose out of the Washington Declaration (or 'Oslo 1') of September 1993, and in accordance with the Declaration of Principles (DOP) signed between Israel and the Palestine Liberation Organization (PLO). It was the first time the PLO had formally established itself (with Israeli consent) inside historic Palestine. The PNA's remit covered the territories agreed on at the secret Israel–PLO talks in Oslo, namely the Gaza Strip and Jericho (although the exact extent of Jericho was a matter of some debate in the months preceding the handover of power from Israeli civilian rule).

Gaza and Jericho were only the first areas in the PNA, and would become the 'test-case' for extending authority to other parts of the West Bank. The Interim Agreement (or 'Oslo 2') of September 1995 set the timetable and modalities for this latter stage [see Chapter 9 for more details]. Final borders will be decided after the 'permanent [or final] status talks', officially scheduled to begin in 1996. In November and December 1995, Israeli troops withdrew from five major Palestinian towns in the West Bank, in preparation for elections to a Palestinian Council. The PNA officially dissolved itself at the start of a three-week election campaign, and polling was held, on schedule, in January 1996. The Council will assume the powers currently enjoyed by the PNA. According to the agreements signed so far, the nominated PNA and its elected successor body, the Palestinian Council, are primarily responsible for the well-being of Palestinians. At least in the interim stage, Israel is responsible for the Jewish settlers in the occupied territories.

Leadership

Head of the PNA   Yasser Arafat (Abu Ammar)
(In 1988 the PNC elected Arafat 'President of Palestine'. Since 1994 he has used the title *Ra'is*, which in Arabic approximates to 'president'; Israel acknowledges this usage.)

Cabinet

Chair; Interior portfolio	Yasser Arafat
Economic Affairs	Ahmad Qurei (Abu 'Ala)
Labour and Social Affairs	Samir Ghosheh
Planning and Economic Co-operation	Nabil Sha'ath
Finance	Mohammad Zuhdi Nashashibi
Justice	Freih Abu Medein
Housing	Zakaria al-Agha
Culture and Arts	Yasser Abed Rabbo
Health	Riyadh Zaanoun
Education	Yasser Amr
Tourism and Antiquities	Elias Freij
Communications and Post	Abdel-Hafidh al-Ashhab
Local Administration	Sa'eb Erekat
Sports and Youth	Azmi al-Shu'aibi
Welfare, Social Affairs	Intissar al-Wazir (Umm Jihad)
Transport and Communications	Abd al-Aziz al-Hajj Ahmed
Minister Without Portfolio	Faisal al-Husseini (effectively Minister for Jerusalem)
Minister Without Portfolio	Munib al-Masri
[Later appointments] Minister for the Palestinian Jewish community	Rabbi Moshe Hirsch
Minister for Islamic Affairs	Sheikh Hassan al-Tahboub

Party in government

The PNA includes officials from most of the main PLO factions, as well as many independents. It is a nominated body. According to the Interim Agreement, there will be elections to a new Palestine Council in January or, failing that, spring of 1996. Below is a list of PLO factions supporting the concept of the PNA, and which are, to a greater or lesser extent, involved in its administration.

Palestine Liberation Organization (PLO)
Fatah (the dominant faction and prime force behind the PNA)

Democratic Front for the Liberation of Palestine (DFLP) [Hawatmeh faction]
Fida (DFLP dissident faction, led by Yasser Abed Rabbo)
Arab Liberation Front (ALF)
Palestinian People's Front (formerly the Palestine Communist Party)
Palestine Liberation Front (PLF)

Opposition

Officially unknown until elections in 1996. In January 1994, ten groups (eight PLO 'rejection-ist' factions and two Islamic fundamentalist organizations) organized themselves into an anti-PNA 'Alliance of Palestinian Forces' or 'National Alliance'. Whether some will break rank, and compete in the elections as anti-PLO parties, remains to be seen.

Alliance of Palestinian Forces
Popular Front for the Liberation of Palestine (PFLP)
Democratic Front for the Liberation of Palestine (DFLP) (anti-Hawatmeh faction)
Palestinian Liberation Front (Talat Ya'qub faction)
Palestine Popular Struggle Front (PPSF)
Popular Front for the Liberation of Palestine- General Command (PFLP-GC)
Palestine Revolutionary Communist Party
Fatah Uprising
Al-Saiqa
Hamas
Islamic *Jihad*

Presidential aides

PNA Secretary-General	Tayyeb Abdul Rahim
Information Department	Ussama Abu Shurab (director-general)
Adviser	Nabil Abu Rudeineh
Spokesperson	Marwan Kanafani
National Security	Gen. Mohammed Yussef Al-'Amla
Police Affairs	Maj.-Gen. Abdullah Al-Farra
Economics	Dr Maher Al-Kurd
TV and Radio	Yussef Hassan Qassaz
Public Affairs	Najib Al-Ahmad
National Institutions	Samir Shehadeh (director-general)
Education	Jarir Numan Qudwa
State Comptroller	Aziz Al-Aklouk (secretary)
Public Relations Officer	Said Salem Sharafa
Personal Representative	Sulleiman Sharafa
Protocol Officer	Khaled Yaziji

Heads of Palestine Authority councils

Jerusalem National Council	Faisal Husseini (president)
Council for Medical Services	Hassan Shrab (director)
Health Services Council	Darwish Nazzal
Higher Council for the Arab Tourist Industry	Hani Abu-Dayyeh
Environment	Jad Ishaq
Palestinian Council of Health	Dr Fathi Arafat
Palestinian Council for Higher Education	Yasser Amr (also Minister of Education) Naim Abu Homus (deputy)
Palestinian Housing Council	Mohammad Shadid (head) Abd-Rahman Hamad [vice-pres.; Gaza]

| Palestinian Oil Council | Said Assaf |
| Supreme Muslim Council | Hassan al-Tahboub |

In addition to these councils, special mention must be made of PECDAR (the Palestine Economic Council for Development and Reconstruction). PECDAR was intended to be the main channel for disbursing international aid to the PNA. Its nominal Director is Farouq Qaddumi, who is based in Tunis, but the more active members are:

Deputy Managing Director	Dr Hassan Abu Libdeh
Co-Director	Ahmad Qurei (Abu 'Ala)
Director of the Planning Unit	Tony Zahlan
Economic Director	Prof Samir Abdullah

COMPOSITION OF THE PNA

The Palestine National Authority (PNA) held its first meeting on May 26, 1994. There were 20 participants, headed by Yasser Arafat. Five places were yet to be filled. Arafat envisaged the PNA as interim cabinet for the self-rule areas. He had also hoped to fill the posts with 12 'insiders' (from the occupied territories) and 12 'outsiders' (from the PLO offices in Tunis). In the event, only three PLO Executive Committee members, apart from Arafat himself, became ministers in the PNA (Muhammad Zuhdi al-Nashashibi, Yasser Abed Rabbo and Samir Ghosheh).

Some of Arafat's closest associates refused to join. These included Farouk Qaddumi (PLO second-in-command and since 1988 its 'foreign minister'), Jamal as-Surani and Mahmoud Abbas (known as Abu Mazen, and a key player in the Oslo talks). Similarly, Hanan Ashrawi, spokesperson for the Madrid talks and a notable Palestinian representative on the media circuit, also refused to join. There was no formal role for Haidar Abd al-Shafi, official head of the Palestinian delegation to Madrid.

Less surprisingly, rejectionist groups (including DFLP, PFLP, PFLP-GC) and Islamic groups (*Hamas* and Islamic *Jihad*) refused to participate in the PNA. In January 1994, these formed a collective opposition group, the Alliance of Palestinian Forces.

Opposition to the PNA

Palestinian opposition to the PNA has broadly taken three forms:

- The Alliance of Palestinian Forces, which vowed to fight it outright
- Internal forces, like Husseini and Ashrawi, who felt it conceded too much on key issues like Jerusalem and borders
- PNC veterans (external PLO forces), like Farouk Qaddumi, and Nasir Aruri, who voted for the establishment of the PNA, but stated that it did not go nearly far enough. 'What we used to consider as [minimal] Palestinian conditions for entering the process seems now to be looking like maximal objectives', Aruri commented.

In time, some members of latter two groups were given a role in the PNA's councils. Qaddumi officially heads the influential Palestine Economic Council for Development and Reconstruction (PECDAR); while Husseini was soon co-opted as the unofficial Minister for Jerusalem. Others, notably Ashrawi, have added a second charge – namely, that the PNA was acquiring draconian powers. It is to the PNA's credit that it has begun to listen to the resultant lively debate, and, in certain cases, it has actually heeded public opinion (such as its decision to amend and liberalize proposed draft legislation on press freedom and and non-governmental groups).

With the advent of elections to a Palestine Council (due in Jan. 20, 1996), opposition forces faced the classical dissenters' dilemma – to participate in elections would mark a *volte face*, a belated acceptance of the legitimacy of agreements with Israel, and hence the appearance of hypocrisy. Not participating, however, could deprive them of influence in a future Palestinian state. Opposition parties considered various ways of squaring the circle. It was thought that the PFLP might put up candidates, to 'test its support', but refuse to take their seats if elected. *Hamas* may split into a political wing (ready to co-operate with the PNA and perhaps compete in elections); and an unreformed military wing. [See p 95, p 165 and Chapter 20.]

THE EARLY RECORD OF THE PNA

The PNA got off to a bumpy start, when initial plans had to be delayed pending agreement between the PLO and Israel on security arrangements. (The original timetable had envisaged final withdrawal from Gaza and Jericho by April 13, 1994; and Palestinian elections by July 13). In the interim, two prominent *Fatah* supporters of the Oslo deal, Muhammed Abu Sha'aban and Asad Siftawi, were assassinated in Gaza. Many Palestinians, not least Haidar Abd al-Shafi, complained of Arafat's draconian and overtly personal style of leadership. Frustrated by the lack of progress, many Palestinians seemed to turn to *Hamas* and other rejectionist forces.

Nonetheless, intensive negotiations in early 1994 began paying off, and on Feb. 9 1994, Peres and Arafat agreed that for security purposes, Gaza would be split into three zones:

- Under Israeli control: Gush Katif and Erez settlement areas; military installations on the Egyptian border
- Under joint control: Access roads and perimeter of settlements
- Under Palestinian control: The remainder of Gaza, including Gaza City

Despite the Hebron massacre in February, which threatened to sabotage the talks, both parties renewed effort at sorting out problems, and this resulted in the Cairo Agreement of May 4, 1994.

Chronology of events in 1994

Jan 7	The PLO and Jordan sign an economic co-operation agreement
Jan. 22–30	Arafat and Peres hold talks in Oslo and later in Davos, Switzerland
Feb. 25	Hebron massacre: Israeli settler kills 29 Muslim worshippers
March 31	Talks resume in Cairo
April 22	*Fatah* Hawks and *Hamas* brigades sign a temporary peace accord
April 29	Israel and PLO sign Economic Protocol in Paris after five months of talks
May 4	Arafat and Rabin sign Cairo Agreement, specifying modalities of granting Palestinian self-rule in Gaza and Jericho
May 11	Deir al-Balah in Gaza becomes the first town to come under Palestinian self-rule
May 17	Israel and PLO agree on transferring to the PNA control of civilian administration's 38 departments in Gaza and Jericho
May 28	Arafat announces the PNA cabinet [see above]
July 1	Arafat enters Gaza
Aug. 29	Israel and PLO sign an 'early empowerment' agreement, transferring new powers to the PNA
Sept 8–9	World Bank-sponsored conference of international donors in Paris collapses after Israel and the PNA argue over the funding of projects in East Jerusalem
Nov 18	*Hamas* and Islamic *Jihad* supporters clash with Palestinian police; 12 are killed

The PNA establishes its authority

After Yasser Arafat's triumphal return to Gaza and Jericho in July, support for the PLO and the peace deal revived. Meanwhile, Nabil Sha'ath, as head of the Palestinian technical committee, continued to negotiate on outstanding aspects of the Cairo Agreement with his Israeli counterparts (he discussed the release of 5,000 Palestinian prisoners and detainees held in Israeli jails with Maj.-Gen. Amnon Shahak; and 'early empowerment' in the rest of the

West Bank, with Maj.-Gen. Danny Rothschild). Throughout June, July and August, the PLO was busy organizing the transfer of 1,200 officials from their headquarters in Tunis.

Within the PNA, there was ambiguity over whether to persecute *Hamas* and other fundamentalists, or woo them. After the Gaza riots in November 1994, Arafat and Justice Minister Freih Abu Medein cracked down on the Islamists, arresting 200 Islamic *Jihad* members. But when Islamic fundamentalists attack buses and other targets in Israel itself, Arafat has been equivocal, condemning them publicly, but allegedly praising their 'heroism' in private. The PNA has clearly been embarrassed by charges that it is doing Israel's bidding in rounding up Islamic suspects. (Although to date they have not extradited a single terrorist suspect to Israel, as provided for in the agreements.) At the same time, it is in its own interests to neutralize this political threat. By 1995, it seemed as if the PNA was at last eroding *Hamas's* role as chief local welfare benefactor in Gaza, and was changing the political culture of the area. The clearest sign of this came when elements within *Hamas* spoke of participating in the forthcoming Palestinian elections.

The establishment of a Palestinian police force has also brought mixed responses. On the one hand, Palestinians feel proud of controlling their own affairs; on the other, there are suggestions that some officers (notably Jibril Rajoub in Jericho) have established their own all-powerful fiefdoms, and are intimidating opponents. By and large, the joint Palestinian–Israeli police patrols have been a success, and have served to break down barriers between officials on both sides.

The question of the exact size of Jericho remained a problem for Israel, but with the onset of Oslo 2 this became largely an academic issue. Of more pressing concern to Palestinians were alleged human rights abuses by the PNA (highlighted by an Amnesty International report in 1995, and various home-grown monitoring groups). Radwan Abu Ayash tried to ensure that the new Palestinian press enjoyed freedom of expression, and popular pressure succeeded in overturning draconian laws. On a less tangible level, returning diaspora Palestinians have experienced something of a culture clash. The realities of life in the territories often seem parochial and humble compared to life in the big capitals of Europe, the USA and the Arab world.

In terms of political personalities, Arafat used his time-honoured technique of incorporating potential enemies into the power structure (for instance, giving Farouk Qaddumi the prestige and authority of heading PECDAR). He also played off one side against the other, maintaining his position as arbiter, and keeping 'above the fray'. Salim Tamari, the respected Palestinian sociologist, notes that in Gaza Arafat used the same techniques to pacify potential foes in *Hamas* as he had used in the PNC with left-wing groups (especially the Popular and Democratic Fronts).

Another prevailing problem was the physical (and hence psychological) separation between Gaza and West Bank. Oslo 1 provides for a 'safe passage' for Palestinians wishing to travel from one area to the other, through the Negev desert; but in practice this has proved difficult to organize. Israel is wary of upsetting its Negev citizens with the prospect of continuous Palestinian traffic through their land. By late 1995, Arafat proposed an ambitious $200 million flyover highway to overcome the problem. The glaring economic and social disparities between the two areas may cause problems in the future. West Bankers on average have double the income of Gazans; their society is more variegated and sophisticated, and the gap between rich and poor is not so stark; Gaza is much more crowded, and has a higher proportion of refugees.

Finally, the PNA faces a potential dilemma over how to react to domestic non-governmental organizations (NGOs) which arose during the *intifada*, and filled the gap left by a retreating Israeli civil administration. If they were co-opted into government, would they not then displace PLO officials from the 'diaspora' (because of their superior local knowledge)? In many cases, NGOs suffer from the same 'crisis of expectations' as shared by the common people; however, this feeling has been exacerbated for *intifada* activists who feel that they have been 'passed over' by the Tunis set.

ECONOMIC POLICY

In order to make the Gaza-Jericho Agreement work, the Palestinian economy had to be set on its feet. Clearly, this would be impossible without an injection of aid. Hence in October 1993,

---

Monitoring the accords, policing the areas

Following an order to administer Oslo 1, a host of commissions were set up to monitor the implementation of the Accords, and to keep lines of communication open with Israel. These included the following organizations, with the names of their directors of heads in brackets:

- Civil Affairs Committee for Negotiations on Transfer of Legal Powers to the PNA (Nabil Kassis)
- Committee to Study Proper Implementation of the Gaza-Jericho First Agreement (Dr Abed al-Razzaq al-Yahya)
- Committee for the Welfare and Support of Prisoners and Detainees (Intissar al-Wazir)
- Liaison Commission with Israel (Jamil Tarifi)
- Negotiations Directorate (Hassan Asfour)
- Palestinian Security Liaison Committee (Maj. Gen. Abed al-Razzaq al-Yahya)
- Palestinian Electoral Commission (Sa'eb Erekat)
- Prisoner Committee (Hisham Abd a-Razzaq)
- Released Prisoner Committee (Abdul Qader Hamed)

In addition, Oslo 1 provided for an extensive Palestinian police force. Most of the initial recruits came from outside the territories, and were Palestine Liberation Army personnel trained in Iraq and elsewhere. Some Israelis complained that the PNA exceeded the number of policemen allocated in the agreement; but most concluded that the joint policing patrols between Israeli and Palestinian forces have been amongst the most successful aspects of the Oslo Accords. The most important leaders of the new force are:

- Public Security Commander of the Police Force Maj.-Gen Nasr Yussef
- General Intelligence Service chief Brig Gen Amin al-Hindi
- Preventive Security, West Bank Col Jibril Rajoub
- Preventive Security, Gaza Col Muhammad Dahlan
- Civil Police (Autonomous Areas) head Ghazi Jabali
- Civil Police in Jericho Hajj Ismail Jaber
- Civil Police in Gaza Gen. Abdel Razzaq Majaydeh
- Border Crossings Abd ar-Rahman Barakat

---

soon after the signing of the Israel–PLO Declaration of Principles, major economic nations met under the auspices of the World Bank to fix plans for disbursing aid. Following the death of the Norwegian Foreign Minister Jorgen Holst, the World Bank instituted the Holst Fund, to marshal the aid. A ministerial level international Ad Hoc Liaison Committee was set up to monitor the disbursement of funds, and on Oct. 31, 1993, the PLO established PECDAR (the Palestine Economic Council for Development and Reconstruction) as the main vehicle of economic policy. A legal framework for PECDAR was finally approved in early May, 1994, as were the first three projects in the World Bank's Emergency Assistance Programme (EAP). These projects were to cost $1.2 billion over three years. The following month, donors pledged an immediate $42 million.

Problems in 1994

Problems arose, however, which hampered the smooth flow of funds to the PNA. One of these stemmed from confusion over who actually controlled economic policy. At various stages, four leaders each claimed responsibility for dealing with the donor community – Planning Minister Nabil Sha'ath, Economics Minister Ahmed Qurei, PLO political department chief Farouk Qaddumi, and Finance Minister Muhammed Nashashibi.

There were also other factors which caused the best laid plans of Washington and Oslo go awry. The Israeli border closures after terrorist incidents deprived Palestinians of employment, reduced Palestinian income and thus cut the tax base which the PNA depended on. The expulsion of Palestinians from the Gulf reduced the remittances flowing into the Palestinian economy, while since 1990 Arab states have cut their funding to the PLO; thus much of the aid flowing into Gaza and the West Bank has been spent on plugging the PLO's own deficit. Donor nations have in turn expressed qualms about the 'transparency' of the PNA's use of their aid, and tended to hold back on granting new sums.

In a bid to restore some confidence, in August 1994 the United Nations Secretary-General appointed Terje Larsen, the 'point-man' in the Oslo talks, as a special envoy in charge of aid disbursement in Gaza. Larsen set about streamlining the procedure whereby aid reached the PNA, and tried to make the accounting procedures more 'transparent' for donors. In November he presented a blueprint for a new structure to a donors' conference in Brussels. This was accepted by both the Palestinians and the donor countries. It consists of a secretariat, comprising himself, the resident World Bank official in Gaza, and the Norwegian ambassador to Israel representing the donor community. The secretariat would steer 12 committees, each devoted to one key issue (such as education or infrastructure). Each committee would be chaired by a donor and would include a Palestinian representative.

The new structure earmarks job creation as its main goal. Larsen suggested that in the medium term this could be achieved by boosting public works, encouraging the Gulf states to use Palestinian labour, and discouraging Israel from sealing off the territories. In the longer term he foresaw special industrial zones with high security and modern infrastructure, as attracting vitally needed private investment to Gaza.

Mixed progress in 1995

In 1995, Israeli Foreign Minister Shimon Peres took Larsen's idea one stage further, by suggesting that Western countries each 'adopt' one of nine industrial parks to be set up in Gaza and the West Bank. The estimated start-up cost would be $200 million per park. The scheme aims to provide the Palestinian entity with a strong industrial base, and is loosely based on Project Renewal (the means by which Diaspora Jewish communities sponsor development in poor Israeli neighbourhoods). Palestinian dissidents regard the scheme not so much as a solution to Palestinian unemployment, but more as another means of maintaining Israeli control of the Palestinian economy. However, Palestinians such as Khaled Abd al-Shafi, Gaza officer for the United Nations Development Programme, have warmly endorsed the scheme. Throughout 1995, Peres and other Labour politicians actively lobbied the US Congress to release more funds for the PNA.

Balanced against this Israeli support is the stark reality is that the number of Palestinians working in Israel has dropped dramatically. In 1985 there were 130,000; in 1995 (estimates the Palestinian economist, Samir Abdullah) Israel could only absorb 30,000. The two main reasons for this shortfall are the long-term effects of the *intifada*, and Israel's policy of 'sealing the border' with the territories after major terrorist incidents. Consequently, Israeli firms have encouraged some 70,000 foreign workers to substitute for the Palestinian 'labour pool'. The net result is massive Palestinian unemployment (especially in Gaza, where it is estimated to run at 50%), and increased political tensions. In addition, Tony Zahlan of PECDAR was angry at the attitude of donor countries, who, he claims, failed to realize that the PNA needed time to set up its institutions. As of the end of March 1995, he said, only 68 construction projects worth $35.7 million had been signed for (although the World Bank put the figure at closer to $245 million).

Palestinian Diaspora and Oslo 2 bring new optimism

Nonetheless, hope seemed to come from an unexpected corner – Palestinian private investors, especially those from Jordan and elsewhere in the 'Diaspora'. In 1993 a number of these businessmen set up Padico (the Palestinian Development and Investment Company) with capital of $200 million. In March a big concrete manufacturing plant opened in Gaza. By mid-1995 a number of other projects were under discussion between Palestinian financiers, Jordanian banks and US and Egyptian companies – hotels, refineries and airports in Gaza, and a stock exchange in Nablus.

But the most significant boost to the PNA came with the long-awaited signing of the Interim Agreement (also known as Oslo 2) between Israel and the PLO, in Washington, on Sept. 28, 1995. To demonstrate the international community's support for the Interim Agreement, US Secretary of State Warren Christopher hosted a ministerial-level meeting of the Ad Hoc Liaison Committee (AHLC) on Palestinian assistance, chaired by Norwegian Foreign Minister Godal, on the same day as the official signing. The AHLC agreed to support projects that addressed basic infrastructure needs and created employment opportunities for Palestinians. A series of follow-up meetings are designed to launch the second phase of the development effort. First, the World Bank chaired a Consultative Group meeting in Paris on Oct. 18–19, 1995, to review projects at a technical level. Then, a ministerial-level Conference on Assistance to the Palestinians was to convene in Europe before the end of the year, where donors could confirm pledges for specific projects.

The day after the signing of Oslo 2, US Secretary Warren Christopher, Israeli Foreign Minister Shimon Peres, and Chairman Arafat convened the first meeting of the US-Israel-Palestinian Trilateral Committee. Hoping to emulate the success of the similar arrangement between Israel, USA and Jordan, it provided a framework for future economic and political co-operation.

Palestine Council elections, 1996

Under the guidance of Sa'eb Erekat, and the supervision of EU monitors, the PNA immediately set about registering voters for the Jan. 20 elections. Reactions were surprisingly enthusiastic, with over a million potential voters joining the rolls in just three weeks. The poll took place on schedule, exactly 22 days after Israeli troops redeployed from Jenin, Tul Karm, Nablus, Ramallah, Qalqilyah and Bethlehem. As expected, Yasser Arafat and most of his supporters scored large majorities. (*Hamas* did not participate in the end, which may explain *Fatah's* exaggerated share of the vote.)

Significantly, the elections were held in Gaza, and all three designated areas in the West Bank, as well as among the Palestinians of East Jerusalem. The Council will enjoy full civic powers and responsibility for internal security and public order in Area A (the major towns). In Area B (the villages, containing 68% of the Palestinian population) it cedes overall security to Israel; and Arafat has accepted responsibility for Palestinian civil affairs in Area C (remaining areas, including Israeli state land, small Palestinian holdings and Jewish settlements).

Critics of Oslo 2 point out that the Council will have no say in foreign relations. But the PNA is determined that this is a temporary condition, to be sorted out during final status talks (scheduled to begin in mid-1996). There are many vexed questions to be sorted out – the place of Diaspora Palestinians in the new dispensation; questions about refugees, Jerusalem and Jewish settlers; and, of course, whether the Palestinian entity will become a fully-fledged State of Palestine. But that is for the future. For the present, what is true is that the assassination of Israel's Yitzhak Rabin in November 1995 shocked the PNA into realizing the high price to be paid for peace. Likewise, the new Shimon Peres administration kept to its promises regarding redeployment and elections. Notwithstanding signs of Israeli interference (like the killing of *Hamas* bomber Yahiya Ayyash in Gaza) Palestinian autonomy in the territories seems to have gone beyond the point of no return.

Political Parties

THE PALESTINE LIBERATION ORGANIZATION (PLO)

The creation of the Palestine Liberation Organization (the *Munazamat Tahrir Filastin*, familiarly known as the PLO) in 1964 marked a crucial break with Palestinian political traditions since the foundation of the State of Israel in 1948. Between 1948 and 1964 the Palestinian position was somewhat ambiguous. Palestinians were considered to be part of the broader Arab nation (*umma*); as such, they were by and large expected to entrust their political future to the established Arab states. These states in turn promised to guarantee their well-being until the liberation of Palestine (i.e. destruction of Israel), when the 'dispossessed' Palestinians could return to their own homeland. In reality many Palestinians felt that, behind such Pan-Arabist rhetoric, they had been relegated to the status of merely a 'refugee problem'.

The *raison d'être* behind the PLO's creation was precisely to give Palestinians control over their own affairs. The authenticity of this rationale is open to question (with first Egypt and then Syria trying to dominate the organization). But the notion of Palestinian aspirations *qua* Palestine was established; and, especially after the Rabat Summit of 1974, it has never been seriously questioned in the Arab world.

Since 1964, and particularly since 1974, the history of the organization has become almost synonomous with the history of the Palestinian nationalist movement as a whole. This realization speaks both of the power of the PLO, but also of its role as an umbrella organization, a 'broad church' which encompasses and represents so many strands of Palestinian political opinion. When Israel recognized the PLO after nearly three decades of belligerency in 1993, it, too, acknowledged the centrality of the organization, and the reality that Palestinians had valid claims to autonomy in their own right.

But equally significantly, in formally recognizing the State of Israel the PLO, in turn, acknowledged that one phase had ended and another had begun. The PLO was transforming itself from liberation movement into proto-government of an area designated for eventual Palestinian self-rule, and perhaps in time full independence, as a new Arab State of Palestine. In one sense, it was a return to the ideas of 1947 – the date when the UN proposed to divide historic Palestine into two states, one predominantly Jewish and the other predominantly Arab.

Landmarks in PLO history until 1982

[For a fuller chronology, see Chapter 2]. The PLO was officially founded in 1964, and together with it the instruments of its organization:

● The Palestine National Covenant (or Charter);
● The Palestine Liberation Army (PLA, or armed wing);
● The Palestine National Council (PNC; in effect, the Palestinian 'parliament-in-exile').

However, groups which later played a major role in the organization had appeared years earlier – notably, *Fatah* in 1958 and the Arab Nationalist Movement (precursor to the Popular Front for the Liberation of Palestine, PFLP) in 1951. After the 1967 war, PLO Chairman Ahmed Shukeiri was forced to resign. Although *Fatah* failed to establish an armed base in the now Israeli-occupied territories, its leader, Yasser Arafat, became Chairman of the PLO in 1969. Soon the Syrian-backed *Al-Saiqa* and other groups joined his Armed Struggle Committee. Arafat has held that position ever since, and similarly *Fatah* has remained the dominant group within the PLO.

With the demise of Shukeiri and the death of Egyptian President Gamal Nasser in 1970, the PLO weaned itself away from Egyptian control. Syria attempted to fill the void, largely through *Al-Saiqa*, but *Fatah* has managed to survive. The PLO Charter was re-written and made more hardline after the Six-Day War. Putting this new militancy into practice, the PLO (and especially the radical PFLP which operated within it) threatened to overthrow the government of Jordan. In response, King Hussein unleashed the 'Black September' crackdown in 1970, and in 1971 expelled the PLO from its bases.

PLO forces fled to Syria, and the Cairo Agreement granted it limited independence in southern Lebanon. The PLO is noted for its level of internal democracy in the Arab world. At the 1974 PNC meeting the PLO adopted a plan for 'liberation in stages'. At the 1977 PNC meeting, this policy developed into acceptance of negotiations with Israel under certain circumstances. Some factions saw this as a betrayal of total liberation; led by the PFLP, they formed a breakaway 'rejectionist front'. Also in 1974, the Rabat summit of Arab leaders recognized the PLO as the sole legitimate representative of the Palestinian people. Arafat addressed the UN General Assembly, saying that he had a gun in one hand, and an olive branch in the other. The early 1970s were characterized by the use of terrorism as a political weapon. Although this strategy was mainly perpetrated by smaller factions, the mainstream PLO effectively endorsed it.

Lebanese war and intifada, 1982 to 1990

After 1976, the PLO became embroiled in the Lebanese civil war, and aligned itself with leftist and Muslim forces, ranged against the Christian Phalange. Meanwhile, the PLO *fedayeen* continued to shell northern Israel; in retaliation, Israel launched Operation Litani in 1978, and the much larger Operation Peace for Galilee in 1982. The latter campaign sought to eradicate the PLO altogether, but only partly succeeded – most PLO fighting units left Lebanon in late 1982, but had returned by the later 1980s. The war also led to a breakdown in relations with Syria, exacerbated when Damascus backed anti-Arafat rebels within the PLO. The PLO headquarters closed in Beirut, opened briefly in Damascus, and then was forced to relocate in Tunis. In 1979, the PLO had rejected the autonomy proposals contained in the

US-Egyptian-Israeli Camp David Accords. But by 1985, events had forced the organization to be more pliable. One sign of this came when King Hussein and Arafat appeared to mend fences and unite behind a joint policy based on a 'land for peace' deal with Israel. A Palestine National Salvation Front was formed to reject this stance, and within a year the Hussein–Arafat alliance had broken down.

The outbreak of the *intifada* (Palestinian uprising) in the occupied territories in 1987 marked a new phase for the PLO. It had begun internally, without input from Tunis. Nonetheless, the PLO realised the importance of the *intifada,* and was soon attempting to direct it. At the same time, it set about recruiting a new batch of young leaders in the territories. In 1988 King Hussein responded to the *intifada* by abrogating Jordan's claim to the West Bank. This opened the way for the 19th PNC session, held in Algiers that year, which openly called for a 'two-state solution' and talks with Israel. Arafat also declared Palestinian 'independence'. By the year's end, the PLO had started its first ever official talks with the USA, but Israel refused to believe that the PLO had changed from being a terrorist organization.

The PLO had little to show for its 'peace initiative', and this led to more support for the hardline Islamic groups, like *Hamas,* which claimed to have inherited the PLO's radical mantle. Meanwhile, radical leftist groups (like the DFLP, PFLP and the Communists) concentrated on 'institution-building', and tackling practical social and economic issues, instead of the previous high profile political broadsides. In 1990 the PLO was split over whether to support Saddam Hussein, with Arafat apparently leading the pro-Iraqi faction. After the Gulf War, oil-producing states which had previously bankrolled the PLO now withdrew their funding. In 1991, the 20th PNC meeting approved of Palestinian participation in the Madrid peace conference, on a majority verdict. The PLO and Israel met face to face, with the signing of the Declaration of Principles in Washington, on Sept. 13, 1993.

Organization and structure of the PLO in 1990s

It is hard to define where the PLO begins or ends. The organization is not so much a single political party, as an umbrella covering a spectrum of Palestinian political opinion, from liberal capitalist to ultra-Marxist, and locally nationalist to pan-Arabist. It also includes many features of a state, with welfare, health and education ministries, and a defence department. At its centre is the Palestine National Council (PNC), in effect the self-styled Palestinian parliament in exile. The PNC has an assembly of between 350 and 650 or more members, drawn from all PLO factions as well as many independents, but this only meets every five years or so. In the interim, it delegates legislative authority to a 40-member Palestine Central Council (PCC), which deals with day-to-day affairs.

The PCC in turn elects the 15-member Executive Committee (Exco), under the chairmanship of Yasser Arafat, which wields the real power. As in a normal government, Exco oversees a number of departments: Health, Information and National Guidance (including PLO news agencies), National Relations, Education, Popular Organizations. But perhaps the most powerful are the Political Department, which controls PLO representatives throughout the world; the Palestine National Fund (PNF), which acts both as the PLO's finance ministry, and its social welfare department; and the Department of Affairs of the Occupied Homeland.

Arafat has direct control over a separate military department, which includes the Palestine Liberation Army and militias of the various factions. The final four 'branches' of the PNC consist of: Palestinian mass unions (including guilds for writers, labourers, women, students, teachers, engineers, lawyers, doctors, artists and peasants); Palestinian diaspora communities and their representatives; independent organizations; and resistance organizations (including *Fatah, Saiqa,* PFLP, DFLP, Arab Liberation Front, Palestine Liberation Front, and the Communists).

Faced with the persistance of the *intifada,* the PNC strove to improve on its earlier 'steadfastness' committees, and build better institutions to represent the 'internal Palestinians'. In 1988, however, Abu Jihad, the chief architect of renewed PLO activities in the territories, and number two to Yasser Arafat, was assassinated.

The decision to sign the Oslo accords almost split the PLO, and prominent figures, such as 'foreign minister' Farouk Qaddumi, technically number two to Yasser Arafat himself, objected to it. Although many Tunis officials and Iraqi-trained PLO troops have returned to the

West Bank and Gaza, thousands of others have not. Amongst these are the National Alliance (a Damascus-based grouping of eight 'rejectionist' PLO groups and two Islamist groups). Even apart from them, there now appears to be a serious split between the internal and external wings of *Fatah* itself. Qaddumi and the al-Hassan brothers remain in PLO, but is the Tunis-based organization being irretrievably sidelined?

To a considerable extent the PNA, and especially since Jan. 20, 1996, the Palestine Council, have superceded the external PLO. PLO institutions still remain intact, however, and so if the peace deal fails, the PLO may be ready to resume its previous leadership role. The current challenge for Arafat is to ensure that the new Council defines its role vis a vis the existing PNC. Below are the main groups which together have constitued the PLO, listed alphabetically.

CONSTITUENT GROUPS OF THE PLO

Democratic Front for the Liberation of Palestine (DFLP)

Leader: Naif Hawatmeh

The DFLP (initially known as the PDFLP) began as a breakaway from the PFLP in 1969, after its members accused the parent organization of not being sufficiently rigorous in its Marxism. It sees the struggle against Zionism as part of a battle against Arab reactionary regimes. The DFLP supports a secular binational Palestine, with Jews as a tolerated minority. Unlike more romantic elements within the PLO, the DFLP proclaimed as early as 1948 that 'liberation of all of pre-1948 Palestine' was impossible, and thereby tacitly accepted the need for negotiations. In fact, the DFLP's lifelong leader, Naif Hawatmeh, has maintained contacts with left-wing Israelis for decades, and believes in solidarity of the working class.

At the same time, the DFLP is responsible for some of the most vicious terrorist attacks, including, in 1974, the Ma'alot school attack, which killed 27 Israelis, mainly schoolchildren. In late 1982 the group joined its erstwhile enemies, the PFLP, in a front which rejected the Reagan peace plan. Two years later, the DFLP escalated attacks on *Fatah* in Lebanon, and on Israelis in Jerusalem. However, by the 18th PNC session in 1987, the DFLP and *Fatah* had mended fences. Alongside the PFLP, *Fatah* and the Palestine Communist Party, the DFLP constituted one of the four wings of the United National Command (UNC) of the *intifada*. Indeed, the Labadi brothers, Mohammed and Majid, both DFLP supporters, are credited with founding the UNC in 1988. DFLP members set up the UNC in Gaza, countering the Islamist opposition with their calls for an 'open strike' against the occupation.

By the late 1980s, Israeli authorities managed to suppress the 'internal' DFLP and its myriad support groups (labour unions and women's organizations). Yasser Abed Rabbo had meanwhile emerged as the DFLP's rising star. He gained a key seat on the PLO Executive Committee, opened the first ever official PLO talks with the USA, and seemed to threaten Hawatmeh's leadership. The DFLP itself split in 1991 when Rabbo led a breakaway and more dovish faction, *Fida*. This group gained support in the West Bank, at the expense of the mainstream DFLP. Hawatmeh's own faction nominally supports the peace process; although a more hardline group opposes it. The DFLP was badly affected by the collapse of the Soviet Union, in terms of lost funding and training (given its Marxist stance, it could not turn to the conservative Gulf states for backing, as *Fatah* could).

Democratic Party of Palestine

(See *Fida*)

Fatah

Chairman: Yasser Arafat

Ever since Yasser Arafat assumed the chairmanship of the PLO, *Fatah* (or *Al-Fatah*) has enjoyed a pre-eminent role within the organization. Despite its militant and often terrorist past, *Fatah* is seen as a moderating influence on the PLO. The group lacks the ideological clarity of Marxist rivals (like the DFLP or PFLP), but offers a platform for mainstream Palestinian nationalism. In 1991 there were only 38 *Fatah* delegates on the Palestine National Council (PNC), which then had 456 seats. Yet most members of the PLO

Executive Committee come from *Fatah*. However, with the Oslo accords and the implementation of the Palestine National Authority, a profound process of realignment has begun within both the PLO and *Fatah*. As a result the old hegemony of the organization cannot be assumed to be intact. Furthermore, open rifts within *Fatah* (especially in southern Lebanon, starting in the late 1980s), have led Arafat to turn to leaders of other factions for support, thus further debilitating *Fatah's* coherence.

Fatah is the reverse acronym of *Tahir al-Hatani al-Falastani* (Movement for the National Liberation of Palestine). The word means 'breach', or, in the political sense, 'conquest'. It was first set up in 1958 by a group of expatriate Palestinian students in Kuwaiti and Egyptian universities. Prominent amongst these were: Yasser Arafat, Abu Jihad (Khalil al-Wazir), Abu Mazen and the al-Hassan brothers, Hani and Khaled. Although *Fatah* members enjoyed ties with the Muslim Brotherhood, it was always an essentially secular nationalist movement, committed to the 'liberation of Palestine', but also independence from Arab governments.

Its first base was in the Gaza Strip (then under Egyptian administration). *Fatah* set up training camps in Algeria in 1962 and Syria in 1964. In 1965 its *fedayeen* (soldiers) began raids on Israel – 31 in all, mostly directed from Jordan). After a left-wing coup in Syria, *Fatah* came increasingly under Syrian control. Analysts point out that with the mainstream PLO (founded in 1964) under strong Egyptian influence, it was natural for Arafat to turn to Syria, Nasser's great rival for leadership of the 'progressive Arab masses'. At the same time the al-Hassan brothers quietly established financial ties with wealthy Saudi Arabia and the Gulf states.

Fatah assumed control of the PLO in 1969, and its head, Yasser Arafat, became PLO Chairman. Throughout the 1970s, *Fatah* wrested control of schools and clinics in refugee camps from the UNRWA. Its armed presence in south Lebanon was such that the area was nicknamed 'Fatahland'. Meanwhile, Arafat allowed certain *Fatah* moderates (like Issam Sartawi and Abu Mazen) to be kite-flyers for the previously blasphemous idea of peace talks with Israel.

In 1983, following the devastation of the Israeli invasion, *Fatah* had to fight for its life against the *Amal* militia and Syrian-backed Palestinian groups in Lebanon. Abu Musa led a group dubbed the *Fatah* Rebels (backed by Syria); while Jordan backed another anti-Arafat *Fatah* faction, led by Abu Attalah. The 'war of the camps' is still simmering today, with a new *Fatah* militia, led by Mounir Makdah, attacking beleagured *Fatah* mainstreamers in Sidon and nearby refugee camps (the latter support the Declaration of Principles with Israel). *Fatah* was depleted by the killings of two founding leaders, Abu Jihad in 1988 and Abu Iyad in 1991. This has left Arafat in prominent control, although after his flirtation with Saddam Hussein, and increased reports of authoritarianism, he faced opposition from *Fatah* leaders like Khalid al-Hassan, Abu Ali Shaheen, and at times his nominal second-in-command, Farouk Qaddumi.

Increasingly, Arafat has bypassed traditional *Fatah* institutions in favour of dealing with forward-thinking leaders in other factions (notably Yasser Abed Rabbo from the DFLP, and Bassam Abu Sharif, formerly from the PFLP). Within the territories, Arafat has tolerated the growing authority of Faisal al-Husseini. But through groups like the *Fatah* Hawks and Force 17, sometimes called his praetorian guard, led by Abu Tayeb (Col Muhammed Natur), Arafat reserves a military option.

Fida

Leaders: Yasser Abed Rabbo (external); Jamal Zakut (internal)

Fida, an acronym for the Democratic Party of Palestine, was launched as a breakaway from Naif Hawatmeh's DFLP (q.v.) in 1991, after the former deputy leader of the DFLP, Yasser Abed Rabbo, was expelled by the mainstream party. It tends to be more willing to back the peace process than the DFLP, although the final split between the two came after Hawatmeh had backed Saddam Hussein. Under Saleh al-Khalili, *Fida* seemed to usurp the DFLP's well developed infrastructure in the territories. Its current 'internal' leader, Jamal Zakut, used to represent the DFLP on the now-defunct Unified National Command of the *intifada*. However, by the mid-1990s, *Fida's* support was somewhat squeezed by competition from a renascent *Fatah* (in the shape of the newly established PNA), and the lure of *Hamas*. It stood in the Palestinian Council elections of 1996, but won few seats.

Palestine Liberation Front (PLF)

Leader: **Muhammed Abul Abbas**

Formed by Talat Yaqub in 1977, in 1984 the PLF split into three factions. Currently, the Yaqub faction supports the National Alliance (anti-Arafat forces), while the larger Abul Abbas faction nominally backs the peace deal (although probably seeks to fight it 'from the inside'). A third splinter operates from Libya. In 1985 the PLF hijacked the *Achille Lauro* cruise ship, winning it international notoriety. Abul Abbas was on the PLO executive committee when PLF forces attacked Tel Aviv in 1990. After Arafat refused to condemn this action, the US suspended its talks with the PLO. Abbas subsequently resigned from the committee to spare Arafat further embarassment. According to some accounts, the Abul Abbas faction is closely affiliated with *Fatah*.

Popular Front for the Liberation of Palestine (PFLP)

Leader: **Dr George Habash**

Once the pre-eminent anti-*Fatah* grouping within the PLO, the PFLP has for a long time led the rejectionist wing in the Palestine National Council. Habash, its leader since the outset, founded the PFLP in 1967 out of his earlier Arab Nationalist Movement (founded in 1951), and other factions. Within two years, the group suffered two major breakaway splits – Ahmed Jibril's PFLP-GC in 1968 and Naif Hawatmeh's DFLP in 1969. Nonetheless, it still enjoys support in the territories, largely through the figure of the young and dynamic Riad al-Malki. But these days *Hamas* tends to eclipse the Popular Front as a repository for militancy. The PFLP follows a vaguely Marxist and partly Nasserist line. During the 1970s, its tactical chief, Wadia Haddad, organized many terrorist acts and hijackings. A PFLP splinter group masterminded the Entebbe hijacking of 1976. The Front also joined forces with foreign terror groups, such as the Japanese Red Army and the German Baader Meinhoff Gang.

The PFLP is renowned for its organization and spread of leadership – Habash in Damascus, Malki in the West Bank, Mustafa Abu Ali in Tunis, and in Jordan, Taysir al-Zibri (head of the *Hashd*, or Jordanian Popular Democratic Unity Party, a PFLP affiliate which was eventually legalized in 1990). The group is traditionally close to Syria, and must take most of the blame for prompting the Jordanian putsch against Palestinians in 1970. The PFLP left the PLO in 1974 to lead a 'rejectionist front'. It spearheaded the Palestinian National Salvation Front in the mid-1980s, leading opposition to the PLO's rapprochement with Jordan's King Hussein, but when that arrangement fell through, it rejoined the PLO in 1987. Its fortunes revived somewhat with the *intifada,* when it played a key role in the United National Command; and its Damascus-based radio station issued orders to activists. The PFLP sought to use Israeli Arabs as 'the lungs of the *intifada*', keeping it 'breathing' when their cousins in the territories were hemmed in. In 1987, the PFLP expelled Bassam Abu Sharif, a former terrorist turned peace campaigner, who had been tipped as a possible successor to Habash. (Later, Abu Sharif became the architect of the PLO's reforming Algiers Declaration of November 1988.)

Habash's acquiescence was an important factor in seeing that the PNC passed the Declaration, which endorsed a 'two-state solution'. In 1991 Habash led 120 other 'anti-imperialist' Arab parties in a Jordanian meeting to support Saddam Hussein. That same year, the PFLP and Israel exchanged fire in southern Lebanon. The PFLP was said to have left the PLO in 1993, in protest at the peace accords with Israel; although recently it has spoken from within the organization. West Bank affiliates spoke of the PFLP 'testing its support' by standing in the 1996 Palestinian Council elections. As it happened, they were forbidden from doing so by the external leadership in Damascus and Amman. At present, the PFLP is probably the strongest non-Islamist party within the Damascus-based National Alliance. But some former supporters interpret its unwillingness to stand for election as a sign that, with the demise of its Soviet sponsors, the PFLP lacks its once legendary grip on the Palestinian left.

Popular Front for the Liberation of Palestine – General Command (PFLP-GC)

Leader: Ahmed Jibril

This group, which split from the PFLP in 1968, has been behind numerous terrorist incidents (including allegedly the Lockerbie bombing in 1988). It virulently opposes the peace deal with Israel, and regards the PFLP as too bourgeois and not sufficiently revolutionary in orientation. Its leader, Ahmed Jibril, has been associated with several terrorist incidents, including blowing up a Swiss airliner in 1970 (47 dead), attacking a settlement in northern Israel in 1974 (18 dead), and killing a former prime minister of Iraq in London, in 1979. In May 1985, the PFLP-GC exchanged three captured Israeli soldiers for 1,155 Palestinian fighters in Israeli jails.

In the week before the *intifada* broke out, a PFLP-GC hang-glider attacker from Lebanon killed six Israeli soldiers, and became a folk hero amongst some youths in the territories. Since the outbreak of the *intifada*, the PFLP-GC co-operated with Islamic *Jihad* in a spate of attacks on Israeli military forces, including some in Egypt. Nonetheless, the organization holds to its original Marxist and secular vision of a revolutionary greater Arab nation. The PFLP-GC is strongly represented in southern Lebanon, but less so in the territories themselves. In August 1995 the Israeli Air Force bombed the PFLP-GC headquarters south of Beirut. Ahmed Jibril remains the group's leader, and through his radio station, *Al-Quds*, denounces the peace process. He was the favourite of Libya's Muammar Ghaddafi, until their major breach in 1988. Since then, Jibril has relied more on Syria and Iran for funding, and is based mainly in Damascus.

Palestine Communist Party (PCP)

[see Palestine People's Front]

Palestine Liberation Army

Officially set up as the armed wing of the PLO in 1964, the PLA was soon eclipsed by *Fatah* and other armed groups. Its fortunes revived somewhat in succeeding decades, when it won Iraqi patronage. Currently, many PLA-trained soldiers form the bedrock for the new police and security forces in the Palestine National Authority-run areas.

Palestine People's Front

Secretary General: Bashir al-Barghouti

Formerly the Palestine Communist Party, now known as the Palestine People's Front. It is renowned for its excellent organization in the territories, which belies its somewhat limited popular support. The Communists' relationship with the mainstream PLO has always been somewhat ambiguous. In the early 1970s Communists dominated the Palestine National Front [see below], a group sponsored by the PNC to operate in the occupied territories. Its popularity grew, especially in the West Bank Communist heartland of al-Birah and Salfit (nicknamed 'Moscow on the West Bank'). But by 1977 it faced crippling Israeli restrictions, and attacks from the mainstream (albeit banned) PLO.

The Palestinian Communists traditionally enjoy links with the sister organization in Israel (both Jews and Arabs, currently organized in *Hadash*). These ties date back to the 1935 Arab Revolt, and the late 1940s, when Palestinian Communists had cautiously endorsed the idea of a partitioned state (unlike the larger groups represented on the Higher Muslim Council). The PCP reconstituted itself in February 1982, in Beirut, but within months suffered the fate of other Palestinian groups in the wake of the Israeli invasion. Communists from the territories only gained a seat on the PNC in 1987. However, in that year the PCP was the main force in unifying the badly split PLO. The following year, Barghouti revived the party's fortunes in the territories, ensuring that Communists participated (and at times dominated) the Unified National Command of the *intifada*. Communist sympathizers usually held positions on the PLO Executive Committee, and in the days of Soviet funding proved a useful bridge between the Eastern Bloc and the PLO. From time to time, Communists have been amongst the most pragmatic forces in the PLO, and even in the 1970s some members were arguing for talks with

Israel. Despite the party's loss of Soviet funding, it enjoys a unique mediatory role within the PLO, as seen in July 1991, when Communist PLO Executive Committee member, Suleiman an-Najjab, led reconciliation talks with Syria (a crucial rapprochement which paved the way for the October Madrid conference).

EXTREMIST PALESTINIAN GROUPS
(Mostly non-Islamist groups within the Alliance of National Forces)

The **Abu Nidal Group** (or Revolutionary Council of *Fatah*, RCF) is named after the *nomme du guerre* of its leader, Sabri Khalil al-Banna. It is perhaps the most notorious Palestinian terrorist group, having carried out more than 250 acts of terror, and killing over a thousand people, in two decades of its existence. Many of its murders, if not most, are directed against fellow Palestinians. The group shifted its allegiance from Iraq to Syria in 1983, but is Damascus offices were shut down in 1987. It currently enjoys support from Libya (after a rift in 1989), Iran and Sudan. In 1985 the group attacked El Al counters at Rome and Vienna Airports, killing 14. In 1991 the RCF assassinated Arafat's deputy, Abu Iyad, presumably because Abu Iyad had criticized Saddam Hussein, the RCF's paymaster at the time. By 1993 a new simmering war of attrition began between the RCF's 1,000 fighters in Lebanon, and *Fatah's* 3,000 fighters, capitalizing on disquiet over the peace process. Once again, the hallmark was political assassination. The Abu Nidal Group lacks a wide support base in the territories, and is clearly in the 'rejectionist' camp. It often acts as a 'hired gun' for various Arab regimes. In a distinctly minority opinion, British author Patrick Seale has suggested that Abu Nidal is an undercover agent for Israeli secret services; but considering how many Israelis have been killed, this appears unlikely.

The **Arab Liberation Front (ALF)** and **Palestine Popular Struggle Front (PPSF)** are both pro-Iraqi groups in the anti-Arafat National Alliance. However, former PPSF leader, Samir Ghosheh, now holds the post of Labour and Social Affairs Minister in the PNA cabinet. **Force 17** began as a breakaway from the Palestine Liberation Front, and acted as a terror group, but usually as Arafat's personal Praetorian Guard. In the 1990s, the group appears less active; former members have returned to the newly autonomous Palestinian areas, and some (notably Col. Jibril Rajoub) hold high office in the new security services). Since 1968, Syria has backed **Al-Saiqa** (The Storm) as a military wing to counteract *Fatah*. In 1978 *Saiqa* set up cells in the West Bank, although today its support there is negligible. *Saiqa* was temporarily allied with *Fatah* in the mid-1970s, but by 1984 it had begun attacking *Fatah* supporters in Lebanon, in what became known as the War of the Camps. *Saiqa* also received assistance from the Lebanese Shi'ite militia, *Amal*; and a group called the **Abu Musa Group,** or the *Fatah* Revolutionary Council, led by Col Said Musa Muragha (Abu Musa). These groups have links with the PFLP-GC (q.v.). Since the Israeli-PLO Declaration of Principles, other *Fatah* rebels dissidents have rebelled against pro-Arafat leaders, like *Fatah* military commander, Mounir Maqdah, in PLO refugee camps near Sidon and elsewhere in Lebanon.

GROUPS IN THE TERRITORIES

The **Palestine National Front** arose in the West Bank in 1972 and soon filled the void left by the banned PLO. The Front backed the nationalist mayors who were elected in the territories in 1976. After that, municipal elections were disallowed. The mayors formed a National Guidance Committee in 1978, to co-ordinate nationalist activity. The committee was itself banned in 1982. When the Front began acquiring its own support base, *Fatah* managed to erode its support (largely through the work of Abu Jihad). Other groups operating in the territories include the **Village League,** a moderate grouping largely discredited when it appeared to be a front for Israeli peace initiatives in the 1970s; and the more radical **Sons of the Village.**

In addition, **Fatah's Shabiba** (Youth Movement) seemed to acquire a life of its own during the *intifada*. They were eventually condemned for corrupting the spirit of the *intifada* by indulging in revenge killings, disguised as 'punishment of collaborators'. **The Unified National Command** was the secret cross-party steering committee of the *intifada*, but repeated Israeli raids and the revival of the PLO seemed to spell its deathknell. Many UNC figures have re-appeared in *Fatah* and other PLO parties. Many of the Madrid conference Palestinian delegates were drawn from a loose group of nominally independent professionals and academics known as the **Shakhsiyat** (General Personalities). In 1991 two new parties, **Palestine National Unity Party** and **Fida** (see above), arose in the territories as moderate opponents of the armed struggle. However, they seem to have been overtaken by events, especially after the PLO signed its historic deal with Israel in 1993.

ISLAMIC MOVEMENTS

Hamas

Spiritual leader: Sheikh Ahmed Yassin

Hamas was founded in February 1988 at the instigation of followers of Sheikh Ahmed Ismail Yassin of Gaza. The word is an acronym for 'Islamic Resistance Movement', but it also means 'zeal' in Arabic. The organization grew out of Yassin's Islamic Congress, itself an offshoot of the Egyptian-based Muslim Brotherhood (*Ikhwan al-Muslimun* – for more on this group, see Chapter 16). Many of its members had belonged to the conservative *Al-Majama* association. According to Israeli security analysts and authors, Ya'ari and Schiff, throughout the 1980s Israel had encouraged the growth of fundamentalists as a counterweight to the secular nationalist PLO. With the *intifada*, however, *Hamas* and its allies joined, and even threatened to hijack, the anti-Israeli struggle. Israel outlawed *Hamas* in September 1989, and imprisoned Yassin himself in 1990. Many other *Hamas* activists were detained; a few were deported (see 1992 incident below).

Today *Hamas* is the pre-eminent Islamic fundamentalist movement in the occupied territories, and is the biggest single rival to the PLO for support amongst Palestinians. Indeed, some analysts foresee that *Hamas* will one day form the official opposition to the PLO in forthcoming elections – if it agrees to participate. *Hamas* stands for *Jihad* for the 'total liberation of Palestine'. It employs its own shock troops (*Al-Suad al-Ramaya*, the Throwing Arm) as well as the Izz al-Din al-Qassem Brigades. These forces (and a morality patrol called *Majd*) have attacked 'erring' Muslims and Christian Palestinians, as well as Israelis. Much of its impetus derives from *dawa* (sermonizing) in sympathetic mosques; and a widespread social welfare network, which filled a void in the occupied territories.

During the *intifada Hamas* rivalled the PLO-dominated United National Command (ad hoc leadership committee, also known as UNLU) in garnering support amongst Palestinian youths. Its influence spread beyond its natural base in Gaza to areas in the West Bank, notably in Hebron (where in 1995 the PLO and *Hamas* formed an electoral non-aggression pact, possibly a harbinger for the future). Opinion polls vary, with some talking of 30–40% support for *Hamas*, and others suggesting it stands at no more than 15%. *Hamas* operates under several other names – the Islamic Stream, or the Islamic Trend (led by Subhi Anabtawi).

During the Gulf War, *Hamas* did not support Saddam Hussein, and thus, ironically, was better thought of by the 'moderate' and conservative Gulf states and Saudi Arabia who until then had largely backed the PLO. In 1991 *Hamas* external leader Musa Abu Marzouk demanded 40% of the seats in the PNC. Arafat refused, and offered them a far smaller percentage, which *Hamas* rejected. A few months after Labour took office in 1992, Shmuel Toledano, an Israeli conscript, was abducted and murdered by fundamentalists. Rabin decided to deport some 415 *Hamas* and affiliated activists to south Lebanon, the biggest such exercise in Israel's history. After a year he had to relent, and gradually repatriated most of the deportees. However, it did signal that Rabin earmarked *Hamas*, and not the PLO, as enemy number one, and was prepared to risk a cabinet split to make this point clear.

Hamas rejected the Israeli–PLO joint accords, which were signed in September 1993. After the Cairo Agreement of March 1994, under which a Palestinian National Authority (PNA) under PLO leadership took over from the Israeli civil administration in Gaza and Jericho, the PNA's newly installed security forces clamped down on *Hamas*. There was a shootout between PNA forces and *Hamas* outside the Gaza Mosque, in which 17 died; although tempers were later calmed, thus averting a potential civil war. Nonetheless, Israelis have chided Arafat for not doing more, especially after a string of *Hamas*-inspired terrorist incidents within the Green Line (Afula, Beit Lid, Tel Aviv and Jerusalem).

Hamas activists gain support through *shahada* (martyrdom, or witness to God). This can take the form of suicide bombings (unusual in Sunni tradition, but presumably copied from *Hamas's* Lebanese Shi'ite allies, the *Hezbollah*); or imprisonment. Various states have incarcerated *Hamas* notables: Sheikh Yassin and the Lebanese deportees leader, Dr Abd al-Aziz al-Rantisi in Israel; Musa Abu Marzuk, head of the political bureau, in the USA; and Sheikh Sayid Abu Masamakh, formerly head of a *Hamas* group which held 'reconciliation' talks with the PNA, is held in Gaza.

Today there is believed to be a division, even a potential rift, between the mainstream political movement and its armed wings, the Izz al-Din al-Qassam and the smaller Abdallah Azzam Brigades. In addition there seems to be a division between the *Hamas* leadership in exile, and young local leaders in Gaza (like Imad Falluji and Khaled al-Hindi), who want to form a political party to participate in elections. Some query whether this stance is merely one of pragmatism regarding the means to achieve 'total victory'. After all, *Hamas* is still committed to Islamic rule over all of Palestine (defined as including present-day Israel).

Not surprisingly, *Hamas* denies all talk of a rift. Nonetheless, by mid-1995 the group appeared to be distancing itself from terror attacks by the Izz al-Din al-Qassam Brigades. Despite the PNA's roundup of 40 *Hamas* activists in Gaza in late 1995, *Hamas* had not shut the door on talks with the PLO. In August 1995 Sheikh Yassin announced from prison that Islamists should participate in the PNA, even if they rejected the concessions made by the PLO. According to the Israeli newspaper, *Ha'Aretz*, some former members of *Hamas* in Gaza had formed a new movement in August. Called *El-Ma'asar*, it 'recognized of the reality created by the Oslo Agreements and opposed using violence to change this reality'.

Hamas and the PLO had formed a joint electoral ticket in Hebron in mid-1995. Meanwhile, the Islamic Movement in Israel, who sympathize with *Hamas*, hinted at new ties with Yasser Arafat's chief Israeli Arab ally, Dr Ahmed Tibi. Later that year, the PNA released from prison the vocal *Hamas* leader, Mahmoud Zahhar, who announced that the group (or at least part of it) would become a 'political party', but later he seemed to retract his statement. In November, Ghazi Hamad, editor of the wide circulation *Hamas* newspaper, *Al-Watan*, admitted that the 'military programme had been a mistake'. The PLO and *Hamas* held 'reconciliation talks', and there were rumours that a *Hamas*-sponsored 'National Salvation Party' would participate in the forthcoming Palestinian Council elections. In the event, this did not happen (the assassination by *Mossad* of leading *Hamas* bomber, Yahiya Ayyash, in early January only inflamed *Hamas* opposition to any aspect of the peace process). Even so, certain *Hamas* supporters (like Falluji) did stand as independent candidates. In February and March 1996, *Hamas* bombings claimed 62 lives in Israel. Israeli and PNA police arrested hundreds of *Hamas* suspects.

Islamic Jihad

Islamic *Jihad* precedes *Hamas,* but is an altogether smaller group with less popular support and a different agenda. It was founded by Sheikh Abdel Aziz Odeh in 1981. Although its members are almost entirely Sunni Muslim Palestinians, it is believed to receive Iranian funds, and may have ties with the Lebanese Shi'ite group which shares its name. Islamic *Jihad* is subdivided into groups, or cells, usually based outside 'historic Palestine' (Damascus and Amman are both said to be home to the group's various leaders). Perhaps the largest cell is the *Beit al-Maqdes* (Temple Mount, or Jerusalem) cell, led by Sheikh Asa'ad al-Tamimi from Amman. Tamimi held talks with Yasser Arafat at the 19th meeting of the Palestine National Council.

The movement suffered a blow with the assassination of its leader, Dr Fathi Shiqaqi, in Malta in October 1995. Shiqaqi had once boasted that peace in the Middle East would only come with the 'disappearance' of Israel. It was assumed that the Israeli secret service, *Mossad*, was behind his death. Islamic *Jihad* seems certain to continue its activities regardless, through such leaders as Abdullah al-Shami in Gaza, and the 'folk hero' Imad Siftawi. On many occasions since the 1980s, it has co-operated in terrorist acts with the secular Marxist, but equally radical, PFLP-GC.

Islamic terror groups

The Izz al-Din al-Qassam Brigade is named after the short-lived 'hero' of the Arab Revolt in Palestine under the Mandate, 1935. This group is nominally under the control of *Hamas,* and is thought to be responsible for most of *Hamas* atrocities. In the late 1990s, the group followed a policy of individual stabbing incidents on Jews (although many such attacks were dismissed as unplanned actions by 'freelance' agents). By 1994, it had adopted the suicide bombing technique (especially directed against Israeli buses) The smaller Abdallah Azzam Brigade also operates under the *Hamas* aegis. For Islamic *Jihad*, the main group is the Fighting Islamic Resistance-Qasam movement.

PALESTINIAN NON-GOVERNMENT ORGANIZATIONS (NGOS)

Palestinian Trade Union Federation (PTUF)

The Palestinian Trade Union Federation began life as the General Union of Palestine Workers. Its first congress was held in Gaza in 1965. It has close affiliations with the PLO (formed in the previous year). However, its roots lie in two much earlier organizations: the Haifa Railway Workers' Union (founded in 1922, and one of the first unions in the Arab world); and the Palestine Arab Workers' Society (PAWS), founded in 1926. PAWS played a key role in the general strike of 1936 (part of the Arab Revolt). The organization largely disintegrated after the events of 1947–49 (including the assassination of its leader).

Since 1965 the PTUF has tried to represent Palestinian workers throughout the world. PTUF also has branches in the occupied territories. In the West Bank it is known as the General Federation of Trades Unions (GFTU) and has more than 100,000 members (belonging to separate unions). Israel restricted the GFTU's activities and tended to ignore its bargaining rights.

In the Gaza Strip the PTUF branch is called the Gaza Palestinian Trade Union. It was banned from 1967 until 1980 (when the International Labour Organization, ILO, forced Israel to allow it to operate). The constituent Gaza unions held elections in 1987. Many union activists were arrested during the *intifada*. In June 1992 the ILO's Geneva conference held a special session on labour in the occupied territories.

The PTUF has been caught up in the considerable changes currently taking place in Israel and the territories. Within Israel, the *Histadrut* labour federation has evidently opened its doors to Arab members, but still maintains its home base amongst 'Hebrew workers'. In the areas controlled by the PNA, it appears that rifts are developing between the 'workerist' viewpoint of the PTUF, and a more free enterprise approach favoured by leading PNA ministers (notably, former businessmen like Nabil Sha'ath and Abu 'Ala).

This trend manifests itself both as a clash of ideology, and in the two sides' differing attitude towards co-operation with Israel. Broadly, the PNA backs enterprise zones in Gaza and Jericho; while trade unionists are more sceptical, seeing this as a ploy for Israel to maintain its dominance over the Palestinian economy. They also suspect that Israel wants to continue sealing off the borders to Palestinian labour entering Israel; and at best is prepared only to use non-unionized and casual Palestinian workers. Finally, Palestinian autonomy is raising profound questions of identity for Israel's own Arab citizens; depending on how matters develop, Israeli Arabs may find themselves allying with fellow Palestinian unionized labour 'across the green line'.

Other PLO affiliates

The Palestine National Council oversees a number of bodies, all to greater or lesser extent affiliated to the PLO. These include: the General Union of Palestinian Students (GUPS); the General Union of Palestinian Women (GUPW); and the Palestinian Red Crescent Society (PRCS). The PRCS is led by Yasser Arafat's brother, Dr Fathi Arafat, and has close ties with the Red Cross and International Red Crescent Society (Muslim sister organization to the Red Cross). The Society is responsible for running many hospitals and clinics for Palestinians in the occupied territories, as well as for refugee camps in the Palestinian 'Diaspora'. In Gaza the society is run by Haidar Abd al-Shafi, a founder member of the Palestine National Council, who became head of the Palestinian delegation to the Madrid peace conference in October, 1991.

Independent NGOs

Two bodies deserve special mention for work done for human rights – *Al-Haq* (Bassam Eid, Raji Sourani and others) and the Palestinian Independent Council for Citizens' Rights (Hanan Ashrawi's group, set up on June 8, 1994). They operate outside the PLO power structure. While secular in orientation, they defend the human rights of *Hamas* members detained by the PNA. This matter became especially sensitive after the Amnesty Reports criticizing the PNA for its record, in 1995. In addition, another group, the Mandela Institute, has also made its voice heard on human rights recently. The Palestine Press Council is an influential force for defending free speech and press, and actually caused the PNA to reconsider some of its draconian press laws. Similarly, Radwan Abu Ayyash, head of the Palestine Broadcasting Corporation, and the lawyer, Jonathan Kuttab, have both criticized PNA shortcomings as they once castigated the Israeli occupation.

Gaza and the West Bank

GAZA STRIP

Total area	360 sq km
Land boundaries	Total 62 km
	Egypt 11 km, Israel 51 km
	Israel 51 km
	Coast 40 km
Population	813,322 (July 1995 est.)
	4,800 Jewish settlers (1994 est.)
Population growth rate	4.55%
Ethnic divisions	99.8% Palestinian Arab
Religions	Muslim, 99%; Christian, 0.7%; Jewish, 0.3%
Trade	Exports $83 million
	Imports $365 million (90% of external trade with Israel)
GDP	$1.7 billion (1993 est.)
National product per capita	$2,400 (1993 est.)

[Figures from *CIA World Factbook*, 1995; *MEED* June 1995]

HISTORICAL PROFILE OF GAZA

The area known as the Gaza Strip is an artificial creation of the 1947–48 war, yet the history of Gaza City itself (the main urban conurbation in a traditionally rural area) goes back several millenia. Gaza become famous as the launchpad of the *intifada* on Dec. 9, 1987. Generally, the PLO has held a more tenuous grip on Gaza than in the West Bank, for in Gaza there is more vocal public support for *Hamas* and other fundamentalist Islamic groupings.

From Israel's perspective, there were good reasons for 'releasing' Gaza as compared with the West Bank. Unlike the West Bank, Gaza is not really part of historical *Eretz Yisrael*. There were Jewish settlements, but these were generally small in size, and somewhat removed from the mainstream of life in the Jewish Commonwealth. The biblical phrase, 'eyeless in Gaza', refers to the plight of Samson, blinded and forced into exile in Gaza. But it also implies a region considered by Jews as unfriendly and hostile, populated as it was then by their Philistine enemies. With the notable exception of the medieval scholar, Nathan of Gaza, the region has produced little of lasting Jewish spiritual worth (in strong contrast with places on the West Bank like Hebron, Shiloh and Shechem near Nablus). With the signing of the peace treaty with Egypt in 1979, it was less easy to argue the case for retaining Gaza as a security buffer zone.

As a wellspring for the *intifada*, Gaza was difficult for the IDF to control. Popular unease grew over the hardship imposed on young Israeli conscripts who had to guard the area. Similarly, as the heartland for *Hamas*, some Israeli analysts felt that bequeathing Gaza to PLO jurisdiction was a clever way of handing them a poisoned chalice. If they could succeed in a challenging test-case like Gaza, they would establish their credentials to rule over more amenable areas where they had more proven support (e.g. Nablus, Jericho, Ramallah, etc.). With a large proportion of refugees amongst its Palestinian population, Israeli security analysts assumed there was less hope of finding stable structures whereby Palestinians could co-operate with Israeli authorities.

As a consequence of the above reasons, fewer than 5,000 Israelis settled in Gaza (as it lacked appeal in terms of economic utility, defensive importance and spiritual attractiveness). And logistically, if it came to the crunch it would be easier to uproot these settlers than their counterparts in the West Bank.

Ancient roots

Gaza is an ancient trading centrè, strategically sited as the last city which travellers and traders visited as they entered the vast Sinai desert en route to Egypt. It marks a nexus between the continents of Africa and Asia. In antiquity Gaza was one of the five 'great towns' of the Philistines (the others being Ashkelon, Ashdod, Ekron and Gath). It was also the centre of pagan worship, and for centuries it defied the monotheistic faith of the Jewish Common-wealth to its north. Gradually, Gaza came under the ambit of Israelite rule, but was never completely expropriated. After a long struggle Alexander the Great took over the city in 332 BC. Thereafter Gaza became a Hellenistic city, and enjoyed a new lease of life as a prosperous seaport by the 2nd century AD.

With the conversion to Christianity of Emperor Constantine (306–337 AD), Gaza, along with other centres in Roman Palestine, adopted the new faith. In the 6th century it came under the influence of the charismatic Bishop Porphyry. Historians describe its population as extremely mixed – descendants of the original Philistines, both pagan and Christianized, living alongside Arab *bedouin*, Romans, Greeks and a small Jewish population. Under Ottoman rule Gaza became something of a backwater, situated as it was so far away from the larger centres of the *vilayet* of Syria (which included Palestine).

Refugee centre after 1948

In a matter of a few months, from November 1948 to January 1949, the Gaza district's population mushroomed from 60,000 to as many as 230,000. This resulted from the so-called 'fourth wave' of Palestinian refugees – those Arabs who fled in the wake of Israel's successful military offensives in the adjoining northern Negev and coastal plain region. Unsurprisingly, the massive influx dramatically altered the character of the region. Eight large organized camps emerged in the Strip: Jabaliyah, Beach, Nuseirat, Bureij, Maghazi, Deir al Balah, Khan Yunis and Rafah. Shelter and food became overriding concerns simply in order to keep the newcomers alive. American Quaker volunteers, UN agencies, the Red Crescent and those Egyptian military authorities who had survived the recent war with Israel struggled and eventually succeeded in saving refugee lives. To this day, however, a disproportionate number of Gazans still live in refugee camps, although solid structures have generally replaced the temporary accommodation of 1948 and 1949.

At tentative peace talks in Lausanne Israel offered to take the Gaza Strip and its refugees under its hegemony, but Egypt rejected this. From 1948 till 1967, Gaza remained under Egyptian jurisdiction. However, unlike the Sinai peninsula, Egypt never formally annexed the Strip as it believed that one day Gaza would be re-absorbed into a renascent Arab Palestine on the ruins of the State of Israel. Nominally, Hajj Amin al-Husseini, the former Mufti of Jerusalem and head of the Supreme Muslim Council, now ruled an All Palestine Government from Gaza. But in reality Husseini was a spent force; many officials deserted to Jordan, and in 1952 the Arab League dissolved his 'government'. Egypt then set up an elected Council of Representatives, but this too was something of a sham, as only powerful Gazan families participated. Refugees were excluded from politics, and instead encouraged to join the Cairo-sponsored *fedayeen* (guerrillas) who periodically attacked Israel. In the course of the

Suez Canal War, Israel briefly occupied Gaza in late 1956, but within months the USA and UN forced it to return the Strip to Egypt. After 1962 Gaza came under military 'emergency law'. Egypt also restricted Palestinian migration from Gaza into Egypt proper. Crowded conditions and the collapse of the local citrus economy led to extreme poverty – one source put annual per capita income at just $80. Nonetheless, Egypt has left its legacy in the shape of two antagonistic political trends – Nasserite pan-Arabism, and Sunni Islamic fundamentalism of the Muslim Brotherhood variety.

Labour pool for Israel after 1967

PLO Leader Ahmed Shukeiri had deployed a few PLA units in Gaza after 1964, with Egyptian approval, but they proved useless against the Israeli forces which invaded in June 1967. Thereafter, *Fatah* tried to forment an armed uprising in the territories, and this was most successful in Gaza. By 1970, however, Israeli forces under Ariel Sharon had largely crushed all resistance. Gaza became an increasingly important source of cheap labour for the Israeli economy, particularly in the construction and manufacturing industries. In turn, many Israelis were attracted by the inexpensive prices of Gazan fruit and vegetables, and used to cross the border to bargain in Gazan markets.

Israeli occupation brought mixed blessings for Gazans. According to Israeli statistics released in July 1994, between 1970 and 1990, the Civil Administration increased the number of community clinics from three to 28; tetanus and polio were virtually eradicated; infant mortality had declined from 85 deaths per 1,000 live births to 26.1; most houses had running water; vegetable and citrus yields had each risen from 40 tons to about 200 tons; and Israel permitted the Al-Azhar University to be built in 1978. At the same time, however, the administration clearly favoured the 5,000 Jewish settlers of the Gush Katif and Netzarim, who had easy access to water and transport. While the 1967 war did 're-unite' Gazan with West Bank Palestinians, in practice they needed special permits to visit each other, so families remained divided. Membership of *Fatah* became a criminal offence; somewhat unwisely, Israeli officials encouraged Islamist movements as a counterweight to the nationalists, until the *intifada* resulted in a boom for *Hamas*, and attacks on Israel.

Intifada and autonomy

The *intifada* began with rioting in Jabaliyah camp in Gaza, and with the resultant increase in terror attacks and worker stay-aways, fewer Gazans travelled to Israel, and vice versa. By the early 1990s, Israel repeatedly 'sealed off' the Gaza Strip after terror incidents in mainland Israel. Recent plans to build a perimeter security fence reinforce the trend towards separation. Furthermore, thanks to increased Soviet Jewish immigration, and foreign imported non-Jewish labour (from Romania, Thailand, Philippines and other places), Israel has learnt to do without Palestinian labour from Gaza. Many economists, however, warn that such a situation cannot endure – foreign labourers lack the specific skills needed in agriculture and construction; new immigrants will soon tire of working in unfamiliar areas; and, both in terms of natural geography and man-made infrastructure, the Israeli and Gazan economies are naturally linked together.

Sheikh Ahmed Yassin and others who studied theology in Egypt (especially at the al-Azhar University), brought the ideas of the Muslim Brotherhood to Gaza. Initially, Israeli civil administration encouraged local fundamentalists as a convenient counterweight to the secular nationalists of the PLO. But by 1988 these groups had coalesced into *Hamas*, now the fiercest foe of peace with Israel. At present, the return of the PLO (especially after Arafat's arrival in July 1994) has begun to change the character of Gaza, away from the fundamentalist domination.

Significantly, it was a prominent Gazan, Haidar Abd al-Shafi, who was chosen to head the first Palestinian delegation to the peace talks in Madrid in 1991. Apart from being one of the founding members of the PLO, al-Shafi is well known as a physician and head of the Palestine Red Crescent Society (equivalent to the Red Cross). His victory in the January 1996 elections, at the head of an independent list, suggests that Gazans want their own interests to be protected.

Under the PNA, Gaza still has enormous problems. The World Bank ordered an Emergency Assistance Programme, with money to come from the Holst Fund. As mentioned above, Arafat was angry that funds arrived piecemeal and too slowly. Palestinians accused Arafat of crushing opposition in Gaza, with strong police forces imported from the Palestinian diaspora, and the use of barely legal 'night courts'. Even so, the peace process has at least ended the *intifada*, and, with it, the nightly curfews that ruined social life in the area. The new mayor of Gaza City, Aoun Shawwa, has enthusiastically set about cleaning up the city; and building ties with Israeli mayors to the north. A private enterprise boom has resulted in new restaurants by the long-neglected beach front, and investment (often from former Gulf Palestinians) in cement plants and other industries. A port and airport are under construction, as are other public works (electricity, sewerage and telephone lines). Still, conditions for Gazans are still several times worse than those of Israelis living across the border. Unemployment remains the chief concern. And above all, Gaza's ultimate future prosperity depends on a solution for the refugees who constitute the bulk of the Strip's population.

THE WEST BANK

Total area	5,860 sq km
Land boundaries	Total 404 km Jordan 97 km Israel 307 km
Population	1,319,991 (1995 est.) Some 122,000 Jewish settlers also live in the area [Another 149,000 live in East Jerusalem]
Population growth rate	3.5%
Ethnic divisions	Palestinian Arab and other, 83%; Jewish settlers, 17%
Religions	Muslim (mainly Sunni) 75%; Jewish 17%; Christian and other 8%
Labour force	Construction 28.2% Agriculture 21.8% Industry 14.5%
National product per capita	$2,175 (1991) $2,800 (1994 est.)
GDP	$1.668 billion (1991 est.) [$4 bn for National product, 1994 est.]

[Figures from *CIA World Factbook*, 1995; *MEED* June 1995]

The idea of 'the West Bank' as a single unit is comparatively recent. It really dates back to 1951, when the area was absorbed into the Kingdom of Jordan. Henceforth, what was previously known as Transjordan became the East Bank, while King Abdullah ensured that 'West Bank' was used as a term instead of 'Palestine'. According to UN 181 (the Partition Resolution) of November 1947, the West Bank was to have made up the bulk of 'Arab Palestine', but most Palestinians had rejected this 'division of the homeland'. Almost 50 years later, after the years of Jordanian annexation and then Israeli occupation, the West Bank is once again cited as the main area for a reborn Palestinian entity.

Before 1951, Palestinians living in the West Bank tended to refer to themselves as citizens of particular cities (like Jerusalem, Nablus or Qalqilyah), or as affiliates of one or other clans. The events of 1947–49 and later 1967, however, have profoundly altered both the demographic and psychological make-up of the area. Most significantly, the population has changed – some 400,000 Palestinians from what is now Israel poured into the West Bank during and immediately after the first war. Many of these people established refugee camps alongside existing cities, and saw themselves as waiting in transit for their imminent return to their original coastal or Galilee towns (for instance, Balata camp in Nablus consists of thousands of refugees from Jaffa). It can be argued that Balata's refugees felt as alien from established Nablus citizens, as Ein al-Hilweh's Palestinian camp-dwellers did from their Lebanese neighbours. On the other hand, the formation of the PLO in 1964, and the advent of Israeli rule in 1967, has fostered a stronger and more unified Palestinian identity.

Under Israeli rule

The Six-Day War of 1967 heralded new changes. After Israel took over control of the West Bank, upwards of 200,000 West Bank Palestinians fled to East Bank Jordan, joining fellow Palestinians who already formed a majority in the Kingdom. And from 1967 to the present, growing numbers of Jewish settlers moved into the West Bank, a land they know as *Eretz Yisrael*. By and large, Jews tended to settle away from large Palestinian conurbations (and the Oslo 2 accord has tried to exploit this fact, by incorporating Arab cities in Area A, Arab villages in Area B, and settlers and other state land in Area C). The more religious settlers moved to places of biblical significance. The more secular tended to settle in 'commuter belt' towns, nearer to the Green Line, which afforded them easy access to the Israeli towns where they worked. But inevitably there were clashes – over water rights, agricultural land, and access to religious sites (notably, the Tomb of the Patriarchs in Hebron and the Tomb of Rachel outside Bethlehem).

Also inevitably, there are two contradictory views of the Israeli occupation. The prevailing Israeli view (at least until the *intifada* broke out) was of benign rule bringing economic and social benefits to an underpriviledged Arab populus. The prevailing Palestinian view, however, painted a picture of an alien and oppressive regime which stifled political independence, and used the threat of armed force to ensure that settlers had access to water, land and security, at the locals' expense.

Major West Bank cities

Nablus

Nablus is the biggest city in the West Bank. For almost 2,000 years it was closely linked with Shechem, which started as a Canaanite town situated in the east-west pass between Mount Gerizim and Mount Ebal (in Arabic, Jabal at-Tur and Jabal 'Aybal). According to the Bible, Jacob bought land there. It later became a walled city, and the site of a revolt by the ten northern tribes of Israel. After the Assyrian conquest of 722BC, Samaritans resettled there, and a small community exists near Mount Gerizim to this day. (Samaritans were guaranteed one constituency in the 1996 Palestine Council elections.)

The Roman Emperor Vespasian built the new city, Neapolis (later rendered in Arabic as Nablus or Nabulus) to the west of Shechem, in AD72. Nablus was conquered by Arabs in 636. Thanks to its springs and strategic position, it soon thrived as a Muslim population centre, apart from an interregnum, from 1099 to 1187, when it was in Crusader hands. Under the Ottoman Empire, Nablus became the capital of a governorate, rivalling the somewhat sleepier Jerusalem as a regional centre. In modern times, Nablus was included in the Palestine Mandate (1923 to 1948), and it became the centre of Arab opposition to Zionists and the British mandate. During the period of Jordanian rule (1948 to 1967), Nablus was the southern anchor of a triangle of Arab guerrilla groups which launched raids and terrorist attacks on Israel (the other two anchors being Jenin and Tul Karm). A large refugee camp known as Balata arose alongside the established city of Nablus. 'Resistance' continued after Israeli occupation, but was quelled by the early 1970s, before re-erupting in the *intifada* of 1987.

The city's economy is based on agriculture, olive oil, soap manufacture and handicrafts. Nablus held the first all-West Bank agricultural fair in 1972. It now has a university, and a small middle class, such as the Abd al-Hadi clan, which has long roots in the city. Nablus traditionally vied with Jerusalem to be the paramount city in old Palestine; by the 20th century, young Nabulsis left what they saw as a 'staid and conservative city', to make their fortune in the booming coastal cities (like Haifa and Jaffa). Since 1948, refugees swelled the city's already considerable numbers, although most live in a separate camp, Balata, and tension between Balata and Nablus itself continues to simmer. In 1980 Jewish terrorists tried to assassinate Nablus' mayor, Bassam al-Shaqa. Nablus became a centre of resistance during the *intifada*. Following the Oslo 2 Accords, Israeli troops redeployed from Nablus and the city is now ruled by a Palestinian governor, Mahmoud al-Aloul.

Ramallah

Situated on the crest of the Judean Hills, Ramallah (or Height of God in Arabic) lies just north of Jerusalem, and is adjacent to the town of al-Birah to its east. The mound of Tel

Mizpe to the south of the modern city is said to be the site of the biblical city of Mispah, although there has been little Jewish habitation in the area for 2,400 years. Ramallah came under Jordanian rule in 1948. Refugees from former Palestine tended to migrate to a camp in nearby al-Birah. Blessed with mountain breezes, and good olive plantations and viticulture, Ramallah used to be a predominantly Christian town, and was once a popular resort. However, an Israeli census, conducted after the conquest of 1967, put the population at 12,314, equally divided between Muslims and Christians. Under Israeli occupation, the Bir Zeit University was built near the city, although for many years during the *intifada* it was closed by Israeli edict. As Jerusalem has expanded, Ramallah is sometimes regarded as part of the larger conurbation. For this reason, it was said, the PLO chose to set up offices in Ramallah during the first stage of the Oslo Accords, as a way of 'staking its claim' to Jerusalem itself. Ramallah won its autonomy in the second phase of the Accords (Oslo 2) following the Interim Agreement of September 1995.

Bethlehem

Best known as the city of Jesus Christ's birth, according to the New Testament, Bethlehem (or *Beit Lahm* in Arabic) means 'house of bread' (i.e. bakery) in Hebrew, and 'house of meat' (i.e. butchers) in Arabic. It lies 15 km south-east of Jerusalem, near the Judean hills, and houses the 4th century Church of the Nativity. The charismatic Christian Palestinian Mayor Elias Freij has ruled Bethlehem for most of Israeli rule (since 1972). Over that period, Christians started to emigrate, leading to a narrow majority of Muslims in the town. In 1987 Freij objected to Israeli plans to pump water from the Herodian reservoir, which he said would deprive his city of access to this resource. Bethlehem has in recent years clashed with the neighbouring Jewish settlement of Efrat. The city still suffers from 40% unemployment, partially a consequence of closures during the *intifada*. Yet Freij and others predict a Christian tourism boom, especially after Bethlehem achieved its autonomy in December 1995 (in time for Christmas). In many ways, Freij has deliberately imitated his rival and friend, the former Israeli Mayor of Jerusalem, Teddy Kollek, setting up a Bethlehem Foundation to encourage economic development; and talking of a Bethlehem 2000 (marking Christ's birth) to rival the controversial Jerusalem 3000 celebrations. Freij's imminent departure leaves the city's future uncertain; but the PLO is sure to exploit to the full Bethlehem's useful symbolic image as a bridge between Palestine and the Christian world.

Jericho

Jericho (*Ariha* in Arabic) is the oldest walled city in the world, and played a pivotal role in the development of culture in the region of historical Palestine. Readers of the Bible know of Jericho as the city whose walls tumbled when the Israelite soldiers of Joshua blew their trumpets. Jericho has never had a strong Jewish presence, and after the Arab conquest of Palestine its population generally adopted the Islamic faith. With its naturally warm climate and plentiful waters, the area (north-west of the Dead Sea) attracted settlers in the 8th millenium BC, who built the first houses and walls in the region. Jericho was conquered in succession by the Hyksos people, Egyptians and Canaanites; and, in about the 12th century BC, by the Israelites. The town was absorbed into the territory of Benjamin, and housed one of King David's storehouses. In 587 BC, Babylonian invaders demolished Jericho, after which few Jews returning from exile in Babylon chose to settle there. A new Hellenistic city was established a mile to the west, but was destroyed during the Jewish War (AD 66–70) against the Romans. Jericho moved to its present location under Byzantine rule, where local Jews built a synagogue in the 7th century.

With the Arab conquest of Palestine, the Ummayad Chaliph, Hisham, built a winter palace near Jericho in 724. By 891 Jericho was the district capital of the Ghauer region (cleft of the lower Jordan). It was captured by European Crusaders in 1099, and was recaptured by Saladin in 1187. Present-day Jericho carries evidence of its Crusader heritage – a monastery on the site where Jesus is said to have fasted for fourty days, three sugar mills, and a Knights Templar fortress. Jericho came under Ottoman rule in 1516, but was allowed to subside into quiet decay. The town was destroyed and rebuilt in 1840, and again in 1871, caught as it was in the crossfire between Egyptians, Ottomans and local Palestinian Arab dissent. In 1918 the British General Allenby captured Jericho from the Turks, thereby securing the eastern front and facilitating the final defeat of the Ottoman Empire. Jericho was now part of British Mandatory Palestine. By the 1940s its population had revived to 3,000.

After the 1947–48 war, Jericho became part of Transjordan (later, the Hashemite Kingdom of Jordan). Arab refugees from Israel fled there, thus boosting its population. In 1949 an apparently stage-managed Palestine 'national congress' in Jericho called on King Abdullah of Jordan to unify the West Bank with Jordan. Jericho began to prosper by cultivating oasis-type farming, including tropical fruits, and exploiting its year-round heat it became a haven for winter tourism. In 1967 Israel won control of the entire West Bank region, including Jericho. Just before the war, Jordan estimated the population of Jericho and its environs at 80,000 (a post-war Israeli census, however, recorded just 6,837 folk in the town proper, 90% Muslim and the remainder Christian; recent figures suggest 7,500).

Unlike Nablus, Ramallah and Tul Karm, Jericho was not renowned as a seedbed of Palestinian dissent. It has a reputation for accommodating bigger powers, whether Israeli or Jordanian; and a tradition of political scepticism vis-à-vis the PLO. Nonetheless, as with all cities in the territories, it became caught up in the Palestinian *intifada* after 1987; though its mayor, Jamil Sabri Khalaf, was one of only two Israeli appointees who refused to resign. Jericho sprang back into the headlines in September, 1993, with the signing of the Declaration of Principles (DOP) between Israel and the PLO. The DOP decreed, *inter alia*, that Jericho and the Gaza Strip would be granted immediate autonomy. This meant that for the first time Israel would cede authority over a part of the occupied territories. Initially, there was some dispute between Israel and the PLO about how big Jericho was (the PLO favoured including the environs, Israel only considered the town centre). In the two years since Oslo 1, Jericho has largely proved itself as a test case for Palestinian self-rule. However, many Palestinians voiced deep qualms about the wide-ranging powers vested in Col Jibril Rajoul's PNA-sanctioned Preventive Security Service. In the January 1996 elections, Jericho returned the PNA Minister of Local Government, a Jericho resident and former *intifada* personality, Sa'eb Erakat, as its MP. Palestinians hope that ultimately Jericho will become part of a fully independent Palestinian state, and (in the words of one resident) 'our window to the Arab world'.

Chapter 15   Jordan

National statistics

Capital	Amman
Official languages	Arabic (English is widely understood)
Ethnic groups	Arab 98%, Circassian 1%, Armenian 1%
	[Approximately half of Jordan's population is Palestinian in origin]
Religions	Islam 92% (Sunni, with Shi'ite minority); Christianity 8%
Total area	89,213 sq km
Population	4,100,709 (July 1995 est.)
Armed Forces	98,000 (1994)
Currency	Jordanian dinar (JD) = 1,000 fils
Exchange rate	US$1 = JD 0.704 (as at Dec 31, 1994)
GDP	[purchasing power parity] $17 bn (1994 est.)
GDP per capita	$4,240 (1994 est.)
Unemployment	16% (1994 est.)
Inflation	6% (1994 est.)
Balance of payments	$765.2 million (1990)
Foreign debt	$6bn (March 1995 est.)

[Figures from *CIA World Factbook*, 1995; and *Keesing's Record of World Events*, Reference Supplement 41, 1995]

Politics in Jordan

POLITICAL LEADERSHIP

King	Hussein ibn Talal
Crown Prince	Hassan ibn Talal
Head of the Royal Court	Field Marshal Sharif Zayid ibn Shaker (since Jan. 8, 1995)
Prime Minister	Abdul Karim Kabariti (since Feb. 1996)
Cabinet (as of Jan. 8, 1995)	
Prime Minister, Defence	Sharif Zayid ibn Shaker
Deputy Prime Minister, Education	Abdel Rauf al-Rawabidah
Deputy Prime Minister, Information	Khaled al-Karaki
Foreign Affairs	Abdul Karim Kabariti
Interior	Salameh Hammad
Finance and Customs	Basil Jardaneh
Agriculture	Mansour bin Tarif
Posts and Communications	Jamal Sarayrah
Culture	Samir Habashneh
Higher Education	Ratib al-Suud
Energy and Mineral Resources	Samih Dawarzah
Health	Arif Bataynah
Justice	Hisham al-Tall
Labour	Nader Abu al-Shaer

Municipal, Rural, Environment	Nader Theirat
Planning	Rima Khalaf
Public Works and Housing	Abdel-Razzaq al-Nusur
Waqf, Islamic Affairs, Holy Places	Abdel-Salam al-Abbadi
Social Development	Salwa al-Masri
Supply	Adil al-Qudah
Tourism and Antiquities	Abdulellah al-Khatib
Trade and Industry	Ali Abu al-Ragheb
Water and Irrigation	Salih Irshaidat
Youth	Awad Khleifat
Transport	Samir Qowar
Administrative Development	Muhieedine Touq
Chief of Royal Court	Marwan Qassim

King Hussein swore in this new cabinet headed by Prime Minister Sheikh Zayid ibn Shaker,on January 8, 1995. This followed the resignation three days earlier of the previous prime minister, Salam al-Majali, who had held the position since May 1993. The January cabinet included two women, and saw three previous ministers take up new responsibilities. Fourteen ministers were new appointments.

In the first week of February 1996, there was another cabinet reshuffle, resulting in Abdul Karim Kabariti, the previous Foreign Minister, replacing ibn Shaker as Prime Minister. Mr Kabariti will continue to serve as Foreign Minister, and will also be Defence Minister. Dr Marwan Muasher, Jordan's first ambassador to Israel, is to take over from Khaled al-Karaki as Information Minister.

POLITICAL PARTIES

Al-'Ahd (Pledge) Party	Sec.-Gen. 'Abd al-Hadi al-Majali
Al-Ahrar (Liberals) Party	Sec. -Gen. Ahmad al-Zu'bi
Al-Hurriyah (Freedom) Party	Sec. -Gen. Fawwaz al-Zu'bi
Al-Watan (Homeland) Party	Leader 'Akif al-Fayiz
Al-Yaqazah (Awakening) Party	Sec. -Gen. 'Abd al-Ra'uf al-Rawabidah
Constitutional Jordanian Arab Front Party	Leader Milhim al-Tall
Democratic Arab Islamic Movement Party (*Du'a'*)	Sec. -Gen. Yusuf Abu Bakr
Democratic Arab Unionist Party (*Wad*)	Sec. -Gen. Anis al-Mu'ashir
Islamic Action Front (IAF)	Sec. -Gen. Ishaq al-Farhan
Jordanian Arab Democratic Party	Sec. -Gen. Mu'nis al-Razzaz
Jordanian Arab Masses Party	Sec. -Gen. 'Abd al-Khaliq Shatat
Jordanian Arab Socialist *Ba'ath* Party	Command 1st Sec Taysir al-Himsi
Jordanian Communist Party (JCP)	Sec. -Gen. Ya'qub Zayadin
Jordanian Democratic Popular Unity Party	Sec. -Gen. 'Azmi al-Khawaja
Jordanian Democratic Progressive Party	Sec. -Gen. 'Ali 'Amir
Jordanian National Alliance Party	Sec. -Gen. Mijhim al-Khurayshah

Jordanian People's Democratic Party (*Hashd*)	Sec. -Gen. Taysir al-Zibri
Jordanian Socialist Democratic Party	Sec. -Gen. 'Isa Madanat
Pan-Arab Action Front Party	Sec. -Gen. Muhammad al-Zu'bi
Popular Unity Party – the Unionists	Sec. -Gen. Talal al-Ramahi
Progress and Justice Party	Sec. -Gen. 'Ali al-Sa'd
Progressive Arab Ba'ath Party	Command Sec. Mahmud al-Ma'ayitah
Al-Mustaqbal (Future) Party	Sec. -Gen. Sulayman 'Arar

The Hashemite Kingdom of Jordan is a constitutional monarchy, in which the King appoints a Prime Minister, who in turn selects a Council of Ministers. This council is responsible to a bicameral National Assembly (*Majlis al-'Umma*) – the House of Representatives (80 elected seats), and the Senate, or House of Notables (40 nominated seats). In the immediate aftermath of the First World War, Transjordan (essentially, land east of the Jordan River) was considered as part of the British Mandate in Palestine. However, after the San Remo conference of 1920, the area was hived off from the rest of Palestine, and three years later Transjordan was recognized as an Emirate. Its ruler was Abdullah, son of Feisal, from the Hashemite family. (Hashemites trace their descent from the Prophet Muhammed; for centuries they ruled the holy cities of Mecca and Medina, until they were displaced by the Saudi family in this century.)

The Kingdom achieved its independence from British mandatory rule in 1946. In 1948, it was involved in a war against the new state of Israel. In the course of this war, Transjordan acquired control of the West Bank of the Jordan River (an area which according to the UN 181 Partition Resolution had been earmarked as the basis of an Arab Palestine). After consultations with pro-Hashemite Palestinians, in 1950 this area was fully absorbed into the Kingdom, which henceforth was known as Jordan. Officially, only Britain and Pakistan recognized this action. After the assassination of Abdullah, his grandson Hussein became king in 1953. King Hussein still rules today, making him the longest-serving head of state in the Middle East.

Jordan lost control of the West Bank to Israel after the Six-Day War in 1967. As a result, King Hussein outlawed political parties and imposed martial law provisions. Constitutionally, the Kingdom argued that as elections could not be held in the occupied West Bank, there should be no elections on the East Bank either. In 1978 King Hussein replaced parliament with a National Consultative Council, but in 1984 he restored the 1967 parliament. In by-elections held in 1984, all Jordanian women were allowed to vote for the first time.

The situation really changed in 1988, however, when King Hussein formally abrogated Jordan's claim to the West Bank. This set in train a series of political reforms, including:

- Nov. 1989   Non-party parliamentary elections
- April 1992   Abolition of martial law
- July 1992   Lifting of the ban on political parties stipulated in new National Charter
- Sept. 1992   Political Parties Law (no 32 for the year) enacted by Royal Decree
- Aug. 1993   King dissolves Parliament, announces new one-person-one-vote system
- Nov. 8, 1993   Multi-party elections to the 80-member House of Representatives

The first parties granted permission to operate were – a Jordan National Alliance (a coalition of central and southern Bedouin tribes); the rightist Pledge Party (*al-Ahd*); the Muslim Brotherhood-backed Islamic Action Front (IAF); the Jordanian Communist Party; the Arab Ba'ath Socialist Party; and two pan-Arab centrist parties, the Popular Union Party and *Mustaqbal*. By July 1993, 20 political parties had applied for licensing and were registered.

The short run-up to elections and continuing debate about electoral reform tended to disrupt political organization. As a result, many parties chose to back independent candidates and tribal representatives, instead of running in their own right. Another complicating factor was the surprise announcement of the Israel–PLO accords, in September 1993. This raised the spectre of Jordanian Palestinians being deprived of their right to vote in Jordan (seeing as they might in time be able to vote for a Palestine Authority). Because of this, some parties asked for the elections to be postponed; but King Hussein nonetheless decided to proceed as planned, and reassured Palestinians that their voting rights remained intact.

The November 1993 elections resulted in a victory for moderate independents and tribal notables loyal to the King (55 out of 80 seats). The IAF emerged as the largest single party, with 16 seats, but the overall strength of the Islamic bloc was reduced. Thus no single party enjoys a majority in the House. The King still wields considerable power through his ability to shuffle his cabinet, and appoint and dismiss prime ministers (which he did in June 1994, and again in January 1995). Even so, Jordan took an important step towards democratic legitimacy when the freely elected House of Representatives approved the peace treaty with Israel (signed on Oct. 26, 1994).

Major political trends

In her booklet, *Jordan's Parliamentary Elections*, Rima Hajjar defines four categories of political parties, each one representing a distinct political trend in the country. These are:

Islamists

Of the two parties in this category, the senior is Ishaq Farhan's Islamic Action Front (licensed on Dec. 8, 1992). The IAF acts as an umbrella for the long-established Jordanian Muslim Brotherhood, which had gained 22 seats in the 1989 non-party elections. The smaller Democratic Arab Islamic Movement Party (*Du'a*) differs from the IAF in supporting peace with Israel, and keeping its distance from the Muslim Brotherhood. Both parties, however, agree that Jordan – and indeed the entire Arab and Muslim world – should return to *sharia* law.

Centrists

Also known as conservatives, this group contains eight parties, the largest of which is the *Al-Ahd* (Pledge) Party, under 'Abd al-Hadi al-Majali. Centrists adhere to the principles of the Great Arab Revolt of World War I, namely an independent and unified Arab state, and the upholding of ancient traditions within the framework of Islamic ideals. Their main support base is tribal, and their leadership includes many former cabinet ministers and army officers. Initially, their biggest challenge was to adapt to modern party politics, and recruit new members. Although many centrist parties belonged to a Higher Committee for Party Coordination, they failed to form a united front on the eve of the elections, and instead chose to back individual candidates.

Leftists

Five parties belong to this group, of which three are essentially sections of the old Jordanian Communist Party. The Communists had split over issues of leadership, and also in the wake of the Soviet Union's collapse. The other two parties in the leftist caucus originally emerged as offshoots of Palestinian parties – not a surprising development when one considers that Palestinians make up approximately half the population of the Hashemite Kingdom. The Jordanian People's Democratic Party (JPDP, or *Hashd*) was set up by supporters of the Democratic Front for the Liberation of Palestine (DFLP) in 1989; the Jordanian Popular Democratic Unity Party was set up by supporters of the Popular Front for the Liberation of Palestine (PFLP) in 1990. All five parties received licenses only after proving their commitment to the Jordanian constitution by omitting such words as 'socialism' from their manifestos; and by persuading the licensing authority that they were set up and financed '[independent] of outside links and parties'.

Ba'athists and Pan-Arabists

The *Ba'ath* (Rennaiscance) Party was originally founded in Syria, and held its first conference in 1947. Socialist, secular and pan-Arabist in nature, its influence soon spread to Iraq, Lebanon and Jordan. Today *Ba'ath* rules in Iraq and Syria, although in practice the two wings are bitter foes, and analysts suggest that the movement is merely a front for military regimes in each country. Since 1992 Jordan has recognized two *Ba'ath* parties – the Arab Progressive *Ba'ath* Party and the Jordanian Arab Socialist *Ba'ath* Party. In addition, there are three other newer parties which tow a broadly pan-Arabist line – the Jordanian Arab Democratic Party, the Jordanian Arab Popular Party, and *Al-Watan* (Homeland) Party.

Developments in 1994 and 1995

EFFECTS OF PEACE WITH ISRAEL

After the Declaration of Principles between Israel and the PLO, Jordan speeded up the negotiations with her neighbour. This culminated in a cessation of a state of war in July, 1994, and a historic peace treaty between the two states, signed on Oct. 26, 1994. [For details of the accords, see Part Two, Chapter Five.] Implementing the treaty took longer than expected, as King Hussein had to win approval for overturning earlier anti-Israeli legislation. Further, throughout 1995 the Islamic Front and radical Palestinian groups formed a strategic alliance to obstruct the peace. They compelled professional bodies to boycott meetings or trade deals with Israel, and tried twice to organize anti-peace rallies – the first unsuccessfully in March, and then in October. Privately, however, businessmen in Amman and Irbid pursued their new contacts; while King Hussein moved to assure Palestinians in Jordan that their future was not prejudiced in any way by the terms of the Jordanian–Israeli peace. In July 1995, the Islamic opposition suffered serious reverses in local elections.

A year on from the signing of the peace treaty, there were some signs of optimism from Israeli quarters. Tourism to Jordan took off, and there was growing co-operation in the economic development of two shared areas – the Jordan River Valley and the Dead Sea Riviera. Similarly, Jordan and Israel began to co-operate on mutual ecological concerns. Much time was spent on building up new institutions, where none had existed before. Here the USA played a crucial role – especially in the Tripartite Committee dealing with the nexus of economics and ecology. In addition, Jordan joined a Quadripartite Committee with Israel, Egypt and the Palestine Authority, to tackle the profound issue of Palestinian refugees and displaced persons.

As 1995 unfolded, Jordanian banks began re-opening in Palestinian territories, building on the trade agreements signed between the PNA and Jordan in early 1994. The improved border links between Israel and Jordan also benefited Amman-based Palestinian businesses, which could now travel to the West Bank far easier. As the full implications of the Israeli–Palestinian Interim Agreement (Oslo 2) become known in 1996, it is almost certain that Jordan will build up strong links with the nascent Palestinian economy of the major West Bank cities.

ECONOMIC IMPROVEMENTS

After two years of cool relations between Jordan and the USA (a consequence of the King's stance during the Gulf War), relations improved markedly in 1994. Jordan benefited economically from improved ties with the USA (itself a by-product of its peace with Israel). This entailed an agreement to write off official debts which Jordan owed to the USA. In addition, an international donors' conference promised $200 in aid, and the IMF a further $181 million in credits, to help Jordan's medium-term adjustment and structural reform programme in mid-1994. The USA eased restrictions on trade to Jordan through the port of Aqaba in 1994; and in July, 1995, the US Congress wrote off Jordan's remaining debt to the USA of $480 million.

In the longer term, Jordan faces the challenge of absorbing into the economy the estimated 300,000 Palestinians who were expelled from Kuwait and other Gulf states during and after the Gulf War. Unemployment remains a serious problem, and similarly the lack of oil industry remittances from expatriate Jordanians has harmed Jordan's revenue. But by the end of 1995, there was renewed optimism, from two quarters. First, Israel and Jordan signed a trade law in October (as stipulated in their treaty a year earlier). The deal had been repeatedly delayed, as Jordanian officials feared that Israel's economy, 12 times the size of Jordan's, would use its high capitilization to dump cheaper products on Jordan. After much negotia-

Figure 12   *Literacy rate in Jordan – a regional comparison*

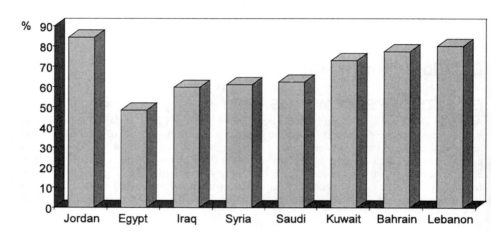

Note: Figures for Jordan are for 1993 (other states' figures are for 1990)

Source: Jordanian Ministry of Education, as printed in Jordan Media Group's publication. *Jordan – Keys to the Kingdom*

tion, the two sides agreed on an equitable mechanism, which freed the way for a host of co-operative projects, not least the mineral exploitation of the Dead Sea. Second, Amman hosted the Middle East and North Africa Conference. Hundreds of delegates from Israel and the Arab world attended this successor to 1994's Casablanca conference. The meeting was seen as a triumph for its organizer, Crown Prince Hassan, and it aired plans for $25 billion in regional investments. Furthermore, Amman was made the headquarters for the increasingly influential Regional Economic Working Group (of the multilateral talks).

FINAL ENABLING TREATIES WITH ISRAEL

On Jan. 18, 1996, Israel and Jordan signed the last of four bilateral agreements in Aqaba, resulting from the peace agreement between the two countries. These were:

- Science and Culture Agreement – A framework for co-operation on projects in the fields of research and development, professional training, and cultural exchanges.
- Communication Agreement – A legal structure for existing postal connections which should facilitate future bilateral and regional co-operation in telecommunications;
- Aqaba–Eilat Agreement – A framework for transforming the Aqaba–Eilat region into a single district for co-operation in the fields of tourism, industry, trade, environment and infrastructure, including setting up an ocean park on both shores of the Gulf;
- Maritime Border Agreement – An arrangement for marking the maritime border between the two countries.

Over the last few months, the following agreements have been signed: Tourism, Border Crossings, Energy, Health, Environment, Police and the War Against Drugs, Trade and Economic Co-operation, Agriculture, Transportation and Civil Aviation. The signing ceremony in January was attended by Prime Ministers Shimon Peres and Zayid ibn Shaker, as well as Foreign Ministers Ehud Barak and Abdul Karim Kabariti, and King Hussein and Crown Prince Hassan.

The signing concluded the process of initial peace-making, and heralded the start of the process of implementation. Thus the joint Supervisory Committee disbanded, its work done; but three permanent working groups will continue to operate: the Jordan Valley Development Committee (JRV); the Water Committee; and the Special Regime for Zofar and Naharayim.

REGIONAL AND INTERNAL POLITICS

In July 1995, Foreign Minister Kabariti visited Saudi Arabia, for the first high level talks since the Gulf Crisis of 1990–91. This marked a significant return to the fold of Arab states, and implied Jordan's belated distancing of itself from its traditional ally, Iraq. Later that year, senior aides to Saddam Hussein began deserting to Jordan, but talk of a Jordanian role in fostering an anti-Saddam resistance appeared premature.

Relations with Syria cooled after Jordan's treaty with Israel. Syrian President Assad felt aggrieved that King Hussein had made peace without his approval. However, since then the two states have restored ties. Internationally, Jordan's standing as a political force for peace in the Middle East grew enormously after the King's moving address at Yitzhak Rabin's graveside, in November 1995.

Within Jordan, the democratic reforms were taking root, but equally the King's government took a hard line against Islamic fundamentalist opposition. Following bomb blasts in early 1994, a state security court passed 11 death sentences on Islamic activists in December. The following June, security forces killed a leading Muslim critic, Sheikh Mohammed Khalifa, in an incident at his home. Similarly, the government seemed to be fighting a running battle against Leith Shubaylat, head of the engineers' professional association, and a leading foe of alleged government corruption, and the peace process.

Prospects for 1996 and beyond

Ultimately, Jordan's future depends as much on external factors as on internal ones. In this regard, the Palestinian Council elections of January 1996, and the final status talks between Israel and the PLO (which will discuss Jordan's role in Jerusalem), will no doubt have profound repercussions for the Hashemite Kingdom. Unlike other Diaspora Palestinians, Jordanian Palestinians on the whole seemed to support the polls with some enthusiasm. Even supporters of *Hamas* appeared to blame their counterparts in the territories for not officially participating in the historic elections.

The King continues to wield ultimate power through the technique of shuffling cabinets. In the first week of February, he replaced Sharif Zayid ibn Shaker as Prime Minister with the younger Foreign Minister, Abdul Karim Kabariti. Shaker had served as Prime Minister for barely a year. King Hussein's new appointments reflected a move away from the caution of the previous 12 months, and heralded a new dynamic approach inside the Kingdom. Kabariti accepted a mandate to root out corruption, and he pledged to launch extensive reforms to all levels of Jordan's bureaucracy. The new prime minister also intends to consult more with Jordan's democratic parliament, and wants to promote free enterprise. With the aid of his new Information Minister, Marwan Muasher, he hopes to 'sell the idea' of peace with Israel, to a still sceptical Jordanian populus.

REDEFINING JORDANIAN IDENTITY

The great challenge for the future is how to redefine Jordanian identity, in the light of five factors: the Palestinian dimension, the diplomatic after-effects of the Gulf War, the economy, the relationship with Israel, and the status of the monarchy.

Because at least half of Jordan's population are Palestinian, the Kingdom fears that Palestinians in Amman and elsewhere may consider that their true political interests lie on the other side of the River Jordan, now that 'self-rule' under the PLO is taking hold there. Jordan's challenge is to guide and co-operate with the new political entity, while also satisfying the remaining demands for reform at home.

At last, Jordan appears to be shaking off the diplomatic effects of the Gulf War. For the first time in five years, King Hussein paid a personal visit to Saudi Arabia in early February 1996. Conceivably, the coming to power of Prince Abdullah in Riyadh has ended the Cold

War between the two monarchies, and allows them to co-operate on mutual interests. A week later, Kuwait and Jordan announced that they would restore relations, though few details emerged. Jordan publicly says it has no intention of toppling Saddam Hussein; but despite new signs of economic co-operation between Iraqi and Jordanian businessmen, relations between the two traditionally allied governments remained tense.

Economically, there were signs of improvement – exports rose by 39% in 1995, and the IMF approved a loan of $295 million. But the Jordanian currency remains weak, and unemployment is still worryingly high as many Palestinians returnees from the Gulf have no jobs. Finally, Jordan's ties with Israel are seen as a double-edged sword. It now appears that while the expected trade boom with Israel is still in its early days, Jordanian and Israeli military officers have rushed ahead with ambitious joint projects. There was talk of Israel training Jordanian soldiers, upgrading Jordanian tanks, even sharing sensitive information. Israeli politicians have begun to act as brokers on Jordan's behalf, and helped to influence the USA to provide the Kingdom with more F-15 fighter aircraft. Yet this very closeness risks antagonizing radicals at home, and rival regimes abroad. However, if Syria does sign a peace deal with Israel, and (as is predicted) a comprehensive 'regional deal' follows, Jordan could well become a crucial conduit for Arab states to Israel – and, in time, to a new state of Palestine.

In the longer term, the monarchy seems likely to continue after Hussein's departure. Prince Hassan has been given ever greater responsibilities, both locally and in the international arena. Now, under Prime Minister Kabariti, Jordan appears set for profound reforms. The question is, can these take place without upsetting the conservative tribal chiefs who underpin the Royal Court? And might not greater democraticization encourage those elements – Muslim Brothers and 'rejectionist' Palestinians – who still question the legitimacy of a Hashemite Monarchy in Jordan?

Chapter 16   Egypt

National statistics

Capital	Cairo
Official languages	Arabic (some French and English also spoken)
Religions	Islam 86% (mainly Sunni); Christianity 11% (mainly Coptic) (est.)
Land area	1,101,499 sq km
Population	62.3m (July 1995 est.)
Armed forces	440,000 (1994)
Currency	Egyptian pound (LE) = 100 piastres
Exchange rate	LE 3.39 per $ (May 1994)
GDP	$151.5bn (1994 est.)
GNP per capita	$630 (1993 estimate)
GNP real growth	4% (1993 estimate)
Unemployment	20% (1993 estimate)
Inflation	15.2% (1993 estimate)
Trade balance	-$5.5bn (1992)
Foreign debt	$30bn (1993)

[Figures from *CNN Middle East Yearbook*, 1995; and *Keesing's Record of World Events*, Reference Supplement 41, 1995]

Politics in Egypt

POLITICAL LEADERSHIP

President	Mohammed Hosni Mubarak
Assistant President	Field-Marshal Mohammed Abdel-Halim Abu Ghazalah
Prime Minister	Atef Sedqi [replaced by Kamal Ahmed Ganzouri in Dec., 1995]
Cabinet [until Dec. 1995]	
Prime Minister, International Co-operation	Atef Sedqi
Foreign Affairs	Amr Mohammed Moussa
Deputy Prime Minister, Planning	Kamal Ahmed Ganzouri
Deputy Prime Minister, Agriculture	Yusuf Amin Wali
Defence	Field-Marshal Mohammed Hussein Tantawi
Interior	Gen. Hussein Mohammed al-Alfi
Finance	Mohammed Ahmed al-Razaz
Information	Mohammed Sawfat al-Sharif
Economy and Foreign Trade	Mahmoud Mohammed Mahmoud
Party in government	
National Democratic Party	Leader: Hosni Mubarak Sec.-Gen.: Yusuf Amin Wali
Other political parties (legal)	
Socialist Labour Party	Leader: Ibrahim Mahmoud Shukri

Figure 13   *Comparative land area of countries in peace talks*

Area in 1,000s of sq km

Egypt	1.001
Israel	21
Jordan	98
Lebanon	10
Syria	185

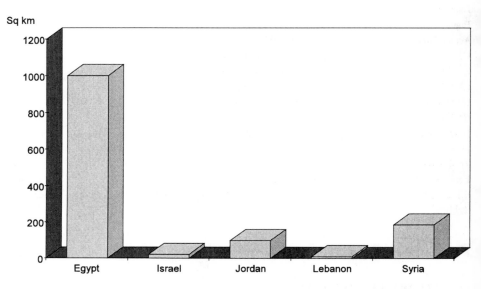

[Source: *WH Smith World Atlas,* 1985]

National Progressive Unionist Grouping	Leader: Khaled Mohiedin
New *Wafd* Party	Leader: Fuad Serageddin
Liberal Socialist Party	Leader:Mustafa Kamal Murad
Umma (National) Party	Chairman: Ahmed al-Sabahi Awadallah
Green Party	Leader: Kamal Kirah
Democratic Union Party	Leader: Ibrahim Abd al-Mun'im Turk
Nasserite Arab Democratic Party	Leader: Diya al-Din Dawud
Egypt's Arab Socialist Party	Leader: Jamal Ribi'i
Social Justice Party	Leader: Mohammed Abd al-Al

Political parties (illegal)

Muslim Brotherhood	(*Ikhwan al-Muslimun*)
Gamaat Islamiya	(Islamic Movement)
Al-Jihad	(Holy War, or Self-Improvement)
Tala'i al-Fath	(Vanguards of Conquest)

The Muslim Brotherhood is the oldest organization, founded in 1922. Although technically illegal, it is tolerated and remains very influential in a number of professional organizations. *Gamaat* and *Al-Jihad* are the principal militant and largely clandestine Islamic opposition groups. *Tala'i al-Fath* is an offshoot of *Al-Jihad*, and is sometimes known as New *Jihad*.

Egypt has perhaps the oldest operating constitution in the Middle East. This is a legacy of its importance in the old Ottoman Empire, and particularly of the dynamic leadership of Mohammed Ali in the early 19th century. The Arab Republic of Egypt became fully independent in 1936. A military coup overthrew the monarchy in 1952, and in 1954 Gamal Abdal Nasser assumed leadership as the President, a position he held until his death in 1970. Anwar al-Sadat replaced Nasser, and in 1980 presided over a new constitution. After Sadat was assassinated in 1981, his deputy, Hosni Mubarak, assumed the presidency. President Mubarak was sworn in for a third term in October 1993.

Constitutionally, the president is nominated by the unicameral People's National Assembly, which has 454 members. The Assembly is elected by universal adult suffrage, and the president is confirmed by popular referendum for a six-year term. A 258-member Consultative Council (*Majlis ash-Shoura*) advises the president, and helps draft legislation. (Since 1989 the Consultative Council has gained 48 new members, including, for the first time, 10 women.)

In practice the president enjoys wide executive powers. He appoints the Council of Ministers and its head, the prime minister. In addition, he can call referendums, issue statutes, and (as commander-in-chief of the armed forces) declare war, with the Assembly's approval. Most importantly, it is he who sets national policy. A Presidential Bureau and special National Councils (including one for national defence and security) aid him in his work. According to the *US Army Handbook*, the presidential aides form the top echelon of political power, and the cabinet the second. The proportion of the military in the cabinet fell from 40% under Nasser to just 10% under Sadat and Mubarak, evidence of the relative decline of the military élite in Egyptian politics. Mubarak seems to favour technocrats and trained engineers or lawyers, like Prime Minister Sedqi. Figures like Field Marshal Abdul Halim Abu Ghazala, the vice-president, loom in the background, but for the moment it appears their wings have been clipped.

During the 1980s, President Mubarak attempted to revive the multi-party system, which had fallen into abeyance under his predecessors. However, the system is still dominated by the ruling National Democratic Party (NDP), which itself was only created in 1978. Parties had to win at least 8% of the vote to be represented in the People's National Assembly. As a result, only two parties won seats in the 1984 elections – the NDP with 391 seats, and the *Wafd* with 57. In elections held over November and December 1990, the NDP won 348 of the 444 elected seats in the Assembly. The three main opposition parties boycotted the poll, and accused the NDP of corruption, electoral manipulation and of monopolizing the tools of state. In June and July 1994, a National Dialogue General Congress was set up to repair some of the damage, and promote dialogue between political parties, government, trade unions and other organizations. But faith in multi-party democracy suffered a major setback during the elections of November and December 1995. Opposition parties accused the government of gross intimidation during the campaign, and decried the NDP's subsequent landslide victory as the result of a rigged poll.

Meanwhile, the principal threat to national security came from clandestine militant Islamic groups, notably *Gamaat Islamiya,* and the smaller *Al-Jihad* and *Tala'i al-Fath.* (The longer established Muslim Brotherhood prefers to wield its enormous influence through domination of professional associations, and largely eschews violence.) After the assassination of the security service's head of anti-terrorism, in April 1994, the National Assembly extended existing emergency laws for another three years. These laws permit security forces wide powers to detain and arrest suspects. Even so, fundamentalists continued to attack tourists, journalists and intellectuals, Christian Copts (especially in the southern town of Assyut), and government officials. Most notably, they tried – but failed – to assassinate Prime Minister Sedqi in 1994, and President Mubarak himself in 1995 (at the time, attending an African leaders' summit in Addis Ababa, Ethiopia).

POLITICAL PARTIES

National Democratic Party

Leaders: President Hosni Mubarak; Deputy Prime Minister Yusif Amin Wali

The National Democratic Party (NDP) was founded in 1978 out of the centrist platform of the Arab Socialist Union (ASU). According to Frank Tachau, an authority on political parties in the Middle East, it was purpose-built as the party of government, and remains the majority ruling party in Egypt today. The NDP arose out of former President Anwar Sadat's desire to dismantle the ASU, which was the power base of his predecessor, Gamal Abdul Nasser. While still deputy president, Hosni Mubarak was given the task of organizing the NDP nationwide. The creation of the party coincided with the restoration of multi-party democracy in Egypt, although critics see it as a mere tool of the presidency. The party aims at prosperity for the individual and nation. Its three weekly newspapers are *Mayo, Shabab Biladi* and *Al-Lewaa al-Islami.* Today, the NDP dominates the upper chamber, the Consultative Council, and through control of voter registration ensures its majority in the Assembly. The party has no clear policy other than that of the president and his advisers. Party membership, says Tachau, is seen as the key to political advancement in Egypt. President Mubarak formally heads the NDP, but party General-Secretary Yusif Amin Wali, Agriculture Minister and deputy prime minister, manages it on a day to day basis.

New Wafd *Party*

Leaders: Fu'ad Siraj al-Din and Ibrahim Firaj

The original *Wafd* (or 'delegation') arose out the group of Egyptian politicians who went to London in 1918 to negotiate greater independence for Egypt. Its pre-eminent politicians in the early years were Al-Nahhas and Zaghlul. From independence until 1952, the *Wafd* and *Sa'adists* (chief rivals) dominated Egyptian party politics. Britain forced King Farouk to accept *Wafd* influence at the highest levels. However, with the overthrow of the monarchy and coming to power of the Free Officers (including Nasser), the *Wafd* party was increasingly blamed for the corruption of the old order, and was eventually banned.

After Nasser's death, President Sadat encouraged the party to re-emerge as a counterweight to the remnants of Nasser's Arab Socialist Union. The new party was legalized in 1978 and fully established in 1983. In 1984 it participated in its first election in 34 years, and, thanks largely to a timely alliance with the officially illegal Muslim Brotherhood, it became the only opposition party in the Assembly (no other party managed to get over the 8% threshold for representation). The New *Wafd* is thought to be the only opposition party with widespread popular support.

By the 1987 elections, the Muslim Brotherhood switched its allegiance to Socialist Labour Party – a relief for the Coptic Christians who make up much of the *Wafd's* traditional support base. The New *Wafd* stands on a platform of political and economic liberalization, and particularly stresses Egyptian identity within the Arab world. Through its widely read party newspaper, *Al-Wafd*, the party has a reputation for muckraking, and keeping the ruling NDP on its toes. However, it has always offered Mubarak loyal support over peace with Israel. In 1990, the New *Wafd* joined other opposition parties in boycotting the elections.

Socialist Labour Party

The SLP was founded in 1978 on a platform of socialism and popular rule. Much of its initial support came from leftists within the old Arab Socialist Union. In 1987 the officially illegal but very influential Muslim Brotherhood switched its allegiance from the New *Wafd* to the Socialist Labour Party, which is headed by the veteran politician, Ibrahim Mahmoud Shukri. The party boycotted the 1990 elections, and clashed with Mubarak over Egypt's participation in Operation Desert Shield and Desert Storm. In 1994 Shukri was served with a libel writ for statements made by his party's popular *Al-Shaab* newspaper, which accused President Mubarak of corruption. He unexpectedly lost his seat in the late 1995 elections, and immediately protested that the polls were rigged.

Liberal Socialist Party

Despite its name, the party (which was founded in 1976) stands for Islamic *sharia* law as the basis of the constitution and legal system. It also supports a strong public sector, and is seen as a front for the Muslim Brotherhood. In 1987 the party formed a temporary alliance with Shukri's Socialist Labour Party. The party organ is *Al-Ahrar*.

Other parties

The National Progressive Unionist Grouping was set up in 1976, and publishes the *Al-Ahali* newspaper. It preaches a socialist doctrine, backed by 'extensive social research'. The New *Misr Al-Fatah* Party, Democratic Unionist Party and the environmentalist Green Party were all founded in 1990. The former believes that prices of goods should vary according to the income of purchasers. Other parties include the Arab Misr Party, the Nasserite Arab Democratic Party, the Democratic People's Party and the Social Justice Party.

Muslim Brotherhood (Ihwan al-Muslimin)

General guide:	**Muhammad Hamid Abu al-Nasr (died in early 1996)**
General secretary:	**Mamoun al-Hudaiby**
Political leadership:	**Mustafa Masshur**

The *Ikhwan al-Muslimin* is the quintessential Sunni Muslim fundamentalist group in the Middle East. Over the years it has spawned numerous branches in many Arab countries. Founded in Egypt in 1928 by Hassan al-Banna, the group favours a return to Islam and the *sharia* law. From the start it opposed political parties as antithetical to true Islam, and regarded itself more as a religious order. Even so, from time to time it has influenced politicians who are swayed by its mass appeal – notably in the period 1945 to 1948, when, through a series of demonstrations and assassinations, it forced King Farouk of Egypt to fight the first Arab–Israeli war. Farouk banned the Brotherhood between 1948 and 1951. Muslim Brothers assassinated the Egyptian Prime Minister Nuqraishi Pasha and, even though al-Banna condemned this act, he was killed on the order of the King.

The Brotherhood was unbanned after Farouk's overthrow in 1952, (especially as Col Sadat liased with the group prior to the successful coup), but his fellow republican Free Officers banned it again in 1954. Six of its leaders were executed following an attempt on President Nasser's life in October of that year. Since that time, the Brotherhood has cast itself as an enemy of capitalism, colonialism, and secular Arab politicians (whether Pan-Arabist, Nasserite or Ba'athist). Sayed Qutb became its chief theorist, and he developed Al-Banna's argument that Muslims were living under a new *Jahiliya* (period of ignorance without Islam). The Brotherhood opposes government corruption, and even while operating clandestinely, it has managed to run a grassroots-based social welfare system for poorer believers which rivals – and often betters – official state structures. In the late 1960s it formented student disturbances in Egypt. Qutb was arrested and hanged in 1966. Similar Brotherhood-inspired actions in Syria led to a brutal crackdown by President Assad in 1982.

Under Nasser's successors, Sadat and Mubarak, it has remained officially banned, although in practice it is tolerated. Partly this is because the Brotherhood wields power through ordinary mosques, and even influences the *ulema* (priesthood) of the esteemed theological centre, the Al-Azhar University.

Initially, Anwar Sadat even found the Brotherhood a useful ally against Nasserite socialists and communists. Much of the Brotherhood's success lies in its remarkable ability to survive persecution, which in turn derives from its tremendous organization. The Brotherhood in effect runs many of the powerful professional associations and welfare support groups in Egypt. Branches of the Brotherhood in Gaza evolved into the *Hamas* movement; but in Egypt, it has mellowed over the years, and is treated differently from the more violent *Gamaat al-Islami*, *Al-Jihad* and *Tala'i al-Fath* groups. After initial opposition, moderates within the Brotherhood tacitly accepted Sadat's peace overtures with Israel in 1977. Umar Tilimsani, leader of the group until his death in 1986, condemned the assassination of Sadat.

Since the re-introduction of party politics in Egypt, the Brotherhood has not been allowed to stand in elections in its own right. Nonetheless, it has participated by backing various other parties – the New *Wafd* in 1984, and the Socialist Labour/Liberal Party alliance in 1987 (when Brotherhood supporters won half of the 61 seats which went to the alliance). In 1988 the Brotherhood responded to the Palestinian *intifada* by calling for the liberation of the territories, as the first step to the liberation of 'all of Palestine' (in other words, Israel). Generally, the Brotherhood stayed aloof from an increase in militant Islamist attacks on tourists, police, government officials and Coptic Christians in the early 1990s. In 1995, the Egyptian government began clamping down on the Brotherhood once again, on the grounds that its members were aiding more militant Islamic groups. As a result, some 200 people affiliated with the Brotherhood were arrested, pending the first mass Brotherhood trial to be held since 1965.

Al-Gama'a al-Islamiyya *(Islamic Group)*

(Also called *Gamaat al-Islami* – written in the plural, as it is really an alliance of student-based groups). *Al-Gama'a* is more militant than the Brotherhood, although in 1972 President Sadat had actually encouraged it as a counterweight to the Nasserites by getting the Religious Affairs Ministry to run summer camps for young Muslims. The group allegedly enjoys financial backing from Saudi Arabia, and offshoots served as *mujaheddin* in Afghanistan. *Al-Gama'a* has attacked Egyptian Christians since 1978, and also has been implicated in numerous political assassinations and attacks on tourists (especially in Assyut). It claimed to be behind the attempted assassination of President Mubarak in June 1995, and was also implicated in the World Trade Centre bombing in New York. The Group's spiritual head, Sheikh Omar Abderahman, is currently in a US prison, facing charges of involvement with the atrocity. *Al-Gama'a* favours an overthrow of the existing government, and its replacement by a regime based on strict adherence to *sharia* law.

Al-Jihad

This militant group made itself known in 1977. It claimed to be behind the assassination of President Anwar Sadat on Oct. 4, 1981. The murder was widely presented as revenge for the 'crime' of making peace with Israel; however, in the dock the accused spoke mainly of the crimes against Islam within Egypt, in particular attempts by the Sadat regime to bring mosques under state control. *Al-Jihad* is smaller than the *Gama'a*, and could well be a front group for the latter. A new offshoot, the New *Jihad*, or Vanguard of Conquest, attempted to kill Prime Minister Atef Sedqi in 1993. Following a major governmental crackdown in 1994, most of its educated top echelon of leaders have either been imprisoned, or fled into exile. As a result, the number of sophisticated terror attacks has virtually ended.

Egypt's role in the peace process

THE CAMP DAVID BREAKTHROUGH

President Anwar Sadat was the first Arab leader formally to visit Israel, in 1977. And following the Camp David talks, Egypt was the first Arab country to sign a peace treaty with Israel, in 1979. As a consequence of this, Egypt recovered the Sinai peninsula, which Israel had captured in the 1967 Six-Day War. (All areas of Sinai were returned by 1982, save for a small piece of land around the Red Sea port of Taba, which was eventually returned in 1988 following international arbitration.) Before the peace treaty, Egypt had been regarded as the leading force in the Arab world's struggle against the Jewish state. It was Nasser who instigated the setting up of the PLO in 1964, and again Nasser who in effect prompted the Six Day War by closing the Straits of Tiran to Israeli shipping in 1967. Likewise, President Sadat was the mastermind of the surprise Yom Kippur War of 1973, in which Egypt gained small pieces of territory.

Some analysts concluded (with hindsight) that the 1973 campaign helped restore some of the national pride Egypt had lost in 1967, and this allowed it to bargain from a position of strength. Others concluded that the crippling cost of the military budget, especially at a time when Egypt was in dire economic straits, acted as a catalyst to conclude a peace treaty. Whatever the case, the treaty itself, and the Camp David Accords which led to it, were milestones in the regional peace process. Egypt was ostracized for 'betraying the Arab cause' by signing a 'separate peace' with Israel. Palestinians felt particularly strongly, as Sadat failed to fulfil his promise of winning them 'autonomy' on the West Bank and Gaza (talks on this aspect collapsed after Israel rejected any deal with pro-PLO forces, and Jordan refused to enter negotiations).

But in the decade and a half since then, Egypt has been fully reintegrated into the Arab political world. Most significantly, Cairo is once again the official headquarters of the Arab League; and former Egyptian Foreign Minister Esmat Ahmed Abdel-Meguid is its Secretary-General. Indeed, some Egyptians maintain that with the current peace negotiations, the rest of the Arab world has caught up with their position. Certainly, the idea of 'land for peace' (established in Israel's return of the Sinai to Egypt) had become a model for Israel's dealings with Jordan, Palestinians, and perhaps in time Syria and Lebanon.

DEVELOPMENTS SINCE 1993

Mubarak was kept informed about the secret Oslo channel talks, whereas King Hussein was not. He hosted the Cairo Agreement of 1994, which set the seal on the Washington Declaration of Principles and provided the modalities for implementing the Gaza-Jericho First plan. Egyptian-ruled Taba was the site of the most sensitive Israeli–PLO talks, both before the Cairo signing (Oslo 1) and the second-stage Interim Agreement of September 1995 (Oslo 2). Cairo and Alexandria also were prominent venues for multilateral talks in 1994 and 1995. Mubarak set up the 'peace bloc' (with Egypt, Israel and the PLO) in the wake of the Hebron massacre to keep the talks going.

President Mubarak has quietly encouraged ties with Israel, and in 1995 hosted a party of Israeli tourists. (The number of Israeli tourists to Egypt rose from 134,000 in 1993, to an estimated 200,000 in 1994.) Israel has a cultural centre in Cairo, and increasing numbers of Egyptian students are studying Hebrew and Jewish studies. However, unlike Sadat, Mubarak is notably cautious of appearing 'out of step' with the rest of the Arab world, and is weary of domestic public opinion. He also led Arab protest at an attempt by Israel officials (since dropped) to 'confiscate' Arab land in East Jerusalem. Israelis have come to call the relationship with Egypt a 'cold peace', as the initial promise of the Sadat–Begin venture never quite materialized. This was symbolized by the fact that Mubarak did not visit Israel for 12 years of his presidency, despite invitations from Prime Minister Yitzhak Rabin soon after he came to power in July 1992. Rabin and Mubarak built a close relationship; but it was only Rabin's funeral which brought Mubarak to Jerusalem, in November 1995.

Cairo is a member of the multilateral talks steering committee, and has also played host to various sessions of the working groups – environment in November 1993, and refugees in

May 1994. In December 1994, it hosted a US-sponsored workshop to define threats to public health in the Middle East. The multilateral talks are on the verge of delivering real benefits to Egypt – including a joint project to combat desertification, and plans to link Egypt's electricity grid with Israel, Jordan and the Palestinians. Egypt serves on a quadrilateral committee (with Israel, Jordan and the PLO) to deal with the issue of refugees. In addition, Egypt has joined a regional tourism board, and is talking of an ambitious pipeline to supply gas to Gaza, and perhaps also Israel.

At the important Middle East/ North Africa (MENA) economic summit, held in Amman, Jordan, in October 1995), Cairo was chosen to be the headquarters for a Middle East development bank. Cairo also won the honour of hosting the follow-up summit, scheduled for November 1996. But to some observers, these were mere sops – by and large, Egypt was excluded from the rapidly developing economic nexus between Israel, Jordan and the Palestinians (what Israeli analyst, Ehud Ya'ari, has called the 'southern triangle'). Evidently, the deadweight of bureaucracy which was handicapping privatization at home, was also discouraging Egypt's role in investment and development projects abroad.

In early 1995, Egypt led Arab protests against Israel's refusal to sign the Nuclear Non-Proliferation Treaty (NPT). Reports that Israel had killed Egyptian prisoners of war in 1956 and 1967 revived tensions between the two countries. However, by late 1995 the new Israeli Prime Minister Shimon Peres and Foreign Minister Ehud Barak reached an accommodation with their Egyptian counterparts, Mubarak and Amr Moussa. Israel promised an investigation into the alleged killings, and US Secretary Christopher has repeatedly assured Cairo of America's strategic support.

If there were doubts about Egypt's centrality in Middle Eastern politics, indeed, its claim to speak on behalf of the Arab *umma*, these were surely dispelled by events in the wake of the May 1996 Israeli elections. One of the first diplomats Israel's new Prime Minister Netanyahu met with, to discuss his views on peace, was Mohammed Bassiouni, Egypt's Ambassador to Israel since 1986. In similar vein, Mubarak acted as de facto chairman of Arab opinion about the new government in Jerusalem; and it was he who hosted the resultant Arab leaders' summit (the first since 1990) in Cairo, in the week that Netanyahu officially took office, to demand that Israel honour its commitments to the peace process.

Other political issues

FOREIGN AFFAIRS

By 1996, Egypt and Sudan had yet to finally settle their dispute over land in the Hala'ib border area. This problem was exacerbated by allegations that Sudan had funded and armed Egyptian fundamentalists. Cairo blamed both Sudan's President Bashir, and the spiritual leader, Sheikh Hasan Turabi. Egyptian relations with Syria have improved since the two states fought on the same side in the Gulf War. According to their post-war Damascus Declaration, Egypt and Syria promised to defend Gulf Arab states from future attack. In part, this was meant to deflect popular Arab criticism that US forces had too much influence in the region. Further, the idea of a joint indigenous Arab defence force tallied with the long established goals of the pan-Arab movement. This co-operation also afforded Egypt some leverage over Syria, especially as a way of persuading Syria to make peace with Israel. In early 1996, President Mubarak started a new flurry of diplomatic activity, meeting visiting US Vice President Al Gore, hosting King Hussein of Jordan and reinforcing Egypt's links with Morocco.

DOMESTIC AFFAIRS

In the early 1990s, the main political challenge facing the Mubarak government was how to counter Islamic militants who threatened to overthrow the state. Cairo took a tougher approach after 1994. Some human rights group said security police were running a 'shoot-to-kill' policy. Furthermore, the comparatively moderate Muslim Brotherhood appeared to lose its immunity from government broadsides, when some 200 members were arrested, and 45 arraigned, for the first trial of Brotherhood supporters in 30 years.

By 1995, however, some analysts noted a reversion to earlier long-term concerns – the population explosion and the economy. Privatization was the key issue, but proved more difficult to implement than was at first planned. Mubarak remembers only too well the consequences of Sadat's over-enthusiastic *infitah* (opening up) to international trade in the 1970s. Sadat wished to slash public expenditure, and spark an economic revival based on Western technology, Arab capital and Egyptian labour. Responding to IMF calls, in 1977 Sadat had overruled his cautious ministers and cut welfare and subsidies on basic goods. This resulted in widespread food riots.

Mubarak has sought to steer a middle course between Nasser's centralized economic control, and Sadat's free enterprise inclinations. Inevitably, external factors have affected his plans. While peace with Israel has allowed Egypt to reduce its enormous military expenditure, the fall in the oil price since the late 1970s has also reduced Egypt's income from the remittances of Egptians working in the Gulf. In addition, the *infitah* led to a huge boom in imports. But without a commensurate improvement in Egypt's own infrastructure, the country is saddled with a high balance of payments deficit.

On the political front, Mubarak's democratization has encountered numerous problems, not least, the traditional enthusiasm of security forces to round up enemies of the regime, liberal as much as fundamentalist. The ruling NDP won a landslide victory in the November and December 1995 elections – but opposition parties charged that there had been blatant ballot rigging and intimidation of voters. In the face of such protests, Atef Sedqi, Egypt's prime minister since 1986, announced that he would resign. In 1996 Mubarak will have to restore the stability which he had worked so hard to achieve. For the present, however, there is no clear successor in sight.

Chapter 17   Syria

National statistics

Capital	**Damascus**
Official Languages	Arabic (Kurdish, Armenian, Aramaic and Circassian also spoken)
Religions	Islam 90% (of which 74% are Sunni and 16% belong to Alawite, Druze and other sects) Christianity, less than 10%; a small Jewish minority
Land Area	184,050 sq km [including 1,295 sq km of the Golan Heights, occupied by Israel]
Population	15,451,917 (UNFPA 9) (July est.)
Armed Forces	408,000 (1994)
Currency	Syrian Pound (S£)
Exchange Rate	US$1 = S£22.7165 (Dec 31, 1994)
GDP — purchasing power parity	US$74.46 bn (1994 est.)
Inflation	11.8% (1993)
Balance of Payments	US$1.875 bn surplus (1990)
Foreign Debt	US$19.4 bn (1993 est.)

[Figures from Keesing's *Record of World Events*, Reference Supplement 41, 1995]

Politics in Syria

Political Leadership (as of December 1994)

President	Hafez al-Assad
Vice-Presidents	Abdel Halim Khaddam Zuheir Masharqa Col Rifa'at Assad
Prime Minister	Mahmoud Zubi
Cabinet	
Foreign Affairs	Farouq ash-Shar'a
Deputy PM/ Defence	Gen. Mustafa Tlass
Deputy PM/ Economic Affairs	Salim Yassin
Deputy PM/ Service Affairs	Rashid Akhtarini
Education	Ghassan Halabi
Finance	Khaled al-Mahayni
Information	Mohammed Salman
Economy and Foreign Trade	Mohammed al-Imadi
Presidential Affairs	Wahib Fadel
Justice	Husayn Hassun
Interior	Mohammed Harbah
Industry	Ahmad Nizam al-Din
Agriculture	Asad Mustafa
Labour and Social Affairs	Ali Khalil
Irrigation	Abd ar-Rahman Madani

Religious Trusts (*Waqf*)	Abdel-Majid Tarabulsi
Culture	Najah al-Attar
Health	Iyad al-Shati
Communications	Radwan Martini
Oil and Mineral Resources	Nader al-Nabulsi
Tourism	Amin Abu al-Shamat
Transport	Mufid Abd al-Karim
Higher Education	Salihah Sanqar
Local Administration	Yahya Abu Asaleh
Internal Trade	Nadim Akkash
Electricity	Mounib Saaem Aldaher
Construction	Majid Izzu Ruhaybani
Housing	Husam al-Safadi
Minister of State, Foreign	Nasser Qadur
Minister of State, Cabinet	Danhu Dawud
Minister of State, Environment	Abd al-Hamid Munajjid

Party in government

National Progressive Front (NPF)

Chairman: Hafez al-Assad
The NPF is led by Ba'ath, or Arab Socialist Rennaiscance Party, and includes five others:

Ba'ath Party

Sec.-Gen.: Hafez al-Assad
Asst. Sec.-Gen.: Abdullah al-Ahmar

Syrian Arab Socialist Party (ASP)

Leader: 'Abd al-Ghani Kannut

Arab Socialist Union (ASU)

Leader: Jamal Atassi

Syrian Communist Party (SCP)

Leader: Khalid Bakdash

Arab Socialist Unionist Movement

Leader: Sami Soufan

Democratic Socialist Union Party

Leader: (not available)

Other political parties (illegal)

Muslim Brotherhood (*Ikhwan al-Muslimun*)

Party of Communist Action

National Alliance for the Liberation of Syria

Patriotic Front for National Salvation

Syrian Liberation Front

Ba'athist dissidents

The Syrian Arab Republic became fully independent in 1946. According to the constitution, the President enjoys full executive powers, and appoints the Vice-Presidents and Council of Ministers. He is elected every seven years by universal adult suffrage, the last being held in December 1991. President Hafez al-Assad first came to power after a coup in 1966. In 1970 he overthrew the civilian Ba'ath leader and his former ally, Salah Jedid; and in 1971 he was appointed president. President Assad was sworn in for a fourth term of office in March 1992. He has never been opposed in national referenda.

The new constitution of 1973 re-affirmed the 'leading role' of Ba'ath in Syrian national affairs. Nominally at least, the 250-member People's Assembly enjoys legislative authority. In practice, the only parties allowed to stand were members of the Ba'ath-dominated National Progressive Front (NPF). As chairman of the NPF and Secretary-General of Ba'ath, Assad keeps an iron grip on internal Syrian politics. No doubt he is wary of the sort of schisms which erupted periodically throughout the 1960s (and indeed brought him to power). The latest Assembly elections (held in August 1994) saw the NPF win 167 seats, with the remaining 83 going to independents.

Disproportionate power of the Alawites

Hafez al-Assad is a member of the Alawite sect, a minority community within Syria, but one which largely controls the political structures of the country. Alawites may be descendants of the ancient Canaanites, who rejected Christianity and mainstream Islam. In the Middle Ages, they adopted Ismaili Shi'ite beliefs, but later forged their own secret credo, based on a trinity of Ali, Mohammed and one of the Prophet's companions. Because Alawites reject the Islamic *sunna* (tradition), and dispute the belief that Mohammed is the last prophet, many other Muslims consider them to be heretics, beyond the pale of normal Islam. France granted Alawites autonomy in their northern regions during their mandatory rule over Syria. They also encouraged Alawites and other minorities to enter the armed forces, as a counterweight to the nationalist Sunni Muslim majority. Alawite autonomy evaporated when France left Syria at the end of World War II. However, Alawite military dominance outlasted the French departure, and helped the community to win disproportionate political power, especially after a Ba'ath-military coup in 1966. Assad's Alawite origin is a sensitive point in contemporary Syria. Many Muslims rejected his 1973 constitution as an attempt to undermine the Islamic nature of the country. In 1979 Sunni fundamentalists killed 50 Alawite cadets, and three years later, Assad gained his revenge by massacring thousands of Sunnis in their southern stronghold, Hama. Since the late 1980s, Assad has brought more members of Syria's Sunni majority into the upper echelons of government. This is reflected even in the delegations sent to negotiate with Israel. Most analysts predict that Alawite supremacy will end with Assad's departure. If that is the case, Alawites fear, the Sunnis may take retribution on the community, for their association with Ba'ath Party excesses during Assad's long reign.

The Ba'ath

The Christian Arab academic Michel Aflaq founded the Ba'ath (Renaissance) Party on a platform combining socialism, secularism and pan-Arabism. It held its first conference in Damascus in 1947, and soon its influence spred to Iraq, Lebanon and Jordan. In 1953 the Ba'ath merged with Akram Hourani's Arab Socialist Party, and the following year it helped overthrow the Syrian dictator, Col Adib Shishakli. During 1957 and 1958 it supported union with Nasser's Egypt, but later opposed this policy.

The Ba'ath took power in its own right in 1963 after an officers' coup led by Maj.-Gen. Salah Jadid, but was split by a schism between its military and civilian wings. Michel Aflaq fled into exile in Iraq, now seat of a rival Ba'ath governing faction, where he became Secretary-General of the Ba'ath National Command in 1970. Jadid was ousted in 1965, but returned to power in another coup as head of the Ba'ath military wing. Once again, new divisions emerged, this time between Jadid's supporters and a nationalist wing led by Jadid's former ally and now Defence Minister, Hafiz al-Assad. Whereas Jadid preferred to build up a neo-Marxist state within Syria, Assad and his cohorts, mostly fellow Alawites, initially favoured better ties with neighbouring Arab states and independence from Moscow. Assad also saw that he could further Greater Syrian interests by sponsoring radical Palestinian factions. Ba'ath and Nasser found themselves 'fighting for the same turf' of leadership in the Arab world, and became bitter enemies, especially after the debacle of the 1967 war against Israel.

In 1968 Assad gained the upper hand in Syria, and in November 1970, his faction overthrew Jadid, who was jailed and died in prison in 1993. In 1972 the Syrian Ba'ath became the leading party in the National Progressive Front (NPF), a coalition with five smaller parties, including Communists. To this day, the NPF remains the sole legal political movement in Syria; although some see it as merely a front for Assad's military regime. The primacy of Ba'ath and Assad was effectively cemented in a new constitution of 1973. Many Sunnis opposed it on the grounds that it did not affirm Islam as the state religion (see box on Alawites, above). From 1976 to 1980, and then again in 1982 and 1986, the Muslim Brotherhood instigated riots against the Ba'ath.

An older clique of Ba'ath also began to resent Assad's personal autocracy, and his deviance from Ba'ath ideology. Initially they were led by Hamud al-Shufi, who spoke on behalf of the National Alliance for the Liberation of Syria (an umbrella group). Another dissident group, the National Salvation Command, set off bombs in Damascus in 1981. Although secular in orientation, Ba'ath dissidents have sometimes found common cause with Sunni fundamentalists, against Assad's regime. In 1989 the National Alliance's secretariat, under Muhammad Umar Burhan, spoke of a broad alliance to overthrow Assad and instal democracy. Certain pro-Western dissidents rallied around the president's brother, Rifa'at al-Assad, but ultimately all attempts at a coup failed. Rifa'at was sent into exile (disguised as a minor diplomatic posting) in 1984. In 1992 he returned to Damascus, and is technically one of Syria's vice-presidents; but he is no longer considered to be a threat to President Assad. Meanwhile, the defeat of Iraq in the1991 Gulf War appears to have dented the opposition Ba'ath forces.

Within Syria, the Ba'ath remains the pre-eminent party, but it has had to play second fiddle to President Assad's ultimate authority. Much of the party's earlier ideological fervour has been eroded by Assad's changing allegiances (from support for radical pan-Arabism and the Soviet bloc, to his new friendship with the USA and conservative Gulf Arab states). It is noteworthy that even in Lebanon, where Syria's influence has, if anything, grown in recent years, the sister Lebanese Ba'ath Party remains as marginal as it ever was.

The Muslim Brotherhood

The Muslim Brotherhood remains the main source of opposition to Hafez al-Assad. It draws on the majority Sunni community's sense of exclusion from top level policy-making, which is dominated by Assad's Alawite community. The movement began in the early 1960s, as an offshoot of the parent group in Egypt. In 1979 it massacred Alawite cadets in Aleppo; the following year, membership of the Brotherhood became a criminal offence, and many affiliated army officers were executed. Disturbances nonetheless spread in Homs, Hama and Aleppo, and a newly constituted Islamic Alliance moved the battle to Damascus itself. In 1982, Assad ordered the bombardment of Hama, after 70 Ba'athists were murdered there. Some 10,000 citizens died in the attack, and the fifth Ba'ath congress, held in 1985, boasted that the Brotherhood had been liquidated. The Brotherhood is currently believed to operate from Aachen in Germany. As of 1991, it was led by a triumvirate headed by Ali al-Bayununi.

Syria today

Hafez al-Assad still dominates Syrian politics. Wiliness and caution may explain his political longevity (as the author Patrick Seale describes him, he is the 'Sphinx of Damascus'). Yet he has also been brutal against perceived enemies, as the massacre at Hama shows. Syria probably still nurtures pan-Arabist dreams, although these were hampered by hard economic realities in the late 1980s. The Soviet Union, its chief patron, could no longer afford to foot Damascus's arms bill; at the same time, Western nations shunned Syria for its role in harbouring terrorists. Added to that, the rise of Saddam Hussein's Iraq in 1990 posed a major threat to Syria's quest for regional hegemony.

Ultimately, Iraq's overweening ambitions served Syria well. Syria joined the anti-Saddam UN coalition in Desert Shield, and Assad had a fruitful meeting with George Bush in November 1990. Evidently, the US gave Syria a free reign in Lebanon, to crush the renegade general, Michel Aoun, in return for its support in the coming battle against Iraq in 1991. After the war, Damascus received large injections of aid and credits from Saudi Arabia, the Gulf States, Japan, the EC, and the USA. Assad and President Mubarak of Egypt signed a Damascus Declaration after the war, whereby they promised to use their combined military might to protect Gulf states from future attack. But in Western eyes, the ultimate test of Assad's newfound 'moderation' – a peace treaty with Israel – remains elusive. Further, Damascus' continuing ties with its traditional ally, Teheran, worries Western policy-makers (see foreign policy, below).

ECONOMICS

In the late 1980s, Syria embarked on a policy of economic liberalization, but for most Syrians it has proved to be chimerical. The recent discovery of oil offered Syria a timely windfall, and has resulted in an annual GDP growth of 8.5%; as production increased, income from oil doubled to $1.5 billion from 1989 to 1990. In 1991 Syria passed Investment Law 10, which sought to encourage private investment. By 1994 this resulted in private business people contributing almost two-thirds of Syria's GDP – a significant change from the centrally-run economy of the 1980s. In 1992 Assad appointed the former chairman of an oil company, Nadir al-Nabulsi, as Oil and Mineral Resources Minister, thus signalling a new effort to properly exploit this sector. By 1994, oil accounted for 16.6% of Syria's GDP.

However, only a few entrepreneurs have apparently reaped the benefits; and grand schemes to encourage more foreign company involvement in oil and gas exploitation have only partially materialized (German exploration in the Jaffra oilfields being an exception). Meanwhile, unemployment will probably increase as long as the population grows at its current rate (3.5% yearly, one of the highest rates in the world). By 1994, in a rare deviance from his usual practice, Assad personally intervened to solve Syria's crippling electricity crisis. Without assured provision of electricity, few of his industrial schemes can hope to succeed.

Between 1992 and the end of 1993, Syria's GDP rose by 8.3%; and expenditure increased by more than 32%. Some $1 billion poured into the country from private investors, some of them expatriates. Despite rising imports, Syria has chosen to lessen import restrictions to encourage trade. Syria still depends heavily on foreign aid, totalling $1.2 billion for investment projects. Most came from Gulf States, but the EC approved two projects for water and infrastructure development, totalling $200 million in 1993. In 1994, Italy overtook the former Soviet Union as Syria's main customer. Syrians are eagerly watching the Jordanians, to see if relations with Israel really do bring a 'peace dividend'. About half of Syria's investment projects concern transport; but as Syria has excluded itself from the Madrid and Moscow track multilateral talks, it risks being left out of helping plan the major cross-national highways, now on the drawing board.

FOREIGN POLICY

Syria's traditional foreign policy has been to achieve ideological leadership of the Arab world. To a large extent, recent events have tempered this ambition, but Syria's stance remains ambiguous – it keeps a healthy dialogue going with the USA (Secretary of State Warren Christopher is a frequent visitor to Damascus); and restored ties with Europe (in November, 1994, the EU lifted an arms embargo which had lasted since 1986). In late 1995, it called for a new push for peace with Israel. But at the same time it is cultivating its links with Iran, a firm opponent of peace with Israel. Some see this policy as merely a counterweight to their mutual enemy, Iraq; others see it as a means of staving off Sunni fundamentalism within Syria.

Whatever the case, Western powers (in particular, the USA) are concerned about Damascus's connection with Teheran's nuclear arms potential. Even Arab states criticized Assad's 'anti-Arab' policy in the 1980s, of supporting Iran in its eight year-long war against an Arab state, Iraq. Syria's approach to Israel seems equally double-headed. At various stages, it has offered 'full peace' in exchange for the return of the Golan Heights; and then has criticized Israel for expansionism, and interference in Syrian affairs.

Analysts suggest that this apparent confusion in policy is really a ploy by Assad to keep power. He allows many parties to comment on policy – Vice President Khaddam, Defence Minister Tlas, Foreign Minister ash-Shar'a and military Chief of Staff Shihabi – but ultimately he controls it. Damascus-watchers often find themselves emulating an earlier generation of Kremlinologists, by trying to 'read between the lines'. They saw the lifting of travel restrictions on Syria's small Jewish community in April 1993 (enacted in February 1994) as one sign of impending peace; likewise with a *fatwa* from Syria's leading imam, calling for peace with the Jews.

But so far there is little tangible to show in terms of a deal. At the base of his approach, Assad seeks to balance his potential enemies. Hence his rapprochement with the Gulf states in 1993, and talks with Turkish leaders (Syria and Turkey have not resolved their dispute over the Latakia area in the north; furthermore, Turkey accuses Syria of harbouring rebel Kurds).

Ties between Syria and Egypt have improved, after they were cemented during the Gulf War. Both states know that their military prowess gives them leverage over oil-rich states, so political co-operation has long term benefits.

Even so, ties with moderate Egypt do not necessarily imply a softer Syrian stance. Since 1992, Syria has refused to participate in the regional multilateral talks. And in 1994 Damascus acted as host to the anti-Arafat Palestinian Alliance, which vows to fight the peace process with Israel. That same year Syria lambasted Jordan for its treaty with Israel, in particular, the 'leaseback' clauses which allow Israeli farmers to work on Jordanian territory. It is an open secret that Assad wanted Arafat replaced in the 1970s and 1980s. Syria openly backed *Amal* in its 'war of the camps' against the PLO in Lebanon; and it disputed the PLO's legitimacy to sign accords with Israel, before settling issues like Jerusalem, refugees and Jewish settlements. Relations with the official PLO remain cool, and have forced Arafat, somewhat ironically, to become closer to Israel and Jordan.

Syrian influence over Lebanon remains a centrepiece of its regional policy. Syria first entered the civil war in 1978 at the head of a supposedly united Arab force, to 'prevent' Israeli invasion. In fact, powerful circles in Syria have long considered Lebanon to be sovereign Syrian territory (as it was under the Ottoman Empire, before France encouraged the creation of a mainly Christian *Grande Liban*). In 1984 Syria forced the Gemayel government in Beirut to abrogate its year-old treaty with Israel. The Taif Accords of September 1989 effectively led to the end of the costly Lebanese civil war, but they also cemented Damascus' power over Lebanese foreign policy. In contravention of Taif, a large Syrian force of 35,000 soldiers remains in north-central Lebanon. Syria is believed to hold sway over *Hezbollah* in the south, who, also in contravention of Taif, have refused to disarm until Israel leaves its 'security zone'. As a potent reminder of Syria's authority, Lebanese politicians travelled to Damascus when a constitutional crisis erupted in 1995. Syria says its troops must stay until there is peace in the south (where Israel and the South Lebanon Army militia are fighting a low-level war against the Shi'ite *Hezbollah*). Meanwhile, Lebanon appears to follow Syria's commands in all dealings with Israel (for more details about this, see Chapter 12).

Assad is looking for a new role (perhaps in Lebanon) for his son and heir apparent, the apparently reluctant Bashar Assad. However, the established military intelligence officer, Gen. Ghazi Kenaan, seems well ensconsced outside Beirut. Significantly, Assad decided that Khaddam and Shihabi, both from the majority Sunni population, should lead the negotiations with Israel. The rationale is that, if they were to produce a peace deal, no-one could suggest that this was an Alawite capitulation.

How much power does Syria have in the region? According to the Damascus Declaration signed with Egypt after the 1991 Gulf War, Syria will protect weaker Gulf Arab states, in return for continued invesment in its economy. But the Declaration has not been fully enacted, partly because of residual Saudi fears of Damascus' regional ambitions. At the same time, most of the Gulf States and other Arabs say they will only sign a full peace with Israel, after Damascus has done so. Thus Assad enjoys considerable political leverage. There are limits to his writ, however, and this mainly stems from the collapse of his former chief sponsor, the Soviet Union. Indeed, this has led to a shortage of military supplies, especially spares; and the main successor state to the USSR, Russia, now wants its earlier loans repaid. In short, the Soviet collapse has meant Syria can no longer attain its dream of 'strategic parity' with Israel. It has to bide its time, improve ties with the USA, and perhaps sign a historic peace with Israel – yet on terms which make it appear like a Syrian moral triumph. In this regard, the unambiguous 'return of territory' (i.e. the Golan) will be a *sine qua non* for Syria, in the eyes of the rest of the Arab world. Syria's foreign policy, then, is a balancing act – it needs to keep ties with as many states as possible, and receive economic assistance, explain its new-found moderation to its former radical allies, and at all costs avoid being cast again as a 'terrorist state', and thus lose its access to US and European aid and investment.

THE QUESTION OF SUCCESSION

Assad's health has long been in doubt, and yet he always seems to recover from illness to reassert his authority. Even so, there is a question mark over who may succeed him. It is doubtful that the Alawite hierarchy can survive intact without his protection. But a greater role for Syria's Sunni majority may bring in its wake a neo-fundamentalist regime (the argument being that the Ba'ath has so successfully stifled opposition, that only the well-organized Muslim Brotherhood could offer an alternative power structure).

At present, the limited economic liberalization does not seem to have brought any significant new democratic freedoms in its wake. It now appears that the release of 4,000 political prisoners in 1992 was a false dawn. Recent Amnesty International reports criticized the poor human rights record which prevails in Syria. Assad still removes potential rivals whenever they appear too powerful. This happened in early 1993 when Gen. Ali Duba was replaced as head of military intelligence. (Duba had been depicted as a counterweight to Rifa'at Assad, but arguably had outlived his utility to the president, and furthermore embarrassed Assad in Western eyes, with his links to terrorist organizations.) For the present, Assad appears unassailable, as does the Ba'ath, which together with its affiliates commands a majority in the National Assembly. But Assad has made the party little more than an instrument of his political whims, so there is some doubt as to whether Syria has the political structures to survive unchanged after he dies.

Chapter 18   Lebanon

National statistics

Capital	Beirut
Official Languages	Arabic (French, Kurdish and Armenian also spoken)
Religions	Islam 57% (Sunni, Shi'ite and Druze)
	Christian 43% (mainly Maronite; smaller numbers of Greek Orthodox and Greek Chatholic, Armenian, Protestant and Syrian sects)
Land Area	10,452 sq km
Population	3,695,921 (July 1995 est.)
Armed Forces	44,300 (1994)
Currency	Lebanese Pound (L£)
Exchange Rate	US$1 = L£1647 (Dec. 31, 1994)
GDP — purchasing power parity	US$ 15.8 bn (1994 est.)
Unemployment	35% of workforce (1993 est.)
Balance of Payments	US$2.246 bn deficit (1990)
Foreign Debt	US$ 765 million (1994 est.)

[Figures from *Keesing's Record of World Events,* Reference Supplement 41, 1995]

Politics in Lebanon

Political leadership

President	Elias Hrawi
Prime Minister	Rafiq al-Hariri *
Deputy Prime Minister	Michel al-Murr
National Assembly Speaker	Nabih Berri
Cabinet	(as of May 25, 1995)
Foreign Affairs	Faris Buwayz
Defence	Muhsin Dallul
Interior	Michel al-Murr (also deputy PM)
Finance	Rafiq al-Hariri (also PM)
Culture and Higher Education	Michel Iddih
Expatriates	Ali al-Khalil
Refugee Affairs	Walid Jumblatt
Justice	Bahij Tabbarah
Health	Marwan Hammadah
Agriculture	Shawqi Fakhuri
Labour	As'ad Hardan
Water and Electricity	Elie Hobeika
Industry and Oil	Shahi Barsumian
Transport	Umar Misqawi
Tourism	Nicholas Fattush
Housing and Co-operatives	Mahmud Abu Hamdan
Municipal and Rural Affairs	Hagop Yarwan Demerdjian

Environment	Joseph Mughayzil *
Vocational Education	Abd al-Rahim Murad
National Education, Youth, Sports	Robert Ghanem
Information	Farid Makari
Social Affairs	Istifan al-Duwayhi
Post/ Telecommunications	Al-Fadl Chalaq *
Economy and Trade	Yassine Jaber
Public Works	Ali Harajli
Ministers of State	
Parliamentary Affairs	Nadim Salem
Administrative Reform Affairs	Anwar al-Khalil
Financial Affairs	Fu'ad Sinyurah
(Without Portfolio)	Qabalan Isa al-Khuri
(Without Portfolio)	Fayiz Shukur

*Joseph Mughayzil, the new environment minister, died four days after taking office. Al-Fadl Chalaq also heads the Council for Development and Reconstruction. Rafiq al-Hariri resigned on May 19, 1995, but was reappointed Prime Minister on May 21.

Lebanon became formally independent from France in 1944. According to a 'National Covenant' agreed the previous year, power was allocated between the various ethnic groups on the basis of their relative numbers in a 1932 census. By convention, the President would be Maronite Christian, the Prime Minister a Sunni Muslim, and the Speaker of the National Assembly, a Shi'ite Muslim. For some time Israel, Lebanon and Turkey were the only true multi-party democracies in the Middle East. However, from 1975 to 1990 a violent civil war disrupted parliamentary life in Lebanon. One of its causes was disagreement over the validity of using a clearly outdated census as a basis for dividing political patronage. (Since 1932, Muslims had overtaken Christians in number, but this was not officially reflected in Lebanon's political dispensation.)

According to the Syrian-sponsored Taif Accord, which prevailed after the war ended in 1990, the National Assembly increased in size to 128 members, this time divided equally between Muslims and Christians. While Lebanon maintained the convention of having a Christian President, Sunni Prime Minister and Shi'ite Speaker, presidential power was reduced at the expense of a strengthened prime minister and cabinet. Furthermore, the president would no longer be voted for by popular franchise, but instead would be elected by the National Assembly for a six-year term.

Before the civil war, there was a wide range of political parties, mostly based on ethnic affiliations. During the war, factions of these parties formed armed militias. In the post-war arena, the new rulers of Lebanon demanded that the militias disarm. As a result, political parties have re-emerged; but the hoped-for creation of intra-communal parties espousing national ideals has not materialized. Elections were held in three stages in 1992 (the first national polls in two decades). However, most Christian parties boycotted the polls, so Muslim (and particularly Shi'ite) factions enjoy disproportionate representation in the National Assembly. This is reflected in the greater real power wielded by the Shi'ite Speaker, Nabih Berri.

It has been said that in the absence of a real government, Prime Minister Rafiq Hariri presides over a coalition of forces, on an ad hoc basis; Nabih Berri, in turn, often acts like a Leader of the Opposition. Three other elements add to the picture of politics in today's Lebanon:

• Syria's role as guarantor of stability (a large Syrian 'peace-keeping' force is still stationed in Lebanon, and Syria maintains a measure of control over Lebanese foreign policy).

• A continuing war in the south between the Shi'ite *Hezbollah*, and a South Lebanon Army

(SLA). The SLA is headed by Christians, in particular Gen. Antoine Lahad, but also includes a number of Shi'ite footsoldiers. The SLA is and backed and armed by Israel, which itself still controls a 'security zone' along the border between the two countries. The zone constitutes 10% of Lebanon's surface area. *Hezbollah* and Israeli forces have clashed repeatedly in the 1990s.

- The presence of 350,000 Palestinians (equivalent to 10% of the total population). Most of them live in refugee camps, but hardly any have Lebanese nationality.

Governing party

There is no one party in government. However, after the 1992 elections two Shi'ite parties, *Amal* and *Hezbollah*, organized as the 'Faithful Resistance Bloc', managed to form the largest single coalition of deputies (largely because of the Christians' electoral boycott).

Amal	Leader: Nabih Berri
Hezbollah	Sec.-Gen.: Sheikh Hassan Nasrallah
	Spiritual head: Sheikh Allamah Mohammed Hussein Fadlallah

Other parties

Progressive Socialist Party (Druze)	Leader: Walid Jumblatt
Al-Kata'eb (Phalangist Maronite)	President: Georges Sa'adah
Bloc National (Maronite)	Leader: Raymond Edde
Parti Tachnag	(Armenian)
Ba'ath Party (Pan-Arab socialist)	Sec.-Gen.: Assem Qansou
Lebanese Communist Party	Sec.-Gen.: Faruq Dahruj
Syrian National Socialist Party	Leader: Dawoud Baz
National Liberal Party (Maronite)	Leader: Dory Chamoun
Marada (Maronite)	Leader: Sulayman Franjiyah
Al-Waad (Phalangist splinter)	Leader: Elie Hobeikah
Lebanese Forces	Leader: Samir Geagea
Al-Dustur (Constitutional Party)	

MAJOR POLITICAL FORCES

Christian

The pre-eminent Christian grouping is the Phalange, founded in 1936 by the Gemayel clan. Its initial aim was to preserve Lebanon, and especially the Maronite Christian community, from Syrian domination. The group enjoyed close ties with France, although since World War II, support from Paris grew more lukewarm because of the Phalange's fascistic tendencies. In later years the political wing of Phalange developed a right-wing militia known as the Lebanese Forces, or the *Kataeb*, which in April 1975 clashed with the PLO and other Muslim and leftist forces, and thus set off the civil war. The Phalange joined other Christian factions in a Lebanese Front in 1976. Syria intervened to stop the war, but has stayed in Lebanon until the present. The 1975 clashes grew into a full-scale civil war, which continued until 1990. At times, Syrians have made deals with elements within the Phalange.

In 1982 the Phalange mainstream welcomed Israel's invasion, as a counterweight to Syrian power. However, the Phalangists suffered a major setback with the assassination of their newly elected president, Bashir Gemayel. His death brought two immediate, yet far-reaching, consequences – the ascendance to the presidency of his younger brother, Amin, who was more pliable to Syria's whims, and less enthusiastic about a strategic pact with Israel; and the Sabra and Chatilla massacre, perpetrated by Elie Hobeikah's wing of the Phalange, under the eye of Israel, in revenge for Bashir Gemayel's death. During the course of the conflict, the once united movement split into different factions – the mainstream *Kataeb,* the pro-Syrian *Al-Waad,* and the dissident anti-Syrian Lebanese Forces (led by Samir Geagea, and banned at Syria's behest in 1994). Damascus capitalized on these divisions to entrench its authority over Lebanon.

The Phalange has thus lost its hegemony over Lebanon, and indeed its monopoly of Christian politics. In the civil war's final stages, the renegade Christian general, Michel Aoun, challenged the Christian Phalange élite by declaring himself president and leading an anti-Syrian campaign (which encompassed attacks on Phalange units). Although his surprisingly effective campaign ultimately failed, it did give Syria the pretext to end the war, with tacit US approval. Other Christian clans have enjoyed authority in their own regional fiefdoms, and often clashed with the Phalange. These include the traditionally pro-Syrian Franjiyahs, with their *Marada* militia; and the Chamouns, with their right-wing National Liberal Party. (At times, scions of these clans have held the presidency – Camille Chamoun from 1952 to 1958, and Suleiman Franjiyah from 1970 to 1976.)

Quite separately from the Phalange, another Christian-led grouping, the South Lebanon Army (SLA), emerged in the south after the first major Israeli incursion into Lebanon in 1978. When Israel withdrew, the SLA set up a 'buffer zone' under its dynamic founder, Maj. Sa'ad Haddad, a former officer of the regular Lebanese army. Following the second Israeli invasion in 1982, and the death of Haddad, Israel continued to give arms, funds and training to the SLA under its new leader, Antoine Lahad. By 1985 Israel had withdrawn from Beirut and other areas of central Lebanon, and returned to the buffer zone. Israeli and SLA forces have co-operated ever since in a simmering war with *Hezbollah.* The SLA (whose actual armed strength hovers between 5,000 and 10,000 soldiers) supports a non-sectarian pro-Western Lebanon, devoid of Syrian domination (according to some reports, most of its privates are actually local southern Shi'ites). For its part, Israel demands that the SLA be re-incorporated into the regular Lebanese Army as a precondition for making peace with Lebanon. But Beirut sees the SLA as an illegitimate force, Israel's 'proxy army', and refuses to negotiate with it. For the present, the stalemate persists, although there are reports of SLA fears that Israel may yet desert them after a Syrian–Israeli peace deal is signed. (The rationale is that once that happens, Syria will discipline *Hezbollah,* Lebanon will obediently make peace with Israel, and Israel will no longer need a security zone – in short, the SLA would have outlived its utility.)

Shi'ite

Two movements vie for power in the Shi'ite community – *Amal* and *Hezbollah.* The former group (which means 'hope' in Arabic, and is an acronym for 'Groups of the Lebanese Resistance') was founded by Imam Musa al-Sadr in 1974. It sought to represent the interests of the large but underprivileged and politically disorganized Shi'ite community of the south, and the Beqa'a Valley in the north. After Sadr disappeared (presumably killed) during a visit to Libya in 1978, *Amal* under Nabih Berri grew more militant and entered the civil war on the side of other Lebanese Muslims (Sunnis) and Druze forces. It also formed close ties with the PLO; but after the Israeli invasion of June 1982, it started to change sides. In 1983 *Amal* improved its links with Syria, and throughout the 1980s attacked PLO refugees (presumably with Syria's compliance). In 1984, Berri joined the cabinet, and in 1989 he went along with the Taif Accords. As Speaker of the National Assembly, Berri now enjoys considerable legitimate power.

The Israeli invasion also coincided with the formation of a new and more radical group, *Hezbollah,* which emerged from the ranks of *Amal.* From the start Sheikh Fadlallah has been its spiritual leader, although a succession of other *imams* have led it politically. *Hezbollah* is backed by Teheran, and looks to Iran as the model of an ideal Muslim theocratic state. It often co-operates with units of Iranian Revolutionary Guards, based in Ba'albek, in the northern Beqa'a Valley. *Hezbollah* vowed to oppose 'Western imperialism' in Lebanon, and this led it to execute the extremely damaging car-bomb suicide attacks on US and French bases. Operating through cover groups (Islamic *Jihad,* Islamic *Amal,* the Revolutionary Justice Organization, and others), *Hezbollah* kidnapped Westerners in Lebanon throughout the late 1980s, bringing it international condemnation.

It also vowed to fight the 'little Satan' (Israel). In the event, *Hezbollah* has proved to be a more lethal foe than the PLO, especially after Israel withdrew to its southern 'security zone'. Israeli redeployment left a power vacuum in southern and western Beirut, and the rest of the south, which *Hezbollah* units from the Beqa'a Valley soon moved to fill. In 1990 and again in 1993, there were bitter clashes between *Hezbollah* and *Amal* units. *Hezbollah* has built a network of support in Beirut and the south. Flushed with Iranian funds, it can afford to pay fighters well, and still provide (some may say 'bribe') local people with much needed medical and welfare provisions. From time to time, Israeli elite units have kidnapped *Hezbollah* leaders (such as Sheikh Obeid and Mustafa Dirani) and assassinated others (Sheikh Abbas Musawwi).

Nonetheless, *Hezbollah's katyusha* rocket attacks on northern Israel escalated after the Madrid peace conference. So in response, Rabin ordered Operation Accountability in July 1993. This armed venture, the largest since the June 1992 invasion, dislodged certain *Hezbollah* units and dispersed many thousands of Lebanese civilians. But it ultimately failed to prevent future *Hezbollah* attacks, nor did it force Syria to disarm the Iranian-backed militia. In fact, the *Hezbollah* trademark suicide bombing has been adopted by Palestinian fundamentalists, *Hamas* and Islamic *Jihad,* against Israeli citizens inside the 'green line'.

In 1995, Eyal Zisser of the Moshe Dayan Center for Middle East Studies at Tel Aviv University, argued that *Hezbollah* was transforming itself from an anti-Israeli militia, into a Shi'ite Muslim political party. As a 'pragmatic organization' it is more interested in survival than pursuing goals such as claiming Jerusalem. Zisser has hinted that *Hezbollah* may even be amenable to a negotiated agreement, which would allow Israel to live without a buffer zone in south Lebanon. It remains an open question as to how much of *Hezbollah's* support is genuine, and how much it is the result of fear.

Sunni

Lebanon's Sunni Muslims were incensed at the disproportionate influence of the Maronite minority in national politics, and left-wingers amongst them formed a National Front in 1969, which joined with Druze and PLO elements in later years. Some also organized themselves into militias, the most notable being *Al-Murabitun* (the armed wing of the Independent Nasserite Movement). In 1982 *Murabitun* members joined the *Tawhid Islami* (Islamic Unification Movement), based in Tripoli. However, by the mid-1980s the alliance with *Amal* (see above), PLO and the Druze had crumbled, and the *Murabitun* and *Tawhid* were effectively destroyed. Today, there appears to be no one strong Sunni party, although Sunni fortunes have revived through the person of the dynamic prime minister since 1992, Rafiq Hariri.

Druze

Lebanon's 200,000 strong Druze community constitutes 7% of the population, but it wields considerable power from its heartland in the Shouf Mountains in central Lebanon. There are also Druze minorities in neighbouring countries, Syria and Israel. Most Muslims do not regard them as part of the Islamic camp (the sect broke away from Ismaili Shi'ism in the 11th century, and has some peculiar practices). However, in political terms the Lebanese Druze have tended to side with Muslims (Shi'ite and Sunni) and leftists, against their traditional enemies, the Maronites. Lebanese Druze affairs are dominated by two rival clans, the Jumblatts and Arslans. For most of this century, the Jumblatts have enjoyed the upper hand. Kamal Jumblatt formed the Progressive Socialist Party (PSP) in 1949, which favours 'the constitutional road to socialism', but is really a vehicle for Druze interests. He also helped found the anti-Phalange National Front in 1969. In the early days of the civil war, Druze fought alongside PLO units. After Jumblatt's assassination in 1977, his son, Walid, succeeded him as *zaim* (feudal chieftain) and PSP president. He led the revolt against President Gemayel in 1983. With the end of the war, Jumblatt was appointed Minister of Public Works and

Transport in October 1990, but left the cabinet in 1991, only to rejoin it later as Minister of Refugee Affairs. The Druze appear to have shelved their earlier desire to form a self-governing fiefdom in central Lebanon.

Non-sectarian

The notion of non-sectarian politics is still something of a novelty in Lebanon, largely due to the divisive nature of the civil war, and the ethnic rivalry which led to it. Yet at the turn of the century, Beirut was known as the source of the Arab world's most progressive ideas, including Pan-Arabism which rejected the significance of division along the lines of religion. The three broad non-sectarian trends are: Pro-Syrian parties such as the Syrian National Socialist Party and the Ba'ath; socialist parties such as the Lebanese Communist Party and the *Al-Najjada*; and Liberal parties like the *Al-Dustur* and the Christian Social Democratic Party.

The Communists have the longest pedigree, having been founded in 1924; followed by the National Socialists (1932), *Al-Najjada* [the Helpers] (1936); *Al-Dustur* [Constitutional Party] (1943). Pro-Syrian parties enjoy disproportionate influence, but lack much autonomy as they usually defer to Damascus. The *Dustur* is probably the best-organized party, with strong support in the business community, but little clout in highly centralized government circles. Rafiq Hariri seems to prefer making appointments from his own circle of friends (who like him tend to be Lebanese expatriates who made their fortunes in the Gulf and elsewhere).

Palestinian

Lebanon also has 350,000 Palestinians, most of whom are refugees and Muslim by faith. From 1970 to 1982, the PLO's headquarters were in Beirut; and parts of southern Lebanon were even dubbed 'Fatahland' because of the PLO's strong military presence there. In retaliation for a Phalange massacre in 1975, the PLO attacked and besieged the Christian town of Damour in 1976, which caused many civilian deaths and exacerbated the civil war. At the time, Syria backed the PLO's actions. In July 1977, Syria, the PLO and the Lebanese government signed the Shtaura Agreement, which sought to 'regulate' the Palestinian camps; although in later years Syria and the Beirut government turned on the PLO. The Israeli invasion of 1982 ensured that most of the PLO leadership fled to Tunis; although PLO fighting units returned as Israel withdrew to its southern security zone. From 1985 to 1987 *Amal* forces, backed by Syria, fought a vicious 'war of the camps' with mainstream PLO forces. In July 1988, Abu Musa, head of the Syrian-backed *Fatah* Rebels, overran Arafat's last stronghold in Beirut.

Today, Palestinians make up fully 10% of the total national population, but their status is ambiguous to say the least. There are three main reasons for this: firstly, Lebanese regard Palestinians as temporary sojourners, waiting to return home; secondly Christian Lebanese fear they would tip the numerical balance towards the Muslim camp; and finally right-wing Lebanese blame them for inflaming the civil war, and drawing Israel into the conflict in the late 1970s and early 1980s.

Thus while most of the major PLO factions are represented in the Palestinian refugee camps, none is represented in the National Assembly. Their main focus is on their own communal affairs, and, increasingly of late, on reactions to the peace process with Israel. In late 1995 there were bitter gun battles between pro- and anti-Arafat forces within the majority *Fatah* group. In addition, certain factions (notably Ahmed Jibril's PFLP-GC) have participated in *Hezbollah* attacks on Israeli troops. But the old alliance of the Lebanese National Resistance (at times including the PLO, *Amal*, *Hezbollah* and other left-wing, Muslim and Druze forces) is no longer in force. Denied Lebanese nationality, and hence a voice in national political affairs, the Palestinians are experiencing enormous problems in safeguarding their interests as the Hariri government sets about 'rebuilding Lebanon' (see below).

Lebanon today

The largest immediate issues in Lebanon today are the restoration of the economy, and finding a solution to the conflict in the south. Over a longer term, Lebanon is committed to re-establishing a new sense of national identity after the ravages of a 16-year civil war.

Ultimately, that means overhauling the party system, which still bears the hallmarks of inter- and intra-ethnic conflict. All this must be done without offending Lebanon's 'protector', Syria, and the Lebanese government is tied to the terms of the Taif Accord (1989) and Brotherhood Treaty with Syria (1991). Direct Israeli–Lebanese bilateral talks broke down in February 1994, and it appears that Beirut is waiting for an Israeli–Syrian breakthrough before they are resumed. So apart from its domestic agenda, Lebanon has to come to terms with the desires of two regional superpowers, Syria and Israel.

ECONOMICS

Beirut was once known as the Paris of the Middle East, a commercial and cosmopolitan capital where Arab businessmen used to spend their vacations. But the civil war ruined the economy, and many of Lebanon's own financial élite had fled into exile. According to *Time* magazine, the war caused $25 billion in devastation, and cost 150,000 lives. While US and Arab humanitarian assistance kept an economy of sorts operating during the fighting, for the most part, central government did not function, and militias set up their own 'tax regimes' wherever they held power.

When Rafiq Hariri became Prime Minister in October 1992, inflation was running at 200%, and the Lebanese pound had declined by 60% in the first nine months of that year. In an unprecedented move, Hariri became Finance Minister at the same time. He had a considerable task on his hands, but as a self-made billionaire he felt he had the credentials to tackle all problems. Immediately, he set about winning $500 million in aid packages from Italy and Arab states, and negotiated for infrastructure repairs with the World Bank. His close links with Riyadh encouraged Saudi investors, who backed an initial $500 million development fund.

By March 1993, this had become the seed for the Council for Development and Reconstruction (CDR). The CDR unveiled its draft plan, Horizon 2000, which was scheduled to run from 1993 to 2002, and was costed at $13 billion (later recalculated at $18.4 billion). The Council began awarding contracts liberally, and building started on new transportation, sewerage, electricity and telephone networks. In addition, Hariri helped to set up Solidere, a nominally private company dedicated to redeveloping Beirut (in Project Elissa). It is chaired by Hariri's close ally, Nasser Chamaa. Solidere sold about $650 million's worth of shares in its first year, and is currently valued at $2.4 billion. Hariri had ignited a small boom, and the governor of the Banque du Liban estimated that annual growth would reach 10%. The 1994 national budget increased expenditure, but also managed to close the size of the budgetary deficit through larger revenues. More than a third of expenditure went on debt service. Although Lebanon still had a collosal trade deficit, this was more than covered by net transfers from abroad of some $6.5 billion.

Initial forecasts proved over-optimistic: only 10% of the initial funding for the CDR's long-term plans had arrived by the end of 1994. Likewise, funding was slow for a $120 million project to turn Beirut into the venue for the 1996 Arab Games. Repairs to electricity and telephone grids have taken longer than expected. Potential American investors are stymied by an eight-year ban forbidding US citizens to travel in Lebanon on their US passports. Other investors, from Europe and Asia, have been scared off by the still simmering conflict between *Hezbollah* and Israel in the south. Lebanon alleges that Israel has been siphoning off water from the Litani River in the south, and that this is impeding national economic reconstruction. And while inflation fell to 50% in 1994, the minimum wage remained frozen.

The Hariri government increasingly came under attack – from politicians who alleged corruption by his business partners, and from public sector unions which went on strike every month (industrial action had ultimately destroyed the government of Omar Karami in May, 1992). Many resented the growing independent power of the CDC, and accused Hariri of running the country 'like the head of a business'. In addition, while the boom has revived a small business élite, two-thirds of the population still live in poverty. Palestinians and West Beiruti Shi'ites claim that 'slum clearance' and 'squatter removal' schemes are destroying their communities. Nonetheless, by January 1996, Lebanon's annual inflation rate had fallen to 10%, and Beirut is now ready to host the Arab Games in its prestigious new stadium in July 1996.

Blessed with good beaches, scenic forests, and a rich archaeological past, Lebanon has enormous tourism potential. However, Lebanon is still not a member of the increasingly influential Mediterranean Tourism Association (MEMITTA), which includes Israeli, Jordanian, Palestinian, Egyptian and Turkish participants. As Lebanon refuses to take part in the multilateral regional talks (following Syria's example), it is effectively excluded from numerous international projects which could benefit the national economy. On the other hand, a number of Lebanese economists, notably Ghassan Ayache, former deputy governor of the Bank of Lebanon, have warned that Lebanon stands to lose its reputation as 'banker to the Arab world' if Israel is allowed free reign in the economic sphere. Israel's GDP is three times that of Lebanon, Syria and Jordan combined, and Lebanese businessmen still smart at what they perceived as Israel's 'dumping' of cheap goods on the fragile Lebanese market in the mid-1980s.

NATIONAL UNITY

The Christian boycott of the elections in 1992 undermined Lebanon's bid to restore national unity (although later by-elections saw some Christian deputies elected). In a reverse of the pre-war situation, Shi'ites were now over-represented in the National Assembly, at the expense of Maronites. Nonetheless, through the Christian-Sunni-Shi'ite triumvirate of Hrawi, Hariri and Berri, the public face of Lebanese politics once again reflects its diverse national origins. Professor Mounir Abou Assali, president of the Education Ministry's research centre, is currently devising a new history syllabus to encourage 'national healing'. Similarly, General Ali Harb, head of army education, has spearheaded the integration of military brigades.

Even so, sectarian conflicts periodically emerge, such as when, in May, 1994, Hariri went 'on strike' over his partners' interference in his choice of cabinet ministers. (Hariri, although himself Sunni, wanted more anti-Syrian Maronites in government). Hariri resigned and was reappointed twice (after Syrian mediation) in December 1994 and May 1995, following similar crises. Certainly, he did not improve matters by restricting press freedoms in 1994 (political pressures forced him to rescind this approach). Most recently, Hariri is trying to reduce Lebanon's 40 privately run television stations to just six. There was also much debate about the implications of political reform.

Within the Christian polity there has been a simmering battle for ascendancy, but it is nothing like the ferocious internecine conflicts of 1975–90. Even so, at Syria's behest the Lebanese government banned the Lebanese Forces in 1994, and sentenced its leader, Samir Geagea, to death in 1995 for assassination and bomb attacks on Maronite rivals (this was later commuted to imprisonment). Palestinians, as stated above, remain in refugee camps but do not participate in mainstream Lebanese politics. There are fears, nonetheless, that conflicts within the camps (between supporters and opponents of Arafat) may spill over once again and embroil the government. Perhaps to prevent this, Walid Jumblatt proposed resettling Palestinian squatters in 1994, although this aroused some controversy.

SECURITY

According to the Taif Accords, all militias were to disarm and allow their units to be dissolved within a new and truly national Lebanese Army. In practice, the disarmament drive was generally successful, and with Syrian help the army eventually managed to disarm even the most resistant Palestinian groups. But *Hezbollah* units were virtually untouched. Indeed, contemporaneously with the Madrid track peace talks, *Hezbollah* has escalated its attacks on Israelis (military and civilian, on both sides of the border). Israel considers that Lebanon and Syria are 'tolerating', and even inciting, *Hezbollah* attacks as a cynical negotiating ploy to force Israel to make peace on their terms.

Taif also stipulated the departure of foreign armed forces from Lebanon. This should by rights apply equally to Syrians, based near Beirut and the Beqa'a Valley; Israelis in the southern security zone; and the smaller units of Iranian Revolutionary Guards, also in the Beqa'a. Damascus and Beirut contend that until and unless Israel leaves the southern security zone, the 'Southern Resistance Forces' are justified to take 'defensive measures'. It remains to be seen whether those forces will indeed disarm, and peacefully integrate into the Lebanese Army, after an Israeli departure.

More successful have been the Lebanese army's own attempts to rebuild itself along non-sectarian lines. The army is still recovering from its virtual collapse in 1984, when Muslim and Druze units defected to the militias. There are also open wounds from the period 1988–90, when Gen. Aoun in effect turned the army into a Christian super-militia under his command. The army appeared to be impotent in the face of Israel's Operation Accountability in 1993. In 1995, UNIFIL agreed to extend its stay in Lebanon, in the light of troubles in the south.

Nonetheless, with some US assistance, Aoun's successor, Gen. Emile Lahoud, has managed to create a truly national army once again, and has increased its numbers from 30,000 in 1990 to 58,000 today. The continued presence of Syrian forces in Lebanon is a constant reminder of Damascus's enduring influence. Yet Lebanon has at least succeeded in ending the domination by militias and repeated kidnappings and assassinations which had eroded its independence for almost two decades. (*For more details on talks with Israel, see Chapter 12.*)

Figure 14 *Comparative population density*

The figures and chart below illustrate how Lebanon has the highest population density in the region. (Statistics from the *World Bank* book of 1994.)

Figures in terms of number of people per sq km

Egypt   42
Israel   184
Jordan   28
Lebanon   316
Syria   49

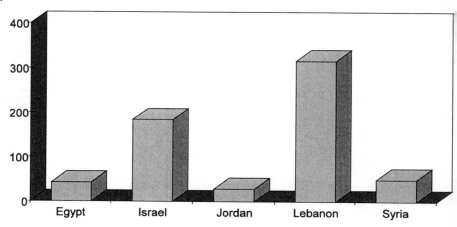

PART FOUR A

BIOGRAPHIES OF PRINCIPAL PARTICIPANTS

Guide to Biography Section

The Biography section is divided into two sections:
A.   The main section, which runs from A to Z.
B.   A listing of personalities grouped according to country

Within the first section, a few particularly important people have large entries, headed by a quick reference summary. Inclusion in this section was on the basis of each individual's contribution to, or opposition against, the peace process; the size of the entry broadly reflects the person's importance in this regard.

Only a few deceased people are listed, because the guide mainly concerns people who are likely to continue playing an important role in the current peace process. Subjects who are no longer alive have their names in italics.

The biography section, as far as is possible, uses a standard form of spelling for often recurring names. However, sometimes local differences mean that the accepted spelling applies (for instance, Gamal Abdul Nasser, and not Jamal).

Note: The biography section was largely completed before the suicide bombings in March, the conflict in Lebanon in April, and the Israeli elections in June.

A

Aas, Evn   Norway

Co-ordinator of the secret Israel–PLO talks at Borregard Manor, in Norway, which eventually led to the Oslo Accords. Aas was a junior official in the Norwegian Foreign Ministry, who also trained the Norwegian women's speed-skating team.

Abbadi, Abd as-Salam   Jordan

Minister of religious affairs, responsible for disbursing the *waqf*. Abbadi may put Jordan's case over Jerusalem's holy sites, when the issue comes up in the final status talks between Israel and the PLO.

Mahmoud Zaidan ABBAS (Abu Mazen)

Nationality	Palestinian
Religion	Muslim
Place of birth	Safad, Palestine
Date of birth	1935
Current position	Head of the PLO Department for National and International Relations since 1980; Head of the Central Election Commission during the campaign for the Palestinian Council elections in January 1996
Previous position	Member of the PNC and PLO Executive Committee; closely involved in the PLO's negotiating team at Oslo
Allies	Formerly close to Yasser Arafat; but in 1995 nurtured ties with anti-Arafat *Fatah* factions in the West Bank
Position on peace	Made contacts with Israeli peace camp when most in the PLO rejected links; key player in steering Oslo talks, but grew disenchanted with the subsequent Oslo Accords
National political importance	Possible bridge between internal and external *Fatah* supporters

Mahmoud Abbas (better known by his codename, Abu Mazen) was a founder member of *Fatah*. Since the early 1970s, he acted behind the scenes in encouraging the PLO to open secret channels to Israelis. He openly advocated negotiations with Israelis, at a time when such an approach was considered heretical. Unusually for PLO officials, Abu Mazen scoured Israeli newspapers to sense the political mood in the country, and wrote reports on his findings. In 1974 PLO officials uncovered a plot by Abu Nidal to murder him. In 1991 Abu Mazen gained responsibility for planning the PLO's negotiating strategy. Assessing that the Madrid talks were leading nowhere in particular, in October 1992 he approached Egyptian Foreign Minister Amr Moussa to arrange a meeting between Israel and the PLO, but Rabin felt this was premature.

In early 1993, he laid much of the groundwork for the secret Israel–PLO talks in Oslo, which eventually developed into the Declaration of Principles (DOP). Although based in Tunis, Abu Mazen was regarded as Arafat's 'eyes and ears' and kept in constant contact with the chief PLO negotiator, Abu 'Ala, in Oslo. Abu Mazen agreed to an Israeli request to defer the question of Jerusalem to 'final status talks', thereby removing a major obstacle at Oslo. And it was he who signed the DOP on behalf of the PLO in Washington, on Sept. 13, 1993. Crucially, Abu Mazen had persuaded an initially sceptical Arafat that the Oslo channel had the support of both Peres and Rabin.

However, after the signing of the DOP, Abu Mazen grew disenchanted with the peace process. He felt Arafat had betrayed some of the commitments which the PLO had made in the secret talks. In particular, he felt Arafat should have demanded that Israel release PLO prisoners immediately. Nonetheless, Abu Mazen headed a delegation to the first Israel–PLO liaison committee on Oct. 14, 1993, and held discussions about the implementation of the accord with Shimon Peres. Subsequently, Nabil Sha'ath, Palestinian co-head of the joint Israel–PLO technical committee, began to enjoy a higher profile at Abu Mazen's expense. Abu

Mazen was also embarrassed when it was rumoured that *Mossad* had planted a spy, Adnan Yassin, in his Tunis office.

Abu Mazen only returned to Palestinian territory on July 14, 1995, when he arrived in Gaza from Egypt after 48 years in exile. He soon established a political bureau in Ramallah, on the West Bank, in 1995; and made useful contacts with local *Fatah intifada* activists who felt excluded from the peace process. Abu Mazen espoused the ideology of Salah Khalaf (Abu Iyad), Arafat's number two, who was murdered in 1991. It was rumoured that Abu Mazen might set up an opposition front to Arafat, possibly to contest the 1996 Palestine Council elections, but in fact Arafat turned this potential poacher into a game-keeper, by making him head of the nominally independent Central Elections Commission. Abu Mazen went on to win one of the two seats reserved for Qalqilyah in the Jan. 20 elections. Wily political survivor that he is, he has created a bridge between his new 'internal' friends, and his older constituency among Diaspora Palestinians. Throughout 1995 Abu Mazen held secret talks with Yossi Beilin; on May 4, 1996, he led the PLO delegation at the first session of "final status talks".

Abbas, Muhammad Abul
(See Abul Abbas)

Abd al-Shafi, Haidar
(See Shafi, Haidar Abd al-)

Abd-Rabbuh, Yasser
(See Abed-Rabbo, Yasser)

Abdallah, Samir
(See Abdullah, Samir)

Abdel-Meguid, Ahmed Esmat   Egypt

Former Foreign Minister and Deputy Prime Minister of Egypt; currently Secretary-General of the Arab League. A cautious and skilful diplomat, Abdel-Meguid, more than any other politician, can take the credit for reintegrating Egypt back into the Arab fold, after it was ostracized following the Camp David treaty with Israel.

He was born in 1923, and trained as a lawyer. From 1950 to 1954, he served as an attaché in the Egyptian Embassy in London. On his return to a new Egypt, headed by Gamal Abdul Nasser and the Free Officers, Abdel-Meguid was put in charge of the 'UK desk' at the Foreign Ministry. Over the next two decades he enjoyed a number of diplomatic appointments, including ambassador to France and, from 1972 to 1982, ambassador to the United Nations. In 1984 he became Egypt's Foreign Minister, and the next year he was made Deputy Prime Minister. For President Mubarak, Abdel-Meguid represented a useful civilian counterweight to his fellow deputy prime minister, Field Marshal Mohammed Abdel-Hakim Abu Ghazala. Abdel-Meguid loyally carried out the terms of Egypt's treaty with Israel, but ensured that it was something of a 'cold peace'. He joined other Arab leaders in castigating Israel's handling of the Palestinian *intifada*.

Abdel-Meguid helped to ensure that Egypt was re-admitted to the Arab League in May 1989, fully ten years after it was expelled. He retired as Foreign Minister to become the League's Secretary-General in May 1991, thus re-establishing the tradition of having an Egyptian as head of the organization (as had been the case from 1945 to 1979), and restoring the League's headquarters to Cairo. During his term in office, Abdel-Meguid rallied Arab nations in the war against Iraq in 1991, despite popular opposition 'on the street'. He was reported to have encouraged Pakistan to recognize Israel in late 1992, as most Arab states were about to do so. In 1995, he noted a voice of dissent by warning Arab states not to rush headlong into economic alliances with Israel. Abdel-Meguid fears that Israel's strong economy, in cahoots with its US ally, may dominate the region, and erode existing inter-Arab institutions, not least the Arab League itself. On other occasions he has called for unity with Israel in the battle against fundamentalism. Abdel-Meguid's five-year term as Secretary-General officially expires in May 1996, but he may be called on to continue for another term.

Abdul Hadi, Mahdi   Palestinian

East Jerusalem academic, and director of PASSIA (the Palestinian Academic Society for the Study of International Affairs). Abdul Hadi comes from an infuential Nablus family, and is regarded as an important opinion-former within what he calls 'the Palestinian house'. Together with Faisal al-Husseini, he favours shared Palestinian–Israeli sovereignty over Jerusalem. To this end, they set up the Jerusalem National Council-Palestine in November 1993, with its headquarters at Orient House. Abdul Hadi says the long-term goal is to extend the political influence of 'the temporary Palestinian government' to Jerusalem; although in the immediate term he favours a lower profile, so as not to antagonize Israeli opinion. He feels that the *intifada* and Oslo Accords gave Palestinians the confidence to formulate a concrete response to Israeli policy, a confidence which they lacked in the aftermath of the June 1967 war. Abdul Hadi will probably be a key figure in final status talks on Jerusalem's future, due to start in 1996.

Abdullah ibn Aziz ibn Saud   Saudi Arabia

Crown Prince of Saudi Arabia; effective ruler of the Kingdom since January 1996. Prince Abdullah has officially been the Kingdom's Crown Prince and Deputy Prime Minister since June 1982. He has also been the Commander of the Saudi National Guard since 1963. Abdullah was born in Riyadh in 1924 and received formal education from religious scholars and intellectuals.

In February 1996, Prince Abdullah hosted Jordan's King Hussein for the first time since the Gulf War of 1991 had strained relations between the two royal states. (Saudi Arabia had accused Jordan of appeasing Saddam Hussein, a charge which King Hussein has always rejected.) Prince Abdullah is known to be cooler towards the USA than King Fahd. This might mean greater Saudi caution over endorsing the peace process with Israel, just when it had appeared relations between Riyadh and Jerusalem were beginning to thaw under King Fahd.

Abdullah, Samir   Palestinian

Economic Director of PECDAR. Born in 1950, Samir Abdullah became Chair of the Department of Economics at an-Najah University, Nablus. He is associated with the Communist Party (now Palestinian People's Party), and during the *intifada* he was a well-known figure in the *shakhsiyat* (academics and professionals who articulated the demands of the uprising). In 1991 he joined the official Palestinian delegation to the Madrid peace talks, but was soon disenchanted with the lack of progress made. As economic director of PECDAR, Abdullah has significant influence over the future economic shape of the Palestinian areas. He also brings a Marxist, and 'internal' Palestinian perspective to economic matters, by contrast with the private enterprise leanings and 'external leadership' viewpoints of PECDAR's effective director, Abu 'Ala. Samir Abdullah has identified mass unemployment as Palestinians' top priority problem, and hopes to generate labour-intensive public works to solve it.

Abdurrahman, Umar

(See Rahman, Omar Abd-al)

Abed-Rabbo, Yasser   Palestinian

Head of *Fida*, the Palestinian Democratic Union (a breakaway from the Democratic Front for the Liberation of Palestine, DFLP); Minister of Culture and Arts in the Palestine National Authority (PNA) since 1994. Yasser Abed-Rabbo was born in Jaffa in 1944, and became a leading figure amongst younger Palestinian activists in the early 1970s. Although his roots lie in the Marxist wing of the PLO, and specifically in Maoism, he soon won a reputation as a pragmatist who was willing to compromise in order to achieve peace with Israel. In August 1973, he first proposed establishing a mini-state in the West Bank, rather than claiming all of 'historic Palestine'. Abed-Rabbo is widely credited with persuading Yasser Arafat to adopt the 'two-state' resolution, incorporated in the PLO's Algiers Declaration in 1988, which *inter alia* also recognized Israel and renounced the use of terror as a political tool.

He served as deputy secretary-general to the Marxist DFLP leader, Naif Hawatmeh, and was appointed head of information on the PLO executive committee in 1977. On Dec. 6, 1989,

Abed-Rabbo headed the first official PLO negotiations with the US government, which began in Tunis. A new 'young democrat' faction within the DFLP tried to install Abed-Rabbo as the front's leader, in place of Hawatmeh. The bid failed, and on April 5, 1991, he was expelled from the DFLP politburo. Abed-Rabbo promptly formed a new group, *Fida*, and remained a close aide to Chairman Arafat. He played an important role in persuading the PLO to back a Palestinian delegation to the Madrid conference in 1991. In 1993 he became involved (albeit somewhat inadvertently) with the secret Oslo negotiations between the PLO and Israel. Abed-Rabbo was one of only four PLO executive committee members in the PNA cabinet. Since 1993, *Fida* has largely eclipsed the DFLP among younger West Bank activists, such as Jamal Zakut and Zahira Kamel. However, although Abed-Rabbo won a seat in Tulkarm in the Palestine Council elections of 1996, *Fida's* overall poor showing suggested that it is still limited to an intellectual élite. In March 1996, Abed-Rabbo led Palestinian calls on Israel to suspend the closure of the territories (which followed *Hamas* bomb attacks in Jerusalem and Tel Aviv).

Abideen, Abdel-Qadir (Sheikh)   Palestinian

Appointed by Jordan as the Mufti of Jerusalem, after the death of Sheikh Sulaiman al-Jabari in October 1994. Immediately, the Palestine National Authority announced their candidate, Sheikh Akram Said Sabri, as the true mufti. Since then, the two *imams* have held separate offices. While most Palestinians seem to favour Sheikh Sabri, Sheikh Abideen still enjoys the financial backing of Jordan.

Abu Adib
(See Za'anoun, Salim)

Abu 'Ala
(See Qurei, Ahmed)

Abu al-Mundhir
(See Qirsh, Subhi Abu)

Abu Ammar
(See Arafat, Yasser)

Abu as-Said
(See Hassan, Khalid al-)

Abu Ayyash
(See Ayyash, Radwan Abu)

Abu Bakr, Tewfiq   Palestinian

Head of Democratic Forum, PLO independents critical of the organization's stance during the Gulf War.

Abu Ghazala, Mohammed Abdel-Hakim   Egypt

Assistant President of Egypt, and a rival to President Mubarak. Born in 1930, Abu Ghazala received military training in the USA and served in all of Egypt's wars against Israel, eventually rising to the supreme rank of Field Marshal. He was Egypt's defence attaché in Washington from 1976 to 1980. On his return to Egypt, Abu Ghazala was appointed Chief of Staff in 1980, and Defence Minister in March 1981. President Sadat valued his contacts with US powerbrokers, and valued too his link with the Egyptian military. In October 1981, Abu Ghazala was wounded when assassins shot and killed Sadat at a military parade.

The new president, Hosni Mubarak, awarded him the additional post of deputy prime minister in 1982. Abu Ghazala improved Egypt's defence capabilities with US aid, and increased the role of the military in the economy. Abu Ghazala's status rose but implication in an arms smuggling scandal gave Mubarak a pretext to demote him. In August 1989, he was made 'assistant to the President', but lost his defence portfolio. In 1990 Abu Ghazala was put in charge of co-ordinating Egypt's controversial privatization programme. Abu Ghazala deserves much of the credit for reviving Egypt's regional military strength, and putting it at the disposal of the Gulf States in the post-war dispensation.

Abu Iyad
(See Khalaf, Salah)

Abu Jaber, Kamal
(See Jaber, Kamal Abu)

Abu Jihad
(See Wazir, Khalil al-)

Abu Libdeh
(See Libdeh, Hasan Abu)

Abu Lutf
(See Qaddumi, Farouk)

Abu Marzak, Musa   **Palestinian**
(See Marzouk, Musa Muhammed Abu)

Abu Mazen
(See Abbas, Mahmoud Zaidan)

Abu Musa
(See Muragha, Sa'id Musa)

Abu Nidal
(See Banna, Sabri al-)

Abu Samer
(See Labadi, Mohammed)

Abu Tayeb
(See Natur, Muhammad)

Abu Za'im
(See Attala, Attala Muhammad)

Abu Zaideh
(See Zaideh, Sufyan Abu)

Abul Abbas, Muhammad   **Palestinian**

Head of Palestinian Liberation Front, mastermind of *Achille Lauro* ocean-liner hijacking, in October 1985. He was a member of the PLO executive committee when another PLF terror act took place, an attack from the sea on Tel Aviv. This prompted the USA to suspend talks with the PLO. He resigned from the committee in September 1991, after the Palestine National Council voted 256 to 58 to support Palestinian participation in the Madrid peace process. The Abul Abbas wing of the PLF is nominally still allied with the PLO, and in the past had good links with *Fatah*; but a rival faction under Talal Yaqub belongs to the rejectionist Alliance of Palestinian Forces (set up in 1994 in protest at the Oslo Accords). Abul Abbas returned to Gaza to join the PNC debate on the Charter in April 1996.

Abul Razak, Hisham   Palestinian

Main spokesperson for Israeli–held Palestinian prisoners in 1995. He led a hunger strike in protest at Israel's unwillingness to release prisoners. This action put pressure on the PNA to demand a response from Israel, before talks on the terms of Oslo 2 could proceed. Abul Razak (alternatively rendered as Abd ar-Razzak) was officially designated the head of the PNA's Prisoners Committee. He liaised with Abdul Qader Hamed, the head of the Released Prisoners' Committee.

Abyad, Darwish   Palestinian

Director, Palestine National Fund (PNF). He took over from Muhammad Zuhdi an-Nashashibi when the latter became PNA Finance Minister in 1994. Abyad administers assets which were once estimated at $5 billion, but which have since been whittled away by declining funding from Arab states, and the need to pay out millions to the new PNA bureaucratic infrastructure. As the PNA finds its feet, and develops its own ability to generate income through taxation, the PNF is expected to shift its emphasis to aid for Palestinian diaspora communities.

Agazarian, Albert   Palestinian

PR officer, Palestinian delegation in Madrid. Agazarian is a Palestinian of Armenian origin, who ran public relations for Bir Zeit University, and acted as a linkman for the media during the *intifada*. He is close to Hanan Ashrawi.

Agha, Zakaria al-   Palestinian

PNA Minister of Housing. Agha was born in Khan Yunis in the Gaza Strip, in 1942. He trained and worked as a physician, was the Chairman of the Gazan Medical Society, and also helps to manage Gaza's private Al-Ahli Hospital. He was a delegate to the Madrid peace conference and subsequent Washington peace talks. Yasser Arafat appointed Agha to head *Fatah* in the Gaza Strip in 1994. Since then, he has succeeded in regaining much of the ground which *Fatah* lost to *Hamas* during the *intifada*. In January 1996 he stood but failed to win a seat in the Palestinian elections.

Ahmed, Abd al-Aziz al-Hajj   Palestinian

PNA Minister of Transportation. A *Fatah* activist and former deportee, Ahmed, now 52, is also the head of the Dentists' Union in Ramallah. During his 18 months in office, Ahmed tried to build up the infrastructure of Palestinian self-rule areas. He negotiated with Egypt about creating new links to Gaza; and lobbied Israel to build a corridor connecting Gaza with the West Bank (as suggested in the Oslo 1 Accords).

Aker, Mamdouh al-   Palestinian

Co-founder (with Hanan Ashrawi) of the Palestinian Independent Commission for Citizens' Rights in 1994. Aker was born in 1943 and works in Ramallah as a urologist. He was a member of the Movement for the Liberation of Palestine. In 1988 Israeli officials accused Aker of belonging to the secret Unified National Command of the *intifada*, and of writing their leaflets. He was detained without charge and placed in solitary confinement for six months. Aker later became a Palestinian delegate in Madrid, and participated in the Washington talks which followed. By 1992, he was the head of a special sub-committee dealing with human rights issues in the talks. Elyakim Rubinstein was his Israeli opposite number. Aker was disillusioned by the Oslo Accords and dropped out of the negotiation process.

Alaf, Muwafak   Syria

Chief Syrian negotiator with Israel (counterpart to Itamar Rabinovitch). Muwafak Alaf was born in 1927 and studied law at the Syrian University of Damascus. From 1950 to 1952 he worked as the commercial attaché in Syria's embassies in Saudi Arabia and Egypt. He served as Foreign Minister from 1960 to 1968, coinciding with the Six Day War of 1967, when Syria was driven off the Golan Heights by Israeli forces. From 1968 to 1974, and again from 1975 to 1978, Alaf was Syria's permanent representative at the United Nations. (In between those postings, he was the director of the department for international organizations, within the Syrian Foreign Ministry.) Throughout the 1970s, President Assad entrusted Alaf with representing Syria at numerous international conferences (UN, trade unions, and the Islamic Conference Organization, amongst others). Alaf also served as a member of the UN Committee on 'the question of defining aggression'.

Muwafak Alaf was recalled from diplomatic retirement to head the talks with Israel throughout 1992 (as part of the Madrid peace process). He was the only non-*Ba'athist* member of the Syrian team, and negotiated together with Syria's Ambassador to Washington, Walid Mualem. In August 1992 Prof. Itamar Rabinovich replaced Yossi Ben Aharon as Alaf's opposite number, and the two men made more progress. However, the twin factors of concern over the Golan in Israel, and the Israel-PLO breakthrough of September 1993, diverted attention from the Syrian talks. Alaf, Mualem and Rabinovich nonetheless achieved their own breakthrough on questions of format in late 1994, and recommended that their respective governments open at military Chief of Staff level. With US support, this happened; but paradoxically the diplomats' very success rendered their role comparitively less important. With the revival of more comprehensive talks in late 1995, Alaf hoped to play a greater role in the unfolding Syrian–Israeli peace process (but Mualem was entrusted with more authority). Alaf subsequently became the number two official in the Arab League.

Alami, Maher al-   Palestinian

Editor of *Al-Quds* (Jerusalem), a leading Palestinian newspaper with occasionally dissident views. In a controversial event on the eve of the January 1996 Palestinian Council elections, Yasser Arafat had Alami detained for not giving greater prominence in his paper to an article about Arafat. Alami also clashed with Jibril Rajoub, the head of the Preventive Security Services in Jericho, and later in the West Bank. The Alami family is a powerful noble clan; some members sold land to Jews in the 1930s, and served as high officials in the Mandatory Palestine; others helped to create *Fatah* in the 1950s.

Alami, Sa'ad al-Din al-   Palestinian

Sheikh Alami was Mufti of Jerusalem until his death in early 1993. During his long term in office, Sheikh Alami, scion of a famous Palestinian family of 'notables', was forced to fight on two fronts – against Israeli government actions, which he said were encroaching on Arab land, and 'Judaizing' the city; and against fellow Palestinians, who felt that the PLO and not Amman should preside over religious affairs in the Holy City, Al-Quds (Jerusalem).

Alawi, Yusuf bin   Oman

Omani Minister for Foreign Affairs since 1982. Yusuf Bin Alawi has taken the lead in opening Gulf Arab states' relations with Israel, and also played a key role in ending the secondary and tertiary Arab boycott of the Jewish state. Born in Salalah, Oman, in 1945, Bin Alawi was educated in England, and from the early 1970s he distinguished himself, first as a member of an Omani council mission to Arab capitals, later as a consul in Egypt and Lebanon, and finally as Ambassador to Lebanon. In 1974 Sultan Qaboos appointed him Under-Secretary in the Ministry of Foreign Affairs; and in 1982, he became Minister of Foreign Affairs, a post he has held to this day.

In April 1994, Bin Alawi welcomed the then Israeli Deputy Foreign Minister Yossi Beilin, who was visiting Oman to attend the fourth session meeting of the multilateral talks water working group. This was the first ever official visit by an Israeli minister to Gulf Arab state. Beilin and Bin Alawi formed a firm relationship, and discussed plans for an ambitious desalination plant in Muscat. Bin Alawi offered Beilin a personal invitation to return, which he did in November 1994. This meeting proved to be a trailblazer for Yitzhak Rabin's own historic visit there in December. On Nov. 5, Bin Alawi flew to Jerusalem to attend Rabin's funeral. As such, he and his Qatari counterpart were the first Gulf politicians to pay a state visit to Jerusalem.

In early December, Bin Alawi announced that Israel and Oman were to open economic missions in Muscat and Tel Aviv respectively in January, 1996. This would be the first Israeli diplomatic mission in the Persian Gulf.

Albright, Madeline Korbel   USA

US Permanent Representative to the United Nations under the Clinton Administration. Madeline Albright was born on May 15, 1937, the daughter of a Czech diplomat of Jewish origin. She arrived in the USA when she was 11, after Communists took power in her native land. Albright is an educator by training, having studied at Wellesley College, and attaining a doctorate from Columbia University in 1976. She worked for two years as an assistant to the liberal Democrat US Senator Edmund Muskie, and then was a staff member of the National Security Council, from 1978 to 1981. From 1982 to 1992 she was Professor of International

Affairs at Georgetown University's School of Foreign Service, and established herself as an expert on Eastern Europe and the former Soviet Union. During her last four years as a professor, she also doubled as President of the Centre for National Policy. Albright acted as foreign policy adviser to the Democrat Party presidential campaigns of 1984, 1988 and 1992.

Her linguistic talents, breadth of experience, patience and ability to reach consensus all commended her for the UN post, which holds cabinet rank in the USA. As the first foreign-born US Permanent Representative, Albright has pursued Washington's traditional support for Israel, often siding with Israel as its only ally in voting against critical UN resolutions. At the same time, she has worked tirelessly behind the scenes, brokering better relations between Israel and its former enemies in the Arab world. In May 1995, Albright led the one-month long conference on the Nuclear Non-Proliferation Treaty (NPT). Despite Egyptian pressure to single out Israel for 'non-compliance', she arrived at a compromise that was acceptable to all sides, and extended the NPT's regime indefinitely. Later, she vetoed a Security Council resolution which condemned Israel's expropriation of land in East Jerusalem, but nonetheless criticized the Israeli action on political grounds.

Shulamit ALONI

Nationality	Israeli
Religion	Jewish
Place of birth	Tel Aviv, Palestine
Date of birth	1929
Current position	Minister of Communications, Science and Technology (1993–96)
	Leader of *Meretz* coalition in Labour-led government until early 1996
Previous position	Minister of Education and Culture (1992–93)
	Founded Citizens' Rights Movement (*Ratz*) in 1973
	Active member of Peace Now
Allies	Amnon Rubinstein, ties with Hanan Ashrawi
Position on peace	Very positive, supports an ultimate Palestinian mini-state
National political importance	Big in left niche; self-styled voice of conscience; foe of orthodoxy, best known campaigner for women's rights
Prospects	If peace is resolved, may gain more national power as womens' advocate

Shulamit Aloni was without a doubt the leading woman politician in Israel, and probably the most influential member of the Peace Now lobby. But her decision to step down as leader of *Meretz*, and possibly to leave politics altogether, announced in January 1996, was interpreted as an admission of her ultimate failure to get her left-wing agenda adopted by the current government.

Born in Tel Aviv in 1929, Aloni was a teacher, lawyer and journalist before entering politics. She joined *Mapai* (which became the main constituent in the Labour Alignment) in 1959 and served as a Labour MK between 1965 and 1969. In 1973 she broke ranks with Labour by opposing its 'Galili Protocols', which facilitated increased Jewish settlement in the occupied territories. She duly formed the breakaway Citizens' Rights Movement (better known by its Hebrew acronym, *Ratz*). The new party advocated electoral reform, separation of religion and state, and a Basic Law protecting human rights. Aloni soon became the *bête noire* of the Orthodox right, and also a champion for the rights of liberated women in Israel. Indeed, Aloni can be seen as the first of a new breed of left-wing Zionists – not raised in the macho environment of the military, nor the old-style socialism of the *kibbutz* movement, she represented a new agenda of women's rights, personal freedoms, intra-communal co-existence, and consumer and environmental issues.

As *Ratz* leader, Aloni has been a Member of the Knesset continuously since 1974. From June to October 1974, she was a minister without portfolio. Outside the *Knesset*, Aloni has been a leader of the Peace Now pressure group, which advocated Israeli withdrawal from the territories, and a lasting peace with Palestinians. Her strong opposition to Israel's invasion of Lebanon in June 1992 gave her a new national platform, especially after the Sabra and

Chatilla massacre (together with Yossi Sarid, she was a lone voice within Labour-affiliated parties in rejecting the extent of the war, even before the massacre in September). Since the outbreak of the Palestinian *intifada*, Aloni appeared on several platforms with Palestinian figures, notably a fellow feminist, Hanan Ashrawi.

In the run-up to the 1992 elections, Aloni helped fashion a new grouping, *Meretz* – a combined list of leftist Zionist parties, namely *Ratz,* the older *Mapam* (United Workers' Party) and *Shinui* (Centre Party). *Meretz* benefited from a national wave against the ruling *Likud,* and by gaining a combined total of 12 seats, it became the third largest party (after Labour and *Likud*). *Meretz* accepted an invitation to join the new coalition government led by Labour under Yitzhak Rabin.

Aloni's first portfolio was as Education and Culture Minister, which she took over from the outgoing Zevulun Hammer, leader of the National Religious Party. However, it was not long before she faced vigorous opposition from her coalition partners in the ultra-orthodox Sephardi *Shas* party, who objected to her strongly secular plans for revising the national syllabus. To prevent a total rift, in May 1993, Yitzhak Rabin moved Aloni from the Education Ministry to her current position as Minister of Communications, Science and Technology.

Despite (or perhaps because of) her peace credentials, Aloni has been largely excluded from the minutiae of the peace process. Even so, while Labour 'securocrats' dominated the negotiations, Aloni and her colleagues acted as a 'voice of conscience' for the Israeli left. Many of her statements make up in frankness what they lack in discretion. Aloni continues to monitor human rights abuses (both by Israel and the new Palestinian Authority under Yasser Arafat). In January 1996, Yossi Sarid displaced Aloni as leader of *Meretz*. It was the culmination of long-simmering rivalry between the two figures.

Aloul, Mahmoud al-   Palestinian

Palestinian Governor of Nablus since December 12, 1995. Mahmoud Aloul was born in the town, which is the largest in the West Bank, with a current population of 130,000. After the Israeli conquest of the West Bank in June 1967, he became a leading activist and was jailed for four years. He was deported on his release in 1971. In October 1995, he returned to Nablus in readiness to take over the district according to the terms of the Israel–PLO Interim Agreement (Oslo 2). In the interim, Aloul had helped to organize the *intifada* in Nablus from abroad. Aloul promised the Israeli head of Central Command, Maj.-Gen. Ilan Biran, that he would place a priority on law and order, and could guarantee the safety of Jewish worshippers at the Tomb of Joseph in Nablus. It remains to be seen how he will deal with a renegade faction of young *Fatah* activists, led by Husam Khader, in the Balata refugee camp, south of Nablus.

Alpher, Joseph   Israel

Former Director of the Jaffee Centre for Strategic Studies, Tel Aviv University; currently Director of the American Jewish Committee's Israel and Middle East office. Alpher is noted for his caution, and has queried Syria's sincerity about making peace. His early 1995 plan for annexing part (11%) of West Bank, and returning the rest to Palestinians, found favour with many left-wing Labour politicians, including Yossi Beilin. In a sense, it revives the principles of the original Alon Plan of 1967, but addresses contemporary concerns (not least, the reality of Israeli settlements, and a new embryonic Palestinian state apparatus). Many aspects of the Alpher Plan map appear in the Interim Agreement, or Oslo 2, which was signed by Israel and the PLO in September 1995. However, Alpher criticized the Oslo 2 on several grounds. It was conceptually flawed, he said, because it returned territory to Palestinians, but also retained the settlements which were set up to prevent just such a scenario. Oslo 2 also restricted Israel's options in the final status talks – Palestinians who gained 'autonomy' (via voting rights) in Zones B and C, were unlikely to accept Israeli annexation of these areas later on. Finally, he felt that Israel's negotiators had very unclear guidelines from the government.

Amir, Yigal   Israel

A law student at Bar Ilan University, 27-year-old Yigal Amir assassinated Prime Minister Yitzhak Rabin on Nov. 4, 1995, at the end of a huge peace rally in Kikar Malchei Yisrael (Kings of Israel Square), Tel Aviv. Although he claimed that he had acted alone, 'perhaps with the help of God', it later emerged that he was affiliated with, if not a member of, the far-right

Jewish opposition group, *Eyal*. Apparently Amir had tried to attack Rabin on two previous occasions, but had been thwarted by security officers.

Amir claimed his action was meant to end the peace process, which was handing over the Land of Israel to Arabs, and was preparing the foundations for a Palestinian state. Claiming justification in the *halakha* (Jewish religious law), Amir, a long-time scholar of religion, said that during war one was permitted to kill any enemy. Other orthodox Jews (including both of Israel's Chief Rabbis, and Yigal's own father, Rabbi Shlomo Amir) said this was a flagrant misinterpretation of the holy texts.

Amir's first hearing took place in December 1995, and his trial reconvened on Jan. 22, 1996. While most Israelis were united in grief and condemnation of the Rabin murder, a small minority saw Amir as a hero, alongside such other 'martyrs for *Eretz Yisrael*' as Rabbi Meir Kahane, leader of *Kach*, and Baruch Goldstein, who caused the Hebron massacre in 1994.

Amirav, Moshe   Israel

Former *Likud* MK turned peace activist, particularly regarding Jerusalem. Moshe Amirav was born in the USSR in 1945, arrived in Israel in 1949, and studied at the Hebrew University, Jerusalem, and New York University. He was a leader in the right-wing *Beitar* youth movement, and in adult life was close to Yitzhak Shamir. However, his experiences in the Lebanon War, and discussions, caused him to accept territorial compromise, if it meant 'peace for his children and Palestinians'. With apparent approval from the *Likud* leadership, Amirav met Faisal al-Husseini for talks on a solution to the *intifada*, and a possible autonomy plan. Aspects of the plan emerged in PLO publications. However, evidently under pressure from hawks, Shamir censured Amirav for these 'illegal negotiations', and he was expelled from the party in 1988.

Amirav joined *Shinui* (now a component in the *Meretz* bloc), and became its secretary general in 1990. In 1991 Moshe Amirav joined forces with Hanna Siniora, the editor of the now defunct Palestinian newspaper, *Al-Fajr*, to formulate a 'blueprint for Jerusalem'. Under their plan, the holy city would be expanded into a vast metropolitan district, and would become the joint capital of two states (*viz.* Israel and Palestine). Amirav and Siniora also favoured putting Jerusalem at the top of the agenda, rather than leaving it to be decided at 'final status talks' between Israel and the Palestinians. Their rationale was, in Amirav's words, 'Once we create peace and justice in Jerusalem, the rest [of the peace process] will fall into place'. He may well participate in the final status talks of Jerusalem, due to start in 1996, as an unoffical consultant.

Yehuda AMITAL (Rabbi)

Nationality	Israeli
Religion	Jewish
Place of birth	Transylvania
Date of birth	1925
Current position	Minister without portfolio in Shimon Peres's new cabinet, Nov. 1995
Previous position	Joint head of the Har Etzion *Yeshiva* (seminary)
	Founder and leader of *Meimad* religious Zionist movement
Allies	Moderate sectors of the settler movement and Orthodox Jews
Position on peace	Favours a secure peace and guarantees for settlers
National political importance	*Meimad* lacks support, but Amital's appointment was symbolic of Peres's desire to take the Orthodox right-wing 'on board'
Prospects	Portfolio is undefined; but Amital bears enormous responsibilities

The appointment of Yehuda Amital to the cabinet in late November, 1995, was the surest sign that Israel's new prime minister, Shimon Peres, was seeking to heal the national wounds caused by the Rabin assassination. It also marked an attempt to define a new consensus, whereby moderate elements in the 'national religious camp' would have a part to play in the unfolding peace process with the Palestinians. However, Amital's appointment was extraordinary in constitutional terms, as his party, *Meimad*, has no *Knesset* members.

Born in Transylvania, Amital came to Palestine in December 1944. He resumed his *yeshiva* studies in Jerusalem, and was ordained as a rabbi. Amital joined the *Haganah* (Jewish defence force) and fought in the battles of Latrun and the Western Galilee in the War of Independence.

Over time, Amital realized the danger to Israeli society if all *yeshiva* students were exempted from military service (as was the case in Israel's first few decades). He consequently formulated the idea of *hesder yeshivot* (literally, 'arrangement seminaries'), which combined yeshiva study and military service. The prototype *hesder yeshiva* was his own Yeshivat Ha-Darom. After the Six Day War of 1967, Rabbi Amital was asked to establish a similar institution in the newly conquered Gush Etzion region of the West Bank (Judea and Samaria in religious Jewish parlance). It opened in 1968, and to this day Amital still heads it, together with Rabbi Aharon Lichtenstein.

In 1988 Amital led a breakaway faction out of the National Religious Party (NRP), when he felt he could not accept the party's increasingly hardline approach on the peace issue. After failing to win *Knesset* seats in the election of that year, nor again in 1992, *Meimad* set itself up as a 'Movement for Religious Zionist Renewal' in 1993. It aimed to 'rejuvenate traditional religious Zionist principles' and address itself to the welfare of all segments Israeli society (including both orthodox and secular Jews). In addition, *Meimad* accepted the need for limited territorial compromise to achieve peace in the territories, a view bitterly rejected by most other national religious factions. Since 1993, Rabbi Amital joined the executive of the Third Way, a cross-party alliance which favours caution in the peace process, especially concerning the Golan Heights issue, and basically steers a middle path between Labour and the *Likud*.

In November 1995, following the assassination of Prime Minister Yitzhak Rabin by a Jewish religious extremist, Yigal Amir, Rabbi Amital was invited to join the government as a minister without portfolio. The rabbi declared that 'this would send a message that it is possible to bridge the gap between religious and secular Jews in Israel'. He also agreed to co-operate with the implementation of the Interim Agreement signed with the Palestinians. One of Amital's first duties in office was to meet the *Yesha* Council executive (a body which purports to represent most Jewish settlers). In January 1996 he was appointed to head a ministerial committee into relations between Israel and Diaspora Jewry, which have been strained in some quarters over the peace process. He later announced his intention to retire from politics.

Amla, Muhammed Yusuf al-   Palestinian

Chief adviser to PNA President Yasser Arafat on matters of 'national security'.

Amr, Yasser   Palestinian

PNA Education Minister, and an independent member of PLO executive committee. In June 1995 Amr hailed the local *Hamas-Fatah* coalition in Hebron as a sign of the 'civilized nature of the Palestinian people'. Amr shares the chairmanship of the National Council for Education with Naim Abu Hommos.

Andersson, Sven   Sweden

Former Foreign Minister of Sweden, who helped to broker the first official talks between the PLO and the USA, in Tunisia in late 1988. Andersson also consulted with his foreign ministry counterparts in neighbouring Norway, and is believed to have influenced the initial stages of the secret Oslo channel.

Annielli, Suzanna   Italy

Foreign Minister of Italy; President of the European Union in early 1996. Suzanna Annielli was ultimately responsible for the EU monitoring presence at the Palestinian elections in January. In February 1996, Ms Annielli reported after a meeting with Syrian President Hafez al-Assad that Damascus felt that Israel was now sincere about peace. She hopes that Syria and Israel will regard European countries as politically neutral brokers; in addition, as ties between the EU and the eastern Mediterranean littoral have grown in recent years, they believe they could offer financial and trading inducements to speed up the peace process.

Aoun, Michel (General)　　　Lebanon

Former Army Chief of Staff. In September 1988 the outgoing President Amin Gemayel appointed Gen. Aoun, a fellow Maronite Christian, as head of a transitional administration. Aoun duly declared himself Prime Minister, from his Baabda Palace headquarters in East Beirut. The official prime minister, Selim al-Hoss, a Muslim, rejected his authority as unconstitutional. For the next two years, Aoun fought with some success against a string of rivals, starting with Samir Geagea's Lebanese Forces (a Christian militia affiliated to the Phalange); and then Sunni and Druze militias. Syria failed to dislodge the renegade general in 1989, and for a while it seemed as if France was supporting him. Aoun refused to sign the Taif Accord between Lebanon and Syria, and was blamed for the assassination of President René Mouawad in November 1989. Gen. Emile Lahoud replaced him as Army Commander in Chief, but it took almost another a year before the Syrian and Lebanese armies and pro-Syrian Phalangists eventually defeated him, with tacit US approval. Aoun currently lives in France, and claims to have no further desires to influence Lebanese politics. Yet in the mid-1990s there were rumours of an imminent comeback as Christians despaired of recovering their former political ascendancy in Lebanon.

Arabi, Nabil al-　　　Egypt

Egyptian Ambassador to the United Nations. Al-Arabi won a 'Seeds of Peace' award for his role in the Oslo Accords (together with Shimon Peres of Israel, and Nasser al-Kidwa, the head of the PLO mission to the UN). He was due to retire in 1996, but his tenure was renewed when Egypt was selected to join the Security Council for two years. Recently, Israel has been worried that Arabi has continued an anti-Israel campaign in the UN, mainly centring on the issue of Israel's nuclear weapons; after President Mubarak had assured Prime Minister Peres that Egypt had, in effect, called a truce in the long-running dispute. Al-Arabi has a wealth of experience, and can be expected to assert Egypt's interests in the UN's highest forum with vigour.

Arabiyat, Abd al-Latif　　　Jordan

Former Speaker, House of Representatives. Considered to be a 'dove' within the strong Islamic Action Front, he approved of the peace deal with Israel, so as to avoid a clash with the government.

Arafat, Fat'hi　　　Palestinian

Head of the Palestinian Red Crescent Society, younger brother to Yasser Arafat. Fat'hi Arafat was a key contact with Terje Larsen in Cairo, and thus acted as an early facilitator for the secret Oslo channel. He now heads the PNA Council of Health.

Arafat, Souha　　　Palestinian

Wife of Yasser Arafat. A somewhat controversial figure, Souha Arafat is the daughter of Raymonda Tawil, a well known poetess and member of the Palestinian elite who lived in Beirut. Journalists thought Arafat was a confirmed bachelor, 'married to the revolution', until he surprised them on Feb. 3, 1992, by announcing his marriage to Souha, an economic adviser, who at 28 was less than half his age. Some saw it as a political union (he is Muslim, and she is Christian). Although they are seldom seen together publicly, she has charmed visitors to the President of Palestine, and, in the media's perception, softened his formerly gruff image. She also encouraged Israeli Arabs to vote for Peres in the Israeli elections in 1996.

Yasser ARAFAT (Abu Ammar)

Nationality	Palestinian
Religion	Muslim
Place of birth	Jerusalem (or Cairo, a disputed point)
Date of birth	Aug. 24, 1929
Current position	President of the Palestine Council and the Palestine National Authority

Previous positions	Declared 'President of Palestine' in 1988 Chairman of the PLO, since 1969 Leader of *Fatah*, since 1956
Allies	Nabil Sha'ath, Faisal Husseini, Hani Hassan, Marwan Kanafani, Abu 'Ala
Position on peace	Positive; accepted DOP; won Nobel Prize
National political importance	Crucially important in Palestinian politics, in the Diaspora, and, increasingly since 1994, also in Gaza and the West
Prospects	Depends on success of PNA; Arafat has many critics, but is known as the quintessential political survivor. His success in the Jan. 20 elections in 1996 gave him a popular mandate to continue in power.

Yasser Arafat's *nomme de guerre* is Abu Ammar, but he is affectionately known by supporters as Mr Palestine, such is his personification with the Palestinian struggle. Since 1993, he has also been the lynchpin of the PLO's historic deal with Israel. Without his approval it would never have taken place. For decades Israel and the USA regarded him as a terrorist; yet in 1994 he shared the Nobel Prize for Peace with Israeli Prime Minister Yitzhak Rabin and Foreign Minister Shimon Peres. Despite numerous challenges to his leadership and several assassination attempts, Arafat has maintained control of his original powerbase, *Fatah*, and the larger PLO. He has weathered many vicious internal conflicts within the PLO, by playing off one group against another, and uniquely sensing the mood of Palestinians dispersed throughout the world. Yasser Arafat is presently the main force behind the creation of a new mini-state in Gaza and the West Bank. It is a far cry from his original goal of the armed liberation of 'all of historic Palestine', yet it is by most accounts still a remarkable tale of the political renaissance of the Palestinian people.

Under Arafat, the PLO moved from being a largely symbolic movement which was subservient to the wishes of Arab nations, to become an independent group, equally feared and respected in the Arab world. In its early days the PLO relied upon terror to attain its maximalist goals of destroying Israel and replacing it with a single Arab Palestine. He later changed the PLO's policy to one of reconciliation, and grudging recognition of Israel, so as to establish a smaller Palestine in the Occupied Territories. Today as *Ra'is* (President) of the Palestine National Authority (PNA), Arafat has become, ironically, a vital ally of Israel's. It remains, however, an open question whether he can achieve his goal of an actual State of Palestine with its capital in Jerusalem, something which Israel still opposes.

Yasser Arafat's paternal family, the Qudwas, hail from Gaza and Khan Yunis, but he was probably born in Egypt two years after his father moved there in 1927. (In other accounts, he claims that he was born in Gaza.) Yasser Arafat's full name is Abd al-Rahman Abd al-Rauf Arafat al-Qudwa al-Husseini, but he became known by his boyhood nickname, Yasser, which means 'easy' in Arabic. The Qudwas were a poorer branch of the Husseini clan, a notable family whose most famous son was Hajj Amin al-Husseini, the Grand Mufti of Jerusalem and effective leader of Palestine's Arabs from 1922 until the foundation of the State of Israel. (During his more revolutionary period, Arafat tended to play down his Husseini connections, and stressed his working class roots.)

Yasser Arafat was the sixth of seven children from his father's first marriage. When he was eight his father remarried and young Yasser returned to Cairo. During the Israeli War of Independence, Arafat was involved in gun-running for the Palestinian forces. He enrolled on a civil engineering course at Cairo University in 1951, and four years later was elected president of the General Union of Palestinian Students, a group which he had helped to form.

At the same time Arafat met two men who would become lifelong comrades, Salah Khalaf and Khalil al-Wazir (Abu Iyad and Abu Jihad, respectively; both since assassinated). In 1956 Arafat left Cairo for Stuttgart, and then for Kuwait, where he set up a thriving construction company. He employed the two Abus, and also other political colleagues, Khalid al-Hassan and Farouq Qaddoumi. Together they formed *Fatah*, or Movement for the Liberation of Palestine. Arafat struggled to wean 'diaspora' Palestinians from supporting Gamal Abdel Nasser's pan-Arabism, to his own more narrowly based Palestinian nationalism. *Fatah* moved to Algeria in 1963, where members received military training, and Arafat opened a bank account for the organization in Beirut. The creation of the Egyptian-sponsored PLO in

1964, however, diverted Palestinian attention from *Fatah* and similarly radical groups. In response, Syria, and particularly its intelligence chief, General Ahmad Sweidani, chose to back Arafat's faction as a counterweight to Nasser.

Fatah's first action was an attack on Israel's National Water Carrier, on Jan. 1, 1965. After the Six Day War of 1967, nearly a million Palestinians living in the West Bank and Gaza came under Israeli control. Arafat claimed victory when, in March 1968, Israeli forces attacked Karameh, a village in the Jordan Valley which served as *Fatah* headquarters (although other accounts say that Jordanian artillery actually repelled the invaders). Arafat personally led cells in the West Bank, but all his attempts at an armed insurrection against the 'occupiers' failed, and he had to escape in disguise.

Even so, *Fatah*'s image gained at the expense of the official PLO. Arafat had long warned that Palestinians should not put their trust in Arab powers, and the defeat of 1967 seemed to vindicate this view. In 1968 PLO Chairman Ahmed Shukeiri resigned, and his successor, Yahiya Humeida, could not hold onto power. In 1969 Arafat staged a bloodless internal coup and was elected PLO Chairman. Immediately, he made his peace with Egypt, which was still the PLO's main backer; and kept a respectful distance from *Ba'athist* Syria. Through the Hassan brothers, Arafat improved his relations with Saudi Arabia and other conservative oil-rich Gulf Arab states. In time this made the PLO the world's wealthiest 'liberation organization'; especially after funding increased following the leap in oil prices after 1973.

To Marxist factions, like George Habash's PFLP and Naif Hawatmeh's DFLP, Arafat lacked ideological rigour. Nonetheless, he skilfully arbitrated between the PLO's contending factions, and promoted the image of the *kaffiyeh*-clad Palestinian *feddah* (fighter). He allowed the militants to launch a series of hijackings and terror attacks, but ensured that *Fatah* controlled Palestinian politics by holding the balance of power in the Palestine National Council (parliament-in-exile). Under Arafat, the PLO amended its Charter to stress the role of armed liberation. Having failed in the West Bank, Arafat made Amman his new headquarters.

However, the increasing militancy of the PLO threatened King Hussein, and he ordered their expulsion. After a clampdown in September 1970, and a civil war in Jordan, the PLO decamped to southern Lebanon. Despite its rhetoric, *Fatah* left most of the terrorist action to the PFLP and similar groups. Arafat began to usurp UNRWA's control of the refugee camps, taking over schools and welfare services. In this way, he created a quasi-autonomous regime, which became known as 'Fatahland', a model for a future 'Palestine'; but to many Lebanese, Arafat's militias posed a threat to their national sovereignty.

After the Yom Kippur War, Arafat reinforced his control over the PLO by heading its Central Committee and Political Department, and becoming Commander of the Palestinian Revolutionary Forces. He also endorsed a slight change in the PLO approach. At the PNC conference of 1974, the PLO agreed to 'liberate Palestine by stages'. Some Israeli liberals detected in this a belated acceptance of the reality of the State of Israel. In the same year, Arafat engineered two major public relations successes. Firstly, a summit of Arab leaders in the Moroccan city of Fez declared the PLO to be the 'sole legitimate representative of the Palestinian people'. Secondly, Yasser Arafat addressed the UN General Assembly, and said he bore an olive branch (for peace) in one hand, and a gun (for war) in the other. Israel and the USA rejected Arafat as a terrorist; but he was now feted in left-wing circles, in the Non-Aligned Movement, and in the UN. In time, the PLO opened more offices worldwide than Israel had embassies. Support for the PLO rose.

However, in Lebanon PLO units (mainly PFLP) began to clash with Christian Maronite Phalangists. Soon Arafat was sucked into a civil war, and he allied the PLO with leftists and Muslims against the Christians. At first Syrian peace-keeping forces seemed to side with the PLO, in 1976; but later they supported the Maronite establishment. The war sapped the PLO's strength; despite some military gains, Arafat realized that Palestinians ultimately had little chance of controlling the balance of power in Lebanon, and far less of winning an outright victory.

Arafat rejected Egyptian President Sadat's peace talks with Israel from 1977 to 1978, when it became clear that its version of Palestinian autonomy fell far short of statehood, and gave no role to the PLO. The USA and Israel resented the way Arafat had apparently marshalled the Arab world to ostracize Egypt. In 1978 Israel raided southern Lebanon (Operation

Litani), in retaliation for Palestinian attacks on northern Israel, sealed the matter. For the next four years, Arafat kept the Palestinian issue alive through his tireless publicity in international forums. In the West Bank, his allies fought off a challenge from Israeli–sponsored Village Leagues (although Israel said the PLO used violent intimidation to defeat opponents). Internationally, Arafat began to distance himself from terrorism, but neither Israel and the USA insisted that he recognize UN 242, and the existence of Israel, before talks could start.

The far greater Israeli invasion of June 1982 resulted in military defeat for Arafat. By September he was forced to leave his Beirut headquarters. This loss marked another turning point for Arafat. It showed that he could not rely on Arab brother nations for military support; nor could the PLO defeat Israel by arms alone. It also brought him into indirect talks with Israeli officials for the first time, as the two sides worked out the modalities of his departure. The Sabra and Shatilla massacre of Palestinian refugees won the PLO sympathy in the West, where before its reputation for terror had made it a pariah. Finally, Arafat's poor treatment by Syria (whence he fled after Beirut) reinforced his desire for political independence.

In 1983 Syria unleashed an anti-Arafat wing of *Fatah*, led by Abu Musa, and virtual civil war reigned amongst the remaining Palestinian fighters in Lebanon. Later, his former Shi'ite allies in *Amal* also attacked his forces (the so-called War of the Camps). Arafat was forced to leave Damascus in June 1983, and he re-established the PLO's new headquarters in Tunis. But Arafat also revealed a pragmatic streak. He mended fences with Sadat's successor in Egypt, Hosni Mubarak – a link which was to prove its significance in the 1990s. In 1985 Arafat angered his radical allies, by signing a Framework for Peace with his old enemy, King Hussein of Jordan. This rapprochement encompassed plans for a Palestinian–Jordanian confederation. As such, it tallied somewhat with Israeli Prime Minister Shimon Peres's own 'Jordanian option', and there was renewed talk of a breakthrough between Israel and the PLO. However, Hussein abrogated the agreement in 1986 when Arafat failed to condemn terrorist incidents by a *Fatah*-related faction (the *Achille Lauro* affair).

The breach with Jordan restored Arafat's 'credibility' amongst leftist factions. But Arafat's semblance of unity with George Habash belied new realities – in Tunis, Arafat no longer enjoyed his intimate relationship with a large Palestinian community, as was the case in Lebanon. There was also a growing rift between the PLO in Tunis, and Palestinians in the Israeli–occupied West Bank and Gaza. A few of them began to criticize the PLO for being out of touch, and cited instances of corruption. In late 1987, for the first time the Palestinian issue did not feature at the annual Arab leaders' summit, a sign that Arafat's hitherto successful publicity machine was not working.

In December 1987, the *intifada* broke out in Gaza and the West Bank. This represented a fundamental challenge to Arafat, from a generation that had grown up under occupation. But it was also an opportunity for him to break the logjam with Israel. Although the *intifada* began spontaneously, Arafat soon adopted it as a PLO policy. Through his number two, Abu Jihad, he made sure that *Fatah* supporters co-ordinated their actions through the clandestine United National Command. He encouraged other Arab states to contribute to a 'steadfastness' fund. But the *intifada* also revealed a new rival for the leadership of the Palestinian movement, *Hamas*. To prevent the fundamentalists from 'hijacking the revolution', Arafat had to deliver something concrete. The opportunity came when King Hussein announced that Jordan was surrendering its claim to the West Bank. Arafat now heeded men like Yasser Abed-Rabbo, Abu Mazen and, from the West Bank, Faisal Husseini. His response was the PNC's Algiers Declaration in 1988, in which he declared himself 'President of Palestine', but also in effect recognized Israel, and renounced terrorism.

In late 1989, the USA opened its first official talks with the PLO, in Tunis. But the Israeli government of Yitzhak Shamir doubted Arafat's sincerity, and regarded the declaration of statehood as a gimmick. Furthermore, his claims to Jerusalem rankled even left-wingers. The collapse of the Israeli National Unity Government in 1990 brought in a more right-wing administration, committed to expanding the Jewish settlements and quelling the *intifada*, so hopes of a Shamir–Arafat summit receded. By this stage, the *intifada* had begun to degenerate into factional fighting. A succession of peace plans (Reagan, Mubarak, Fez summit, Baker and Shamir's response) all came to nought. Palestinians blamed Arafat, and some called for his resignation; Israelis blamed him for apparently condoning the killing of 'collaborators'.

It was in this atmosphere that Arafat responded to Saddam Hussein's 'call to arms' on behalf of Palestine, in early 1990. After Iraq invaded Kuwait instead in August of that year, Arafat offered his 'good offices' to negotiate an Arab solution. When this fell through, Arafat appeared to side with Saddam. It restored his popularity on the 'Palestinian street', but it was a major miscalculation. Syria, Egypt and Saudi Arabia joined a US-led coalition which soundly defeated Iraq in early 1991. Kuwait was restored to independence, and duly expelled some 350,000 Palestinians for alleged 'collaboration'. On a personal level, Kuwaitis found Arafat's behaviour reprehensible, considering the generosity and tolerance they had shown him in the 1950s. Soon all the Gulf states cut off their funds to the PLO. Meanwhile, Arafat could no longer turn to the USSR, as it had too many problems of its own. Finally, Israeli peace activists condemned Arafat as irresponsible.

Thus the PLO was considerably weakened after the Gulf War. US Secretary of State James Baker revived his peace plans, and this time sought to exploit the new regional military authority of the USA, and the unity between Syria, Egypt and Saudi Arabia. Arafat succeeded in placing the Palestinian issue at the centre of a comprehensive peace deal. But Israel would not accept PLO delegates, so Baker arranged a compromise – a Palestinian delegation consisting only of 'insiders', without PLO members, assembled under a Jordanian 'umbrella', but representing the PLO agenda. In September Arafat persuaded the PNC to accept this format as the best in the circumstances. So began the Madrid peace summit of October 1991, the first official meeting of Israelis and Palestinians – but without 'Mr Palestine' present.

As the talks progressed, Arafat's influence over the Palestinian delegation became more evident. His allies in the steering committees and technical committees ensured that nothing the delegates said would contradict PLO policy. Right-wing parties in Israel realized this, and deserted Shamir's government in protest. This prompted an Israeli election in mid-1992, and Labour returned to power on a platform of accelerating the peace process, offering Palestinians limited autonomy, and freezing 'political settlements'. On a personal level, Arafat announced his marriage to Souha Tawil, in February 1992. Two months later he survived an air crash over the Libyan Sahara. Until then, Arafat had enjoyed a near-mythical status – the man who worked 14 hour days for 'the struggle'; a man who had survived assassination attempts by Israel in 1982 and 1987. Both these new events, in their different ways, made Arafat's admirers realize that he was very human, and mortal. Israelis, too, realized that he was the lynchpin to a peaceful solution, especially as *Hamas* threatened to usurp the PLO's leadership role.

In early 1993 Labour rescinded a six-year ban on contacts with the PLO, but it still refused to accept the PLO as a legitimate organization. Meanwhile, the Madrid talks became bogged down, with neither side trusting the other, and little concrete being decided. Arafat once again saw an opportunity, and gave a green light to secret talks with Israel in Oslo. Gradually, Prime Minister Rabin was convinced that only the PLO could 'deliver' an agreement on the future of the territories, and thus end the *intifada* which was draining the Israeli budget and sapping national morale. The Oslo talks revealed many of Arafat's familiar trademarks – his ability to balance his team (with young *intifada* activists from the inside, like Hassan Asfour, and seasoned PLO career politicians, like Abu 'Ala); his secrecy and discretion (getting Abu Mazen to restrict news of the negotiations to a small cabal); his ability to persuade opponents to accept a *fait accompli* (when he cajoled a sceptical PNC to endorse the agreement); his sensitivity to political moods (noting Rabin's willingness to leave Gaza, but realizing that Palestinians would expect at least a token concession in the West Bank, like Jericho); and his cautious retention of the armed option (while explicitly renouncing terrorism, he stopped short of calling off the *intifada*). Most of all, Arafat knew the symbolic value of meeting Rabin in person, and shaking his hands on the Washington Lawn, on Sept. 13, 1993.

Yet some of Arafat's characteristics also had detrimental aspects. By keeping both King Hussein and the official delegation out of the picture, he alienated himself from natural allies. Hanan Ashrawi criticized him for making too many concessions, like postponing the issues of Jerusalem and Jewish settlements, and not insisting on the release of prisoners. In her view, one shared by PLO veterans like Mahmoud Darwish and Farouk Qaddumi, Arafat had sacrificed principles for short-term political gain. Dr Haidar Abd al-Shafi, head of the official

Madrid delegation, thought that Arafat was showing autocratic tendencies. This was especially noticeable after he set up the Palestine Authority, when he clamped down on press criticisms, and gave priority to organizing squads of armed units. Later, Israel would criticize him for duplicity, when he reneged on his promise to extradite suspected terrorists, and made incendiary anti-Israeli remarks in private.

In his defence, Arafat knew that in order to survive, he had to build a consensus, yet also take executive decisions. He had to satisfy Palestinian aspirations, but also assuage Israeli fears. On a cultural level, he had to transform the PLO from a liberation organization, full of grand dreams, into a working bureaucracy. In short, he had to manage an all too understandable crisis of expectations. The practical difficulties of meeting the rigid timetable led to several missed deadlines, and disappointment in the territories. The Hebron massacre of early 1994 exacerbated matters, but Arafat now had too much at stake to pull out of the process. So he personally started negotiations with Israeli Foreign Minister Shimon Peres, in Paris and Davos. He also visited King Fahd in Saudi Arabia in January 1994, and began to revive relations. In late April, Israel and the PLO signed their first economic protocol; on May 4, Arafat and Rabin signed the Cairo Accords, to implement the first stage (Gaza-Jericho) of the Declaration of Principles.

Arafat chose his new cabinet, balancing old PLO stalwarts from Tunis with newer blood from the 'inside'. On July 1, 1994, he arrived in Gaza and stepped onto Palestinian soil for the first time in 25 years. Some cynics thought the event was stage-managed, but few could deny the adulation that greeted his 'return'. Confounding the sceptics, Arafat made Gaza his chief base, despite its reputation as a *Hamas* stronghold He used young *intifada* men, like Asfour, and older soldiers like Agha, to reclaim support for *Fatah*. In late August, the new Palestine National Authority, with Arafat at its head, signed a 'further empowerment' agreement with Israel, which extended Palestinian powers to Israeli–ruled areas. However, violent clashes broke out between *Hamas* and the newly established Palestinian police in November, and Arafat had to intervene to ward off civil war. A spate of *Hamas* bombings in Israel also worsened his relations with Rabin and Peres. Finally, reports came out that Arafat promised to bring Jihad to Jerusalem, which revived Israeli mistrust. Much of this coincided with the Nobel Prize ceremony, where the three men were to share the prize for peace.

To revive the flagging peace process, President Mubarak launched the 'peace bloc' between himself, Arafat, Rabin, and King Hussein, on Feb. 2, 1995. But a private meeting between Arafat and Rabin less than a week later broke down when Rabin refused to lift the 'closure' on the territories. Success against terror was the Israelis benchmark for success; Arafat looked instead towards greater political rights, and economic autonomy. He fell out, too, with Western donor nations. They said his accounting was 'not transparent'; he said they had broken their promise on funding. When Rabin turned to the recently revived Syrian talks, Arafat feared that the Palestinian issue was once again being eclipsed. Nonetheless, Arafat gained a new lease in April, by relaxing his draft press laws, and pushing ahead with an investment law (by April). He personally took part in the talks on the Interim Agreement (Oslo 2). After much arm-twisting of his executive committee in Tunis, he won concessions from Israel, and made large concessions in turn (like delaying IDF redeployment, and accepting a staggered timetable for release of Israeli–held Palestinian prisoners). Israeli Foreign Ministry Director Uri Savir applauded his pragmaticism, without which, he said, there would have been no Oslo 2. Yet within a month of the signing ceremony (again in Washington, in September 1995), Arafat used the Amman economic summit as another platform to blame Israel for setbacks.

Yasser Arafat was clearly shocked by Yitzhak Rabin's assassination on Nov. 4, 1996. He wanted to attend the funeral in Jerusalem, but was told by Israeli intelligence services that they could not guarantee his security. Instead, he travelled secretly to Tel Aviv a few days later, to pay his condolences to Rabin's widow, Leah Rabin. This was his first legal trip to the state of Israel. Just a week earlier, this would have aroused fury in Israel, but the *Likud* right joined with Labour in praising his gesture.

Arafat met the new Prime Minister, Shimon Peres, who kept his promise to accelerate the redeployment of forces, with IDF units leaving Jenin a week before schedule (Jenin was the first of the seven Palestinian cities to gain autonomy under Oslo 2). Peres also saw that Israel vacated Bethlehem before Christmas – another significant gesture and a boost to Arafat's authority. But Peres expected something in return, and warned that unless Arafat get rid of anti-Israeli clauses in the Palestinian Charter, the whole peace process could be brought to a halt.

The election campaign for the Palestinian Council proved to be a success. Barring some accusations of vote-rigging, and of sinecures for Tunis faithfuls, Arafat was pleased with the turnout; and pleased as well that Samiha Khalil had stood against him in the presidential election. But the boycott by *Hamas*, after months of 'reconciliation talks', was a disappointment.

As a directly elected president, Arafat has new powers – *vis à vis* Israel, but also with regard to the increasingly marginalized PNC. In the longer term, he has to persuade the Diaspora that he has not ignored them. By the same token, in 'importing' cadres from Tunis, local Palestinians feel he has ridden roughshod over them. Palestinians in the camps in Lebanon and Syria worry that Arafat may abandon their long-cherished 'right to return', as he builds a local mini-fiefdom. At the end of March, Arafat faced four enormous challenges: choosing his new cabinet in the light of the Palestinian Council election results; convening the PNC to debate amendments to the National Covenant; responding to Israeli calls to clamp down on *Hamas* and Islamic *Jihad*, after bomb attacks in Jerusalem; and most crucially, defining the Palestinian negotiating stance for the 'final status talks' with Israel.

In the longer term, Arafat needs to define his relationship with Israel and Jordan, and hopes to create real economic autonomy in Council-ruled areas. His success at persuading the PNC to amend the Council showed his skills remained intact. Yet the fundamentalist bombings proved how fragile peace still was; and how much might be lost. Yasser Arafat has ruled the PLO for 27 years, and there is no obvious successor who can symbolize the Palestinian nation as he has.

Arens, Moshe   Israel

Former Defence Minister under Shamir. He was once tipped as possible *Likud* leader and prime minister, but was thwarted by Benjamin Netanyahu, his one time protegé, and retired from active politics after *Likud's* electoral defeat in 1992.

Arens was born in Kovno, Lithuania, in 1925. After his education in the USA, he became a professor of aeronautical engineering at the Haifa Technion in Israel. A lifelong member of *Herut*, he joined government of *Likud* (*Herut* alliance with other parties) under Menachem Begin and Yitzhak Shamir. He was Israel's ambassador to the US between 1982 and 1983 (coinciding with Israel's invasion of Lebanon). From 1983 to 1984 he was Defence Minister, taking over from the more hardline Ariel Sharon. Arens, once a dedicated ideologue, became increasingly the pragmatic technocrat in latter years. In 1983 he advocated a unilateral Israeli withdrawal from the Shouf mountains in northern Lebanon to the Awali River.

From 1988 to 1990 he was Israel's Minister of Foreign Affairs, and helped Prime Minister Shamir formulate his peace proposals, as a response to the Baker Plan and the PLO's Algiers Declaration. As Defence Minister again from 1990 to 1992, Arens supported Shamir's Land of Israel policy, but strongly opposed Jewish vigilante groups operating in the territories. He was apparently on the verge of launching a counter-attack after Iraq fired Scud missiles at Israel during the Gulf War; but was dissuaded from doing so after what he later deemed were misleading US promises of military aid and access to sensitive satellite footage of enemy movements. Arens played an important behind the scenes role during the 1991 Madrid peace talks, where his quiet skills as a technocrat were valued by fellow party members. After *Likud's* electoral defeat in 1992, he criticized the party for being out of touch with the public, and for putting the interests of settlers above that of the mainstream Israeli population.

Asaad, Asaad   Israel

Sole Arab *Likud* MK. Asaad Asaad was born in 1944, a member of the Druze minority community in Palestine (now Israel). After a distinguished military service in the Israel Defence Forces, he became the only Arab member of Israel's initial 14-member delegation to the Madrid conference. He entered the *Knesset* for the first time in 1992. Asaad lives in Beit Jan, and also served as the Prime Minister's Adviser on Druze Affairs.

Asfour, Hassan   Palestinian

Close aide to Arafat. Asfour hails from Gaza, and studied in Moscow and Baghdad. After 1987 he became a leading young *intifada* activist with strong Communist sympathies. He was deeply involved in the secret negotiations in Oslo, as an assistant to chief PLO negotiator, Ahmed Qurei, and official record-keeper for the PLO. Afterwards, he admitted that the talks had changed his mind about the possibility of making deals with Israelis. Asfour was known to be close to Hanan Ashrawi. After the signing of the Declaration of Principles in Washington, he returned to Gaza to negotiate the modalities of Gaza-Jericho First, as head of the PLO's Negotiations Directorate, but encountered opposition from former allies in leftist Palestinian factions. On Jan. 20, 1996, Asfour was elected to represent the Khan Yunis refugee camp in the Palestinian Council, as an independent.

Ashhab, Abd al-Hafiz al-   Palestinian

PNA Minister of Posts and Telecommunications. Ashhab, 69, comes from a Communist family and is affiliated with the Palestinian People's Party (successor to the Communists). He was born in Hebron, worked as a physician, and was a founding member of the Palestinian Red Crescent, which is currently directed by Fat'hi Arafat, Yasser Arafat's younger brother.

Ashkar, Ihab al-   Palestinian

Young *Fatah* leader in Gaza. Ashkar was the first Gazan representative of *Fatah* in the Unified Command of the *intifada*, and thus a bulwark of the PLO in region which was, by the early 1990s, increasingly dominated by *Hamas*. Ashkar declined a post in the PNA, and went into business instead. He manages a large insurance concern, which hopes to benefit from economic reconstruction in Gaza. He was nonetheless in favour of eletions in the territories, and, unlike some other *intifada* veterans, did not campaign against the Oslo accords.

Hanan ASHRAWI

Nationality	Palestinian
Maiden name	Hanan Mikhael
Religion	Anglican Christian
Place of Birth	Nablus, West Bank
Date of Birth	Oct. 8, 1946
Current position	Founder of Palestinian Independent Commission for Citizens' Rights
Previous positions	Spokesperson for the Palestinian delegation to Madrid; Professor of English at Bir Zeit University since 1974
Allies	Moderate intellectual West Bankers, like Nusseibeh and Husseini
Position on peace	Initially enthusiastic, now sceptical, of both Israel and the new PNA
National political importance	Influential amongst Western opinion formers; less so amongst Palestinians
Prospects	Now playing a monitoring role; potential leader of Palestinians who oppose the Oslo Accords but equally oppose *Hamas*

Hanan Ashrawi is one of the best-known and most controversial of Palestinian figures. She rose to prominence in the West as international spokesperson for the *intifada* on television. Blessed with natural intelligence and articulacy, she soon won the attention of a public which had grown weary of less glamorous and apparently more belligerent Palestinian leaders. In October 1991 she became the effective spokesperson for the Palestinian negotiating team in Madrid, although she was upset not to be given a more direct role in the talks themselves. Detractors have condemned her for suffering delusions of grandeur while being no more than a figurehead. As an educated Christian woman with strong opinions and expertise in English literature, she certainly does not fit the usual stereotype of a Palestinian politician. But she also has a strong and loyal following outside the PLO hierarchy, as seen during the *intifada*, which she may draw on in possible political bids in the future.

 Born in Ramallah to a wealthy and well-educated Christian Palestinian family, Hanan

Ashrawi has held many important positions in the Palestinian hierarchy. She was a leader in the General Union of Palestinian Students in Beirut, 1967–70; and in the General Union of Palestinian Women, 1967–72. She headed the Palestinian Information Office, Beirut, 1968–70, and founded the Legal Aid Committee in 1974, which she has directed ever since. Returning to academia, she became Dean of Arts at Bir Zeit University, 1986–90, specializing in Medieval English literature. Her period as dean coincided with the *intifada*, and she soon won a reputation for resisting and publicizing infringements of human rights by the Israeli occupying forces. At the same time she built up valuable links with Israeli peace groups (including Peace Now and Women in Black). Ashrawi was often sought after, publicly as a speaker and privately as a representative of the Palestinian 'insiders' (that is, those actually living on the West Bank, as opposed to the PLO, which was based in Tunis).

Having said that, she maintained close links with Tunis, and indeed with Yasser Arafat himself. Her meetings with PLO officials often led to clashes with Israeli administrators, who tried to restrict her movements. During the Gulf Crisis, former admirers amongst the Israeli left were angered by her apparent sympathy with Saddam Hussein. Likewise, her premature praise for the attempted Soviet coup of August 1991 also brought her moderate credentials into question. Even so, at the Madrid peace conference of October 1991 Hanan Ashrawi was the natural choice as spokesperson for the Palestinian delegation.

In fact, her role was more critical, both in voicing Palestinian objections to Israeli intransigence, and in preparing the moving opening speech by the 'official delegation' head, Haider Abd al-Shafi (which set the tone for the talks). In addition, Hanan Ashrawi kept lines of communication open between al-Shafi's delegation, an 'advisory' delegation led by her long-time colleague, Faisal Husseini (who was excluded from direct participation because Israel refused to deal with east Jerusalem Arabs), and the PLO in Tunis.

Ashrawi played a facilitating role in Oslo peace talks, but only in their later stages. She objected to what she saw as Arafat's capitulation to Israeli terms, and particularly fell out with Nabil Sha'ath, a former ally, who drafted the Palestinian proposal for framing the Declaration of Principles. After the Palestine National Authority was set up (after many delays) in May 1994, Ashrawi rejected the proffered post of Head of Information. Instead, on June 8, 1994, she set up the Palestinian Independent Commission for Citizens' Rights (PICCR). Using the commission as a platform, Ashrawi was determined to monitor human rights abuses by the PNA with as much vigour as she had scrutinized the Israeli Civil Administration.

She criticized the PNA for doing Israel's security work for them, and furthermore accused the PLO (which effectively ran the PNA) of dictatorial tendencies, over-centralization and nepotism – such as is practised in other Arab states. Consistent with her previous stance, Ashrawi criticized the PNA for not giving women a greater role in the new dispensation.

Yet despite these feelings, Ashrawi still supports the peace process, and believed that the forthcoming Palestine Council elections could 'start a new dynamic of political structures', giving 'substance to statehood'. She called on *Hamas* to participate, and predicted that the settler issue could be resolved. On a personal level, she saw her role as one of helping transform democratic rhetoric into creating 'a civil society under the rule of law'. In the summer of 1995, Ashrawi resigned as head of the PICCR in favour of Dr Iyad Sarraj. She stood as an independent candidate in Jerusalem for the Palestinian Council elections in January 1996, and scored the highest poll of any candidate in the district.

Hafez al-ASSAD

Nationality	Syrian
Religion	Alawi Muslim
Place of Birth	Qardaha, north-west Syria
Date of Birth	1930
Current position	President of Syria since 1970; also, Secretary General of the Ba'ath Party, and President of the National Progressive Front (a ruling umbrella group consisting of the Ba'ath and five smaller parties).
Previous position	Defence Minister

Allies	Vice-President Khaddam, Foreign Minister Farouq ash-Shav'a
Position on peace	Cool – but reputedly willing to accept Israel if Syria can retake Golan
National political importance	Very influential; holds many portfolios
Prospects	Stable, if his health holds out, and he can stave off economic strife and a threat from Sunni Muslim fundamentalists

Hafez al-Assad has dominated the politics of Syria for more than two decades. Although Syria is nominally a *Ba'ath*ist regime, the party clearly plays a subordinate role to the President himself. Often depicted as a shadowy figure, Assad can be ruthless, as in his violent suppression of Muslim fundamentalists in 1982. He has managed to hold on to power, despite his minority origins, a heart attack in 1983, and threats to topple him from such varied sources as the Muslim Brotherhood and his own brother, Rifaat.

With respect to the peace process, Hafez al-Assad has long supported 'rejectionist' factions within the PLO, and has taken a hard line regarding relations with Israel. Only in 1994 did he hint that Syria may recognize Israel. His ambitions clearly extend beyond Syria's borders (witness his effective hegemony over neighbouring Lebanon); and until recently he has demanded strategic parity with Israel. However, with the collapse of his chief sponsor, the Soviet Union, in the late 1980s, Assad has come to realize that it is time to compromise. In terms of regional strategy, Syria under Assad has mended fences with Jordan and Egypt, but continues to mistrust his traditional local rival, Iraq.

Some contend that Assad's true aim was never to foster Palestinian victory and statehood, but rather to replace the PLO under Arafat with a more pliant group which accepts the idea that Palestine should be part of a Greater Syria. Assad's rift with Arafat was a feature of PLO–Arab relations for most of the 1980s. In the 1990s, Jordan has acted as a broker between the two men, but both remain wary because of past disputes. Furthermore, ever since the collapse of the union between Syria and Egypt (called the United Arab Republic), Syria has harboured resentment against Egypt; and, in the absence of a Pan-Arab nation (a dream of Egypt's Gamal Abdel Nasser), Syria has wished to be the *primus inter pares* amongst Arab states.

Assad still refuses to formally recognize Israel, and is determined not to appear weak in future negotiations with the state. Nonetheless, Syria did participate in the Madrid peace track, and continues to hold on-off talks with Israel on the Golan Heights issue, which is the main obstacle to full diplomatic relations between the two countries. A strong streak of pragmaticism characterizes Assad's nature, and he is on record as saying that he does not wish to be 'left behind', now that the PLO and Jordan have begun making their peace with Israel. At the same time, caution and patiences are also hallmarks of Assad's personality, and he is known to be an obdurate bargainer.

Hafez al-Assad was born to an Alawite family in Qardaha, north-west Syria, in 1930. After forging a distinguished career in the military (a typical path for young male members of minorities, like Alawites and Druze), Assad tasted political power in 1966 following a coup within the ruling *Ba'ath* government. After the disastrous 1967 war, Assad, then Defence Minister, led a renegade military faction opposed to the government of his erstwhile ally, ex-colonel Salah Jedid. In November 1970 Assad ousted the civilian rulers and appointed himself prime minister. He assumed presidential powers on Feb. 22, 1971, and was confirmed as president in the March 12 elections of that year.

Attala, Attala Muhammad   Palestinian

Former head of PLO military intelligence in Lebanon. When the PLO–Jordan accord broke down in February 1986, King Hussein encouraged Col Attala (also known as Abu Zaim) to form a rival faction of *Fatah*.

Atrash, Ziyad al-   Palestinian

Chair of the PNA's Higher Military Liaison Committee (with Israel). He helped to oversee the redeployment of IDF forces from Palestinian cities according to Oslo 2, but later criticized Israel for not releasing more political prisoners.

Aviram, Ram   **Israel**
Foreign Ministry official, in charge of co-ordinating Israel's delegations to the various multilateral talks working groups. In effect, Aviram 'shadows' the multilateral steering committee. His brief is to detect strategic problems and, if possible, minimize them before they reach the negotiating phase. The 'multilateral section' is one of five specialist units within the Israeli Foreign Ministry (the other four units cover relations with the Palestine Authority, Egypt, Jordan and the Maghreb, or North Africa). The section is in turn subdivided into five sub-groups, each one of which 'shadows' one of the five working groups involved in the multilateral track (namely, water, economic development, environment, arms and security, and refugees).

Before taking up his current post in August 1995, Aviram was chief of the press office at the Israeli embassy in London, where he enjoyed a reputation as a convivial and astute aide to journalists. Aviram is one of the new generation of young Israeli diplomats who tend to look beyond security matters. He hopes Israel and its Arab neighbours can transcend ideological and cultural barriers, and could instead devote more time to solving common regional problems dispassionately. Aviram was closely involved with the water issue when he took up his current post. He was a prime mover in achieving the Water Resources Working Group's historic joint Declaration of Principles on Co-operation, which was announced in February 1996.

Avner, Yehuda   **Israel**
Prime Minister's adviser on Diaspora affairs. Yehuda Avner, 67, was born in Britain, and fought with the *Haganah* in the 1948 battle for Jerusalem. He helped to found an Orthodox Jewish *kibbutz* in the Lower Galilee, and later served as Israel's ambassador to Britain and Australia. Avner had advised Yitzhak Rabin on Diaspora affairs in the mid-1970s, during Rabin's first stint as Prime Minister. In late 1995, Rabin decided that his services were needed again, in the light of the deepening schisms between right-wing and religious Jews in the Diaspora, and the Labour government, particularly over the question of peace. After Rabin's assassination, Shimon Peres reconfirmed his appointment, and charged him with organizing the centenary celebrations of Theodor Herzl's First Zionist Congress, for 1997.

Avneri, Uri   **Israel**
Radical journalist, former MK, veteran Peace Now activist. In the late 1950s, Avneri set up *Ha'olam Hazeh* (This Day), a dissident weekly which addressed the 'Arab question'. In the late 1960s Avneri set up an independent party, and agitated in the Knesset for peace with the Palestinians. Avneri co-founded the pro-peace *Sheli* Party, with Zichroni and Yair Tsaban (currently a *Meretz* minister in Peres' cabinet). *Sheli* won two seat in the 1977 elections, but it later disbanded and its members joined Labour, or the Progressive List for Peace.

Awad, Marwan   **Jordan**
Finance Minister since February 1996. Marwan Awad is one of the younger generation of Jordanian politicians who swept to power in the latest cabinet reshuffle. He was born in Jerusalem in 1951, and took his postgraduate studies at Vanderbilt University, in the USA. In 1979 he left his position as an executive manager with Jordan's Central Bank to serve as Deputy Minister of Trade and Industry from 1992 to August 1994. In the 18 months since then, he was the general manager of the Middle East Investment Bank. He also helped to arrange the private sector preparations for the successful Middle East and North Africa summit which was held in Amman during October 1995. His immediate task is to negotiate with the IMF on further structural reforms. In the longer term, his Palestinian origins, enthusiasm for privatization, and experience in attracting investment, will all count in his favour, as Jordanians, Palestinians and Israelis begin to redraw the economic map of their shared region.

Awad, Mubarak   **Palestinian**
Veteran West Bank Palestinian peace campaigner. In the early years of Israeli occupation, Awad was arrested for organizing commercial strikes. He then spent 15 years in the USA, where he gained an American passport, and took a doctorate in psychology at Ohio University. Awad returned to Jerusalem in 1983, and soon personified *samud* (steadfastness) under

the Israeli occupation. After a year of the *intifada*, he adopted a policy of assertive non-violence and 'civic non-co-operation' with Israel. He wrote copious leaflets calling on Arabs to boycott the Civil Administration schools and centres, and set up alternative institutions, instead of just demonstrating. More militant figures favoured armed resistance. Gradually, the Unified National Command of the *intifada* adopted aspects of the 'Awad Doctrine'. Despite protests from US officials in Israel, and a coterie of Jewish supporters, the government deported him back to the US in May 1988.

Awartani, Hisham   Palestinian
West Bank economist and Palestinian negotiator. Awartani lectures in economics at al-Najah University in Nablus. In June 1993 he and other Palestinian, Israeli, Jordanian and US economists produced an influential report, under the auspices of Harvard University. Called 'Securing Peace in the Middle East; Project on Economic Transition', it envisaged free trade and co-operation in the Jordan–Israel-Palestinian triangle, as a prelude to a broader Middle Eastern economic community.

Ayalon, Ami   Israel
Head of Israel's *Shin Bet* intelligence service since Jan. 10, 1996. Ayalon's predecessor, Carmi Gilon, formerly known only by his code-name, Kaf (the Hebrew letter 'K'), resigned after the *Shin Bet* and other branches of the General Security Services were blamed for the lapse in security which led to Prime Minister Yitzhak Rabin's assassination. Rear-Admiral Ayalon is the first *Shin Bet* chief to be publicly named. He was regarded as a leading navy commando, and is said to be creative, intelligent and discreet.

Aynan, Sultan Abu al-   Palestinian
Head of pro-Arafat *Fatah* forces in Lebanon. Aynan is based at the Rashidiyah refugee camp outside Tyre. Aynan's chief foes are the *Fatah* rebels led by former commander, Mounir Maqdah.

Ayoub, Fouad   Jordan
Ambassador to London since 1991. Ayoub was born in 1944, studied philosophy at California State University, and became a fellow of Harvard. From 1977 until taking up his current appointment, Ayoub was King Hussein's press secretary. He also was a member of Jordan's delegation in talks with Israel, after the Madrid summit conference.

Ayyash, Radwan Abu   Palestinian
Head of the Palestinian Broadcasting Corporation, formerly founder of the Palestinian Journalists' Association, director of the Arab Media Centre in Jerusalem, and head of the Democratic Forum. Abu Ayyash was born in 1950, in the Askar refugee camp, near Nablus. His parents had fled from Deir Yassin, the site of a massacre by *Irgun* forces in 1947. Abu Ayyash has worked as a school teacher and journalist, becoming editor of *Al-Shaab* and *Al-Awla* in turn. From 1985 to 1991 he was president of the Arab Journalists' Association, which won international aclaim for its 'work for peace'. Although associated with the PLO, for a long time he made illicit contacts with Israeli and US officials. Through his Democratic Forum, Abu Ayyash criticized the official PLO stance on the Gulf War. He subsequently served on the Palestinian advisory (or steering) committee during the Madrid and Washington talks. Since the Gaza-Jericho Accord of 1994, Abu Ayyash has been the most vocal defender of press freedom in the new Palestine Authority. His public protests helped to overturn the PNA's draconian draft press law. Abu Ayyash, a published poet, advocates 'two states for two peoples' and a shared Jerusalem, and believes an independent Palestine would not compromise Israeli security. As head of the Palestinian Broadcasting Corporation, Abu Ayyash has to steer a narrow path between journalistic independence, and serving the Palestine Authority.

Ayyash, Yehiya   Palestinian
Master bombmaker for *Hamas*; assassinated on Jan. 5, 1996. Ayyash, nicknamed 'The Engineer', was responsible for terrorist attacks which killed at least 40 Israelis and injured 430. He was the Israeli security services' 'most wanted man' for three years; but a hero to many *Hamas* youth, especially in Gaza and his native West Bank village of Rafat. As an electrical

engineering graduate from Bir Zeit University, Ayyash actually constructed the bombs, trained others in their manufacture and use, and planned 'operational logistics'. Israeli operatives began searching for him in 1992, but he continually eluded them. On the morning of Jan. 5, 1996, Ayyash died in a bomb blast in Beit Lahiya, Gaza. Israeli anti-terrorist forces had probably killed him, by implanting a miniature boobytrap device in his mobile telephone, and detonating it by remote-control. At Ayyash's funeral, enormous crowds of angry Palestinians called for revenge against Israel. Suicide bombers acted on this call in Feb. and March; one cell was named the Yehiha Ayyash Brigade.

Azoulei, André   Morocco
Economic adviser to King Hassan; Jewish proponent of Israeli–Palestinian dialogue. Azoulei, 54, was born in Mogador, now called Essaouira, and studied journalism in Paris, where he now resides. For over 20 years he worked for Paris-Bas, a leading European bank. In 1974 he set up *Identité et Dialogue*, a Paris-based group of mainly North African Jews dedicated to dialogue with Arab states. He has often met PLO officials, and also owns a villa in Israel. Azoulei was close to King Hassan for many years, and became his adviser in late 1991. His brief includes public relations for the monarchy, and nurturing Morocco's generally congenial ties with its former Jewish citizens in Israel, France and elsewhere.

B

Badran, Mudar Muhammad   Jordan
Prime Minister of Jordan from 1976 to 1979; 1980 to 1984; and 1989 to 1991. Mudar Badran was born in Jerash in 1934 and studied law at Damascus University. A close ally of King Hussein's, he was head of Jordan's military and general intelligence before becoming prime minister for the first time in the 1970s. He also served as Minister for Education and Defence, and headed the Royal Court. In the mid-1970s Badran was briefly responsible for the Jordanian interests in the West Bank. In 1989 he started reforming the *mukhabarat* secret police, in preparation for democratization. Critics accused him of encouraging Islamic fundamentalism as a counterweight to Jordan's leftist and Palestinian groups.

Bajolet, Bernard   France
French diplomat. In April 1993 the Refugees Working Group (part of the multilateral talks format) sent Bajolet on a fact-finding mission to the Middle East. There he met experts on family re-unification (Jordanian, Israeli, Palestinian and Egyptian), and made a series of recommendations, most of which were accepted by the group's next meeting, held in Oslo.

James A BAKER III

Nationality	United States
Religion	Christian
Place of birth	Houston, Texas, USA
Date of birth	1930
Current position	Senior partner in law firm of Baker & Botts
Previous position	US Secretary of State in the State Department
Allies	Close to former President George Bush
Position on peace	James Baker was the major initiator of the Madrid peace conference
National political importance	Of crucial influence in US foreign policy under the Republicans
Prospects	No longer in active party politics, although once suggested as a possible presidential candidate; nonetheless, his opinion is sought by politicians interested in US foreign policy

James A. Baker, III, was the United States' 61st Secretary of State, from January 1989 until August 1992 in the Bush administration. During his tenure in office he travelled to 90 foreign countries, but in the Middle East he will be best remembered as the chief architect of the Madrid peace talks. Indeed, it was his peace plan, first proposed in 1989, which set the agenda for the current peace process; and it was his intensive 'shuttle diplomacy' after the Gulf War which ensured that all the parties attended the Madrid summit of October 1991.

James Baker graduated from Princeton University in 1952. After two years active service in the US Marine Corps, he entered the Austin School of Law. On qualifying in 1957, he practiced law until becoming President Gerald Ford's Under Secretary of Commerce in 1975.

From 1981 to 1985 Baker was the White House Chief of Staff under President Ronald Reagan. Then from 1985 to 1988 he served as Reagan's Secretary of the Treasury, and also chairman of the President's Economic Policy Council. His appointment to the senior post of head of the State Department in January 1989 fortuitously coincided with the end of the Cold War and the collapse of the Warsaw Pact. In this 'New World Order' (as the new president, George Bush, was to dub it) Baker played a key role in redefining America's global role. Perhaps his greatest test was in organizing the UN coalition ranged against Saddam Hussein, after the latter had invaded Kuwait in August 1990. Baker used his considerable organizational skills to steer public opinion in favour of a war to punish Iraq, at a time when many Americans were sceptical about US international obligations.

Whereas President Reagan and Secretary of State George Bush repeatedly assured Israel that it was the USA's foremost ally in the Middle East, under Baker, US policy towards Israel cooled considerably. Although Baker accepted Shamir's May 1989 plan for peace in principle, he was adamant about Israel putting a halt to new settlements in the occupied territories. In December 1989 he launched his own plan, which synthesized Shamir's plan with a ten-point clarification proposal from Egyptian President Mubarak. Baker's plan envisaged a central role for Egypt, and a Palestinian delegation drawn from the territories. With the collapse of the Labour-*Likud* government, Shamir responded with another plan, which this time sought to demote the Palestinian question to a subsidiary issue, and only discuss it in terms of the Camp David provisions for autonomy. Baker denounced Shamir as 'not being serious about peace'.

In August 1990, Iraq invaded Kuwait, and the Israeli–Palestinian question was placed on hold. Baker was persuaded to forge an anti-Saddam coalition, and military plans went ahead after his last minute talks with Iraqi Foreign Minister Aziz broke down in January 1991. After the US success in the Gulf War, President Bush mandated Baker to canvas opinion in the Middle East for a new peace initiative. This resulted in probably Baker's greatest achievement, the Madrid peace conference of October 1991. It came after months of shuttle diplomacy by Baker to Middle Eastern capitals, in which he met a Palestinian delegation in Jerusalem, dissuaded Shamir from his policy of only conducting separate bilateral negotiations, and persuaded Syrians to meet Israelis publicly for the first time in four decades. A key to his success was the way he involved the USSR as a 'co-guarantor' of the peace process. However, this very success was almost destroyed by the dissolution of the USSR on the eve of the conference. Relations with Palestinians and Israel became strained — the PLO resented US pressure to have Israel 'vet' its delegates, and Israel resented US pressure to freeze new settlements. When Israel continued with its policy, Baker decided to 'punish' it by suspending a $10 billion loan guarantee – a hitherto unprecedented action.

Baker ended his service as White House Chief of Staff, this time for President Bush, from August 1992 to January 1993. He was also the president's senior counsellor during this period, and oversaw the Bush election campaign in its final stages. Despite his proven powers of persuasion, Baker failed to sway the US electorate from electing a Democrat, Governor Bill Clinton, as president. James Baker left office to return to law.

Bakshi-Doron, Eliahu   Israel

Sephardi chief rabbi since 1993. Bakshi-Doron joined his Ashkenazi counterpart, Rabbi Yehuda Lau, in condemning the assassination of Yitzhak Rabin. Since late 1995, the two have worked hard to restore national unity, and to prevent antagonism against religious sectors. He is not known to have strong views for or against the peace process.

Balawi, Hakam   Palestinian
PLO ambassador to Tunis (site of the PLO's headquarters). A loyal Arafat lieutenant, his name was put on the electoral list for the Jan. 20 elections in Tul Karm, after local *Fatah* activists had rejected his candidature.

Bandar ibn Sultan al-Saud   Saudi Arabia
Saudi Ambassador to Washington. Prince Bandar is regarded as being one of the most pro-Israeli figures in Saudi politics. In January 1992, he arranged the first trip by an official Jewish delegation to Saudi Arabia. The delegation was led by the executive director of the American Jewish Congress, Henry Siegman. Prince Bandar is also a member of the Maimonides Foundation, a UK-based body dedicated to dialogue between Jews and Muslims. Prince Bandar is the son of Sultan ibn Abdul Aziz al-Saud, the Second Deputy Prime Minister and Minister of Defence in the Kingdom.

Bani-Hadi, Muhammad   Jordan
Head of the Jordan Valley Authority, a member of the 1991 Jordanian delegation to the Madrid peace conference, and a influential source regarding the water terms of the Israel-Jordan peace treaty.

Sabri Khalil al-BANNA (Abu Nidal)

Nationality	Palestinian
Religion	Muslim
Date of birth	Jaffa, Palestine
Place of birth	1937
Current position	Head of the Abu Nidal Group (*Fatah* Revolutionary Council)
Previous position	Until 1974 a member of PLO and *Fatah*
Allies	Currently based in Libya; alleged ties with Iraq and unspecified wealthy backers; broke long ties with Syria in 1987
Position on peace	Totally opposed; long history of terrorism, including assassinations of PLO moderates
National political importance	Marginal, but still has the power to disrupt
Prospects	Negligible in current political arena; but still feared

Sabri Khalil al-Banna (better known as Abu Nidal), is the most notorious Palestinian terrorist, and as much the scourge of PLO officials as of Israeli and Western targets. He has little direct bearing on the peace process, other than being able to sabotage negotiations through the use of assassination. His 'Abu Nidal Group' (officially known as the *Fatah* Revolutionary Council, or FRC) has carried out more than 250 acts of terror since it was founded in 1974. But its actual base of supporters is small, with a few armed units in Lebanon and the FRC headquarters in Tripoli, Libya.

Abu Nidal was the last of 12 children, born (in his case, illegitimately) into the wealthy landowning al-Banna family in the Ajami quarter of Jaffa. They fled to Nablus in 1948, and later moved to Beirut. Abu Nidal studied engineering in the mid-1950s in Cairo, but interrupted his degree to become an electrician and building contractor in Saudi Arabia. He later worked for a trading firm in Amman, Jordan. There he met and came under the influence of Abu Iyad, Yasser Arafat's closest ally at the time. In 1971 Abu Nidal went to Baghdad as the *Fatah* representative, but once there he started to set up his own opposition force. He remained in Iraq for more than a decade, and served its interests by attacking Syrian embassies throughout Europe and in Turkey. In 1974 the PLO sentenced Abu Nidal to death in absentia for plotting to kill Abu Mazen. He later succeeded in killing three PLO moderates, including Issam Sartawi, the first official to openly call for recognition of Israel.

The Abu Nidal group attempted to assassinate Israel's Ambassador to London, Shlomo Argov, in June 1982, an event which prompted Israel's invasion of Lebanon. Expelled from Iraq in 1983, he left for Damascus. In succeeding years, his group killed scores of people at airports in Rome and Vienna, and a synagogue in Istanbul. By this stage his Syrian sponsors were weary of his actions, and in 1987 he was forced to flee to his current location, Tripoli in Libya. This breach led to a vicious civil war within the group, which was still simmering in the 1990s. In January 1991, Banna's operatives in Tunis killed Abu Iyad, his former mentor and by now Arafat's second in command. Since the Madrid Summit, Abu Nidal's 1,000 fighters in Lebanon have regularly assassinated pro-Arafat officials.

Abu Nidal poses as the quintessential freedom fighter for Palestine. But in reality, he often acts as a hired gun for different Arab regimes, and certainly does not restrict his killing sprees to Palestinian causes. In a recent biography of Abu Nidal, Patrick Seale suggested that he worked for *Mossad*. While there is no firm evidence for this view, Abu Nidal has certainly both embarrassed and threatened the PLO.

Barak, Aharon   Israel

Appointed Chief Justice of Israel's Supreme Court in August 1995. Aharon Barak replaced the outgoing Meir Shamgar, and was first appointed to the Supreme Court in 1978. Born in Kovno (Kaunus), Lithuania, in 1936, Barak immigrated to Palestine in 1947 with his parents. He took law degrees at the Hebrew University, Jerusalem, and Harvard, USA. From 1974 to 1978 he was Israel's attorney-general. During this period, Barak became known for his scrupulousness as he pursued ministers accused of corruption.

In 1977 the new prime minister, Menachem Begin, co-opted Barak to lead the legal team attached to the Israeli delegation at the Camp David peace talks in 1978. Barak drafted a key part of the resultant accords, and managed to persuade Begin to change his mind on a number of issues.

In his 17 years at the Supreme Court, Barak has imitated the American tradition of rigorous judicial review. He ruled that anyone should be allowed to petition the Supreme Court to challenge government actions, and not only those directly effected. Likewise, he has irked politicians by challenging 'unconstitutional' legislation eminating from the Knesset; and in many cases has forced politicians and civic officials to resign. Barak has also fiercely defended individual civil rights (enhanced by the Human Dignity and Freedom Act, passed in 1992), often to the point of offending Orthodox Jewish institutions and religious political parties. Many of the latter group tried, unsuccessfully, to block his appointment as chief justice in 1995.

Even so, left-wing critics say he has shown less concern over Palestinian rights in the territories. He has upheld decisions to demolish the homes of convicted terrorists, and allowed military authorities to close down Palestinian newspapers on the grounds that their owners had 'connections with a terror organization'. In December 1992 Barak issued a temporary injunction to stop the government's mass deportation of *Hamas* activists to Lebanon, but a month later allowed the deportation to proceed. As chief justice, Barak now enjoys wide-ranging powers to determine which judges will review which cases; he also heads the committee which appoints and promotes judges. He is expected to remain in his post for 11 years, until his mandatory retirement at the age of 70. That means he will probably be ruling in cases involving interpretation of the Interim Agreement with the Palestinians, and whatever agreements emerge from the final status talks.

Ehud BARAK

Nationality	Israeli
Name at birth	Ehud Brog
Religion	Jewish
Place of birth	*Kibbutz* Mishmar Hasharon, Palestine (now Israel)
Date of birth	1942
Former position	Foreign Minister Nov. 21, 1995 to June 1996
Previous position	Interior Minister since July 1995. Before that, military Chief of General Staff, and chief negotiator on security matters with Syria
Allies	Very close to the late Prime Minister Yitzhak Rabin; Eitan Haber

Position on peace	Cautious, with a hardline approach on combatting Muslim extremists; offended Syrians by suggesting they reduce army size
	As Foreign Minister, more willing to take risks for peace
National political importance	Influential over Rabin's policy, set to grow once in office
Prospects	Very ambitious, and is tipped by many to be prime minister but potentially stymied by an accident at a military base in 1992

Ehud Barak was widely tipped as Yitzhak Rabin's heir apparent. In many respects, his career even mirrored Rabin's – rewarded for outstanding military service, he went on to become military chief of staff and a key negotiator with Israel's military enemies, and was finally drafted into Labour party politics and even the cabinet just 100 days after retiring from the military. Unlike the Gang of Seven (young dovish 'technocrats' from Tel Aviv who saw Shimon Peres as their mentor), Barak was very much a man in Rabin's image, a throw-back to the older Labour party ties with army leadership and the *kibbutz* movement. However, after the assassination of Rabin in late 1995, it was Peres who became Prime Minister, and Barak was appointed Foreign Minister.

Barak took degrees in mathematics from the Hebrew University, Jerusalem, and systems analysis from Stanford University, USA. Friends say he his tough exterior belies a more sensitive private side, a lover of poetry and philosophy. Even enemies admit his rare powers of insight (in early 1990 he warned US National Security officers that Saddam Hussein was planning to invade Kuwait, and not Israel, as most believed).

As Chief of Military Staff, Barak concocted a plan to assassinate Iraqi leader, Saddam Hussein, using advanced missiles and an élite commando unit in revenge for the Scud missile attacks during the Gulf War. However, six Israeli soldiers died and five were wounded when a dummy run for the mission went horribly wrong, on Nov. 5, 1992. Barak was present at Tze'elim training camp, the site of the accident. The media soon learnt about it and accused him of callousness for allegedly leaving the disaster site early. These charges were subsequently disproved by a commission of inquiry. However, the taint of recklessless and arrogance has hovered around Barak ever since (although if the project had succeeded, he would have been hailed as a national hero).

Barak was also the brain behind expulsion of 413 Muslim fundamentalists from Gaza in December 1992. The exercise ultimately backfired, leading to UN resolutions of condemnation and a suspension of the Madrid peace process. It also marred the new Labour government's carefully nurtured relations with Palestinians in the territories, and resulted in a new-found sense of unity between *Hamas* and the PLO.

In July 1993 Barak authorized Operation Accountability, the biggest Israeli incursion into Lebanon in a decade. The exercise aimed to punish *Hezbollah* for an escalation of attacks on northern Israel. Further, by creating an exodus of an estimated 300,000 homeless Lebanese civilians, Barak intended to force Syria and Lebanon to discipline *Hezbollah* and other 'terrorist groups' in southern Lebanon. US Secretary of State Warren Christopher brokered a 'ceasefire' between the parties concerned. However, it only partly succeeded, as attacks on Israeli military personnel and civilians across the border continue to this day. In late 1994, Barak negotiated with his Syrian counterpart, Hikmat Shihabi, on matters of security. Talks broke down after Barak insisted on warning stations in the Golan, and called for reductions in the Syrian army. Some say Barak's style was to blame; others say he was only doing Rabin's bidding, or that Syria was not sincere about the talks.

On Jan. 1, 1995, Barak retired as Chief of Staff, and handed over the reigns to his deputy and ally, Amnon Shahak. Following the statutory lapse of time needed before a military officer can enter politics, Ehud Barak signed up as a member of the Labour Party on July 16, 1995. The following day he entered the cabinet on July 17, 1995, as Minister of the Interior. Sceptics questioned Barak's peace credentials when he abstained from voting with most of the cabinet in favour of Oslo 2. However, his past record suggested that he was no friend of the settlers (in the 1980s he had blocked plans to create government-backed armed settler units, and in 1994 he was willing to expel Hebron's 450 Jewish settlers, following the massacre at the Ibrahimi Mosque).

After the assassination of Yitzhak Rabin, Barak was tipped for high office, possibly the defence portfolio. In the event the new prime minister, Shimon Peres, assumed this post, and made Barak Foreign Minister. Barak was also assigned a key role within a newly constituted inner cabinet 'peace process team'. It was thought that only a 'tough man' like Barak could persuade doubters to except a territorial compromise on the Golan Heights — the necessary outcome of a future peace deal with Syria. Labour supporters said he had the military credentials to disprove Benjamin Netanyahu's charges of 'Labour softness' (in the 1970s, Barak was commando leader of the élite unit in which Netanyahu served as a junior officer).

Since November 1995, Barak has worked hard to achieve Rabin's peace goals. He shared a platform with Syrian Foreign Minister Farouk ash-Shar'a at the Barcelona conference on Mediterranean states. There he vowed to work towards 'making war impossible', and to 'build bridges' of economic development, interdependence, and human dignity. Barak identified three paths towards regional peace – education, technical co-operation, and developing new sources of water. Later he travelled to Washington for detailed negotiations with Syrian officials, and predicted a 'warm peace' with Syria. In January he held high level talks with US Vice-President Al Gore (an Israel–US strategic pact was rumoured to be on the agenda). He also signed an agreement on co-operation in science and culture with Jordan, on Jan. 18, 1996. More recently, he has bolstered Israeli ties with Tunisia, attended a summit of European defence chiefs, and contacted Russia's new Foreign Minister Yevgeny Primakov. Critics had suggested that Barak's lack of diplomacy might ill suit his new office, but he seems to have proved otherwise. Barak led Peres's prime ministerial campaign in the elections on May 29, 1996. Although blamed for schisms which led to Labour's defeat, he is tipped to succeed Peres as party leader.

Baram, Uzi   Israel

Tourism Minister since 1992; in 1995, interim Interior Minister until Ehud Barak took the post. Uzi Baram, 56, was known as a leading dove within Labour, and an ally of Shimon Peres; but he backed Rabin to lead Labour in 1991, reasoning that only he could win the 1992 elections. Baram was born in Jerusalem in 1937, and holds a degrees in political science and sociology. A veteran MK of 18 years' standing, he was chairman of Labour in Jerusalem, from 1975 to 1981, and national Party Secretary General from 1984 to 1988.

In office, he discussed post-peace tourism potential with Arab states, especially Egypt (where he lobbied for a gas pipeline with Israel). Baram believes that tourism is set to boom with the advent of peace. He particularly wants more Muslim tourists to visit Jerusalem's holy sites. He also spearheaded plans for the tourism ministry to co-operate with the ministries of finance and transport. In July 1994 Baram became the first Israeli minister to meet his Palestine National Authority counterpart (Elias Freij). The two ministers discussed the formulation of joint projects, and joined forces in late 1995 in a new regional tourism organization, MEMITTA. Although avuncular in personality, Baram is also a fierce critic of increased settlement, and led calls for a crackdown on the far right.

Barghouti, Bashir al-   Palestinian

General Secretary, (Communist) People's Party; one-time East Jerusalem member on the PLO executive committee. Barghouti was held in a Jordanian desert detention camp when the Kingdom still ruled the West Bank, and only returned to his native Ramallah in 1974. He revived the Communist Party's fortunes in the territories, organizing an ironcast cell structure, and returning it to its earlier stance of recognizing pre-1967 Israel and condemning terrorism. Working closely with Dr Taysir al-Arouri, Barghouti was active in the *intifada,* although he initially castigated the Unified Command as a puppet of the Tunis-based PLO. As editor of *a-Taliah* and contributor to *Al-Watan,* Barghouti stressed the need to build autonomous institutions, rather than only fight the occupation with stones.

Barghouti, Hassan   Palestinian

Director of the Democracy and Workers' Rights Centre (DWRC). In mid-1995, Barghouti led a campaign to assert workers' rights under Palestinian rule. He criticized the official PLO–backed Palestinian General Federation of Trade Unions (the GFTU, led by Shahar Said) for its excessive factionalism. Instead, he saw in the spontaneous growth of workplace committees, a new nucleus for organized Palestinian labour. Barghouti also attacked the PNA's draft Basic Law, which permits payments in kind, instead of wages. While suspicious of attempts by Israel's own *Histadrut* to co-opt Palestinian workers, he feels these developments ironically offer Palestinians a chance to organize themselves better, against what he sees as the exclusively 'bourgeois' Palestine Authority elite. Barghouti regarded the Israel-PNA plans for industrial zones in Gaza and the West Bank, as a way of generating profits for investors (including expatriate Palestinians), while exploiting cheap Palestinian labour.

Bargouthi, Marwan   Palestinian

General Secretary of the High Command of *Fatah* on the West Bank. Bargouthi is an enthusiastic supporter of Oslo 2, and headed a drive to recruit supporters in preparation for the Palestine Council elections, scheduled for early 1996. He is a major force for 'democratization' within *Fatah*, and encouraged a series of primary elections, prior to the 1996 Council elections. In the Council elections, Barghouti narrowly defeated his cousin, Mustafa, to win a seat in Ramallah.

Barghouti, Mustafa   Palestinian

Head of the Palestinian Health Development Information Project, and the Union of Palestinian Medical Relief Committees. He is typical of Palestinians from the territories who chose the path of non-governmental organizations to serve their community. Defeated as an independent for Ramallah in the January 1996 Palestinian Council elections, Barghouti warned that without an effective secular opposition, the Council would become a rubber stamp for the PLO, and *Hamas* would gain support.

Baz, Osama al-   Egypt

Head of President Mubarak's Office for Political Affairs, and regarded as the most influential Egyptian adviser on foreign policy. Osama al-Sayed al-Baz was born on July 6, 1931, in a town in the Daquahlia governorate. For many years he lectured at the Ministry of Foreign Affairs training school. A conservative figure, he only joined the ruling Arab Socialist Union's youth secretariat after left-wingers were expelled in 1971. He was appointed as deputy head of Foreign Minister Ismail Fahmi's private office in 1974, and the following year he became full head of the office. After Fahmi resigned in protest at Sadat's peace initiative with Israel, in 1977, Baz continued to serve under a succession of foreign ministers (Muhammad Ibrahim Kamel, Mustafa Halil and Kamal Hassan Ali). At the same time, Vice-President Hosni Mubarak made al-Baz head of his bureau. Osama al-Baz was intimately involved in the peace talks with Israel, and helped to repair Egypt's ties with the USA. Hosni Mubarak replaced Anwar Sadat as President, after the latter's assassination in late 1981. Still trying to 'find his feet' politically, he relied very heavily on Baz's advice. As a result, Mubarak weaned Osama al-Baz away from the Foreign Ministry, to make him chief of the President's Office for Political Affairs in 1981, a position Baz has held ever since. In 1992, Osama al-Baz and the new Foreign Minister Amr Moussa worked as behind-the-scene intermediatories in various attempts to achieve talks between Israel and the PLO. Throughout 1993, he was apprized of developments in Oslo. Osama al-Baz remains an influential figure, and it is said that President Mubarak relies on his advice far more than Anwar Sadat did.

Begin, Menachem   Israel

Prime Minister of Israel from 1977 to 1983. Born in White Russia in 1913, and educated in Poland, Menachem Begin led the Revisionist Zionist movement since the State of Israel's inception, and became the first *Likud* prime minister in 1977. He is probably best remembered for the peace treaty with Egypt, signed in 1979, and Israel's invasion of Lebanon in 1982. After arriving in Palestine in 1942, having narrowly escaped the Nazi Holocaust, Begin soon took over leadership of the right-wing *Irgun* underground. He was held responsible for the King David Hotel bombing, Deir Yassin massacre and several acts of terror against British Mandatory forces, which to some extent hastened Britain's departure from Palestine. From 1949 he led the opposition *Herut* Party in the first Israeli *Knesset*. On the eve of the 1967 war, he entered a government of national unity, but left in 1970. Harnessing the votes of disgruntled Sephardim, Begin eventually succeeded in defeating the dominant Labour Party in 1977. He committed his government to encouraging Jewish settlements on the occupied West Bank and Gaza (which tallied with his earlier belief in a Zionist state on both banks of the Jordan).

However, he confounded his critics by negotiating and signing the Camp David Accords with Egypt in 1978, and the subsequent Israel–Egypt peace treaty of 1979. Within weeks of returning the last part of the Sinai to Egypt in 1982 (according to the treaty), Begin turned his attention to the northern border and sanctioned a full-scale invasion of Lebanon. He succeeded in seeing Yasser Arafat and the PLO hierarchy expelled from Beirut; but ultimately Begin failed to remove the PLO presence from Lebanon. Israeli opposition to the war grew, and his ambitious plans for privatization failed to reverse a serious economic decline. These factors, combined with concern over his wife's health, forced his resignation in August 1983. In his remaining years, Begin was often consulted as the charismatic godfather of the Israeli right, during the comparitively lacklustre rule of his chosen successor, Yitzhak Shamir. Menachem Begin died in 1992. His son, Binyamin Ze'ev Begin, is a prominent *Likud* MK, whose politics is very much cast in his father's mould.

Begin, Ze'ev Binyamin 'Benny'   Israel

Likud MK, son of former Prime Minister Menachem Begin, and tipped as a possible future leader of the party. Begin was born in Jerusalem in 1943, is married and has six children. He holds a PhD in geology from the University of Colorado, and has been an MK since 1988. Begin tried to establish a middle ground within *Likud,* based on respect for the party's traditions. He lacks his late father's charisma, but is respected for his honesty and intelligence. Despite his own right-wing inclinations, he objected to the militant *Moledet* party joining the Shamir government in 1991, and in 1995 advised against *Likud's* participation in anti-Rabin rallies, alongside radical settlers. Begin failed in his 1993 bid to replace Yitzhak Shamir as *Likud* leader. He objected to Benjamin Netanyahu's 'Americanization' of *Likud*, and opposed his flirtation with right-wing extremists. However, in early 1996 Begin was one of a minority of *Likud* MKs who rejected a new party platform which accepted Oslo 2 as a fait accompli. In his view, Oslo 2 was fundamentally 'evil'. In June 1996 he became Minister of Science.

Yossi BEILIN

Nationality	Israeli
Religion	Jewish
Place of birth	Israel
Date of birth	1948
Former position	Minister without Portfolio in the Prime Minister's Office (since Nov. 1995)
Previous positions	Deputy Foreign Minister (1992–95) Minister for Economics and Social Development (July 1995) Head of the Israeli delegation to the multilateral talks steering committee
Allies	Protege of Foreign Minister Shimon Peres; Avraham Burg
Position on peace	Very positive, was the key initiator of the Oslo peace talks
National political importance	Extremely influential in steering the peace process
Prospects	Tipped for high office within Labour, although prone to speaking his mind, which has offended Israeli right-wingers and Diaspora Jews

Yossi Beilin is one of the most influential of Labour's younger generation. As Deputy Foreign Minister, he was initially seen as Shimon Peres's chief aide. But while it is true that the two men share a similar political vision, Beilin has certainly made his own mark. He is credited with initiating the Israeli government's involvement in the secret Oslo talks (which eventually resulted in the Israeli–PLO Washington Declaration of September 1993). Beilin currently holds a purpose-built post – Minister Without Portfolio within the Prime Minister's Office – from where he holds tremendous infuence over the future direction of Israel's peace inititiative with the Palestinians.

Beilin was born in 1948, and thus is as old as the state of Israel itself. He began his career as a journalist, writing for the prestigious *Davar* newspaper. He later received a PhD in political science from Tel Aviv University. He served as spokesman of the Labour Party from 1977 to 1984 and was the Government Secretary from 1984 to 1986 (during the first two years of the

Likud-Labour government). During this period he strengthened his ties with Shimon Peres, then Labour leader and Prime Minister. From 1986 to 1988 Beilin was the Director-General for Political Affairs of the Israeli Foreign Ministry. He was elected to the Knesset in 1988, and served as Deputy Minister of Finance from 1988 to 1990, under Shimon Peres.

In 1992 Beilin entered the new Labour-led government as Deputy Minister of Foreign Affairs. Through his contacts with the Norwegian social researcher, Terje Larsen, Beilin launched the Israeli end of the secret Oslo talks. In fact, the initial Israeli negotiators, Pundak and Hirschfeld, worked for Beilin's private research institute. Although he was mistrusted by Rabin, Beilin ensured through his mentor, and now Foreign Minister, Shimon Peres, that the talks resulted in a breakthrough agreement with the PLO, the Gaza-Jericho First plan, encapsulated in the Declaration of Principles (as signed in September 1993). Beilin built good relations with the chief PLO negotiator, Abu 'Ala, but he was diverted from pursuing the 'Palestinian track' by new commitments in the regional sphere.

In December 1993 Beilin headed the Israeli delegation to the steering committee of the multilateral talks, in Tokyo. This afforded him the power to determine Israel's relationships with the Arab world. He called for open borders, economic co-operation, the harnessing of modern technology, rehabilitation of refugees, tackling the sources of armed conflict, and a new system to distribute water throughout the region, on the basis of real needs. In April 1994 he became the first Israeli minister to officially visit a Gulf Arab state, when he travelled to Oman to participate in the multilateral water working group's fourth session.

A man who combines strong liberal instincts with pragmatism, Beilin has made intra-regional co-operation on the environment a centrepiece of his political strategy. At the same time, he has offended many Diaspora Jews with his frank pronouncements about their relationship to Israel. (Traditionally, Israel has welcomed money from Diaspora Jewish communities; Beilin, however, in effect told them that Israel was a sophisticated country which could stand on its own two feet. Rather than give money, Diaspora Jews should immigrate to Israel to participate in the exciting path the new state was embarked upon.) Cynics countered that it was easy for him to 'score points' with such bravado, as Diaspora Jewish charities contribute only a fraction of the amount Israel regularly receives in aid from the US government. Even so, Beilin's speech marked a psychological watershed in Diaspora–Israel relations, and many of his points were amplified by Israel's President, Ezer Weizmann.

Beilin's maverick nature was also seen during the peace process, such as in early 1995, when he advised missing out the interim phase in talks with the Palestinians, and starting immediately with final status negotiations. In July 1995, Yossi Beilin entered the cabinet as Minister of Economics and Social Development. His triumphs in the multilateral arena seemed to bode him well in this new post, from which he could pursue Israel's economic openings to the Arab world. Beilin showed his mastery of regional politics at the Middle East and North Africa Economic Summit, held in Amman, Jordan, in October. His hand (and that of his mentor, Shimon Peres) was behind many of the ambitious schemes for regional economic co-operation approved by summit delegates.

In November 1995, following the assassination of Yitzhak Rabin, he was appointed Minister without Portfolio in Prime Minister Peres's Office (his old ministry was dissolved). Some had tipped him for as Foreign Minister, but this post went to the more hardline Ehud Barak. Analysts felt that Shimon Peres had to reassure the political right. Nonetheless, as right-hand man to Peres, and a key figure in the newly established inner cabinet 'peace team', Beilin wielded enormous influence over Israeli policy in the run-up to Israeli elections in 1996. In December 1995 Beilin was sent to assure West Bank settlements, like Ofra, that the government 'did not ignore their existence'; equally, he asked them to accept the 'facts on the ground' about the peace process.

In February 1996, the Israeli *Ha'aretz* daily reported that Abu Mazen and Yossi Beilin had led teams of negotiators in some 20 secret meetings, held over 12 months. These talks took place in Britain, Sweden, Cyprus, Holland and Jerusalem, and began after the cabinet had turned down Beilin's suggestion to 'leap ahead' to final status talks, in early 1995. Evidently, they produced a blueprint for a final settlement, which included Israeli recognition of Palestinian statehood, in exchange for a Palestinian promise to leave most settlements in place. Beilin reportedly proposed a corridor to link Gaza with the West Bank, but ruled out a Palestinian proposal to make Jerusalem into the 'twin capital of two states'.

Beltagi, Mamdouh el-   Egypt

Tourism minister, and deeply involved in multilateral negotiations on the issue. He was instrumental in convening the World Tourism Organization conference in Cairo, in October 1995. He also played a part in setting up the regional MEMITTA organization, which includes Egyptian, Israeli and Palestinian representatives.

Ben Ali, Zide el-Abidine   Tunisia

President of Tunisia since 1987. Ben Ali was born in 1936, joined the army when 22, and rose to the rank of general. He served two stints as Director-General of National Security, before joining the cabinet in 1985. In October 1987 he was promoted from Interior Minister to Prime Minister. One month later he replaced the ageing president and founding father of Tunisian independence, Habib Bourguiba. Ben Ali had enjoyed a hardliner's reputation, but on taking office he launched major political reforms, by talking to the opposition, releasing political prisoners and encouraging exiles to return. He enjoys close ties with the PLO (which have used Tunis as their headquarters since 1983 and played an important mediatory role in PLO–Israel talks. In 1994, Tunisia agreed to open an interest office in Tel Aviv. Ben Ali is believed to favour eventual full diplomatic relations with Israel.

Ben-Aharon, Yossi   Israel

Director-General of the Prime Minister's office under Shamir. By 1992 he had become the head of Israel's delegation to the Washington peace talks (after the initial Madrid summit conference). Ben-Aharon, who was born in 1932, had a reputation as a tough negotiator. Critics blamed his approach for stifling progress on the Syrian front. When Yitzhak Rabin became Prime Minister, he replaced Ben-Aharon with Shimon Shevis.

Ben-Ami, Shlomo   Israel

Ambassador to Spain, 1987 to 1991; elected to the Knesset as a Labour MK in the 1996 party primaries. He is widely tipped as someone who could contribute to the peace process. Shlomo Ben-Ami was born in 1943 and is currently based at Tel Aviv University, where he lectures in modern Spanish history. He joined Labour in 1977, and quietly but effectively helped to prepare the ground for Israeli participation in the historic Madrid peace conference of October, 1991. According to reports, he was about to be made cabinet secretary in 1992, but upset Prime Minister Rabin by demanding control over peace talks with Jordan and the Palestinians. He subsequently acted as adviser to 'Salaam 2000', a project dedicated to fostering Israel's economic co-operation with the Arab world.

Ben-Eliezer, Binyamin   Israel

Housing Minister, Labour MK. Binyamin Ben-Eliezer took over the portfolio from his Likud predecessor, Ariel Sharon, and immediately began a change of policy. While Sharon concentrated on diverting funds to subsidize new settlements, Ben-Eliezer emphasized the need to house some 500,000 new immigrants. He worked jointly with Treasury Minister Avraham Shohat to this end. He also greatly increased budgetary allocations to Arab town halls. Sharon's legacy still lingered, however, and Ben-Eliezer (known by his Arabic nickname 'Fuad') found that his ministry owed $2 billion to contractors who had built on Sharon's orders in places (like the Negev) where there was little or no demand.

Ben-Eliezer was born in Iraq in 1936 and emigrated to Israel in 1949. He was a commander in the Six-Day War (1967) and the Yom Kippur War (1973). From 1978 to 1981 he was the IDF Commander in the West Bank, and from 1983 to 1984, Government Co-ordinator of Activities in the Administered Areas.

Ben-Eliezer's hopes of using the Housing Ministry as a launchpad to the premiership were thwarted by allegations of corruption and vote-buying, plus a failure to stop a 30% rise in house prices over one year. On the peace process, Ben-Eliezer generally supports the government, although he has qualms about the prospect of dismantling of settlements and towns on the Golan Heights (as part of a possible peace deal with Syria). Together with Rabin's adviser, Noah Kinarti, he apparently allowed a secret fund to sidestep restrictions on expansion of settlements; until left-wing protests within the cabinet closed this channel. Prior to Oslo 2, Ben-Eliezer was hard-pressed to ensure that settler bypass roads were built in time for Israeli troop redeployments. Somewhat controversially, he favours better relations with his native

Iraq. In early 1996 he continued discussions with settler leaders who had broken away from *Yesha,* and were prepared to co-operate with the new Palestinian rulers of West Bank towns.

Ben-Elissar, Eliayahu   Israel
Formerly Director-General of Prime Minister Begin's office. Born in Poland in 1932, he emigrated to Israel and trained as a historian. After managing Begin's political affairs, he became the first Israeli Ambassador to Egypt. Ben-Elissar entered the Knesset as a *Likud* member in 1981. Ben-Elissar was an Israeli delegate to the Madrid peace conference in October 1991, and still holds a Knesset seat.

Ben-Tsur, Eitan   Israel
Deputy Director-General of the Israel Foreign Ministry. Born in 1948, Ben-Tsur was tipped to become director general in 1993, but lost out to a younger man, Uri Savir. Since then the two have formed a close working partnership. Ben-Tsur is first and foremost a career diplomat, without strong party affiliations. In 1991 he joined the Israeli delegation to the Madrid peace conference. In 1995 Ben-Tsur was given special responsibility to get talks moving again with Syria. In November he met a senior Syrian official privately in Belgium, prior to the European-Mediterranean Barcelona Conference, and this led directly to the Wye Valley talks between Israel and Syria, in Maryland, USA.

Ben-Yair, Michael   Israel
Attorney-General. Ben-Yair, 53, is of Sephardi origin, and replaced the outgoing Yosef Harish in November 1993. He was born in Jerusalem, and was a Tel Aviv District Court judge before taking up his current appointment. Some interpreted the replacement of Harish as a political move, prompted by *Shas* party leader, Aryeh Deri, who alleged that Harish was persecuting him over corruption charges. Ben-Yair is a declared foe of *Yesha* and militant settlers, who tried to block his appointment. In office he took a strong stand against rabbis (including the former Chief Rabbi Moshe Goren) who advised soldiers to disobey orders if they were asked to dismantle settlements.

Bentsen, Lloyd   USA
Secretary of the Treasury in the Clinton administration. Lloyd Bentsen became the co-sponsor of the Conference to Support the Middle East Peace, in October 1993, together with US Secretary of State Warren Christopher, Russian Foreign Minister Andrei Kozyrev and Russian Finance Minister Boris Fedorev. He called on the UNRWA, UNDP and IMF to help with meeting commitments to the Israeli–Palestinian totalling over $2 billion over five years. Bentsen stressed the need to co-ordinate private and public investment, in the short term providing immediate relief, and in the medium term, building up infrastructure in Palestinian self-rule areas.

Berri, Nabih   Lebanon
Leader of the pro-Syrian *Amal* Shi'ite group, and Speaker of the Lebanese National Assembly. According to the Lebanese constitution, the post of Speaker is traditionally held by a Shi'ite. The Taif Accords of 1989 continued with this convention, although Berri has moulded the office into a powerful political platform. Some say that in the absence of a fully restored party system, Berri has made himself in effect the Leader of the Opposition (*vis-à-vis* his colleagues in the ruling triumvirate, President Elias Hrawi, a Maronite Christian, and Prime Minister Rafiq Hariri, a Sunni Muslim). The two Shi'ite parties, Berri's *Amal* and their bitter enemies, the Iranian-backed *Hezbollah,* currently hold the largest bloc of seats in parliament. This followed elections in 1992, which the Christian parties largely boycotted. Berri is currently a staunch defender of the constitution, although he made his political career in the service of an armed militia.

Berri trained as a lawyer in Beirut, and in 1978 was called on to take over as head of *Amal* ('Hope', or the Movement of the Deprived). *Amal's* founder, the religious leader, Imam Musa Sadr, had disappeared (feared killed) during a trip to Libya. Under Berri, *Amal* became a powerful military force amongst the underprivileged Shi'ite community, and threatened the supremacy of both Sunni Muslims and Christians. In 1982 it clashed with the invading Israelis, but by the following year it forged a new alliance with Syria, and with their blessing attacked PLO units. *Amal* also had to fight for its survival with a new and more militant group, *Hezbollah*, which enjoyed considerable military and financial support from Iran.

Berri turned *Amal* into a mainstream political party, and in 1984 it joined a National Salvation Front, with other sectarian movements. By 1985, Israeli forces had withdrawn from Shi'ite areas in West Beirut and the Beqa'a Valley. As the official Lebanese army was too weak to take over, *Amal* and *Hezbollah* clashed repeatedly in a bid to fill the political vacuum. Berri was re-appointed leader of *Amal* in 1986, and entered the national cabinet as Minister for Water, Electrical Resources and Justice. He also assumed responsibility for reconstruction and southern affairs. He has been Lebanon's parliamentary Speaker since 1992, replacing Hussein al-Husseini. This followed a strong showing by *Amal* in national elections. The official Lebanese-Israeli bilateral talks ceased in March 1994, but in 1995 there were many reports of secret meetings between Berri and Israeli chief negotiator, Uri Lubrani. At the same time, Berri did little to stop *Amal* attacks on Israel in the south (an apparent attempt to match *Hezbollah*). Berri appears to have lost a lot of his earlier grassroots support (other *Amal* leaders, like Ahmed Dya, are more popular in the *Shi'ite* heartlands). However, he has more than compensated for this deficit by forging an important role as a powerbroker in Lebanese national politics; and there is little doubt he wishes to wield equal influence over Lebanon's future relations with its two powerful neighbours, Israel and Syria.

Bessmertnykh, Alexander   Russia
Former Foreign Minister of the Soviet Union. Together with US Secretary of State James Baker, Alexander Bessmertnykh was instrumental in organizing the historic Madrid peace summit on Middle Eastern peace, in October 1991. He paid visits to Israel in May 1991, which helped to pave the way for the talks. However, it was his successor, Boris Pankin, who actually attended the summit, and who formally restored diplomatic relations between the Soviet Uinon and the state of Israel.

Besseiso, Fuad Hamadi (Dr)   Palestinian
Head of the PNA's Monetary Authority (PMA). Besseiso has led criticism of Jordanian banks for allegedly siphoning off funds from Gaza and the West Bank, and investing them elsewhere. At the same time, he signed an economic agreement with Jordan in January 1995; and was preparing a financial framework for the Central Bank of Jordan, as of August 1995. On Dec. 18, 1995, the Bank of Israel turned over responsibility for banking supervision in the PNA-controlled areas to Dr Besseiso. Dr Besseiso, who was consulted during the Paris, Oslo and Taba talks, will also oversee foreign currency regulations and ensure stability in banks' liquidity. Analysts expect Besseiso's real powers will increase as Palestinian self-rule extends to new areas in the West Bank (according to Oslo 2). Until such time as there is a Central Bank of Palestine, Besseiso and the PMA will continue to work closely with the central banks of Israel and Jordan, and with his counterparts in those countries, Ya'akov Frenkel and Bassam Saket.

Bin Alawi, Yusuf   Oman
(See Alawi, Yusuf bin)

Bin Shaker, Sharif   Jordan
(See Shaker, Sharif bin)

Bin-Nun, Yoel (Rabbi)   Israel
Prominent figure on *Yesha* – the Council of Jewish Settlements in Judea, Samaria and Gaza; a respected rabbinical teacher and former founder of the right-wing religious *Gush Emunim* movement; now seen as a leading 'dove' amongst settlers. Rabbi Bin-Nun lives in the West Bank settlement of Ofrah. He has been ostracized by more right-wing figures for suggesting some territorial compromise on the territories may be necessary in order to achieve peace with Palestinians. He has proposed his own map of pockets of settlements which Israel should annex, leaving the rest of the West Bank under largely Palestinian sovereignty.

Biran, Ilan (Maj.-Gen.)   Israel
Israeli Defence Forces Officer in Command of the Central Command. Maj.-Gen. Ilan Biran was intimately involved with the negotiations which led to the Interim Agreement (or Oslo 2)

in September 1995. He also had the duty of explaining to worried Jewish settlers how the IDF would deploy, and where the new 'bypass roads' would run. Biran relayed new orders to IDF soldiers on when to open fire in the West Bank, taking into account the three different zones in the West Bank, and the views of Palestinian police. One of Biran's tasks is to vet PNA officials on security grounds. In March 1996, Biran led the operational crackdown on *Hamas*, following the suicide bomb attacks in Jerusalem, Tel Aviv and Ashkelon.

Biran, Yoav   Israel
Deputy Director-General in the Israeli Foreign Ministry, with special responsibility for overseeing the peace process. Yoav Biran was born on July 17, 1939. He studied history and international relations at the Hebrew University, Jerusalem, and then entered the Ministry of Foreign Affairs in 1963.

Yoav Biran was Israel's Ambassador to the UK from 1988 to 1993, a testing assignment considering that it coincided with the *intifada* in the territories, and the outbreak of the Gulf War. Biran also distinguished himself as a liaison with British officials during the Madrid summit in October 1991. Yoav Biran was recalled to Jerusalem as Deputy Director-General for the peace process in 1993. In April 1995, he wrote a report which warned that the multilateral talks were stagnating because of insufficient funds to back the myriad of projects proposed during working group sessions; setbacks in Israel's bilateral talks with Syria and the Palestinians; and confusion caused by external organizations which overlap too much with multilateral institutions. In January 1996, Biran signed an agreement to set up commercial interest offices in Muscat and Tel Aviv, with Omani Foreign Minister Yusuf Bin Alawi.

Birnawi, Fatmeh   Palestinian
Commander of the Palestinian women's police force, and effectively the second highest ranking woman in the Palestine National Authority (PNA) after Umm Jihad. Fatmeh Birnawi was born into a small Palestinian community of African descent, which for centuries has lived in the Old City of Jerusalem, alongside the Temple Mount. While still a teenager in the 1950s, Birnawi worked as a nurse in Qalqilyah (then under Jordanian rule). When Israeli forces captured East Jerusalem in 1967, Fatmeh, then aged 25, was a key member of the *Fatah* cell in the Old City. A few months later, following orders from her superiors, she planted a bomb in a Jerusalem cinema mainly frequented by Jews. No-one was killed in the blast, but many were injured. After she was eventually caught, Birnawi was sentenced to life imprisonment, but released in 1978 on health grounds and deported to Jordan. From there she went to Lebanon, and ultimately to the new PLO headquarters in Tunis in the early 1980s.

As women's police commander, General Birnawi initially found herself inundated by prospective candidates. The policewomen under her charge work in administrative posts at customs and border crossings; a few also serve in intelligence and anti-drug squads. During 1994, they trained at police academies in Jordan, Egypt and Tunisia.

Boueiz, Fares   Lebanon
Minister of Foreign and Expatriate Affairs since 1990. According to the Taif and other accords, Lebanese foreign policy must be vetted by Syria. This consideration has restrained Boueiz from taking an independent line. With regard to the peace process, his main concern is to ensure Israel's departure from its 'southern security zone' in accordance with UN 425. Only then would Lebanon enter the multilateral talks, and consider a peace treaty with Israel. Boueiz, a Maronite Christian, represented Lebanon at the Madrid conference in 1991. However, there were deep differences in policy between Boueiz and Suheil Shammas, Secretary-General of the Foreign Ministry and head of Lebanon's bilateral talks delegation. In March 1993, Shammas resigned his posts. In late 1992 Boueiz had protested vehemently against Israel's decision to deport over 400 Palestinian *Hamas* members into Lebanon. He saw it as a violation of Lebanon's territorial integrity. In February 1992, however, Boueiz said Lebanon would accept their returning to Gaza and the West Bank 'within an acceptable period of time'. Bilateral talks broke down in April 1994, and have not yet been resumed. Analysts believe Boueiz is waiting for a signal from Syria. In the interim, the Lebanese Army has neither disarmed nor disciplined *Hezbollah* units, which it sees as fighting a legitimate war of self-defence.

Boutros Ghali, Boutros   Egypt

Secretary-General of the United Nations since Jan. 1, 1992; former Deputy Foreign Minister of Egypt. He was heavily involved in the Camp David peace talks with Israel. Boutros Ghali was born in 1922, studied at Cairo University and received a PhD in international law from Paris University in 1949. From 1949 to 1977, he was professor of law and international relations in Cairo.

Politically, Boutros Ghali joined the Arab Socialist Union Central Committee in 1974, was Minister of State for Foreign Affairs from October 1977 until 1991, and was briefly Deputy Prime Minister for Foreign Affairs, before he was elected to replace Javier Pérez de Cuellar as Secretary-General of the United Nations. He played a central role in the Camp David peace talks with Israel in 1978. He became an MP in 1987, and helped to steer the ruling National Democratic Party after 1980.

With his African, Arab and Christian background, and his wealth of experience, many hailed him as possessing the ideal ingredients to represent the world body. The UN's effectiveness during the Gulf War also raised expectations. However, Boutros Ghali has had his hands full with many simultaneous crises (Bosnia, Rwanda, Somalia, and others); while at the same time, the general economic downturn has depleted the UN's coffers.

In August 1993 he held a tense meeting with the new Israeli Deputy Foreign Minister Yossi Beilin. Beilin accused him of being 'unbalanced and one-sided' in his criticism of Israel's Operation Accountability in southern Lebanon, earlier that year. Boutros Ghali had also opposed a greater UNIFIL peace-keeping role in southern Lebanon (part of an Israeli request for a Lebanese army redeployment there). After the meeting with Beilin, he agreed to adopt a more flexible approach, and allow UNIFIL officers more leeway to make operational decisions.

In August 1994 Boutros Ghali addressed a four-day UN and European Non-Governmental Organizations (NGO) Symposium on the Question of Palestine, held in Geneva. He said the international community and NGOs were responsible for ensuring the success of Palestinian self-government, through funding economic and social development in Gaza and the West Bank. He praised the 'further empowerment' measures agreed between Israel and the PLO, and said they were 'milestones on the way to a comprehensive and lasting peace'. Boutros Ghali accompanied President Mubarak to Jerusalem and delivered an oration at Yitzhak Rabin's funeral in November, 1995. Boutros Ghali is a Coptic Christian, and is married to a Polish Jewish woman who later converted to Christianity. According to some observers, these factors prevented him from becoming Egypt's Foreign Minister. His tenure as head of the UN is due to end in 1996. Boutros Ghali is seeking re-appointment but faces US oppositon.

Boutros Ghali, Youssef   Egypt

Minister of State for International Co-operation (an economics portfolio). Boutros Ghali is a nephew of UN Secretary-General Boutros Boutros Ghali, and is regarded as one of the leading 'new generation' of Middle Eastern politicians. He was appointed Minister of State for Cabinet Affairs on April 18, 1993, and presented Egypt's case to the IMF, at high level talks on the reducing the national deficit and restructuring the economy. Boutros Ghali was given his current portfolio on Oct. 13, 1993, where he serves as effective deputy to Foreign Minister Amr Moussa.

Since then he has played an active role in improving relations between Egypt and Israel. In early 1995, he represented Egypt at the newly created Quadrilateral (or Quadripartite) Commission, a special forum set up with American encouragement, to tackle the specific problems of the displaced Palestinians of 1967. The commission's other members are Israel, Jordan and the Palestine National Authority. At the MENA economic summit held in Amman in October and November 1995, Boutros Ghali said that regional 'openness' and reductions in bureaucracy would bring economic development to the region. Appearing to differ from the cautiousness of other Egyptian politicians, he called for a regional economic bloc, including Israel, to 'stand up to the giants of the USA, the EU or the Far East'. In January 1996, it appeared that Boutros Ghali was being moved to a new post as Minister without Portfolio.

Brodet, David　　　　　　**Israel**
Former Budget Director, and since January 1995, Director General of the Finance Ministry. Brodet was the chief negotiator of the Israel–PLO economic accord, which was signed in Paris in April 1994. He is an ally of Shimon Peres, and has improved ties with the IMF and World Bank, so much so that in early 1996 Israel hosted a board meeting and seminar of their leading officials. Brodet is cautiously optimistic about the Palestinian economy, but feels that Israel should do more to encourage foreign donations and investment, and ought to start planning ahead for mutually beneficial joint ventures.

Brown, Ron　　　　　　**USA**
Commerce Secretary under the Clinton administration. Following Egyptian President Mubarak's historic Cairo meeting, which set up a regional 'peace bloc', Brown convened a meeting in Taba (along the Egyptian-controlled Sinai coastline with Aqaba) on Feb. 7 and 8, 1995, to cement the understanding with US economic assistance. He met senior Egyptian, Israeli, Jordanian and Palestinian trade officials there, and secured agreements to end the boycott of Israel, and accelerate regional co-operation on economic development. Brown is a firm believer in the power of free trade to guarantee international peace. Following the MENA economic summit in Amman, in October 1991, Ron Brown went to Gaza and, together with PNA President Yasser Arafat, signed a symbolically important agreement for US private capital to finance a bottling plant there. On April 3, 1996, Ron Brown died in an airplane crash over Bosnia. Mickey Kantor replaced him as Commerce Secretary.

Burg, Avraham　　　　　　**Israel**
Head of the Jewish Agency, and chairman of the *Knesset* Education and Culture Committee. Burg is one of the most outstanding of the younger generation of Labour MKs. The son of former National Religious Party leader, Yosef Burg, Avraham Burg is himself an observant Jew. Yet he is also the leading enemy of religious 'interference' in government, and suggests that distinct religious parties are detrimental to both the Jewish faith and Israeli politics. Burg is a keen and vocal supporter of the peace process, and opposes the settler movement. However, when thwarted in his ambitions for a cabinet post, he accepted the post of chief executive officer of the Jewish Agency and World Zionist Organization in June 1995. In July he gave up his *Knesset* seat so as to devote all his energies to his new position. It was a testing political baptism, as the Agency was going through a severe crisis over alleged mismanagement and financial corruption. Part of his job there has been to 'sell' the peace process to an often sceptical Diaspora Jewish audience. As of 1996, Burg was hoping to return to high government office, but several of his former allies in the new generation appeared to have taken most of the available positions.

Bush, George　　　　　　**USA**
President of the USA, from 1989 to 1993; before that, Vice-President, from 1981 to 1989. In terms of the Middle East, George Bush is best remembered as the leader who used military might to force Iraq out of Kuwait; and who, as a world statesman, organized the Madrid summit, which in turn began the current Middle East peace process. George Bush was born in 1924 in Massachusetts and educated at Yale. During World War II, he served with distinction in the Pacific Navy, and in the 1950s he made his fortune as an oil executive in Texas. He entered local Texan politics in 1967, for the Republican Party. In 1980 he was chosen as Ronald Reagan's running mate at the Republican Party's convention, and went on to win two four-year terms as the loyal Vice-President to President Reagan.

In 1988 he won his party's verdict, and the nation's vote, to become President of the USA. However, even during his nomination campaign it became clear that he would have to work hard to escape the shadow of Reagan's awesome reputation. In less than six months, economic realities forced him to renege on his election-time promise, 'Read my lips: no new taxes'. Instead, Bush concentrated on his proven strong suit, foreign policy. When Communist regimes toppled one by one in eastern Europe, in 1989, Bush offered America's full support to their democratic successors.

Bush replaced George Schultz with James Baker as US Secretary of State, which marked a distinctly cooler attitude towards Israel, and especially the *Likud* government of Yitzhak

Shamir. Bush seemed to incline more naturally towards conservative and oil-rich Arab states in the Middle East region. He also placed a higher priority on addressing the Palestinian issue, and continued with the US–PLO dialogue, which had started in the last days of the Reagan administration, in December 1988. In May 1989, Baker cautiously welcomed Shamir's first peace plan, but warned that the USA would not tolerate a permanent Israeli presence in the occupied territories. In December, Baker arrived at his own formulation, essentially a synthesis between Shamir's proposals, and a set of clarifications raised by Egyptian President Hosni Mubarak. After much deliberation, Shamir objected to aspects of the Baker Plan in March 1990. This split the Israeli government, and led to Shamir's creation of a more right-wing administration. Meanwhile, in May 1990 Bush suspended the USA's dialogue with the PLO, when Arafat seemed unwilling to condemn a terrorist incident. Next, in June, Baker charged Israel with 'not being serious about peace', when Shamir coupled his second peace plan, with an accelerated programme for building new settlements.

Saddam Hussein's invasion of Kuwait on Aug. 2, 1990 presented Bush with the opportunity to make his own mark on world politics – although initially, his chief concern was to protect the world supply of oil, which Iraq now threatened to dominate. When Iraq refused to leave Kuwait, Bush launched Operation Desert Storm, and defeated Saddam. After the US victory, he proclaimed a New World Order, and identified three issues for immediate action in the Middle East – arms reductions, democratization, and a solution to the Israeli–Palestinian problem.

Of these, the last was most successful. Bush mandated James Baker to prepare potential participants for a conference. Eventually, Israel, Jordan, Egypt, Syria, Lebanon and a Palestinian delegation all attended the Madrid Conference in October 1991. Bush also succeeded in drawing the USSR into the talks as a 'co-guarantor' of the peace process. By the middle of 1992, however, it appeared that the various bilateral talks were hitting deadlock. But Bush had to devote his attentions to his re-election campaign. In the event, his foreign policy successes were not enough to save him from electoral defeat by the Democrat candidate, Bill Clinton, in November 1992.

Buwayz, Faris
(See Boueiz, Fares)

C

Carmon, Yigal   Israel
Adviser on terrorism to former premier Shamir; leading Israeli analyst of terrorist groups. In the mid-1980s, Carmon advised the West Bank Civil Administration on 'Arab affairs'. As a colonel in the National Defence College, he wrote that Israel should focus less on terrorism, and more on an all-out war against the PLO's political arm in the territories. Carmon led a three-man team of right-wing security experts on a tour of US Jewish communities in 1994 and decried the shortcomings of the Oslo Accords. He is close to the new Prime Minister Netanyahu.

Carter, James Earl (Jimmy)   USA
President of the USA from 1977 to 1981. Jimmy Carter, born in 1924, became Governor of Georgia after a career as a scientist and peanut farmer, and in 1979 won the Democratic Party nomination for presidency. He went on to defeat the Republican candidate, incumbent Vice-President Gerald Ford. As a Southern Baptist, Jimmy Carter believed that a Jewish homeland in Israel was ordained by God, and he saw Israel as a strategic bulwark against Soviet designs in the Middle East. At the same time, he was the first US president to openly call for a Palestinian homeland, and suggested that the Palestinian people deserved compensation for past losses. Following Anwar Sadat's historic visit to Israel in 1977, Carter encouraged the Camp David peace talks the following year. Utilizing the unique rapport he had built with Begin and Sadat, Carter brokered the accords, which led to a full peace treaty between Israel and Egypt. However, he was upset when the second round of talks in Washington failed to result in an autonomy arrangement for the West Bank and Gaza.

Under Carter, the US made Egypt one of its firmest allies in the region. At the same time, he maintained the USA's special ties with Israel, and refused to recognize the PLO until it renounced terrorism. He also demanded that the USSR allow its Jewish citizens the right to emigrate to Israel. Carter's foreign policy was initially committed to furtherance of human rights globally, but in practice his administration found it had to pursue the USA's traditional alliances with undemocratic regimes.

In 1982 Jimmy Carter and his wife, Rosalynn, set up the Carter Centre in Atlanta, Georgia, a non-profit public policy institute dedicated to fighting disease, poverty and conflict through collaborative initiatives. Carter maintained his keen interest in Middle East peace, and in 1993 Carter was a guest of honour at the Washington ceremony where Israel and the PLO signed their Declaration of Principles. In January 1996, Jimmy Carter and many Carter Centre workers acted as observers at the Palestinian Council elections. On polling day, he protested that Israel's *Shin Bet* were obstructing East Jerusalem Palestinians from casting their vote. Many original Carter appointees, notably Secretary of State Warren Christopher, are key figures in the present Clinton administration.

Celli, Claudio Maria   Vatican
Under Secretary for foreign affairs, negotiated with Israel. Representative of the Holy See in Jerusalem. He currently serves on a joint committe with Israeli Deputy Foreign Minister Eli Dayan.

Cetin, Hikmet   Turkey
Former Foreign Minister. Cetin visited Israel in mid-November 1993, in the wake of the Israel–PLO breakthrough, and signed a memorandum of understanding with his opposite number, Shimon Peres. Despite traditionally cordial Israeli–Turkish relations, it was the first official written document exchanged between the two countries. Cetin's political career stretches back for at least three decades. In September 1990 he had become secretary general of the Social Democratic Populist Party (SHP), then in opposition. In November 1991, the SHP joined the government, after elections held the previous month, and Cetin became Foreign Minister under Prime Minister Tansu Ciller. Hikmet Cetin resigned his post on Nov. 28, 1994, in the wake of an escalating war against Kurdish PKK rebels in southern Turkey.

Chahid, Leila   Palestinian
(See Shahid, Leila)

Chamoun, Dory   Lebanon
Heads National Liberal Party (Christian) and Lebanese Front. Scion of an established Maronite family, he chose to boycott the first Lebanese elections in 20 years, which were held in late 1992, as 'the conditions were not right'.

Chazan, Naomi   Israel
Meretz MK. Chazan is a vocal dove who favours a Palestinian state. She has often criticized her *Meretz* cabinet colleagues for not being more assertive about keeping the peace process on track. She also met with PLO officials, including Nabil Sha'ath, when this was still illegal under Israeli law. Chazan was formerly a lecturer at the Hebrew University, and is an acknowledged expert on Israel's relations with African countries.

Chomsky, Noam   USA
Left-wing commentator, linguistics professor at Columbia. He is the foremost American Jewish critic of Israeli policy, and accuses Congress and US liberals generally of being deluded by the pro-Israeli lobby. Yet he also has criticized the PLO's 'dictatorial tendencies', and has warned that the US political elite will desert Israel if it no longer serves US business and military interests. Chomsky has accused Israel of racism, but supports the *kibbutz* system as a model for 'true libertarian socialism'.

Warren CHRISTOPHER

Nationality	United States
Religion	Christian

Place of birth	Scranton, North Dakota, USA
Date of birth	Oct. 27, 1925
Current position	United States Secretary of State (foreign minister)
Previous positions	Chairman of the law firm, O'Melveny & Myers; formerly, Deputy Attorney-General under the Johnson adminstration, and Deputy Secretary of State under the Carter administration
Allies	President Clinton, Martin Indyk, 'peace co-ordinator', Dennis Ross
Position on peace	Supports a strong US role in the peace process; especially active on the Syrian–Israeli negotiating front
National political importance	Acts as 'chairman of the board' at the state department, but other international problems have diverted his attention from the Middle East. He has little impact on domestic policy.
Prospects	Despite rumours of his imminent dismissal, Christopher seems set to stay on as a 'safe pair of hands', steering US foreign policy though some difficult challenges.

Warren Christopher was sworn in as 63rd Secretary of State on Jan. 20, 1993, and since then has headed foreign policy in the Clinton administration. While lacking the high public profile and the assertiveness of his predecessor, James Baker, Christopher has been as active in pursuing the USA's interests abroad, and particularly in the Middle East. He brings to the job a wealth of experience in legal and public service, and particularly from his role as the man who negotiated the release of 52 American hostages in Iran in 1980–81.

Warren Christopher graduated from the University of Southern California in 1945, and spent the next three years in the Naval Reserves. After that he studied law at Stanford University, and served as a law clerk to a Supreme Court Judge. Christopher then worked for the law firm O'Melveny & Myers, from 1950 to 1977, becoming a partner in 1958; he left them temporarily to serve as Deputy Attorney General of the USA from June 1967 to January 1969. In February 1977, Christopher joined the Carter admnistration as Deputy Secretary of State, under Secretary Cyrus Vance. Highlights of his time in the State Department included normalization of relations with China, ratification of the Panama Canal treaties, and setting up the first inter-agency group on human rights. Christopher also skillfully negotiated the release of 52 American hostages held in Iran. But it was too late to save Jimmy Carter's chances of re-election, and Christopher left office in January 1981, as Ronald Reagan entered the White House.

Warren Christopher became an ally of Governor Bill Clinton during the election campaign of 1992, and he was put in charge of the period of 'residential transition' from the outgoing Bush administration. Christopher ensured continuity of foreign policy, but unlike his predecessor, James Baker, he preferred the carrot to the stick in relations with Israel. In July 1993 he promised Rabin 'security guarantees' on the Golan Heights if there was progress in talks with Syria. He was only informed about the secret Oslo channel in its final weeks. Nonetheless, he arranged the official signing ceremony in Washington, in September 1993, and agreed to restart the USA's own talks with the PLO (which had been suspended since 1990). Encouraged by the peace deal, he appointed Dennis Ross as the USA's 'peace co-ordinator'.

Christopher tried to use the momentum to press for similar breakthroughs with Syria and Jordan. In December he met President Assad personally, and both he and Ross became virtual conduits for information from Damascus. In April 1994, Christopher conveyed information from Israel, and presented Assad with the first plans for a staged Israeli withdrawal from the Golan Heights. Simultaneously with this, he fostered better ties with Jordan, and pledged to excuse its large debt. Negotiations speeded up, and in October 1994 Christopher witnessed the signing of the peace treaty between Israel and Jordan. After both the Jordanian and Palestinian agreements, he set up an apparatus for US financial backing, and sent secretaries Spero and Brown to finalize new trade agreements. But much of his work also involved shoring up talks after disasters, such as the anger caused by the Hebron massacre of early 1994.

On Feb. 12, 1995, Christopher addressed the Blair House Joint Communiqué in Washington, which reaffirmed the undertaking to continue with the peace process at the earlier Cairo summit. The USA, Egypt, Israel, Jordan, and the Palestinian Authority all accepted this move. Christopher revived the stalled talks between Israel and Syria in 1995, but little progress was made. By August 1995, he was in constant telephone contact with Peres, Arafat and Rabin during the Taba negotiations over the Interim Agreement. He requested US airspace over Israel in the event of an Iraqi attack on Jordan. Then he backed a US-Israeli–Palestinian committee to investigate water sharing between Israel and the PNA.

When the agreement was finalized, he organized a signing ceremony for Oslo 2, in Washington, on Sept. 28, 1995. Warren Christopher attended the funeral of Yitzhak Rabin in November, and took the opportunity to meet Israel's new Prime Minister Shimon Peres, and assure him of American support. He also welcomed the new prime minister's multi-polar strategy *vis-à-vis* Syria. Christopher acted as the main intermediatory in the renewed Israel–Syria initiative in mid-December 1995, which resulted in the Wye Valley talks. With the demands of Bosnia apparently reduced, following his encouragement of the successful Dayton Agreement, he felt ready to devote more of his time to the Middle East.

Observers noted a new assertiveness in Christopher's approach. In January 1996, he met President Assad and asked him to grant his negotiation team more authority to address outstanding issues with the Israelis. He also issued his sternest warning yet to the PLO, and threatened to freeze $500 million in annual aid if the Palestine National Council did not revoke clauses in the Palestinian Covenant which call for the destruction of Israel. After the terrorist outrages of late February and early March in Israel, he and President Clinton convened an extraordinary meeting of top US security personnel. They devised a new strategy to counter terrorism, and offered Israel $100 million in technological help to this end.

Ciller, Tansu   Turkey

Former Prime Minister of Turkey, and the first woman to hold the post. Tansu Ciller is believed to favour full diplomatic relations between Turkey and Israel, but is constrained by domestic opposition from Islamic parties. She visited Israel in 1994 and discussed the need to fight religiously inspired violence in the Middle East. She has also appeared at meetings of Diaspora Jewish communities in the West. Under Ciller, Turkey has played an active role in the multilateral talks (especially in the fields of arms control and, more recently, human resource training for refugees). Domestically, she leads the True Path Party, which follows the secular traditions of Kemal Attaturk, but in addition stresses the need for economic liberalization. Ciller assumed the premiership in June 1993. She narrowly avoided defeat in Turkey's general elections, which were held in December 1995. In early 1996, the possibility of a new coalition, between the resurgent Islamist Welfare Party and the right-wing secular Motherland Party, threatened to remove her from power. As of March 1996, it appeared that Ciller had at last arranged a 'rotation' coalition deal with Mesut Yilmaz's Motherland Party; he would be Prime Minister for the first two years, and Ciller for next two, commencing in 1998.

Clayman, David   USA

Israel office director of the American Jewish Congress. In his frequent visits to Jordan, Clayman helped to prepare the way for a full Israel–Jordan peace treaty, which was signed in October 1994.

Bill CLINTON

Nationality	United States
Religion	Christian
Place of birth	Hope, Arkansas
Date of birth	1946
Current position	President of the United States
Previous positions	Attorney-General of Arkansas in 1976; Governor of Arkansas in 1978 (defeated in 1980, re-elected in 1983)
Allies	(In Middle East) Martin Indyk, Dennis Ross, late Prime Minister Rabin, Jordanian King Hussein

Position on peace	Supports a strong US role in the peace process
National political importance	Constitutionally very powerful; commander-in-chief of the US military; Reputedly hindered by a Republican-dominated Congress, but managed something of a comeback in late 1995
Prospects	Good prospects for re-election for a second term as President

Since taking office in early 1993, Bill Clinton has come to symbolize America's pledge to guarantee the Middle East peace process. He has reinforced the traditional US alliance with Israel, which seemed to be wavering during the Bush administration. At the same time, he has improved relations with Syria, and has put pressure on both Damascus and Jerusalem to sign a historic peace accord. This would complement the historic Declaration of Principles, signed in Washington in September 1993; and the Israel–Jordan peace treaty, signed in October 1994. President Clinton shared the stage with the peace-makers at both those ceremonies, and made clear that the USA intended to be the ultimate guarantor of peace in the region.

Bill Clinton was born in 1946, and became a Rhodes scholar to Oxford University during the period of the Vietnam war. He returned to his native Arkansas, worked as a lawyer and law professor, joined the Democratic Party, and became the state's attorney general in 1976, and its governor in 1978. As governor he pressed forward new legislation in education, economic development, criminal justice reforms and equal opportunity programmes. Although he chose not to run in the 1988 presidential elections, he won the Democratic nomination for President in 1992, and surprised many pundits by defeating the incumbent George Bush to become the USA's first Democrat President since Jimmy Carter.

The reaction in the Middle East to Clinton's election was decidedly mixed. Israelis tended to welcome a change from the Bush administration, which some depicted as antithetical to Israeli national interests. They noted that many of Clinton's advisers were generally pro-Israeli US Jews (Martin Indyk, Aaron Kurtzer, Steven Spiegel and Sarah Ehrman, amongst others). For the same reason, Arab states and the PLO were wary of him. However, during his three years in office, Clinton has gone out of his way to befriend the growing Arab and Muslim community in the USA, and as of March 1996, the American Muslim Council seemed prepared to endorse him for a second term in office. At the same time, Clinton has never shirked from declaring his support for Israel; nor for heeding US Jewish political interests, such as concern over the New Right's agenda for mandatory school prayer.

In the 1992 election campaign, he attacked George Bush for paying too much attention to foreign affairs, while ignoring domestic economic and social problems. However, in office Clinton has found (as all Presidents seem to do) that foreign policy is a major prerogative of the US President, and a source of his authority. One of the highlights of his administration was the ceremony in Washington on Sept. 13, 1993, where Clinton joined Yitzhak Rabin and Yasser Arafat for the signing of the historic Israel–PLO Declaration of Principles.

Clinton has tried to set up a 'domino effect' for peace, and his presided over the Dayton Accords on Bosnia; and a new initiative on Northern Ireland. In January 1994 he met Syrian President Assad, to capitalize on the impetus of the Israel–PLO peace deal. Yet generally Clinton prefers to delegate much of the detailed work in the Middle East to trusted officials – like Secretary of State Warren Christopher and peace process co-ordinator Dennis Ross, or, in the economic sphere, Janet Spero and Ron Brown, and lately Vice-President Al Gore. Another feature of his administration is his tying in of economic aid with political initiatives, most clearly seen in the Trilateral Commission which he created for US-Jordan–Israel relations.

By 1994, Bill Clinton appeared to have run into enormous problems at home. His personal rating dropped alarmingly, as he was tainted with alleged corruption in the Whitewater Affair, and the Republican Party captured both Houses of Congress. Since then, however, he seems to have wrongfooted his opponents, even the wily Leader of the House of Representatives, Newt Gingrich. As the 1996 presidential election campaign began, Democrats seemed to agree that he should be nominated unopposed; meanwhile, the Republicans appeared to struggle to find one candidate behind whom they could rally.

The Israel–Jordan peace treaty of 1994, and the signing of Oslo 2 in Washington, in September 1995, were major triumphs for Clinton. Similarly, his 'hands-on' style was seen at the MENA economic summit in October 1995, where one-third of the business and political delegates were American. Nonetheless, problems remained, and the PLO in particular has criticized him for not putting enough pressure on Israel over issues like land encroachment in Jerusalem. Clinton vetoed a Congressional bill to move the US Embassy in Israel to Jerusalem, but his own views seemed ambiguous on the issue.

After the shock of Yitzhak Rabin's assassination, Clinton articulated his personal sense of loss for a trusted ally. Clinton played an important symbolic role in brokering the Wye Valley talks between Israel and Syria. In 1996, he responded firmly to the bomb blasts in Israel, by sending special bomb-detecting equipment, and vowing to shut off funds for fundamentalist groups. Bill Clinton seems to have 'grown into the role' of a President with international authority, and, as of February 1996, has a good chance of being elected for a second term.

Cohen, Ra'anan   Israel
Chairman of the Labour faction in the *Knesset*. In 1995 Cohen caused some controversy by suggesting that Israeli Arab villages straddling the 'green line' could be 're-united' with their other halves in the West Bank. He proposed amending the 1967 border, thereby extending PNA sovereignty into Israel itself, in exchange for a deal with the PNA which would allow Israel to annex certain adjoining Jewish settlements.

Cohen, Ruth   Israel
Leader of Women in Black. The group consisted of Israeli women who protested in favour of peace, occasionally together with Palestinian women sympathisers, including Hanan Ashrawi. Women in Black was disbanded after the Washington Declaration in September 1993, as it had achieved its goal of direct talks between Israel and the PLO.

Cohen, Ya'akov   Israel
Head of Foreign Ministry's economics department during the Madrid talks.

Coopersmith, Esther   USA
Former UN representative. A well-known society hostess, Coopersmith often acted as a behind-the-scenes diplomatic 'fixer' for Israeli and Arab diplomats and negotiators to meet.

Craig, James (Sir)   UK
President, Middle East Association. Sir James is a former British Ambassador to Syria and Saudia Arabia. His lobby organization influences British foreign policy in the Middle East, by airing the Palestinian issue, but concentrates mainly on maintaining Britain's traditionally close and financially lucrative ties with Saudi Arabia and the Gulf states.

D

D'Amato, Alfonso   USA
New York Senator. This Republican politician of Italian Catholic extraction has joined forces with right-wing Jewish lobbies (like the Zionist Organization of America) and Israel's *Likud* party, to frustrate US President Clinton's support for Israel's peace process. In particular, he opposes US funding of peace-keeping operations on the Golan Heights, in the eventuality of an Israel–Syria agreement on its future.

Dahlan, Muhammad   Palestinian
Pro-Arafat Gazan 'strongman', head of the Preventive Security Forces in the region. A former deportee, Dahlan has clamped down hard on *Hamas* activities in the area. Some regard him as the main conduit for economic deals with Gaza, because, according to the Oslo Accords, his units control access to the area through their border crossing points. Dahlan has co-operated successfully with Israeli security forces, and the two forces regularly run joint patrols. But this has led Islamic fundamentalists, and other Palestinian dissidents, to accuse him of collaboration. Unlike Jibril Rajoub, his counterpart in the Jericho annex, Dahlan has perforce to share authority with other Palestinian proto-military entities, notably police forces under Col Nasser Yusuf.

Dalloul, Muhsin   Lebanon
Defence Minister, Shi'ite. In 1993 he criticized Israel for deporting more than 400 *Hamas* deportees, and leaving them on Lebanese territory.

Dalton, Richard John   UK
British Consul General in Jerusalem, and senior FCO diplomat in charge of relations with the PLO. Richard Dalton was born in 1948, educated at Magdalene College, Cambridge, and joined the diplomatic service in 1970. From 1983 to 1987, Dalton was deputy head of the UK mission to Oman, in Muscat. His next three positions saw him working on the FCO's southern Africa desk, for the Ministry of Agriculture, and as head of the FCO unit which deals with the Conference on Security and Co-operation in Europe (CSCE). Richard Dalton took up his current post in 1993. This coincided with the change in relations between Israel and the PLO, and made him the 'point man' for Britain's contribution to the peace process. Despite official Israeli disapproval, he has often held talks with Faisal al-Husseini at Orient House, the PLO's *de facto* headquarters in Jerusalem.

Daoudi, Muhammad Omar   Palestinian
Senior Adviser to the Programme for Assistance to the Palestinian People (PAPP), in its Jerusalem office. PAPP is a UN Development Programme (UNDP) project that has run since 1980, and currently disburses $30 million annually for a range of economic and social projects in the territories. Daoudi advises PAPP Special Representative Edouard Wattez, and his deputy, Oscar Fernández-Taranco. He also liaises with the Palestine National Authority.

Darawshe, Abdul Wahab   Israel
Founder and leader of the Arab Democratic Party (*Mada*). Darawshe used to be a Labour MK, but left to form the ADP as an Israeli Arab nationalist party in 1988. The ADP gained two seats in the 1992, whereas before they had one. (The other major Arab–dominated non-Zionist party, the Democratic Front for Peace and Equality, *Hadash,* gained three seats, compared to four in 1988). Together, *Mada* and *Hadash* agreed to back the governing Labour-led coalition, but only 'passively' (that is, they tend to vote against the *Likud,* especially on questions of the peace process, but are not technically in the government). Wary of accusations that Labour relied on Arab votes to stay in power, Rabin chose not to include Darawshe in the cabinet, as many predicted he might.

Darawshe believes in pushing ahead with the peace process, and ultimately favours an independent Palestinian state in the (currently) occupied territories. In March 1994, Darawshe led a group of 57 Israeli Arabs to meet Syrian President Assad. In May 1995 *Mada* and *Hadash* tabled a motion of no-confidence over Labour's plan to expropriate 54 acres of Arab land in East Jerusalem. *Mada* (unlike *Hadash*) persisted with the vote, even after Labour agreed to suspend the expropriation, but lost. In 1996, Darawshe visited Yemen and reported back to Shimon Peres that President Saleh was keen to meet him, and forge better ties with Israel. Darawshe joined with the Islamic Movement to create a United Arab List; he kept his Knesset seat in the June 1996 elections.

Darwish, Abdallah Nimr (Sheikh)   Israel
Leader of the Islamic Movement, a fundamentalist grouping amongst Israeli Arabs. Darwish was an ardent Communist until the 1967 war changed his outlook. In 1968 he enrolled in the Islamic College in Nablus. In the early 1980s he was arrested and jailed for activities in a radical and armed Islamic group. Prison changed him again, and he adopted a philosophy of non-violence 'to suit Israel's democratic conditions'. Since then he has co-operated with Israeli authorities in order to improve Arab municipalities. He formed particularly close links with Rabbi Aryeh Deri, former Interior Minister and leader of the *Shas* Party.

Darwish operates from Kafr Qasm, and under his guidance the Movement has grown over the last five years. However, he faces rivalry from a more radical faction led by Sheikh Khatib Kamal. In 1995 Darwish narrowly failed to persuade a caucus of the Movement that it should stand as a political party in forthcoming Israeli general elections. Nonetheless, the Movement does participate in local authority elections, and now controls a number of Arab town councils. Darwish often participates in meetings of the National Union for Arab Local Councils and Mayors, in which forum he advocated shows of sympathy for the *intifada*.

He also reputedly acts as a go-between whenever Israeli officials wish to talk to *Hamas,* the main Palestinian Islamist grouping in the territories. In November 1994, Darwish and Dr Ahmed Tibi, a fellow Israeli Arab and close adviser to Yasser Arafat, joined forces and helped to broker a reconciliation between the PLO and *Hamas,* after clashes in Gaza. Since then, the two men have talked of setting up a joint electoral list to contest the forthcoming Israeli elections. Such a party would combine the 'credibility' of the PLO with the Islamic *caché* of *Hamas.* In the event, Darwish approved a joint link with his former rivals in the Arab Democractic Party.

Darwish, Mahmoud   Palestinian
Renowned Palestinian poet and commentator. Darwish resigned from the PLO Executive Committee over disagreements with the concessions made by the PLO in the Oslo Accords.

Dayan, Eli   Israel
Deputy Minister of Foreign Affairs in Israel, July 1995 to June 1996. Eli Dayan was born in Morocco in 1949 and immigrated to Israel in 1963. After taking a law degree at the Hebrew University in 1971, and serving in the Israeli army as a first lieutenant, he ran a private law practice in the southern coastal town of Ashkelon. He also became chairman of the *Oded* Movement, and was elected Mayor of Ashkelon in 1978, which post he held until 1991.

In 1988 he was elected to the Knesset as a member of the Labour Party, and was re-elected in 1992. He served as Chairman of the Parliamentary Group of the Labour Party, in effect its chief whip. Even so, opponents accused him of playing a mischievous role and undermining the government in a debate over education (Dayan backed a longer schoolday, to boost the educational standing of poorer Sephardi children, although this would have added over a billion dollars to the budget). In early 1995 David Levy tried to woo Dayan into his new *Derekh ha-Hadash* party (a breakaway from the *Likud* which particularly appeals to Moroccan Jewish voters). But Dayan resisted the call, and in July 1995 he was appointed Deputy Minister of Foreign Affairs. He took over from the active dove, Yossi Beilin, who went on to become Minister of Economics in a cabinet reshuffle.

Dayan is the co-director of an Israel–Vatican Committee, with the Vatican Under-Secretary for Foreign Affairs Mgr Claudio Maria Celli. He is also responsible for planning a transport connecton between Gaza and the West Bank, and has discussed the issue with PNA Minister Nabil Sha'ath and Norway's ambassador for the peace process, Rolph Trolle Andersen.

Dayan, Moshe   Israel
Minister of Defence, June 1967 to 1974; Foreign Minister, 1977 to 1979. Moshe Dayan, famous for his eyepatch (the result of fighting against the Vichy French in Lebanon, in 1941), was born in 1915, served in the *Haganah* in the 1930s, masterminded Israel's 1956 campaign, and oversaw the Six Day War in 1967. He joined Ben-Gurion in the breakaway *Rafi* Party, but rejoined the *Rafi-Mapai* union of 1968, which became today's Labour Party. Dayan was known as a maverick, but was also far-sighted in his appreciation of the need for a 'good fences' policy in the West Bank, and limited Jewish settlement, in recognition of Palestinian sensitivities. Others, however, criticized him for merely sugaring the pill of occupation. Dayan was an important figure at the Camp David peace talks, but resigned as Foreign Minister in 1979 over Begin's unwillingness to grasp the nettle of Palestinian political aspirations. Moshe Dayan died in 1981.

Dayan, Uzi   Israel
General, head of IDF planning. A nephew of the late Moshe Dayan (*q. v.*), Uzi Dayan was an important figure in Israeli negotiations on security issues with the PLO and Syria. In early 1995 he criticized the PLO for not doing more to quell terrorism, which won him plaudits in right-wing sections of the Israeli media. In late January 1996 he was sent as a military expert to negotiate with his Syrian counterparts in Wye Plantation, Maryland, USA.

Dayan, Yael   Israel
First Israeli MK to meet Arafat, thereby defying a legal embargo at the time. She represents the left-wing of the Labour Party, and is also the daughter of the late former Defence and

Foreign Minister Moshe Dayan. She had close ties with the Peace Now movement, and often clashes with Orthodox Jewish MKs in the Knesset.

Deri, Aryeh   Israel

Leader of *Shas*, the *Sephardi* religious party; formerly Interior Minister. Aryeh Deri has proven to be a political phenomenon, who left his *yeshiva* (orthodox Jewish seminary) to found a new party, harnessed the political might of his fellow *Sephardim*, and soon reached ministerial rank in Yitzhak Shamir's *Likud* coalition government in 1988, and in Yitzhak Rabin's Labour government in 1992. Defying the stereotypical image of *Sephardi* Jews, Deri has always espoused peace with the Palestinians as a *sine qua non* of his participation in government. At the same time, he supports social legislation which secularists fear would turn Israel into a theocracy. He is currently in opposition, and the whiff of corruption has harmed his chances to return to power.

Aryeh Deri was born in Meknes, Morocco, in 1959. In 1968 he emigrated with his family to Israel, where he went to ultra-Orthodox *yeshivas* in Haderah and later Jerusalem. In 1983, when only 25, Deri persuaded the former Sephardi Chief Rabbi of Israel, Ovadiah Yosef, to help transform *Shas* (an acronym for *Sephardi* Torah Guardians) from a municipal list in Jerusalem into a fully fledged national party. In 1984 *Shas* won four seats in the Knesset, and in 1986 Deri became Director-General of the Interior Ministry in the National Unity Government. *Shas's* influence grew under the tutelage of the Lithuanian-born nonagenarian Rabbi Menachem Eliezer Shach, and it gained another seat in the 1988 elections, at the expense of the National Religious Party. In 1988 Deri became Interior Minister, and impressed his political colleagues with his dynamism. Deri proved himself gifted and articulate; some said he had the qualities to become a future prime minister.

In March 1990, *Shas* and Labour left the coalition government, because, in his own words, '*Likud* wanted to kill the peace process'. However, Deri soon rejoined the *Likud* coalition after Rabbi Shach branded Labour as apostates. In effect, Deri had scuttled Shimon Peres' hopes for setting up a Labour-led coalition. Later, Deri switched allegiances from Rabbi Shach to Rabbi Yosef. Deri further claims that pressure from *Shas* led to Israel's participation at the Madrid peace conference of October 1991. That same conference, however, caused a fatal split in Shamir's coalition, and this in turn led to the 1992 elections, which Labour, now under Yitzhak Rabin, won. Deri became the only minister from Shamir's cabinet to survive into the new administration.

However, his political career has been blighted by allegations of misappropriating public funds, and siphoning them off to religious endowments under his patronage. Since June 1990, Deri has been under severe legal pressure. He also clashed with coalition allies in 1992, in particular after he objected to Education Minister Shulamit Aloni's attempt to secularize the Israeli school syllabus. Deri effectively forced Aloni to resign in May 1993. Later that year, he engineered the removal of his chief legal foe, Attorney General Yosef Harish. But persistent charges of corruption strained his relations with Prime Minister Rabin. Deri promised Rabin that he would step down if charges were brought against him. On Sept. 8, 1993, the Supreme Court ruled against Deri and his *Shas* colleague, Raphael Pinhasi, and they duly resigned. *Shas* left the government on the eve of the PLO–Israel signing ceremony in Washington.

Since then, he has not re-entered the government, as initially suggested, and seemed to drift towards a loose alliance with the opposition *Likud*. Deri broadly supports the rights of Jewish settlers in the territories, and 'values every inch of the Land of Israel'. But at the same time he favours limited territorial compromise for the sake of peace, and believes 'true [Palestinian] autonomy [would] build confidence and get rid of suspicion and lack of trust'. Deri rejected the religious extremism which led to Rabin's assassination. He is an important member of the Knesset Foreign and Security Affairs Committee. *Shas* increased its seat tally in 1996, and now holds two cabinet posts in the new Netanyahu government; thus effecting Deri renewed influence.

Dib, Roger   Lebanon

Former aide to Geagea. In 1991 he deserted the militant Geagea to sign a peace agreement with Syria on behalf of *Kataeb*, the armed wing of the Christian *Phalange* movement.

Din, Muhammad Mandi Shams ad-   Lebanon
Sheikh, and Principal Controller of the Command Council of *Amal*, a prominent Shi'ite group. Sheikh Shams ad-Din was once regarded as the *mujtahid*, or supreme religious authority, of Lebanon's Shi'ite community, although in recent years Sheikh Fadlallah, the spiritual leader of *Hezbollah*, has claimed the mantle. In 1992 he supported extending the Syrian presence in Lebanon beyond the terms of the 1991 agreement to redeploy.

Dirani, Mustafa   Lebanon
Hezbollah leader kidnapped by Israeli special forces on May 21, 1994. Dirani was the head of intelligence for the Shi'ite group, *Amal*, until he broke away and formed a group which affiliated with *Hezbollah* in 1989. Dirani had allegedly captured the downed Israeli Air Force pilot, Ron Arad, in 1986, and Israel claimed it had kidnapped Dirani in order to ascertain Arad's fate. Meanwhile, the Lebanese government insists on Dirani's safe return, as one of the conditions for an ultimate peace deal with Israel.

Divon, Haim   Israel
Deputy Director-General of the Foreign Ministry, and head of Israel's Centre for International Co-operation, known as *Mashav*. One major by-product of the current peace process, in particular the Madrid conference and the Oslo Accords, has been a restoration of Israel's traditionally good relations with developing countries. Haim Divon has responded by reviving Israel's foreign aid and expert help programme, especially in agriculture and the sciences, to some 140 countries in Asia, South America, sub-Saharan Africa, and more recently closer afield, in Tunisia, Mauretania and Egypt. In February 1996 Divon and James G Speth, the Administrator of the United Nations Development Programme (UNDP), signed an agreement to join forces and train people in these countries to 'reach self-sufficiency through the development of human resources'.

Edward DJEREJIAN

Nationality	United States
Religion	Armenian Christian
Place of birth	New York
Date of birth	1939
Current position	Director of the James A. Baker III Institute for Public Policy at Rice University, since Aug. 15, 1994.
Previous positions	US ambassador to Israel until 1994; before that, US ambassador to Syria; negotiator in Middle East; assistant secretary of state for Near Eastern and South Asian affairs
Allies	Warren Christopher
Position on peace	Enthusiastic about a Syrian deal with Israel
National political importance	Influential over US Middle East policy

Edward Djerejian was the first American to be ambassador to Syria and subsequently ambassador to Israel. As such he has a unique insight into the mentalities of the two still-belligerent countries, and has played an important behind-the-scenes role in facilitating a rapprochement, especially on the issue of the Golan Heights.

Born in New York 1939 to Armenian parents who had fled from Turkey to Syria and Lebanon and finally the US, Djerejian graduated from Georgetown University in 1960 with a BSc in foreign service. After a stint in the US Army, Djerejian joined the Foreign Service in 1963. Over the years he has gained useful experience in the Middle East (serving in Jordan, Morocco and Lebanon), as well as in the Soviet Union and France. He was the White House foreign affairs spokesman during Ronald Reagan's second term. There he proved to have excellent public relations skills (unlike some colleagues who fell foul of the US administration through making gaffes).

Fluent in Arabic, Djerejian was posted to Syria in 1988, where he soon struck up a rapport with President Hafez al-Assad. Although known to be soft-spoken and easy-going, he can also be blunt, which won Assad's respect. Djerejian must therefore take some of the credit for wooing Assad into the Western camp – a key strategic success which paid dividends in the Gulf War of 1991. Djerejian was also pivotal in persuading Assad to participate in the the Madrid peace conference. After the Gulf War he was recalled to Washington as assistant secretary of state for Near Eastern and South Asian Affairs (within the Near Eastern Affairs, or NEA, wing of the State Department). He replaced John Kelly, who had been blamed for the pro-Iraq policy of early 1990 which, some say, gave Saddam Hussein the green light to invade Kuwait.

Djerejian became intimately involved in the Madrid peace track, and won a reputation on all sides as an 'honest broker', especially in Israeli–Palestinian talks. In June 1992 he warned against Islam being seen as the new ideological enemy to replace communism in US political demonology. Partly because of this, and his allegedly 'rosy-tinted' optimism about Assad's enthusiasm for making peace, some Israeli officials expressed qualms about his appointment as US ambassador to Israel in January 1992. However, Djerejian has a reputation for affection towards Israel, and already has built up good relations with several Israeli officials. He denies being 'a typical NEA Arabist'.

In 1994 Martin Indyk replaced Djerejian as US ambassador in Israel. However, Djerejian is likely to play an important part in framing US policy in the region, especially regarding the possible deployment of US troops in the Golan if Israel and Syria sign an agreement about the area. Edward Djerejian became the first Director of the James A. Baker III Institute for Public Policy at Rice University, on Aug. 15, 1994.

Dole, Bob   **USA**
Senator for Kansas, US Senate Majority Leader and, as of June 1996, the front-running presidential candidate for the Republican Party. Bob Dole was born in 1923 in Kansas, and served with honour in World War II. He practised as a lawyer before being elected Senator in 1968. From 1985 to 1986 he was Congress majority leader. In 1988 he ran in the Republican primaries against Ronald Reagan's Vice President, George Bush. Although Dole broadly backed Reagan's policies, he fought an irascible campaign against Bush, and failed to generate enough party support to displace the incumbent. Nonetheless, Bush re-appointed Dole's wife, Elizabeth, as Labour Secretary.

In 1989 he called for a 5% cut in foreign aid to Israel, to release funds for other aid programmes. He is believed to favour stationing US peace-keeping troops on the Golan Heights (as part of an Israeli–Syrian peace deal). In 1995 he tabled a bill to recognize Jerusalem as the capital of Israel, a move which embarrassed the Clinton administration (the final status of Jerusalem is due to be decided in 'final status talks' between Israel and the PLO, due to commence in mid-1996). As of March 1996, Dole had survived an initially disappointing campaign to become the Republican Party's front-runner in the race to stand as a presidential candidate against the incumbent Democrat, President Bill Clinton.

Domb, Aharon   **Israel**
Settler leader in Kiryat Arba, chief spokesman for the settlers' council, *Yesha*. Domb initially favoured violent protests against government, but after the Hebron massacre of 1994, he appeared to moderate his stance. It prompted him to write a letter to Yitzhak Rabin, warning that settlers' 'alienation had been translated into despair', and might lead to assassination. More radical figures accused him of 'betraying' them to the *Shin Bet*. After the Rabin assassination, Domb was one of the few settler leaders to admit that rash rhetoric had led to an atmosphere of inevitable violence.

Dromi, Uri   **Israel**
Head of the Israel Government press office.

Drori, Mordechai   **Israel**
Ambassador to the European Union. Drori helped to negotiate Israel's ground-breaking trade treaty with the EU, of Nov. 20, 1995. The treaty bars customs duties on all Israel–EU imports and exports.

Druckman, Haim (Rabbi)   Israel

Heads *Matzad*, religious nationalist splinter party on the far right. Rabbi Druckman was formerly a National Religious Party MK, and is now a prominent settler activist. In November 1993 he was attacked by Palestinians near Hebron. Druckman was involved with the Rabbinical Authority, which called on IDF soldiers to disobey orders if they were asked to dismantle settlements. Israel's GSS is investigating his possible role in events leading to the assassination.

E

Eban, Abba   Israel

Longest-serving Foreign Minister, from 1966 to 1974; a Labour centrist who later became a dove. Born in South Africa in 1915 and educated at Cambridge, Eban was Israel's first Ambassador to the United Nations, from 1949 to 1959. During most of that period, he was also Israel's Ambassador to Washington. In the three years preceding his appointment as Foreign Minister, Eban served as deputy to Prime Minister Levi Eshkol. At the time of the Six Day War he once again doubled as Israel's ambassador at the UN. After the war, and he delivered an impassioned plea for peace, but at the same time told Arab states to come to terms with the State of Israel. Eban was involved with the Jarring peace mission. In 1977 he favoured a substantial Israeli withdrawal from the West Bank, yet at the time he also rejected the idea of a Palestinian state.

In the late 1980s, Eban met visiting US Secretaries of State, and suggested a greater role for the Soviet Union in the peace process. Eban aspired to be prime minister, and had been the *Mapai* faction's candidate for Labour party leader in 1974. But he always enjoyed more prestige amongst Diaspora Jewry and the international political community than he did in Israel. He was effectively dropped from the Labour Party's electoral list in 1992, but occassionally comments on political events from outside the Knesset. Regarded as a dove, his most important recent contribution is his plan for a Levantine 'Benelux option', whereby Israel, Jordan and the Palestinian entity would form a no-tariff customs union. To a large extent, this became Israeli policy under Labour, as witnessed in the Paris Protocols signed with the PLO, and the peace treaty (1994) and subsequent free trade agreement (1995) signed with Jordan. In early 1996, warned the Labour Party not to shy away from the issue of Palestinian statehood. Quoting Talleyrand, he said Israel should 'co-operate with the inevitable'.

Egeland, Jan   Norway

Deputy Foreign Minister at the time of the secret Oslo talks between Israel and the PLO. Jan Egeland is a true idealist in the Scandinavian tradition. In his youth he worked for Amnesty International and the International Red Cross in Geneva. He also spent a period studying at the Hebrew University in Jerusalem, which engendered in him a deep sympathy for the State of Israel. At the same time, Egeland made excellent contacts with the PLO; and in 1992, after he had been Deputy Foreign Minister for a year, they approached him to see if Norway could arrange a 'back channel', which might achieve the breakthrough which had so far eluded the official Palestinian delegation in Washington. Egeland persuaded his boss, Foreign Minister Thorvald Stoltenberg, to provide a secret venue, and by early 1993 the talks were underway. After the breakthrough was achieved, Egeland described Norway as a small yet temperamentally progressive country, which understood the needs of both Israelis and Palestinians, in a way which larger powers perhaps could not. By the end of 1994, Egeland had been promoted to Trade and Industry Secretary; by 1996 he was State Secretary of the Norwegian Ministry of Current Affairs. Egeland has an important overseeing role in the multilateral talks on water resources, and other matters. He is currently working on an international campaign to eradicate the use of anti-personnel landmines.

Eitan, Raphael   Israel

Head of the right-wing *Tsomet* party, former general and Chief of Staff of the Israel Defence Forces (IDF). Eitan was largely responsible for planning Operation Peace for Galilee, Israel's invasion of Lebanon in 1982. His chief ally at the time was Defence Minister Ariel Sharon. Like Sharon, Eitan believes in an extremely tough approach to Palestinians in the territories. He subsequently formed an alliance with Benjamin Netanyahu prior to the 1996 elections, and won the posts of Deputy Prime Minister, Agriculture and Environment.

Raphael Eitan, familiarly known as 'Raful', was born in 1929 in a farming village near Nazareth. Eitan has spent most of his life in the military, distinguishing himself in the 1967 and 1973 wars. In 1978 he became a surprise appointment as Chief of Staff. Despite his roots in the Labour movement, he was notorious for his hawkish views. Eitan was stripped of his post in 1983, following the Kahan Commission of Inquiry into the Sabra and Shatilla massacre in 1982 (Christian Phalangists had killed more than 800 Palestinian refugees in a camp outside Beirut, which was supposed to be guarded by Israeli forces).

The following year he entered politics, as the head of the *Tsomet* Party, in alliance with fellow right-wingers in *Tehiya*. In a pattern that was to repeat itself several times, as he made and broke allegiances with other politicians. Eitan's political authority increased in 1990, when his party joined a new coalition with *Likud* (to keep the party in power after Shimon Peres led Labour into opposition). He lambasted the autonomy plans for Palestinians at the Madrid track talks, and this led to the fall of the Shamir government in 1992. In the June 1992 elections, Eitan enjoyed a renaissance, on a platform of 'clean government', assertive secularism (he opposed 'kickbacks' to the Orthodox community), and support for retaining all of 'Greater Israel'. *Tsomet* increased its seats tally from two to eight, but found itself in opposition to Labour. For much of the following two years, Rabin tried to woo him to join the government, but *Meretz* vetoed a draft deal in March 1994 – one month after internal party clashes led to the desertion of three MKs, to form *Yi'ud*.

In 1994 Eitan was embarrassed by revelations that he had diverted government campaign funding to a charity run by his mistress. His 'clean' reputation was further tarnished by revelations that he had broken promises to political allies. Eitan is a fierce opponent of the Oslo accords, and is extremely wary of deals with Syria. He eventually forged a deal with the opposition *Likud* in February 1996, whereby he would step down as a candidate in the forthcoming direct prime ministerial elections, and pledge his support for the candidacy of *Likud* leader, Benjamin Netanyahu. In return, *Tsomet* would be guaranteed eight seats on a joint *Tsomet-Likud* list. Eitan is sometimes depicted as a securocrat in the Labour tradition, but his overtly antagonistic views towards Palestinians may alienate more pragmatic *Likud* supporters, who read in Rabin's assassination signs of danger in flirting with the far right.

Eliav, Arie 'Lova'   Israel
Early advocate of direct talks with PLO. A Labour Party veteran, he ran as a presidential candidate in 1993, but ultimately lost to Ezer Weizman.

Elitzur, Uri   Israel
Editor of *Nekuda*, the settlers' bulletin. In December 1995, Elitzur became one of the first leaders of *Yesha* Council to recommend negotiations with the Palestine National Authority, in the light of Oslo 2's implementation.

Elmusa, Sharif S.   Palestinian
Expert on Middle East water issues. Elmusa calls for a reassessment of the 'factors' determining water allocation, as defined in the doctrine of 'equitable apportionment' according to international law. These factors include prior use of water, economic and social needs of the disputants, and 'avoidance of appreciable harm'. Elmusa considers that such factors favour Palestinians; yet at the same time, such reallocation need not harm Israel, and could even bring benefits, in terms of improved regional co-operation and trade. Elmusa has been a consultant at the World Resources Institute and the Library of Congress. In 1993 and 1994, he was a senior Fulbright Fellow pursuing research on water and irrigated agriculture in the West Bank. He holds a PhD from the Massachussetts Institute of Technology (MIT), taught courses on Arab agrarian development at Georgetown University, and is currently a research fellow at the Institute of Palestine Studies in Washington, DC. Elmusa has written numerous articles and a few books on technology, agriculture, and water resources (especially in the Jordan Valley).

Elon, Benny   **Israel**
Rabbi, in 1992 head of *Gush Emunim* messianic religious settlers' movement.

Epstein, Haim   **Israel**
Secretary-General, *Degel Hatorah* (Flag of the Law) Party. This ultra-Orthodox group was
set up by its spiritual leader, Rabbi Eliezer Shach, as a breakaway from *Agudah Yisrael*. It later
rejoined *Agudah* in a coalition called United Torah Judaism. Since 1992 it has been in
opposition, and tends to oppose territorial compromise.

Sa'eb Mohammed ERAKAT

Nationality	Palestinian
Religion	Muslim
Place of birth	Jerusalem (while under Jordanian rule)
Date of birth	28 April 1955
Current position	PNA Minister for Local Government
Previous position	Vice-chairman of Palestinian delegation to Madrid peace talks, Oct 1991; Professor of political science at A-Najah University; Secretary-General, Arab Studies Society
Allies	Faisal Husseini, Hanan Ashrawi, Muhammed Ishtiyeh; at times, Yasser Arafat
Position on peace	Initially positive, turning to scepticism; major role as negotiator
National political importance	Influential in territories and in PLO 'internal' wing
Prospects	Wields considerable grassroots power as local government minister

Like Faisal Husseini, Sa'eb Erakat (sometimes rendered as 'Uraykat') is one of the generation
of internal PLO leaders who made their reputation during the *intifada*. He is currently
Minister for Local Affairs in the Palestine National Authority, and is the main PNA cabinet
member to actually live in Jericho.

Sa'eb Erakat was born in Jerusalem as one of seven children, and moved to Jericho when
he was young. He took his BA and MA in international relations at San Francisco State
University, in 1977 and 1979 respectively. In 1983 he completed his PhD in peace studies and
conflict resolution at Bradford University, in Britain. Since 1979 Erakat has been an associate
professor of political science at A-Najah University (from 1982 to 1986 he also headed its
public relations division). Israel banned him from travelling abroad for five years, from 1985,
because of his pro-*Fatah* political activities. He was arrested and detained briefly during the
early days of the *intifada*. Erakat joined the Palestinian Cultural Council in 1989, and became
Secretary General of Faisal al-Husseini's influential Arab Studies Society in 1992.

As deputy head of the official Palestinian delegation to the Madrid peace talks, beginning
in October 1991, Erakat caused a stir in Israel by wearing his *kaffiyeh*, a symbol of the
Palestinian struggle. He later acted as a go-between in the early stages of the secret Israel–
PLO talks. However, in August 1993, Erakat joined Husseini and Hanan Ashrawi in protesting their mistreatment, when the Oslo Accords effectively nullified their own negotiations
with Israel. As a consolation, Arafat appointed the trio to a 'Higher Committee for the Peace
Talks'. Since this rapprochement, Erakat continues to be a key lynchpin in the negotiations.
As a prominent 'internal' PLO member, Erakat is a useful counterweight to the perceived
domination of the PNA's high offices by 'external' men and women from Tunis.

Erakat is considered to be on the moderate intellectual wing of the PLO. He won
widespread praise for his management of the Palestine National Authority's electoral preparations, in conjunction with Muhammed Ishtiyeh. By the end of November 1995, fully a
million Palestinians had registered to vote. Erakat has also liaised with local *Fatah* members
and Israeli officials, in the arduous process of extending the PNA remit beyond the borders of
Jericho. On Jan. 20, 1996, Erakat won the sole seat for the district of Jericho ('Ariha) in the
Palestine Council elections. Ever pragmatic, Erakat believes a strong economic base is a *sine*

qua non for Palestinian political independence. He has often criticized *Hamas* and other fundamentalists for threatening the peace process with their acts of violence.

Eran, Oded   Israel
Head of the Foreign Ministry's economic department. Eran proposed various Middle Eastern projects to the World Bank, and was influential in setting the agenda for the MENA Amman economic summit of October 1995. Eran broadly shares Shimon Peres's vision of a new Middle East based on economic co-operation between Israel and its Arab neighbours.

F

Fadlallah, Muhammad Hussein   Lebanon
Spiritual head of *Hezbollah*, Iranian-backed Shi'ite group. Sheikh Fadlallah is one of the leading exponents of an Islamic fundamentalist solution to the Middle East's problems. Despite his militant views, however, Sheikh Fadlallah has recently given the faintest hints of compromise, and a willingness to curtail *Hezbollah* activities if Israel truly withdraws from southern Lebanon. If that is the case, he may hold the key to an eventual peace deal between Lebanon and Israel.

Born in Najaf in Iraq, Fadlallah, now 60, arrived in Beirut with a reputation as an outstanding Koranic scholar. Using the mosque pulpit as his platform, Fadlallah inspired the creation of *Hezbollah* after the Israeli invasion of 1982. Soon the new group began to eclipse the established Shi'ite *Amal* in southern Lebanon. Fadlallah is said to have personally blessed the suicide bombers who decimated US, Israeli and French military stations in 1983. Nonetheless, he publicly condemned the kidnapping of Western hostages later in the decade. In 1990, he went to Teheran to plan their successful release. The Sheikh enjoys close relations with Iran's leading radical cleric, Ayatollah Ali Akbar Mohtashami, and has upheld a fragile truce with Syria. But while other Shi'ite leaders, such as *Amal*'s Nabbih Berri, have opted for overt political power, Sheikh Fadlallah seems content to wield his considerable influence through his Friday sermons, and closed-door consultations.

Fahd ibn Abdul Aziz ibn Saud   Saudi Arabia
King of Saudi Arabia since 1982; initiator of the Fahd Plan for Middle East peace. Born in 1923, he is the eldest of the seven sons of King Abdul Aziz's favourite wife. This afforded him an early *entrée* into Saudi politics, and in 1953 he became the kingdom's Education Minister, despite his reputation as a playboy. When King Faisal, his half-brother, was assassinated in 1975, another half-brother, the health-troubled Khaled, became king. But it was Fahd who effectively ruled Saudi Arabia, and on Khaled's death in 1982 Fahd became king. With bitter irony, Fahd suffered a stroke in November 1995, and another half-brother, Abdullah, took over the reigns of political power in January 1996.

Fahd showed his political flair in August 1981 with a plan for Mid-East peace, while still Crown Prince. Soviet leader Leonid Brezhnev and the European Community (in the Venice Declaration) had suggested peace conferences earlier in the year; but Fahd realized that the Arab world needed its own formulation. The so-called Fahd Plan called for a Palestinian state with Jerusalem as its capital, but it also seemed to recognize the legitimate existence of Israel. It initially won support amongst Arab League states; but soon the League was divided over the Israeli clause. The PLO felt this conceded too much. It also felt it should enjoy a more central role. However, while the plan was formally shelved, it formed the basis of the Fez Plan a year later.

As king, Fahd has quietly espoused better relations between Israel and Arabs, and backs Saudi involvement in the multilateral talks that arose from the Madrid summit in 1991. Saudi Arabia represents the Gulf Co-operation Council on the multilateral steering committee. It also concurred with the GCC decision in 1994 to drop the secondary boycott of Israel, and participated in security talks with Israel and other Arab states, within the multilateral framework. Yet Fahd seemed content to let other Gulf states (notably Oman and Qatar) take the initiative with Israel.

After the Gulf War, Fahd curtailed his normally cordial relations with the PLO, because of

Arafat's sympathies for Saddam. After Saudi Arabia cut off funds to the PLO, Arafat lost much bargaining power and was forced to accept Palestinian participation at the Madrid conference on unfavourable terms. Poor health forced Fahd to yield power to Crown Prince Abdullah, but by mid-1996 he seemed to have recovered his authority.

Fahmi, Nabil   Egypt

Important Foreign Ministry official and diplomat. Dr Fahmi formulated detailed proposals for regional disarmament, and presented these at the opening Moscow session of the multilateral talks, in January 1992. His paper included a demand to discuss Israel's nuclear potential (Israel's unwillingness to discuss the issue became a big source of friction between it and Egypt, on the eve of the Nuclear Non-Proliferation Treaty conference). Fahmi is the son of a former Egyptian Foreign Minister Ismail Fahmi.

Faluji, Imad   Palestinian

One of four *Hamas* members who were elected to the Palestine Council on Jan. 20, 1996. As *Hamas* officially refused to participate in the poll, Faluji had to stand as an independent. He is one of seven representatives for the Shamil Gaza district. Faluji is often touted as typical of the more acquiescent younger 'internal' leadership of *Hamas,* prepared to co-operate with the PLO's institutions, and possibly in time with Israel itself.

Faqih, Hassan   Lebanon

Amal leader in the south, regarded as a potential rival to *Amal's* overall leader, the Parliamentary Speaker Nabih Berri. Faqih may have been behind renewed *Amal* attacks on Israeli troops in the south, in 1995.

Farhan, Ishaq (Dr)   Jordan

Secretary-General of the Islamic Action Front, the largest single political party in the Lower House of Parliament. Farhan is also a leading force in the opposition to the Israel–Jordan peace treaty. Born in 1934 in Ain Karem, Jordan, Farhan studied chemistry to a doctorate level. He then joined the Jordanian Education ministry, and between 1965 and 1969 was in charge of defining the national education syllabuses. In the early 1970s Dr Farhan served as a junior education minister, and became director of the Royal Scientific Society. Farhan enjoys close ties with the Muslim Brotherhood. Indeed, opponents of the Islamic Action Front (IAF) contend that it is no more than a political wing of the Brotherhood in Jordan. Farhan registered the party in February 1992, and it received its licence in December of that year. At the multi-party elections held in November 1993 (the first since the 1960s), the IAF has become the largest voting bloc in the National Assembly. Farhan approved of holding the elections, regardless of the new circumstances of the Israel–PLO deal in September 1993, which threatened to disrupt the vote. However, he has aggressively opposed changes to the electoral law, which could erode the IAF's vote tally.

Fatah, Ali Abed al-   Egypt

Health Minister. In early 1994, Dr al-Fatah signed a bilateral agreement to improve co-operation in health matters with his Israeli counterpart, Dr Ephraim Sneh.

Fattah, Zia Abd al-   Palestinian

Editor, Palestine News Agency (WAFA). Fattah gives the official PLO line on current affairs.

Fayyad, Sharif (Lieutanant-Colonel)   Lebanon

Secretary-General of the Druze PSP's 'assembly of guides'. Fayyad manages Druze local affairs while the PSP leader, Walid Jumblatt, concentrates on matters of national concern.

Feiglin, Moshe   Israel

Head of *Zo Artzeinu* (This is Our Land), a radical settlers' group opposed to the peace deal. Feiglin was born in Australia and immigrated to Israel, where he founded *Zo Artzeinu* with an American, David Romanov. In late 1993, Feiglin responded to the Washington Declaration with 'Operation Double', a campaign to double the number of Jewish settlements in Gaza and the West Bank. Throughout 1995, he led many of the hilltop protests against Israeli governmental blocks on building. The group began attracting formerly moderate settler voices, including Rabbi Riskin. After the Rabin assassination, Feiglin is being investigated for incendiary remarks.

Feldman, Avigdor   Israel

Co-founder of *B'Tselem*, Israel's leading human rights group, and litigation director for the Association of Civil Rights in Israel (ACRI). Feldman is a lawyer who has often defended Palestinians in military court. In 1991 he shared the Robert F. Kennedy Human Rights Award with the Palestinian lawyer, Raji Sourani.

Filali, Abdelatif   Morocco

Prime Minister of Morocco. Abdelatif was appointed to this position by King Hassan on May 25, 1994, taking over from the veteran Prime Minister Lamrani. Filali has a long diplomatic and political career, stretching back to 1968, when he was first appointed Minister of Higher Education. In 1971 he became Foreign Minister for a year. After holding several important ambassadorial posts, he returned to head the Foreign Ministry in 1985. Both as Foreign Minister and Prime Minister, Filali has quietly nurtured Moroccan ties with Israel. In October 1994 Morocco agreed to open an interest office in Israel, and Israel opened a liaison office in Morocco. However, the two countries have yet to enter full diplomatic relations. In November 1995 Filali attended Yitzhak Rabin's funeral in Jerusalem, on behalf of the King. Filali's son is a son-in-law to the King.

Freij, Elias   Palestinian

Mayor of Bethlehem, and PNA Minister of Tourism and Antiquities. Freij was born in 1920, and over the years has come to be known as one of the leading Christian Palestinian figures in the occupied territories. He is politically independent, yet enjoys close ties with both Jordan and the PLO hierarchy. Freij has often protested at Israeli interference in his West Bank city, which is famous as the birthplace of Jesus Christ. On the other hand, he was also an early proponent of talks with sympathetic Israelis.

Elias Freij became Mayor of Bethlehem in 1972, and has held the post ever since. As a successful businessman who runs a family souvenir-producing factory, he has always emphasized the virtues of free enterprise. From the outset of his mayoralty, his Bethlehem Foundation has encouraged local economic development. Freij showed his pragmatic streak during the height of the *intifada*, when he opposed Hana Siniora's scheme for boycotting Israeli goods as risking 'starvation in the territories'. In 1988 Siniora and Freij mended fences and joined a team of Palestinian 'insiders' who were to meet visiting US Secretary of State George Schultz, but were ultimately dissuaded from doing so by orders from the PLO in Tunis. Freij was a member of the official Palestinian delegation to the Madrid peace talks. In early 1994, after the Israel–PLO breakthrough the previous September, Freij was appointed Tourism Minister on the PLO–backed Palestine National Authority. In July he became the first minister to meet his Israeli counterpart (Uzi Baram), and discuss joint projects. Freij has predicted that up to five million tourists will visit Israel and the territories by the year 2000; at least a million would come to Bethlehem, which could help solve the town's 50% plus unemployment problem. Throughout 1994 and 1995, Freij visited Italy, Spain and France to encourage Christian tourism to the 'Holy Land'.

The departure of Israeli troops from Bethlehem in December 1995, ahead of the schedule as laid down in the Interim Agreement (Oslo 2), was clearly a personal triumph for Freij. It was also a public relations boost for both Israel and the Palestinian Authority – an autonomous 'Palestinian Bethlehem' in time for Christmas. Deciding to leave local politics while still on a crest, he announced that he did not intend to stand in the next mayoral elections. However, he scored another success in the first week of 1996, this time wearing his Tourism Minister's hat, by hosting the second meeting of the newly established Middle East Mediterranean Tourism Association (MEMITTA) in Bethlehem. Delegations from Egypt, Jordan, Morocco, Tunisia, Turkey, Israel, Cyprus and the PNA all attended the event.

Frenkel, Ya'akov   Israel

Governor of the Bank of Israel. Immediately after the signing of the Declaration of Principles, Frenkel offered the embryonic Palestine Authority his professional co-operation. On Dec. 18, 1995, following the PLO–Israel Interim Agreement of September, he turned over responsibility for banking supervision in the PNA-controlled areas to Dr Besseiso, the head of the Palestine Monetary Authority (PMA). Frenkel is credited with shepherding economic expansion in Israel, but by 1996 he had to face the consequences of mounting deficits (the result of boom-fed expenditure on imports) on the value of the shekel.

G

Ghaddafi, Muammar   Libya

Ruler of Libya since 1969. Muammar Ghaddafi, born in 1942, has long sought the mantle of 'leader of the Arab masses', and for a time was the USA's 'enemy number one'. But today he has been largely marginalized by other Arab leaders, and plays only a spoiling role in the unfolding peace process. He joined the Libyan Army in 1965 after studying history, and formed a version of the Egyptian Free Officers Movement, which overthrew King Idris in 1969. Establishing his lifelong ally, Abdel-Salam Jalloud, as prime minister in 1972, Ghaddafi began preaching his Third Universal Theory, a revolutionary conflation of Islamic elements, *bedouin* folk wisdom and socialism, which he promulgated through the *Green Book*. He proclaimed the Socialist People's Libyan Arab Jahamariya in 1976, and three years later gave up his official post to become 'leader of the revolution'. Even so, he has held absolute power ever since. The mid-1970s oil price boom fuelled his overseas operations and sponsorship of revolutionary movements, including factions of the PLO. He became notorious for sending hit squads to kill enemies of the regime in overseas capitals.

Ghaddafi sponsored his own Palestinian groups and vowed to fight Israel. He also gave refuge to Abu Nidal, and was accused of being behind the 1988 Lockerbie bombing, although some security sources point the finger at Syria. Ever mercurial, in June 1993, Ghaddafi allowed 192 Libyan Muslim pilgrims to visit the holy sites in Jerusalem, and promised to follow this up with a state visit. However, in August 1995, he began expelling thousands of Palestinians from Libya, which he justified as an exercise to 'prove' that the PLO's pact with Israel had not created a truly autonomous Palestine. Ghaddafi currently faces grave domestic threats from Islamic fundamentalists.

Gal, Yossi   Israel

Foreign Ministry Director General (before Yossi Hadas). He laid the groundwork for talks with Gulf states, which led to visits by Yossi Beilin and Yitzhak Rabin to Oman, gas deals with Qatar, and the partial lifting of the Arab boycott of Israel.

Gammo, Sami   Jordan

Former Finance Minister. Gammo helped to define the new role of Jordanian banks in the Palestine Authority, and worked with Palestine Monetary Authority chief Besseiso.

Ganzoury, Kamal Ahmad al-   Egypt

Prime Minister since December 1995. Before that, Kamal Ahmad Ganzoury was Deputy Prime Minister and Minister for Finance, Economy and Planning in the cabinet chosen by Egypt's President Hosni Mubarak. He succeeded the outgoing prime minister, Atef Sedki, who had resigned in the wake of protests surrounding allegedly rigged national elections. Dr Ganzoury was born in 1933, and educated at Cairo University, and Michigan University, in the USA, where he took his PhD. He was the Governor of Beni Suef, an area in southern Egypt. In 1975 he became Under Secretary at the Ministry of Planning. Later Ganzoury worked as a consultant on development issues at the United Nations. He returned to Cairo to head the National Planning Institute within the Ministry of Planning, from 1982 to 1985. Ganzoury was appointed Deputy Prime Minister, and Minister of Planning and International Co-operation in 1985. He led Egypt's negotiations with the IMF in 1991, and again in October 1995, when he firmly opposed suggestions to devalue the Egyptian currency. Like his predecessor, Ganzoury has proven his economic skills and demonstrated his loyalty during his many years of service under President Mubarak.

Garg, Prem C.   India

Co-ordinator of the World Bank's 'task-force' on the Occupied Territories. Garg helped devise, and prepare the report into, the Emergency Action Programme (EAP). The EAP arose out of the September 1993 Oslo Accords and the international donors' conference in Washington which followed. Its purpose has been to direct priority investments in the West Bank and Gaza, and to channel donor funds most effectively over three years (1994 to 1996). Garg recommended a two-track approach – achieving immediate short-term results, like reducing chronic Palestinian unemployment through public works; while at the same time aiming at the longer term goal of a thorough economic infrastructure. He worked closely with Samir al-Khouri, a Lebanese-born economist who subsequently joined the IMF. Prem Garg is a graduate of the Indian Institute of Technology in Delhi, and holds a PhD in Engineering Economic Systems from Stanford University, USA.

Gazit, Shlomo   Israel
Former head of Israeli military intelligence, and the first co-ordinator of the occupied territories, from 1967 to 1974. Shlomo Gazit was born in Istanbul, Turkey, in 1926 and came to Palestine in 1932. He served in the *Palmach* before and during the first Arab–Israeli war; and then studied at the French Military Academy and Harvard, where he became a fellow. He oversaw affairs in the occupied territories for most of the post-1967 Labour administration, and sought to implement an 'invisible occupation', restricted to a few military settlements. From 1974 to 1979 he was the head of Israeli military intelligence. As such, he authorized numerous attacks on suspected PLO terrorists.

Gazit was a right-hand man to Defence Minister Moshe Dayan, but later criticized his former mentor for policies which perpetuated the status quo in the territories. He used to believe in 'containing' Palestinian aspirations, but in 1980 he began investigating ways of improving the West Bank economy; and in 1986 he and Binyamin Ben-Eliezer called for a new approach to Palestinians. Less than a year after the *intifada* broke out in 1987, Gazit advised Prime Minister Shamir to invite Yasser Arafat to Jerusalem; he also favoured a unilateral Israeli withdrawal from Gaza. Gazit is now respected as a doveish security analyst and since 1988 has been a senior research fellow at the Jaffee Centre.

Geagea, Samir   Lebanon
Head, Lebanese Forces (*Kataeb*), military wing of Maronite Phalange. Geagea was one of the most feared militia chiefs during the Lebanese civil war. An enemy of Syria, he was sentenced to death in 1994 for involvement in bombing of Christian rivals in Jounieh, and the murder of Danny Chamoun. This sentence was later commuted to life imprisonment.

Gheit, Ahmed Abul   Egypt
Egyptian Ambassador to Rome. As Director of the Foreign Minister's Bureau before his current appointment, Abul Gheit has been at the centre of important decision-making on the peace process. He was born in 1942, graduated with a BA in Commerce from Ain Shams University, in 1964, and has done diplomatic service in Nicosia, Moscow and New York. Abul Gheit acted as deputy head of the Egyptian 'observer' delegation at the Madrid peace conference of October 1991.

Ghosheh, Samir   Palestinian
PNA Minister of Labour and Social Affairs. Now 54, Ghosheh was born in Jerusalem but left in 1967 after the Israeli victory there. He spent many years in Damascus and Beirut as the head of the Palestinian Popular Struggle Front, a rejectionist movement which was founded in 1967. However, by the late 1980s he had also begun supporting Arafat. By backing the Oslo Accords, Ghosheh sent an important sign to fellow radicals that their could be a place for them in the new dispensation.

Ghussein, Jawid   Palestinian
Chairman of the Palestine National Fund. A PNC member and businessman, Ghussein has welcomed the Oslo Accords. Following talks with Israel's giant Koor Industries group in October 1993, Ghussein founded a joint Israeli–Arab investment fund to help finance new projects in Gaza and the West bank.

Gillerman, Dan   Israel
President, Israel Chambers of Commerce. He attended the Casablanca economic summit in 1994, and made close contacts with Arab businessmen.

Gilon, Carmi   Israel
Former head of the Israeli General Security Services (GSS). Gilon offered his resignation a few days after the assassination of Prime Minister Yitzhak Rabin, as the GSS came under severe pressure over its fatal lapse in security. The new prime minister, Shimon Peres, refused his offer at first, and later publicly praised Gilon (who was only known by the Hebrew letter, Kaf) for the stability he brought in the aftermath of the assassination. Carmi Gilon also felt obliged to see through the supervision of Oslo 2, at a sensitive time, as Israeli troops redeployed from five major Palestinian towns on the West Bank. He co-operated with the Palestinian Authority, and can be presumed to be behind the remote-control assassination in January 1996, of Yehiya Ayyash, the infamous *Hamas* 'Engineer', number one on the GSS hit-list for his string of bus-bombings in Israel. Only belatedly did Peres accept Gilon's resignation, and in a ceremony held in February 1996 Gilon handed over to the incoming chief, Ami Ayalon. In a breach with tradition, Ayalon was named publicly. There was a suggestion that Gilon may become Prime Minister Peres's private adviser on terrorism, but that would depend on the outcome of the Shamgar Commission of Inquiry into security lapses concerning the Rabin assassination.

Ginnosar, Yossi   Israel
Yitzhak Rabin's chief liaison with Yasser Arafat in late 1994 and 1995. Yossi Ginnosar is officially the chairman of Amidar, the Israeli government housing company. But he works more actively as a 'fixer' for Israeli–Palestinian deals, often acting in cahoots with his Palestinian counterpart, Muhammed Rashid. According to the *Jerusalem Report* magazine, in 1994 the two men arranged for the Israeli company, Dor Energy, to supply the autonomous areas with fuel. Evidently they did so by 'freezing out' possible competitors, and in exchange they won handsome commissions. Rashid, it was said, passed on part of his commission to a fund controlled by Arafat, which pays salaries and relief to *intifada* orphans. In November 1995, Ginnosar arranged and took part in Yasser Arafat's historic visit to Tel Aviv. Ginnosar was previously a senior official in *Shin Bet*, Israel's internal security services. He first came to public attention when he was accused of 'obstructing justice' in an investigation into the murder of two captured terrorists. He was also accused of perjury in a case involving the torture of an alleged spy, but was never tried. In 1993 the Supreme Court blocked Ginnosar's appointment as Director-General of the Housing Ministry, citing his dubious record.

Glaspie, April   USA
Co-ordinator of UNRWA (United Nations Relief and Works Agency) in Gaza since early 1995. Ms Glaspie was the USA's Ambassador to Iraq in 1990. After Saddam Hussein invaded Kuwait in August of that year, Glaspie was criticized for not having warned him of the consequences of this action. UNRWA has been the main aid agency supporting Palestinian refugees for almost 50 years. But there were reports of clashes between Glaspie and Terje Larsen, the UN Secretary-General's special envoy responsible for aid disbursement in Gaza. Some said that their rift was merely a symptom of UNRWA's declining authority, as the Palestine Authority (close to Larsen and his aides) gradually takes over more of UNRWA's traditional functions, in looking after refugees' social welfare and health needs. By the end of 1995, UNRWA was due to relocate its headquarters from Vienna to Gaza.

Godal, Bjorn Tore   Norway
Foreign Minister of Norway, and Chairman of the Ad Hoc Liaison Committee (AHLC), an inter-ministerial apparatus to oversee donor states' contributions to the Palestinian economy. The AHLC was set up in 1993, in the aftermath of the Israel Palestinian Declaration of Principles. Godal assumed the chairmanship on taking over as foreign minister when Johan Jorgen Holst died on Jan. 13, 1994. A special fund was named in Holst's honour, and administered by the AHLC; it was meant to cover the nascent Palestine Authority's current expenditures.
    In December 1994, Godal told Israeli Palestinian donor representatives in Brussels, that

the Holst Fund would allocate $102 million to the Authority, and give a further $23 million for short-term employment projects. Following suggestions from Larsen, the donors adopted a new mechanism to improve co-ordination with Palestinians. Godal hoped this would answer Palestinians who had complained that pledged sums had still not arrived. However, a follow-up meeting held in Jericho in May, 1995, was told that the Holst Fund had run dry. Under Godal, the AHLC held a special session simultaneously with the signing of the Israeli Palestinian Interim Agreement, on Sept. 28, 1995. It committed itself to an expanded programme of granting further aid to Palestinian self-rule areas, and fostering economic co-operation between Israel and the Palestinians, particularly in the form of cross-border 'industrial parks'.

Golan, Daphna   Israel
A founder of *B'Tselem*, the prominent Israeli human rights group; and head of *Bat Shalom* (Daughter of Peace) an Israeli womens' peace group. Together with Rada Zughaier, she is also the joint head of the Jerusalem Link, a group which unites Palestinian and Israeli women who share common goals concerning the peace process and womens' rights.

Goldmann, Nahum   USA
Late head of the influential World Jewish Congress (WJC) during the 1970s. Goldmann was one of the first Zionists to criticize Israeli policy *vis-à-vis* the Palestinians. He enjoyed close ties with Israeli politicians, yet insisted that the USA should offer Israel 'strong advice' on talking to the PLO, along with its aid donations.

Goldstein, Baruch   Israel
US-born settler who killed 29 Arab worshippers in March 1994 in the Hebron massacre and died himself. He opened fire on Muslim worshippers in the Ibrahimi Mosque, which adjoins the Cave of Machpelah Synagogue. Goldstein worked as a medical doctor, and was a prominent demonstrator against the Rabin government's policies. Goldstein was an Orthodox Jew, and served as the sole councillor for the racist *Kach* group on the Kiryat Arba town council. (Kiryat Araba is a Jewish settlement situated near Hebron). Although most settler leaders condemned his action, a minority said it was revenge for a Muslim massacre of Hebron's Jews in 1929. His grave became a place of pilgrimage for many far right extremists, including members of *Eyal*, who were reputedly behind the assassination of Yitzhak Rabin in November 1995.

Gonen, Eli   Israel
Director-General of the Israeli Tourism Ministry. Gonen has worked closely with Tourism Minister Uzi Baram to foster ties with sister ministries in neighbouring Arab countries and the Palestine National Authority. He headed an Israeli delegation at a planning meeting for the newly established Middle East Mediterranean Tourism Organization (MEMITTA), held in Bethlehem in the first week of 1996.

González Márquez, Felipe   Spain
Prime Minister of Spain from 1982 to the present. In October 1991, and at very short notice, González successfully hosted the international peace conference in Madrid, which for the first time saw Israel sharing a podium with a Palestinian delegation. In December of that year he visited Israel and chided the *Likud* government for not freezing settlements, nor for endorsing a 'land for peace' approach. Since Labour took power in Israel in 1992, relations between Spain and Israel have improved, partly because of ties formed over the years between the two ruling socialist parties. In November 1995 González represented the European Union at Yitzhak Rabin's funeral. However, González has not been able to play as an active a role in the peace process as he might have wished, because in recent years he has faced political turmoil at home (following allegations of corruption).

Goodman, Hirsh   Israel
Editor in chief of the *Jerusalem Report*, a leading English language Israeli magazine. Born in Port Elizabeth, South Africa, Goodman emigrated to Israel and served as a journalist with Israel Army Radio. He broke away from the established *Jerusalem Post* when it adopted a

more right-wing editorial policy, and founded the *Report*, which articulates Israeli and Middle Eastern affairs to a large readership of Diaspora Jews. Goodman supports the Labour camp, but often takes a maverick stance, and is not above criticizing Labour politicians for serious shortcomings. In the early 1990s, he opposed deals with the PLO, which he saw an increasingly 'irrelevant' institution; by 1995, he was a firm supporter of the Oslo 2 Accords. He also warned against Israeli over-optimism regarding ties with Jordan; but also belatedly praised Arafat for his achievements in setting up the PNA, and proposed a solution to the Jerusalem issue.

Gorbachev, Mikhail   Russia

Leader and later President of the Soviet Union from 1986 to 1992. Under his rule the Soviet Union ended the Cold War with the USA, espoused the new philosophies of *perestroika* and *glasnost*, and ended aid to Syria (its traditional ally in the Middle East). Gorbachev also began a rapprochement with Israel, two decades after the Soviet Union had severed relations at the time of the Six Day War in 1967. This change was sealed by the restoration of diplomatic relations on Oct. 24, 1991, which in turn facilitated the Madrid peace conference less than a week later. However, the dramatic changes within the Soviet Union ultimately destroyed the union itself, and, with it, Mikhail Gorbachev's political career.

Mikhail Gorbachev was born in 1931 in the Stavropol region of north Caucasus. He took degrees in law and agriculture, and worked his way up the Soviet Communist Party (CPSU) ladder to become a member of the CPSU central committee in 1971, a full member of the Politburo in 1980, general secretary of the CPSU in 1985, and Chairman of the USSR Supreme Presidium in 1988. In 1989 he set up new legislative structures which ended the CPSU's constitutional guarantee of power. In 1990 he won the Nobel peace prize for his international diplomatic offensive to end the Cold War and loosen the USSR's bonds to eastern Europe.

Middle East foreign policy was never Gorbachev's prime concern, but he certainly had an influence. In July 1987 a Soviet consular delegation arrived in Israel. In 1989 Soviet Foreign Minister Eduard Shevardnadze allowed a similar delegation from Israel to operate in Moscow. Gorbachev called on Yasser Arafat to recognize Israel, in 1988, while at the same time promising Israel 'full normalization' if it allowed the PLO to participate in a peace conference. In time the barriers came down for Russian and Soviet Jewry generally, and hundreds of thousands emigrated to the USA and Israel.

Arab allies voiced their disappointment with these developments but Gorbachev pressed ahead. In 1989 Gorbachev gave a lukewarm reaction to the Shamir-Rabin peace plan of May 14 that year. In September, Israel turned down a Soviet offer to meet PLO officials on Soviet soil. Meanwhile, Shevardnadze nurtured relations with Israeli Foreign Ministers Moshe Arens and David Levy. Gorbachev and US President George Bush jointly sponsored the Madrid peace conference. He also made Moscow the launchpad of the multilateral branch of the negotiations, and promised to sponsor the working group on arms control and regional security. But by this stage, Gorbachev had been fatally weakened by a failed coup against him in August 1991, and retired at the end of the year with the collapse of the USSR.

Gore, Albert R. ('Al')   USA

Vice-President of the USA. A close ally of Israel, Gore has been involved at the highest level with the peace process, on occasion deputizing for President Clinton. Gore opened the economic donors' conference after the signing of the DOP in September 1993. He endorsed 'Builders for Peace', a major private enterprise initiative by prominent Jewish and Arab Americans, which sought to increase investment in the West Bank and Gaza. In late 1995 and early 1996, Gore met Israel's new Prime Minister Shimon Peres and foreign minister, Ehud Barak, and also spoke with PNA President Yasser Arafat. Gore emphasized the USA's commitment to Israel's security, and praised progress on negotiations with Syria. He has also led the USA's campaign against Iran and Iraq's acquisition of nuclear weaponry.

Al Gore was born in 1948, educated at Harvard and the Vanderbilt Law School, and worked as an army journalist in Vietnam, before being elected to the House of Representatives in 1976. In 1984 he became a Democrat Senator for his native Tennessee. He is a passionate advocate of arms control and protecting the environment, while being conservative on social issues.

Green, Andrew   UK
Assistant Under-Secretary of State in the UK Foreign and Commonwealth Office (in the permanent diplomatic service), and hence main steward of British foreign policy in the Middle East, since 1994. Andrew Green became the UK Ambassador to Saudi Arabia in March 1996.

Green joined the diplomatic service in 1965 and spent a year at the Foreign Office language school in Lebanon. He later served as a assistant political agent in Aden and Abu Dhabi, before becoming a ministerial private secretary in the mid-1970s. Green left Washington in October 1984, and from 1985 to 1988 he was head of chancery in the British mission in Saudi Arabia. For three years thereafter he worked in London on 'the international aspects of the Lockerbie affair'.

When Britain resumed diplomatic relations with Syria in 1991, Green became the UK ambassador in Damascus. Once the dust settles on Riyadh's internal politics, Green may well play a more assertive role in the peace process; and help to steer Saudi Arabia into a new relationship with Israel, Syria, Jordan and the Palestine National Authority.

Grossman, Steve   USA
President of AIPAC, the American-Israel Public Affairs Committee, the main pro-Israeli Congressional pressure group. Grossman is a young Boston businessman who broadly supports the peace process, although many of his AIPAC colleagues are lukewarm about it (reflecting a growing scepticism by American Jewry generally). In December 1993 he found himself in the curious position of opposing pro-Israel US Congress members who wanted to link US aid to Palestinian areas, with the lifting of the Arab boycott of Israel. Rabin and the Israeli government felt it was better to keep the peace process on track, with US aid assured, rather than risk this by demanding an immediate end to the boycott, and Grossman concurred.

Gur, Mordechai   Israel
Deputy Defence Minister until his death on July 16, 1995. Mordechai 'Motta' Gur was born in Jerusalem in 1930, and fought alongside Yitzhak Rabin in the 1948 war. In 1967, as commander of Israel's 55th paratroop brigade, he was the first Israeli soldier to enter the Old City of Jerusalem. Gur then briefly became commander of the now occupied Gaza Strip, an assignment which started him thinking about Israel's need to reach a solution with the Palestinian people. He was military chief of staff in 1974, and in 1978 led Operation Litani (Israel's limited invasion of southern Lebanon). He joined the Knesset as a Labour MK in 1981, and later served as Minister for Health under his ally, Shimon Peres, in the National Unity Government. In 1989 Gur said that the time was right for opening talks with the PLO, but his *Likud* cabinet colleagues rejected this call. After Labour's victory in 1992, Gur deputized for Defence Minister Yitzhak Rabin, who often deferred to him when his prime ministerial duties proved too pressing. Gur kept important lines of communication open with Israeli settlers, who were worried about the ramifications of the Oslo Accords on their future. He also helped the Rabin administration through his connections with the USA, nurtured during an earlier tenure as military attache in Washington. Mordechai Gur committed suicide after a long battle with cancer, and his death was widely mourned in Israel.

Gutman, Shaul   Israel
Leader of a breakaway from the right-wing *Moledet* party, since 1994. Called 'Peace Guard', it proposes the 'transfer' of Palestinians from the West Bank. Gutman was tipped as a future leader of *Moledet*, until clashes with its current leader, Rechavam Ze'evl, proved too great.

Guvendiren, Ekrem Esat   Turkey
Charge d'affairs in Tel Aviv since 1991. Guvendiren won an Israeli prize for improving ties between the two nations, which has resulted in more trade and tourism, plus Turkish offers to play the host in peace talks.

H

Haass, Richard   USA

Top Middle East specialist on the USA's National Security Council under President Bush. Haass was a key consultant in planning the US response to Saddam Hussein's invasion of Kuwait in August 1990. After the war, he formulated Bush's strategy of withholding loan guarantees unless Israel agreed to freeze its settlements.

Habash, George   Palestinian

Head of Popular Front for the Liberation of Palestine (PFLP), and for decades the best known rival to Arafat as leader of the Palestinian cause. Habash was born in 1926 in the village of Lydda (now Lod in Israel). He was brought up in a Greek Orthodox Palestinian home, and, while still a schoolchild, he won a scholarship to the American University in Beirut (AUB). He entered the AUB Medical School in 1944, and formed the radical Arab Nationalist Movement (ANM) with Wadia Haddad, a fellow Palestinian, and Hani al-Hindi, a Syrian, in 1951. With his home now part of Israel, Habash decided to move to Jordan in 1956, but was soon arrested for political activities. He left for Damascus, but was expelled in 1963 and relocated in Lebanon.

Throughout the 1960s, Habash opposed those in the ANM who advocated a separate Palestinian military role; instead, he favoured a pan-Arab revolution, within which the Palestinian struggle was just one facet. The June 1967 war changed his mind, however, and in December he formed the PFLP as a rival to the PLO (which was then effectively under Egyptian control). Habash now became the leading ideologue on the Palestinian left; he aimed to emulate the Vietcong, and form a workers' fighting force to topple Israel. He soon won Soviet sponsorship, and formed a working alliance with Abu Jihad, number two to Arafat within *Fatah*. By late 1968, the PFLP began a campaign of airplane hijackings and terrorism. It also started widespread unrest in Jordan, which eventually led to 'Black September' in 1970 – the crushing of all PLO forces in Lebanon. Many PLO veterans have never forgiven Habash for giving King Hussein this pretext to defeat the PLO.

After the October 1973 war, the PLO showed the first signs of coming to a possible accommodation with Israel, perhaps through the offices of Jordan. Habash rejected this, and led a 'rejectionist' front within the PLO. By this stage, he had strong rivals on the left, Ahmed Jibril of the PFLP-GC, and Naif Hawatmeh of the DFLP, both groups which had left the parent PFLP for not being sufficiently Marxist. Habash and Arafat staged a reconciliation in 1979, and two years later the PFLP joined the PLO Executive Committee. In 1982 Habash left for Damascus, as Israel invaded Lebanon. Although he was now pro-Syrian, Habash did not join other Palestinian radicals in attacking Arafat during the Syrian–inspired war of the camps. However, he did lead a National Salvation Front, in protest at the PLO's short-lived consensus with Jordan. Habash rejoined the PLO at the PNC conference of 1987, after the PLO–Jordan alliance had collapsed. The following year, he gave tacit approval to the Algiers Declaration (endorsing a two-state option and renouncing terrorism).

But when this peace initiative failed to bear fruit, Habash reverted to his hardline stance. He allowed PFLP supporters in the territories to take a leading role in the *intifada*, yet kept a firm grip on the group's affars. In late 1990 he headed an alliance of 120 groups which supported Saddam Hussein. Habash has rejected the Oslo deal, and refuses to return to the Palestinian self-rule areas. He is currently a member of the radical National Alliance coalition; but with his failing health, the collapse of his Soviet mentors, and his increasing isolation from politics in the West Bank, his political authority is much reduced. It was said of Habash that he provided the 'checks and balances' of an opposition to Arafat; now it seems as if other groups, liberals on the one hand, and fundamentalists on the other, have usurped his place.

Haber, Eitan   Israel

Chief of Bureau and special adviser to the late Israeli Prime Minister Yitzhak Rabin, from July 1992 until the prime minister's assassination in November 1995. Together with the Director General of the Prime Minister's Office, Shimon Shevis, Eitan Haber acted as a gatekeeper to Rabin, and crucially tested the mood of the Israeli public for peace. Born into a right-wing Zionist family, and now 56, Haber first established his friendship with Rabin while writing for the IDF magazine, *Bamahaneh*, in the 1950s. In the late 1970s he co-operated with the recently ousted Rabin in writing up interviews with famous people, while at the popular *Yediot Aharanot* newspaper. At the same time he also wrote a biography of Menachem Begin. Haber served as Rabin's Defence Ministry spokesman from 1984 to 1990, during the national unity government. As bureau chief since 1992, Haber was very protective of Rabin, and also sought to 'soften' his gruff image. He is not thought to have political ambitions of his own, but as one of the keepers of Rabin's legacy and an expert political analyst, he remains an important asset to the Labour Party as it negotiates future peace deals.

Hadas, Shmuel   Israel
Israel's first Ambassador to the Vatican, and one of the main negotiators of the Fundamental Agreement between the Vatican and Israel.

Hadas, Yosef 'Yossi'   Israel
Former acting Director-General of the Foreign Ministry; currently head of the Foreign Ministry's department monitoring the multilateral working group on refugees. Yossi Hadas, born in 1928, co-ordinated Israel's various multilateral talks teams between 1992 and 1993, and deserves much of the credit for improving relations with Arab nations. But neither he nor Uri Lubrani made much headway in bilateral negotiations with Suheil Shammas and the Lebanese delegation in Washington over the same period. During his tenure of office, Israel established diplomatic relations with Russia, China and India. In 1993 he handed over the director-generalship to Uri Savir. In June 1995, Hadas headed the Israeli delegation to the first meeting of a 'committee of experts', which was set up by the quadripartite committee (Israel, the PNA, Jordan and Egypt) to look into the question of the 1967 Palestinian refugees (or 'displace persons').

Haddadin, Munther   Jordan
Head of Jordan's water delegation at peace talks. A development planner by profession, he has served for more than 15 years as president and vice-president of the Jordan Valley Authority (JVA). During that period, he helped to persuade Jordanians to relocate from the cities to irrigated rural areas, like the JVA's project north of the Dead Sea. However, the JVA's plans were often stymied by lack of water. Haddadin once offended Palestinian refugees by saying that they used up too much of this precious resource. Long before the signing of Israel–Jordan Common Agenda in 1993, and subsequent peace treaty, Haddadin used to hold meetings with Israeli officials under the auspices of the UN commission overseeing the armistice agreement of 1949 (the ceasefire line which followed the Jordan River). Haddadin registered little progress in the first two years of the Madrid track talks. However, in the peace treaty negotiations of 1994, he succeeded in winning significant Israeli concessions on the distribution of the Jordan headwaters.

Ha'etzni, Elyakim   Israel
Kiryat Arba settler, formerly an MK and leader of the (now defunct) far-right *Tehiya* Party. Ha'etzni was born in Kiel, Germany, in 1926. His family fled Nazi persecution to arrive in Palestine in 1938. Ten years later he joined *Haganah* and fought in the first Arab–Israeli war. After 1967, he settled in Kiryat Arba, outside Hebron, which he maintains is as much part of Israel as Tel Aviv is. Ha'etzni blames the PLO for the failure in Arab–Jewish co-existence in the territories, and for decades has warned of the danger of war (both civil, and against the Palestinians) in those areas. He currently leads the Struggle Command Against Autonomy, a violent group which protests against the peace accords and their effects on settlers. He became notorious for demanding the 'transfer' of all Palestinians from Israel and the occupied territories (Judaea and Samaria, in the settlers' vernacular). As other settlers have come to accept Oslo 2 as a *fait accompli*, Ha'etzni remains steadfast in his beliefs, which ultimately rely more on his own uncompromising analysis of Jewish history, rather than on Messianic or religious doctrines.

Hahsana, Duryad   Jordan
Director-General of the Jordanian Environment Ministry, and chief negotiator on environ-mental affairs with Israel. On May 8, 1995, Dr Hahsana signed an environmental co-

operation agreement with his Israeli counterpart, Dr Yisrael Peleg. It drew up a framework for ambitious joint projects to counter pollution, protect joint natural resources, and fight against natural disasters; and enacted the principles of the previous year's peace treaty.

Halevy, Ephraim   Israel
Deputy Director of *Mossad*. Halevy, whose father is British, helped broker the Israel–Jordan peace treaty, working in tandem with Elyakim Rubinstein. He was tipped to be Israel's first ambassador to Jordan, but his *Mossad* connections proved to be a barrier, and Shimon Shamir was chosen in his stead.

Hamad, Ghazi   Palestinian
Editor of *Al-Watan* (The Homeland), a *Hamas* weekly printed in Gaza. Hamad argued unsuccessfully against the use of suicide bombers, and said this 'mistaken' programme had given Israel and the PNA the pretext to clamp down on *Hamas*. Hamad thought there was no alternative to reconciliation with the PNA, and he favoured *Hamas's* participation in the Palestinian Council elections, but was overruled.

Hammer, Zevulun   Israel
Chairman of the National Religious Party (NRP). In previous *Likud*-led administrations, Hammer held the Religious Affairs portfolio. Zevulun Hammer was born in Haifa in 1936, and entered the cabinet in 1977 as Education Minister. He took over from the veteran Yosef Burg as party leader and Religious Affairs Minister in 1986, but returned to his education portfolio in 1990. The NRP stands for the 'modern orthodox' trend, also called the national religious camp. In Hammer's words, it sees Israel's capture of the territories as being 'the beginning of redemption'. The party was closely allied to the *Gush Emunim* settler movement, although in the 1980s more extreme NRP members left to join other right-wing parties (*Moledet, Tsomet, Tehiya, Matzad* and the now-defunct *Morasha*).

Hammer represents the more moderate centre of the party, but he has been bedevilled by radical factions which favour open defiance and civil disobediance on the question of the territories. Three weeks after Yitzhak Rabin's assassination, Hammer announced that the NRP accepted the Interim Agreement (Oslo 2) as a *fait accompli*. He asked his party's settler supporters to stop fighting it, and instead try to seek some accommodation within its parameters, so as to present a good case at the final status talks with the Palestinians. 'Of course we will not return to Gaza and Jenin [areas handed over to Palestinian rule under Oslo 1 and Oslo 2]', he said. 'We are not giving up our rights to the Land of Israel, but there is a different reality on the ground and we should do our best to make the most of the situation'. Hammer held talks with Shimon Peres, but has thrown his weight behind a united right-wing prime ministerial candidacy. Since June 1996, Hammer is Netanyahu's Minister of Education.

Hanegbi, Tzachi   Israel
Young *Likud* MK, right-hand man to party leader, Benjamin Netanyahu. Hanegbi was born into a highly politicized home in Jerusalem, in 1957. Both his parents had been prominent members of *Lehi*, or the Stern Gang, a far-right militia headed by Yitzhak Shamir in pre-state days. Hanegbi's mother, Geula Cohen, went on to become a leading maverick right-wing MK, from 1975 until 1992.

Campaigning on a right-wing ticket, Hanegbi became president of the National Students' Union in Israel. Afterwards, he joined the *Likud* as an aide to the Transport Minister, and ran the party's successful publicity campaign in the 1984 elections. He was close to Yitzhak Shamir, his godfather, and advised him when he was Foreign Minister, between 1984 and 1986. When Shamir resumed his job as Prime Minister in 1986, he made Hanegbi, then only 29, chief of the Prime Minister's Bureau.

In 1988 he became a *Likud* MK in his own right, and joined the prestigious *Knesset* Foreign Affairs and Defence Committee. Hanegbi formed close ties with Benjamin Netanyahu in the late 1980s, when the latter was Israeli Ambassador to the US, and is now his closest adviser.

Although he claims to respect Israel's democratic procedures, and will not officially revoke agreements with the PLO, his actions and statements often seem to belie this. If *Likud* returned to power, he promised, it would freeze the Palestinian autonomy process. And if the *intifada* were to re-erupt as a result, soldiers should seal the territories absolutely, expel agitators and perhaps even arrest the PNA leadership. Hanegbi was blamed for inflaming the 'street protest' atmosphere which preceded the Rabin assassination in November 1995. He has been notably contrite since the Rabin tragedy.

Hanieh, Akram   Palestinian

PLO press representative in Tunis; liaison between PLO Chairman Yasser Arafat and the media during the Madrid peace talks. Akram Hanieh had edited *As-Sha'ab* (The Masses) in East Jerusalem, and lived in nearby Ramallah. He was also a clandestine organizer for the PLO in the West Bank since the late 1970s, guiding his protegees through the unions and the media; co-ordinating demonstrations at the Bir Zeit University; and advising leaders in the *Shabiba* youth movement. Hanieh was never associated with any of the PLO's guerrilla or terrorist wings, and depicts himself as a Palestinian who supports co-existence with Israel. Israeli authorities used to censor his work, but generally turned a blind eye to his politicking.

In November 1986, however, he was arrested under a new Israeli law which allowed detention without charges, and was deported early the following year. Hanieh soon linked up with the PLO in Tunis, and proved to be an invaluable asset. Through his communicative skills and huge network of contacts, he bridged the gap between Tunis and the 'internal' Palestinians like Faisal Husseini and others. His role proved crucial in the run-up to the Madrid Conference in October 1991, when he advised Arafat on who to pick for the Palestinian delegations. Hanieh was later kept informed of the secret Oslo talks, in 1993. Akram Hanieh has a wide circle of friends, including Radwan Abu Ayyash, Hanan Ashrawi and Bassam Asfour.

Harel, Yisrael   Israel

Chairman and founder of *Yesha*, the settlers' council. Harel was a founding member of *Gush Emunim*, but left to set up *Yesha* in the 1980s, as a more broad-based group, encompassing secular as well as religious settlers. He once described 'co-existence [as] the best guarantee for our survival here', but in the same breath ruled out any return of land to Arabs. As the former editor of *Nekuda*, the main settlers' newspaper, Harel positioned himself as a foe of the peace process. However, he also criticized violent opposition to the ruling Labour government. Since 1994, he led delegations to the government, to put *Yesha's* 'case'. Since the Rabin assassination, Harel has suggested that settlers should accept the terms of Oslo 2 as a *fait accompli*.

Hareven, Alouf   Israel

Co-director of *Sikkui*, a pressure group which promotes equal opportunities for Israeli Arabs. Hareven is himself Jewish, and is involved with the New Israel Fund, which seeks to redirect Diaspora Jewish money to worthy projects within Israel.

Rafiq HARIRI

Nationality	Lebanese
Religion	Sunni Muslim
Place of birth	Sidon, Lebanon
Date of birth	1934
Current position	Prime Minister of Lebanon since October 1992
Previous position	Businessman in Saudi Arabia
Allies	Close ties with Saudi Arabia
Position on peace	Lukewarm; grievances with Israel in South Lebanon persist Hariri depends on Syria for guidance in foreign policy
National political importance	Hariri is largely responsible for Lebanon's recent economic revival; but has offended several vested interests
Prospects	Has offered to resign in past; mercurial and charismatic

Rafiq Hariri has had a profound impact on contemporary Lebanese politics. Appointed prime minister in October 1992, after Lebanon's first elections since 1972, he has spearheaded attempts to revive the Lebanese economy to its pre-war heyday. His first task was to impose some stability in the aftermath of civil war.

For most of the civil war, he lived in Saudi Arabia where over the years he made $3 billion in contracting and investment. He is charismatic and often controversial. Twice in 1994 and once again in 1995 he threatened to resign over charges of corruption and nepotism. Opponents accuse him of 'running the country like a business'. In 1995 the National Assembly Speaker, Nabbih Berri, said Hariri was flouting the constitution by trying to extend President Hrawi's five-year term. Rafiq Hariri has *inter alia* revived the fortunes of Lebanon's Sunni Muslim community (during the latter stages of the civil war, Sunni militias were largely eclipsed by fighting between, and within, the Shi'ite and Christian Phalange camps).

Hariri has cleverly used his Saudi patrons as a useful counterweight to Syrian pressure. He has also placed close aides in key positions, such as Nasser Chamaa as head of Solidere, a holding company valued at $2.4 billion, which promises to turn Beirut into 'a city of the future'. However, Syria remains the main powerbroker in Lebanon, and Hariri has tried (not always successfully) to steer the narrow path between Lebanese economic autonomy and obediance to Damascus on foreign affairs. In 1992 he said he looked forward to peace with Israel, but since then he has avoided strong rhetoric on relations with Israel. Given his pragmatic record, Hariri will probably welcome economic ties with his southern neighbour 'when the time is right'. Hariri hopes that he has made himself indispensable to Lebanese politics. By the same token, if the economic promise does not materialize, Hariri will most likely be made the scapegoat. Paradoxically Israel's attack in April boosted his prestige as a 'national leader'.

Harish, Michael 'Micha' Israel

Industry and Trade Minister. On Oct. 26, 1995, Harish signed a historic trade accord with his Jordanian counterpart, Ali Abu al-Ragheb, which allowed for the first movement of goods between the two countries in 46 years. He is also credited with Israel's trade boom, and to some extent, for Israel's diversification into new markets and technologies. Born in Romania in 1936, Micha Harish immigrated to Israel as a teenager and studied economics and political science at the Hebrew University. He founded the Labour Party's Young Guard in 1966. Over the next 15 years he directed the party's international department. During this period he worked to persuade world socialists to block the Arab boycott (Gulf States announced an end to the secondary and tertiary boycott in September 1994). He was also instrumental in establishing Israel's diplomatic relations with Spain.

At various stages in his career, Harish has chaired the Labour Party's political committee, the *Knesset* Finance Committee and the Israel Centre for Energy Policy. As Secretary-General of the Labour Party, from 1989 until he joined the cabinet in 1992, Harish oversaw far-reaching reforms within the party, including the introduction of primary elections to decide on *Knesset* candidates. Many political analysts believe that these reforms helped revive the Labour Party's fortunes on the eve of the 1992 elections. In office, Harish has concentrated on opening up new areas for Israeli business, in the Arab world, Germany and Argentina. However, he has also struggled to reduce Israel's enormous $7.5 billion trading deficit with the EU. (On Nov. 20, 1995, Israel signed a Treaty of Association with the EU, which considerably expanded free trade and co-operation between the two parties; although this was ultimately a foreign ministry venture.)

HASSAN bin Talal al-Hashimi (Crown Prince)

Nationality	Jordanian
Religion	Sunni Muslim
Place of birth	Amman, Jordan
Date of birth	March 29, 1947
Current position	Crown Prince of the Hashemite Kingdom of Jordan
Previous positions	Responsibilities for developing the country; patron of numerous national institutions and societies

Allies	Closely allied to King Hussein; supports better contacts between Christians, Muslims and Jews; backed by tribal leaders
Position on peace	Enthusiastic; played a key role in peace negotiations, and as host of the Amman regional economic conference, held in October 1995
National political importance	Since 1971, supervised the Kingdom's national development planning
Prospects	Likely to succeed King Hussein as head of state

Crown Prince El-Hassan of Jordan is one of the most active proponents of peace in the Middle East. As heir apparent to his brother, King Hussein, Prince Hassan has been well groomed to succeed him as the head of the Hashemite monarchy and the government of Jordan. In the absence of parliamentary elections, Hassan assumed many of the roles normally assigned to an elected prime minister. He won widespread praise in 1989 for dealing with food riots while his elder brother was away.

Prince Hassan's broad interests in arts, sciences, education, economics and religion are reflected in his support for a range of institutions. In the 1990s, Prince Hassan turned his attention to interfaith meetings between Muslims, Christians and Jews. He is regarded as an authority on Islamic law, and as such he acts as a counterweight to those Islamic fundamentalists who regard the Hashemite Kingdom as an impediment to *sharia* law. He has also taken more overtly political decisions of late. After the Gulf War, Kuwait expelled thousands of Palestinians from its land, many of whom were expatriate professionals who ran the economy. After some 300,000 fled to Jordan, Prince Hassan called for a regional and international social charter to protect the rights of migrants and refugees. His views on refugees aroused some controversy amongst Palestinians at the October 1993 donors' conference in Washington. Prince Hassan likes to see them as examples of lateral thinking – moving beyond Arab demands for compensation or repatriation, to a more flexible concept of citizenship, and acknowledging Arab state harrassment of their Jewish minorities (most of whom fled to Israel since 1948).

Hassan has also played a direct role in the peace process with Israel. On Oct. 1, 1993, he met Israeli Foreign Minister Shimon Peres for the first time at the White House. This cemented the Common Agenda agreed between the two nations the previous month, and prepared the way for King Hussein to sign the Washington Declaration (ending the state of war) with Israeli Prime Minister Yitzhak Rabin, the following July. On Aug. 8, 1994, Prince Hassan and Rabin inaugurated the first border crossing between Israel and Jordan, north of Aqaba. Jordan and Israel signed their full peace treaty on Oct. 17, 1994.

Hassan has also been intimately involved in problems arising out of the implementation of the treaty. Addressing Palestinian fears that the treaty guaranteed Jordan sole rights over Jerusalem's holy sites, he assured them that Jordan's custodianship was temporary, but would last until the final status talks between Israel and the PLO settled the status of the city. In March 1995, Hassan and Peres met again in Amman to formulate a common position on projects for creating sources of water for Jordan (as specified in the Israel–Jordan Peace Treaty). The two men also discussed joint projects in the Jordan Valley program, establishing a regional educational committee, free trade in the the Aqaba-Eilat-Taba triangle, the establishment of a Europe-Jordan–Israel economic committee, plans for the forthcoming Amman Conference, establishing a regional development bank and promoting the idea of creating a regional security structure.

As chief planner and sponsor of the Amman economic conference of late October, 1995, Prince Hassan gained much credit for its success. But Jordanians opposed to the peace with Israel attacked him for allegedly giving Israel an open door to regional economic domination. Hassan acknowledges this fear, and has repeatedly called for economic parity between Israel and the Arabs. In this respect, he feels the USA should engage the 'human resource-rich countries' of the Middle East, rather than only the oil-rich states. Hassan has been cushioned from many of the more controversial aspects of Jordan's evolution towards multi-party democracy. However, his broad experience, amiable manner and the trust he engenders amongst the Hashemite loyalists, Israeli officials and Palestinian negotiators, all should count in his favour. He may well be called on to act as an unofficial mediator on the refugees issue, in the forthcoming 'final status talks' between Israel and the PLO.

King HASSAN II

Nationality	Morocco
Religion	Sunni Muslim
Date of birth	July 9, 1929
Current position	King of Morocco since 1961
Position on peace	Openly backed the Arab League line, but privately maintained close contact with Israel for many years; acts as broker for peace initiatives
National political importance	Most powerful force in Morocco, influential in the *Maghreb* region
Prospects	Despite rumours of opposition, likely to maintain power

King Hassan II ascended the throne after the death of his father, King Muhammed V, in 1961. Hassan's reign has been characterized by generally benevolent autocracy, with some political liberalization at the margins. His Alaouite dynasty claims descent from the house of the Prophet Muhammed. Between 1965 and 1970, Hassan imposed a state of emergency on the country; he survived assassination attempts in 1971 and 1972. Partially to divert attention from Morocco's own internal problems, the king spearheaded a popular 'green march' on the Western Sahara (formerly Spanish Sahara). Morocco claims it as its own; local Sahrawis oppose them. Since then Morocco has fought a long-running war in the area.

With regard to the broader Middle East, Morocco is physically far removed from Israel, Palestine, and has contributed little more than token divisions to the conflict there. Nonetheless, the king is still held in high regard by many of the Morrocan Jews who immigrated to Israel (Morocco is the largest single 'donor country' of Sephardim to Israel). Generally, Jews were better treated in Morocco than in most other Arab countries, and a significant Jewish community remains there to this day. Officially, King Hassan toed the Arab League line on Israel. Unofficially, he has played a key backstage role in facilitating peace: in 1977 he helped path the way for Sadat's visit to Jerusalem; in July 1986 he hosted Shimon Peres (then Israeli Foreign Minister) at his Ifrane Palace for talks on Palestinian autonomy; and in September 1993 he was the first leader to host Israeli Prime Minister Rabin and PLO Chairman Yasser Arafat after the Washington signing. It is also said that King Hassan persuaded Jordan's King Hussein to loosen his ties with the West Bank. This proved to be an important step towards the PLO's Algiers Declaration in 1988, and, in turn, the current peace process.

In the past, other Arab states had criticized Hassan for his ties with Israel (especially his alleged use of *Mossad* intelligence in the war against the Saharans). But in the new post-Gulf War atmosphere, Morocco's approach has been accepted, even considered to be useful as a precedent for other Arab states to follow. Hassan opened the Casablanca MENA economic summit in October 1994. This was seen as an outstanding by-product of the multilateral talks initiative, in which Morocco plays an important role. For the first time, Israeli businessmen and politicians were seen openly discussing common concerns with their Arab counterparts. In late 1994, Morocco opened a special interest office in Tel Aviv, but has yet to embark on full diplomatic relations with Israel. Since 1996, Rabat has become the headquarters of the MENA summit secretariat.

Hassan, Hani al-   Palestinian

Founding member of the PLO. Hassan was born in Haifa in 1937, and studied engineering in Germany. He was an ally of the first PLO Chairman, Ahmed Shukeiri; but adjusted easily to Arafat's take-over of the organization in 1969, and rose to the position of European chief of *Fatah* in 1970. That same year he was cast as PLO spokesman during the crisis in Jordan, which eventually led to near civil war and the PLO's expulsion from the Kingdom. Like his brother, Khalid al-Hassan (*q.v.*), Hani has fostered close ties with Saudi Arabia; he also opened up PLO channels to China in the 1970s. Hani al-Hassan was the long-serving deputy to Salah Khalaf (Abu Iyad). After Abu Jihad's assassination, Abu Iyad assumed the number two position in the PLO, and this increased Hassan's status within the organization. Hassan depicted himself as a 'realist' since the mid-1970s, and opposed those who rejected peace with Israel. However, he has criticized aspects of the Oslo Accords, and the managerial style of Yasser Arafat.

Hassan, Khalid al-   Palestinian

PLO chief theoretician and one of the founders of *Fatah*. Born in Haifa in 1928, he was one of the first *Fatah* leaders to favour a two-state solution in the 1970s. Together with his brother, Hani (*q.v.*), Khalid al-Hassan managed to persuade oil-rich Gulf States, including Saudi Arabia, to bankroll the PLO (which made it at one stage the wealthiest liberation movement in the world). In the 1960s, Hassan held a senior position in the Kuwaiti ministry for development. He joined the PLO Executive Committee in 1969, and later became the head of its political department. Hassan broke with Arafat over the Gulf Crisis. He regarded Arafat's support for Saddam Hussein as misguided, and chose to remain in Kuwait during the war. Events proved Hassan right, as the Gulf states cut off funds to the PLO, and Kuwait expelled up to 350,000 Palestinians. Unfortunately for Hassan, as the senior PLO representative in Kuwait, he was strictured by the Kuwaiti regime once it returned to power.

Hassan unequivocally recommended PLO support for the Madrid peace track formula, at the PNC's 20th conference in 1991. However, in January 1992, he criticized the PLO and the Madrid delegates for short-sightedness and point-scoring, instead of planning long-term goals. His own vision of a solution encompasses a Swiss-style 'canton system', incorporating Israel, the Palestinian territories and Jordan in a tripartite confederation. It would enjoy free internal trade and a single external trade policy, with Hebrew and Arabic as official languages. Hassan also chided Palestinian delegates for not demanding adherence to UN 194 (which offers refugees the right of return or compensation). Since the Declaration of Principles, in September 1993, he has refused to participate in the Palestine National Authority, and has continued to criticize Arafat from outside. While some observers see him as a possible successor to Arafat, if the peace process were to collapse, it is more likely that PLO members would choose a younger substitute.

Hawatmeh, Naif   Palestinian

Head of Democratic Front for the Liberation of Palestine (DFLP). Naif Hawatmeh was born in 1935 into a Christian family which lived near Salt in Jordan. In a political sense, he became a Palestinian by adoption. His Marxist views were forged by the experience of his family, who had to leave their land and become manual labourers after a series of bad crops. In the 1950s Hawatmeh joined the Arab Nationalist Movement. Sentenced to death after plotting the overthrow of the Hashemite monarchy, he fled to Iraq, but was forced to leave there too after more revolutionary activity in 1963.

In 1967 he co-founded the Popular Front for the Liberation of Palestine (PFLP) with his mentor, George Habash. Two years later he led a breakaway from the PFLP, and formed the DFLP, after accusing Habash of ideological impurity. Habash in turn has long charged the DFLP with 'infantile leftism'. Like Habash, Hawatmeh chose to live under the broad PLO umbrella. He upholds (indeed, probably inspired) the *Fatah* goal of a democratic and secular Palestine (incorporating present-day Israel), in which Jews, Muslims and Christians would live as equal citizens. Hawatmeh sees the struggle against Zionism as only part of the broader struggle against 'imperialist and reactionary Arab regimes'. To this end, he made several contacts with 'progressive' Jews in Israel, and even gave interviews with the Israeli press. He believes that Jews should be allowed to preserve their separate identity within his utopian Palestine.

At the same time, Hawatmeh's DFLP was also responsible for a number of vicious terrorist attacks. The most notable was an attack on a school in Ma'alot, northern Israel, in 1974, which killed 27 Israelis. But in keeping with his belief in a 'people's war', he forbids cadres from indulging in terror outside 'historic Palestine'. Throughout the 1970s and 1980s, DFLP enjoyed a large basis of support in the West Bank, to the chagrin of *Fatah*. However, recently tensions built up between the 'internal' comrades, and the somewhat distanced leadership, including Hawatmeh, based in Damascus.

Even within the 'external wing' there were divisions. These were exacerbated as Hawatmeh's deputy, Yasser Abed Rabbo, a close aide to Arafat, began to steal with limelight. Abed Rabbo's younger supporters failed to unseat Hawatmeh, and in 1991 the rising star was expelled from the DFLP. The peace process and collapse of Hawatmeh's chief sponsor, the Soviet Union, has placed an enormous strain on the organization. Today it is split three ways – between FIDA, which supports the Oslo deal quite overtly; a renegade faction in the rejectionist National Alliance; and the rump DFLP under Hawatmeh, which occupies the middle ground, waiting to see how Palestinian autonomy turns out.

Heiberg, Marianne   Norway
Co-leader of a Norwegian social study of living conditions in Gaza and the West Bank. Heiberg worked together with the Director of the FAFO research institute, Terje Larsen, and as the wife of Norway's Foreign Minister Johan Jorgen Holst, she became a crucial link in setting up the secret Oslo channel for talks between Israel and the PLO. After the break-through of August 1993, negotiators on both sides praised her and her husband for providing the relaxed but worklike environment for the talks to succeed.

Heikal, Mohammed   Egypt
Prominent journalist and author. Born in 1924, he edited the prestigious *Al-Ahram* newspaper between 1957 and 1974. He served briefly as a minister in 1970, and advised Nasser and Sadat in turn, until the latter constrained him for opposing his policies. Heikal advocates peace, but on Egypt's terms. He wrote of the Gulf War as a missed opportunity to redress the social divisions in Arab society, and warned of American domination in the region.

Hendel, Zvi   Israel
Campaigner for Jewish settlers in the Gush Katif coastal region of Gaza. Israeli officials consulted him when drawing up the security provisions of the Cairo Accords (the implementation of Oslo 1).

Hertzog, Haim   Israel
State President from 1983 to 1993. Haim Hertzog was born in Belfast (now Northern Ireland) in 1918. His father became Chief Rabbi of Ireland in Dublin. In 1935, the family emigrated to Palestine, and Hertzog's father became the first Ashkenazi Chief Rabbi of Israel after 1948. The younger Hertzog was educated at universities in Dublin, London and Cambridge, and studied at Hebron's *yeshiva* (talmudic academy). He served as a major with British forces in World War II, and was the Jewish Agency's head of security in 1947 and 1948. During the Israeli War of Independence, Hertzog was the chief of Israeli military intelligence. He became the first military governor of the West Bank, after the 1967 war. From 1975 to 1978, Hertzog was Israel's Ambassador to the United Nations, and then entered the Knesset as a Labour Party MK.

Despite his Labour credentials and moderately dovish reputation, he was elected to succeed Yitzhak Navon as President by a Knesset led by the *Likud* in 1983. He proved to be a popular President, and was re-elected in 1988, when he had the difficult task of repairing national morale in the wake of the *intifada* and international opprobrium. Hertzog used his talmudic training to counter the arguments of militant religious settlers. However, former liberal allies were disappointed by what they saw as his leniency towards convicted members of the terrorist Jewish Underground. Ezer Weizman succeeded Haim Hertzog as President in 1993. Hertzog favoured peace talks with Arab nations, but generally confined his politics within the mainly titular strictures of his office.

Hindi, Amin al-   Palestinian
Senior PLO intelligence officer; implicated in 1972 Munich Olympics massacre.

Hirsch, Moshe (Rabbi)   Israel
Secretary of *Neturei Karta* and Palestine National Authority 'Minister for the Jewish Community of Palestine'. *Neturei Karta* is a small and militantly anti-Zionist ultra-orthodox Jewish group based in the Me'ah She'arim district of Jerusalem. Rabbi Hirsch rejects the State of Israel and has long enjoyed cordial relations with the PLO. In his view, until the Messiah arrives, Jews in 'Palestine' should live as a non-political community under benign Muslim rule.

Hirschfeld, Yair   Israel
Academic active in secret pre-Oslo facilitating talks with Abu 'Ala. Yair Hirschfeld was Professor of Middle Eastern History at Haifa University, who also worked for a research body backed by Yossi Beilin, when the latter was still an opposition MK. In 1989 he and his

colleague Ron Pundak met Hanan Ashrawi for 'proximity talks' in East Jerusalem. In 1992 he was involved with a European Community-sponsored study on political and economic conditions in the occupied territories. His initial liaison with Abu 'Ala in a London hotel, with Terje Larsen acting as a go-between, and Ashrawi as another contact, set in train what became known as the secret Oslo channel. It was Hirschfeld who outlined the broad terms of a joint programme, which later developed into the Declaration of Principles. Together with Ron Pundak and Abu 'Ala, Hirschfeld devised the concept of 'gradualism' to keep the talks moving.

In time Hirschfeld and Pundak agreed to take a secondary role, as professional politicians and diplomats joined the negotiations. Since the successful outcome (the Declaration of Principles in September 1993), Hirschfeld and Pundak have returned to the quieter life of academia. Hirschfeld combined his naturally genial nature with dogged persistance. This, and his appreciation of the economic and psychological ingredients for make a lasting peace deal, all contributed to the ultimate success of the Oslo talks, where so many other 'secret channels' failed.

Hobeika, Elie   Lebanon

Minister for Electricity and Water Resources. Hobeika's faction of the Christian Phalange militia was responsible for the Sabra and Shatilla massacre of Palestinians in 1982. At the time he was allied with Israel, but later switched allegiances to Syria. In October 1990 his forces helped the Syrians crush the renegade Christian Gen. Michel Aoun. Hobeika's *Waad* Party strongly opposes his former ally in the Phalange, Samir Geagea.

Holst, Johan Jorgen   Norway

Foreign Minister from April 1993 until his death in early 1994, and facilitator of the Oslo peace talks. At a crucial stage mid-1993, when it appeared the secret Oslo channel talks were reaching deadlock, his personal intervention ensured that they continued. Johan Holst was born in 1937. After studies at Oslo University and Columbia in the US, he worked at the Norwegian Institute for International Affairs (NUPI). He was defence secretary from 1976 to 1979, foreign secretary from 1979 to 1981, and then defence minister in Gro Harlem Brundt-land's Labour government, from 1986 to 1989. After a year as director of NUPI, he returned to the cabinet in late 1990 as defence minister in a new minority Labour government.

Holst became Foreign Minister in April 1993, when the tentative Israel–PLO 'secret channel' was already underway. However, his predecessor, Thorvald Stoltenberg, and his deputy, Jan Egeland, had briefed him well about developments. Added to that, Holst's wife, Marianne Heiberg, worked together with Terje Larsen in FAFO, the body under whose auspices the first Israeli–PLO contacts were made. In Jane Corbin's book, Holst, Heiberg and even their young son were credited with helping to pull back the talks from the brink of disaster on many occasions. It was Holst who spoke to Yasser Arafat on Shimon Peres's behalf in August, 1993, an act which set the seal on the channel developing into the full Declaration of Principles. Holst became an official co-ordinator of the peace process. Arafat and Rabin addressed letters to him as an intermediatory. In one significant instance, Shimon Peres promised Holst that Israel would address the issue of Jerusalem's future in its fullest extent. Johan Jorgen Holst died of a brain tumour in January 1994, aged 56, and Bjorn Tore Godal took over as Foreign Minister. A World Bank channel for aid to the Palestinian Authority was named the Holst Fund in his honour.

Elias HRAWI

Nationality	Lebanese
Religion	Maronite Christian
Place of birth	Zahle, Beqa'a Valley
Date of birth	1930
Current position	President of Lebanon since November 1989
Previous position	Deputy for Zahle in the Lebanese National Assembly
Allies	Close ties with the Maronite establishment and Syria

Position on peace	Cautious; favours peace with Israel only after its troops leave the southern buffer zone; toes the Syrian line
National political importance	Has helped to restore some unity and stability after the civil war
Prospects	Simmering battle for influence with Prime Minister Hariri; no obvious successor in sight as president

Elias Hrawi came to power in difficult circumstances, but while some saw him as merely an interim president, he has proved his staying power, and shown some skill in reconciling his nation after the bitterness of a 16-year-long civil war. Although the Lebanese National Assembly effectively dissolved in 1975, Hrawi continued to represent his constituents from Zahle. Like his predecessor as president, Rene Mo'awad, Hrawi is a Maronite Christian. Unlike other Maronites, however, Hrawi is not a Phalangist, and has assiduously nurtured his contacts with Syria. Thus Hrawi played a central role in drafting the Syrian–backed Taif Accords of 1989, which redefined the future relationship between Syria and Lebanon, and which introduced the prospect of significant political reforms within Lebanon.

Assembly deputies (survivors of the parliament of 1972) met in Taif, Saudi Arabia, and nominated Rene Mo'awad as president on Nov. 5, 1989. But the new head of state was assassinated by car-bomb while returning from Independence Day celebrations on Nov. 22; two days later the deputies reconvened and elected Hrawi as his successor. By tradition, the Lebanese president is always Christian; also following tradition, Hrawi nominated Salim al-Hoss, a Sunni Muslim, as his prime minister. Hrawi's first major act on taking office was to dismiss the renegade Christian general, Michel Aoun, from his post as commander-in-chief of the Lebanese Armed Forces. (Aoun claimed Hrawi was an imposter, and instead called himself the true legitimate president of Lebanon.)

Steering a narrow path between Lebanon's Maronite establishment and Damascus, in September 1990 Hrawi signed into law the reform policies as stipulated in the Taif Accords. In October, he authorized his armed forces (now under the more loyal commander, Gen. Emile Lahoud) to defeat Aoun. This they did, with Syrian armed support and US approval. Hrawi's authority was further bolstered by the implementation of a security plan which forced the various armed militias to vacate Beirut.

In 1991, Hrawi agreed to Lebanese participation in the Madrid peace conference. However, he was careful not to move faster on the peace track than his partners in Damascus. Hrawi maintained that there could be no peace with Israel until Israeli forces left the southern 'security zone'. He was less exacting on the Syrians, who, contrary to the Taif Accord, did not leave their posts in Hrawi's native Beqa'a Valley. It is an area with a mixed Christian and Shi'ite population, so Hrawi appreciated the need for a government which represented a broad cross-spectrum of ethnicity. However, even though his own wife is half-Palestinian, Hrawi is adamant that Lebanon's Palestinians should not become citizens, nor should they 'interfere' in national politics.

Since 1992 he has clashed repeatedly with the new prime minister, Rafiq Hariri, whose dynamic approach has apparently enhanced the premiership at the expense of the presidency. Even so, in 1995 Hariri joined supporters of Hrawi to demand that Hrawi's term of office be extended for another five years (it was due to expire in November 1995, according to Article 42 in the revised Lebanese constitution). Many former Hrawi allies, including Salim al-Hoss and Assembly Speaker Nabih Berri, resented this attempt to tamper with the constitution. In the end, Syria affected a last-minute compromise, and Hrawi was appointed for a further three years. Some may see the outcome a backhanded compliment to Hrawi, for the way in which he brought a much-needed sense of stability in Lebanon. But, as with so many political issues in Lebanon, it also served to remind everyone of the ultimate power that Syria wields in the nation's affairs.

Hulleileh, Samir   Palestinian

Director-General of the Palestine Authority's trade department within the Economic Ministry. Hulleileh is also head of aid co-ordination for PECDAR, and was responsible for drafting a new private investment law. However, he agreed to delay its implementation until Palestinians can apply it to the West Bank as well as Gaza. In June 8, 1995, Hulleileh announced that Israel and the PNA would set up nine industrial zones, each valued at up to $100 million, with six in the West Bank and three in Gaza. Palestinian leftists and trade union activists challenged him to prove that the scheme did not mean a return to the exploitation of non-unionised cheap Palestinians, this time by the PNA instead of Israel. Hulleileh remains a political pragmatist, and backed *Hamas* participation in the scheduled Palestinian council elections. He is a close aide to Yasser Arafat and Economics Minister Abu 'Ala.

Hurd, Douglas   UK

Foreign Secretary from Oct. 26, 1989, until his resignation in July 1995. Douglas Hurd served in this capacity during the Gulf War, Madrid peace talks, and Oslo Accords. During his earlier tenure as a junior Foreign Office minister, he had shown great interest in Middle Eastern affairs; but as Secretary most of his time was devoted to redefining Britain's role in the European Community, and trying to solve the Bosnian crisis. When he left office, he was praised for his excellent command of Britain's foreign affairs, during the last years of Margaret Thatcher and the first years of John Major.

Douglas Hurd was born in 1930 in Wiltshire, and educated at Eton and Trinity College, Cambridge. After serving in the Royal Horse Artillery, he spent 14 years as a career diplomat, and rose through the ranks as his superiors recognized his qualities of discretion and intelligent analysis. From 1970 to 1974 he was political secretary to Conservative Party leader, Edward Heath, who was then Prime Minister. Douglas Hurd was elected to Parliament himself in 1974, in the year that Heath lost power to a Labour administration. Within the Conservative Party, Hurd was known as a patrician, and somewhat at odds with the harder monetarist approach called 'Thatcherism'. Nonetheless, Thatcher made him her Northern Ireland Secretary, and, in 1985, Home Secretary.

As Foreign Secretary, Hurd used his mandarin's background to defeat more right-wing colleagues on issues like Hong Kong and relations with Europe. He became a central figure in determining US, UN and Western policy during the Gulf Crisis of 1990. Hurd also restored diplomatic relations with Syria in the same year. When Mrs Thatcher was forced to resign during these developments, Douglas Hurd entered the race to succeed her, but finished third. The successful candidate, and now Prime Minister, John Major, re-appointed Hurd as Foreign Minister. Following the signing of the Israel–PLO Declaration of Principles, Hurd visited Syria to discuss the new developments and reaffirm the two nations' improving ties. With junior minister Douglas Hogg, Hurd arranged for British seminars in policing and finance for the new Palestinian Authority (PNA). On the whole, Hurd channeled donations to the PNA via the European Union. In May 1995, he criticized Arab states for not matching the Western funding; he also opposed Israel's expropriation policy in Jerusalem, as being contrary to the spirit of the peace agreements. Douglas Hurd retired in July 1995, and was replaced by Malcolm Rifkind.

Hurd, Maher al-   Palestinian
(See Kurd, Maher al-)

King HUSSEIN ibn Talal al-Hashimi

Nationality	Jordanian
Religion	Muslim
Place of birth	Amman
Date of birth	Nov. 14, 1935
Current position	Head of State and King of the Hashemite Kingdom of Jordan
Previous position	Crown Prince of Jordan
Allies	Prime Minister al-Majali; younger brother, Crown Prince Hassan; Prime Minister Kabariti
Position on peace	Positive, unofficial ties with Israel long before the formal peace treaty Initially wary of the Israel–PLO Declaration of Principles Signed full peace treaty with Israel on Oct. 14, 1994
National political importance	Most powerful man in Jordan

Prospects   Survived many assassination attempts in past; now secure

King Hussein of Jordan has enjoyed the longest reign of any major political figure in the Middle East. As the last remaining Hashemite monarch in the area, he controls a nation which is economically poor, but remains vitally important in terms of regional politics. For decades he was an enthusiastic supporter of peace with Israel, but felt constrained by more powerful Arab states, and his commitments to the Palestinian people. On Oct. 14, 1994, Hussein signed a full peace treaty with Israeli Prime Minister Yitzhak Rabin (only the second such treaty between an Arab state and Israel).

Hussein was born in Amman and educated largely in England. His family were forced to leave what is now Saudi Arabia, when the Ibn Saud family usurped their centuries-old rights as Custodians of Mecca and Medina, the holiest sites of Islam. King Hussein is a descendant of the prophet Muhammed. In 1951 Hussein witnessed the assassination of his grandfather, King Abdullah, by a Palestinian in Jerusalem. Hussein's father, Talal, was appointed king, but was removed in 1952 because of reported mental illness. The young Hussein was designated his successor, and became king in 1953. In his first decade in office, Hussein encouraged slow but steady economic development.

Nonetheless, these were difficult years for the teenage monarch. Jordan's Palestinian majority, many of them refugees from the 1948 war with Israel, felt little loyalty to the Hashemite throne. Hussein relied heavily on the support of indigenous bedouin tribesmen, and they formed the core of Jordan's military establishment. Political unrest led him to dismiss the British head of the Jordan Arab Legion, General John Bagot Glubb (Glubb Pasha) in 1956. Hussein also tightened his grip on Jordan's parliament, and clamped down on anti-monarchist forces, inspired by the *Ba'ath* in Syria and Iraq, and Egyptian President Gamal Abdul Nasser's pan-Arabism.

During the 1960s, King Hussein fostered ties with the USA, and Washington provided huge amounts of aid to this potentially useful conservative ally in the Middle East. Somewhat reluctantly, Hussein joined Syria and Egypt in the 1967 Six Day War with Israel. The result was the loss of the West Bank and East Jerusalem, which Jordan had formally annexed in 1951. During the years of Israeli occupation, the King continued to support civil servants in the territories, and spent some $500 million on the upkeep of the Mosques of the *Haram al-Sharif* in Jerusalem. The war also had deep ramifications for Jordanian politics. As the West Bank was now 'in enemy hands', King Hussein suspended parliamentary elections and effectively dissolved the national legislature. Multi-party elections were only restored in 1993. For the next 25 years, Hussein held supreme authority, assisted by a consultative council and his Royal Court officials.

In addition, up to 300,000 Palestinians had fled from the West Bank to the East Bank (Jordan proper). Amongst them were PLO forces, which used Jordan as a launch-pad for raids on Israel and the territories. Matters came to a head in September 1970, when radical PLO elements threatened to topple the monarchy and, in effect, turn Jordan into a Palestinian state. The resultant bloody civil war ended with PLO forces being expelled from Amman and elsewhere, in July 1971; martial law was imposed in Jordan. On March 15, 1972, King Hussein suggested a Jordanian federation, whereby Jordan would reincorporate the West Bank, and grant it quasi-autonomous status. The PLO rejected this, but it marked the first of many Jordanian initiatives to solve the Palestinian–Israeli conundrum. King Hussein deliberately kept out of the 1973 Yom Kippur War with Israel, but he also slowly mended fences with the PLO. In 1974 the King backed the Arab summit resolution in Fez which made the PLO the 'sole legitimate representatives of the Palestinian people'. At the same time, he maintained a 'custodial' role over the Palestinians, who constituted at least half of his population. Israeli politicians sought to exploit this as a means of excluding the PLO from a permanent settlement in the territories. However, in the 1976 West Bank municipal elections, pro-Hussein candidates were largely defeated by PLO sympathizers.

King Hussein was invited to join the peace talks between Israel and Egypt, after 1977, but regarded Menachem Begin's plans for Palestinian autonomy as wholly inadequate, and so declined. As terrorism mounted in the Middle East, Britain and the USA identified King Hussein as a source of moderation, and improved political and economic ties with Jordan. Hussein also repaired relations with his traditional royal enemies, the Saudis, and the Gulf

States. Expatriate Jordanians (mainly Palestinians) generated vast remittances for the King-dom while working in the oil-rich states. At the same time, Hussein forged closer ties with Saddam Hussein's Iraq, as a counterweight to Syrian ambitions on the Hashemite Kingdom. In the early 1980s, the King improved ties with Egyptian President Hosni Mubarak, at a time when most of the Arab world still shunned Cairo over its 'separate' peace treaty with Israel.

On Feb. 11, 1985, King Hussein and Yasser Arafat signed a surprise 'Framework for Peace' plan for a confederation between a PLO–ruled West Bank and the Kingdom. Palestinian leftists rejected it, but the USA lent its support, hoping it would lead to direct talks with Israel and a joint Palestinian–Jordanian delegation. In the event, Hussein dissolved the agreement within a year, as he felt Arafat was not sincere about ending terrorism or openly endorsing UN 242. In April 1987 the King secretly met Israeli Foreign Minister Shimon Peres in London, but their resultant London Plan (for talks between Israel and a joint Palestinian–Jordanian delegation) were scuppered by conservatives in each camp.

The outbreak of the *intifada* in the Israeli–occupied territories in late 1987 led to sympa-thetic riots in Palestinian refugee camps in Jordan. In a historic declaration the next year, King Hussein formally abrogated Jordan's claim on the West Bank. This paved the way for the PLO's Algiers Declaration, and a flurry of new peace initiatives in the region. It also meant that King Hussein could revive democracy within his own 'East Bank' Jordan. In November 1989 Jordan held non-party parliamentary elections, and the newly elected representatives gradually acquired political power at the expense of the nominees.

Mindful of his ties with Iraq, King Hussein refused to join an anti-Saddam coalition after Iraq's invasion of Kuwait in August 1990. After Saddam's defeat, the Gulf states, Saudi Arabia and the USA ostracized Jordan, and imposed a virtual blockade on the port of Aqaba, to prevent goods from reaching Iraq. Once again, Hussein had to deal with an influx of Palestinian refugees, this time some 350,000 expatriate Jordanian citizens who were expelled from Kuwait after its liberation from Iraq. These factors combined to seriously damage the fragile Jordanian economy – unemployment mounted, and debts rose – which in turn threatened Hussein's political survival.

The Madrid peace summit of October 1991 offered Hussein an opportunity to restore his ties with the West, and formalize a peace accord with Israel. He agreed to provide an 'umbrella' for Palestinian delegates, under the chairmanship of his Foreign Minister Kamel Abu Jaber, but when the Palestinians wished to negotiate separately, he supported their wishes. Talks continued in Washington, but little real progress was made, as all the Arab parties waited for a breakthrough in the Palestinian talks. By mid-1992, it was clear that until the PLO was directly involved, this would not occur.

Meanwhile, Hussein pressed ahead with democratization at home. In April 1992, he abolished martial law, and by September had allowed for the creation of legal political parties according to a new National Charter. In August 1993 he dissolved Parliament, in preparation for multi-party elections on a one-person-one-vote basis. Hussein was angry when he learnt that the PLO had decided to make an agreement with Israel that same month, without consulting him, but nonetheless proceeded with elections in November. Some senior advisors had tried to dissuade him from allowing them, citing the rise in fundamentalist support, and the uncertainties over Palestinians' political future. The results, however, confirmed Hussein's judgement – although the Islamic Action Front became the largest single party, it was outnumbered by MPs loyal to the King. This gave him a mandate to make peace with Israel.

In September 1993 Israel and Jordan signed a Common Agenda, which identified water, borders, refugees and security as the four main areas for negotiation. Hussein appointed Abdul Salam al-Majali as Prime Minister, who used his experience in the Madrid/Washington talks to speed up negotiations. At the same time, Hussein assuaged Palestinian fears that they were being 'left out' of his new rapprochement with Israel, firstly by creating a trading agreement with the nascent Palestine National Authority in early 1994; and secondly by persuading the Palestinian refugees in Jordan that they were safe under Jordanian protection. In July 1994 Hussein met Rabin pubicly for the first time, and this was followed by a Declaration of Non-Belligerancy in Wasington, and in October 1994, a full peace treaty.

Although Parliament ratified the treaty, there was a backlash from Islamist and radical Palestinian elements. Over the next 18 months, Hussein responded with a typically double-pronged strategy – promoting young elected democrats who supported the peace, while using his earlier powers of detention to quell the dissidents. By replacing Majali with the more cautious Zayid Ibn Shaker as Prime Minister, Hussein signalled that the peace process should not be rushed. Some Israelis were disappointed that their longed-for 'warm peace' with Jordan was taking so long to implement, but Hussein realized that he had to cater to popular fears of 'Israeli domination'. However, the signing of a trade agreement in October 1995 marked a significant breakthrough, and there followed a flurry of similar agreements (including culture, the environment, police, borders and tourism) which at last helped to implement the terms of the peace treaty.

October 1995 also saw the launch of the second Middle East and North Africa (MENA) economic summit, in Amman, which placed Jordan and the King at the centre of bold new economic ventures for a post-peace Middle East. It also allowed Hussein's younger brother, Crown Prince Hassan, to prove his mettle as heir apparent to the Hashemite throne. However, the assassination of Yitzhak Rabin a week later temporarily threw all peace plans into doubt. King Hussein's moving eulogy at Rabin's funeral was broadcast throughout the world, and endeared him to a grieving Israeli nation. Hussein assured Rabin's successor, Shimon Peres, of his full support, and this definitely helped Israel to continue with the peace process, and the implementation of Oslo 2. Hussein's visit to Jerusalem was doubly poignant, for it was his first since witnessing the murder of his grandfather, Abdullah, in 1951, just metres from Rabin's graveside.

In early 1996, Hussein made sure that Jordanian politics had entered a new dynamic phase. He paid his first official visit to Israel, and was warmly welcomed there. He then replaced Ibn Shaker with the younger Abdel Karim Kabariti, and quickly moved to restore relations with Kuwait and Saudi Arabia, which had been severed since their rift over the Gulf War in 1991. At the same time, he distanced himself from his former alliance with Iraq, and for a while hosted two sons-in-law of Saddam Hussein who took refuge in Amman. Most strikingly, he encouraged close co-operation between his own military forces and the Israelis' – an arrangement unprecedented in the Arab world. President Clinton has come to regard King Hussein as one of his firmest allies in the region.

Over the years, the King has survived numerous assassination attempts, to become accepted and even loved by most elements of his population. He has also transformed Jordan into a true constitutional monarchy, and against the odds he has defined a sense of Jordanian patriotism that can accommodate the aspirations of the majority of his subjects who are Palestinian. Although question marks remain over Jordan's 'special interests' in Jerusalem, Hussein will probably play an important, albeit unofficial, moderating role in Israeli–Palestinian final status talks. Crown Prince Hassan is almost certain to succeed Hussein as monarch, and will continue with his path.

Faisal Abdul Qader HUSSEINI

Nationality	Palestinian
Religion	Muslim
Place of birth	Baghdad, Iraq
Date of birth	July, 1940
Current position	Chairman, Arab Studies Society; *Fatah* affiliated leader in territories
Previous position	Head of Palestinian delegation to Madrid peace talks, Oct. 1991
Allies	Sari Nusseibeh, Hanan Ashrawi; at times close to Arafat
Position on peace	Initially positive, turning to skepticism; left out of DOP track
National political importance	Influential in territories; both a moderate and a critic of Oslo
Prospects	Uncertain, although at times touted a successor to Arafat

Faisal al-Husseini comes from the most prominent family of Palestinian *ayan* (notables). His uncle was the Grand Mufti, Hajj Amin al-Husseini, and his father (who was killed in the 1947–49 war) was Abd-al Qader al-Husseini, the leading military foe of Israel. Notwithstanding his aristocratic origins, Faisal has built a considerable wellspring of support amongst common folk in the West Bank. In addition, during the *intifada* he became one of the most respected of all 'internal' Palestinian leaders, and his many talents were put to the test in his role as head of the Palestinian steering committee in the Madrid track peace talks. Technically, he is a Minister without Portfolio (widely seen as the PNA Minister for Jerusalem). In addition, he is the head of the PNA's Jerusalem National Council. Although his role is somewhat covert within the PNA, he is still considered a leader-in-waiting, and is the doyen of *Fatah* opinion in the territories.

Faisal Husseini was born in Baghdad, but returned to the family home in Jeruselam when he was one. In 1959 he helped establish the General Union of Palestinian Students in Cairo, and over the next four years he studied science there and in Baghdad.

In 1964 Husseini returned to Jerusalem, and at 24 became deputy manager of the public organization of the newly created PLO. Later he joined the Palestine Liberation Army following military training in Aleppo, northern Syria. In October 1967, after the Six Day War, Israeli authorities imprisoned him for a year on charges of arms possession. From 1969 to 1977 he worked as an X-ray technician in Jerusalem, and then studied history at the University of Beirut, in Lebanon. Back in Jerusalem, Husseini founded and became chairman of the Arab Studies Society in 1979, which has been the base of his influence ever since. Since 1982 he has also been a member of the Higher Islamic Council, following a longstanding family tradition.

During that period he began putting out feelers to Israeli peace groups, but was placed under house arrest between 1982 and 1987. Between April 1987 and January 1989 he was again imprisoned, under Israel's laws of 'administrative detention'. This effectively removed him from the day-to-day leadership of the *intifada*, although on his release he soon rose to prominence as a media spokesperson for the uprising, and helped set up the political committees which provided an organized focus for Palestinian opinion.

By the 1990s Husseini had become the first contact for Israeli politicians seeking a deal with pro-PLO Palestinians, during a period when open talks with PLO officials were still banned by Israeli law. He also built up his connections with like-minded Palestinian intellectuals and fellow 'moderates', such as the editor Hanna Siniora, and the Bir Zeit academics, Hanan Ashrawi and Sari Nusseibeh. However, he was bedevilled by attacks from, on the one hand, militant Palestinian 'rejectionists' (extreme leftists and Islamic fundamentalists alike), and on the other, Yitzhak Shamir's Israeli administration (even though he reputedly preferred talking to *Likud* Israelis rather than Labour supporters).

In the aftermath of the Gulf War, Husseini helped marshal support for a historic peace with Israel. In October 1991 he attended the Madrid peace conference. Because he was registered as living in East Jerusalem, however, Israel refused to accept him as an official delegate. As a result, Haidar Abd-al Shafi led the official delegation, while Husseini headed the ultimately more influential but unofficial steering and technical committees. It was widely believed that Husseini had the ear of Arafat. In effect he became the transmission mechanism whereby Tunis determined the stance of the Palestinian delegation. One of Prime Minister Rabin's first acts on coming to power, was to allow Husseini to head the 'steering committee' to the official delegation at the talks in Washington.

However, as the negotiations became increasingly bogged down, Husseini began to feel frustrated at the lack of consultation between his 'internal' wing and the 'external' wing of the PLO based in Tunis. Matters came to a head in August 1993, when Husseini and his colleagues realized that they had been largely bypassed in the implementation of the Washington/Oslo accords, even though they had played a considerable role in laying the groundwork for it. As a concession, Husseini, Hanan Ashrawi and Sa'eb Erakat were nominated to the PLO's Higher Committee for the Peace Talks.

Today Husseini is a Minister without Portfolio in the Palestine National Authority. According to some accounts, he is not considered to be in the inner circle. Instead, he appears to be dallying with a new role as an outside critic of human rights abuses by Palestinian authorities, through the Palestine Human Rights Information Centre, which he set up with Hanan Ashrawi. Others say that from his headquarters at Orient House, in Jerusalem, he acts as the PNA's unofficial 'foreign minister' to visiting politicians. Husseini has called for a strictly juridical constitution to safeguard nascent Palestinian democracy. His ultimate goal is a free market Palestinian economy which can fully integrate into the regional Middle Eastern economy, but only after it has successfully established its own infrastructure. Husseini believes that 'absolute justice' entails a Palestinian 'right to return'. Nonetheless, he is committed to the pragmatic acceptance of a 'relative just peace', which means attaining the possible, even if that falls short of a 'really just peace based on absolute justice'.

On June 28, 1995, Husseini went on a hunger strike in sympathy with Palestinian prisoners held by Israel (the PLO was accusing Israel of failing to honour its promise to release some 3,000 Palestinian political prisoners). After the signing of Oslo 2, Husseini appeared to score a success, by ensuring that East Jerusalem was included as an electoral district in the Palestine Council elections of January 1996. Through his Jerusalem National Council-Palestine, which he and Mahdi Abdul Hadi set up in November 1993, Husseini has already begun the debate on Jerusalem's future status. He envisages shared Israeli–Palestinian authority, and appears to be prepared to accept Jewish neighbourhoods in East Jerusalem as *de facto* realities, and not 'settlements' to be dismantled, as other Palestinians suggest. Faisal al-Husseini is sometimes spoken of as the effective leader of *Fatah* in the West Bank. He certainly has a number of enemies who resent his noble origins and present position, but he could yet become the future leader of Palestine.

Hussein, Saddam   Iraq

Saddam Hussein is one of the most controversial, complicted and feared figures in the Middle East. To Western powers and many of his own population he was (and is) a brutal dictator. Yet to large numbers of disgruntled people across the Arab world, he represented – briefly – a new champion of the pan-Arab cause. In early 1990, having spent two decades cementing his power in Iraq, and eight years fighting a costly war against Iran, Saddam Hussein adopted the mantle of the late Gamel Abdul Nasser, and threatened to lead a united Arab army to win back Jerusalem from Israel, and 'burn half of [that country]'. But ironically, within 18 months his actions actually led to the reverse situation – a new peace process, as the USA used its new power in the region to push forward the Madrid peace conference of 1991. Iraq currently is still held under a strict sanctions regime, imposed by the United Nations, and Saddam's ambitions for regional superiority have been effectively spiked.

Saddam Hussein was born in 1937 near Baghdad. He belongs to the Takriti clan, part of the politically dominant Sunni minority, in a country where the majority population is Shi'ite. At 20, Saddam joined the Ba'ath Party. In 1959, he was involved in the attempted assassination of Prime Minister Abd al-Karim Kassem. He returned to Iraq from exile in Egypt in 1964, after army officers in league with the *Ba'ath* had toppled and killed Kassem. Saddam quickly rose through the ranks of *Ba'ath* to become Vice-Chairman of the ruling Revolutionary Command Council in November 1969. On July 16, 1979, he finally defeated rivals to become President of Iraq. His rule is typified by draconian repression of all opposition (in particular, of the *Dawa* Shi'ite fundamentalists). He encouraged a personality cult, to such an extent that the *Ba'ath* hierarchy seems to have lost all its former autonomy.

In 1980 Saddam called for Arab unity, and launched a war with the new Islamic revolutionary government in neighbouring Iran. The war was to last eight years and cost over 500,000 lives. After the war ended in virtual stalemate, Iran and Iraq maintained an uneasy truce. Meanwhile, in 1981 Israeli aircraft had destroyed Iraq's French-built nuclear reactor at Osirak, which Tel Aviv claimed was really producing material for Baghdad's secret atomic arsenal.

In 1990 Saddam Hussein attempted to sway the Arab masses by posing as their saviour against 'US and Israeli imperialism'. A dispute over oil pricing policy gave him the pretext to invade and annex Kuwait, in August 1990. Saddam proclaimed that the invasion would focus attention on the Palestinian question. Arab leaders rejected this 'linkage' of the two issues as a flimsy and hypocritical ruse. However, many Palestinians, including Yasser Arafat, were frustrated at the sparse gains after three years of *intifada,* and Israel's rejection of the PLO's Algiers Declaration, and so climbed onto the Saddam bandwagon.

In 1991, the US forged an 'anti-Saddam' coalition of forces (including many Arab states), nominally under the aegis of the United Nations. When Saddam refused to vacate Kuwait, they counter-attacked from Saudi Arabia, liberated Kuwait, and soundly defeated the Iraqi army by using the latest high techonology weapons. During the war, Iraq had fired Scud missiles at Israel, in an ultimately unsuccessful bid to shatter the unity of the coalition.

Despite claims of internal army coup attempts, Saddam remains firmly ensconced in power. While Iraqi citizens still suffer the effects of UN sanctions and poor internal food distribution, Saddam has rebuilt the army, and clamped down on opponents.

Hut, Shafiq al-   **Palestinian**

PLO representative in Lebanon. Hut was at various stages a journalist and a science teacher, who made Beirut his base from the early 1970s. He founded the *Abtal al-Awla* (Heroes of the Return) group, before joining the Democratic Front for the Liberation of Palestine. In later years he served as a loyal independent member of the PLO Executive Committee, but in 1993 resigned in protest at the PLO–Israeli Declaration of Principles.

I

Ilan, Baruch   **Israel**

Director of the Israeli Foreign Ministry's [Palestinian] Autonomy Department. Ilan helped to negotiate the Oslo 2 accords with his Palestinian counterparts. In July 1995, he also participated in the first 'committee of experts' on the issue of Palestinian refugees of 1967 (the displaced persons), together with Palestinian, Egyptian and Jordanian officials.

Martin INDYK

Nationality	USA
Religion	Jewish
Place of birth	England, brought up in Australia
Date of birth	1952
Latest position	US Ambassador to Israel since 1994
Previous position	National Security Council adviser to President on Middle East
Allies	Close to Clinton; and long associations with Israeli causes
Position on peace	Enthusiastic about the peace process; stresses role of trade
National political importance	Was influential in shaping US Mideast policy; as ambassador he is an active protagonist; knowledge of Syria

Martin Indyk's ascent in the US State Department has been meteoric. As US Ambassador to Israel since late 1994, he has had great influence on US policy in the area, and especially regarding the direction of the peace process. However, it was as National Security Advisor to the President on Middle Eastern foreign policy that he first made his mark.

Born in England, he arrived in Australia when he was one and spent most of his life there. He took his PhD at the Australian National University on Israeli and Egyptian foreign polices *vis-à-vis* the superpowers. Later he worked as a senior researcher in Australian intelligence, and between 1979 and 1982 lectured at Macquarie University on Middle Eastern politics.

On moving to Washington DC in 1982, he joined AIPAC (the main US pro-Israel lobby group) and set up its research department. In 1992 Indyk joined the Bill Clinton election team as chief Middle East advisor. In January 1993 he became Special Assistant to the President and chief of the Middle East section of the National Security Council (NSC). Just before assuming this post, Indyk was granted US citizenship.

Certain prominent Arab Americans have objected to his ambassadorial appointment to such a strategically sensitive position. However, Indyk rejects accusations of a clear pro-Israel bias, and instead describes himself as pro-American. In numerous journal articles, he espoused the view that the end of the Cold War presented the USA with a 'window of opportunity' to restructure the Middle East order. He favours a permanent US presence in the Persian Gulf and eternal vigilance regarding both Iran and Iraq. Indyk has been an enthusiastic backer of Arab–Israeli peace talks. He places a particularly high premium on a Syrian–Israeli rapprochement, and has a good relationship with Syria's ambassador to

Washington, Walid Mualem. Close US ties with Egypt forms a centrepiece of his Middle Eastern vision. Yet Indyk's tendency towards 'interventionism' in foreign policy has upset some Clinton administration officials, who favour caution and 'isolationism' – in short, a more domestically based political agenda. Similarly, Indyk upsets the Israeli right when he appeared to intervene in domestic debates about the Golan issue in 1995.

Iryani, Abdul-Karim al-   Yemen

Deputy Prime Minister and Foreign Minister. In late 1995 Abdul-Karim al-Iryani told an Israeli journalist and representatives of Jewish organizations in New York that Yemen had lifted its secondary and tertiary boycotts of Israel. However, he added that full diplomatic relations between Sanaa and Tel Aviv would only follow a 'comprehensive peace agreement' with the Arab states. Iryani studied in the USA, joined the North Yemeni cabinet in 1976, and became Prime Minister in 1980. In the wake of internal divisions, he lost his post in 1983, but returned as Foreign Minister and deputy prime minister the next year. In May 1990 conservative North Yemen and Marxist South Yemen successfully re-united as one state. A new civil war threatened to erupt in 1995, but was later brought under control. Iryani's main concern is to redefine Yemen's relations with its giant neighbour, Saudi Arabia (the two have clashed over land and access to oil reserves, as well as Yemen's unenthusiastic support for the Gulf War).

Ishaq, Jad   Palestinian

Co-founder with Jonathan Kuttab of the *Al-Haq* civil liberties group; prominent Palestinian peace activist during the *intifada*; lecturer at Bethlehem University. Jad Ishaq (also Isaq or Isaac) was born in 1947 into a Christian family in Beit Sahur which traces its origins back to 1635. He studied biology to postgraduate level at Rutgers University, New Jersey, and the University of East Anglia. Ishaq is currently the director of the Applied Research Institute, which is based in Bethlehem in the West Bank. During the *intifada* he turned his gardening hobby into an exercise in agricultural self-reliance, and founded a seed and livestock centre in Jericho. Ishaq was jailed for six months and in 1992 was put under a restriction order, for allegedly 'subversive activities'. Since 1989 Jad Ishaq and his wife, Ghada Andoni, have been involved in an Israeli–Palestinian dialogue group in Beit Sahur. In 1996 Ishaq and Kuttab published an analysis of the need for an equitable solution to the Israeli–Palestinian dispute over water.

Ismail, Mahmoud   Palestinian

Leader, Arab Liberation Front, an Iraqi-backed PLO faction, reputedly affiliated to *Fatah*.

Ivri, David (Maj.-Gen.)   Israel

Director-General of Israel's Defence Ministry since 1986. Regarded as one of Israel's main strategic decision-makers, Ivri was born in 1934, studied at the Haifa Technion and entered the IDF in 1952, later serving as a pilot. He was commander of the Israeli Air Force from 1977 to 1982.

David Ivri has also spearheaded Israel's successful overtures to help Jordan's armed forces. In 1996 he visited military installations in Jordan, and lobbied on Jordan's behalf with US Defence Secretary William Perry, to ensure that the US provided Jordan with F-15 fighter aircraft. Ivri has discussed proposals for a formal strategic alliance between Israel and the USA, but is thought to favour the current dispensation, which allows Israel more political autonomy.

J

Ja'abari, Muhammed Amin   Palestinian

Representative for Hebron on the Palestine National Council (PNC), the PLO's 'parliament in exile'. Ja'abari returned in mid-1994 after 25 years in exile. He has represented Hebron for eight years, and now calls for 'both sides (Israel and the PLO) must pay the price for cancelling the [Palestinian] Charter'. He believes Israel should release political prisoners, lift the occupation of Hebron, address the issue of Jerusalem's Arabs, and ease the closure. In return, Palestinians would co-operate with Israel, and end the armed struggle forever. The Charter issue is a major stipulation of Oslo 2. As other PNC members return from exile to debate it, Ja'abari was well-placed as an early returnee to influence their decisions.

Ja'abari, Suleiman al- *(Sheikh)*   Palestinian
Appointed Mufti of Jerusalem by Jordan in 1993, when he was 81. Sheikh Ja'abari hailed from Hebron, where his traditionally pro-Jordanian family were prominent *ayan* (notables). Ja'abari was also a fierce opponent of what he saw as Israeli encroachment on, and 'Judaization' of, the Old City of Jerusalem. When Sheikh Ja'abari died in October 1994, a mini-crisis erupted over who his successor should be. Jordan appointed Sheikh Abideen, but the Palestine National Authority under the PLO decided on Sheikh Ikram Sabri. Currently, the two men hold rival offices, although the latter is felt to be more popular amongst Palestinians.

Jaber, Hajj Ismail   Palestinian
West Bank Palestinian Police Chief in 1995. Jaber liaises closely with Maj.-Gen. Gabi Ofir, the IDF Commander in Judea and Samaria (West Bank), on redeployment of IDF forces from major West Bank towns, including Qalqilyah and Nablus, according to Oslo 2. He is also involved with the setting up of liaison and co-ordination offices in the towns concerned.

Jaber, Kamal Abu   Jordan
Head of the 'umbrella' joint Palestinian–Jordanian delegation to the Madrid peace conference in October 1991. Born in 1932, Jaber became Foreign Minister in 1991. His job as joint delegation head ultimately became redundant in 1992, when the Palestinians (with full Jordanian agreement) began to negotiate in their own right with Israelis. Jaber currently heads Jordan's World Affairs Council.

Jahshan, Khalil   USA
Director, National Association of Arab Americans (NAAA). Khalil Jahshan is a Christian Arab from Nazareth who immigrated to the USA in 1969. The NAAA was set up in 1972 as an Arab lobby, on the model of the Jewish community's successful American-Israeli Political Action Committee (AIPAC). The NAAA supports the peace process, and wants an independent PLO–led state alongside Israel, and a 'negotiated solution' to the question of Jerusalem.

Jarrar, Bassam (Sheikh)   Palestinian
Islamist intellectual from Ramallah. In December 1995, Sheikh Jarrar became the main spearhead of *Hamas* opposition to the scheduled January 1996 Palestine Council elections. He called them a 'laughing stock . . . aimed at legitimizing the Oslo Accords and [perpetuating] Israeli occupation of our land'.

Jauda, Hisham   Palestinian
Commander of *Fatah* Hawks, the PLO's operational arm in territories. Israel insisted that the PNA restrict the Hawks' activities, but recent reports suggest that they were still active in Nablus, and especially in the adjoining Balata refugee camp.

Jazzar, Majdi   Syria
Director of the Syrian Foreign Ministry's department for international affairs in 1991. Born in 1936, Jazzar was a leading member of Syria's delegation to the Madrid and subsequent Washington peace talks.

Jibril, Ahmed   Palestinian
Head of PFLP-GC (Popular Front for the Liberation of Palestine – General Command) since 1968; member of the anti-Oslo Alliance of Palestinian Forces since 1994. Ahmed Jibril was born in 1936 in Yazur, near Tel Aviv. In 1948 he fled with his family to Beirut and then Damascus, where he became an expert in explosives in the Syrian Army. In 1967 he joined George Habash's PFLP, but broke away the following year. Since then, he has become one of the most active terrorists, starting with a mid-air explosion on a Swiss airliner over Israel, which killed all 47 passengers, in 1970. Since 1976 PFLP-GC units have fought alongside Syrian army regulars, against Arafat's forces in Lebanon. In 1985, Israel exchanged some 500 Palestinian prisoners a deal with Jibril, in exchange for three Israeli prisoners-of-war. During the 1980s, Jibril received funding from Libya and Iran in turn. While his radio station,

Al-Quds, beams into the territories with regular denunciations of the peace process, Jibril is not thought to enjoy much popular support. Over the last decade, however, he has formed a functional alliance with the Palestinian Islamic *Jihad*, despite the ideological gulf between them, leading to a spate of attacks on Israelis in Israel and Egypt.

Jinnah, Zuheir   Syria
Syrian spokesman at Madrid.

Jiryas, Sabri   Palestinian
PLO leader and journalist. Jiryas used to head *al-Ard* (The Soil), a group of Israeli Arabs who protested at the expropriation of their land in the Galilee region. He later became Director of the PLO Research Centre in Beirut.

John Paul II (Pope)   Vatican
Pope and Vatican head of state since Oct. 16, 1978; first non-Italian head of the Roman Catholic Church since 1523. John Paul II is known for his high-profile world tours, and his willingness to comment on political affairs. Some Catholics were disappointed with his doctrinal orthodoxy, but on the whole he has been one of the most popular popes this century. There was immense relief when he survived attempts on his life, in 1981 and 1982. Regarding interfaith matters, John Paul II has improved relations with world Jewry more than any other papal predecessor. He was also the first Pope to grant a private audience with Yasser Arafat, in 1982, for which he was roundly criticized at the time by Israel and many Diaspora Jews. In 1987 he announced that there was no 'theological obstacle' to relations between the Holy See and the State of Israel.

Pope John Paul II was born Karol Wojtyla in Wadowice, Poland, in 1920, and was ordained in 1946. He taught ethics at the universities of Lublin and Krakow, and became a cardinal in 1967. The pope has nurtured a good relationship with Italy's Chief Rabbi Elio Toaff, and some believe this personal bond smoothed the way for the signing of the Fundamental Agreement between the Vatican and Israel in December 1993. It actually followed some 18 months of negotiations, with the Israeli team led by Yossi Beilin. The real breakthrough was the Israel–PLO deal, which satisfied the Pope that the issue of Jerusalem, Palestinian national rights and borders would be discussed (conditions for his recognition of Israel). In March and June of 1994, the Pope authorized the establishment of full diplomatic relations with Jordan and Israel respectively. In early 1994 Prime Minister Rabin held discussions with Pope John Paul II, and asked him to use his influence to restart the stalled peace talks.

Jones, Richard   USA
Ambassador to Beirut, since 1996, replacing Maeve Fort. In March 1996, Lebanese Prime Minister Hariri summoned Jones to find out if Israel intended to bomb Lebanon, in the wake of renewed *Hezbollah* violence in the south.

Juan Carlos (King)   Spain
King and host of Madrid peace talks. The king later paid a historic trip to Israel, which had deep significance because of the legacy of the Jewish expulsion from Spain in 1492.

Jubran, Salem   Israel
Co-director of the Jewish-Arab Centre for Peace at the Givat Havivah Institute. Jubran is a former Communist who now campaigns for equal civil rights for his fellow Israeli Arabs within the State of Israel.

Jumblatt, Walid   Lebanon
State Minister for Displaced Persons and Refugee Affairs; head of the Progressive Socialist Party (PSP); clan leader of the Druze community. Walid Jumblatt was born on Aug. 7, 1949. In that same year, his father, Kamal Jumblatt, founded the political party which Walid would one day lead. The younger Jumblatt studied politics at the American University of Beirut.

Kamal Jumblatt created a left-wing front, the Lebanese National Movement (LNM), which was the main enemy of the Christian Maronite Phalange in the first years of the civil war. Kamal was assassinated on March 16, 1977, allegedly by Syrian agents; and Walid immediately succeeded him as the Druze communal leader. Two years later, Walid Jumblatt became head of the LNM and the PSP, beating off opposition from members of the Arslan clan. Jumblatt also formed links with the PLO and Syria, in opposing President Elias Sarkis. Four months after Israel launched its June 1982 invasion of Lebanon, Jumblatt arranged a *modus vivendi* with the new force. Israel tried to hold him in check, in his Shouf Mountain heartland, with the 'carrot' of ties with Israeli Druze notables, and the 'stick' of threatening to unleash right-wing militias. By late 1983, however, Jumblatt relaunched his local war, clashing first with Christian forces, and then with his former allies in the Shi'ite *Amal*. The ensuing instability ended the fragile Israel–Lebanon treaty. From 1984 to 1987 Jumblatt joined the Karami cabinet as Tourism Minister. When Syrian forces entered Beirut in 1987, they encouraged *Amal* forces to attack Palestinians, and Jumblatt re-entered the fray. By 1991, however, he agreed to disarm most of his militia. In 1995 he stoked up new controversy by suggesting that Palestinian refugees should be removed from certain camps. Jumblatt's main interest, as ever, is to protect his community, and their virtual fiefdom in the centre of Lebanon.

Juul, Mona   Norway
Senior diplomat, assistant to former Foreign Minister Thorvald Stoltenberg. Mona Juul is also the wife of Terje Larsen, whose FAFO institute provided the 'cover' for the secret Oslo talks. While working in Cairo, Juul had met PLO figures like Ahmed Qurei and Yasser Arafat's brother, Fat'hi, and persuaded Stoltenberg that the PLO was keen to open talks with Israel. She and Larsen chose the initial venue, Borregard Manor, outside Oslo; and during the talks Juul acted as the liaison to the Norwegian Foreign Ministry.

K

Kabariti, Abdul-Karim   Jordan
Foreign Minister of Jordan; and since February 1996, also Prime Minister and Defence Minister. Kabariti, now 46, played an important part in drafting the peace deal with Israel. At the same time, he called for rapprochement between Jordan and other Arab nations. Speaking with Israeli Foreign Minister Ehud Barak in January 1996, Kabariti said of Jordan's new links with Israel, 'This is a warm peace [and] an example for a real peace in the region'. On Jan. 18, 1996, he joined King Hussein and Crown Prince Hassan at a ceremony in Aqaba to mark the signing of four agreements with Israel, regarding maritime borders, developing the Aqaba-Eilat area, communications, and science and culture. This marked the completion of the terms of the peace treaty of 1994, and the beginning of increased political, economic and military co-operation between the two states.

Kabariti comes from a well known Jordanian business and political family. He was educated in the USA, and elected to parliament in 1989. Before becoming Foreign Minister, Kabariti held the labour and tourism portfolios. By replacing the sitting prime minister, Sharif Ziyad ibn Shaker, with a younger man, King Hussein signalled that a new generation of Jordanians was in the ascendant. The King gave Kabariti a mandate to root out corruption (a charge frequently levelled by the Islamic opposition) and launch sweeping reforms of Jordan's bureaucracy. Kabariti immediately promised to promote the role of parliament, and set up a new 'executive mechanism to achieve change in all state institutions'.

Kabariti favours free enterprise and closer ties with the West. He has also called for reconciliation with Saudi Arabia, and, in contrast with many 'old guard' politicians, he favours isolating Iraqi President Saddam Hussein. Kabariti also has strong links with Syria, which Israel and the USA hope could smooth the path to peace between Jerusalem and Damascus. Finally, with the aid of his new Information Minister Marwan Muasher, Kabariti hopes to 'sell the idea' of peace with Israel, to a still sceptical Jordanian populus. In April 1996 he attempted to broker a cessation of Israel's Operation Grapes of Wrath, but with little success.

Kahalani, Avigdor   Israel
Head of the Third Way, formerly a hawkish Labour MK. Avigdor Kahalani was born into a Yemenite Jewish family in Nes Tziona, a poor neighbourhood south of Tel Aviv, in 1944.

After attaining a BA in history and an MA in political science, he joined the IDF armoured brigades. His tank was the first to cross into Egypt in 1967; in 1973 he won a medal for blocking the Syrian advance into the Golan. Since then, retaining the Golan has remained a cornerstone of his political outlook, and ultimately caused his rift with Labour. Kahalani was accused of fighting an unnecessary battle at Fort Beaufort in Lebanon, in 1982, and was never promoted to brigadier-general, as many predicted he would be. He failed to become mayor of Tel Aviv. After Labour's electoral victory in 1992, Kahalani and fellow MK Emanuel Zismann formed a middle ground 'Third Way' caucus within the party (the movement began in 1994 as an extra-Knesset Labour faction led by the kibbutznik, Yehuda Harel). It opposes returning Golan to Syria, and favours continuing peace talks with Palestinians, but at a slower pace. By late 1995, the group voted with *Likud* on many security issues. After the assassination of Yitzhak Rabin, the Third Way split, with former supporter, Dan Shomron, leaving its ranks. However, Kahalani officially became leader of the Third Way when it set itself up as a political party in 1996. In June 1996 he was made Minister of Public Security.

Kahane, Benyamin   Israel
Head of *Kahane Chai*, racist right-wing Jewish group. The son of the late US-born Rabbi Meir Kahane, founder and leader of *Kach,* Benjamin Kahane aspired to succeed him as leader. He set up Kahane Chai when other figures, like Rabbi Toledano and Baruch Merzel, took over *Kach*. Like his father, who was killed in New York in 1990, he believes in armed force against Arabs, and the establishment of a non-democratic Jewish theocracy in all of biblical Israel (that is, including the entire West Bank, and possibly areas beyond it).

Kahane, Meir   Israel
Leader of the racist *Kach* party between 1984 and 1988, chief demagogue on the Israeli far right until his assassination in 1990. Rabbi Kahane was born in 1932 in the USA, and founded the Jewish Defence League (JDL) in the late 1960s as a militant Jewish group in Brooklyn, New York. Kahane evidently worked for *Mossad* before he arrived in Israel in 1971. He soon found a receptive following amongst some poorer Sephardim, and ideological settlers. The result was a new party, *Kach* (or 'Take') which advocated the expulsion of Israeli Arabs and Palestinians in the territories, who were not prepared to accept Israeli hegemony. Kahane also favoured eradicating Israeli democracy and replacing it with a Jewish theocracy. Nonetheless, he was elected to the Knesset in 1984. The US State Department stripped him of his US citizenship in 1985, and Israel banned his party for being 'racist and fascist' prior to the 1988 elections. Kahane still managed to raise enormous funds for his West Bank ventures (including terror attacks on neighbouring Palestinians) at meetings in the US. It was at one such meeting that he was shot and killed by an Egyptian assailant. Kahane's grave is a place of pilgrimage for radical right-wingers, and many of his ideas were incorporated into the platforms of more conventional parties.

Kahane, Shamai   Israel
Foreign Ministry's veteran expert on refugees. In 1992 Kahane was recalled from retirement to lead Israel's delegation at the multilateral talks working group on refugees.

Kahn, Jean   France
President of CRIF, French Jewry's umbrella group.

Kamail, Ahmed Awad   Palestinian
Commander of the Black Panthers since the early 1990s. This pro-PLO hit squad began to act as an *intifada* vigilante force against collaborators, but since the peace process began in 1991, they are widely seen as mavericks.

Kamal, Sa'id   Palestinian
PLO ambassador to Cairo, involved in drafting the Israel–PLO Declaration of Principles (DOP).

Kamel, Zahira   Palestinian
DFLP member of the Palestinian advisory delegation at the Madrid and Washington peace talks, and founder of the Women's Work Committee. Kamel has fought against moves to

subordinate women's issues within the Palestinian national cause. Born in 1945 to a middle-class family in Wadi Joz, East Jerusalem, Zahira Kamel (or Zuheira Kamal) studied in Cairo, from 1963 to 1968. She then returned to Jerusalem, now under Israeli control, and worked as an instructor at the Teachers Training College in Ramallah (run by UNRWA). There she came into contact for the first time with refugee women, which altered her political outlook. She became a member of a women's charity help-group, *In'ash al-Usrah*, which was, and still is, run by Samiha Khalil (in 1996 Mrs Khalil challenged Arafat in the Palestinian presidential elections).

But Kamel soon grew disenchanted with *In'ash's* unwillingness to address women's issues directly, and in 1978 she founded the Women's Work Committee. It later split into four separate organizations, each one affiliated to one of the PLO factions. Kamel's group, the Federation of Palestinian Women's Action Committee (FPWAC) is the largest, and has ties with the Democrat Front (DFLP). She has more recently been associated with *Fida* (the Palestinian Democratic Union), a less doctrinaire offshoot of the DFLP which has gained support at the latter's expense in the territories. After narrowly losing a seat in Jerusalem at the January 1996 Palestinian Council elections, she claimed that there were irregularities and called for a recount.

Kana'an, Sameh   Palestinian

Palestinian delegate to the Madrid Conference in 1991. Kana'an was born in Irbid, Jordan, in 1954. His father was a Muslim Palestinian from Jerusalem, and his mother, Mazal Maiman, is a Jew from Morocco. In 1964 Kana'an returned to the family home in Nablus. After the Israeli occupation of 1967, Kana'an joined *Fatah*. In 1972 he was sentenced to 20 years for allegedly throwing a hand grenade, but released in a massive Israeli prisoner exchange in 1985. He mastered Hebrew while in prison, and has since expressed his admiration for Israeli democracy. Kana'an was active during the *intifada*, and currently works for the Nablus Chamber of Commerce. Although he was reported to distrust the PLO old guard in Tunis, he accepted a position on the official Palestinian delegation to the Madrid and Washington peace talks. He warned that unless Israel gave something tangible to 'moderate Palestinians', they would have to deal with *Hamas* in the future.

Kanafani, Marwan   Palestinian

Chief spokesman for the PNA and *inter alia*, for Yasser Arafat. Kanafani spent much of 1994 and 1995 defending Arafat from accusations of autocracy; and kept media pressure on Israel to make more concessions to the PNA. Invariably frank in his opinions, in March 1996 Kanafani admitted that both the PNA and Israel 'had been caught with their pants down' by the *Hamas* bombings, but that they could only eliminate the threat to peace by working together.

Kantor, Micky   USA

Former US Trade Representative. Micky Kantor announced in October 1995 that the USA had agreed to sign a free trade agreement with the Palestinian Authority, in order to boost the Palestinian economy. He also reached a 'framework agreement' with Israel, which facilitated better access for US agricultural products to Israeli markets. He negotiated with Israel's Trade Minister Micha Harish, and Agriculture Minister Ya'akov Tsur. He is a close political ally of Bill Clinton's, and chaired his election campaign staff, before joining the cabinet as trade representative. Kantor replaced the late Ron Brown as Commerce Secretary in April 1996.

Karas, Attar Abu   Palestinian

Leader of *Fatah's intifada* committee in Gaza; 'unemployed' since Oslo deal.

Kashdan, Bruce   Israel

US-born backroom diplomat and general 'trouble-shooter' for the Israeli Foreign Ministry.

Kashriel, Benny   Israel

Mayor of Ma'aleh Adumim, the largest Jewish settlement outside Jerusalem. Kashriel has predicted a population of 50,000 settlers by 2005. Ma'aleh Adumim is designated as Area C under the Oslo 2 agreement. While its future is yet to be determined in the 'final status talks' between Israel and the PLO, some analysts predict that it may be subsumed into Greater

Jerusalem and annexed to Israel. Kashriel is a member of the *Yesha* Council, which represents settlers in the territories. However, in early 1996 there were hints that Kashriel may join other settler leaders in a more moderate breakaway from *Yesha*.

Kassem, Anis   Palestinian
Member of the steering committee shadowing the Palestinian delegation to the Madrid talks; after the 1993 Declaration of Principles, he was the main force behind a Draft Basic Law for the PNA in the transitional period. Born in 1925, Kassem (or Qassem) is an acknowledged expert on international law, and was an adviser to the Libyan Ministry of Justice in 1959. He later was affiliated with the DFLP. At the time of the Madrid and Washington talks, Kassem was based in Amman, Jordan, from where he edited the *Palestine Yearbook of International Law*. He was also the Chairman of the PNC Legal Committee, and, as such, had considered the notion of a basic law after the PLO declared 'Palestinian independence' in Algiers, in 1988.

In November 1993, the PLO Executive Committee mandated him to investigate such a law, as the recently signed DOP stipulated a transitional period of Palestinian self-rule. Kassem duly travelled to Jerusalem, for the first time in 30 years, in early 1994, and presented his proposals at a Palestinian NGO conference. He soon consulted with a range of groups, including diplomats from the USA, UK, Germany and France, and local Palestinian human rights and womens' groups. Kassem's main challenge was to create a document that reflected the myriad legal structures of the territories (Ottoman, British Mandate, Egyptian, Israeli and Jordanian law); but which also addressed the Palestinian people's own concerns. The result was a draft which included stipulations about protecting human rights, establishing legislative and executive authority, independent judicial review and legal accountability, the status of Jerusalem, as well as provisions for religious freedom and protection from torture. Kassem hoped that, although transitional in nature, his draft law might serve as a basis for a future Palestinian constitution. During the period of PNA rule, many Palestinians used the draft law to argue against alleged abuses by the new authority. Kassem is currently working as a barrister in London; although he may be asked to contribute to the 'final status talks' between Israel and the PLO in 1996.

Kassis, Nabil   Palestinian
Palestinian delegate at Madrid. Born in 1947, Kassis (also spelt Qassis) is the vice-president of Bir Zeit University, where he also worked as a professor of physics. Kassis currently heads the Civil Affairs Committee for Negotiations on Transfer of Legal Affairs to the Palestine National Authority.

Kattan, Shlomo   Israel
Mayor of the settlement of Alfei Menashe. In December 1995 he became the first settlement leader to open talks on regional development with the PLO–appointed mayor of a neighbouring Palestinian town (Kattan met Maruf Zahran, mayor of Qalqilyah, and they discussed water supply).

Katz-Oz, Avraham   Israel
Head of the Israeli delegation to the multilateral water resources working group; former Agriculture Minister and Labour MK until 1996. Delegates last met in June 1995 in Amman, in a joint session with the environment working group. Katz-Oz estimated that annual funding of Middle Eastern water projects would come to $200 million. He negotiated with the Palestinian Water Commissioner, Nabil Sharif, and they may well meet again when water comes onto the agenda of the final status talks between Israel and the PLO.

Katzover, Zvi   Israel
Kiryat Arba mayor, settler activist. In the early 1990s, Katzover claimed that settlers had the right to organize vigilante 'self-defence' units to ward off attacks from Palestinians. He implied that if peace went too far, settlers would start their own 'Jewish *intifada*', if need be, against the IDF. Since the Hebron massacre of 1994, Katzover has clashed with less fanatical leaders, like Aharon Domb.

Kawwar, Samir
(See Kuwar, Samir)

Kenaan, Ghazi (General) Syria
General and Syrian military supremo in Lebanon. Gen. Kenaan is a close ally of President Assad, and has much experience in military intelligence. Israel protested when Kenaan refused to remove his 35,000 troops from northern Lebanon, as specified in the Taif Accords. US intelligence sources believe that Kenaan has secretly sponsored terrorist groups, ranging from *Hezbollah* to the Ahmed Jibril group, the PFLP-GC.

Kessar, Yisrael   Israel
Transport Minister, former Secretary General of *Histadrut* (Israel's powerful Labour Federation). Kessar was one of the early wave of Yemenite Jews to immigrate to Palestine. He arrived in 1933 when he was two year's old. He studied economics and sociology, and then joined the *Histadrut* in 1966. Kessar gradually rose up through its ranks to become Secretary-General from 1984 to 1992. Kessar was elected as an MK in 1984. Although he does not share the typical Labour 'profile' (stereotypically Ashkenazi, with a *kibbutz* and military background), Kessar nonetheless has come to represent the 'old guard' approach on matters of domestic policy. His attachment to state ownership and traditional structures has led to many a clash with younger Labour politicians, notably Haim Ramon. In 1991 Kessar made a bid for party leadership, but ultimately lost and backed the victor, Yitzhak Rabin. Kessar has not played a major role in the peace process. However, on Jan. 16, 1996 he and his Jordanian counterpart, Samir Kuwar, signed a historic transport agreement. This enacted the terms of the October 1994 Israel–Jordan peace treaty, and should at last open the way to bilateral trade. The new agreement applies to land, sea and air routes, and also regulates shipment of goods to Palestinian self-rule areas. Kessar announced in early 1996 that he would be leaving the cabinet. Nonetheless, in his final months in office he considered plans for Arab air links to Israel and witnessed the first bus route between Israel and Jordan.

Khaddam, Abd al-Halim Syria
Vice-President of Syria, regarded by most observers to be second-in-command to Hafez al-Assad. He is in charge of foreign affairs, probably more so than Foreign Minister Farouk ash-Shar'a. Born in 1936 in Banyas, he studied law at Damascus university and in 1964 became governor of the province of Damascus. After a brief period as Economy and Trade Minister, Khaddam served as Deputy Prime Minister and Foreign Minister from 1970 to 1984. During this period he proved his loyalty to President Assad, and fought off an attempted coup by President Assad's brother, Rifa'at al-Assad. In 1984 he was rewarded with the post of Vice-President for Political and Foreign Affairs.

Khaddam was given special responsibility for developing relations with Lebanon, and is known to be on good terms with Iranian President Rafsanjani. In 1994 he attacked Arafat over the Declaration of Principles. As a Sunni Muslim married to an Alawite women, and with his 'tough man' reputation, Khaddam has been tipped as a possible successor to President Assad. In 1995, however, there were reports that he had to surrender some of his powers to the President's son, Bashar, who, following the death of his favoured brother, Basil, was apparently being groomed to succeed Assad.

Khader, Asma   Jordan
Head of Jordan Women Union. She is a well-known voice in the fight against gender discrimination.

Khader, Husam   Palestinian
Fatah leader in Balata refugee camp, south of Nablus. Khader, born in 1961, and seasoned by years of *intifada* activities, welcomed the Oslo 2 agreements which led to the departure of Israelis from Nablus, on Dec. 12, 1995. But he also warned that Oslo 2 has not satisfied the refugees and their desire to 'return home'. Furthermore, Khader blames Arafat for unilaterally backing PLO 'external' politicians, and 'notables', as candidates in the January 1996 Palestinian elections, instead of relying on *Fatah's* grassroots local supporters.

Khalaf, Salah   Palestinian
Second-in-command of the PLO after the assassination of Abu Jihad. Better known as Abu
Iyad, Khalaf was a founder member of *Fatah,* and later gained a reputation as a hardliner
within the PLO. He was Yasser Arafat's lifelong aide-de-camp. Khalaf helped formulate the
PLO's belief in the Palestinian people forging their own destiny; in latter years, he seemed to
veer towards a deal with Israel. Salah Khalaf warned against PLO support for Saddam
Hussein in late 1990. He was assassinated in early 1991, reputedly at the hands of Iraqi agents,
possibly by Abu Nidal operatives.

Khaled, Leila   Palestinian
Former hijacker for the Popular Front for the Liberation of Palestine (PFLP), and member of
the Palestine National Council. Leila Khaled was born in Haifa in 1944, and as a four-year-
old fled with her family to Lebanon during the first Arab–Israeli war. She was recruited into
George Habash's PFLP in the late 1960s, and in August 1969 she hijacked a TWA flight from
Los Angeles to Tel Aviv during a stopover in Rome. The plane was diverted to Damascus and
destroyed; after a 44-day stand-off, Israel released two Syrian prisoners of war in exchange for
two Israeli hostages held by Khaled. In 1970 she hijacked another airplane, but the plan
backfired and she was arrested in London. She was freed when Britain, West Germany and
Switzerland exchanged captured Palestinians for 310 civilian hostages who were held in four
simultaneous hijackings in Jordan. Striking in appearance, Leila Khaled became a revolutionary icon for many young radicals worldwide. She later turned away from terrorism and entered
mainstream Palestinian politics, where she passionately defended the rights of women. In
1996 Israel agreed that she could return to Palestinian territory, so as to debate the proposed
amendments to the PLO Covenant (as stipulated in the Oslo 2 agreement).

Khalefeh, Khaled   Israel
Director, National Union for Arab Local Councils and Mayors. The union is the main forum
for Israel's Arab community, and includes Communists, radicals, liberals, Islamists and Arab
MPs from many Israeli parties.

Khalidi, Rashid   Palestinian
Professor of Mideast History at Chicago University. Khalidi was a member of the Palestinian
steering committee following the Madrid peace summit of 1991.

Khalil, Joseph Abu   Lebanon
Leading figure in the *Kataeb* (military wing of the Maronite Christian Phalangist, also known
as the Lebanese Forces); and a sworn enemy of Prime Minister Rafiq Hariri.

Khalil, Mustafa   Egypt
Prime Minster of Egypt from 1978 to 1980, doubling as Foreign Minister for the last year,
under the late President Anwar Sadat. Khalil is now the Chairman of the Arab International
Bank, and supports the peace process as a means to improving the regional economy.

Khalil, Samiha   Palestinian
Sole candidate opposing Yasser Arafat in the presidential poll part of the Palestine Council
elections of January 20, 1996. Arafat pronounced himself glad that the election was to be
contested; others in *Fatah* were relieved that his opponent was relatively unknown, and so
could not seriously threaten his chances of victory. Samiha Khalil, 73, and affectionately
known as Umm Khalil, comes from a middle-class refugee family. In 1965 (two years before
the Israeli occupation of the West Bank) she founded *In'ash al-Usra* (roughly, 'family
support network'). The group runs training projects for women, and employs them in
workshops which produce traditional crafts and textiles. Khalil is based in Al-Birah,
although her group has branches throughout the West Bank. She announced her candidacy
at a hastily organized press conference in late December 1995. Later she said she had been
inspired to do so after she had joined women who were protesting at the imprisonment of
their relatives in Israel. Passionate and charismatic, Khalil's political position was not clear,
other than criticizing shortcomings in the Oslo Accords (she used to have ties with the
DFLP). In the event, Samiha Khalil obtained about 11% of the vote. She gave voters the
chance to register their protest, but was not a candidate behind whom many Islamist or

leftist 'rejectionists' could rally. Nonetheless, her courage and spirit has guaranteed her a place in modern Palestinian history.

Khalili, Saleh al-   Palestinian

Founded Democratic Party of Palestine in 1991 as moderate alternative to PLO. It may have connections with FIDA, the Palestinian Democratic Union.

Khameini, Seyed Ali   Iran

Vali Faqih, or supreme spiritual leader of Iran; President of Iran from 1981 to 1989. Ayatollah Khameini was born in 1940, and established the Council of Militant Clerics in his home town of Mashad in the 1960s. A lifelong ally of Ayatollah Khomeini, Khameini became the supreme leader after Khomeini's death in 1989. Since then he has steered a narrow path between the more radical clerics, and his more pragmatic successor as President, Ali Akbar Hashemi Rafsanjani. Khameini opposes any concessions with Israel, and is believed to have put pressure on Syria not to sign a peace treaty with Israel.

Khatib, Ghassan   Palestinian

Ghassan Khatib was born in Nablus and after school became involved in political activities which landed him in an Israeli jail. After his release he studied economics, eventually becoming an economics lecturer at Bir Zeit University.

In 1987 he established the Jerusalem Media and Communications Centre, which soon developed into a conduit for Western media personnel to 'gain access to a deeper level of [Palestinian] society' during the *intifada.* Since 1988 Khatib has also been the director of the United Agricultural Company, which provides marketing support, technical assistance and credit-free loans to Palestinian small farmers. Despite his strong affiliations with the Palestine Communist Party (since renamed the People's Party), Khatib concedes that private enterprise will play a crucial role in reviving the economy of the West Bank and Gaza.

In 1991 Ghassan Khatib was a member of the Palestinian delegation to the Madrid peace talks. He became involved with forging diplomatic contacts and was influential in the steering committee, although he dropped out of the negotiations after the eighth session in protest at Israeli policies, and lack of progress in the talks. Khatib's Jerusalem Media and Communications Centre often conducts polls, which observers regard as an accurate barometer of Palestinian feeling. Khatib himself favours closer ties with Jordan, as a means to establish Palestinian economic security, and loosen the territories from Israel's grip. Still a lecturer at Bir Zeit University, he is now prominent in leftist opposition to Arafat and Gaza-Jericho First plan.

Khawaja, Azmi Abdul Aziz al-   Jordan

Secretary-General of the Jordanian Democratic Popular Unity Party. Khawaja was a founding member of the Popular Front for the Liberation of Palestine (PFLP), and is also a member of the Popular Front for supporting the *intifada* in the Israeli–occupied territories. His party is widely seen as a front for George Habash's PFLP. As such, it supports a Marxist Leninist line, and opposes peace talks until Israel adheres to UN Resolution 799.

Khoury, Michel Bechara   Lebanon

Leader, *Al-Dustur* (Constitutional Party). The party is backed by Lebanon's business élite, and espoused a non-sectarian vision. However, Khoury does not see eye to eye with Prime Minister Rafiq Hariri, who also draws support from the business community.

Khreisheh, Mijhim al-   Jordan

Secretary-General of the Jordanian National Alliance. Khreisheh's party was the first to be licensed after King Hussein announced a new period of multi-party democracy. It supports the Hashemite establishment, and favours a congenial relationship between Palestinians and Jordanians. Most of Khreisheh's supporters are tribal leaders in the south and central regions of the kingdom.

Khuri, Ahmed   Palestinian

(see Ahmed Qurei)

Kidra, Khalid al-   **Palestinian**
Attorney-General of the Palestine National Authority. Kidra has faced a difficult task in
drafting new laws for the PNA, and consults with PNA Justice Minister Freih Abu Medein.
He is also accused of turning a blind eye to PNA human rights abuses. In particular, the head
of the Palestine Commission for Citizens' Rights, Dr Iyad Sarraj, blames him for allowing the
new Palestinian judiciary to become subservient to the PNA's political diktat.

Kidwa, Nasser al-   **Palestinian**
310PLO observer to the UN. He argued and voted against overturning the 'Zionism is Rac'
resolution. He also opposed the US Congressional decision to move the US embassy to
Jerusalem, in 1995.

Kilani, Sami   **Palestinian**
Member, Palestinian delegation in Madrid; physics professor at Nablus University.

Kinarti, Noah   **Israel**
Prime Minister Rabin's adviser on settlements, and one of Rabin's 'inner circle'. Kinarti, 53, is
a leading figure amongst Labour's more hawkish MKs. While accepting the broad principles
of the peace process, he sidestepped the official government policy of freezing funding for new
building in the territories, by creating a 'special cases committee' to grant building permits.
Together with Housing Minister Binyamin Ben-Eliezer, Kinarti ensured that between September 1993 (the signing of the DOP) and February 1995, enough new houses were built in
the territories to accommodate a 10% expansion of the settler population. In late 1993 he
persuaded Rabin to allow the expansion of Efrat (when builders began encroaching on the
neighbouring Arab village of Al-Khader in 1995, it sparked a crisis which threatened to
stymie the peace negotiations).

Kissinger, Henry   **USA**
Assistant to the President for national security affairs (1967–75) and Secretary of State
(1973–75), under Presidents Richard Nixon and Gerald Ford. Henry Kissinger was the chief
architect of US foreign policy in the 1970s, and is best known for his espousal of *détente*
between the superpowers. Yet to many liberals, he also typified a policy of pursuing the Cold
War through proxy wars, whether in Vietnam, Cambodia or the Middle East.
  Born in Germany in 1926, he fled Nazi persecution with his Jewish family, and emigrated to
New York in 1938. Kissinger served in World War II, and later received a PhD from Harvard
University. He became a leading authority on international relations in the nuclear age, and
influenced President Kennedy's policy of 'flexible response'. After joining the Nixon adminis-
tration, he helped to forge US rapprochement with China in 1972, and negotiated the
withdrawal of US troops from Vietnam. In 1973 he won the Nobel Peace Prize. As the
Watergate scandal mounted, Kissinger assumed an even more powerful profile in determining
US foreign policy. His famous 'shuttle diplomacy' succeeded in achieving delimitation
agreements between Israel and Egypt after the 1973 Yom Kippur War (known as Sinai I and
Sinai II). It also laid the groundwork for the Camp David agreements of 1978–79.
  Kissinger's Geneva peace conference of 1973 ultimately failed, and Palestinians still regard
his exclusion of the PLO from those talks as a slight. In 1975, Kissinger ruled that the US
would neither recognize nor negotiate with the PLO until it accepted UN 242. This remained
US policy ever since, and 14 years later the US kept to its pledge when it opened talks with the
PLO on those terms. Overall, Kissinger remained a close ally of Israel (despite the anger felt
by some right-wing Israelis and US Jews over the concessions which he demanded from
them). At the same time, he never firmly closed the door on the PLO, and indeed mandated
staff to keep open unofficial contacts.

Kleibo, Mounir   **Palestinian**
Palestinian co-ordinator of TOKTEN, the Transfer of Knowledge through Expatriate Palestinians. TOKTEN is a United Nations Development Programme (UNDP) initiative, set up
originally in the late 1970s as a means of channelling the skills of Diaspora Palestinians towards
projects in the territories. To date, more than 2,000 assignments have been completed. Under
phase one of the programme, which was sponsored by the Norwegian government, 21 TOK-

DEN technical assistance missions worked hand-in-hand with PNA institutions. These covered 13 subject areas, including computer sciences, finance, education and agriculture. Kleibo was appointed co-ordinator in August 1995, which marked phase two of the TOKTEN programme. His job is to co-operate with the UNDP, the PNA Planning Ministry, private enterprise and research institutions. Phase two also signals a broadening of TOKTEN's scope, to tally with the increased responsibilities of Palestinian politicians as Oslo 2 takes effect.

Koch-Weser, Caio   Brazil

Vice President of the World Bank, responsible for the Middle East. In January 1994, Koch-Weser estimated that donor nations and organizations would contribute $300 million in actual disbursements to the Palestinian National Authority in 1994. This would cover the initial needs of the $1.1 billion three-year Emergency Assistance Programme (EAP), as well as a $35 million Technical Assistance Programme (TAP). Koch-Weser administered what became known as the Holst Fund, a mechanism for aid disbursement that arose out of the Conference to Support the Middle East Peace Process, held in October, 1994. One of his top priorities was to identify areas for immediate relief work.

Kohl, Helmut   Germany

Chancellor of West Germany since 1982, and first post-war Chancellor of a united Germany since 1990. Kohl is not regarded as an expert in foreign affairs, and during the years of Germany's conciliation with the Soviet Union, he often deferred to the expertise of his Foreign Minister and deputy chancellor, Hans-Dietrich Genscher. Since the collapse of the eastern bloc and the re-unification of Germany, Bonn's main concerns have been the Bosnian crisis and Germany's role in the European Union (EU). Under Kohl's rule, Germany has also participated in many aspects of the multilateral peace talks, hosting a session of the Economic Working Group, and providing intersessional plenaries on matters concerning security. In early 1996, Shimon Peres met Kohl and the two men reportedly discussed Germany's leading role in a possible European Union deal to foster a Syrian–Israeli peace.

Kollek, Teddy   Israel

Mayor of Jerusalem from 1965 to 1992 (Mayor of West Jerusalem from 1965, and the whole city after 1967). Teddy Kollek was elected for seven terms in succession, but was finally defeated when right-wing secular Jews and ultra-Orthodox Jews formed an alliance against him. As mayor, Kollek always proclaimed the unity of the city under Israeli rule. He approved the demolition of the Moghrabi neighbourhood (described as a slum) which had obstructed the Western Wall (one of the holiest sites in Judaism, which had fallen into disrepair under 19 years of Jordanian rule). At the same time, Kollek stressed the trilateral religious significance of the city, to Jews, Muslims and Christians. Kollek permitted East Jerusalem Arabs to set up memorials to their own war dead. He also ensured that many of them served in the municipal bureaucracy. Although no Arab stood for election, about a third traditionally exercised their right to vote. Invariably, they cast their ballot for Kollek, who over the years rose above party politics and became as much an institution as the city's venerable buildings. However, years of alleged neglect of the Arab sector took their toll, and Arabs largely boycotted the 1992 mayoral elections, leading to Kollek's first defeat. He had misjudged the growing strength of ultra-Orthodox Jewish Jerusalemites, who voted in droves for the successful candidate, former *Likud* Minister Ehud Olmert. Finally, Kollek was harmed by allegations of disputes with his much younger running mate, Nachman Shai. Political observers noted that Kollek's defeat was a sign of disatisfaction with Labour's peace initiative, coming, as it did, only months after Labour's national electoral victory.

Palestinian critics accused Kollek's initiatives of being the acceptable face of Zionism, and what they saw as the Judaization of traditionally Muslim areas of Jerusalem. During the height of the *intifada*, Kollek kept lines of communication open with Palestinians, in particular, Faisal al-Husseini. He never backed down on the idea of Jerusalem as Israel's capital, nor Israeli sovereignty over the whole city; but was prepared to accept a measure of Arab autonomy ('cantons') in their suburbs.

Kozyrev, Andrei   Russia

Foreign Minister of the Russian Federation from 1992 to 1996. His role was somewhat ambiguous from the start, being responsible for Russia's concerns, but also to some extent presiding over those of all the states within the former Soviet Union (which in December 1991 was dissolved and reconstituted as the Confederation of Independent States). Nonetheless, Kozyrev inherited the role of co-sponsor with the USA of the Middle East peace process, which had begun at the Madrid summit. Soon after Russian President Boris Yeltsin appointed him Foreign Minister in 1992, Kozyrev signed a financial and cultural treaty with Israel. In that year, Israel restored ties with all the states of the former Soviet Union. Moscow also hosted the opening session of the post-Madrid multilateral talks, and Russia joined the steering committee as co-chair with the USA. Kozyrev continued with the policy of allowing many thousands of Soviet Jews to emigrate to Israel.

Russia's ties with its former allies in the Middle East cooled under Kozyrev, partly because of the financial and inter-ethnic crisis in Russia itself, and partly because the end of the USA–USSR Cold War meant that Russia no longer needed its alliance with 'progressive states' like Syria. In September 1993 Kozyrev officially witnessed the signing of the Declaration of Principles in Washington; in October, he and Finance Minister Boris Fedorev acted as co-chairs of the follow-up economic Conference to support the Middle East Peace. Kozyrev also witnessed the Israel–Jordan Treaty of 1994. In January 1996 Yevgeny Primakov succeeded him as Foreign Secretary.

Kurd, Maher al- (Dr)   Palestinian
Economist and aide to the PLO's chief negotiator in Oslo, Abu 'Ala. Kurd (whose name is occassionally rendered as 'Hurd') is a graduate of the American University in Cairo. At Oslo, Kurd particularly sought assurances that a new Palestinian self-governing entity would get economic support. Currently, he acts as a chief economics aide to Yasser Arafat.

Kurtzer, Dan   USA
Deputy Secretary of State for Near Eastern affairs. Kurtzer, 45, was involved as a backroom consultant during the the later phases of the secret Oslo peace talks. An Orthodox Jew and former dean of undergraduate studies at Yeshiva University in New York, he joined the US diplomatic service in 1976. He is fluent in Hebrew and Arabic, which served him well when he served in Cairo and Tel Aviv. After that, he returned to Washington to work at the Egypt Desk during the Reagan administration. During the Lebanon war and early days of the *intifada*, Kurtzer incurred he wrath of *Likud* leaders who disliked his government's criticism of their policies. He kept his position after Bill Clinton became president, and helped to steer US involvement in the Mideast multilateral talks.

Kuttab, Daoud   Palestinian
Influential Palestinian journalist, and a critic of infringements on press freedom by both Israel and the PNA. Kuttab was born in 1955 and grew up in Bethlehem. He emigrated to the USA in 1969, where he was educated, and returned to Jerusalem in 1979. He has written for the *Al-Quds* and *Al-Fajr* newspapers, and was a stringer for many US and Japanese publications during the *intifada*. Since 1990 he has been a leading television documentary film-maker, and is also Secretary of the Palestinian National Theatre. He won the Andrew Stern Annual Award for Arab–Jewish Understanding. Kuttab is a committed democrat and a leading figure in the Palestinian intelligentsia.

Kuttab, Jonathan   Palestinian
US-educated lawyer; co-founder with Jad Ishaq of *Al-Haq* civil liberties group. Kuttab has criticized human rights abuses by Israeli occupiers before 1994, and Yasser Arafat afterwards. He stood as an independent candidate in Jerusalem during the January 1996 Palestine Council elections, and warned that a new Palestine should not emulate the example of Arab dictatorships. Kuttab and Ishaq are also influential in the Bethlehem-based Applied Research Institute, and in early 1996 submitted a considered analysis on the legal aspects of the conflict on water rights in Palestine/Israel. In the paper, Kuttab concluded that the water dispute was soluble, and could foster wider regional co-operation in the field; but only if the parties adopted a strictly legal and equitable framework.

Kuwar, Samir   Jordan
Transport Minister of Jordan until February 1996. Samir Kuwar served as Minister of Water and Irrigation in the years 1991 and 1992, a testing assignment, considering the scarcity of

water in the Kingdom. Since then, Israel and Jordan have agreed a new and more equitable mode of distributing water from the Jordan River, in their mutual peace treaty of October 1994. On Jan. 16, 1996, Samir Kuwar and his Israeli counterpart, Yisrael Kessar, signed a far-reaching transportation agreement, which at last enacts the terms of the peacy treaty. The new agreement applies to land, sea and air routes, and also regulates shipment of goods to Palestinian self-rule areas. It should open the way to bilateral trade, which has been hitherto blocked. In 1996 Nasser al-Lawzi replaced Kuwar in a major cabinet reshuffle.

L

Labadi, Mohammed   Palestinian

Activist in the Democratic Front for the Liberation of Palestine (DFLP), and regarded as the founder of the secret United National Command leadership during the early years of the *intifada*. He was based in Ramallah, and together with his family, Labadi brought the *intifada* to Jerusalem in February 1988. This he achieved largely through the device of promoting a stream of handbills to co-ordinate the insurgency. He later moved from a policy of 'mass attack' to the longer-term expedient of 'civil disobediance' (as proposed by Mubarak Awad and Hanna Siniora). He was briefly imprisoned, interrogated and then released by Israel, but has not been heard of since.

Lahad, Antoine   Lebanon

Commander of the South Lebanon Army (SLA). Antoine Lahad began his 'second career' in 1984, when he took over over the command of the southern militia troops (later known as the SLA) of the late Gen. Haddad. Before that, he had served as the regular Lebanese Army's commander of the Mountain region. Lahad used to support Camille Chamoun's National Liberal Party; but since the Israeli invasion of 1982, Tel Aviv has backed his forces financially and militarily. SLA units operate from the safety of the Israeli–controlled southern 'security zone'. For more than a decade the SLA has fought a vicious, albeit low-level, war with *Hezbollah* forces. Lahad is currently resisting Lebanese calls to disband his units. Israel promises not to sign a peace accord with Lebanon until the latter guarantees the political security and well-being of the SLA. Nonetheless, there may soon be rifts between Israel and Lahad, as Israel favours the SLA's absorption into the regular army, whereas Lahad seems to prefer his cherished independence.

Lahat, Shlomo 'Chich'   Israel

Former mayor of Tel Aviv who left *Likud* over its opposition to the peace treaty. His sometimes tempestuous, sometimes friendly relationship with Jerusalem Mayor Teddy Kollek symbolized the traditional rivalry between their two cities. Often controversial, Lahat favoured legalizing prostitution, and called for Israel to withdraw from occupied territories. He organized the peace rally on Nov. 4, 1995, attended by 100,000 people, at which Yitzhak Rabin was assassinated.

Lahoud, Emile   Lebanon

Army Chief of Staff and general. In November 1989 President Elias Hrawi formally dismissed the renegade Gen. Michel Aoun as Commander of the Lebanese Army, and appointed Emile Lahoud in his stead. Since then Gen. Lahoud, a Christian, has forged a more united Lebanese Army out of the ethnically fragmented force left him by years of civil war. The army has expanded from 20,000 then, to more than 54,000 today. Lahoud works closely with Syria, and co-operated with the final assault against Aoun, in late 1990. The army also successfully disarmed most militias in early 1991, according to the Taif Accord. However, Lahoud has tended to leave *Hezbollah* to its own devices, on the grounds that it was waging a defensive war in the south against Israel. Lahoud is a career soldier, and is not thought to harbour political ambitions.

Lake, Anthony   USA

Assistant to the President for Nationa! Security Affairs, in the Clinton administration. Anthony Lake was born in 1939, and was educated at Harvard and Princeton, where he took his doctorate in international affairs in 1974. He was a personal assistant to Henry Kissinger from 1969 to 1970, and Director of Policy Planning in the State Department under the Carter administration. During this time tenure, he worked alongside Secretary of State Cyrus Vance, and Deputy Secretary Warren Christopher (who is now Bill Clinton's Secretary of State). He was also deeply involved in the Camp David peace talks. Anthony Lake impressed Bill Clinton with his analysis of the need to redefine US security policy, in the more complicated post-Cold War era; and became Clinton's top foreign policy advisor during the election campaign.

Landau, Uzi   Israel
Likud MK since 1984. Born in 1943, Landau trained as an engineer and was director general of the Ministry of Transportation. He was a member of Israel's delegation to the Madrid and subsequent Washington peace talks. Landau represents the 'hard right' within *Likud*. In June 1996, *Likud* chose him to chair the Knesset Foreign Affairs Committee.

Lang, Bob   Israel
Chief spokesman and deputy director of Peace Watch, an organization which aims to monitor Israeli and Palestinian compliance with the peace process. Bob Lang is an Orthodox Jewish settler, and was previously well known amongst foreign correspondents as the main spokesman for *Yesha*, the settlers' council. He left *Yesha* in 1995, after reports of a schism with more right-wing leaders.

Terje Rod LARSEN

Nationality	Norwegian
Religion	Christian
Place of birth	Bergen, western Norway
Date of birth	1947
Current position	Special UN envoy for aid disbursement to Palestinians
Previous positions	Initiator and convener of the secret Oslo peace talks Executive Director of FAFO
Allies	Close to Arafat, Abu 'Ala, Yossi Beilin, Uri Savir, Bjorn Tore Godal
Position on peace	Very positive; helped steer peace talks; fashioned a compromise blueprint for donors to PNA in 1994
National political importance	Influential in achieving Oslo Accords; small role in Norwegian politics
Prospects	Enjoys a pivotal role in Gaza, as interface with international community

Terje Larsen emerged from relative obscurity in late 1993 as the prime mover behind the Oslo peace talks. Without his persistence and patient chiding they may well have broken down. A social scientist by profession, in 1981 he founded the FAFO (Fagbevegelsens Foskning Organisasjon) research institute, backed by the Norwegian Trade Union movment. In 1989 he and his wife Mona met Yasser Arafat's brother, Fat'hi (head of the Palestinian Red Crescent in Cairo, and as a result of that meeting they decided to set up a survey of living conditions in Gaza. This in turn provided him with an entrée to join the Norwegian team at the multilateral peace talks which stemmed from the Madrid conference.

When the Madrid track peace talks between Israel and a Palestinian negotiating team became increasingly bogged down in 1992, Larsen approached Yossi Beilin in Tel Aviv, then a backbench opposition Labour MK, with close ties to Shimon Peres. Together, the Norwegian researcher and the Israeli politician began a 'secret track' to open the way for direct talks between Israel and the PLO. The initial participants were the Larsens, Abu 'Ala and Hasan Asfour for the PLO, and the Israeli academics, Yair Hirschfeld and Ron Pundak. Working under the guise of his social research unit in Gaza, Larsen acted as middle-man between the PLO and the Israelis. In time leading Israeli politicians joined in. While other secret channels were blown by leaks, Larsen succeeded in keeping his quiet. He won the backing of the Norwegian government, largely through the influence of his wife, Mona Juul, who was the assistant of the then Foreign Minister Thorvald Stoltenberg. Later, the Larsens became firm partners of Stoltenberg's successor, Johan Jorgen Holst.

Labour took power in Israel in July 1992, and Beilin became Deputy Foreign Minister, which provided an added impetus to the negotiations at a country house in Boergerard, outside Oslo in Norway. The ultimate result was the famous Oslo Accords, revealed to a surprised world in August 1993, and signed in Washington on Sept. 13, 1993. Larsen still maintains that the Declaration of Principles and the Oslo process (Jericho and Gaza First) provides the best framework for ensuring continuing peace between Israel and the Palestinians.

In August 1994 the United Nations Secretary-General Boutros Boutros Ghali posted Larsen to Gaza as a special envoy in charge of aid disbursement. Larsen was also made a special adviser to the Norway's Foreign Ministry. One of his first tasks was to streamline the procedure whereby aid reached the PNA, and to make the accounting procedures more 'transparent' for donors. In November 1994 Larsen attended a donors' conference in Brussels, where his blueprint for a new structure won the backing of both Palestinians and donor countries, as well as Jordan and Egypt. It consists of a secretariat, comprising of himself, the resident World Bank official in Gaza, and the Norwegian Ambassador to Israel representing the donor community. The secretariat would steer 12 committees, each devoted to one key issue (such as education or infrastructure). Each committee would be chaired by a donor and would include a Palestinian representative.

Since taking office, Larsen has made job creation a main goal. His medium-term solution to mass unemployment in Gaza has three components: boosting public works, encouraging Gulf states to use Palestinian labour, and discouraging Israel from sealing off the territories. He repeated this last point in March 1996, and said that closure (following *Hamas* bomb attacks in Jerusalem and Tel Aviv) had led to a near collapse of the economy in Gaza and the West Bank. In the longer term Larsen envisages special industrial zones with high security and modern infrastructure, to attract the private investment which Gaza so desperately needs. In mid-1995 he praised the Palestinian National Authority for building up and maintaining new institutions, despite the odds. Larsen has crossed swords with other aid co-ordinating agencies in Gaza, not least the well-established UNRWA. Meanwhile, he continues to chivvy participants in the peace process, as he did during the secret Oslo talks.

Le Baron, Richard   USA
Gavel-holder (chairman) of the Multilateral Working Group on Water Resources. In February 1996, Le Baron presided over the signing of a Declaration of Principles on co-operation regarding water-related matters between the 'core parties' in the Middle East peace process (Israel, the PLO and Jordan). The declaration set out a framework for exploiting new and additional water resources, to the benefit of all the parties.

Leibler, Isi   Australia
Co-chairman of the governing board of the World Jewish Congress. Leibler often acts as a diplomat on Israel's behalf, with countries or organizations which do not have diplomatic ties with Tel Aviv. In October 1991 he paid an official visit to China, which helped to seal the latter's establishment of full diplomatic relations with Israel a few months later. Leibler is a leading businessman, and President of the Executive Council of Australian Jewry.

Levin, Aryeh   Israel
Former Ambassador to the USSR. Levin was responsibile for setting up diplomatic relations with 14 former Soviet republics, including many Muslim states, in the wake of the Madrid Conference. He left his ambassadorial post in 1992. Aliza Shenhar was the successor.

Levine, Amiram   Israel
Head of army's Northern Command; has to counter *Hezbollah* in Lebanon.

Levinger, Moshe   Israel
US-born rabbi, founder of Kiryat Arba settlement, leader of Hebron settlers in 1968. Levinger aspired to Kahane's leadership after the latter's assassination, but others on the far right accused him of splitting their vote when he stood in the 1992 elections. During the 1980s Levinger was described as the leader of the *Gush Emunim*. He was also charged with murder after he shot and killed a Palestinian shopkeeper.

David LEVY

Nationality	Israeli
Religion	Jewish
Place of Birth	Rabat, Morocco
Date of Birth	1937
Current position	Founder and leader of Gesher (Bridge); Foreign Minister since June 18 1996
Previous positions	Minister for Immigrant Absorption, 1977–78 Minister for Housing and Construction, 1978–90 Deputy Prime Minister from 1981–92 Minister of Foreign Affairs, 1990–92.
Allies	Close aide, Uri Oren; Shalom Shitreet; Dimonah Mayor, Gabi Laloush ex-Israeli ambassador to France, Yehuda Lankri
Position on peace	Pragmatic and conciliatory; took principled opposition to right-wingers when in *Likud*; however, his strongest suit is internal social policy, rather than foreign affairs
National political importance	Very influential amongst Sephardi voters, and particularly amongst the 800,000 Israelis of Moroccan origin. Strong in the uncharted centre of Israeli politics
Prospects	Harbours ambitions to be Israel's first Sephardi prime minister; but his ethnic support base is both a help and a hindrance. If security is not the main electoral issue, his social concern ticket may gain national following; otherwise, his new grouping could still be influential in holding the balance of power post-1996 elections.

David Levy's political 'rags to riches' story is one that he hopes many fellow Sephardi Jews could emulate. He is probably the leading Sephardi politician in a country which is half Sephardi, and has confounded critics, who mocked his humble origins and supposed lack of knowledge by building up tremendous experience in a number of key portfolios. This included a stint as Foreign Minister between 1990 and 1992, during which time Levy steered Israeli foreign policy in hitherto uncharted waters in the negotiations with the Palestinians in the Madrid peace track.

David Levy was born in Morocco in 1937. When he was 19 he emigrated to Israel with the other nine members of his family . They started in Beit She'an, a somewhat rundown town where Levy, true to his populist roots, still lives. Menachem Begin, *Herut* leader and Levy's idol, hand-picked the young Moroccan as a national vote-winner for *Herut*. At only 31, Levy was elected as a *Gahal* (*Herut*-Liberal) MK in 1969.

In June, 1990 Levy became Israel's Foreign Minister, to the derision of many within *Likud* who felt he lacked the sophistication and diplomacy necessary for the post. In the event, Levy's straight-forward approach soon won new allies for Israel in the international community. Despite his rivalry with Prime Minister Yitzhak Shamir, Levy acted as a moderating influence on his leader, and was at least partly responsible for getting Shamir to agree to Israel attending the Madrid peace conference in October 1991. Hence his displeasure when Shamir took upon himself the honour of making Israel's opening statements in Madrid (all other national delegations were headed by their foreign ministers). Levy felt increasingly sidelined by Shamir's nominee as deputy foreign minister, Benjamin Netanyahu. In January 1992 he regained prestige by securing full diplomatic relations with China and India.

Bolstered by these diplomatic triumphs, he beat off a challenge from Defence Minister Moshe Arens to secure the number two slot in the *Likud* list, prior to the June 1992 elections. *Likud* lost the election, however, and Levy was demoted within the party hierarchy. On March 24, 1993, Levy lost a bruising battle for party leadership succession to his arch-rival, Netanyahu. Their rivalry persisted during *Likud*'s life in opposition, culminating in June 1995 with Levy's decision to leave the party.

By forming a largely Sephardi breakaway party, *Derech Ha-Hadash*, Levy took a big political gamble. Levy also intends running in Israel's first direct elections for the prime ministership (scheduled to coincide with general elections in 1996). This too is seen as a gamble, as Levy would be pitted against heavyweights in the larger parties. Furthermore, for any chance of success, Levy would have to firm up his stance on peace (currently he has eked out a position midway between Rabin and Netanyahu). Even so, Levy has mustered a strong core of supporters, including many municipal and labour leaders, and another former *Likud* minister, David Magen.

For Levy it is a particularly bitter irony that, after leaving *Likud* because of perceived anti-Sephardi bias, he is now accused of formenting ethnic divisions by founding a new party. Many Sephardim criticize him for hindering their cause by splitting the traditional Sephardi vote between Likud loyalists, *Shas,* and his new party. Others observed that Levy and *Derech Ha-Hadash* (since renamed *Gesher*, or bridge) may join the Labour government in the event of a national crisis. But in March *Gesher* rejoined *Likud*. Thus Levy won back his old post as Foreign Minister when Netanyahu took power in June 1996.

Liba'i, David   Israel

Justice Minister since 1992. David Liba'i was born in Tel Aviv in 1934, practised as a lawyer, becoming head of the Israel Bar Association, and then became a law professor and Director of the Institute of Criminology at Tel Aviv University. Liba'i first entered the *Knesset* in 1984. For the next eight years chaired the State Audit Committee. As a Labour minister, he supported, albeit reluctantly, Prime Minister Rabin's decision in late 1992 to deport 413 Palestinian fundamentalists for alleged involvement in terror incidents. Yet he also clashed with Rabin over other issues, and the prime minister often relied on Police Minister Moshe Shahal to enact policy which should have been Liba'i's domain. David Liba'i presented the bill in December 1992 which aimed to revoke the ban on meetings with the PLO. Liba'i's bill became law in 1993, and paved the way for open peace talks between Israel and the PLO. At the end of 1995 Liba'i was responsible for determining which Palestinian prisoners could be released in terms of the Interim Agreement.

Libdeh, Hassan Abu   Palestinian

Deputy director of PECDAR, and head of the Palestinian Bureau of Statistics. Abu Libdeh effectively runs the PECDAR under the direction of PNA Economy Minister Abu 'Ala. He submits expenditure schemes to aid donors, including donor states, the World Bank and the UN Development Programme. Before the establishment of the PNA, Hassan Abu Libdeh was the deputy director of the technical committees which supported the Palestinian negoti-ating team during the Madrid/Washington talks. In 1993 he stated his belief in an ultimate federation between Jordan and a Palestinian entity. In 1994 Abu Libdeh began implementing an Emergency Assistance Programme (EAP), containing technical assistance (TAP) and rehabilitation projects (ERP). Abu Libdeh currently backs the projected industrial zones on the Gaza-Israel border. In September 1995 he signed a declaration that his Jerusalem-based statistics bureau had no 'official function' within the PNA. This followed a warning from Israeli Police Minister Moshe Shahal to close down the office (according to the Oslo Agreements, the PNA was not to operate in Jerusalem as the city was under Israeli jurisdic-tion).

Lidbom, Carl   Sweden

Head of the team of European Union observers to the January 1996 Palestine Council elections. In early January, Lidbom complained of 'serious irregularities' in the electoral process, which had to cease if the elections were to 'retain credibility'. He criticized the PNA's decision to add seats by 'presidential decree', which would lead to over-representation in Gaza, Arafat's base. After the elections, Lidbom pronounced himself satisfied with the overall conduct of the campaign.

Linowitz, Solomon   USA

US special envoy to the Israel–Egypt Camp David negotiations. In 1982 he drafted a compromise proposal on a 'self-governing authority' for Palestinians (halfway between the plans of Begin and Sadat). In the end, the talks fell apart as neither the PLO nor Jordan were involved. But aspects of Linowitz's scheme resurfaced in the 1992 Washington talks (part of the Madrid track); and later, in the Oslo Accords of 1993.

Lubrani, Uri   Israel

Co-ordinator of Israeli Government Activities in Lebanon, Prime Minister's adviser on affairs concerning the security zone in southern Lebanon. Lubrani played a role in negotiations which saw the release of Western hostages held by *Hezbollah*. He was disappointed when Western states did not reciprocate by helping Israel get back IDF officers held by *Hezbollah* In 1992 and 1993, Lubrani and the acting Director-General of the Foreign Ministry, Yossi Hadas, negotiated with their Lebanese opposite numbers, Suheil Shamas and Jihad Murtada. Although the two sides made some progress on small points of procedure, Lebanon refused Israel's offer of a six-month ceasefire prior to withdrawal, and also refused to accept the Israeli–backed South Lebanon Army (SLA) militia as a legitimate part of the Lebanese Army. It soon became clear that Lebanon was not willing to move faster than Syria in its talks with Israel, nor was it willing to disarm *Hezbollah*, as Israel demanded. Lubrani approved Israel's strong counter-response against Hezbollah in July 1993, which led to a mass flight by an estimated 300,000 southern Lebanese villagers.

To seek a way out of the impasse, Lubrani is believed to have held secret talks with Lebanon's National Assembly Speaker Nabih Berri, who is also the head of the Shi'ite *Amal* party, and a rival of *Hezbollah*. In December 1995, Lubrani concluded that Syria had the power and the willingness to stop, or at least minimize, *Hezbollah's* military actions. One of Lubrani's chief roles is to liaise with the SLA, and reassure the militia that Israel will not 'sell it out' in peace talks with Syria and Lebanon.

M

Ma'aruf, Lamia   Palestinian

Woman political prisoner who became a *cause célébre* amongst radical Palestinians in late 1995. Ma'aruf worked for a cell directed by Mahmoud al-Alloul, currently Governor of Nablus. She was arrested on charges of driving a car in a kidnap heist that resulted in the murder of a captured Israeli. According to the terms of Oslo 2, she was due for release; but Israeli officials, quoting domestic law, stated that she and five other imprisoned women would stay incarcerated because they had 'blood on their hands'. Ma'aruf was released from Tel Mond Prison on Oct. 22, 1995, after mounting protest from Palestinian politicians and liberal Israelis, on the grounds that she held Brazilian citizenship, and immediately returned to Brazil. Before her release, she wrote a bitter letter to Yasser Arafat, accusing him of deserting women activists and treating them as 'a losing card in the game of peace'.

Majali, Abdul Hadi al-   Jordan

Secretary-General of the centrist and pro-monarchy Pledge Party (*al-Ahd*). Majali is a Hussein loyalist, and his party is the largest of the centrist bloc. The Pledge Party makes a clear distinction between the Palestinian and Jordanian political entities, and opposes Palestinian 'interference' in Jordanian politics. It supports both the PLO–Israel and Jordan–Israel agreements. Majali tried but failed to get King Hussein to delay the November 1993 elections.

Abdul Salam al-MAJALI

Nationality	Jordanian
Religion	Muslim
Place of birth	Kerak, Jordan
Date of birth	1925
Current position	President of the University of Jordan, since 1981
Previous position	Prime Minister, Foreign Minister and Defence Minister, 1993–95 Medical physician and Director of the Royal Medical Services
Allies	King Hussein, tribal support
Position on peace	Enthusiastic support; credited with planning Jordan–Israel peace treaty

National political	
importance	Influential on the centre-right; good image in Western media
Prospects	Poor at present, but as ever in Jordan, he may be recalled

A former Prime Minister of Jordan, and chief architect of Jordan's peace treaty with Israel, Abdul Salam al-Majali comes from a prominent East Bank political family, renowned for their loyalty to the monarchy. Majali's earlier career combined prowess as a doctor, administrator and a military man. He studied medicine at the Syrian University of Damascus, graduating in 1949, and specialized in ear, nose and throat medicine in London. Majali worked mainly within the Jordanian military establishment, and held several prominent positions, including commanding officer of the main hospital, before becoming Director of Royal Medical Services between 1960 and 1969. Majali was Jordan's Health Minister from 1969 and 1971.

He became Foreign Minister succeeding Kamel Abu Jaber, and served as head of the Jordanian delegation at the Madrid peace conference in October 1991. At first, there was little progress at the resultant talks in Washington, as Jordan took the side of Palestinians who wished to negotiate separately (Israel had insisted that Palestinians be contained under a Jordanian 'umbrella'). However, by the end of 1992, and with a Labour government in Israel, Majali seemed to be making more progress than the other Arab delegations. Younger men, like Faiz Tarawneh and Marwan Muasher, ably assisted Majali, who won the affectionate nickname Al-Basha (the pasha). In May 1993 Majali was appointed Prime Minister, Defence Minister and Foreign Minister – an extraordinary range of responsibilities, which was interpreted as a reward for his role in the bilateral talks. King Hussein charged him with accelerating the peace process, and also of preparing Jordan for multi-party elections. Faiz Tarawneh assumed day-to-day responsibility for heading the talks with Israel's chief negotiator, Elyakim Rubinstein.

On Sept. 14, 1993, Majali oversaw the Common Agenda, signed between Israel and the Hashemite Kingdom. This came a day after the Declaration of Principles (DOP) between Israel and the PLO. Meanwhile, on Aug. 4, 1993, King Hussein had announced the first multi-party elections in 35 years, to be held on Nov. 8. Majali faced enormous pressure to postpone the elections, from both Islamic fundamentalists and more moderate forces in the Pledge Party. Nonetheless, on Sept. 28, 1993, Majali announced that they would go ahead as scheduled. In the event, the exercise proved successful, with the Islamic opposition failing to capitalize on their support, and this strengthened Majali's hand within Jordan. Majali went on to negotiate the details of a peace with Israel in 1994. In July he met Israel's Foreign Minister, Shimon Peres, and from their discussions emerged the Washington Declaration, on July 25, 1994, which ended the state of war between Israel and the Kingdom. Although there was domestic opposition to the deal, Majali ensured that the Jordanian Assembly passed it on Nov. 6, by 55 votes to 23. He nonetheless resigned on Jan. 5, 1995, at the King's request, after his deputy had earlier criticized him for 'lacking a clear agenda'.

Majid, Ismat Abd al-   Egypt
(See Esmat Abdel-Meguid)

Major, John   UK
Prime Minister of the United Kingdom, from 1990 to the present. John Major was born in 1943 and, after leaving school early, he became a banker and later a Tory MP. He served briefly (for 93 days) as Britain's Foreign Secretary in 1989, and then as Chancellor of the Exchequer before replacing the ousted Margaret Thatcher as Conservative Party leader and Prime Minister. He took office during the build-up to the Gulf War, and continued his predecessor's approach by working closely with the US administration when the defensive Operation Desert Shield evolved into the offensive military operation, Desert Storm. In January 1991 he called for a post-war international conference on the Palestinian issue.

John Major used his nation's influence in the region to support US President George Bush and his plans for an international peace conference (which was eventually held in Madrid, in October 1991). He also supported the 1993 Israel–PLO Oslo Accords, and committed Britain to training members of the new Palestinian police force. John Major became only the second major national leader to visit Yasser Arafat at his Gaza seafront headquarters, during a four-day trip to Israel, the territories and Jordan in March 1995. He attended Yitzhak Rabin's funeral in November, and spoke with Yasser Arafat and Israel's then Prime Minister, Shimon Peres, about a private enterprise scheme to introduce Palestinian produce to UK supermarkets.

Makkawi, Khalil   Lebanon
Lebanese Ambassador to the UN. He unsuccessfully opposed repeal of 'Zionism is Racism' motion in 1991, as an act that would 'hinder the peace process'. He frequently protests against Israeli incursions in southern Lebanon at the General Assembly.

Malki, Riyad Najib al-   Palestinian
Chief spokesperson and possibly leader of the Popular Front for the Liberation of Palestine (PFLP) on the West Bank. He was born in Bethlehem in 1953, and later returned to his parents' birthplace, Ramallah. He founded the civil engineering department at Bir Zeit University, and has lectured there from 1981 to 1983, and from 1986 to the present. Riyad Malki's specializes in transport policy, and the role of artificial intelligence.

Malki is an erstwhile friend, but now political foe, of fellow lecturer, Hanan Ashrawi. He rose to prominence during the *intifada* (for which he was interned for a month in 1989) and founded PANORAMA, the East Jerusalem Centre for the Dissemination of Alternative Information, to provide Western news media with news about the uprising. He refused to join the Palestinian delegation to talks in Washington in 1992, and in September 1993 he opposed the Oslo Accords as conceding too much to Israel. Articulate and handsome, Malki became popular with journalist as an instant barometer of the mood of the 'rejectionists' and leftist in the territories. Despite his antipathy to Oslo, he frequently discusses political matters with Israelis and foreign visitors. He remains sceptical about the record of the PNA, and blames it for ignoring women's issues and social problems. Some see Malki as a potential leader of Palestinians who oppose Oslo, but who seek an alternative to *Hamas*.

By early 1996, however, it seemed a rift was growing between Malki, who favoured PFLP participation in the Palestine Council elections; and George Habash, and other leaders of the PFLP in exile in Amman and Damascus, who favoured a boycott. In the end Malki did not stand for election.

Manning, David   UK
Ambassador to Israel since December 1995. David Manning, 46, was the head of the Foreign Office's planning unit and served in Moscow. He pledged his 'total support' for the peace process, and promised to continue sending aid to the Palestinians. He welcomed the boom in trade between Britain and Israel, which is now only second to Saudi Arabia as Britain's favourite client in the Middle East.

Mansour, Camille   Palestinian
Member of the Palestinian steering committee during the Madrid track talks. Camille Mansour is a professor of political science at the Sorbonne in Paris, and a former director of research at the Institute for Palestine Studies in Beirut. Unlike Faisal Husseini, Hanan Ashrawi and other 'internal' Palestinians who were involved in the Madrid track talks Mansour welcomed the Israel–PLO breakthrough of September 1993.

Maoz, Moshe (Professor) Israel
Professor at the Hebrew University, and widely acclaimed as Israel's number one expert on Syria. Prof. Maoz is optimistic about the chances for peace, and is said to harbour ambition to become Israel's first ambassador to Damascus, if or when the two states make peace.

Maqdah, Mounir   Palestinian
Top military commander of *Fatah* in Lebanon. Maqdah used to defend the Arafat wing of *Fatah* in a simmering war with dissidents in the Lebanese Palestinian refugee camps. On Aug 23, 1993, Maqdah changed his mind after the PLO announced its impending peace deal with Israel, and he called on Yasser Arafat to resign as PLO Chairman. Fighting between Maqdah and his many enemies continued, and even escalated, after the signing of the Declaration of Principles the next month. Mounir Maqdah, also known as Abu Hassan, was born in Acre in the 1950s, and controls 3,000 armed men from his base in the Ein al-Hilweh refugee camp near Sidon. Although a religious Muslim himself, Maqdah decries the influence of Iranian

sponsored fundamentalists, who have sought to exploit the financial crisis in the PLO, to win support in the camps.

Marín Gonzales, Manuel   Spain

Vice-President of the European Commission, and Commissioner for Co-operation, Development and Fisheries. Marín has chief responsibility for EU ties with Israel, Palestinians and the Middle East. In 1996 he expressed satisfaction with the Palestinian Council election results, and pledged $1.2 billion of EU money for the Palestinian economy.

Marzouk, Musa Muhammed Abu   Palestinian

Reportedly head of the *Hamas* politburo, or political wing (as distinct from the military wing). Dr Abu Marzouk was credited with re-establishing *Hamas* after Israel had arrested or deported its main leaders, including Sheikh Ahmed Yassin, in the 1990s. For a while he was based in Damascus, before moving to the USA. He takes a hard line against any co-operation with the PLO or Israel. In July 1995, US authorities arrested Abu Marzouk on charges of plotting acts of terrorism. Much of the evidence came from a former *Hamas* member who was arrested in Israel on returning from the USA in 1993, Muhammed al-Hamid Salah. He said that Abu Marzouk had raised funds and recruited volunteers for terror activities. But in the apparent absence of firm proof, there were rumours that Abu Marzouk was being held on the vaguer charges of 'seditious conspiracy'. Israel requested his extradition, and solicited the help of New York's deputy US attorney, Shirah Nieman to this end; yet US authorities seemed determined to prosecute Abu Marzouk in the USA.

Masri, Munib Sabih   Palestinian

PNA minister without portfolio. Masri, now 47, was born into an established Nablus family (some of whose members have been prime ministers of Jordan). He left Nablus in the early 1960s, and went to Saudi Arabia, where became a millionaire from his work in construction and investments. Later, Masri was based in London. He is closely associated with Padico, a private Palestinian investment corporation, set up in 1993 with capital of $200 million.

Massalha, Nawaf   Israel

Deputy Health Minister since 1995. Massalha is an Israeli Arab and a Labour MK. He is associated with the Group of Seven (young labour reformers, including Yossi Beilin and Haim Ramon).

Medein, Freih Abu   Palestinian

PNA Justice Minister. Born to a bedouin family in Gaza in 1944, Medein trained as a lawyer, became head of the Gaza Bar Association, and was active in local politics. He soon became known as an uncompromising *Fatah* supporter, and the passion of his views helped in some way towards curbing the growing influence of *Hamas* in the Gaza Strip. Abu Medein was a member of the official Palestinian delegation to the Madrid and Washington peace talks. Since the Israeli–PLO Declaration of Principles in 1993, and the subsequent Gaza-Jericho implementation agreements (the Cairo Accord) of 1994, Medein has played a central role in drafting many new laws in the PNA. He upset Israeli politicians by refusing to extradite any Palestinian terrorism suspects to Israel (as the Cairo Accords provide for). In similar vein, he angered Israeli Justice Minister David Liba'i in late 1995, when he said Palestinian victims of the *intifada* deserved compensation from Israel, just as Holocaust survivors got reparations from Germany. Until the dissolution of the PNA (pending Palestine Council elections), Medein negotiated with Israel about the release of Palestinian prisoners from Israeli jails. On Feb. 12, 1996, it was announced that Freih Abu Medein had topped the list of five legislators who will represent Deir al-Birah in the Palestine Council.

Medhat, Kamal   Palestinian

Head of *Fatah*'s intelligence service in Lebanon. A supporter of Arafat, Medhat has fought a running battle with Mounir Maqdah in the Lebanese refugee camps since the 1993 peace accords were announced. He is believed to have close ties with Lebanese Army intelligence, and the Lebanese Christian community.

Meirom, Hagai   Israel
Labour MK, and head of the party's strategy committee. As one of the Labour Party's Group of Seven (also characterized as the North Tel Aviv yuppies), Meirom favours an eventual Palestinian state, although this view is still not official party policy. As of July 1995, Meirom was chairman of two of the most influential *Knesset* committees – Foreign Affairs and Defence.

Merhav, Reuven   Israel
Former Director-General of the Foreign Ministry. Merhav served as the head of Israel's liaison bureau in Beirut, during the short-lived Israel–Lebanon treaty of the early 1980s. In 1985 he was posted to Hong Kong, and used it as a springboard for a diplomatic initiative to China itself. Merhav fostered scientific and academic ties with the People's Republic, and laid the groundwork for the November 1991 visit of Defence Minister Moshe Arens to Beijing. In early 1992 he saw the fruition of his work – full diplomatic relations between the two countries. But by this stage, he had already resigned as Director-General (in July 1991) in frustration with Foreign Minister David Levy's approach. Merhav has since been the president of the International Centre at Beit Gavriel, which hosts international seminars on the shores of the Sea of Galilee. The Centre was a key venue during the Israel–Jordan negotiations, before and after the signing of their peace treaty in October 1994.

Meridor, Dan   Israel
Appointed Minister of Finance in June 1996. Dan Meridor is the leading moderate in the *Likud.* Some fellow MKs urged him to challenge Benjamin Netanyahu for the job of party leader, after the latter found his reputation tarnished by association with far-right elements in the aftermath of the Rabin assassination. Like Netanyahu, Meridor was one of *Likud's* eminent 'young princes' in the 1980s – new leaders espousing modern ideas, but with the dynastic blessing of being members of the Revisionist movement's founding families. Born in Jerusalem in 1947, Meridor practised law before serving as Government Secretary from 1982 to 1984. He entered the *Knesset* in 1984, and went on to serve as Justice Minister under Yitzhak Shamir.

Former prime minister, Menachem Begin, said he wanted Meridor to head the party one day. However, right-wing elements in the party (increasingly influential in the 1990s) attacked Meridor for taking a pro-human rights stance during the *intifada.* In 1991 Meridor launched secret talks with the Bush administration, which contributed to Israel's participation in the Madrid summit that October. However, tensions within *Likud* meant that Meridor was demoted to the 15th slot on the party's 1992 electoral list. In 1993 he chose to stay out of the race to replace the outgoing Shamir as party leader.

Merzel, Baruch   Israel
Leader of *Kach*, right-wing banned Jewish terrorist grouping. Merzel bitterly opposes the autonomy plans of Oslo 1 and 2. He has openly advocated that settlers take the law into their own hands, and even supported murdering Islamic students in Hebron. Merzel was placed under house arrest in Kiryat Arba after the Rabin assassination.

Miller, Aaron   USA
Deputy Assistant Secretary of State, and a Pentagon official on the Mid-east desk. Miller played an important role behind the scenes in the Israeli–Palestinian peace talks. Now 45, Miller moved from the US State Department's historians' office to intelligence analysis of Lebanon. He joined the Department's policy planning unit in the 1980s, after writing two books on Palestinian affairs. He ultimately failed to realize the Schultz blueprint for a Lebanese settlement, and the Reagan peace plan. But Miller did impress players on all sides with his grasp of detail, and to some extent he set the parameters for the more successful initiatives of James Baker. Miller is Jewish and broadly supports an Israeli Labour line (on territorial compromise and peace with security). At the same time he is said to appreciate Arab political sensitivities.

Mitterand, Francois   **France**
President of France from 1981 to 1995. Francois Mitterrand, born in 1916, revived the Socialist Party in the 1970s, and as President became known as one of the most consumate

politicians in Europe. Mitterand enjoyed cordial relations with Israel, especially the Labour Party, and had close ties with the French Jewish community. He also began his first seven-year presidency with a call for Palestinian statehood, and in late 1982 he used his good offices to help Arafat leave Beirut, after the Israeli invasion of that year. In 1989 he became the first Western head of state to receive Yasser Arafat, in the wake of the PNC's Algiers Declaration. In the run-up to the Gulf War, Mitterrand favoured a diplomatic settlement, and commentators felt he was concerned not to risk France's lucrative contacts with Iraq. However, he contributed French military airplanes to Operation Desert Storm, and was present at the Madrid peace talks nine months later. Mitterand supported the Oslo Accords, and provided the Parisian venue for the conclusion of the Economic Protocol between Israel and the PLO, in 1994. Mitterrand finally succumbed to cancer and died in January 1996.

Moddalal, Sa'id   **Palestinian**
PNA director of employment services. Moddalal has criticized Diaspora Palestinians for not investing more in the new Palestinian self-rule areas.

Mohtashami, Hojatoleslam Ali Akbar   **Iran**
Radical politician, Islamic authority, and a major patron of the Lebanese Shi'ite *Hezbollah* movement. Mohtashami was born in 1946, and worked in Ayatollah Khomeini's Paris office before the 1979 revolution. He was Ambassador to Syria from 1982, and Interior Minister from 1985, until he was dismissed by Iran's new President Ali Akbar Hashemi Rafsanjani in 1989. He leads the Council of Radical Clerics, and forms a focus of opposition to the more pragmatic President Rafsanjani.

Moussa, Amr Mohammad   **Egypt**
Foreign Minister, and a close ally of President Hosni Mubarak. Born on Oct. 3, 1936, in Cairo, Amr Moussa qualified as a bachelor of law from Cairo University, and in 1958 joined the Foreign Ministry. Moussa became Egypt's ambassador to India in 1987, and three years later returned to the UN as Egypt's permanent representative. He replaced the veteran Ahmad Esmat Abdel-Meguid as Egypt's Foreign Minister in 1991, and attended the Madrid peace conference as a high-ranking observer.

After Labour took power in Israel in July 1992, Moussa paid a surprise visit to Israel in October, spoke to Prime Minister Rabin and Foreign Minister Peres, and agreed terms for diaspora Palestinians to participate in multilateral forums. Meanwhile, Moussa and his colleague, Presidential Adviser Osama al-Baz, worked behind the scenes as intermediatories in the first tentative contacts between Israel and the PLO. After the Israeli–Palestinian breakthrough in September 1993, part of Moussa's job was to assure the new Palestinian Authority of Egypt's loyal support (when many other Arab states were crying 'betrayal'). On Jan. 25, 1994, he signed a five-year technical and economic co-operation agreement with the PLO (represented by the head of the PLO Political Department, Farouk Qaddumi). Egypt and the Palestinian entity granted each other 'most favoured nation status' in matters of trade; they also studied possible joint projects, and considered the option of making Rafah (on their mutual border) a free trade zone. Further afield, Moussa worked to improve Egypt's relations with Syria, Jordan and Iran.

In August 1995, Moussa said that the reality of peace with Israel was taking hold in Egypt, and by extension, in the whole Middle East. However, he felt Israel should make more than statements, and should engage fully with her Arab neighbours. He also criticized Israel for not signing the Nuclear Non-Proliferation Treaty; and accused Israel of covering the alleged killing of Egyptian prisoners-of-war in 1956 and 1967. In late October 1995, Moussa addressed the MENA economic summit in Amman and chided Jordan for racing ahead too quickly in its peace with Israel. Moussa accompanied President Mubarak to Yitzhak Rabin's funeral on Nov. 5, 1995. Unfortunately for Israeli–Egyptian relations, his contacts with Shimon Peres have often been frosty. In early 1996 the two men were accusing each other of interfering in internal affairs. However, they seemed to mend fences with a new understanding on the issue of nuclear arms in the Middle East.

Mu'alam, Walid   **Syria**
Syrian Ambassador to Washington. Walid became Syria's unofficial peace negotiator with

Israel. Together with delegation head, Mu'afaq Alaf, he held talks with Israel's Yossi Ben-Aharon, and, after August 1992, with Professor Itamar Rabinovich. US Secretary of State Warren Christopher, and US 'peace co-ordinator' Dennis Ross, have often used Mu'alam as a crucial 'point-man' in talks with Damascus as does the current US Ambassador to Israel, Martin Indyk. Mu'alam led Syria's delegation to the Wye Valley peace talks in December 1995 and early 1996.

Muasher, Marwan   Jordan

First Jordanian Ambassador to Israel; appointed Jordan's Information Minister in February 1996. Born in 1954, Muasher was head of Jordan's information office in Washington when he joined the Jordanian delegation at the Madrid peace conference, in October 1991. He was intimately involved in the negotiations towards the Jordan–Israel peace treaty, and set up Jordan's temporary embassy in Israel on Dec. 11, 1994 (his official appointment was delayed until Israel decided on Shimon Shamir as replacement for its first choice of ambassador, Efraim Halevy, in early 1995). Muasher protested at Israeli government expropriation of Arab land in East Jerusalem. He had been in Tel Aviv for ten months, when he was recalled to Amman, as one Jordanian analyst put it, 'to explain the benefits of peace, and how Israelis think'. Together with the new prime minister, Abdul Karim Kabariti, Muasher represents the more pro-Western 'new generation' of Jordanian leaders.

Mohammed Hosni MUBARAK

Nationality	Egyptian
Religion	Muslim
Place of birth	Kafr al-Museilha, Governate of al-Menufiya, northern Egypt
Date of birth	1928
Current position	President of the Arab Republic of Egypt
Previous position	Deputy to late President Anwar al-Sadat
Allies	Foreign Minister Moussa Amr
Position on peace	Positive; stewardship role for other Arabs; but wary on NPT
National political importance	Very influential
Prospects	Stable, if he can stave off economic strife and fundamentalists

Mohammed Hosni Mubarak has ruled Egypt ever since the assassination of former President Anwar Sadat, in 1981. Although at first he seemed to lack Sadat's charisma, Mubarak has over the years created a stable leadership by cautiously fostering democracy, clamping down on corruption and reinforcing Egypt's ties with the USA. In the regional arena, he has re-integrated Egypt into the Arab world after years of ostracization because of the Camp David accords.

More than that, he has exploited his links with Israel to act as an 'honest broker' in negotiations between other Arab states, the PLO and Israel. He played a crucial role in convincing Yitzhak Rabin to accept Yasser Arafat's *bona fides* in the prelude to the Oslo accords of 1993; and later hosted the Israel–PLO ratification of the Oslo/Washington accords on May 4, 1994. However, Mubarak has been bedevilled by domestic problems, including economic strife and the associated growth of violence by Islamic fundamentalists.

Hosni Mubarak was born in 1928 in Kafr al-Museilha, a village in northern Egypt. He joined the Egyptian air force in 1950 and saw service in the Yemen civil war. Following special training in the Soviet Union, Mubarak became director of the air academy in November 1968, and as such was entrusted with the task of rebuilding Egypt's air force, which Israel had largely destroyed in the 1967 war. On 23 June 1969 he became Air Force Chief of Staff, and from 1972 to 1975 he was overall military commander-in-chief and Deputy Minister of Defence. Sadat appointed him Vice-President on 16 April 1975 with responsibility for Egypt's national security apparatus. On 15 Aug. 1978 he was chosen as Deputy Chairman of the newly constituted ruling National Democratic Party (NDP), thus giving him a clearer role in national politics. He also played an important part behind the scenes in negotiating the Camp

David accords, and became friendly with his opposite number in the Israeli Air Force, Ezer Weizman (now President of Israel). Anwar Sadat was killed on Oct. 6, 1991, and later that month Mubarak took over as president. Immediately he re-committed Egypt to maintaining her ties with Israel. For this he won considerable international praise, as it was assumed (probably incorrectly) that disfavour with the peace deal had led to Sadat's untimely death.

Through careful diplomacy, Mubarak succeeded in getting Egypt re-admitted to Arab political forums in 1987, although arguably at the expense of cooling relations with Israel. In 1990 and 1991 Egypt under Mubarak was a leading member of the UN coalition of states opposed to Iraq's invasion of Kuwait (his personal intervention failed to reach an Arab diplomatic solution). However, there was a cost to pay at home, as many in 'the street' detested what they saw as Mubarak's connivance with the US against an 'Arab brother' (Saddam Hussein). In 1993 Egypt was blighted by fundamentalist violence directed against foreigners, members of Egypt's Coptic Christian minority, state officials and secular political and literary figures. In response Mubarak imposed tougher security laws and set up military courts to deal with the threat. Since then, terrorist violence has been largely forced underground. Mubarak narrowly survived an assassination attempt while attending an OAU summit in Ethiopia in 1995. He blamed Sudan for formenting extremism, which has led to over 1,000 deaths in recent years.

At the end of 1995, there was widespread anger at the suspect general election results. The NDP recorded a near total victory, and opposition forces say the election was rigged. Hosni Mubarak has been elected president three times in a row – in 1981, 1987 and most recently in October 1993. His long-awaited third term cabinet reshuffle, however, delivered fewer changes than were initially promised (although this was rectified in January 1996).

Once ostracized by Arabs generally, and the PLO in particular, for his peace agreement with Israel, in the new political dispensation Mubarak has managed to turn his ties with Israel to his distinct advantage. In fact, the thaw with the Arab world had begun earlier. After the PLO leadership was expelled from Beirut in 1982, Mubarak was one of the first leaders Yasser Arafat visited. Observers claim that he 'threw Arafat a lifeline', when other more vociferously 'pro-Palestinian' Arab states did little to help. Egypt was re-admitted to the Arab League in May 1989, where it soon assumed its traditional role as leader.

At the same time, by retaining the services of men like Deputy Foreign Minister Bhoutros Bhoutros Ghali and his adviser, Osama al-Baz, Mubarak ensured a sense of continuity from the Camp David days. These twin factors gave Mubarak the authority to devise an Arab formula for a lasting regional peace. In August 1989 he submitted a ten-point peace plan in the form of questions and clarifications on Yitzhak Shamir's response to the Baker Plan. At the time his plan bore little fruit; but it did restore Arab unity, and after the Gulf War, many of its recommendations were incorporated in the Baker initiative, which resulted in the Madrid conference.

Newcomers to the current 'peace track' often use Mubarak as an intermediatory. He sent Foreign Minister Amr Moussa to head an 'observer delegation' at the Madrid talks, and was kept informed about the secret Oslo channel talks, whereas King Hussein was not. He had the honour of hosting the Cairo Agreement of 1994, which set the seal on the Washington Declaration of Principles and provided the modalities for implementing the Gaza-Jericho First plan. Egyptian-ruled Taba was the site of the most sensitive Israeli–PLO talks, both before the Cairo signing (Oslo 1) and before the second-stage Interim Agreement of September 1995 (Oslo 2). Cairo and Alexandria also were prominent venues for multilateral talks in 1994 and 1995. In December 1994, he delivered an impassioned plea for Muslim unity, defiance of terrorism, and confidence in making peace with the non-Muslim world, at the 25th anniversary summit of the Organization of Islamic Conference. Mubarak set up the 'peace bloc' (with Egypt, Israel and the PLO) in the wake of the Hebron massacre to keep the talks going.

President Mubarak has quietly encouraged ties with Israel, and in 1995 hosted a party of Israeli tourists. He also favoured low-key cultural interchanges, and trade between the two states has grown. However, unlike Sadat, he is notably cautious of appearing 'out of step' with the rest of the Arab world, and is weary of domestic public opinion. In April 1990 Mubarak launched an initiative which called for the Middle East to be a region free of weapons of mass destruction. In 1994 he took this a stage further, by explicitly criticizing Israel's possession of nuclear weapons; and in 1995, he insisted that Israel ratify the Nuclear Non-Proliferation Treaty in 1995. He also led Arab protest at an attempt by Israel officials (since dropped) to 'confiscate' Arab land in East Jerusalem.

Israelis have come to call the relationship with Egypt a 'cold peace', as the initial promise of the Sadat–Begin venture never quite materialized. For six years, between 1982 and 1988, Israel and Egypt argued about sovereignty over the Sinai port of Taba. International arbitors eventually awarded it to Egypt, and although Mubarak praised it as an example of how 'fruitful and civilized dialogue' could settle differences peacefully, others saw the 'Taba Dispute' as both a cause and a symptom of the frosty ties between Cairo and Jerusalem. This was further symbolized by the fact that Mubarak did not visit Israel in 12 years of his presidency. (The newly elected Israeli Prime Minister Yitzhak Rabin had invited him to come in July 1992. Mubarak accepted, but later postponed his visit in the light of events at home, and Israel's deportation crisis of December 1992. However, in their many telephone conversations, and meetings in Egypt and the USA, Rabin and Mubarak formed a close partnership).

Hence the significance of Mubarak's attendance at Yitzhak Rabin's funeral in Jerusalem, in November 1995. Commentators praised his courage, in the light of the threat of Muslim fundamentalists assassinating him as they did his predecessor, Anwar Sadat. Ironically, the coolness between Israel and Egypt has revived Egyptian fears of being left out of economic boom, as new parties (Palestinians, Jordan, and perhaps even Syria) rush to form bonds with Israel. This was certainly true of the regional economic summit, held in Amman in late October 1995. But even there, Mubarak scored a success by assuring Cairo as headquarters for the new Middle East Development Bank. In early 1996 Mubarak appeared to have weathered the storm of criticism about the controversial national elections. He accepted Prime Minister Sedki's resignation, and replaced him with Kamal Ahmad Ganzouri. Mubarak also re-established the pivotal nature of Egypt, by hosting an extraordinary conference of world leaders in March (this followed the terrorist atrocities in Israel. In June 1996 he hosted the first Arab leaders' summit since 1990, in light of Netanyahu's election win.

Mufleh, Jhassan   Jordan
Director-General of the Tourism Ministry, and an enthusiast for deals with Israel.

Muragha, Sa'id Musa   Palestinian
Chief of the PLO's campaign to defend their headquarters from Israeli attack in 1982. Also known as Abu Musa, from 1983 till the present he has headed a group of Syrian–backed anti-Arafat rebels within *Fatah*. Muragha is opposed to the peace deal with Israel, and, especially after 1993, his group has joined with the Abu Nidal Group and others in a campaign of assassination, directed against *Fatah* forces in Lebanon.

Musa, Sharif al-   Palestinian
(See Elmusa, Sharif)

Musallum, Sami   Palestinian
Head of Yasser Arafat's office in Jericho. As such, Mussalum wielded considerable influence in implementing the PLO chairman's writ during stage one of the Oslo peace process (Gaza and Jericho First).

Musamih, Sayyid Abu   Palestinian
A prominent *Hamas* leader, currently held in PNA detention in Gaza.

Mustafa, Abu Ali   Palestinian
Deputy leader (to George Habash) of the PFLP. Based in Tunis during the *intifada*, Mustafa has been cautious on supporting PLO negotiations with Israel.

N

Nabulsi, Muhammad al-   Jordan
Governor of the Central Bank of Jordan. Nabulsi arranged a moratorium on currency with

Palestinians, and co-operates with the head of the Palestinian Monetary Authority, Fouad Besseiso.

Nachman, Ron   Israel
Mayor of Ariel and a *Likud* MK since 1992. Ariel is the largest West Bank settlement, a town of more than 10,000 residents. Nachman represents the many largely secular 'commuter belt' settlers who live in the territories. He was determined to build good relations with Salfit, the neighbouring Arab village, and encouraged its residents to work in Ariel, while Ariel residents taught in Salfit schools. Salfit benefited from Ariel's boom, with new houses and electrification. However, many in Salfit resented Ariel's 'carrot and stick' approach, and an abortive PLO bomb attack on Ariel in 1986 cooled relations between the two municipalities. Nachman hopes that Ariel will expand into a city of 100,000 by the year 2000, and by then will entirely absorb Salfit. At present, access to water rights is a burning issue for the two communities, and will surely be discussed in both the water resources and settlements sessions of the final status talks between Israel and the PLO, scheduled for 1996.

Nahhas, Salem   Jordan
A leader of Jordanian opposition to the peace treaty with Israel. Salem is a prominent Islamic fundamentalist who opposes any normalization of relations with Israel. In September 1995 he addressed the first legally allowed meeting of an 11-party anti-peace front. Some 330 representatives of the parties attended, and included many prominent Islamists and Palestinian leftists. The meeting followed an earlier incident, when local businessmen in Irbid had invited Israeli ambassador Shimon Shamir to address a meeting, but were prevented from doing so by raucous anti-peace demonstrators. An earlier attempt to hold an anti-peace rally failed in May 1995, when the government declared that it was indulging in anti-democratic incitement.

Najjab, Suleiman an-   Palestinian
Prominent supporter of the Palestine People's Party (formerly Communist). Najjab heads the Social Affairs Department on the PLO executive committee. In July 1991, he engineered the restoration of links between the PLO and Syria.

Najm, Raef   Jordan
Former government minister, and, since November 1995, deputy chairman of a special 'Higher Committee to Defend Jerusalem'. The committee reportedly includes three ministers from the Palestine National Authority, in Gaza; and is chaired by the Speaker of the Palestine National Council. Najm accused Israel of delaying talks on Jerusalem to the final stages, as a ploy to buy time so that it could 'Judaize' the city with new settlers.

Nashashibi, Muhammad Zuhdi an-   Palestinian
Independent member of PLO executive committee, and PNA Finance Minister. Nashashibi is not affiliated to any particular faction. He comes from a famous *ayan* family in Jerusalem, traditional rivals to the Husseini clan. He was once a member of Syria's *Ba'ath* Party, and a leading Palestinian official in Damascus. He later became Director of the Palestine National Fund in Amman and Tunis. As such, he encountered enormous difficulties after the Gulf War, when the Gulf states, traditional donors to the PLO, cut off funds in protest at Arafat's apparently pro-Saddam stance. Nashashibi is known for his administrative prowess, and was secretary to the PLO Executive Committee. As Finance Minister, Nashashibi has fought a low-key battle for influence with foreign investors, against his PNA colleagues, Ahmed Qurei (in effect the head of PECDAR), and Planning Minister Nabil Sha'ath.

Nasrallah, Hassan   Lebanon
Secretary-General of *Hezbollah*. Sheikh Hassan Nasrallah was born in the south Lebanese village of Bazouriyeh, and grew up in Beirut. He claims to be a Sayid, a direct descendant of the Prophet Muhammed, and his fluency in Persian has helped to make him one of Iran's most trusted allies in the organization. After Israeli forces assassinated *Hezbollah's* secretary-general, Abbas Musawi, on Feb. 16, 1992, Sheikh Nasrallah and Sheikh Subhi Tufeili both claimed his mantle. However, Nasrallah was officially elected, and in recent years has gained the upper hand. Both men ultimately defer to the Shi'ite community's chief *mujtahid* (spiritual leader), the veteran Sheikh Muhammad Hussein Fadlallah.

Nasrallah's first speech as leader condemned Israel as 'a cancer that has to be removed', and he has maintained the 'armed struggle' against Israel in the south, with tacit approval from Beirut and Damascus. Nasrallah's stronghold lies in the Beqa'a Valley, east of Beirut; his chief lieutenant in the south is believed to be Khalil Kharb. At the same time, he allowed *Hezbollah* to participate in the August 1992 general elections. After fighting escalated between Israeli and South Lebanese Army forces, and *Hezbollah*, in late 1995, Nasrallah threatened more Katyusha rocket attacks on Israeli soldiers and settlements across the border. Under Nasrallah, *Hezbollah* has begun to mend fences with the rival *Amal* group, and it enjoys greater independence from Iran on the battlefield. It has also expanded its social welfare programmes, and, according to Lebanese and Israeli academics, Nizar Hamzeh and Eyal Zisser, it is showing a new pragmatism, and willingness to compromise, borne out of its new parliamentary experience. However, Nasrallah has not abandoned his military options, nor his policy of forcing local Shi'ites into his group. His own personal political survival still depends on keeping Teheran's favour.

Nasser, Maha   Palestinian
Chair, Palestinian Women's General Union. She is a member of the Popular Front for the Liberation of Palestine (PFLP), a Marxist faction which usually opposed the Arafat line in the PLO throughout the 1970s and 1980s. Nasser is believed to have clashed with Umm Jihad, who as the PNA Welfare Minister is the leading woman in the Palestinian political hierarchy.

Natsheh, Mustafa   Palestinian
Mayor of Hebron. A pro-*Fatah* member of the Palestinian delegation in Madrid, Natsheh was born in 1930. He trained as an engineer and was elected mayor of Hebron in the 1980s, but deposed by Israel and deported to Jordan in 1983. Subsequently re-appointed, Natsheh was intimately involved in the sensitive negotiations about Hebron preceding the Oslo 2 agreement. Natsheh is ultimately determined to see the 450 Jewish settlers in central Hebron leave, but for the present he has accepted the compromise deal, involving joint Palestinian and Israeli security patrols in the city.

Natur, Muhammed a-   Palestinian
Head of Force 17, pro-*Fatah* Praetorian Guard, occasionally operating as a terror group. Under his *nomme du guerre*, Abu Tayeb, Col. Natur took over Force 17 from Ali Hassan Salameh, whom *Mossad* assassinated in Beirut in 1979 for his involvement in the Munich Olympics massacre. Force 17 was initially created as an élite unite within the Palestine Liberation Army, and included Jibril Rajoub, now head of Palestinian security in Jericho.

Nazzal, Muhammed   Palestinian
Hamas representative in Jordan. In 1993 he suggested that Palestinians should accept a mini-state as a first step towards a fully Muslim Palestine (presumably swallowing up Israel). In 1995, Nazzal and the Amman wing of *Hamas* have tended to be less compromising than many internal factions, and *Hamas* exiles based in Sudan.

Binyamin NETANYAHU

Nationality	Israeli
Religion	Jewish
Place of Birth	Jerusalem, Israel
Date of Birth	1949
Current position	Prime Minister of Israel following the May 1996 elections
Previous positions	Leader of the Opposition in Knesset; Head of Likud since 1993
	Deputy Minister of Foreign Affairs (1988–91)
	Deputy Minister in the Prime Minister's office (1991–92)
	Ambassador to the United Nations (1984–88)
Allies	Tsachi Hanegbi, Ariel Sharon, Rafael Eitan, Uzi Landen, Limer Livnet
Position on peace	Lukewarm, rejects Arafat, but accepts peace process as *fait accompli*

National political	
importance	Very influential on the centre-right; good image in Western media
Prospects	Enjoys narrow but decisive popular mandate as PM

Binyamin (also known as Benjamin) Netanyahu, currently head of the *Likud* and Leader of the Opposition, was born into a prominent Zionist Revisionist family which originally hailed from Russia. From early on, Benjamin was groomed as one of *Likud's* 'Young Princes'. His earliest field of expertise was in fighting terrorism, and he served as a soldier and officer in an elite unit in the Israeli Defence Forces from 1967 to 1972.

Netanyahu made the most of his American education and his natural articulacy while serving as Deputy Chief of Mission to the United States from 1982 to 1984, and Israel's Ambassador to the UN from 1984 to 1988. He has been a *Knesset* member for *Likud* since 1988, and became Deputy Minister of Foreign Affairs in the same year. During the Gulf War in 1991, Netanyahu acted as Israel's principal television spokesman, where he proved himself to be a master of the soundbite. It is widely thought that his media exposure increased his support within *Likud*, and amongst the influential pro-Israel lobby in the US. In 1991 he formed part of Israel's delegation to the Madrid peace conference, which was under the direct leadership of Prime Minister Yitzhak Shamir. Netanyahu was clearly at odds with his senior, Foreign Minister David Levy, who conspicuously was not included in the Madrid delegation. In part this resulted from a clash of personalities; but also Netanyahu tended to take a more hawkish approach, more akin to that of former Prime Minister Yitzhak Shamir. Some analysts have blamed failure in the negotiations on the mixed messages emanating from Jerusalem because of the Levy–Netanyahu clash.

By 1992 Netanyahu had become Deputy Minister in the Prime Minister's Office. When Yitzhak Shamir resigned the *Likud* party leadership in 1993, Netanyahu won the resulting poll, displacing more seasoned *Likud* figures like David Levy, Ariel Sharon and Benny Begin (son of the late Menachem Begin).

The gist of his world view is that Israel represents the summation of Jewish power, and must remain ever vigilant to guard against another disaster like the Holocaust; the idea that the 'Palestinian problem' is central to Middle East affairs is a myth concocted by the PLO and cynical Arab states; the PLO's two-state solution is in essence a two-stage solution, where negotiations are merely a 'Trojan horse' behind which PLO officials hide, while planning the total conquest of Israel and its absorption into a greater Palestine. True peace with Arabs will only come when they realize Israel is a 'wall', which will not yield an inch in its fundamental right to exist within its present borders. In his view, the West Bank gives Israel vital 'strategic depth'. Similarly, he believes Israel should not give up the Golan Heights for a peace with Syria. Having said that, he enthusiastically backed Israel's peace treaty with Jordan, and has held several meetings with King Hussein. He also promised that under *Likud*, Israel would not 'return to Gaza'.

By the latter half of 1995, Netanyahu was leading large protest rallies against the Oslo 2 peace accords. His close aide-de-camp, Tzachi Hanegbi, seemed to push him towards more radical views. Although Netanyahu objected to demonstrators who called Rabin a traitor, some fellow *Likud* MKs, notably Dan Meridor, warned him against a stance which gave credence to right-wing extremist views. As a result, after the assassination of Yitzhak Rabin on Nov. 4, 1995, Netanyahu faced fury from certain quarters in Labour. Rabin's widow, Leah, even refused to shake his hand at the late prime minister's funeral. Zalman Shoval was drafted to restore Netanyahu's image, but his poll ratings plummeted in the wake of sympathy for Rabin. Netanyahu sagely refused to demand a general election, saying that an assassin's bullet should not determine politics in a democracy.

Since the atrocity, Netanyahu has appeared more muted in his pronouncements. He even persuaded the *Likud* caucus to accept Oslo 2 as a reality in early 1996, whereas a year earlier he said that autonomous Palestinian regions were 'seedbeds for terrorism'. In February 1996, Netanyahu signed a pact with the right-wing *Tsomet* Party, guaranteeing it a share of the seats on a joint list with *Likud,* and winning *Tsomet* leader Raphael Eitan's backing for his prime ministerial candidacy for the May 1996 elections (the first with direct election of the prime minister). Pundits felt this gesture would only further ostracize potential centrist voters, and hasten Netanyahu's slide in the opinion polls (where he lagged up to 20% behind Shimon Peres, the sitting Prime Minister and chief Labour candidate). However, a new spate of terrorist attacks in February and March knocked public confidence in the peace process, and this helped Netanyahu to defeat Shimon Peres (by scarcely 20,000 votes) in Israel's first direct elections for the Prime Ministership.

Nevo, Danny   Israel
Israeli Co-ordinator of the Multilateral Working Group on Refugee Affairs. In June 1995, Nevo took part in the first meeting of a quadripartite (Israel, PNA, Egypt and Jordan) 'committee of experts', to investigate the issue of the Palestinian refugees of 1967 (also known as 'displaced persons').

Nofel, Mahmoud   Palestinian
Member, PLO economic advisory committee to Palestinian delegation in Madrid.

Novick, Nimrod   Israel
Shimon Peres' 'ambassador at large', and secret negotiator. Novick is also Vice-President of the Hertzliyah-based Merhav Group, which in February 1994 was negotiating with an Egyptian firm to build a $1 billion oil refinery in Alexandria.

Sari NUSSEIBEH

Nationality	Palestinian
Religion	Muslim
Place of Birth	Jerusalem
Date of Birth	1949
Current position	Professor of Philosophy at Bir Zeit University
Previous positions	Head of the Holy Land Press Services; leader during the *intifada* Prominent member of political advisory committee at Madrid talks
Allies	Hanan Ashrawi, Faisal Husseini, Jibril Rajoub
Position on peace	Enthusiast of a two-state solution; initially wary of Oslo Accords
National political importance	Influential in academic circles; good image in Western media
Prospects	After returning from a two-year sabatical, Nusseibeh appears to be poised to play a renewed role in final status negotiations

Nusseibeh, a leading *Fatah* moderate in the West Bank, was born into a family of Jerusalem notables. Although Muslim, since the 12th century they have had the honour of keeping the keys of the Church of the Holy Sepulchre. Sari Nusseibeh grew up on the border between Israeli West Jerusalem and Jordanian East Jerusalem. He studied at Christ Church, Oxford University, and graduated in 1971. After working in Abu Dhabi, he spent four years at Harvard, where he gained a PhD in Islamic studies, and returned to the West Bank in 1978. He was a visiting professor at the Hebrew University, and taught Islamic philosophy to Jewish students; at the same time, he took up a post of Professor of Philosophy at Bir Zeit University, near Ramallah. Nusseibeh was a virulent opponent of the Israeli occupation, but also kept open channels of communication with left-wing Israelis, such as the Peace Now group. In July 1987, members of the *Likud* government approached him for talks. Nusseibeh brought Faisal Husseini into these private negotiations. However, Palestinian radicals accused him of 'selling out', and beat him up in September. He made his name politically during the *intifada*, as a leading spokesman for the *shakhsiyat*, or 'personalities', a group of Palestinian intellectuals and professionals who articulated the cause of the uprising. Nusseibeh fostered longstanding ties with Hanan Ashrawi and Faisal Husseini. During this period he and Ziyad Abu Zayyad set up some 200 'technical committees' throughout the West Bank, in the name of *Fatah*. These attempted to restore a Palestinian infrastructure that had been damaged by years of occupation, and now, potentially, by the uprising itself. The committees reflected his own political analysis: either Palestinians make an effort to create their own state, or they must accept annexation by, and integration into, Israeli society. His controversial views have often caused him to clash with the Tunis-based PLO, which feared he was severing ties with the 'external' wing of the Palestinian movement. Yet they also led to problems with Israel. In 1989

Israeli military authorities indicted Nusseibeh for allegedly formenting violence and siphoning funds into the territories to keep the *intifada* alive; they also shut down his Holy Land Press Service, and banned his English language newsletter, *Monday Report*. In January 1991, he was accused of 'spying for Iraq', and spent three months in jail. His arrest and imprisonment sparked protests from the USA, UK and Israeli peace activists.

Nusseibeh played an important role on the Palestinian advisory committee to the Madrid and Washington peace talks (1991 to 1993), but he lost a good deal of his influence and international standing when the Madrid track was eclipsed by the Oslo deal. Since then, Nusseibeh has maintained a lower profile, and left Bir Zeit for an extended sabbatical in 1994. Nonetheless, more recently he returned formed a close alliance with Jibril Rajoub, the Palestine National Authority's security chief in Jericho (and increasingly, in the rest of the West Bank). Nusseibeh designed the programme for Rajoub's elite police academy. Some former allies criticized him for co-operating with a man who was accused of flouting human rights. Nusseibeh is expected to return to prominence when the issue of Jerusalem comes up for discussion at the final status talks in 1996. He has one of the keenest intellects in the Middle East, and inherited from his father the ability to work within existing systems of political power, whether Jordanian, Israeli or now the PNA. Yet his intellectual honesty has led to rifts with less patient or scrupulous activists.

O

Obeid, Abd al-Karim   Lebanon
Sheikh, *Hezbollah* leader in Jibshit, south Lebanon. The Sheikh is currently being held captive by Israel in Khiam prison, in the southern security zone. In the early 1990s, following *Hezbollah's* release of Western hostages, Uri Lubrani, Israel's co-ordinator for the zone, proposed to release Obeid in exchange for the captured Israeli airman, Ron Arad. So far there has been no concrete information about Arad's whereabouts, and Obeid remains incarcerated, a *casus belli* between Israel and Lebanon. In 1996 there were new rumours that Obeid may be released in exchange for the bodies of Israelis killed in action.

Odeh, Abd al-Aziz   Palestinian
Muslim law lecturer, and co-founder of Islamic *Jihad* with Dr Fat'hi Shiqaqi. Obeid graduated from an Egyptian University, and brought the message of the Muslim Brotherhood to Gaza. After Shiqaqi's assassination in October 1995, Odeh could well experience a political revival amongst disaffected Muslim fundamentalists.

Ofir, Gabi   Israel
IDF Commander in Judea and Samaria (West Bank), and co-ordinator of Israeli activities in the territories. Maj. Gen. Ofir was intimately involved with the negotatiations surrounding the Interim Agreement (Oslo 2). He has liaised closely with West Bank Palestinian Police Chief Hajj Ismail Jaber on the redeployment of IDF forces from major West Bank towns, including (in December 1995) Qalqilyah and Nablus. Ofir is also involved with the setting up of liaison and co-ordination offices in the towns concerned. He joined a joint Israeli–Palestinian security patrol in Jericho, and was encouraged by the way it worked. He firmly believes that many misunderstandings can be resolved through 'one-on-one' communication, out of the limelight.

Ogata, Sadako   Japan
United Nations High Commissioner for Refugees. Sadako Ogata was born in 1927 and became dean of the Faculty of Foreign Studies at Tokyo University, before working as a diplomat and chairing the executive board of UNICEF. She is the first woman to head a major UN agency, and assumed the post for an initial three-year period in January 1991. At the end of 1993 she was re-appointed for another five years. Given that Japan is the second biggest contributor by country to the UNRWA (the premier relief fund for Palestinian refugees), Ogata can be expected to be a valuable expert adviser to the final status talks on refugees, between Israel and the PLO.

Ehud OLMERT

Nationality	Israeli
Religion	Jewish
Place of birth	Binyaminah, south of Haifa, Palestine
Date of birth	1945
Current position	Mayor of Jerusalem
Previous position	Health Minister in Shamir's *Likud* administration, 1988–92
	A successful corporate lawyer before he entered politics
Allies	Strong ties with *Likud* aparatchiks
Position on peace	Although considered to be on the left of the *Likud*, Olmert has been notably antagonistic towards PLO attempts to set up office in Jerusalem
National political importance	Influential in Likud, although sidelined by radicals in 1995
Prospects	Probably still harbours national ambitions, especially after *Likud's* electoral victory in May 1996; certain to play a key role when 'final status' talks begin on Jerusalem

Ehud Olmert ended 28 years of rule by the Labour veteran, Teddy Kollek, as Mayor of Jerusalem. It was interpreted as a protest against the peace process, coming as it did just months after the nation had voted out a *Likud* government in national elections. Olmert's victory owed much to his wooing of the ultra-Orthodox constituency. Most importantly, he will be the city's mayor when its future is discussed in the final status talks with the Palestinians. He is known as one of *Likud*'s leading 'young princes', but untypically he is friendly with many left-wingers in Israel's bohemian circuit. Within *Likud*, Olmert has been characterized as a pragmatic centrist. He toed the party line in voting against the Israel-PLO agreement in 1992. Yet in 1990 he abstained in protest when Rechavam Ze'evi, leader of the *Moledet* party, joined the Shamir cabinet (Ze'evi had called for the 'transfer' of Palestinians from the territories).

Ehud Olmert worked as a lawyer and newspaper columnist before entering the Knesset as a *Likud* member in 1973. From 1988 he served as Minister Without Portfolio and Minister of Health in the outgoing Shamir government. In 1992 he surprised many by defeating Jerusalem's veteran mayor, Teddy Kollek, who had held the post continuously since 1965.

As mayor, Olmert has fiercely opposed the establishment of PLO institutions anywhere in Jerusalem, and in 1995 condemned visitors to Orient House, the putative headquarters of the PLO in Jerusalem. However, he refused to take part in the virulent *Likud*-led anti-peace process rallies of 1995. In 1996 Olmert plans to devote much of his energy on Jerusalem 3000, a festival to mark the holy city's trimillenial celebrations. Inevitably, perhaps, the festival has been seen as a political gesture by left-wing Israelis and Palestinians. Evidently, Olmert disappointed his ultra-Orthodox allies (notably Meir Porush) by not delivering on his promises. However, in May 1996 he was elected as a *Likud* MK, which will strengthen his hand in Jerusalem's affairs.

Olmert, Yossi   Israel

Spokesman for Israeli negotiating team in Madrid; brother of Jerusalem Mayor Ehud Olmert (*q.v.*). Yossi Olmert stressed in 1991 that Israel would not go beyond the Camp David plans for Palestinian autonomy. He won a place on the *Likud* party lists for the May 1996 elections, but failed to enter the Knesset.

Ophir, Gabi

(see Ofir, Gabi)

Orr, Ori   Israel

Deputy Minister of Defence since 1995. Ori Orr was the Chairman of the Knesset Foreign Affairs and Defence Committee prior to taking up his ministerial appointment. Before entering politics, Orr had a distinguished military career, notably as a tank commander in the 1973 war, when he helped to recapture the Golan Heights after initial gains by Syria. As the head of the IDF Northern Command, he set up Israel's south Lebanese security zone in 1985. Later, as the head of the Central Command during the height of the *intifada*, Orr clashed with settlers who wanted to set up autonomous local militias. Orr entered the *Knesset* as a Labour MK, and took over the deputy defence portfolio after the assassination of Yitzhak Rabin prompted a cabinet reshuffle in late November 1995.

Orr is a close ally of Yossi Beilin, and is very positive about the peace process, although he acknowledges the need for caution regarding security matters. He favours returning Golan to Syria as a price worth paying to achieve a real peace with Syria. Orr's own political future depends on the prospects of Syrian negotiations, but it is thought he may seek the Labour Party leadership in the future. As deputy defence minister, Orr served under Shimon Peres (who has added the defence portfolio to his prime ministerial obligations). Immediately on taking office, Orr faced the sensitive task of overseeing the Israeli end of the implementation of the Oslo 2 agreement, in particular, ensuring a relatively trouble-free redeployment of Israeli troops from Palestinian cities and towns in the West Bank. In February 1996, he was given overall responsibility for implementing the 'closure' of PNA areas, following *Hamas* bomb attacks in Jerusalem and Ashkelon.

P

Peled, Rafi   Israel
Appointed Israel's Chief of Police in March, 1993. Peled served in the *Shin Bet* (internal security police) before joining the regular force in 1975. He took over the post of police chief from Ya'akov Terner, who left office under a cloud of scandal. He has since resigned from his post.

Peled, Matityahu   Israel
Member, Israeli Council for Israeli–Palestinian Peace. A retired general, he sought to achieve reconciliation with the Palestinians, as a means of assuring Israeli long-term security.

Peleg, Yisrael   Israel
Director-General of the Israeli Environment Ministry, and head of peace talks on environmental issues. In May 8, 1995, Dr Peleg signed a far-reaching environmental co-operation agreement with his Jordanian counterpart, Dr Duryad Hahsana. The agreement amplified the commitment to protecting joint natural resources, fighting pollution, and countering natural disasters, as set out in the previous October's peace treaty. Peleg was optimistic about future joint development projects in the Gulf of Aqaba, the Arava, the Dead Sea and the Jordan Valley.

Pelletreau, Robert H. Jr   USA
Robert H. Pelletreau, Jr. was sworn in as Assistant Secretary for Near Eastern Affairs on Feb. 18, 1994, thus crowning an illustrious career in the service of the US Department of State (equivalent to foreign office). Since July 31, 1991, he had served as Ambassador Extraordinary and Plenipotentiary to the Arab Republic of Egypt from July 31, 1991. However, it was during his stint as Ambassador to Tunisia (from 1987 to 1991), that Robert Pelletreau first made international news. With the full approval of US Secretary of State George Schultz, Pelletreau launched the first official negotiations between the US government and the PLO, on Dec. 6, 1989. Pelletreau's stewardship of this sensitive role was a mark of the rapport he had built up over many years in the Middle East, and also a sign of the trust his political masters had invested in him.

Shimon PERES

Nationality	Israeli
Religion	Jewish
Place of birth	Vishniva, Poland

Date of birth	1923
Current position	Leader of the opposition Labour Party
Previous positions	Prime Minister of Israel November 1995 to May 29, 1996
	Foreign Minister, Deputy Prime Minister, 1992–95
	Leader of Labour Party when in Opposition, 1990–92
	Foreign Minister, 1986–88 (under Labour-*Likud* rotation agreeement)
	Prime Minister, 1984 to 1986 (under Labour-*Likud* rotation agreeement)
Allies	Yossi Beilin, Avraham Burg, Amnon Shahak
Position on peace	Very positive; helped frame DOP; won Nobel Prize
National political importance	Very influential; was close to Ben Gurion; left of PM Rabin
Prospects	Remains Labour leader, but is likely to face challenges from younger aspirants

Shimon Peres has played a key role throughout Israel's comparitively short history. Most recently, he was the dynamo behind the secret Oslo channel, which led to Israel's historic deal with the PLO in 1993. Peres has been described as 'Israel's only world-class statesman, perhaps Zionism's last pragmatic visionary' (*Jerusalem Report*, July 25, 1991). Technically, he is Prime Minister for the third time, but on none of these occasions has he won the post in the way he would have wished. His narrow electoral defeat in 1996 was interpreted as a rejection of Labour's peace policies; on the personal level it may mark the end of his political career.

He first became caretaker prime minister in 1977, after Yitzhak Rabin, head of government since 1974, was forced to resign after corruption allegations. Peres led the Labour Party and the nation for a few months, only to preside over Labour's first defeat to the *Likud* in general elections. He next became Prime Minister in 1984, after an inconclusive election resulted in a hung parliament, and necessitated an awkward 'government of national unity' with Yitzhak Shamir's *Likud*. Once again, Peres felt hamstrung by having to compromise in government with his natural enemies. All hope of Peres winning outright power seemed dashed in 1992, when, having led the Labour Party for almost two decades, he was ousted by Yitzhak Rabin in party primaries. Rabin went on to win the general election, and Peres had to settle for the role of deputy, and Foreign Minister.

On Nov. 4, 1995, Yitzhak Rabin was killed in Tel Aviv, and Shimon Peres immediately became caretaker prime minister. The Labour Party caucus and the Knesset approved his appointment as full Prime Minister later that month. In 1996, Israel held its first direct elections for prime minister, and Shimon Peres, as the chosen Labour candidate, once again failed to win the commanding public mandate which had so long eluded him.

Although today he is considered as a leading dove, Shimon Peres's earlier years were characterized by hawkishness mixed with pragmatism and much political guile. Born in Poland in 1923, Peres (originally Perski) immigrated to Palestine when he was 13. At 19 he became general secretary of the *Hano'ar Ha'oved* Zionist socialist movement and founded Kibbutz Alumot, where he married Sonia Gelman in 1945. In 1947 he became manpower chief of the *Haganah* (Labour Jewish underground).

Peres soon became a protege of David Ben-Gurion, Israel's first prime minister. After developing a penchant for arms-purchasing, so vital in Israel's War of Independence, Peres rose from defence ministry representative in North America in 1950, to Director General of the entire ministry in 1953. Shimon Peres was elected to the Knesset for the first time in 1959, and immediately became deputy defence minister. In 1965 he joined his mentor, David Ben-Gurion, in a new party, *Rafi*, a hawkish breakaway from *Mapai* (the main Labour group). During the mid-1960s, Peres persuaded the USA to end its arms embargo of Israel, and supply the IDF with vital tanks and planes. From 1969 till 1974, Peres held office as Minister of Immigrant Absorption, Transport and then information in successive governments led by Golda Meir. But national anger over Israel's poor performance in the 1973 Yom Kippur War led to Meir's resignation. In the ensuing Labour leadership elections, Peres lost to Yitzhak Rabin who, thanks to his posting as ambassador to the USA, was not tainted with responsibility for the 1973 war. Nonetheless, Peres continued in office as Defence Minister, and played a leading role in planning the daring rescue of hostages from Entebbe in 1976. When Rabin was forced to step down in 1977, Peres took over as acting prime minister and Labour Party leader. However, his reign was short-lived as Menachem Begin's *Likud* convincingly defeated Labour for the first time in elections that year.

In opposition, Peres campaigned against Begin's policy of expanding settlements. Nonetheless, he supported the Israeli government when it struck a peace deal with Egypt at Camp David (although with some bitterness, as he had assumed this honour should have been his). After Labour narrowly lost the 1981 national election, he fought off calls for resignation, although by now his rivalry with Rabin was out in the open. During the Lebanese war, Peres moved from loyal support of the campaign in 1982 to principled opposition, as it rapidly turned into a quagmire.

With *Likud*'s fortunes on the wane, due to Lebanon and an ailing economy, it lost support, resulting in a 1984 election result of complete deadlock. The only way out was a government of national unity. Under a 'rotation' arrangement, Shimon Peres and Yitzhak Shamir each agreed to be prime minister for two years. Peres was the first prime minister, and during his tenure he succeeded in withdrawing most Israeli troops from Lebanon, and slashing annual inflation from 400% to less than 20%. He went on to act as Foreign Minister from 1986 to 1988, with *Likud's* Yitzhak Shamir as Prime Minister. During this period, Peres made strenuous efforts to achieve the elusive peace breakthrough with the Palestinians.

As Foreign Minister he pursued a more dovish and adventurous course. In 1987, he signed a London Agreement with King Hussein of Jordan, which appeared to offer Palestinians an 'umbrella' under which they could negotiate terms of autonomy with Israel. Unfortunately for Peres, Shamir and his *Likud* allies dashed these plans. Labour lost the 1988 election, and Peres had to accept the lesser portfolio of Finance Minister in a new unity government where *Likud* held the upper hand.

By this stage the *intifada* had taken hold of the territories. While Labour Defence Minister Rabin adopted a hardline approach, Peres positioned himself on the left of the Labour Party and called for compromise and negotiation. In 1990 the tensions between Shamir and Peres became unbearable, and Peres pulled Labour out of the unity government, accusing *Likud* of blocking the peace process. But his attempts to set up a Labour-led coalition were scuppered at the last moment when religious parties, like the Sephardi *Shas*, deserted his cause, following the intervention of the nonagenerian Rabbi Eliezer Shach. For the next two years, Shimon Peres led the Labour Party in opposition.

Shimon Peres lost his fourth encounter with Yitzhak Rabin for party leadership in early 1992; partly as a result of a new system of opening up voting to all Labour party members, which demonstrated Rabin's populist advantages over Peres. It was a particularly galling event for Peres, as Labour went on to win the election of that year. Nonetheless, he settled into his new role as Foreign Minister under Prime Minister Rabin, and confounded sceptics by forming a good working relationship with his longtime arch-rival. By and large, Peres has acted as the more accommodating of the two on the peace process, and it was largely thanks to his pressuring and manoeuvring that Israel signed the historic Oslo accord with the PLO in 1993. It was Peres who gave the go-ahead to his deputy minister and protégé, Yossi Beilin, to initiate the secret talks with the PLO; and Peres again who had to persuade Rabin that the responses from Tunis seemed genuine.

Since then, invariably Peres has been sent in to deal with problems whenever they threaten to destroy the peace process. Unlike the dour, cautious and meticulous Rabin, Peres enjoyed grand gestures and bold ideas, such as his call for Israel to join the Arab League. He has often relied upon what cynics may call 'miracle cures' to achieve peace – developing the Negev Desert at the expense of the Occupied Territories; or relying throughout the 1980s on a 'Jordanian option' to solve the Palestinian problem.

Drawing on his reputation for financial acumen, as seen in his success against hyperinflation, Peres was given the major responsibility of steering the negotiations towards an economic arrangement with the embryonic Palestine Authority. These culminated in the Paris Protocol of April 1994. On Dec. 10, 1994 Peres shared the Nobel Peace Prize with Rabin and Yassir Arafat of the PLO. In 1995 Peres personally negotiated with Yasser Arafat at Taba about Israeli troop redeployment in the territories prior to Palestinian elections. Problems led to repeated missed deadlines, but eventually the two teams reached a compromise, which became known as the Interim Agreement, or Oslo 2.

On Nov. 4, 1995, Yitzhak Rabin was assassinated at a peace rally in Tel Aviv. Peres, who was the other intended target of the assassin, immediately became interim Prime Minister, and was installed as full Prime Minister by unanimous acclaim by the Labour Party and the Knesset. Despite the shock of Yitzhak Rabin's assassination, Peres ensured that Oslo 2 was implemented on schedule, and rejected calls to capitalize on the 'sympathy vote' by calling an early election. He also won unprecedented support in opinion polls for the way in which he sought to heal the nation; and graciously had a public reconciliation with Opposition leader, Benjamin Netanyahu. In reshuffling his cabinet, Peres showed his acumen by balancing hawkish figures (like the new Foreign Minister Ehud Barak) with young left-wing Labourites, like Haim Ramon and Yossi Beilin. In addition, he held out an olive branch to the religious sector, which had felt ostracized after the Rabin assassination, and brought Rabbi Yehuda Amital into his cabinet.

With regard to the Palestinians, Peres proved accommodating, allowing Yasser Arafat to increase the number of Council seats to 88, and redeploying the IDF from six Palestinian cities ahead of schedule. On other matters, Peres has shown a steely side which has surprised critics who felt he was too 'soft' on peace. He insisted on the annulment of the Palestinian Covenant as a precondition for further talks with the PLO, and demanded that Israeli political sovereignty over all of Jerusalem would remain intact. He forced concessions from Egypt on the nuclear arms issue, approved the assassination of *Hamas* bomber, Yehiya Ayyash, and pledged that no settlers would be forcibly removed. Peres ensured that the Oslo 2 impetus carried over to relations with Jordan. The last 'enabling' agreements were signed in January, in time for Israel to host its favourite new ally, King Hussein of Jordan. Peres approved close military ties with the Hashemite Kingdom, and suggested a 'Middle East NATO' with Israel and Jordan at its centre, to isolate Iran and curb Islamic fundamentalism. Peres also showed courage, by addressing head-on the hoary question of Israel's nuclear weapons, and pledged to 'give up the bomb' in exchange for a comprehensive regional peace.

Most surprisingly to some, he restarted the stalled talks with Syria. His ten-point plan spelt out a new 'multipolar' approach, which went beyond the issues of security on the Golan Heights. Above all, he built on the close ties which Rabin had formed with US President Bill Clinton. There was talk of a new strategic pact between the two nations. With the Israeli right apparently stricken with guilt, Peres used his first three months as prime minister to achieve notable breakthroughs – an upgrading of relations with Tunisia and Morocco, a clampdown on Israeli right-wing extremists, a partial rapprochement with the National Religious Party. He also forged new links with the Jewish Diaspora, and hosted state visits by a stream of international leaders. Throughout the peace process, Peres had to steer a narrow path between meeting Palestinian aspirations, ensuring Israel's security, and appeasing the understandable fears of Jewish settlers. He was relieved by the results of the Palestinian election on Jan. 20, 1996, and announced new concessions which allowed PNC figures like Naif Hawatmeh and George Habash to return to the territories.

Shimon Peres believes Israel can play an active role in the Middle East as a technological nexus, a Singapore of the region. His office drew up the grandiose plans for $25 billion investment in the region, unveiled at the MENA economic summit in October 1995 in Jordan. But critics accuse him of naiveté, of failing to recognize the realities of fundamentalists on all sides. Many call him hypocritical, for in the past he was every bit as security-conscious as he condemns his foes for being now. Several Labourites still could not trust him after the apparently devious way in which he undermined Yitzhak Rabin during the 1970s crises.

However, the *Hamas* suicide bombings of February and March roused national despair and anger against the peace process. Peres responded by declaring war on the fundamental-ists, demanding greater action by Arafat, and imposing a total closure on the territories. Once again, he was risking on the one hand offending the Israeli right who accuse him of passivity; and on the other, of undermining the credibility of his peace ally, Arafat, in the supposedly autonomous Palestinian areas. Most painfully for Peres, he found himself compelled by military advisers to impose precisely the separation between Israel and the Palestinians which he had so long opposed, although he stopped short of making it permanent, as Police Minister Shahal seemed to recommend. In April Peres accepted military advice and attacked Lebanon. Ultimately the failure to break Hezbollah, the mission's prime goal, undermined Peres and contributed to his narrow election defeat.

Perry, William J.   **USA**
Defence Secretary in the Clinton administration after Les Aspin resigned in 1994. In 1995 he was given a bigger role in the peace process, as talks between Israel and Syria raised the issue of the Golan Heights. Perry visited Israel and Syria in early 1996, to further the talks between the two countries. He is concerned about how Israel may withdraw from the Golan Heights in a possible peace deal with Damascus, and is responsible for deciding on a role for US troops who may be stationed there as peace-keepers. At the same time, he has to take into account Congress's growing unwillingness to sponsor US forces abroad, especially when US obligations in Bosnia have put a drain on resources, and when huge budget cuts are planned.

Perry favours a ban on nuclear weapons in the Middle East region, but at the same time does not wish to see Israel bereft of defences if Iran possesses nuclear arms. In January 1996 he told Arab ambassadors and journalists in Washington that he was committed to Israel's 'qualititative military edge'. In a meeting with Israel's newly Foreign Minister Ehud Barak, the two men discussed the possibility of a formalized strategic alliance between the USA and Israel; although for the moment this seems like a remote possibility.

Polisar, Dan   **Israel**
Founder of Peace Watch. Dan Polisar was born in the USA and immigrated to Israel, where he worked as a political scientist. In October 1993 he set up Peace Watch as a purportedly dispassionate body to monitor the implementation of the Oslo Accords, and modelled it on Helsinki Watch.

Powell, Colin   **USA**
Chief of Staff during Gulf War and Madrid peace talks. Powell, who was a distinguished soldier in Vietnam, favoured caution initially, and wanted to give sanctions against Iraq 'time to work'. In the end, he directed a successful military campaign, Operation Desert Storm, with General Norman Schwartzkopf; and was praised for his organizational and public relations skills. He is known as a friend of Israel, and enjoys cordial relations with the US Jewish community; he also believes in fostering closer ties with the Arab world. Powell may yet play an important consultancy role in guiding future US foreign policy on the Middle East.

Pressburg, Gail   **USA**
Jewish communal leader and co-director of Peace Now's Centre for Israeli Peace and Security. Pressburg has championed the cause of a two-state solution to the Israeli–Palestinian conflict in the USA.

Preston, Lewis   **USA**
Eighth President of the World Bank, ultimately responsible for the bank's extensive funding programme. The bank pledged an immediate $50 million to the Palestinians in October 1993 as a concessionary credit, and sent experts to investigate the economic situation in the territories. Preston stressed the value of private investment and steered the bank towards funding the development of 'human resources'. He resigned in 1995 while suffering from cancer, and was ultimately replaced as President by James Wolfensohn.

Primakov, Yevgeny   **Russia**
Foreign Minister of Russia since January 1996. Officials in Jerusalem feared that his 'pro-Arab' credentials would reverse Russia's recently improved relations with Israel. Yevgeny Primakov was born as Yona Finkelstein, the son of Jewish parents, in 1929. However, his father died when he was two, and he was not raised as a Jew. After studying Arabic at the Institute for Middle East Studies in Moscow, Primakov (his newly adopted name) worked at the Communist Party newspaper, *Pravda*, notably as its Middle East correspondent in the late 1960s.

After 1970 he became director of the Institute of World Economy and International Relations within the Academy of Sciences. Throughout the 1970s, he held clandestine meetings with Israeli officials, including Prime Minister Rabin. In 1978 he wrote 'The Anatomy of the Conflict in the Middle East', in which he exonerated the PLO's record of violence because of the attitude of Israel's leadership. He also drafted what became known as the Brezhnev Plan for Middle Eastern peace of 1981.

Primakov survived the transition from Brezhnev to his successors, Yuri Andropov, Mikhail Gorbachev and Boris Yeltsin. In June 1989 he was appointed chairman of one of the two USSR Supreme Soviet chambers. In March 1990 he left that post to join Mikhail Gorbachev's short-lived Presidential Council, and was a candidate politburo member. Primakov became known as Gorbachev's main foreign 'trouble-shooter' in the Middle East. Before replacing Andrei Kozyrev as foreign minister, he was the head of Russia's foreign intelligence services, although he had no KGB background.

At his first press briefing since becoming Foreign Minister, Primakov stressed that Russia was still a 'great power'. He is expected to continue with the cooler approach to the West which his predecessor espoused in his final months. Primakov also promised to renew ties with traditional partners in the Middle East, especially Syria, which had lapsed with the collapse of Communism. With his obvious interest and expertise in the region's affairs, Primakov is expected to push for a more active Russian role in the peace process.

Pundak, Ron   **Israel**
Academic active in secret pre-Oslo facilitating talks with Abu 'Ala. Pundak worked with Yair Hirschfeld before the talks, and was closely associated with Yossi Beilin. At the actual Oslo talks, he helped to draft the first version of the Declaration of Principles. He returned to academia after the Washington signing ceremony.

Q

Farouk QADDUMI

Nationality	Palestinian
Alternate spellings	Farouq Qaddumi, Faruq Khaddoumi
Nomme du Guerre	Abu Lutuf
Religion	Muslim
Current position	Nominally second in command of PLO; head of PECDAR
Previous position	Elected Palestinian 'foreign minister' in April 1989
Allies	At times close to Arafat, although currently seen as critic within Fatah
Position on peace	Sceptical; proposed two-state compromise in early 1970s, but in 1980s grew more hardline
National political importance	Functionary role in PNA; but enjoyed prestige in PLO old guard
Prospects	Unlikely to succeed Arafat, but may become figurehead for non-fundamentalist opponents of the Oslo accord

Farouk Qaddumi, like Yasser Arafat, is one of the few remaining founding fathers of *Fatah*. Their partnership goes back to the late 1950s, when Qaddumi worked for the construction company which Arafat formed in Kuwait. He was partly responsible for helping his old colleague and political master forge vital links with Egypt's Gamal Abdel Nasser in 1967. After the assassinations of Abu Jihad in 1988 and then Abu Iyad in 1991, Qaddumi moved into the second place to Arafat himself. When Hafez al-Assad expelled Arafat from Damascus in 1983, he offered to crown Qaddumi as head of the PLO in his stead. Loyally, Qaddumi refused.

Qaddumi's position has often been at variance with Arafat's. In the early 1970s he leaned towards a minimalist two-state option (and *de facto* recognition of Israel), at a time when the rest of the PLO was determined to maintain the armed struggle. In September, 1982, for instance, he openly welcomed aspects of the Reagan Plan while most Damascus-based PLO factions rejected it. However, in recent years he has taken a harder line against deals with Israel. As head of the PLO's political department, his ideological purity contrasted with Arafat's willingness to reach a pragmatic solution. Throughout the 1980s, Qaddumi received ambassadors and even foreign ministers from many Western countries, including Norway, France and Italy. He was formally elected Palestine's 'foreign minister' in June 1989 by a 60-member PLO central council meeting in Tunis.

Qaddumi was notably absent from the podium at the signing of the Declaration of Principles in September 1993. He also abstained from voting for the accords at the PLO Central Committee meeting, held in Tunis in October; and he refused to be a member of the Palestine National Autonomy's cabinet when Yasser Arafat was chosing his ministers in May 1994. Qaddumi nonetheless accepted a post as formal head of PECDAR (the Palestine Economic Council for Development and Reconstruction). On Jan. 7, 1994, Qaddumi signed an economic co-operation agreement on behalf of the PLO with Jordanian Deputy Prime Minister Sa'id al-Tal, which allowed the Central Bank of Jordan supervisory powers over Jordanian banks operating in the West Bank. On Jan. 25, he signed a similar agreement with Egyptian Foreign Minister Amr Moussa. Egypt and the Palestinian entity would treat each other as 'most favoured nation status' in matters of trade; they also studied possible joint projects, and considered the option of making Rafah (on their mutual border) a free trade zone.

But Qaddumi has failed to generate a support base in the territories. Meanwhile, PECDAR's real political power resides with Abu Ala, the PNA Economics Minister, who, unlike Qaddumi, has managed the transition from Tunis with some skill (Abu Libdeh is the PECDAR's effective day-to-day director). Analysts suggest that Qaddumi is 'waiting in the wings' in case the PNA experiment collapses. He will then be ready to restore the PLO to its former role as a liberation organization. As for the present, Qaddumi speaks for the many diaspora Palestinians who feel Oslo 1 and 2 has excluded those living outside 'historic Palestine'.

Qassim, Marwan al-   Jordan

Chief of the Royal Court. Qassim was born in 1938, and after studying at various US universities, he joined the Jordanian Foreign Ministry. He served as Chief of the Royal Court, until becoming foreign minister and deputy prime minister in December, in 1988, returning to the court in the 1990s.

Qichen, Qian   China

Foreign Minister. He visited Jerusalem and forged links with Israel, which culminated in full diplomatic relations in 1992. Born in 1929, he worked as a diplomat in the USSR and Africa, and then joined the Foreign Ministry in 1977, becoming its minister eleven years later. Qian Qichen was a leading figure in the restoration of relations with the USSR. China has yet to play a significant role in the multilateral peace process.

Qirsh, Subhi Abu   Palestinian

PLO deputy representative to Saudi Arabia in 1989; influential in restoring ties with Gulf states after the 1991 war.

Ahmad Suleiman QUREI (Abu 'Ala)

Nationality	Palestinian
Religion	Muslim
Alternative spellings	Kriah, Khreih, Khuri
Place of birth	Safad, Palestine
Date of birth	1935
Current position	Minister of Economic Affairs in the Palestine National Authority
	Elected as Palestinian Council representative in Jerusalem
	Palestinian representative on Oslo 2 Steering Committee
Previous positions	Co-director of PECDAR
	Co-manager with Yasser Arafat of the PLO's finances
	Leader of the PLO negotiating team at secret Oslo peace talks
Allies	Yasser Arafat, Abu Mazen; Israeli opposite number, Uri Savir
Position on peace	Favourable; crucial role in steering initial Oslo talks; with PNA cabinet post, he has a vested interest in seeing peace succeed

National political
importance   Architect of Oslo 2; proponent of private business's role in Gaza and
                                  West Bank economy

Ahmad Qurei (better known by his codename, Abu 'Ala) led the PLO negotiating team during
the secret Oslo talks. From 1994 he held an influential position in the resultant PNA
administration, as Minister for Economic Affairs. Most recently, he led an expanded Palestinian negotiating team in the gruelling talks which culminated in the Israel–PLO Interim
Agreement (Oslo 2), and attended the signing ceremony on Sept. 13, 1995. He is also the
Palestinian representative on the Steering Committee which monitors the implementation of
Oslo 2.

Qurei was earlier based in Beirut, where he headed SAMED, the PLO's employment
project for helping the families of refugees and 'PLO martyrs'. He accompanied Yasser
Arafat to Damascus in 1983, and after 1984, to Tunis. Arafat soon recognized his financial
expertise, and made him head of the PLO's economic department. He relied on Qurei to sort
out the PLO's ailing accounts after Gulf States cut of funds in the wake of the Gulf War.
Arafat posted him to Washington as a member of the PLO steering committee which advised
the official Palestinian negotiators in 1992.

Later that year, Abu 'Ala (Qurei) met Terje Larsen and Yair Hirschfeld in London, and out
of this encounter arose the seeds of the secret Oslo talks. Abu 'Ala gained a reputation as a
tough negotiator in Oslo, but also as someone who was prepared to compromise. Abu 'Ala
initialled the final version with Israeli Foreign Minister Shimon Peres on Aug. 20, 1993. In
subsequent talks, Abu 'Ala conceded Israeli responsibility for the Jordan passage; but
problems about defining the size of the Jericho enclave were posponed until the Cairo and
Taba talks in 1994.

Since the establishment of the Palestine National Authority (PNA) in Gaza and Jericho,
there have been reports of rivalry between Abu 'Ala and Nabil Sha'ath. Both men hold
economics portfolios in the PNA, but it is uncertain which one should be the conduit for
donors seeking to invest in the PNA area. Abu 'Ala's main source of authority lies in his
co-directorship of PECDAR, the Palestinian Economic Council for Development and Reconstruction. Nominally, Farouq Qadummi is its head, but with the assistance of Dr Hassan
Abu Libdeh, Tony Zahlan, and Prof. Samir Abdullah, Abu 'Ala really runs the organization,
and determines priorities for investment in the PNA. Abu 'Ala was largely responsible for the
Palestinian Investment Law, ratified by the PNA on April 30, 1995. He also set up a Higher
Agency for the Promotion of Investment.

Typically, Arafat has played off the two rivals, Sha'ath and Abu 'Ala, and in the process has
made them work hard for their privileged status. Sha'ath was prominent in the first stage
negotiations (over Gaza and Jericho), while Abu 'Ala was the main negotiator in the second
stage (interim self-rule in the West Bank, and preparation for Palestinian Council elections).
The latter agreement owes much of its success to the bond which Abu 'Ala had formed with
his opposite number, Israeli Director General Uri Savir, during the Olso talks. So intense were
the Oslo 2 talks, that Abu 'Ala physically collapsed on the final day. On Aug. 11, 1995, the two
men initialled agreements which settled area demarcations for West Bank villages and the
second stage of IDF redeployment; prisoner release; taxation; a committee on water; amending the Palestinian Covenant; and an understanding on a redeployment in Hebron.

Together with Uri Savir, Abu 'Ala heads the committee which monitors the implementation of Oslo 2. Savir was promoted to chief co-ordinator for the peace process, following the
Rabin assassination, and, because of their connections, this has probably bolstered the status
of Abu 'Ala within the PLO hierarchy. Abu 'Ala almost certainly harbours higher political
ambitions, but he is not thought to enjoy a mass support base in the territories. He nonetheless
was placed top the list of Palestine Council members for Jerusalem, when final results were
announced on Feb. 12, 1996 (immediately after the Jan. 20 poll, Hanan Ashrawi was believed
to have come first). Abu 'Ala is expected to be a major force during final status talks, which are
due to start after May 1996. He holds strong views on the issue of equitable distribution of
water. Back in April 1993, he told delegates to multilateral talks in Geneva that there shoud be
an international commission to investigate the issue, before dealing with any other areas.

Economic management remains his strong suit. By supporting private enterprise industrial zones in Palestinian territories, Abu 'Ala has endeared himself to expatriate Palestinian

and other private investors. He also favours closer links with Israel. On both these issues, he has antagonized the strong leftist caucus within the PLO. His future thus very much depends on the fate of the unfolding peace process, and the fortune of his main mentor, Yasser Arafat.

R

Rabie, Mohammed   USA

A Palestinian American who launched a private initiative in 1988 to achieve talks between the USA and PLO. Rabie acted in response to King Hussein's announcement that Jordan would sever its legal ties to the West Bank. He took his proposed conditions for talks (with US State Department responses, stipulating PLO adherence to UN 242, recognition of Israel and renunciation of terrorism) to Arafat in Tunis. He later dovetailed with the Swedish Foreign Minister, Sven Anderssen, and ultimately, he helped to set the ball rolling for the first US–PLO talks in Tunis in late 1989.

Rabin, Leah   Israel

Widow of the late Prime Minister Yitzhak Rabin. Since the assassination of her husband, Leah Rabin came to symbolize the nation's grief, especially through her stoic presence at the funeral, accompanied by her grandaughter, Noa Ben-Artzi Philosof.

Yitzhak RABIN

Nationality	Israeli
Religion	Jewish
Place of birth	Jerusalem, Palestine
Date of birth	March 1, 1922
Position	Prime Minister of Israel since July 1992
Previous positions	Chief of Staff, 1964 to the end of 1967
	Israeli Ambassador to Washington, 1968–73
	Prime Minister of Israel, 1974–77
	Defence Minister
Allies	Closest advisor, Shimon Shevis; Ehud Barak
Position on peace	Positive; accepted DoP; won Nobel Prize
National political importance	Very influential; holds many portfolios

Yitzhak Rabin, twice prime minister of Israel, will be remembered as one of the chief architects of the Middle East peace process. His assassination on Nov. 4, 1995, also made him the first major martyr of the cause of peace in recent years. In the aftermath of the shocking event, Israelis and Palestinians have come to realize what a crucial role Rabin played in the region's affairs, a role which went back to the very creation of the Jewish state. To many observers, Rabin's transformation from soldier to peace-maker symbolized the profound changes taking place in the contemporary Middle East. An unprecedented gathering of international leaders came to Jerusalem to pay homage to the man at his funeral. Nonetheless, he had his detractors. His murder by a right wing Jewish opponent marked the depth of division in Israeli society over the peace process. And while Arab leaders, like King Hussein, Hosni Mubarak and Yasser Arafat, mourned Rabin's departure, in 'the street' there remained large numbers who could not forgive him for his role during the *intifada* and the various Arab–Israeli wars.

Yitzhak Rabin enjoyed the distinction of being Israel's first native-born prime minister. He was born in Jerusalem into a Socialist Zionist family, and raised in Tel Aviv. After studying at the Kadoorie Agricultural College, he joined the *Haganah* (Jewish military guard) under Moshe Dayan.

During the first Arab–Israeli war (known in Israel as the War of Independence), Yitzhak Rabin led the Harel Brigade in an operation which relieved an Arab blockade on the road to

Jerusalem. He then took over the formerly Arab neighbourhoods of Katamon and Sheikh Jarrah. Later in the war, Rabin saw action in Lod and Ramle, and also led a counter-offensive against the Egyptian Army, which gained the Negev and the Red Sea port of Eilat in the south. When he was just 26, Lt-Col Rabin was entrusted with negotiating a post-war armistice with Egypt in 1949. This marked the beginning of his long career in Israeli politics.

However, for the next two decades, the military remained his chief domain. In Israeli lore, his finest hour came in June, 1967, when he oversaw Israel's decisive victory in the Six Day War.

Yitzhak Rabin retired from the military on Jan. 1, 1968, and for the next five years he served as Israel's ambassador in Washington. There he built up vital ties with US politicians and leaders of the powerful US Jewish community. The posting also groomed him for political life; and fortuitously meant that he was 'otherwise engaged' during the 1973 Yom Kippur War. Thus while other Labour figures, including Prime Minister Golda Meir and Defence Minister Moshe Dayan, were blamed for not foreseeing a war which Israel almost lost, Rabin had clean hands. In barely six months, Rabin rose from Knesset novice (he was elected as a Labour MK in December 1973) to Prime Minister. In April 1974 he became Minister of Labour, and after Meir was forced to resign, it was Yitzhak Rabin who took her place on June 2, 1974, beating off a challenge from the politically more experienced Shimon Peres.

As Prime Minister, Rabin signed disengagement agreements with Egypt and Syria in 1974, and an interim agreement with Egypt in 1975. In that same year, Israel and the USA signed their first Memorandum of Understanding, in part a by-product of Rabin's excellent relations with Washington. In June 1976 Rabin signed the order for 'Operation Entebbe', which freed hijacked air passengers in Uganda. However, his premiership was blighted by problems inherited from his predecessors, notably, a string of economic scandals, and national malaise after the Yom Kippur War. When the press leaked the news that his wife, Leah, kept a bank account in the US (a practice which was banned under contemporary Israeli law), Rabin resigned in April 1977. He handed over the Labour leadership and acting premiership to his deputy and long-time foe, Shimon Peres, only to see Labour lose the elections to Menachem Begin's *Likud*, in May 1977.

Many now considered Rabin a spent force, but he continually challenged Peres for the Labour leadership, wrote his memoirs, and gradually rebuilt his power-base amongst Labour hawks while the party languished in opposition. Rabin entered the National Unity Government (or *Likud*-Labour coalition) as Minister of Defence, in September 1984, serving initially under Prime Minister Peres, and then, after, 1986, under Yitzhak Shamir. In January 1985 he proposed the withdrawal of IDF forces from most of Lebanon, and helped to establish an Israeli–controlled 'security zone' in the south. After the outbreak of the Palestinian *intifada* in Gaza and the West Bank in December 1987, Rabin won a new reputation for toughness. He told troops to 'break the bones' of stone-throwers, which brought him plaudits from conservatives and brickbats from liberals. Defending his stance, Rabin said this was a more humane alternative to the usual approach, employed throughout the world, of using live ammunition against demonstrators and insurgents. In 1989 he published a programme for phased negotiations with the Palestinians, which Shamir adopted as the basis for his first peace plan.

In 1990 Rabin returned to the opposition benches, when the coalition government collapsed over differences regarding the peace process. He was elected Chairman (leader) of the Labour Party after the party held its first nationwide primaries, in February 1992. It was Rabin's fourth attempt to unseat Peres for the leadership, and demonstrated his widespread support amongst the Labour rank and file. Four months later, in June 1992, Yitzhak Rabin led the party to victory in national elections, returning Labour to overall power for the first time in 16 years.

Yitzhak Rabin proved to be a political phoenix; on returning to power, he was determined to make up for lost time. His political persona had not essentially changed – he still combined toughness, pragmatism and dedication to Israel's security with an unwillingness to delegate difficult decisions. Friends often worried about his stressful lifestyle – working up to 12 hours a day, eating sporadically and chain-smoking – yet he would confound them with his extraordinary energy, and grasp of details.

His first task was to fashion a coalition government out of very differing elements. His own

Labour party had won a convincing but not an absolute majority. Thus Rabin was forced to incorporate into his cabinet both the *Meretz* grouping (secular and left-wing), and the *Shas* party (ultra-Orthodox Sephardi). In ensuing years Rabin found himself playing the role of broker between these ill-suited political bedfellows. Usually, internal issues of religious policy, labour relations and education formed the battleground for intra-governmental strife, rather than the peace process.

In addition, Rabin relied on the tacit support of left-wing and anti-Zionist Arab parties, a situation which prompted the right-wing opposition to question his 'patriotism'. Rabin also faced opposition, both internally and externally, for assuming several ministerial portfolios (initially defence and interior, and later, for a while, religious affairs) in addition to the premiership. But he left the Foreign Minister portfolio to his former rival, Shimon Peres, who also served as deputy prime minister. Indeed, the Rabin–Peres axis, often depicted as the union of opposites, proved to be one of the strongest features of his rule. By and large, Peres was seen as the visionary, and together with his dynamic deputy, Yossi Beilin, he was given a broad brief to pursue avenues for expanding the peace process. Rabin, meanwhile, stood for extreme caution, and with his deputy Defence Minister Mordechai Gur, he tried to reassure the right that security remained Israel's top priority.

Palestinians in the territories cautiously welcomed Rabin's election, but were keen to see action rather than words. In December 1992 Rabin upset them, and some members of his own cabinet, by deporting to Lebanon some 415 alleged Muslim fundamentalists from Gaza. Rabin eventually backed down in the face of international condemnation, and effectively rescinded the deportation orders within a year. Many Palestinians felt the deportations belied Rabin's dovish election promises, and showed that his peace policy lacked substance. However, Rabin did manage to wrong-foot his right-wing foes; he seemed to be true to his word about not compromising on security (the deportations followed a string of *Hamas* kidnappings and killings).

Rabin continued with the Madrid peace track, but largely kept the same officials who had negotiated for the previous Shamir government. Significantly, however, he replaced the hawkish Yossi Ben-Aharon with the more moderate Prof. Itamar Rabinovich at the talks with Syria, signalling a new desire for a breakthrough over the Golan issue. Similarly, Rabin accepted Faisal al-Husseini as part of the official Palestinian delegation; until then, the *Likud* had blocked Husseini's participation, because he was from East Jerusalem, and was an open supporter of the PLO. Even so, the deadlock in the Washington talks led to fury in the territories, and a revival of the *intifada* in 1993. Rabin somewhat grudgingly realized that Israel's only alternative to the cycle of violence was talks with the PLO. He lifted the ban on contacts with the PLO, and cautiously approved of Yossi Beilin's secret channel talks in Oslo.

As with the expulsions, many of Rabin's biggest decisions were taken unilaterally. These included closing the territories in March 1993, and Operation Accountability against *Hezbollah* in Lebanon, in July 1993. His most momentous decision was his recognition of the PLO in September 1993, by signing the Declaration of Principles in Washington. (The story of the secret Oslo talks which led to the signing is dealt with elsewhere in this book.) Rabin also aided the process, by accepting immediate autonomy for Jericho, in exchange for a PLO promise to delay talks on final borders, Jerusalem, refugees and settlements until 1996. Peres sealed the Oslo agreement, but Rabin's handshake with PLO Chairman Yasser Arafat in Washington came to symbolize the breakthrough that had been achieved. Finally, the mutual trust between President Bill Clinton and Yitzhak Rabin, as well as the growing friendship between Rabin and Egyptian President Mubarak, were all crucial factors in Rabin's decision to bury the hatchet with the PLO.

In 1994, Yitzhak Rabin played an active role in implementing the peace process. He held direct talks with Yasser Arafat whenever the process seemed to be flagging. He also involved the army at the highest level, making IDF Deputy Chief of Staff Amnon Shahak a chief negotiator, so as to allay the security suspicions of the Israeli public. The Hebron massacre of February threatened to stop the talks altogether (numerous deadlines had been missed, and Palestinian frustration was growing). But Rabin's swift action to ban *Kach* and other extremist Jewish groups persuaded the PLO and Arabs to resume talks, and in May he joined Arafat on a new podium, in Cairo, to initial the Gaza-Jericho Accords. On July 25 he held his first public meeting with King Hussein of Jordan, and on Oct. 26, he signed the historic peace treaty between the State of Israel and the Hashemite Kingdom at Wadi Araba. In December Rabin shared the Nobel Prize for Peace with Shimon Peres and Yasser Arafat.

By late 1994, Rabin had earmarked peace with Syria as his next target. He sent his trusted Chief of Staff Ehud Barak to negotiate with his Syrian opposite number, Hikmat Shihabi Rabin devised a plan based on 'four legs of a table', but primarily emphasized the need for ironcast security guarantees before Israel would withdraw from the Golan Heights. President Assad baulked at what he saw as 'intervention' in Syria's internal affairs, and called off the talks. US Secretary of State Warren Christopher engineered a revival of talks in April 1995 but these too failed to make much headway. Rabin offered to hold a national referendum in Israel before conceding the Golan to Syria, but this also offended Damascus, and he later dropped the plan. By August, Rabin in effect placed the Syrian talks 'on hold', after only narrowly defeating a Knesset vote which would have placed huge restraints on his ability to sign a peace treaty with Syria.

Increasingly, Rabin relied on advice from the military establishment and tended to sidestep his cabinet colleagues. His bureau chiefs, Shimon Shevis and Eitan Haber, protected him from unwelcome intrusions, and planned his increasingly hectic timetable. When Ehud Barak entered the cabinet in July, 1995, many saw him as Rabin's chosen heir. By late 1995, Rabin concentrated on achieving the often delayed Interim Agreement (Oslo 2) with the PLO Shimon Peres led high-level negotiations but, once again, Rabin's personal intervention proved crucial in seeing that the agreement was signed, on Sept. 28, 1995. The reams of stipulations on security in the 350-page document seem to bear Rabin's hallmark.

Oslo 2 went considerably further than Oslo 1 in extending real power to the PNA. As a consequence, a new mood of militancy swept the settler community of the West Bank. They held hilltop demonstrations in the territories, and huge anti-Rabin rallies in Israel proper Increasingly, their protests took the form of personal attacks on Rabin as a 'traitor' and even 'murderer'. At the same time, Rabin had to fight a rearguard action within his own party, led by MKs in a group called The Third Way. They threatened to desert and thus deprive Labour of its narrow majority, if it 'compromised' on the Golan.

On Nov. 4, 1995, Yitzhak Rabin attended a huge rally in Tel Aviv, organized by Peace Now supporters. It was the first time in months that the normally dour and cautious Rabin had come out so unequivocally on the side of the 'peace camp'. On returning to his car, Rabin was shot and fatally wounded by three gunshots. He died hours later in the Ichilov Hospital Rabin's assassin was Yigal Amir, a young law student and sympathiser of the far right religious settler movement.

The murder created a sense of national trauma which will probably last for years to come Ironically, it also gave Rabin's successor, Shimon Peres, an enormous mandate for carrying on with the peace process – something which Rabin never really enjoyed in his lifetime, and precisely the opposite to what Amir had intended. Yitzhak Rabin's grave has become a place of pilgrimage for many young Israelis, who saw in his death the importance of the peace process.

Rabinovich, Itamar   Israel
Ambassador to the USA since early 1993; and chief negotiator with Syria on political issues Itamar Rabinovich was born into a highly politicized Jerusalem family in 1942.

He studied at UCLA in Los Angeles and later became a visiting professor at Cornell University. Through his attendance at academic conferences, he became friendly with a range of political and diplomatic figures. This served him well during his tenure as head of the newly established Tel Aviv University Dayan Centre for Middle Eastern Studies, from 1983 to 1989 Colleagues nicknamed him 'the Senator' because of his tall and dignified appearance, and the charm with which he persuaded donors to fund the prestigious centre. Meanwhile, he revealed his interest in the current peace process, through his 1992 book, *The Road Not Taken* (an analysis of missed diplomatic opportunities during Israel's early years).

After Labour's electoral victory, Prime Minister Rabin chose Rabinovich to replace Yoss Ben-Aharon as Israel's chief negotiator with the Syrian delegation, at the sixth round of their bilateral taks in Washington, in August 1992. Syrian negotiators reported an immediate improvement in atmosphere, and praised Rabinovich for his astuteness and sensitivity However, right-wing politicians in Israel criticized him for not raising the issue of *Hezbollah* attacks with Syria; and academic rivals said he was too self-serving and compliant to his political masters. In early 1993 Rabinovich took over from another *Likud* appointee, Zalman Shoval, to become Israeli Ambassador to the USA, while retaining his role as negotiator. Rabinovich enjoyed good relations with both Peres and Rabin; in fact, he was the latter's Sunday tennis partner for many years. Nonetheless, the early promise of a 'Syrian breakthrough' failed to materialize, and Rabinovich was somewhat sidelined when, from late 1994, Rabin chose to concentrate on the security aspects of a possible Golan deal with Damascus. While Rabinovich concentrated on nurturing Israel's ties with the Clinton administration, Israel's military chiefs of staff (first Ehud Barak, and later Amnon Shahak) enjoyed the limelight in talks with their Syrian counterpart, Hikmat Shihabi. With the appointment of Shimon Peres as Prime Minister in November 1995, Israel launched a new 'multipolar' offensive to achieve peace with Syria. Rabinovich was sure to play a larger role in talks during 1996, but after *Likud's* victory in May he was said to be considering resigning.

Rafsanjani, Ali Akbar Hashemi   Iran

President of Iran since August 1989. Rafsanjani was born in 1934, in Iran's south-eastern desert region, near Kerman. He studied theology under Ayatollah Khomeini at the seminary in Qom, and supported the ayatollah after he was exiled in 1963. In 1977, Rafsanjani began organizing opposition movements in preparation for Khomeini's return from Paris, and in July 1979 he entered the cabinet of the new revolutionary Shi'ite fundamentalist regime. From 1980 to 1989 he was the Speaker of the Islamic Consultative Assembly, the *Majlis*.

Technically, Rafsanjani took over as president from the more militant cleric, Ayatollah Seyed Ali Khameini. (The latter assumed the late Khomeini's mantle as *Vali Faqih*, or supreme spiritual leader.) In practical terms, Rafsanjani has turned the presidency into the main source of authority in Iran. President Rafsanjani has been markedly more conciliatory towards the West than his predecessor. In 1990 he became the central figure in ensuring the release of Western hostages who were held in Beirut. Rafsanjani has cautiously encouraged free enterprise inside Iran, to alleviate the country's economic problems, and satisfy a nation which has grown weary of an revolutionary fervour.

In recent years, Rafsanjani has cemented ties with Syria, especially with General Khaddam. Iran continues to condemn any peace deal with Israel; and the West remains fearful of the Islamic republic's nuclear potential, and sponsorship of terror organizations (like *Hezbollah* in Lebanon, and *Hamas* amongst the Palestinians). Yet for the same reason, optimists suggest that Rafsanjani and his loyal ally, the Foreign Minister Ali Akbar Velayati, may use their influence to achieve a breakthrough in Israel's peace talks with Syria and Lebanon, by reining in *Hezbollah* – provided that Iran gets something in return. Rafsanjani is due to stay in office until 1997. He may well be called on to continue, if no one else is found to bridge the emerging schisms in the once monolithic edifice of Teheran's Islamic revolution.

Rahim, Tayyeb Abd al-   Palestinian

Secretary General of the PNA. Rahim, now 51, is responsible for 'presidential affairs' in the Palestine Authority. Although something of a surprise appointment, he has a long record of loyalty to Yasser Arafat, which made him a 'safe pair of hands' in the interim phase of Palestinian self-rule. Rahim is a *Fatah* veteran, and served as the PLO envoy to Jordan, where he was regarded as Arafat's 'point man'. He now represents Tulkarm in the Palestine Council.

Rahman, Ahmed Abd al-   Palestinian

Official spokesman of Yassir Arafat.

Rahman, Hassan Abd al-   Palestinian

Former PLO 'ambassador' in Washington, replaced in 1992. Rahman worked at the PLO's United Nations office, and by the early 1980s had replaced the less telegenic Hatem Husseini as the PLO's spokesperson and unofficial representative in US political circles. When the Reagan administration shut down the PLO's offices, Rahman worked under the auspices of the Arab League. Part of his job was to sound out the US Jewish community about its possible role as a bridge to Israel. Rahman, a close ally of Farouk Qaddumi, left for Canada in 1992, having been accused of nepotism and embezzlement. He subsequently returned to Washington, although his current role is not well defined.

Ragheb, Ali Abu el-   Jordan
Jordanian Minister of Industry and Trade. On Oct. 26, 1995, after months of hard negotiation, Ragheb signed a trade accord with his Israeli counterpart, Micha Harish. He secured safeguards against 'dumping' and unfair competition due to Israeli subsidies (many Jordanians had feared that Israel's heavily capitalized industries would overwhelm the weaker Jordanian economy). The agreement allowed for the first exchange of goods between the two countries in 46 years, and opened the door to joint ventures, as promised in the peace treaty signed a year earlier. The trade deal was signed on the eve of the economic summit in Amman. Ragheb survived the cabinet reshuffle of February 1996, and holds a seat in the Jordanian Assembly.

Jibril RAJOUB

Nationality	Palestinian
Religion	Muslim
Place of birth	Hebron (Palestinian land, then under Jordanian rule)
Date of birth	1953
Current position	Head of the Palestinian Preventive Security Apparatus in Jericho, and effectively security boss-in-waiting for all of the West Bank
Previous positions	*Fatah* activist since 1970; head of *Fatah* in West Bank, 1985–88; assistant to the late Abu Jihad, in Tunis
Allies	Locally, Sari Nusseibeh; trusted by Arafat as main figure in Jericho
Position on peace	Pragmatic – sees peace with Israel as framework to build local Palestinian strength in the West Bank
National political importance	Regarded by some as the most powerful *Fatah* figure in West Bank; established local credentials during *intifada*, and is also trusted by Tunis-based external PLO
Prospects	Wields considerable effective power; political ambitions outside security

Colonel Jibril Rajoub probably wields more real power than any other Palestinian in the West Bank. As head of Jericho's Preventive Security Apparatus, he is responsible for maintaining law and order in the area. During his two years in charge, Rajoub has established a reputation for toughness and innovation. Critics accuse him of exceeding his brief and kidnapping suspects from elsewhere in the West Bank. However, he is clearly trusted by Arafat, and has been given a virtually free reign to set up an indigenous police force in the area. The Colonel takes pride in his record of preventing terror attacks on Israel by dissident Palestinians (unlike his counterparts in Gaza). He is also a *Fatah* man through and through, who earned his spurs as an *intifada* activist in the late 1980s.

Born in Hebron in 1953, Jibril Rajoub joined the 'armed struggle' against Israel in 1970 and spent 17 years in Israeli prisons. There he rose to the top of Fatah's prison committees, where he learnt Hebrew and English. After his release in 1985, as part of the 'Ahmed Jibril exchange', he became head of *Fatah* in the West Bank. Israel deported him in 1988 for his role in the early days of the *intifada*. He moved to the PLO headquarters in Tunis, where he served as assistant to Abu Jihad, who was in effect Arafat's second-in-command, and who was responsible for the territories. After the latter's assassination, Rajoub assumed many of his late master's duties. Together with Akram Haniyeh, Rajoub acted as a middleman between Faisal al-Husseini and Yasser Arafat, during the fraught negotiations over who should be in the Palestinian delegation to the Madrid talks, in October 1991. Rajoub returned to the territories in late 1993, and was given the post of head of security for Jericho; he is also regarded by many as effectively head of *Fatah* in the West Bank.

Rajoub has stamped his authority on Jericho, and his authority has extended beyond its borders. He has deliberately used mainly local Palestinians ('insiders'), allies from his *intifada* days, rather than soldiers from the official Palestine Liberation Army (who have spent the last three decades in exile, and thus are less familiar with local realities). Rajoub quickly outlawed illegal possession of arms, confiscating from some users and granting permits to others. He played no role in negotiations with Israel, but is committed to obeying the stipulations of the interim agreement, including not removing Jewish settlements or settlers. However, he is sure that they cause trouble in the area and should go; although he has said that Israeli visitors or tourists to Jericho and the West Bank have nothing to fear.

At his headquarters in Akbat Jaber, a half-abandoned refugee camp outside Jericho, Raboub is planning an élite military academy. He chose the respected philosopher and seasoned political activist, Professor Sari Nusseibeh, to design the two year programme for this 'West Point' of Palestine. Nusseibeh's sophistication and dovish reputation contrasts with Rajoub's brusqueness. Nonetheless, the two have forged a strong alliance, together with Abed Alloun, a psychology graduate, *Fatah* activist in East Jerusalem and public relations officer for Rajoub. Jewish settlers may fear his expansionist ambitions, and many Palestinians fear his alleged abuse of democratic rights in the area; nonetheless, with his charisma and the backing of Arafat, Rajoub seems set to wield enormous influence in years to come.

Ramon, Haim   Israel

Rising Labour politician, dovish aspirant for party and national leadership. Haim Ramon was born Haim Vishnia in a poor neighbourhood of Jaffa in 1950. He served in the Israel Air Force from 1968 to 1973, and then studied law at Tel Aviv University. From 1978 to 1984 he led the Israel Labour Party Young Guard, and first entered the Knesset in 1983. Two years later he founded the dovish *Kfar Hayarok* group with Nissim Zvilli. After the 1988 elections, Ramon became chairman of the Labour Knesset faction. He also unofficially led a group of young technocratic Labour MKs, known as the Group of Seven. Fellow members included Yossi Beilin, Avraham Burg and Hagai Meirom. As the *intifada* took its toll on national morale, and relations with Egypt worsened, the group attempted to right matters with a trip to Cairo, where they met leading Egyptian government figures. Ramon and his allies threatened to leave the party and join the embryonic *Meretz* group, unless certain reforms were adopted at the November 1991 party conference. In response, the party formulated a more assertive pro-peace stance, and Ramon's group stayed in the party. After Rabin defeated Peres in the party primaries, Ramon joined the 'inner circle' and, with his populist support, helped assure Labour victory in the 1992 elections.

Haim Ramon was made Minister of Health in the new cabinet. He tried but failed to introduce a national health law. Resigning his seat in protest, he led a campaign against the *Histadrut* labour federation and Labour establishment, and blamed them for a doctrinaire attitude which had ossified the Israeli socio-economic system. Efraim Sneh became Health Minister in his place in June 1993. Ramon led two other MKs in a Labour breakaway, called the *Ram* or New Life List, after he was expelled from the party in April, 1994. In May, Ramon won a surprise victory against a Labour old guard, to become chairman of the *Histadrut*. After Yitzhak Rabin's assassination in November 1995, Ramon's group decided to rejoin the main Labour caucus. Ramon became the new Interior Minister under Prime Minister Shimon Peres, on Nov. 21, 1995. He also joined an inner cabinet 'peace process team', together with fellow ministers, Ehud Barak, Moshe Shahal, Yossi Sarid and Yossi Beilin. Some blame Ramon for mismanaging Labour's 1996 election campaign.

Abdul Aziz Ali RANTISI

Nationality	Palestinian
Religion	Muslim
Place of Birth	Yebna (Jibna), Palestine
Date of Birth	1947
Current position	Lecturer in the science faculty, Islamic University of Gaza; leading spokesman for *Hamas*
Previous position	Chief paediatrician, government hospitals, Khan Yunis, 1976–86
Allies	Sheikh Yassin; Islamists within Israel proper
Position on peace	Rejects Oslo peace deal; but may a favour political role for *Hamas*
National political importance	Influence has diminished since the deportations

Prospects   Important in Gaza; fundamentalist who may co-operate with PNA

Abdul Aziz Ali Rantisi leapt into the world's headlines when he and 413 other alleged members of Palestinian Islamic militant groups were deported to south Lebanon by the new Rabin regime in Israel. Soon he became well known as official spokesman for the deportees' camp, and was released later in 1993.

Rantisi was born to a poor family in Jibna in 1947. They were displaced in the war which began that year, and moved first to a tent-site in Khan Yunis, and later to various UNWRA camps in Gaza, which is where he made his home. Rantisi studied medicine at the University of Alexandria in Egypt, graduating in 1971. There he was greatly influenced by the Muslim Brotherhood. Embued with his new Islamist beliefs Rantisi returned to Gaza, where he worked as a general practitioner in government hospitals from 1972 to 1974.

Rantisi spent about four years in jail during the *intifada* for helping to set up *Hamas*, the fundamentalist organization which challenged the hegemony of the PLO in the Gaza uprising. On his release from prison in December 1991, Rantisi resumed his political activities, leading a protest against Palestinian participation in the Madrid peace track. He helped lead a local campaign to protest against the lack of paediatric facilities in Gaza, and claims that Israel has refused to allow Gazans to run their own private hospitals.

Rantisi was one of more than 400 Islamic fundamentalists who were deported to a camp in Marj al-Zahour in south Lebanon, and soon became the *de facto* spokesman for the group. As such he managed to keep international pressure on Israel to rescind the deportation order. In April 1993 he called Hanan Ashrawi and Faisal al-Husseini 'traitors' for returning to the Washington peace talks while most deportees were still in Lebanon. (Since then, he seemed to offer the PLO an olive branch, by calling it 'a national Palestinian achievement' whose structure should be 'redefined on a democratic basis'.) An embarrassed Prime Minister Rabin of Israel was forced to allow the last deportees to return by the end of 1993 (although Rantisi was immediately placed under six months' administrative detention). Rantisi is committed to a theocratic Muslim Palestinian state and remains determined in his opposition to Israel. Within *Hamas*, he was regarded as a supporter of the organisation's participation in the promised Palestinian elections; but in recent years he appeared to have been eclipsed by other spokesmen, notably Mahmoud al-Zahar.

Rashid, Muhammed   Palestinian

Influential broker for deals between Israeli companies and the PNA. Rashid, who also is known as Khaled Salaam, or Kurd Islam (a reference to his Kurdish roots) works closely with Yossi Ginossar, a former *Shin Bet* official. Critics accuse the pair of questionable behaviour such as 'freezing out' rival companies, awarding unfair monopolies to others, and siphoning off hefty commissions. Rashid enjoys close personal ties with Yasser Arafat, and accompanied him in Beirut and Tunis, at one stage serving as his press secretary. He is also close to Col Muhammed Dahlan, head of Preventive Security in Gaza, who effectively controls entry points to the area. Officially, Rashid is the head of the Palestinian Commercial Services Corporation, which was set up by the PNA to centralize the import of major commodities and thereby control taxation better. Rashid often travels to Europe and the USA on business as a senior PNA 'economics adviser', he has a VIP pass from Israel. Several Palestinians notably Samir Hulleileh and Hanna Siniora, have criticized Rashid for impeding free trade and establishing unfair monopolies in the autonomous areas.

Raviv, Avishai   Israel

Head of *Eyal,* Jewish underground anti-peace deal group. A law student at Bar Ilan University, he had been expelled from Tel Aviv University for organizing demonstrations. Raviv was arrested in November 1995 on charges in connection with the Rabin assassination. He denied any knowledge of the event, and rejected accusations of being behind a conspiracy.

Rawabdeh, Abdul Raouf al-   Jordan

Deputy Prime Minister and Education Minister until February 1996. Rawabdeh is also Secretary-General of the centrist Reawakening Party. He represented the governate of Irbid in the Lower House, and ran in the 1993 elections. Apart from that exception, the party chose not to nominate other members for the elections. Although he supported the peace treaty with Israel, he was subsequently cool on fostering educational ties with the Jewish state.

Reagan, Ronald USA
Two-term President of the USA, who held office from 1981 to 1989. Ronald Wilson Reagan was born in 1911, acted in Hollywood films, and became a Republican Governor of California. He won the Republican Party's nomination for president in 1980 and convincingly defeated the incumbent Democrat President Jimmy Carter at the polls. He is best remembered for his right-wing political agenda, which called for a return to family values at home, and American strength against the Communist 'evil empire' abroad. In economic terms, he sought to cut back on 'big government' and reduce taxes; but by the time he left office, he had bequeathed to the nation its largest balance of payments deficit in history.

On the Middle East, he was, according to his first Secretary of State, Alexander Haig, Israel's greatest friend ever. In 1982 he assured Menachem Begin that the US would guarantee Israel's military superiority. Arab commentators believed he had given Israel the 'green light' to invade Lebanon that year. At the same time, President Reagan promulgated several plans for peace in the Middle East, including his own 'Reagan Plan' in September 1982, and the Schultz Plan of May 1985 (George Schultz being the US Secretary of State at the time). Both plans envisaged Palestinian autonomy, possibly in a federation with Jordan; they also demanded that Arab states recognize Israel. These initiatives resulted in a new dialogue of proposal and counter-proposal with Israel and the Arabs, but ultimately floundered in the wake of the Lebanese war. Reagan sent US troops into Lebanon, but after a series of suicide bomb attacks on their barracks, they withdrew in 1984.

Towards the end of his second term, Reagan adopted stances which worried his Israeli allies. In December 1988 he sanctioned the first official talks between the USA and the PLO, in Tunis. He also waived objections from Congress and the pro-Israel lobby, by supplying advanced AWACS surveillance aircraft to Saudi Arabia. When American citizens were held hostage by Shi'ite radicals in Lebanon, Reagan arranged a secret 'arms for hostages' deal with Iran, the paymasters of *Hezbollah*. This flagrantly contradicted his stated policy of 'no deals with terrorists'. The affair was known variously as Irangate, or Contragate (as it also involved illegal US arms supplies to right-wing guerillas in Nicaragua). Evidently Israel acted as a broker between the USA and Iran, although Israel and Iran were supposed to be sworn enemies.

Rhein, Eberhard Germany
Head of the European Union's department for the Mediterranean, Near and Middle East. At the Mediterranean conference held in Barcelona in late November 1995, Rhein proposed a free trade zone covering 30 countries, to come into effect by 2010. The plan involves Israel and Arab coastal states, and intends to harmonize rules on currency, banking and intellectual property. Rhein was a professor at Hamburg University, and now co-ordinates EU involvement in the multilateral peace talks.

Rifai, Omar Abdul-Monem Jordan
Omar Abdul-Monem Rifai replaced Marwan Muasher as Jordan's Ambassador to Israel, in February 1996. Rifai, 43, was educated at Harvard and Georgetown Universities in the USA. His father and cousin were prime ministers. Rifai served in Jordanian embassies in Cairo, Berne, London and Washington, and he was a member in Jordan's peace delegation. Before taking up his current appointment, Rifai was the co-ordinator for the Middle East peace process and director of the Foreign Minister's special bureau.

Dennis ROSS

Nationality	USA
Religion	Jewish
Current position	US overall co-ordinator for the Middle East peace process
Previous position	US State Department chief of policy planning under President Bush
Allies	Very close aide to US Secretary of State Warren Christopher
Position on peace	Positive, and hard-working to achieve Israeli–Jordanian peace

**National political
importance**   A career diplomat who handled the transition from Bush to Clinton
easily

Dennis Ross was the man who convinced US Secretary of State James Baker to launch the Madrid track Middle East peace process. Although said to be a Democrat by political persuasion, he worked comfortably with successive Republican administrations. Ross held office at the Pentagon and National Security Council under Ronald Reagan, as an expert on US–Soviet relations, but with a special interest in the Middle East. In 1988 he advised the Bush presidential campaign on foreign policy, and after Bush became president, he headed James Baker's Policy Planning Staff. At the same time, he was also a key member of an independent 'Presidential Study Group'. In the group's pamphlet, *Building for Peace,* Ross endorsed an incrementalist approach to Arab–Israeli peace-making. Unlike earlier activist US initiatives, this one would favour caution; the US should only intervene if conditions were 'ripe' for peace. Meanwhile, the US State Department would mind the 'garden', while the fruits of potential peace would ripen naturally, through direct talks between Arabs and Israelis. The pamphlet stressed that the USSR should be excluded from intefering with the balance of power in the Middle East.

After 1988, however, two events changed Ross's approach – the Gulf War and the demise of the Soviet Union. Ross felt the time was right for US action, and he led the US diplomatic team at Madrid. The team, which embraced most members of the Presidential Study Group, consisted of Ross, his deputy, William Burns, and two Middle East experts, Aaron Miller and Daniel Kurtzer. Ross won plaudits for persuading Israel and the Palestinians to join the talks; yet his approach focused on letting the contending parties make up their own rules. While the US 'facilitatory role' succeeded in keeping the talks going, it also failed to nail down points of agreement, so that little concrete was achieved.

When Bill Clinton became president, Ross stayed on at the State Department, acting as special assistant to the new Secretary of State Warren Christopher. Ross was scheduled to leave the service in June 1993, to become director of the Washington Institute for Near East Policy, an influential think tank; but was then appointed 'overall co-ordinator' for the US involvement in the peace process. Some Israeli and Palestinian officials favoured a more senior figure in the post, but the State Department favoured a more measured approach. Since 1994, Ross has taken a leaf out of Henry Kissinger's book, and embarked on frenetic shuttle diplomacy to achieve the long-desired peace between Israel and Syria. Together with Christopher, Ross was a crucial player in reviving the peace process after the Hebron massacre of February 1994 had threatened to end it.

He also responded to a new Syrian desire to make peace, as voiced after the assassination of Yitzhak Rabin. This resulted in the Israel–Syria talks, held in the Wye Valley, Maryland, USA, in December 1995 and January 1996. Now 46, Ross was primarily concerned with organizing a summit meeting between Syrian President Hafez al-Assad and Israeli Prime Minister Shimon Peres. Ross invariably suffers the fate of all intermediatories, being accused by by both sides of being too lenient on the other. He also evidently upset Shimon Peres by casting doubt on his abilities in briefings to US intelligence staff, before the Rabin assassination. Nonetheless, Ross's persistance has been a key factor in keeping peace talks going during difficult times.

Rothermel, Timothy   USA

Director, Programme of Assistance to the Palestinian People (PAPP). PAPP is a UN Development Programme (UNDP) project that has run since 1980. Its current yearly budget is $30 million, and this includes funds from the UNDP and donor countries. Since 1994, PAPP has co-operated with the Palestine National Authority in the fields of water and sanitation, health, agriculture, public administration.

Rothschild, Danny (Maj.-Gen.)   Israel

Israeli general currently dealing with security negotiations with Syria over the Golan. Danny Rothschild was the co-ordinator for military activities in the territories. As such, he was involved with the Madrid peace process, which continued in Washington, DC. In 1992 Rothschild recommended re-opening Bir Zeit University, which the *Likud* government considered to be a hotbed of the *intifada*; but the then Defence Minister Moshe Arens overruled him. After the Oslo breakthrough, he negotiated directly with the newly appointed Palestine National Authority (PNA) Planning Minister Nabil Sha'ath over 'further empowerment' for Palestinians. Their talks culminated in the Preparatory Transfer of Powers agreement, signed by Israel and the PLO on Aug. 29, 1994.

Rubinstein, Amnon   Israel

Education and Culture Minister, and head of *Shinui* (Centre Party) within *Meretz*. Amnon Rubinstein was a leading intellectual and author before entering politics. Rubinstein was born in Tel Aviv in 1931. He studied economics, international relations and law at the Hebrew University in Jerusalem, became a member of the Israel Bar in 1963 and received a PhD in law from the London School of Economics in 1966. Rubinstein was a law professor at Tel Aviv University from 1961 to 1975. He founded *Shinui* in 1974, on a platform of free enterprise and electoral reform. In the 1977 elections, Rubinstein became an MK, and joined the Democratic Movement for Change, but went independent in 1978.

In 1992 *Shinui* joined *Mapam* and *Ratz* to form the left-wing Zionist *Meretz* bloc, which won 12 Knesset seats. Rubinstein entered the cabinet as Energy Minister, although he would have preferred to be Justice Minister. After the religious *Shas* Party threatened to leave the coalition over the secular policy of his fellow *Meretz* MK, Shulamit Aloni, Rubinstein was called in to replace her as Education Minister in late 1992. As a minister, he has had his hands full trying to satisfy the demands of teachers for pay increases, and continuing rumblings from the religious sector. Rubinstein has been largely excluded from the inner cabinet dealing with the peace process. It was feared that his left-wing sympathies may have antagonized the Israeli right. He hoped that as peace bore fruit, especially in cultural and educational co-operation between the Israel and the Palestine Authority (as per Oslo 2), and Israel and Arab states (following multilateral agreements), that he would gain more responsibility and influence beyond the borders of Israel; however, he was voted out of office in 1996.

Elyakim RUBINSTEIN

Nationality	Israeli
Religion	Jewish
Date of Birth	1947
Current position	Defence Ministry legal adviser; in late 1995 he became a district court judge in Israel
Previous position	Head of Israeli negotiating team with Palestinians at Madrid in 1991 Chief negotiator with Jordan in 1993 and 1994
Allies	Initially appointed by Yitzhak Shamir for Madrid talks posting; remained for a year in same posting under Rabin administration
Position on peace	Positive; key role in facilitating the peace treaty with Jordan; but wary of conceding too much 'land for peace'
National political importance	Influential in diplomatic circles
Prospects	Not thought to harbour political ambitions; may retain influence as an expert adviser

Elyakim Rubinstein was propelled from the world of backdoor diplomacy to become a figure of international prominence after the Madrid talks. He is renowned as a tough negotiator, but his ready sense of humour and pragmatic nature successfully defused many potential sources of conflict. He can justifiably can take much of the credit for the successful peace treaty with Jordan. Somewhat unusually for one of Israel's diplomatic corps, Rubinstein is an observant Orthodox Jew and often brings his Talmudic insights to bear during difficult junctures in negotiations. Perhaps even more anomalously, Rubinstein believes that Jews have a divine right to the biblical *Eretz Yisrael*; yet equally he is a firm adherent of peace talks with Palestinians.

In 1974, Defence Minister Moshe Dayan picked the scholastic legal expert, then 26, as his counsel for an inquiry into Israel's errors in the 1973 Yom Kippur War. In 1977, Moshe Dayan, now Foreign Minister, remembered Rubinstein's rare talents, and made him his bureau chief. In 1978 and 1979, Rubinstein was a delegate to the Camp David talks between Israel and Egypt. By this stage he had mastered Palestinian Arabic, and as the question of Palestinian autonomy came onto the agenda, he accompanied Dayan on a series of meetings with Palestinian leaders in the territories. Most significantly, in retrospect, Rubinstein met and struck up a relationship with Dr Haidar Abd al-Shafi in Gaza.

Rubenstein survived Dayan's resignation as Foreign Minister and led the first stage of negotiations with Egypt over the disputed Sinai enclave of Taba. But talks reached deadlock and the issue was only resolved in 1989, after international arbitration, with the town returning to Egyptian rule. Following Israel's invasion of Lebanon in 1982, it was Rubinstein who in 1983 helped to fashion Israel's short-lived peace treaty with the Gemayel government after hours of arduous talks with officials in Beirut. Enormous Syrian pressure ensured that the treaty was abrogated a year later.

In 1984 Prime Minister Yitzhak Shamir offered Rubinstein the post of Israel's Ambassador to the UN, which he accepted. However, elections that year resulted in a *Likud*-Labour coalition government. With Shimon Peres as Prime Minister, and Shamir as Foreign Minister the offer was withdrawn, and the more telegenic Benjamin Netanyahu took up the UN post instead. For the next two years Rubinstein worked as political counsellor in the Israel embassy in Washington. During this period Rubinstein led Shamir's rearguard campaign against Peres plans for an international peace conference. In 1986 Shamir succeeded Peres as Prime Minister (according to their 'rotation agreement') and Rubinstein became cabinet secretary.

The outbreak of the *intifada* in 1987, and the PLO's Algiers Declaration of 1988 convinced Rubinstein that Israel needed to overhaul its tough policy *vis-à-vis* the Palestinians. Consequently, in 1989 he and Justice Minister Dan Meridor persuaded Yitzhak Shamir to respond to the PLO with a peace initiative of his own. In 1990 Shamir agreed to name him deputy attorney general. Once again, however, Rubinstein's career was 'overtaken by events' and he was chosen to head negotiations with Jordan and the Palestinians at the Madrid conference of 1991, and the subsequent peace talks in Washington. In May 1993 he jointly headed two working committees which emerged out of the Washington talks – a self-rule committee (where his Palestinian opposite number was Sa'eb Erekat) and a human rights committee (opposite Mamdouh al-Aker).

Ultimately his work here was superceded by the events of September 1993 (the Oslo Accords); but Rubinstein soon found himself immersed in talks with Jordan. He formed a good working relationship with his opposite number, Faiz Tarawneh, the Jordanian ambassador to Washington. Indeed, the two men became the subjects of a popular political satire in Amman. Rubinstein's legal handicraft is seen in the intricate lease-back stipulations for Israeli farmers living and working on what is now Jordanian sovereign territory. In January 1996 the two negotiators received special awards at a ceremony in Beit Gavriel, next to the Sea of Tiberias, for their role in achieving the Israel–Jordan peace treaty. While he has become an expert on military and security matters, his real ambition has always been to become a Supreme Court judge. In late 1995, Elyakim Rubinstein was appointed a district court judge, thus ending, for the moment at least, some 20 years' 'interruption' in the cause of making peace.

S

Sa'ade, George   Lebanon
President of the Maronite Phalange Party. Sa'ade has steered the Phalange movement out of the shadow of the Gemayel family, and now favours greater pluralism.

Sabbah, Michel   Palestinian
Latin Patriarch of Jerusalem. Monsignor Sabbah is the first Palestinian to hold the 800-year old post. He opposes sole Israeli sovereignty over Jerusalem, and feels it should be shared between Jews, Muslims and Christians. In similar vein, he has called for a Law of Return to

apply to all three monotheistic faiths. Sabbah declared in January 1996 that only a Palestinian state could guarantee Israel's security.

Sabri, Ikirmeh (Sheikh)   Palestinian

PLO–chosen mufti of Jerusalem. The PLO quickly moved to appoint Sheikh Sabri (also rendered as Akram Said Sabri) as mufti on Oct. 16, 1994, after the death of Sheikh Suleiman al-Ja'bari. An official Jordanian-backed candidate, Sheikh Abd al-Qader Abdeen, took office at the same time, but was largely ignored by most Palestinians. Sabri is known to be close to Arafat, and has castigated east Jerusalem Arabs who, he says, want to become 'new Israelis'. On other occasions, Sabri has called for the Muslim liberation of Jerusalem.

Sacks, Jonathan Henry (Rabbi)   UK

Rabbi Sacks succeeded Lord Jakobovits as Chief Rabbi of Great Britain and of the United Hebrew Congregations of the Commonwealth in 1991. As such he is regarded by many in the broader populus as a *de facto* spokesman for the Jewish community in the UK.

Sadat, Anwar el-   Egypt

President of Egypt from 1970 until his assassination in October 1981. Anwar Sadat was born in 1918, and graduated from the Egyptian military academy in 1938. As an anti-British Egyptian nationalist, he spent the war years working in a pro-German underground movement. Sadat was a member of the Free Officer coup of 1952, which removed King Farouk from power and ultimately saw Gamal Abdul Nasser become President of Egypt. From 1959 to 1969 he was chairman of the National Assembly. He became Vice-President in 1969, and became President when Nasser died the following year. President Sadat shifted Egypt's alliance from the USSR to the USA, and removed one by one the Nasser old guard. In October 1973 he launched the Yom Kippur War with Syria, against Israel. Although the war ultimately failed to recover the Sinai peninsula (lost to Israel in 1967), it did restore some of Egypt's military pride.

After his surprise visit to address the *Knesset* in Jerusalem, in 1977, Sadat negotiated with Israel's new Prime Minister, Menachem Begin, and US President Jimmy Carter, at the Camp David peace talks in the USA. On March 26, 1979, he signed a historic peace treaty with Israel, thus breaking a 30-year Arab taboo. In subsequent years, Sadat recovered all of the Sinai; but Palestinians felt he had betrayed them by not fighting harder for a genuine autonomy in the Israeli–occupied territories. Egypt was ostracized by most of the Arab world for its treaty with Israel, while at home Sadat clamped down on growing unrest, as the economy showed few signs of recovery. Despite his earlier alliance with the Muslim Brotherhood, Sadat became a hate figure for Islamic extremists, who eventually killed him as he reviewed a military march-past. His trusted deputy, Hosni Mubarak, took over as President, and has since maintained Sadat's twin legacies, peace with Israel, and privatization at home. In the light of the current peace process, several Arab leaders are now re-appraising Sadat's place in Middle East history.

Sadi, Ghazi al-   Palestinian/Jordanian

Director and founder of the Al-Jalil Research Centre in Amman, which provides information on Israel and runs the first Hebrew language training institute in Jordan. Ghadi al-Sadi was born in Acre, now in Israel, and read Middle Eastern studies at Tel Aviv University in the 1950s. He has been a *Fatah* member since the 1960s. Sadi was deported for 'organizational activities' in 1977, and toured the Arab world as a member of the Palestine National Council. After the Madrid peace conference opened up the possiblity of a peaceful contacts with Israel, Sadi started his Hebrew classes. Al-Jalil is funded by the PLO, and Sadi writes a weekly newsletter in Arabic, which circulates in Arab countries.

Afifi SAFIEH

Nationality	Palestinian
Religion	Roman Catholic
Place of birth	Sheikh Jarrah district, Jerusalem

Date of birth	1950
Current position	Palestinian General Delegate (PLO representative) in London, since 1990
Previous positions	President, General Union of Palestinian Students in Belgium and France
	Deputy Director of the PLO observer mission to the UN, 1976–78
	Headed PLO unit on European Affairs and UN, in Beirut, 1978–81
	PLO representative to the Netherlands, 1987–90
Allies	Mahdi Abdul Hadi, Faisal Husseini, close to Yasser Arafat
Position on peace	Influential in brokering US–PLO dialogue, and communicating with British Foreign Office; facilitated several secret peace initiatives; critical of Israeli position on Jerusalem and settlements
National political importance	Respected amongst Jerusalem Palestinians, prominent amongst Palestinian intellectuals and in the Palestinian diaspora
Prospects	Tipped as Palestinian General Delegate to the Holy See; Expected to play a key role in forthcoming talks on Jerusalem's status

Afif Safieh is a seasoned PLO diplomat, and one of the organization's most articulate spokesmen. Charming yet forceful in his opinions, he has long advocated dialogue with Israel and with Diaspora Jewry, reasoning that Palestinians and Israelis are 'in a situation of unavoidable co-existence'. Although he was one of the catalysts for the current peace talks, he has equally never shirked from criticizing its shortcomings, nor from pointing out what he sees as acts of Israeli bad faith.

Afif Safieh was born in 1950 into a Christian Palestinian Jerusalemite family. He studied at the College Des Frères in Jerusalem, and in 1972 he completed a licence in Political Science and International Relations from the Catholic University of Louvain in Belgium. However, as he was not in Jerusalem at the time of the Israeli take-over of eastern sector of the city in 1967, he lost his residency rights according to Israeli law, and was compelled to travel on a Belgian passport. Safieh was the President of the Belgian section of the General Union of Palestinian Students (GUPS) from 1969 to 1971. From 1976 to 1978 he was the deputy director of the PLO observer mission to the UN in Geneva. For the next four years, Safieh was a staff member in Yasser Arafat's office in Beirut. In 1980 was sent to the Vatican as a special envoy and the following year he helped to negotiate the UN-brokered ceasefire in Lebanon.

Safieh returned to academia from 1981 to 1987, initially as a researcher at his *alma mater* in Belgium; and later as a visiting scholar at the Centre for International Affairs, in Harvard University. From 1987 to 1990, he was the PLO's representative in the Netherlands. During this period, he was involved in the Stockholm negotiations which led to the direct US–PLO dialogue in Tunisia, starting in 1989. In September 1990 he took over from Faisal Aweida as the PLO representative in London. He soon began breaking down longstanding barriers between the PLO and the Anglo-Jewish community (in particular, forging cordial relations with former President of the Board of Deputies, Greville Janner, and the editor of the *Jewish Chronicle*, Ned Temko).

Safieh acted as an early go-between for the Oslo talks, arranging a crucial meeting between the Israeli intellectuals, Yair Hirschfeld and Ron Pundak, and a PLO group led by Abu 'Ala, in London in 1992. In December 1993, Safieh became the first high-ranking PLO official to return to his native land, after the signing of the Declaration of Principles in Washington. He visited Jerusalem to celebrate Christmas, and to see his daughter confirmed by the Latin Patriarch Michel Sabah. In early 1996 Safieh joined the Palestinian Authority in calling on Israel to apologize for its treatment of Palestinians. He has often defended Arafat's reputation from criticism by other Palestinians. Safieh said the Authority would allow 'certain Jews' to become residents, but only after the refugee issue had been solved. He also feels a golden opportunity was missed by Europe and the USA, by not putting more pressure on Israel when it would have produced mutually beneficial results.

Saguy, Uri   Israel

Former head of Military Intelligence, and a major-general in the IDF. Saguy, 51, was widely tipped to succeed Amnon Shahak as Deputy IDF Chief of Staff, but in November 1994 Maj.-Gen. Matan Vilna'i assumed the post. Saguy was well respected as chief of military intelligence, and was the first high-ranking Israeli official to discern a Syrian inclination towards peace in the early 1990s. However, his former ally, Amnon Shahak, also blocked his appointment as head of the team to negotiate security matters with Syria. An ally of Ehud Barak, Saguy shares many of his political concerns. His advice smoothed the path for Israel's acceptance of the security terms in Oslo 1. Even so, he warned that terrorism could still endanger the entire peace process. Saguy left the army in June 1995, after 33 years' service. Political observers believe his growing ties with Peres will help his chances to join the Labour Party's electoral list, and, in time, possibly the cabinet too.

Said, Edward W.   Palestinian
Prominent Palestinian intellectual, former member of the Palestine National Council (PNC); Professor of English and Comparative Literature at Columbia University, USA. Edward Said is the best known spokesperson in the USA for the Palestinian cause. His numerous publications attempted to 'debunk myths' about what he saw as Palestinian expulsion from their homes in 1948. He accuses the US liberal establishment of bias and double standards regarding its unquestioning support for Israel. Said has argued that without US aid, Israel could never have come about. To Said, this alleged negation of Palestinian rights fits firmly within the broader 'Orientalist' view of Arabs and Muslims, which he sees as patronizing at best, and racist at worst. In 1983 he was a consultant to the UN for its International Conference on the Question of Palestine.

He has long favoured a peace deal with Israel, and in the early 1980s was a key member of American Professors for Peace in the Middle East. However, he rejected the Declaration of Principles as PLO capitulation – 'a Palestinian Versailles' – and in 1993 resigned his seat on the PNC in protest. In 1994, he criticized Palestinian negotiators, particularly Yasser Arafat, for overly fulsome rhetoric, while the Israeli team 'outsmarted' them through their superior planning and grasp of details.

Saket, Bassam Khalil   Jordan
Leading economist and proponent of Jordanian modernization; close adviser to the Jordanian Royal Family. Bassam Khalil Saket was born in 1944 and studied at the Universities of Baghdad, Oxford and Keele (in Britain). He took his BSc in Economics in 1966, and went on to attain a diploma from the IMF in Washington, in 1973, and a PhD in 1976. Saket began his career as an analyst with the Central Bank of Jordan, where he worked from 1966 to 1970. He was designated Head of the Domestic Economy of Jordan, from 1970 to 1973. He served as chief economic adviser to Crown Prince Hassan from 1978 to 1984, and has been the Managing Director of the Government Investment Corporation since 1984. Saket is also a member of several influential national bodies, including the executive committee of the Royal Scientific Society.

Saleh, Abdel Jawad   Palestinian
Bir Zeit politics professor, Independent MP for Ramallah in the Palestine Council since 1996. Abdel Jawad Saleh was born in Ramallah in 1932, and educated at the American University of Cairo. He returned to the West Bank where he worked as a teacher. In 1967 he was elected Mayor of El-Bireh. Israel deported him to Jordan in 1973, after he expressed overt sympathies for the PLO. He joined the organization, and soon became head of the Executive Office for Home Affairs, deputy head of the Occupied Homeland Department, and a member of the committee which handled the Palestine National Fund (PNF). Saleh moved to the PLO's headquarters in Tunis, but in the 1990s he grew disenchanted with corruption within the organization. In the Palestinian Council elections of Jan. 20, 1996, Saleh stood as an independent in Ramallah and topped the poll of seven elected candidates.

Salman, Muhammad   Syria
Information minister. Following the *Hamas* deportation, Salman attacked Israel's 'Nazi practices' in 1993. Since then, he has considerably softened Syria's public stance on Israel, and cautiously provided an atmosphere which encourages public acceptance of possible peace with Israel.

Samiah, Yom Tov   Israel
Brigadier-General in charge of Gaza Strip just before the Oslo Accords were announced in
September 1993. Samiah, 42, was born to Libyan Jewish immigrant parents. He was given the
Gaza command in 1991, and clamped down hard on unrest. In March 1993, he imposed a
total closure on the Strip, and arrested many Palestinian activists; human rights groups in
Israel blamed him for using excessive force (some 70 people were killed in the first six months
of 1993). Samiah thought industry should be encouraged in Gaza itself, to minimize its
workers' dependence on the Israeli economy.

Sandler, Deborah   Israel
Ecologist and lawyer. The US-born Sandler is currently the co-ordinator for a joint Egypt-
Israel-Jordan ecological project in the Gulf of Aqaba.

Santer, Jacques   Luxembourg
President of the European Commission, former Prime Minister of Luxembourg. Under
Santer's stewardship, the European Union (EU) has developed the links between its southern-
most member states, and Turkey, Israel, and the Maghreb and Mashreq Arab nations, which
border on the Mediterranean. This was most clearly seen in the Barcelona conference of
December 1995. The EU also drafted a low-barriers trading agreement with Israel. Jacques
Santer was born in 1937 and became leader of the Christian Social Party. He entered
Luxembourg's cabinet in 1979, and five years later became Prime Minister.

Sarid, Yossi   Israel
Minister of the Environment, *Meretz* MK; since January 1996, leader of the *Meretz* coalition.
Before entering the cabinet, Sarid was regarded as the *enfant terrible* of the Israeli Zionist left.
However, his roots are very much within the Labour establishment, and with the responsibil-
ity of office, Sarid has maintained his reformist zeal while still toeing the official line.

   Yossi Sarid was born into a staunchly Labour family in Rehovot, Palestine, in 1940. He was
originally a Labour MK, first elected in 1974, when he was closely associated with Pinhas
Sapir, Finance Minister at the time. Sarid then backed Yitzhak Rabin and Shimon Peres in
turn, but fell out with both of them. In 1984, he left the Labour *Knesset* faction, in protest at
its decision to form a coalition government with Yitzhak Shamir's *Likud*. He joined *Ratz*
(Shulamit Aloni's Citizens' Rights Movement), where he enjoyed more freedom to speak out
on issues like opposition to the Lebanon war and Israel's treatment of Palestinians. In 1990 he
backed Shimon Peres in his ultimately unsuccessful bid to form a new government, after the
Labour-*Likud* pact collapsed over disagreements on the peace process.

   He has also been chairman of the *Meretz* Knesset faction since 1992. A long-time
supporter of Peace Now, and regarded by the right as an arch-dove, Sarid and his family have
often received death threats from extremists. At the same time, he became disillusioned by
Palestinian support for Saddam Hussein during the Gulf War. Since then he has mended
fences with his allies in the Palestinian camp, but tends to hold a middle ground in the *Meretz*
faction.

   On Jan. 1, 1993, he was appointed Minister of the Environment, making him the fourth
Meretz MK to hold a cabinet post. He played a behind-the-scenes role as advocate for talks
with the PLO, and tried to open an unofficial channel with the PLO via Nabil Sha'ath, when
the PLO official was attached to the Washington talks. After the Oslo breakthrough, some
leftist allies blamed Sarid for not being more vocal about the need to accelerate the peace
process with Palestinians. When others in Labour (notably Yossi Beilin) favoured accelerating
the talks to the final stage, Sarid recommended the step-by-step approach.

   Although Sarid played little part in the Israeli–Palestinian negotiations, he was given
ample scope to develop new links with Arab states within the less contentious multilateral
track framework. Sarid addressed a conference of Middle Eastern environment ministers in
Casablanca in May 1993. He was also the first Israeli minister to visit Bahrain as head of the
Israeli delegation to the Working Group on the Environment in October 1994. In November
he broke similar new ground, by attending the Conference of Environment Ministers from
Mediterranean States in Tunisia, and meeting his Tunisian counterpart, Mohammad Mahdi

Malika. The two men discussed a programme to exchange environmental experts and reaffirmed their nations' improving ties.

In early 1995, Sarid praised the PNA for its crackdown on suspected *Hamas* bombers, but also called for the dismantling of Israeli 'flashpoint settlements' in the Gaza Strip, such as Netzarim. After the Rabin assassination, Sarid joined the five-man inner cabinet 'peace team', headed by the new Foreign Minister Ehud Barak, in late November. It appears that Shimon Peres felt the time was right to include a committed dove like Sarid at the highest echelons of government. Sarid has since been an active participant in talks on releasing Palestinian prisoners (in accordance with Oslo 2). In late January 1996, Sarid took over from the outgoing Shulamit Aloni as leader of the *Meretz* coalition, the culmination of years of inner party (and often personal) acrimony between the two politicians.

Sarraj, Iyad (Dr)   Palestinian

Head of the Palestine Independent Commission for Citizens' Rights (PICCR). Sarraj is a respected doctor in Gaza, and also heads the Community Centre for Mental Health. In July 1994, he and Hanan Ashrawi helped to co-found the PICCR, with the apparent blessing of Yasser Arafat. Since then, the PICCR has waged a fierce campaign for freedom of speech, and has publicized human rights abuses by the Palestine National Authority (PNA). But its complaints were largely rebuffed, and on Dec. 6, 1995, Sarraj (who has led the PICCR since Aug. 31, 1995) was himself arrested and detained when he refused to sign a pledge not to criticize the PNA in public. As of mid-December, Sarraj was threatening to sue the PNA attorney-general, Khalid al-Kidra, for not responding to the PICCR's allegations of 'death by torture' in PNA detention cells.

Saud al-Faisal ibn Abdul Aziz ibn Saud   Saudi Arabia

Foreign Minister since 1975. Born in 1942, Prince Saud graduated with a BA in economics at Princeton University. He was deputy governor of the oil company, Petromin, from 1970 to 1971, and served as deputy minister of petroleum and mineral resources until 1975. Prince Saud is the eldest son of the late King Faisal's last wife. Saud believes in economic modernization, and has successfully presented the kingdom's case to Western allies. In November 1995 he hosted a delegation of leading Jewish Americans, and impressed them with his commitment to the peace process. Since Prince Abdullah took over effectively from King Fahd in January 1996, Saud probably has a closer ally as his new boss. Politically, however, Saud's pro-Western stance may not agree with Abdullah, who seems to prefer the *bedouin* traditions of self-sufficiency and austerity.

Uriel 'Uri' SAVIR

Nationality	Israeli
Religion	Jewish
Place of birth	Jerusalem, Israel
Date of birth	1953
Current position	Director General of the Israeli Foreign Ministry
Previous position	Joined Oslo secret talks after the sixth round
	Consul-general in New York, heading relations with US Zionists
Allies	Shimon Peres, Yossi Beilin, and Yitzhak Rabin
Position on peace	Architect of Oslo 1 and Oslo 2
National political importance	Key role in determining peace accords with Palestinians on both macro and micro levels
	Responsible for Oslo 2 implementation with PLO's Ahmed Qurei
Prospects	Increased role after Rabin's assassination, when Prime Minister Shimon Peres appointed him the government's 'special peace process co-ordinator' in November 1995; future in doubt after *Likud* victory

Uri Savir has been at the very centre of Israel's talks with the Palestinians since the outset of the Oslo initiative. At just 40, he took over as Director-General of the Israeli Foreign Ministry, and immediately instigated some far-reaching structural changes. When Shimon Peres became Prime Minister in November 1995, he appointed his protégé, Savir, as the official Israeli 'peace process co-ordinator', thus formally acknowledging his crucial role. Savir helped to set the tone for Oslo 1, and was a key player in the drafting of Oslo 2. His current job is to turn the theory into practice by overseeing the implementation of Oslo 2. As such, he acted as a bridge between Palestinian leaders on one side, and an inner cabinet ministerial 'peace team', headed by Foreign Minister Ehud Barak, on the other.

Savir's first choice of career was academia, and not the diplomatic service, but decided to join its 'cadet course' in 1975. Savir worked in the legal and press divisions, until, quite by chance, a ministry spokesman overheard him speaking fluent German (which he had learnt at home) and assigned him to the ministry's overseas press division. His first international posting was in Canada, where he served from 1980 to 1983, and then in New York. When newly appointed Prime Minister Shimon Peres arrived in the US without a spokesman in 1984, Uri Savir was asked to 'fill in'. The two men struck an instant rapport, and within two days the 31-year-old Savir returned to Israel as Peres's media adviser. By 1986 Savir was Chief of the Foreign Minister's Bureau under the now Foreign Minister Shimon Peres. One of Peres' last acts as minister was to appoint Uri Savir as Consul-General in the Israeli embassy in New York, in 1988.

As a natural Labourite and Peres protégé, Savir found it a challenge to represent the more hardline Shamir-led *Likud* administration dispassionately. The consul is often called 'ambassador to the American Jewish community', and it proved a particularly testing assignment, given the controversy over Israel's handling of the *intifada* (which had broken out the previous year). Savir drew on his reserves of wit and intellect to win important friends, and open new channels of communications to business figures and US ethnic minorities, especially the African-American community. His power breakfasts at the Regency Hotel became renowned in diplomatic circles.

He returned to Israel in June 1992, to head the West Europe section of the Israeli Foreign Ministry, and become deputy director general. On May 1, 1993, he became the ministry's director-general, taking over from the outgoing Yossi Hadas. The more widely tipped candidate, the 53-year-old Eitan Bentsur, became his deputy. Immediately, Savir proposed drastic departmental reforms, by increasing the ministry's role in policy-making, re-directing PR at the media rather than élite groups, and stressing the use of diplomacy as a tool for economic development. He also upgraded the international co-operation unit (reflecting Israel's many new relations forged since 1991); split the Africa-Asia department for 'clearer focus'; and set up two new research centres. Continuing his predecessor's work, he encouraged a special subsection to 'mirror' the various multilateral track working groups.

Savir felt the Madrid peace track had reached terminal deadlock. So two weeks after taking up his post, he went to Oslo as the first official Israeli government representative at the secret peace talks with the PLO. His presence there at a stroke raised the status of the talks and showed Palestinians that Israel was serious about this channel. (Until then, two academics, Yair Hirschfeld and Ron Pundak, had represented the Israeli side.) Uri Savir soon found common ground with chief PLO negotiator, Ahmed Qurei (Abu 'Ala), and, with the aid of Israeli lawyer, Joel Singer, they thrashed out a formulation which later became the Declaration of Principles, which was signed in Washington on Sept. 13, 1993.

In 1994 Savir concentrated on consolidating the ministry's gains, and left detailed negotiations on implementation to security experts (like Amnon Shahak and Danny Rothschild), and leading politicians (Arafat, Peres, Rabin and Mubarak). From January to March 1995 Savir was engaged in an intense secret dialogue with PNA negotiators to assess the 'mutual mistakes' both sides made in implementing the Gaza-Jericho Accord. He determined to remedy this in Oslo 2 (Israeli redeployment in preparation for Palestinian elections) by ensuring closer co-operation with the Palestinians. Although Yasser Arafat and Shimon Peres ironed out the final stages of the Interim Agreement, it was Savir and his Palestinian counterpart, Abu 'Ala, who had prepared much of the groundwork.

In October 1995, addressing a Conference of Presidents of Major American Jewish Organizations, Savir was frank in admitting past errors, but optimistic about the importance of 'graduality' – the step-by-step method of enacting peace through a process of 'confidence-building measures'. He praised Chairman Arafat for taking some hard decisions, in the face of PLO opposition.

Savir and Abu 'Ala are joint heads of the committee to monitor the implementation of the interim plan. Savir has played a very important role behind the scenes in formulating Israel's stance on peace. After the assassination of Yitzhak Rabin, Prime Minister Shimon Peres raised his status to 'special peace process co-ordinator'. His special responsibilities included overseeing the Interim Agreement with Palestinians, and liaising with five cabinet ministers, now constituted as a 'peace team'. Netanyahu's victory led Savir to hint that he would have to resign.

Sawalha, Kasem   Palestinian
Head of the Izz al-Din al-Qassam brigades, military wing of *Hamas*. The group is responsible for terrorist attacks on Israelis. Sawalha reportedly escaped to London in 1992.

Sayeh, Abed al-Hamid a- Palestinian
Chairman of the PLO's Palestine National Council (PNC). In the late 1940s, Sayeh was the leading *sheikh* (Muslim religious leader) in Nablus. After the January 1996 Palestine Council elections in Gaza and the West Bank, Sheikh a-Sayeh, 93, could play a role in determining the shared areas of authority between the new 'internal' Council, and the long-established 'external' PNC. Sayeh accepted Israeli Prime Minister Shimon Peres's offer to return to Jerusalem, although he still opposes the Oslo Accords.

Schach, Eliezer   Israel
Nonagenarian spiritual head of ultra-Orthodox MKs. In 1990 he ensured the collapse of the Labour-*Likud* coalition government, and stymied Shimon Peres's attempts to form a Labour-led government, when he instructed his supporters not to co-operate unless their religious agenda was addressed. Rabbi Schach was born in Lithuania. After fleeing the Nazi Holocaust, he arrived in Israel to become head of the esteemed Ponevezh Yeshiva (rabbinical seminary) in Bnei Brak. In political terms, this has meant he has enormous powers of patronage within the *haredi* (ultra-Orthodox) community, and especially among those Jews who follow the so-called Lithuanian anti-Hassidic trend. All told, the 300,000 potential *haredi* voters make up 8% of the Israeli electorate, and hence often hold the balance of power.

In the mid-1980s, Schach helped to found *Shas*, the Sephardi Orthodox Jewish political party led by Rabbi Aryeh Deri. It was an astute move, for, despite his own Ashkenazi origins, Schach realized that there was a niche for a party which combined orthodoxy with Sephardi ethnic interests. In later years, Rabbi Schach and Deri fell out, and *Shas* came under the sway of Ovadiah Yosef, former Chief Sephardi Rabbi of Israel. Schach then became 'spiritual head' of the United Torah Judaism Party. His favourite faction within this uneasy coalition is *Degel Hatorah* (Flag of the Torah), which has lost support in recent years. Rabbi Schach remains agnostic on the peace issue – while believing in the ultimate sanctity of *Eretz Yisrael*, he rejects the militancy of religious Zionist settlers, and instead concentrates on a range of religious issues within Israel itself (like Sabbath observance, Orthodox conversions, and funds for Orthodox institutions). In late 1995, he instructed Orthodox Jews to support a peace treaty with Syria if it would save lives in the future, according to the *halachic* (Jewish legal) principle of *pikuach nefesh*. Once again, with elections pending in Israel, *Likud* and Labour politicians have been sounding out the rabbi.

Schultz, George   USA
US Secretary of State under Ronald Reagan. In September 1982, George Schultz helped to draft the Reagan Plan for peace in the Middle East. Later that month, he praised the Fez Summit proposals for a Middle East peace as containing the seeds of a possible breakthrough. Under Schultz, the US sent a contingent to Lebanon, as part of the multilateral peace-keeping forces there. He also instructed a special US envoy, Philip Habib, to intercede in an ultimately unsuccessful attempt to end the civil war in Lebanon. Following costly bomb attacks by *Hezbollah*, Schultz ordered that US forces be withdrawn in 1984. Schultz was re-appointed Secretary in Reagan's second term, but chose to concentrate more on improving relations with the USSR under Gorbachev, while leaving local forces to devise a Middle East settlement. Responding to the Framework for Peace proposals, as drafted by King Hussein and Yasser Arafat in February 1985, Schultz suggested that PNC members could join a joint

Palestinian–Jordanian team to negotiate team with Israel. (At the time Israeli Prime Minister Shamir rejected this formulation because it gave a role to the PLO; however, the idea of a Jordanian 'umbrella' delegation was to re-emerge at Madrid in 1991.) In December 1989, Schultz gave the go-ahead to the first ever official talks between the US government and the PLO, which led to strains in US–Israeli relations (the talks were suspended in May 1990 when Arafat failed to condemn a terrorist attack by one of the PLO factions). After George Bush was elected President, James Baker replaced George Schultz as Secretary of State.

Sedqi, Atef   Egypt

Prime Minister of Egypt from 1986 to 1995; also Minister of International Co-operation. Atef Mohammed Naguib Sedqi (also spelt Sidki, Sidky, Sidqi or Sedki) was born on Aug. 21, 1930. He graduated as a Bachelor in Law from Cairo University in 1951, and after further studies in law and economics, he gained his PhD in Economics from Paris University in 1958. Sedqi's first taste of politics came in 1959, when he was briefly appointed Deputy Head of the State Council. He then returned to academia, and by 1981 was Professor in the Economics and Finance Department of Cairo University. The following year he became head of the Central Authority for Accountancy.

Between 1980 and 1986, Sedqi was a member of the *Shura,* or president's consultative council. He impressed President Hosni Mubarak with his technical adeptness as chairman of its economics committee, especially during a period when Egypt was attempting to solve its economic problems through politically sensitive reforms. Like Mubarak, Sedqi eschewed the socialist path of Nasser, and the capitalist path of Sadat, for a more ideologically neutral centrist position. He is an acknowledged expert on taxation, and enjoys close ties with France (from whom he received the Order of Merit and the French Legion of Honour). At the same time, his lack of military connections meant he posed no great threat to Mubarak's rule, unlike some other appointees. For these reasons, Mubarak appointed Sedqi his prime minister in November 1986. He has held that position since, and has led Egypt's important negotiations with creditors, both bilaterally and through the IMF. At the same time, he was charged with reducing state control of the economy. In both spheres, his task has been daunting, especially when one considers that in 1990 Egypt's non-military debt came to $50 billion – more than its total Gross National Product.

Sedqi spent much of 1993 improving ties with Syria, in 'higher joint committee' talks with his Syrian counterpart, Mahmoud Zu'bi. On Oct. 13, 1993, President Mubarak invited him to form a new cabinet, although he made few major changes, despite rumours that Mubarak was thinking of appointing ministers from the Muslim Brotherhood group. Sedqi survived a fundamentalist assassination attempt on Nov. 25 of the same year. Five members of the Vanguard of Conquest were executed for this crime in December 1994. At the end of 1995, Sedqi agreed to resign, after controversy surrounding the general election results.

Segev, Gonen   Israel

Energy Minister, appointed in 1995. Segev created a new party, *Yi'ud,* as a splinter offshoot from Raphael Eitan's nationalist *Tsomet* party. He favoured a more conciliatory approach on peace than that espoused by *Tsomet.* When Prime Minister Yitzhak Rabin failed to woo Eitan's party into government (having faced strong opposition from his *Meretz* colleagues), the two-member *Yi'ud* MKs joined in its place. Nonetheless, Segev was the sole member of the cabinet to vote against the Oslo 2 (Interim Agreement between Israel and the Palestinians). In January 1996 he travelled to Cairo to negotiate a deal to build a pipeline to pump gas from Egypt to Israel.

Serri, Robert   Netherlands

Emissary who promoted a European Community scheme to finance the transfer of Mediterranean waters to Jordan, and desalinate them, at the multilateral talks.

Sfeir, Nasrallah Pierre   Lebanon

Patriarch of the Lebanese Maronite Church. In the late 1980s he acted as a broker between warring Christian factions. After General Aoun's forces attacked his palace, the patriarch joined other Maronite leaders in seeking a deal with Syria. Sfeir participated in the drafting of the Taif Accords in 1989, and its implementation in 1991.

Nabil SHA'ATH

Nationality	Palestinian
Religion	Muslim
Date of birth	1938
Place of birth	Safad, Galilee region of Palestine (now Israel)
Current position	Minister for Planning and Economic Co-operation Palestinian negotiator in setting up the Cairo Accords of 1994 (Oslo 1)
Previous position	Member of the PNC; successful businessman in Cairo
Allies	Close adviser to Yasser Arafat; support from moderates within the PLO Ministry director general, Walid Siam
Position on peace	Enthusiastic, a patient yet often stubborn proponent of peace
National political importance	Key role in PNA, but is not tied to any particular faction
Prospects	Vital to success of PNA, although grassroots popularity questionable

Nabil Sha'ath is a close ally of Arafat, and was an early proponent of talks with Israel and territorial compromise. His current title is Minister for Planning and Economic Co-operation within the Palestinian Authority. But it has been his role as chief negotiator with Israel which has made him such an influential figure – and a source of envy for members of the PLO old guard, some of whom fear he has conceded too much to Israel in his bid to 'make a deal'.

Sha'ath first came to public attention as the suave PLO 'point-man' who negotiated Yasser Arafat's withdrawal from Lebanon following the Israeli invasion of 1982. His career path is markedly different from mainstream PLO figures, who made their names in the cause of one or other of the guerrilla factions. Nabil Sha'ath was born in Safed to a middle-class family of bedouin origin. His father was a school principal. The family moved to Hebron and later Jaffa, but became refugees in 1948 and fled to Alexandria, Egypt. The young Sha'ath studied business administration at Alexandria University, and took his PhD at the University of Pennsylvania. From 1959 to 1965 he was a professor of business management at the latter university's prestigious Wharton School.

Sha'ath began his political career in 1969, when he was asked to represent Palestinians at a conference 'in support of the Arab people', organized by Egyptian President Anwar Sadat. He said he developed a special empathy with left-wing European and US Jewish delegates there, especially a writer who had survived the Holocaust. Since then, he says, he tried to 're-educate Palestinians' away from an alien European anti-Semitic depiction of Jews. But Sha'ath failed to convince Israelis to support a binational secular state for both peoples. Instead, since 1974 he espoused the 'two-state solution', for which he received death threats from Abu Nidal and other radicals. He also endorsed the Palestinian armed struggle, but opposed terrorism against civilians. By this stage Sha'ath was teaching economics at the American University in Beirut. He became head of the Advisory Council for the *Fatah* Central Committee, dealing with foreign information, and later, director of the PLO Planning Centre in Tunis. Sha'ath was based in Cairo at the time of the Oslo deal, A well-known figure in the Egyptian business community, he was President of TEAM, a successful management consultancy firm, which specializes in computer and management training.

In 1985 Yasser Arafat nominated him as one of four Palestinians to talk to US Secretary of State Richard Murphy, but his obvious PLO affiliations prompted right-wing Israelis to veto his participation, thus effectively scuppering this secret 'peace channel'. During the 1991–93 Madrid and Washington peace process, there were really three Palestinian delegations present – the 14-strong 'official' team led by Haidar Abdel Shafi; a Steering Committee of advisers from East Jerusalem and the Occupied Territories, led by Faisal Husseini and represented by Hanan Ashrawi; and an unofficial delegation which represented Yasser Arafat's viewpoint, led by Nabil Sha'ath. Only the first was recognized by Israel, because of the Shamir administration's strictures on talking with PLO personnel, or any Palestinians from East Jerusalem. However, it is widely accepted that Sha'ath's team ensured that whatever the official delegation said fell in line with Arafat in Tunis.

Throughout this period, Sha'ath nurtured unofficial (and, according to the current Israeli laws, illegal) ties with members of Israel's Labour Party and the Peace Now movement (including Shulamit Aloni, Ephraim Sneh, Ora Namir, Abba Eban and Yair Tsaban). In 1992 he opened a secret 'peace channel' with Yossi Beilin (who later became Labour's deputy foreign minister) in Washington, but this was jeopardized by leaks. He did not play an active part in the secret Oslo talks, but was very influential in its final stages by drawing up the Palestinian position, which led in turn to the Declaration of Principles and the Washington signing in 1993. Signs of a schism, however, with other Palestinians had already begun to show. Hanan Ashrawi, a longtime friend of Sha'ath's, objected to his draft response to the American position on territorial jurisdiction and the issue of Jerusalem. She believed it conceded too much, particularly regarding Israeli settlements. This dispute prompted Ashrawi's resignation from the official Palestinian negotiating team. In similar vein, Sha'ath has been criticized for not insisting on protection of Palestinians from Israeli settlers, until after the Hebron massacre in early 1994.

Following the Washington signing, Sha'ath was the first external PLO leader to relocate to Gaza. On June 26, 1994, he presided over the first council meeting of the Palestine National Authority. As head of the Palestinian 'technical committee', he held detailed talks with his Israeli counterpart, deputy chief of staff, Maj.-Gen. Amnon Shahak, in the Egyptian Sinai resort of Taba. Ever the astute judge of the media's power, Sha'ath encouraged television crews to picture the obvious rapport which the two men had struck. The initial round of talks ended in on Jan. 13, 1994, with agreement on 35 out of 38 subjects, including security issues, regarding the transfer of administrative power from Israel to the PLO in the self-governing areas. Eventually, Sha'ath and Shahak reached a compromise on the remaining question of releasing 5,000 Palestinian prisoners held in Israeli jails. On May 4, Nabil Sha'ath appeared on stage at the Cairo ceremony marking the transfer of powers, with Arafat, Rabin, Peres and Egyptian President Hosni Mubarak. When Arafat apparently baulked at signing one of the maps (contained in the treaty), it was Sha'ath who helped persuade him to do so.

On May 28, 1994 Yasser Arafat appointed Nabil Sha'ath as Minister for International Co-operation in the newly established Palestine National Authority (PNA), later expanded to a full economics ministry. As the PNA finds its feet, there has been some confusion about who has the final say about financial matters. Consequently, Sha'ath has faced rivalry from Ahmad Qurei (Abu 'Ala), Economic Affairs Minister; Mohammad Zuhdi Nashashibi, finance minister; Jaweid Ghussein, head of the Palestine National Fund; and Farouk Qaddumi, formally number two to Arafat and in charge of PECDAR (the Palestinian Economic Council for Development and Reconstruction). However, all these men did at least agree on the need for a a mixed economy or free enterprise formula for sustaining the new Palestinian entity – in contrast to the more Marxist or 'workerist' leanings of those in the Palestinian trades union movement, or in the minority Popular or Democratic Fronts.

Sha'ath was soon recalled to the negotiating table, this time with Maj.-Gen. Danny Rothschild as his Israeli counterpart, in talks on 'early empowerment' for Palestinians in the occupied territories outside Gaza and Jericho. Eventually, a Preparatory Transfer of Powers Accord was signed in October 1994. He played a smaller role during the talks which resulted in the Interim Agreement of September 1995. Instead, Arafat encouraged Sha'ath's rivals, Abu 'Ala, and Jamil Tarifi, to negotiate on the PLO's behalf.

Sha'ath is an acknowledged master of detailed negotiations. Yet he can also see matters strategically, and predicted that *Hamas* members would participate in Palestinian elections. Probably less quiescent than his critics make out, he has strongly criticized foreign donors for not honouring their pledges to provide £2.2 billion in aid to help the fledgling Palestinian Authority. Detractors accuse him of feathering his own nest, by getting TEAM to take over the computer infrastructure of the now defunct Israeli Civil Administration in Gaza (Sha'ath says that he has divested himself of all interests in the business). In the longer term, his ties with Arafat ensure him a continued top role in the Authority, and his commonsense approach has averted many a disaster. On Jan. 20, 1996, he was elected to the Palestine Council for a seat in Gaza Central. But his lack of a powerbase in the refugee camps and PLO factions may prevent him from achieving his ultimate ambitions.

Shaban, Sayed   Lebanon
Sheikh and leader of *Tawheed* (Islamic Unification Movement). Shaban founded *Tawheed* in

Tripoli in 1982, and together with the PLO this Sunni movement resisted the Syrian offensive of November 1983. However, after suffering a number of defeats, he formed an alliance with Syria and 'normalized' relations.

Shachor, Oren   Israel

Major-general, Co-ordinator of Government Activity in the Territories. Since Oslo 1, Jamal Tarifi, the PNA's 'liaison minister', and Shachor have headed the Civil Affairs Committee (CAC), an Israeli–Palestinian liaison forum. Shachor was in charge of the logistics of IDF redeployment, which he negotiated with Tarifi, as one by one major Palestinian cities (Tul Karm, Nablus, Ramallah and Bethlehem) achieved autonomy in late 1995.

Haidar Abd al-SHAFI

Nationality	Palestinian
Religion	Muslim
Place of Birth	Gaza
Date of Birth	1919
Current position	Palestinian leader in territories, loosely affiliated to *Fatah* Head of the Palestinian Red Crescent Society
Previous position	Head of the official Palestinian delegation at the Madrid peace talks
Allies	Sari Nusseibeh, Hanan Ashrawi; at times close to Arafat
Position on peace	Initially positive, now critical of PNA
National political importance	Influential in territories; both a moderate and a critic of Oslo
Prospects	Unlikely to succeed Arafat, but respected by friend and foe

Little known outside the Palestinian community, Dr Haidar Abd al-Shafi was chosen as head of the first Palestinian delegation to negotiate directly with Israel, in the Madrid peace conference of October 1991. He also led the delegation during the protracted negotiations with Israel in Washington. Abd al-Shafi soon impressed an international audience with his quiet dignity and frankness in representing the Palestinian cause. Yet in succeeding years he grew frustrated with lack of progress at the talks, and effectively dropped out of the process when the Oslo Accords supplanted the bilateral negotiations in Washington. Dr Abd al-Shafi is a critic of the Israel–PLO accords of Oslo and Washington, which he believes conceded too much to Israel, and which have delivered even less than they promised.

Abd al-Shafi studied medicine in Beirut and the United States, after which he returned to work as a community physician in Gaza. He is said to have been a founder member of the Palestinian National Council, but was never actually a card-holding member of the PLO. In 1948 he was one of the few leading Palestinians who accepted the UN partition plan. In the 1960s, Arab press articles attacked him for recognizing Israel's right to exist, and calling for a peaceful solution with the Jewish state. Israeli sources say that the Egyptians, who ruled Gaza from 1948 until 1967, had imprisoned him for political dissent, although al-Shafi denies this.

Abd al-Shafi maintained a position roughly in line with the Communist Party, and after 1967 opposed the excesses of Israeli rule in Gaza, but never condoned the use of terror. Israel banished him to Sinai and later to Lebanon. On his return he continued to run the Palestinian Red Crescent Society. In the absence of the PLO (banned by Israel), the society became a hub for leftist nationalists, and acted as a counterweight to the growing support for Islamist groups like *Hamas* in the territories. In 1980 young fundamentalists tried to burn down its headquarters. Since then, Haidar Abd al-Shafi has maintained a truce with *Hamas* followers, and won their respect if not their political support.

It was significant that the PLO approved Abd al-Shafi, a Gazan, to head the Madrid team. Most of the other delegates came from Ramallah and other areas in the West Bank. However, as the talks progressed, Abd al-Shafi was frustrated by the higher profile enjoyed by the technical advisory 'unofficial' team, headed by Faisal al-Husseini. Renowned as a stubborn negotiator, al-Shafi presented the first plans for Palestinian self-government (PISGA), al-though neither the Shamir nor Rabin administrations accepted their terms. In early 1993 he suspended talks with Israel over the deportation of 413 *Hamas* supporters, but agreed to return to the ninth session in March of that year, after Yitzhak Rabin promised to implement a phased return. He accused the Rabin government of not fulfilling its promise to freeze new settlements, and asked for an Israeli gesture that it was 'negotiating in good faith'. To some extent his scepticism was later justified, when details emerged in August 1993 of the secret Israel–PLO talks in Oslo. But Abd al-Shafi was equally angry with the PLO for not informing him of these developments.

Since the implementation of the Gaza-Jericho Accords, Abd al-Shafi has not been assigned any specific role in the Palestine National Authority. In 1994 he criticized what he saw as a disturbing lack of democracy within the PLO–led government of Gaza and Jericho. He called for a collective leadership to curb Yasser Arafat's autocratic tendencies and the domination by the formerly Tunis-based *Fatah*. In the 1996 Palestinian Council elections he stood as head of an independent list. In the new dispensation there is no question mark on his credibility, and he is freer to express his independent views. His latest campaign was to oppose amending the Palestinian Covenant, as a bargaining chip in talks with Israel on matters concerning refugees, Jerusalem, settlements and borders. Some predict he may become the Council's Speaker. Dr Haidar Abd al-Shafi always said he was first and foremost a physician, and only a politician out of duty; now he may have found a new role, as loyal opposition to the professional politicians of the PLO.

Shafi, Khaled Abd al-   Palestinian

Gaza officer for the United Nations Development Programme (UNDP), and a leading Palestinian economist. Shafi sees a strong economic link between Gaza and the West Bank as the key to Palestinian development. To this end he believes a land-link between the two areas (as stipulated in the DOP) is 'a matter of economic survival'. He also supports the joint Israel-PNA-World Bank plan to build industrial zones on the border between Israel and the self-rule areas. To Shafi, this will boost local business and end the security problem. Shafi co-operates with UN representative Terje Larsen and UNRWA chief, April Glaspie.

Amnon Lipkin SHAHAK

Nationality	Israeli
Religion	Jewish
Date of birth	1944
Place of birth	Tel Aviv, Palestine
Current position	Chief of Staff since January 1995
Previous position	Deputy Chief of staff to Ehud Barak
Allies	Ehud Barak, Rafi Peled, Binyamin Ben-Eliezer, Shimon Shevis, Ya'akov Peri, Moshe Levy, Amos Yaron, Yitzhak Rabin
Position on peace	Played key role in negotiating with PLO in Taba, and now re-Syria
National political importance	Important as a negotiator
Prospects	Future political aspirations depend on success of current talks

Amnon Shahak was made Chief of Staff on Jan. 1, 1995 and was immediately propelled into high-level talks on security matters in the Golan Heights with his Syrian opposite number, Hikmat Shihabi. Despite the sensitivity of the negotiations, observers had great faith in Shahak because of his long experience, outstanding military record and proven ability to achieve results in negotiations.

Shahak is the only Israeli soldier to have been decorated twice for bravery. On both occasions this came after actions against Palestinians (for operations against bases in Karameh, Jordan, in 1969, and Beirut in 1973). In the aftermath of the 1982 war in Lebanon, Shahak was commander of the Beirut and Shouf areas. From 1983 to 1986 he was head of Central Command. For the next five years he was Israel's chief of military intelligence, and carefully studied key figures in enemy countries. Shahak has said that ultimately people, rather than processes and interests, make history. In 1987 Shahak predicted that serious disturbances could break out in the territories, but after the *intifada* actually began, Shahak admitted that the authorities had erred by not discussing the issue with more vigour when it was presented to the Israeli cabinet.

Amnon Shahak has a reputation for combining flexibility with ruthlessness. Although he is quietly spoken he is also not afraid to come out in the open on sensitive issues. In 1988, at the height of the *intifada*, he told Prime Minister Yitzhak Shamir that the PLO was the main powerbroker in the territories, and that only by talking to the organization could Israel hope to stem the violence. That same year, he planned the assassination of Yasser Arafat's number two, Abu Jihad.

Shahak assumed the post of deputy chief of staff, under Ehud Barak, in 1991. In October 1993 he was sent to Taba to head the Co-ordinating Committee, where he discussed implementation of the Declaration of Principles with his PLO counterpart, Nabil Sha'ath. Shunning advice that he should keep the discussions secret, he allowed cameras to cover the talks, stating that public symbols of reconciliation were necessary to achieve peace. In the event Sha'ath and Shahak built up a warm mutual respect which helped to break the deadlock in talks and cleared the way for the handover of powers to the new Palestinian Authority in March 1994. Arafat's advisor Ahmed Tibi described him as the most honest and respectful Israeli negotiator. He was praised for the successful redeployment of IDF forces from Gaza and Jericho. This became a model for the larger IDF redeployment from other towns in the West Bank in late 1995, for which Shahak secured some $300 million from the government.

The restarted talks between Syria and Israel, held in mid-1995, largely centred on the issue of the Golan. Shahak took over the security brief from Ehud Barak, who retired to enter mainstream politics. Hikmat Shihabi, Shahak's opposite number and negotiating partner, has effectively headed the Syrian army since 1974 and thus has much experience. Israel decided not to demand reductions in the Syrian army (which had stymied Barak's efforts in late 1994). This made Shahak's task somewhat easier. Even so, the talks failed in mid-1995.

After the Rabin assassination, Barak became Foreign Minister, and mandated Shahak to renew talks with Syria, which took place in Maryland. Shahak has devised plans to pre-empt a nuclear threat to Israel, and envisages a reformed army, with fewer conscripts and more specialist units. In March 1996, Shahak presented Yasser Arafat with a list of 15 *Hamas* names, after a new spate of suicide bombings threatened to wreck the peace process, and demanded that the PNA arrest them. In April he lobbied for, and planned, Operation Grapes of Wrath in Lebanon, and so bears some responsibility for its shortcomings. In the longer term, Shahak may enter politics, like Barak, but at present his main concern is to guard Israeli security against a resurgence of *Hamas* attacks.

Moshe SHAHAL

Nationality	Israeli
Religion	Jewish
Birth name	Morris Fattal
Place of birth	Iraq
Date of birth	1934
Current position	Minister of Internal Security (after November 1995)
Previous position	Minister for Energy, Infrastructure and Police (since 1992)
Allies	Security-conscious Labourites, Yitzhak Rabin
Position on peace	Cautious support; credited with the 'separation plan'
National political importance	Influential on the centre-right; good image in Western media
Prospects	Important Labour Sephardi politician, but support base is questionable

Moshe Shahal is a veteran of Israeli politics who has long harboured desires to become prime minister. He was born in Iraq in 1934, and emigrated to Israel in 1950. Shahal is a lawyer by profession, and holds degrees in economics, sociology and political science from Haifa

University; and a law degree from Tel Aviv University. Shahal was a member of the Haifa Labour Council from 1964 to 1971, and he served on the Haifa City Council from 1965 to 1969. Since 1971 he has been a Labour Party MK. From 1974 he was Israel's Permanent Observer to the Council of Europe; after that he served as Permanent Representative to the Inter-Parliamentary Union (from 1976 to 1984).

Between 1981 and 1984 Shahal was a Deputy Speaker and Chairman of the Labour Party faction in the Knesset. In the National Unity Governments (1984 to 1990) he served as Minister of Energy and Infrastructure. Within the party, Shahal was a Peres loyalist until Rabin's comeback in late 1991. Following the Labour victory in 1992, Shahal entered the cabinet as Police Minister. He was given a broad brief to investigate opportunities for Israel in the multilateral talks, and negotiated with Egyptian counterparts on energy co-operation between the two countries. Rabin often bypassed Justice Minister David Liba'i and relied on Shahal to carry out difficult policies.

In office, Shahal has overseen the growth of the Israeli police force. While some analysts have blamed him for not doing more to improve traffic policing, and for the poor state of many prisons, he has won some praise for the success of joint Israeli–Palestinian patrols (a feature of Oslo 1). More controversially, he supported the building of a multi-million dollar 'security fence' to divide the territories from Israel proper. The plan aimed to formalize the frequent 'sealing of the territories'; but curiously, right-wingers began to oppose it, because it seemed to acknowledge the division of *Eretz Yisrael* from the State of Israel (they feared it was the first step towards establishing a separate Palestinian state). Yitzhak Rabin agreed to drop the scheme.

In August and September 1995, Shahal ordered three Palestinian bodies in Jerusalem (including a broadcasting corporation and statistics bureau) to close down, as their presence, he felt, contravened Oslo 1's restriction on PNA bodies in the Israeli capital. After the assassination of Rabin on Nov. 4, 1995, Shahal's departmental brief was expanded, and he became Minister of Internal Security. Shahal avoided blame for the security lapse which led to Rabin's death. Some critics feared that his extended ministerial powers could become draconian. Significantly, Shahal joined the small inner cabinet 'peace team', which oversees the day-to-day implementation of Oslo 2. He is also known to favour closer ties between Israel and his native Iraq, although this is very much a minority view. In the light of renewed *Hamas* bombings in 1996, Shahal has called on Arafat and the PNA to eliminate terrorist groups.

Shahid, Leila   Palestinian
Chief PLO representative in Paris. In the early 1960s she studied at the American University in Beirut, and became active in Lebanon's exile Palestinian community. She later left for Morocco to pursue a quieter academic life, but was hand-picked by Yasser Arafat to head the PLO offices, first in the Hague and later in Paris. Shahid is a descendant of the Mufti of Jerusalem, Hajj Amin al-Husseini, and is a cousin of East Jerusalem PLO leader, Faisal al-Husseini. She is also known as a close friend and ally of Hanan Ashrawi. In 1995 Shahid was guest of honour at the annual conference of CRIF, the main French Jewish communal organization.

Shaiah, Khalil   Palestinian
Gaza's chief justice.

Shaikholeslam, Hussein   Iran
Iranian Deputy Minister of Foreign Affairs, with responsibility for relations with the Arab world. Shaikholeslam is also believed to be the deputy head of Iranian military intelligence, and a major conduit of aid to *Hamas, Hezbollah* and other radical groups. In December 1995, the London *Independent* reported that in October he had met Fathi Shiqaqi, leader of the Palestinian Islamic *Jihad* group, in Libya, allegedly to plan the murder of Yasser Arafat. (Shiqaqi was assassinated in Malta later in October, reputedly by the Israeli *Mossad*, following a tip-off from the PLO.) In 1979 Shaikholeslam had helped to take over the US embassy in Teheran. He is also believed to have planned the suicide truck bombing which killed 241 US Marines in Beirut, in 1983. Currently, Shaikholeslam liaises between the Iranian Foreign Ministry and the *Vezarat-e-Ettelat* (the Information Ministry, but in effect the intelligence agency). In the week after *Hamas* resumed its bombing campaign in Israel, Shaikholeslam

attended a meeting of Palestinian and Lebanese 'peace rejection front' groups, in Damascus. He promised these groups Teheran's 'full support, and with all means at our disposal'. Teheran officially denies being involved in the suicide bombings.

Shaka'a, Bassam al-   Palestinian

Former elected Mayor of Nablus. Bassam al-Shaka'a was born in Nablus in 1930, as one of 11 children. After the 1948 war he left for Syria, where joined the *Ba'ath* Party. He returned to Nablus, but spent two years in hiding while Jordanian authorities were looking for him. By the mid-1970s he was back in Nablus, now under Israeli occupation, and was elected mayor on a pro-PLO platform. Shaka'a made contacts with left-wing Israelis, but was harried by the *Likud* government, which sought his deportation. Shaka'a lost both his legs after members of the Jewish Underground detonated a car-bomb in 1980. Mayor Karim Khalaf of Ramallah and the Mayor of Jenin suffered a similar fate. Shaka'a was later deported, and went to Damascus, from where he criticized the Oslo accords. Now back in the West Bank, he denounced King Hussein and President Hosni Mubarak for attending Yitzhak Rabin's funeral in November 1996, as this marked 'a tacit recognition of Israeli sovereignty over Jerusalem'; and called Arafat a 'dictator without a philosophy'.

Shaka'a, Ghassan al-   Palestinian

Mayor designate of Nablus, West Bank, as of late 1995.

Shakaki, Fathi   Palestinian

(See Shiqaqi, Fat'hi)

Sharif Zaid bin SHAKER

Nationality	Jordanian
Religion	Muslim
Date of birth	1934
Place of birth	Near Amman, Jordan
Current position	Prime Minister of the Kingdom of Jordan since January 1995 Replaced by Abdul-Karim Kabariti in February 1996
Previous positions	Several stints as prime minister and chief of the Royal Court
Allies	Strong family and personal connections with King Hussein
Position on peace	More cautious than his predecessor, Abdul Salam al-Majali

Sharif Zaid ibn Shaker (sometimes also rendered as Bin Shaker or Ibn Shakir) is one of the most seasoned politicians in the Hashemite Kingdom, and is on excellent terms with King Hussein. His father accompanied Hussein's grandfather, Emir Abdullah ibn Talal, when the Saudi family deposed the Hashemites and expelled them from Mecca and Medina, in Arabia. Bin Shaker was educated at Victoria College in Amman, and at two prestigious military establishments in the USA, as well as at Sandhurst in Britain. When the young king was finding his feet, it was Bin Shaker who acted as his Royal Companion, from 1955 to 1957. Sharif bin Shaker became assistant military chief of staff in 1970, and Commander of the Jordanian Armed Forces, before becoming entering mainstream politics as Chief of the Royal Court.

When he was chosen as Prime Minister in January 1995, taking over from Abdul Salam al-Majali, it was actually his third stint in the office. He first led a caretaker government from April 1989 to November 1989, and was entrusted with overseeing the first general parliamentary elections held in Jordan since 1966. However, he was forced to resign in the wake of incessant price riots, and the unexpectedly good results for the Muslim Brotherhood in the November elections. He was recalled to office in November 1991, coinciding with Jordan's participation at the Madrid peace conference, and served until May 1993.

Abdul Salam al-Majali, former chief negotiator in peace talks with Israel, took over from Shaker in May 1993, and continued his work in driving ahead with Jordan's constitutional reforms and democratization drive. In October 1993, Shaker replaced Khaled al-Karaki as Chief of the Royal Court. When Shaker replaced Majali as prime minister in 1995, some analysts interpreted it as a sign that King Hussein wanted to slow down the peace process

(Majali had signed the peace treaty with Israel in September 1994). Other analysts, however, feel that Shaker was a 'trusted pair of hands', and so a necessary force as Jordan embarked on the difficult task of actually implementing peace with the former enemy, Israel. After overseeing the completion of numerous agreements with Israel, which flowed from the 1994 peace treaty, Shaker was in turn replaced as Prime Minister by a younger man, Abdul-Karim Kabariti. Shaker was named a prince, but his departure was widely seen as the sign of a profound 'generational shift' in Jordanian politics.

Shallah, Ramadan Abdullah   Palestinian
Said to be the leader of Islamic *Jihad* in Gaza, after the death of Dr Fath'i Shiqaqi. Shallah, a one-time student in the UK, consulted with Iranian First Vice President Hassan Ebrahim Habibi in March, following the Tel Aviv suicide bomb attack. That atrocity was claimed to be an Islamic *Jihad* revenge operation for the assassination in 1995 of Dr Shiqaqi.

Shamas, (Muhammed) Suheil Lebanon
Chief Lebanese negotiator at the Washington peace talks in 1992 and 1993. He was called in after the opening session in Madrid, in October 1991. Shamas is a seasoned diplomat, and Secretary-General of the Foreign Ministry. Together with his deputy, Ambassador Jihad Murtada, he established a reasonable working relationship with his Israeli counterparts, Uri Lubrani, the co-ordinator of Israeli government activity in Lebanon, and Yossi Hadas, then the Director-General of the Israeli Foreign Ministry. However, Shamas was hampered by the need not to steal a march on his Syrian partners. His main stance was to demand Israeli withdrawal from south Lebanon, and then to talk about the modalities of a real peace treaty. He also stressed the need to settle disputes about water. In March 1993 he resigned his posts after 'differences' with Foreign Minister Faris Boueiz.

Shamgar, Meir   Israel
Chief Justice on Israel's Supreme Court until August 1995; judge in charge of commission into Hebron massacre, 1994. On his recommendations, Israel tightened restrictions on Jewish settlers who wished to worship at the Cave of Machpelah (alongside the Ibrahimi Mosque) in Hebron. Shamgar also approved the presence of The International Peacekeeping Force in Hebron (known as TIPH), despite initial objections from Jerusalem. After the Rabin assassination of November 1995, Shamgar was recalled to head a commission of inquiry into the murder. In the light of his preliminary findings, the head of the General Security Services and other officers in the organization resigned. Meir Shamgar won the prestigious Israel Prize for contributions to Israeli society, in January 1996.

Shamir, Shimon   Israel
Israel's first and current ambassador to Jordan; formerly Israeli ambassador to Egypt. Shimon Shamir was born in Satu Mare, Romania, in 1933. He immigrated to Palestine in 1940, and studied at the Hebrew University in Jerusalem, and later at Princeton, USA. From 1966 to 1972 he was the director of the Shiloah Institute. Until his ambassadorial appointments, Shamir was Professor of Middle East History in Modern Times at Tel Aviv University. He also headed the university's Centre for Peace Research. Shamir wrote 'Arabs in the Middle East', and has written copiously on the role of Arab intellectuals in the political process, as well as heading an interdisciplinary research unit into aspects of Palestinian society. He once proposed a compromise solution for the problem of Jerusalem, with autonomous Palestinian boroughs in a united city.

Shimon Shamir became ambassador to Egypt in 1988. This proved a testing assignment, as relations between Cairo and Tel Aviv had cooled over Israel's handling of the *intifada*. Shamir was called on to defend Israel's policies. In early 1995 he became ambassador to Jordan, after Jordanian officials had raised qualms about Israel's first choice appointee, the negotiator Ephraim Halevy, because of the latter's *Mossad* connections. Shamir soon nurtured contacts with Jordanian intellectuals and professionals who were keen to work on joint projects with Israelis. However, he was doubly handicapped in his efforts as mediator, by delays in the signing of an Israel–Jordan trade agreement, and by a mounting campaign of 'non-co-operation' with Israelis, led by the Islamic Action Front (IAF) and 'rejectionist' Palestinians. In September he was forced to abandon a public meeting in Irbid, after intimidation by demonstrators, and a boycott by IAF-dominated professional associations. The eventual signing of a trade deal and the successful Amman regional economic conference, which both took place in late October 1995, thus marked something of a breakthrough for Shamir, who is well regarded in Jordanian government circles.

Yitzhak SHAMIR

Nationality	Israeli
Religion	Jewish
Place of birth	Poland
Date of birth	1915
Current position	MK for the *Likud*
Previous positions	Prime Minister (1983–84 and 1986–92)
	Foreign Minister (1980–86)
	Knesset Speaker (1977–80)
Allies	Ariel Sharon, Dan Meridor, Benjamin Begin, Yossi Avimeir
Position on peace	Approved Israeli participation in the Madrid peace conference
	Rejected talks with the PLO, and any territorial compromises
National political importance	Dominant political force of the 1980s
	Power diminished as *Likud* suffered from schisms in the 1990s
Prospects	Age precludes hope of a comeback; his opinion is still sought on political issues

Although originally depicted as the most right-wing prime minister in Israel's history, it was Yitzhak Shamir who gave the green light to talks between Israel and a Palestinian delegation, at the Madrid peace conference, starting on Oct. 31, 1991. Shamir also turned out to be one of the longest-serving Israeli prime ministers, yet when he took office, in 1983, he was seen as something of a compromise candidate.

Born as Yitzhak Yazernitsky in Poland, he joined the local youth branch of the Revisionist Zionist Movement, and emigrated to Palestine in 1935, aged 20. In 1941 he broke away from the right-wing *Irgun* underground (led by Menachem Begin) to co-found the more extreme *Lehi* (better known as the 'Stern Gang', after its charismatic leader, Avraham Stern). Unlike mainstream Zionist groups, *Lehi* continued to fight the British Mandate for the duration of the war. Shamir personally planned a number of assassinations (of Lord Moyne and Count Bernadotte, amongst others). After British forces shot Stern dead, Shamir became *Lehi's* effective leader. Britain twice arrested Shamir, but on both occasions he escaped (the second time from a military camp in Ethiopia). After Israel achieved independence, Shamir returned from exile in France, and temporarily withdrew from politics to run a chain of cinemas.

From 1955 to 1965, Shamir worked for *Mossad*, reputedly overseeing its European sphere of operations. He only joined *Herut* (successor to the Revisionist Movement) in 1970, and entered the Knesset in 1973. Shamir proved to be cautious, loyal and hard-working, and Prime Minister Menachem Begin chose him as Knesset Speaker in 1977. Though at the time he had opposed the Camp David accords with Egypt, he became Foreign Minister in 1979 after Moshe Dayan resigned the post. In 1982 he sided with Ariel Sharon and Chief of Staff Eitan Rafael in planning the invasion of Lebanon, and ensuring that it became a far bigger operation than most cabinet ministers had intended it to be.

Shamir succeeded Menachem Begin as Prime Minister and *Likud* chairman in 1983. However, widespread disillusionment with the Lebanese war and the ailing economy led to *Likud* failing to win the 1984 Israeli general elections outright. Instead, Shamir was forced to form a government of national unity with the opposition Labour Party. According to the deal, Shimon Peres (Labour's leader) would act as prime minister and Shamir would be foreign minister for two years; in the following two years (1986 to 1988) they would swap positions. The 1988 elections, fought with the Palestinian *intifada* as a backdrop, was equally inconclusive, but Shamir retained the premiership in another coalition with Labour. Compelled to respond to the PLO's Algiers Declaration, Shamir surprised his right-wing allies with plans for Palestinian local elections. However, he was forced to shelve them in 1989 after internal party opposition.

In March 1990 the *Likud*-Labour coalition eventually split after Shamir rejected US Secretary of State James Baker's plans for peace talks with the Palestinians. The resultant new government (without Labour) relied on support from ultra-right parties and religious factions. Shamir did little to stem growing calls by right-wing factions for 'transfer' of Palestinians from the territories. *Likud* was also increasingly fraught with rivalries (between Moshe Arens, Ariel Sharon and David Levy, all of whom felt they ought to succeed the ageing Shamir). Once again, Shamir proved to be the quintessential political survivor, playing off one faction against the other; but the cost to the country was considerable. During the Gulf War, Shamir showed remarkable restraint in not responding to Iraqi Scud attacks on Israel. He eventually agreed to send a delegation to the Madrid peace talks in October and November 1991, but only after stipulating restraints on the composition of the Palestinian delegation. Shamir bolstered the rising Deputy Foreign Minister Benjamin Netanyahu, at the expense of the more moderate Foreign Minister David Levy. He also antagonized the Bush administration by refusing to freeze new settlements.

After the 1992 defeat, Shamir resigned as Prime Minister and party leader. In a subsequent interview, he admitted that he had intended to drag on autonomy talks with the Palestinians without conceding anything substantial. As a backbench MK, Shamir adopted a lower profile. Despite his many achievements, *Likud* supporters could not easily forgive his vacillations and incessant rivalries, which, they believe, ultimately cost their party the election. Even so, Shamir will be remembered as a staunch defender of what he saw as Israel's security needs. He ensured that Jewish settlement in the territories (or *Eretz Yisrael*) became a fait accompli. At the same time, he succeeded in absorbing 600,000 new Soviet immigrants into Israel; and, while rejecting 'territorial compromise', he did plant the seeds in Israeli minds for some form of Palestinian interim self-government. In December 1995, Yitzhak Shamir announced that he would not be standing for re-election.

Shanab, Ismael Abu   Palestinian

Declared the head of the political bureau of the Islamic National Salvation Party, on Nov. 19 1995. The new party was seen by many as a wing of *Hamas*. It sought a political entity based on *sharia* law, and *shura* (consultation or democracy); it also vowed to 'struggle against the Israeli occupation by employing all political means'. In the event, the party did not contest the Palestinian Council elections of Jan. 20, 1996, although individual members may have been numbered amongst elected 'independent Islamist' candidates. Abu Shanab has been held in an Israeli prison since 1989, when he was arrested for a *Hamas* office in Gaza during the *intifada*.

Shar'a, Farouq ash-   Syria

Foreign Minister, wily diplomat. Shar'a is seen as the 'cosmopolitan' face of Damascus in the post-Gulf War period, and was charged with improving relations with the United States and European Union. He delivered Syria's opening statement at the Madrid peace conference which reiterated his nation's demand for a total Israeli withdrawal from the Golan Heights before it would consider peace with Israel. He also took the opportunity to launch a fierce personal attack on the leader of the Israeli delegation, Prime Minister Yitzhak Shamir, calling him a 'terrorist who kills peacemakers'. Shar'a claims to favour a 'comprehensive peace', and on that basis criticized the PLO's Yasser Arafat and Jordan's King Hussein in turn for signing 'separate peaces' with Israel, in 1993 and 1994 respectively.

Later, Shar'a appeared to soften his line, and in 1993 took charge of a new Syrian diplomatic offensive. In January he led a Syrian delegation to Iran. Ties between the two states improved, to the chagrin of Syria's new ally, the USA. However, the following month he told visiting US Secretary of State Warren Christopher that he thought the peace talks with Israel were 'broader and more important' than the deportation issue (Israel's decision the previous year to expel more than 400 Islamic militants from Gaza had angered Arab leaders, and threatened to halt the peace process). Shar'a bolstered ties with Cairo in March; and in October he hosted UK Foreign Secretary Douglas Hurd, who described UK–Syrian relations as 'strong and growing'.

In January 1994, Shar'a claimed that Yitzhak Rabin's plan to hold a referendum on returning the Golan Heights to Syria was 'against international law'. In February he suspended bilateral talks with Israel over the Hebron massacre, but assured Warren Christopher that this was 'a pause, not a retreat'. Shar'a broke new ground a few months afterwards, by granting Israeli television its first interview with a Syrian minister. Later that year, Syria resumed talks with Israel, but Shar'a chose not to be directly involved, lest their failure may harm his political standing. In the event, the talks broke down when Israel's negotiator, Ehud Barak, insisted that Syria reduce the size of its standing army as part of a Golan deal.

On May 27, 1995, Shar'a expressed satisfaction with a new US–brokered 'framework of understanding' between the two countries, which they had signed three days earlier. Talks resumed, this time between Israeli and Syrian military chiefs of staff, Amnon Shahak and Hikmat Shihabi respectively; but by August they had stalled again, over the issues of security and the future of the Golan Heights. The assassination of Yitzhak Rabin in November appeared to shock Syria into reviving talks. In December 1995, Shar'a met Israel's new Foreign Minister, Ehud Barak, at a Mediterranean conference in Barcelona. Through the offices of Warren Christopher, he ensured that talks resumed, this time in the Wye Valley in Maryland, USA. Israel was disappointed that Shar'a did not personally take part in negotiations. However, in a symbolic breakthrough, Shar'a did suggest publicly that *Hezbollah* terror was impeding the peace process. Israel praised Syria for evidently quelling *Hezbollah* activity, but Iran, chief paymasters of the group, warned Syria that this could spoil their relationship. Farouq ash-Shar'a is a skilful political operator. Yet Syria-watchers say his apparent independence is illusory, and that President Assad makes all the main decisions.

Sharansky, Natan   Israel

Former Russian Jewish refusenik, and now leader of the *Aliyah Leumi* party. During the 1970s and 1980s Sharansky was internationally regarded as the symbol of the refuseniks, those Soviet Jews who were denied the right to immigrate to Israel. He was imprisoned for years, but the personal intervention of Mikhail Gorbachev ensured his eventual release in 1986. In retrospect, this marked the beginning of a new flood of immigration from Russia and its immediate satellites. After arriving in Israel, Sharansky changed his first name from Anatoly to Natan, and became active as a political commentator. In the early 1990s he was elected president of the Zionist Forum, a pressure group for the rights of immigrants. He also set about learning Arabic, which he saw as essential if Jews wished to make peace with their Arab neighbours. In 1995, Sharansky founded a political party, *Aliyah Leumi* (also called *Yisrael B'Aliyah*), which in Hebrew means Immigration for the People, or National Renaissance, depending on interpretation. Israel has more than 700,000 citizens of Russian or former Soviet descent; by tapping into this ethnic vote goldmine, Sharansky holds the balance of power in the Netanyahu government. He also benefits from the great affection of Diaspora Jews, which he has cultivated by addressing numerous communal meetings in London, New York and elsewhere. Sharansky broadly supports the current peace process, although he criticizes the Palestinian Authority for not complying to the Oslo Accords; and criticizes Israel for encouraging 'non-democratic' aspects of Arafat's rule.

Sharif, Bassam Abu   Palestinian

A leading light within the Popular Front for the Liberation of Palestine (PFLP), who changed to become a proponent of the 'two state solution' within the PLO. Bassam Abu Sharif (sometimes known as Abu Omar) was born in 1946 in Irbid, Jordan, to a family which came from Jerusalem. He moved to Amman aged four, and in 1963 he began his studies at the American University in Beirut, where he joined the Movement of Arab Nationalists (MAN), led by the Palestinian leader George Habash. Later he worked in the Suweileh refugee camp in Jordan, and in December 1967 became a founder member of MAN's successor group, the PFLP. Abu Sharif was the deputy editor of the PFLP newspaper, *Al-Hadaf,* and became 'the public face of the PFLP' as it stepped up its campaign of hijackings after 1968.

Abu Sharif was wounded at the newspaper offices by a letter-bomb, planted by Israeli security forces, in 1972. In his recent book, *Tried By Fire,* which he co-authored with the Israeli journalist and former intelligence operative, Uzi Mahnaimi, Bassam Abu Sharif describes how his brush with death persuaded him that constant war was not the answer to the Palestinian problem. In 1982 he warned the PFLP of Israeli plans to attack Lebanon, but was ignored. It was during this period that he grew closer to PLO Chairman Yasser Arafat. Bassam Abu Sharif was finally expelled from PFLP in 1987. Now an Arafat aide, he advocated a two-state solution, and opened negotiations about this with Egyptian President Mubarak. Abu Sharif mobilized the PLO publicity machine in Baghdad, to stress the PLO's support for the *intifada* in the occupied territories. Privately, he began persuading Arafat to drop his opposition to UN 242, and to renouced terrorism openly. Abu Sharif arranged for the Mitterrand–Arafat meeting in the wake of the Algiers Declaration in 1988.

He also penned an influential document, *Prospects for Peace in the Middle East; the Two-State Solution*, which in many aspects pre-empted the terms of the Oslo Accords. In mid-1991, months before the Madrid peace conference, Abu Sharif reiterated the necessity for activists in the territories to co-ordinate their activities with the PLO headquarters in Tunis. He condemned 'unjustified killings' in the *intifada*, but admitted some punishment of 'collaborators' was legitimate (in many cases, suspects were arrested by *shabib* and tried before local lawyers in unofficial Palestinian courts). Abu Sharif was one of the initiators of contacts with the Norwegian Foreign Minister Stoltenberg in September 1992, but was not intimately involved with the secret Oslo talks. He returned to the territories in 1996, in preparation for the PNC debate on the Palestinian Covenant. Abu Sharif does not hold any official position, but his influence with decision-makers in Washington will probably count in his favour in years to come. Above all, he remains an optimist about peace, and believes that 'Palestine is Israel's bridge to the Middle East'.

Sharif, Mohiedin   Palestinian

Hamas master bomb-maker and co-ordinator of terrorism. Suicide bombings in Israel killed about 70 people in late February and early March 1996, and threatened to sabotage the peace process. Sharif's name topped the list of 15 *Hamas* leaders, whom Israel blame for the atrocities. IDF Chief of Staff Amnon Shahak submitted the list to Palestinian President Yasser Arafat, and demanded that the Palestine Authority capture and detain them without delay. Sharif lives in Beit Hanina, Jerusalem. He is regarded as a disciple of Yehya Ayyash, the *Hamas* 'Engineer' who was assassinated on Jan. 5, 1996.

Sharif, Nabil   Palestinian

Water Commissioner for the Palestine National Authority. Sharif is an engineer by training. In July 1995 he represented the Palestinians for the first time at the water working group, within the multilateral framework, at its session in Amman, Jordan. There he negotiated with the head of the Israeli delegation, Avraham Katz-Oz, over possible joint projects. Sharif ensured that the Interim Agremeent (Oslo 2), signed between Israel and the PLO on Sept. 28, 1995, included provisions for Israel to allocate a further 28 million cubic metres of water to Palestinians. A tripartite US–Israeli–Palestinian forum was to convene after Oslo 2 was signed. He also drafted proposals for a $65 million project for water management and sanitation services in Gaza. However, Sharif will probably be most busy in 1996, when the issue of water comes onto the table during the 'final status' talks between Israel and the Palestinians.

Sharon, Ariel   Israel

Right-wing *Likud* politician, former Defence Minister, and one-time leading proponent of the Greater Israel philosophy. Ariel Sharon was born on a *moshav* in 1928, and while still a teenager he impressed his *Haganah* superiors as an outstanding officer. After Israeli Independence, Ben-Gurion made him head of Unit 101, a special force dedicated to eradicating threats from Palestinian *fedayeen,* who werê launching frequent attacks on Israel from bases in Gaza and the West Bank. Sharon's retaliatory raid on Qibya, Jordan, in 1953, became notorious in Palestinian circles for its ruthlessness, and marked Sharon as a feared enemy. Although his paratroopers failed to hold a key pass in the 1956 war, Ariel Sharon became commander of the IDF's armoured brigades in 1962. He led a division during the 1967 war and was seen as a military hero. Immediately afterwards, Sharon enthusiastically crushed Palestinian resistance in the newly occupied Gaza Strip.

After a dispute with fellow officers, Sharon left the military to become a *Likud* MK in 1973.

although he had no strong prior party political affiliations. In 1974 he left *Likud* to become Labour Leader Yitzhak Rabin's special security adviser. But after the *Likud* victory of 1977, he switched sides again, and served under Menachem Begin as Agriculture Minister until 1981. Although Sharon has never been religious, he keenly supported the *Gush Emunim* movement, and used his ministry as a means to encourage intensified Jewish settlement on the West Bank. At the same time, this bulky and bullish personality nurtured a growing populist support base, especially amongst poorer Sephardi Jews (notwithstanding his own typically Ashkenazi background, and the fact that he is Israel's wealthiest cattle farmer).

In 1982 he became Defence Minister, and, together with Chief of Staff Raphael Eitan, they masterminded Israel's huge invasion of Lebanon in June of that year. The Kahan Commission report into the subsequent Sabra and Shatilla massacre blamed Sharon for culpable negligence, and he was forced to resign as Defence Minister in 1983. However, Begin insisted that he remain in the cabinet as a Minister without Portfolio. From 1984 to 1990 he was Minister of Trade and Industry; and from 1990 until *Likud's* electoral defeat in 1992, Sharon was Minister for Construction and Housing. Once again, he bypassed normal ministerial strictures by injecting funds into a renewed settlement drive. This led US Secretary of State James Baker to 'punish' Israel by suspending $10 billion in loan guarantees.

Sharon has proposed radical schemes for 'solving the Palestinian problem'. One was an alternative to the Allon Plan, whereby Israel would annex 75% of the West Bank, and post armed settlers on the higher ground. Palestinians would have limited autonomy over the remaining 25% (mainly towns near the 'green line' and northern Samaria). In another plan, Sharon gave a new and sinister twist to Peres's 'Jordanian option', by suggesting that the PLO overthrow King Hussein, and declare Jordan as their Palestinian state (thereby foregoing any claims on 'the territories'). Sharon also stirred controversy in his personal life, when he broke a government taboo by occupying property in Jerusalem's Muslim Quarter.

After Labour took power, Sharon was accused of mismanaging the housing department. His ill-considered project for development dwellings to house Soviet Jewish immigrants to Israel left his successor, Binyamin Ben-Eliezer, with billions in unpaid debts. At various stages, Sharon had tried to replace Prime Minister Yitzhak Shamir as party and national leader. Their rivalry sapped *Likud's* strength, and contributed to its defeat in 1992. In 1993 Sharon was upset when the younger Benjamin Netanyahu succeeded Shamir as party leader. However, their philosophies largely tallied, so he reconciled himself to this *fait accompli*. In December 1995 Sharon announced that he would not be standing as a candidate for the prime ministership in the first direct elections for the post in 1996, as had been expected. Instead, he called on the entire right-wing opposition to stand behind Netanyahu's candidacy. Labour hoped that Sharon was a spent force, but after June, he is vying for high office in the new *Likud* government, and many still regard him as the genuine voice for the dreams of a Greater Israel.

Shawwa, Mansour Aoun al-   Palestinian

Mayor of Gaza. Yasser Arafat personally appointed Shawwa, a well-known local businessman and economist by training, as mayor in December 1994. (He had effectively held that post since July.) Opponents criticized his appointment as 'undemocratic', and Shawwa announced he would not hold office until guaranteed a consensus of support. The crisis soon blew over, however, and Shawwa is now credited with improving conditions in Gaza, making it cleaner and better organized, where many said he would fail. He strongly criticized Israel's policy of 'sealing the territories' after terror incidents, which he blames for the estimated 60% unemployment rate in Gaza. He welcomed the $90 million already received from US, Norwegian and French donors, but called for $500 million over five years to build up infrastructure in Gaza.

Nonetheless, he is optimistic about Gaza's tourism potential, citing the beautiful coastline and the pending setting up of a new Marriott Hotel as arguments in his favour. Agriculture was his initial concern, but lately Shawwa has been seeking ways of winning economic independence from Israel, mainly through plans to build a small container port and a $200 million 180 MW electricity power station. Foreign investors have already pledged $300 million for the former, while four overseas groups are tendering for the latter.

Shawwa believes a regional peace will bring real economic benefits to Gaza. In December

1995, he met several mayors from Israeli coastal towns, at a European Union backed conference held in Limassol, Cyprus. He signed co-operation agreements with Amram Mitzna (mayor of Haifa), Tzvi Tzilker (mayor of Ashdod) and the mayor of Limassol. This forms part of a joint project under the aegis of the Cyprus Development Bank. Shawwa also managed to get Tzilker to agree to a Gazan representative at the Ashdod port (to the north, in Israel), to resolve any problems that may arise concerning Gaza-bound containers.

Shawwa, Rashad   Palestinian
Former Mayor of Gaza. Rashad Shawwa was born into a prominent Palestinian land-owning family. After a youth spent as a playboy and fashionable sportsman in Amman, Beirut and Cairo, he returned to his native Gaza in 1949, and began a political career. Shawwa helped Gaza's new Egyptian rulers to use the Strip as a launchpad for *fedayeen* (guerrilla) raids into Israel. He made himself equally indispensable to Israel, after it conquered and occupied Gaza in the 1967 war. They appointed him mayor in 1972, but deposed him in 1981. During this period he established himself as a political independent, but always kept lines of communication open to King Hussein of Jordan (his natural ally) and the PLO. The British television journalist, David Smith, says that Shawwa was optimistic about a regional settlement, and, while dissuading the PLO from several plots to kill him, also lent the organization his support. His influence spred beyond Gaza to the West Bank.

Lamenting the desperate poverty and mounting frustration of youths in Israeli–occupied Gaza, in 1985 he predicted fundamentalist suicide attacks from the area; and was proved sadly correct within a decade. In July 1986 he broke with his earlier loyalties, and announced that 'the PLO is leading us blindly into disaster'. He denounced Arafat's decision to break the two-year pact he had made with Jordan, and called for a new Palestinian leadership that was more in touch with realities on the ground. Once again, his predictions came true, for within 18 months 'internal' Palestinians launched the *intifada* from Gaza, independently of any orders from Tunis.

Shehadah, Raja   Palestinian
Co-founder of *Al-Haq*, Palestinian human rights organization. Throughout the 1980s Shehadah, a lawyer, made his mark by publicizing what he claimed were illegal Israeli activities in Gaza and the West Bank. In particular, he condemned Israel's alleged transgressions of the Geneva Convention pertaining to governance under occupied territories. In 1994 Shehadah criticized the PLO negotiators of the Cairo Accords for being obsessed with grand symbolic legal aspects, such as Israeli adherence to UN 242, while ignoring the local details. As a result, he said, the Accords allowed Israel to maintain an economic grip on the territories, and a de jure security presence in Gaza and Jericho. He also blamed fellow Palestinian legalists for being too wedded to the culture of resistance. Instead, he said, they should concentrate on replacing the existing Israeli military and civil legal apparatus with a cohesive Palestinian legal code.

Shehadah, Samir   Palestinian
First *Fatah* representative on the United National Command (*intifada* secret steering committee). Shehadah is currently a 'presidential aide' to Yasser Arafat for National Institutions. His task is to recreate the organizational infrastructure which Palestinians claim Israel eroded during the years of occupation.

Shek, Danny   Israel
Foreign Ministry spokesman. At the time of the Oslo talks, Shek was the spokesman at the Israeli embassy in Paris. Regarded as a protege and confidante of Shimon Peres, Shek worked as a liaison during secret talks in Paris, leading to the Israel-PLO recognition.

Shetreet, Shimon   Israel
Minister of Religious Affairs under Rabin and Peres; formerly, Economics Minister and a leader of hawkish Labour Mks opposed to aspects of peace. Shimon Shetreet was born in Morocco in 1946 and emigrated to Israel as a child. Shetreet became a Labour MK in 1988 and Economics Minister in 1992. But his hawkish views, especially concerning the Golan Heights, have probably precluded him from playing any meaningful role in the peace process.

Shetreet stepped into the breach when the orthodox Jewish party, *Shas*, left the coalition government. He soon won praise for restoring stability at the Department of Religious Affairs, even at the risk of offending powerful rabbinical fiefdoms. He was the only Labour minister to abstain from the cabinet's vote in September, 1993, on the Oslo Accords with the PLO. He also held secret talks with the far-right *Tsomet* Party, in a bid to draw them into the coalition government. In the wake of the Rabin assassination, Shetreet and his new cabinet colleague, Rabbi Yehuda Amital, were charged with repairing the government's strained relations with Israel's religious community, and with Diaspora Jewry.

Shevis, Shimon   Israel

Director-General of the Prime Minister's Office under Yitzhak Rabin. Together with Rabin's bureau chief, Eitan Haber, Shevis acted as a 'gatekeeper' to the prime minister, and skilfully planned his busy agenda. He was also Rabin's most intimate adviser, and assessed the Israeli mood for changes in relations with Palestinians. Shevis, 44, comes from a *kibbutz* background, and was a member of Labour's 'Young Guard'. A hawk by inclination, and a campaigner for the rights of Golan settlers, Shevis nonetheless was extremely loyal to Rabin as the government adopted the policy of territorial compromise. He joined Rabin's entourage as a volunteer in 1984, and in 1992 took over from Shamir's director general, Yossi Ben-Aharon, who was seen as too right-wing to carry out Labour's vision of the peace process. Shevis is thought to harbour political ambitions of his own, although his impatience and tendency to secrecy have made him a few enemies.

Shihabi, Hikmat   Syria

Syrian military Chief of Staff since 1974; in 1995, the highest ranking Syrian negotiator with Israel. Hikmat Shihabi is close to Hafez al-Assad, and analysts suggest that, as head of the Syrian army, he is in effect the second strongest figure in Syria next to the president himself. Before his current posting, he ran Syrian military intelligence. He was given the huge responsibility of negotiating about security concerns with his Israeli counterparts (Ehud Barak in 1994, and Amnon Shahak in 1995). In December 1994, after Barak called for reductions in the Syrian army, Shihabi was instructed by Assad to suspend the talks. Determined action by US Secretary of State Warren Christopher helped revive the talks in March 1995, but they collapsed again in August after Shihabi rejected Shahak's demand for early warning systems to be placed on the Golan.

Israel's top 'Syria-watcher', Prof. Maoz, has described Shihabi as the 'professional' in Assad's ruling coterie, with Abd al-Halim Khaddam as the tough man, and Foreign Minister Farouk al-Shar'a, the cosmopolitan charged with cultivating Israel and the West. His political future may depend on his continuing alliance with Assad, and the success of the peace process. He enjoys the advantage of being a Sunni Muslim, and thus being part of the majority community in Syria.

Shiqaqi, Fat'hi   Palestinian

Islamic *Jihad* leader until his death on Oct. 26, 1995. Shiqaqi was born in 1949, and trained as a doctor in Egypt. Inspired by the Muslim Brotherhood, he returned to the territories and, together with Sheikh Odeh, founded Islamic *Jihad* in the early 1980s. The group predates *Hamas,* but has never won as a large a support base. Where *Hamas* has an advanced ideology and a well-developed social welfare structure for its supporters, Islamic *Jihad* specializes in the 'grand gesture' (terrorist attacks, often planned in tandem with Ahmed Jibril's PFLP-GC). On spiritual and theological matters, Shiqaqi deferred to Sheikh Tamimi and other *Jihad* supporters amongst the *ulema* (Islamic scholars).

After Israel deported Shiqaqi from the territories in August 1988, he moved to a new base in the Yarmouk Palestinian refugee camp, outside Damascus, where he enjoyed the patronage of President Assad. In January 1994, Shiqaqi was a key player in the setting up of the National Alliance, a coalition of eight PLO rejectionist groups and two fundamentalist groups (Islamic *Jihad* and *Hamas*). The Alliance rejected Arafat's peace deal with Israel, and Shiqaqi vowed to oppose it by any means. He boasted that his forces were behind the Beit Lid bus-bombing in January 1995, which killed 21 Israelis. Later, he told interviewers that the only way to make peace with Israel was if Israel were to 'disappear'. At the same time, he said he had nothing against Jews *per se*. In early October 1995, Fat'hi Shiqaqi met Iranian Deputy

Foreign Minister Hussein Sheikholeslam, reportedly to plan the murder of PLO leader Yasser Arafat. Later that month he was assassinated in Malta, allegedly by Israeli *Mossad* agents acting on a tip-off from PLO intelligence.

Shiqaqi, Khalil   Palestinian
Director of the respected Centre for Palestine Research and Studies, in Nablus; younger brother of the late Fath'i Shiqaqi, former leader of Islamic *Jihad*. By contrast with his brother Khalil Shiqaqi broadly supports the peace process. He believes that if borders were agreed to then settlers could remain as Jewish citizens resident in Palestine, but still holding Israeli passports. He would define the settlements themselves as Palestinian property, but welcome the potential input of economically productive Israelis into joint ventures with Palestinian neighbours. He is specifically investigating the relationship between the commuter belt settlement city, Ariel, and its surrounding Arab villages, as a useful model.

Shitrit, Shimon
(See Shetreet, Shimon)

Shohat, Avraham   Israel
Minister of Finance, Labour MK. Avraham 'Beiga' Shohat negotiated on behalf of Israel with his PLO equivalent, Abu 'Ala, to create the Paris Economic Relations Pact (also known as the Economic Protocol). The two men first met on Nov. 16, 1993, and signed the agreement on April 29, 1994, in the French capital. In this respect, Shohat helped to define the economic relations between Israel and the Palestinian Authority over a five-year interim period. The Protocol was the product of five months' negotiations, but had to be finalized before Israel and the PLO could go ahead with self-rule in Gaza and Jericho.

In addition, the subsequent Interim Agreement (Oslo 2) signed between Israel and the PLO on Sept. 28, 1995, actually contains the economic protocol. With hindsight, this seems to demonstrate the protocol's durability and veracity, although at the time the Israeli and Palestinian negotiating teams had quite different views of the economic future. While the PLO wanted an independent trade policy (fearing Israeli economic domination), Shohat wanted a customs union (fearing Israel being flooded by cheap Palestinian goods). In the end Shohat and Abu 'Ala agreed on a compromise, after Israeli Foreign Minister Shimon Peres flew to Paris and lent some weight to the proceedings.

Shohat was born Tel Aviv in 1936, and is a construction engineer by profession. He was a paratrooper in the IDF, and later worked as a branch director of the giant *Histadrut*-backed Solel Boneh construction company. He helped found the city of Arad in Israel's south, and was its mayor from 1967 to 1989. Shohat has also been chairman of the Development Towns Council and deputy chairman of the Union of Local Authorities. Shortly after entering the Knesset as a Labour MK in 1988, Shohat became chairman of first the Committee on the Economy, and then the Finance Committee. He currently works closely with the Director General of the Finance Ministry, David Brodet. Shohat is particularly keen to turn Israel into a hub of IT expertise. Western financial analysts credit him with the recent boom in the Israeli economy.

Shoval, Zalman   Israel
Effectively spokesman for the *Likud,* but unofficially he leads a pragmatic *Likud* faction which favours a compromise on the West Bank. Born in 1930, Shoval served as Ambassador to the UN and USA in succession, and in 1991 joined the Israeli delegation at the Madrid and Washington peace talks. In 1994 Shoval proposed a 'damage limitation exercise' to save part of Greater Israel, and avoid the costs of military redeployment. This would entail establishing 'defensible settlement blocs' and annexing them, in return for waiving Israeli sovereignty over the rest of the West Bank. After the Rabin assassination, Shoval defended party leader Benjamin Netanyahu from accusations that his rhetoric provided the atmosphere of violence which led to the atrocity.

Shtayyeh, Muhammed   Palestinian
Deputy head of Palestinian Electoral Commission. Shtayyeh (whose surname is sometimes rendered as Ishtiyyeh) worked under Sa'eb Erekat since the middle of 1994. He initially had

hoped that elections would be held in October of that year. In the event, elections took place on Jan. 20, 1996, and Shtayyeh was praised for the way in which he and Erekat had managed to register so many people in such a short space of time. He also upset some Tunis stalwarts by organizing exhaustive primaries to choose local *Fatah* candidates for the elections. Earlier, Shtayyeh had worked as an aide to Arafat, who had recognized his organizational skills, and put him in charge of day-to-day expenses for the Palestinian delegation during the Madrid track talks.

Shueibi, Azmi   **Palestinian**
PNA minister of Youth and Sports. A dentist by profession, Shuebi used to head the Democratic Front (DFLP) underground in the territories until Israel deported him in 1987. He was a member of the Palestinian negotiating team in the Washington peace talks (which followed the Madrid conference). After the Oslo Accords were signed, Israel allowed Shuebi to return to Ramallah. Together with fellow minister, Yasser Abed-Rabbo, Shuebi (who is now 44) founded the DFLP breakaway group, *Fida*. He is currently the group's head in the West Bank.

Shukeiri, Ahmed   **Palestinian**
First Chairman of the Palestine Liberation Organization (PLO). Shukeiri was born in Acre in 1907, and trained as a lawyer. He was a senior official in the Arab League during the 1950s, and served as Saudi Arabia's Ambassador to the United Nations from 1957 to 1962. On Jan. 13, 1964, Egyptian President Gamel Abdul Nasser appointed him as the chief Palestinian delegate to an Arab leaders summit meeting in Cairo; and as a consequence of decisions taken there, Shukeiri called the founding conference of the PLO four months later. Shukeiri's main achievement was to set up a Palestinian Liberation Army (PLA), which had units in Gaza. However, he never managed to quell disputes within the new organization, nor to break free of Nasser's control. Shukeiri was forced to resign in December 1967, following the Six Day War, which was a calamity for Palestinians. Yahya Hammuda replaced him as head of the PLO, but he in turn was replaced *Fatah* Chairman Yasser Arafat in February 1969. Ahmed Shukeiri died in 1980.

Siam, Walid   **Palestinian**
Deputy Director-General for the Palestinian Ministry of Planning and International Co-operation (MOPIC). Walid Siam was raised and educated in the USA, and returned to Gaza to serve as chief aide to Planning Minister and leading PLO negotiator, Nabil Sha'ath. Siam is one of the main conduits for foreign donor aid to Palestinian self-rule areas, and is typical of the younger breed of technocrats in the PNA. He believes the solution to the problem of a link between Gaza and the West Bank lies in sharing existing highways with Israelis.

Sibiud, Jean-Luc   **France**
Head of EU delegation co-ordinating observers to Palestinian elections; deals with the peace process at the French foreign ministry.

Sidki, Atef   **Egypt**
(See Sedqi, Atef)

Singer, Joel   **Israel**
Legal Adviser to the Israeli Ministry of Foreign Affairs. Joel Singer was a Washington-based Israeli lawyer, when he was called in on June 11, 1993, to participate in the secret Israel–PLO talks in Oslo. The talks were entering their final stages, but Israel needed a legal expert to scrutinize the draft document which the negotiators had prepared. Singer also served as the eyes and ears of Prime Minister Yitzhak Rabin (Uri Savir, Israel's chief negotiator, was seen as Foreign Minister Shimon Peres's man, and the PLO feared he did not carry the prime minister's blessing).

Singer, the son of an Austrian-born Israeli actor, had been a colonel in the Israeli army, and a member of the military advocate's unit specializing in international law. He was part of the team which drafted the disengagement agreement with Egypt in 1974, and which later helped settle the legal aspects of the Camp David accords. For 12 years he helped to draft many of the laws for the military government in the occupied territories. He was also involved in several

Israeli 'peace missions', which still remain secret. For the last five of those 12 years, Singer worked directly with then Defence Minister Yitzhak Rabin, during the *Likud*-led national unity government. The two became firm friends. In 1988, Singer left the army and settled in New York; but Rabin hinted at the time that he might be called on later.

At Oslo, Singer showed his renowned courtroom manner by interrogating the negotiators at length to pin down the details of agreements. His twin concerns were to win full Palestinian agreement, while at the same time providing Israel with ironcast guarantees on security. The Norwegian hosts found his approach too aggresive at first, and the Palestinians under Abu 'Ala rejected his proposals. Even so, Singer did eventually succeed in winning Palestinian approval for what became the Declaration of Principles. In 1994 he officially joined the Foreign Ministry as a special legal adviser.

Siniora, Hanna   Palestinian

Editor of the leading Palestinian newspaper, *Al-Fajr*, until it was closed down. Siniora became a prominent figure during the *intifada*. He repeatedly called for direct talks with Israel, coupled with disciplined 'civic non-co-operation' until Palestinian demands were met. Siniora towed a broadly pro-*Fatah* line while editor of *Al-Fajr*, but on occasion criticized Arafat. He received death threats from within the PLO for voicing dissent. As a moderate and a Christian, Siniora became a target of *Hamas* invective. Hana Siniora remained a leading force in the 'internal' PLO, but the ascendance of Hanan Ashrawi somewhat eclipsed his status amongst the Western media. He was generally excluded from both the Madrid and Oslo peace tracks. Siniora currently heads the International Palestine Bank.

Ephraim SNEH

Nationality	Israeli
Religion	Jewish
Place of birth	Tel Aviv
Date of birth	1944
Former position	Health Minister May 1994 to June 1996
Previous positions	Brigadier-general in the army Commander of the South Lebanon security zone Head of the West Bank civilian administration
Allies	Formerly in Peres camp, managed Rabin's 1992 election campaign; allies on the moderate left of the Labour Party
Position on peace	Very positive
National political importance	Influential on centre-left
Prospects	If peace is resolved, he may gain more national power

By all accounts, Palestinians regarded Sneh as the most sympathetic Israeli chief civil administrator of the West Bank, a position he served from 1984 to October 1987. After graduating in internal medicine in 1972, Ephraim Sneh rejoined the army as medical officer of the Paratrooper Corps, and saw action in the 1973 war. He headed an elite rescue commando unit from 1978 to 1980.

Sneh went on to become commander of the South Lebanese security zone in 1981, and accepted the civil administrator's post after Yitzhak Rabin took over from the *Likud's* Moshe Arens as Defence Minister. He left the job after repeated clashes over policy with the more rigid Defence Ministry co-ordinator for the territories, Shmuel Goren.

After retiring from the military in 1987, Sneh became director of the Golda Meir Association for the education and promotion of democratic values. He entered the Labour Party in 1988 and served as Shimon Peres's adviser on the territories. In 1990 he made a strategic shift by backing Rabin's challenge for the party leadership. Throughout 1991 Sneh attacked the *Likud* government in the press for risking the relationship with the USA over increased funds for settlements. He called for immediate peace talks with Palestinians, a total freeze on settlements, and diverting much-needed funds to help absorb Russian and other immigrants.

In 1992, Sneh managed the successful Labour election campaign, and entered the *Knesset* for the first time. Unofficially, he sounded out Palestinian opinion for Rabin, and held meetings with the PLO's Nabil Sha'ath, in parallel with the secret Peres-backed Oslo initiative. In May 1994 Sneh became Health Minister, after Haim Ramon resigned the post. He inherited a colossal health service crisis, centred on the near bankruptcy of the dominant health fund. One of his first acts in office was signing a bilateral agreement to improve co-operation in health matters with his Egyptian counterpart, Dr Ali Abed al-Fatah. Sneh describes himself as a 'dove with claws', but so far his skill in matters concerning peace have not been fully tested in government.

Somekh, Sasson   Israel
Director of the Israeli Academic Centre in Cairo, and formerly Professor of Arabic Literature at Tel Aviv University. The centre was set up in 1982, and it acts as an unofficial liaison office to facilitate the peace process through 'normalizing' relations between Israelis and Egyptians. However, sections of the Egyptian press have attacked the centre as a 'Zionist spy satellite on the banks of the Nile', a charge Somekh rejects as ridiculous.

Sourani, Raji   Palestinian
Leading Gazan human rights lawyer. Raji Sourani was born into one of Gaza's leading land-owning families. In 1967 he joined the PLO, when Israel began its occupation of Gaza. Ten years later he set up an office to give legal aid to Palestinians who were charged with being members of the PLO. In 1979 Sourani himself was sentenced to two and a half years in prison for belonging to the Marxist PFLP. He became the leader of the prisoners' 'political wing' and claimed to have created there 'another generation of *fedayeen*'. Sourani was released in 1982, but placed under administrative detention in 1985, and forbidden from defending Palestinians in the Israeli military courts, in 1986. He rejected an Israeli offer of a permit to leave Gaza and return within three years. Raji Sourani is now the director of the Gaza Centre for Rights and Law, and is proving to be as much a thorn in the flesh of the PNA as he was when Gaza was under Israeli rule.

Souss, Ibrahim   Palestinian
Former head of PLO office in Paris. A brother-in-law of Yasser Arafat, he kept channels of communication open with top French officials. In the late 1980s, he gave an interview with Israel's *Jerusalem Post*, in which he said he sympathized with Jews about the Holocaust, and was prepared to recognize Israel if Israel recognized the PLO. However, in 1993 he criticized the Declaration of Principles. His successor in Paris is Leila Shahid.

Speth, James Gustave   USA
Administrator of the United Nations Development Programme (UNDP), one of the chief agencies involved in the economic dimensions of the peace process. Speth's appointment in June 1993 coincided with the initial Israeli–PLO breakthrough (the DOP was signed less than three months later). He responded by enhancing the UNDP's existing programmes, and adapting them to the new conditions. These included the UNDP's Programme of Assistance to the Palestinian People (PAPP). Speth represented UN Secretary-General Boutros Boutros Ghali at the Middle East and North Africa economic summit in October 1994, and welcomed the economic and political rapprochement between Israel and the Arab nations.

In February 1996, James Speth and Haim Divon, the head of Israel's foreign co-operation division, signed an agreement to run joint training programmes for people in developing countries. They ultimately hoped to 'develop human resources towards self-sufficiency'; but another stated goal to reinforce the improving ties between Israel and the Third World. This was the first purpose-built co-operation between Israel and the UNDP, or, indeed, Israel and any UN agency.

Spiegel, Baruch   Israel
Brigadier-General in the Israeli Defence Forces, and chief liaison officer with UN and other forces. Spiegel has held secret talks with Syrian officials, in an attempt to break the deadlock about security concerns on both sides. He was a key negotiator for Israel in the run-up to the Interim Agreement (Oslo 2) which Israel signed with the PLO in September 1995.

Stoltenberg, Thorvald   Norway

Foreign Minister during the first four months of the secret Oslo talks. Thorvald Stoltenberg was born in 1931 and joined the Norwegian foreign service in 1959. He entered government as a junior minister for the Labour Party, and became Defence Minister from 1979 to 1981, and Foreign Minister from 1987 to 1989. In his latter position, Stoltenberg forged a good relationship with another Labour Foreign Minister, Shimon Peres of Israel. When Labour lost power in Norway, Stoltenberg went to the UN, serving first as Norway's Ambassador and then briefly as the UN High Commissioner for Refugees in 1990. At the end of that year, however, he returned to serve another term as Foreign Minister. In 1992 Shimon Peres approached him to act as a possible broker in peace talks with the PLO; Stoltenberg's assistant, Monica Juul (the wife of Terje Larsen), responded by 'sounding out' PLO opinion. Together with deputy minister Jan Egeland, the Norwegian quartet engineered the first secret talks, which were held in a manor house outside Oslo. A consensus-seeker and pragmatist by nature, Stoltenberg allowed them to take their own course, but always was on stand-by in case they hit deadlocks. He was trusted by both sides, and kept the talks a closely guarded secret. Stoltenberg returned to the UN in April 1993, and Johan Jorgen Holst, the new Foreign Minister, inherited the mantle of arbitor of the 'Oslo Channel'.

Sultan, Khaled   Palestinian

Khaled Sultan is responsible for Palestinian border police, and is a brigadier-general.

Surani, Jamal as-   Palestinian

Secretary-General of the Palestine National Council, and member of the PLO Executive Committe since 1966. Jamal as-Surani was born in Jerusalem in 1923, and worked as a lawyer in Gaza. He became chairman of the Palestinian Lawyers' Association in 1959, and joined the PLO Executive Committee in 1966. Throughout the 1970s he was the PLO's point-man with Warsaw Pact countries, and led several missions to the eastern bloc. He also served as the PLO representative in Cairo, and official delegate to the Arab League. In 1974 he visited London while *en route* to the UN Conference on Palestine, in an ultimately unsuccessful attempt to get Britain to support the PLO. Surani became head of the PLO Executive Committee's admin stration in 1987, and was a close aide to Yasser Arafat. He was instrumental in ensuring the safe passage of the Algiers Declaration at the 19th PNC session in 1988. However, he refused to participate in the setting up of the Palestine National Authority in 1993.

T

Tahboub, Hasan (Sheikh)   Palestinian

President of the PLO–backed Supreme Muslim Council, and Palestine National Authority (PNA) Minister of Islamic Affairs. In autumn of 1994, Tahboub established his offices on the *Haram al-Sharif* (Temple Mount) in Jerusalem. This technically broke the terms of the May agreement between Israel and the PLO, which initially limited PNA institutions to Gaza and Jericho. Tahboub's Council wrested control of the Jerusalem *awkaf* (religious trusts) from pro-Jordanian elements. He claimed responsibility for overseeing the Muslim shrines and paying the salaries of religious functionaries. On Oct. 16, 1994, when the Mufti of Jerusalem, Sheikh Sulaiman al-Jabari, suddenly died, Tahboub agreed to a Palestinian replacement, Sheikh Akram Said Sabri, in opposition to Jordan's appointee, Sheikh Abdel-Qadir Abideen.

In practice, while the Palestinian mufti enjoyed more popular support, harsh economic realities forced Tahboub to turn once again to Jordan as paymaster. Tahboub will play a key role in articulating Palestinian interests in Jerusalem during the 'final status talks', scheduled to begin in 1996 and be fully implemented by 1999. He resents what he sees as a cozy deal between Israel and Jordan, contained in the peace treaty of October 1994, which apparently entrenches Jordan's claims to Hashemite custodianship of the holy sites. Sheikh Tahboub has promised that Jews will still be able to worship at 23 designated holy sites in the Palestinian ruled teritories, as designated in the Oslo 2 accords. However, when pressed, he said this could happen only where there was not an existing mosque, which effectively rules out such famous sites as the Caves of Machpelah in Hebron. Meanwhile, Tahboub also has to fight a rearguard action against *Hamas*, and prove to the Palestinian public that the PLO has not abandoned its Islamic roots.

Tamari, Salim (Dr)   Palestinian
Professor of Sociology at Bir Zeit University on the West Bank. Salim Tamari will serve on the Palestinian negotiating committee for refugees, an issue which was scheduled to be discussed at the final stage talks between Israel and the PLO in 1996. Born in Jaffa in 1945, Dr Tamari received his PhD from Manchester University in England, and is currently the editor of a journal, *Afaq* (Horizons). Tamari is an acknowledged expert on Palestinian non-governmental organizations, and the role which they played in re-establishing a Palestinian civic society during occupation and the *intifada*. In the early 1970s Tamari backed the leftist vision of a single democratic state for Jews and Arabs. Since then, he has come to accept a two-state solution, and welcomed the PLO's adoption of this policy in 1988.
Long before the 1993 breakthrough, Tamari had regular contacts with Israeli intellectuals. He believes that the American public can wield much influence on Israeli politics. With respect to Palestinian affairs, he warns of the dangers of rifts in the future – between 'internal' Palestinians and those in the 'diaspora'; between an impoverished Gaza and a more socially variegated West Bank; and between the '*intifada*' generation, yearning for empowerment, and the PLO's 'Tunis set', which is only slowly learning how to act democratically. Nonetheless, in contrast with many fellow Palestinian academics, Tamari is optimistic that all problems can be solved, and is proud of the steps towards autonomy which have already been achieved.

Tamimi, Asa'ad Bayoud al-   Palestinian
Leader of Islamic Jihad – *Beit al-Maqdes* ('Jerusalem') faction. A religious sheikh, he was deported from Hebron for incitement in 1980. He wrote a book, *The Disappearance of Israel: a Koranic Imperative*, which became 'required reading' for young Islamic militants in the territories. Sheikh Tamimi formed close ties with *Hezbollah's* leader, Sheikh Mohammed Hussein Fadlallah, with Egypt's Muslim Brotherhood, and in particular with the Iranian government under Ayatollah Khomeini. In 1988 Jordanian authorities arrested him when he returned to his base in Amman from Teheran, replete with fresh funds. Sheikh Tamimi held meetings with Yasser Arafat at the 1991 PNC conference, although he disapproved of the PLO's endorsement of the Madrid talks. The *Beit al-Maqdes* group is responsible for a number of terror attacks on Israel, usually co-ordinated with the PFLP-GC (Ahmed Jibril group). After the assassination of the Islamic *Jihad's* leader, Dr Fat'hi Shiqaqi, in October 1995, Tamimi is expected to wield more influence in the movement.

Tarawneh, Faiz   Jordan
Jordanian Ambassador to the US, and the Kingdom's chief negotiator with Israel. Tarawneh established a good working relationship with his Israeli opposite number, Elyakim Rubinstein, at the Washington talks (following the Madrid summit of October 1991). He became head of the Jordanian negotiating team at the 10th round of talks, after Abdul Salam al-Majali left to become Jordan's new prime minister. On Sept. 14, 1993, Tarawneh signed a Common Agenda with Israel, which provided a framework within which talks could be accelerated. The agenda was signed the day after the Israeli–PLO Declaration of Principles, and marked the formal separation of the Jordanian and Palestinian delegations. Once again, Tarawneh and Rubinstein concentrated on the details (water rights, border demarcation, cessation of war, and plans for future co-operation) in busy talks held alternatively on the Israeli and Jordanian coasts of the Dead Sea. Meanwhile, King Hussein, Prince Hassan and Foreign Minister Kabariti, and Shimon Peres and Yitzhak Rabin, met in a series of public arenas to set the seal on their agreements. The process culminated in the full Israel-Jordan peace treaty of October 1994. In early January 1996, Tarawneh and Rubistein were awarded special honours at a ceremony at Beit Gavriel, next to the Sea of Kinneret (Tiberias), for their role in achieving the peace treaty.

Tarbuk, Ahmad   Palestinian
Leader of the *Fatah* Hawks, a militant offshoot of *Fatah*. The Israeli press has accused him of running a vigilante force set on 'disciplining' foes of *Fatah,* even resorting to murder of 'collaborators'. While Arafat officially distances himself from their operations, the Hawks

remain active in the Balata refugee camp outside Nablus. Tarbuk became a prison leader, and then joined the PNA's Preventive Security Forces under Jibril Rajoub, before deserting in 199. to set up his own independent militia. Observers are keenly watching to see whether he can reach an accommodation with the new Palestinian governor of Nablus, Mahmoud al-Aloul.

Tarifi, Jamil al-   Palestinian
PNA minister for liaison with Israel. Born in 1947 near Lydda (present-day Lod in Israel) Tarifi was one-year-old when his family fled to Ramallah, in what was then soon to become the Jordanian-ruled West Bank. He trained as a lawyer and worked as a successful director of a Ramallah contracting firm. In 1989, he was threatened by PFLP members for taking a moderate stance on talks with Israel. In 1992 he served on the Palestinian steering committee (or advisory committee) at the Madrid track peace talks. Israeli negotiators turned a blind eye to the fact that he was a well known *Fatah* activist in the territories.

After the Oslo Accords and Cairo Agreement, Tarifi became a key negotiator for the Palestinian Authority in 1994. On Aug. 27, 1995, he signed with his Israeli counterpart, Oren Shahor, an agreement to transfer eight further 'civilian powers' to the PNA. These were – fuel transport, postal services, statistics and census, insurance, agriculture, local government. The deal was interpreted as a sign of satisfaction with the success of the original transfer agreement, of 1994. Tarifi was also closely involved in the arduous negotiations which resulted in the Interim Agreement (Oslo 2) of September 1995. Jamil al-Tarifi became one of Ramallah's seven MPs following the elections for the Palestinian Council, which was held on Jan. 20, 1996.

Terzi, Zehdi Labib   Palestinian
Head of the PLO observer mission at the UN.

Thani, Sheikh Hamed bin Jassem bin Jabir al-   Qatar
Foreign Minister of the Emirate of Qatar. Sheikh al-Thani met with Israel's Foreign Minister and Energy Minister (Shimon Peres and Moshe Shahal) on several occasions during 1994. He was a major player in lifting the Arab boycott of Israel, and approved plans to sell natural gas to Israel.

Thatcher, Margaret Hilda   UK
Prime Minister of the United Kingdom from 1979 to 1980. Mrs Thatcher is best remembered as the British Conservative leader who tried to overturn years of overspending, and the perceived excesses of the welfare state, with a more decidedly right-wing and free enterprise economic policy. On foreign affairs, she formed a close partnership with the United States, especially during the Reagan years. However, on occasions she followed a more independent policy on the Middle East, and was prepared to go further than the US administration. In September 1985, she told a banquet in Amman that a Middle East peace settlement should take into account 'the legitimate rights of the Palestinians'. She later invited two PLO Executive Committee members to meet the Foreign Secretary, but cancelled the meeting after the *Achille Lauro* terrorist incident, and strong US pressure.

In 1989 Mrs Thatcher condemned Yitzhak Shamir's plans for elections in the occupied territories as not going far enough. She also condemned Israel's handling of the Palestinian *intifada.* The following year, she sent UK troops to Saudi Arabia, in response to Saddam Hussein's invasion of Kuwait. Throughout her rule, Mrs Thatcher managed to balance cordial relations with the British Jewish community, with a more sympathetic approach to the PLO than her predecessors had shown. Ultimately, however, UK Middle East policy under Mrs Thatcher never assumed the independence which it had enjoyed before the Suez Crisis of 1956.

Tibi, Ahmad   Israel/ Palestinian
Yasser Arafat's main adviser on Israeli affairs, and a rising Israeli Arab politician in his own right. Born in 1957 in Taibeh, an Arab town north-east of Tel Aviv, the young Tibi studied medicine at the Hebrew University in Jerusalem. He graduated in 1983, and specialized as a gynaecologist. Later, he worked at Israel's prestigious Hadassah Hospital on Mount Scopus, until he was fired after a confrontation with a hospital guard. Tibi first met Yasser Arafat

when he joined Raymonda Tawil (a Palestinian poet and mother of Yasser Arafat's wife, Susha) in 1984, on a trip to Tunis. Arafat and Tibi have been in constant contact ever since. At the time, it was illegal for Israeli citizens to meet PLO officials; but Tibi nonetheless served as a conduit for Israeli government officials who wished to 'sound out' the PLO. In September 1993, after Israel and the PLO recognized each other, Tibi formally became known as Arafat's adviser.

In 1987 Tibi and his family (wife and daughter) moved to East Jerusalem. He failed to win a place on the left-wing *Ratz* slate for election to the Knesset in 1988. Since late 1993, Ahmad Tibi has instead started to carve out a niche for himself in Israeli Arab politics. His main enemies were the established Arab parties, the communist *Hadash* (with three MKs) and the nationalist Arab Democratic Party (with two MKs) led by Abdul Wahab Darawshe. Tibi has accused them of kow-towing to the Israeli government of the day, although his political agenda is not so different from theirs. He wants to see Arab directors of Israeli government ministries, and demands a five-year plan for integrating Arabs into the Israeli mainstream. Tibi believes that Israeli Arabs have been sidelined in Israel's bid to make peace with their Palestinian cousins, and hopes to capitalize on this grievance. He is expected to stand in the 1996 Israeli elections, on a slate informally sponsored by the PLO.

Somewhat surprisingly for someone of his secular background, Tibi has struck up a firm friendship with Sheikh Abdallah Nimr Darwish, leader of the Israeli Arab Islamic Movement. In November 1994 the two men joined forces in the mediation between the PLO and *Hamas*, following the riots outside Gaza City's Palestine Mosque. Tibi is convinced that with Arafat's backing, and a strategic alliance with the increasingly popular Islamic Movement, his party could displace the older generation of Israeli Arab politicians, and win at least six Knesset seats – possibly enough to be a powerbroker in the next Israeli government. His enemies claim he has 'no following' (being the son of a wealthy landowner might not endear him to poorer Arab town-dwellers). Nonetheless, he has managed the transition from back-door diplomat to crowd-pleaser with aplomb. Observers say he is articulate, confident, fluent in Hebrew and Arabic, and has a distinct political advantage in being married to a Palestinian woman from Tul Karm in the West Bank.

Tlass, Mustafa al-   **Syria**
Defence Minister. Mustafa al-Tlas is the archetypal Syrian hardliner when it comes to matters of peace with Israel. Born in 1932 in Rastan City, near Homs, he was educated at the Syrian Military Academy and law college, and later at the Voroshilov Academy in Moscow. Tlass joined the Ba'ath Party in the 1960s, and served as Chief of Staff and Deputy Minister of Defence from 1968 to 1972. He helped to restore much of the military prestige of the Syrian armed forces after their humiliating defeat by Israel in 1967. Tlas exploited popular anguish against the Jadid regime to install Hafez al-Assad's 'correctional movement' in 1970. In 1973 he led Syrian forces in the October, or Yom Kippur, War. They initially overran the Golan Heights, but within three weeks an Israeli counter-attack forced them to retreat to the outskirts of Damascus.

In 1984 Tlass became First Deputy Prime Minister, responsible for defence. He also played a key role in thwarting Rifa'at al-Assad's bid to replace his brother as President in the same year. In the 1990s, however, his trademark belligerency seems out of step with new mood of *détente* with the West and Israel. Tlass's ties with Moscow count for less now that the Soviet Union has collapsed, and he has lost much of authority to two fellow-Sunnis in the otherwise Alawite-dominated regime, Military Chief of Staff Hikmat Shihabi and Vice-President Abd al-Halim Khaddam.

Tsaban, Yair   **Israel**
Former Minister of Immigrant Absorption, and one of four *Meretz* MKs in the cabinet. Tsaban is primarily responsible for Soviet *olim* (immigrants) – a colossal task, seeing as fully 600,000 have entered Israel in under five years. At the same time, he has faced criticism from new Ethiopian Jewish immigrants who feel the Ministry could do more to help their transition to life in Israel. He is one of the strongest cabinet supporters of the peace process, and opposes making excessive concessions to the religious right. He particularly lambasted certain settler rabbis, such as Dov Lior, as 'racists'.

Born in Tel Aviv in 1930, Tsaban is by profession a teacher and journalist, with a degree in philosophy. He was one of the founding members of Kibbutz Tzorah, and from 1965 to 197 held a seat on the political bureau of *Maki* (the Israel Communist Party), acting as it chairman in the last two years. In 1977 he co-founded *Sheli*, a peace list which ran for th Knesset. In 1980 he joined *Mapam*, serving as its Political Secretary and the head of its factio in the *Histadrut*. As *Mapam* Chairman he persuaded others in the party to form the *Meret* coalition (with *Shinui* and *Ratz*), prior to the 1992 elections. Tsaban has been an MK sinc 1981. In early 1996 he announced that he intended to retire from the cabinet.

Tsedakah, Binyamin   Israel
A leader of Israel's Samaritan minority community. He welcomed the PNA's special provisio for West Bank members of his community, who live around Mount Gerizim, near Nablus, t vote in forthcoming Palestinian elections.

Tsur, Ya'akov   Israel
Agriculture Minister until June 1996. Ya'akov Tsur was born in Haifa in 1937 and has lived o Kibbutz Netiv Halamed-Heh since 1957. Tsur is a teacher by profession. Between 1976 an 1980 he was the Secretary-General of the United Kibbutz Movement. He was an MK from 1981 to 1992. Between 1984 and 1988 he was the Minister of Immigrant Absorption; from 1988 to 1990 he was Minister of Health. Although he failed to win a seat in 1992, Rabin mad him Agriculture Minister. Tsur backed a desalination solution to water problems in Israel an the Middle East generally, and has offered Israeli technical expertise to Tunisia, Oman Mauretania and Egypt.

Tufeili, Subhi   Lebanon
Former Secretary-General of *Hezbollah*. Sheikh Subhi Tufeili is a learned Shi'ite cleric, base in the Beqa'a Valley, who first became the operative head of *Hezbollah* in the mid-1980s. Hi manifesto of 1985 stated that the 'liberation of Palestine' was a prerequisite for the creation o a truly Islamic Lebanon. Tufeili has been associated with taking Westerners hostage i Lebanon, and of being behind the bombings of Jewish and Israeli institutions in London an Buenos Aires. In the early 1990s. Sheikh Abbas Musawi replaced Tufeili as secretary-genera in 1989, but after an Israeli helicopter raid killed Musawi, in February 1992, he returned to th post. In recent years it appears that Sheikh Hassan Nasrallah holds the real reigns of powe although both Tufeili and Nasrallah ultimately defer to *Hezbollah's* veteran spiritual leade Sheikh Muhammed Hussein Fadlallah.

Turkmen, Ilter   Turkey
Commissioner General of the United Nations Relief and Works Association for Palestin Refugees in the Near East (UNRWA). He delivers an annual report to the UN Genera Assembly, and oversees the operations of the group, which since 1950 has looked after th needs of Palestinian refugees in Jordan, Syria, Lebanon, the West Bank and Gaza. On Jun 24, 1994, Turkmen exchanged letters with PLO Chairman Yasser Arafat to facilitate th continued provision of UNRWA services to Palestine refugees in areas under the control o the Palestinian Authority. This included land and buildings, temporary shelter and emergenc humanitarian aid. Turkmen also involved UNRWA in the mulitlateral working group o refugees. He ordered the relocation of UNRWA's headquarters from Vienna to Gaza by th end of 1995, and pledged his full support to the peace process. This has entailed paying th salaries of 9,000 PNA policemen, and funding the development of infrastructure and jo creation, and building houses and a new hospital in Gaza. Ilter's largest challenge wa balancing his new responsibilities, with his standing commitments to refugees in Lebanon Syria and Jordan, including providing education for 410,000 refugee children.

Tzilker, Tzvi   Israel
Mayor of Ashdod, a major Israeli port city along the country's southern Mediterranea coastline. Tzilker formed a close tie with Aoun Shawwa, mayor of Gaza, at a European Unio conference, held in early December 1995 in Limassol, Cyprus. The two men signed co operation agreements to develop the region; and also agreed that a Gazan representativ

should sit on the Ashdod port authority, to ensure that any problems concerning transport between the two ports were quickly resolved.

U

Umm Jihad   Palestinian
(See Wazir, Intissar al-)

V

Van den Broek, Hans   Netherlands
Former Foreign Minister. Van den Broek represented the European Community at the opening of the Madrid peace conference in late October 1991. He was born in 1936, studied law, worked in industry, and was first elected to parliament as a Christian Democrat in 1976. Van den Broek became Foreign Minister under Prime Minister Ruud Lubbers in 1982. He served three terms in this post, the last one beginning in November 1989. Criticized for inactivity, and for showing a supine attitude towards the whims of NATO and the EU, he took a more authoritative political stance during his third term, and to some extent his honour at Madrid reflected this. Van den Broek was appointed to the European Commission in January 1993, with responsibility for foreign and security affairs, and expansion of the Community.

Vance, Cyrus   USA
United States Secretary of State under President Jimmy Carter, from 1977 to 1980. Vance deserves much of the credit for marshalling the Camp David talks, which led to the Israel-Egypt peace treaty. He proclaimed that depriving Palestinians of rights was 'contrary to moral or ethical principles'.

Velayati, Ali Akbar   Iran
Foreign Minister of Iran since December 1981. Velayati is often depicted as a 'moderate' who favours closer ties with the West. However, he is also committed to ostracizing Israel, and forging links with fundamentalist groups in the Middle East. He was born in Teheran in 1945, and taught hygiene sciences before the revolution of 1979. President Ali Akbar Rafsanjani maintained Velayati's services when he took office in 1989. Suave and congenial, Velayati skillfully manoeuvred Iran into a neutral position during the 1991 Gulf War, and has nurtured Iran's traditionally close ties with Syria.

Vilna'i, Matan (Maj.-Gen.)   Israel
Deputy Chief of Staff, and head of the IDF operations branch. Matan Vilna'i became Officer Commanding Israel's Southern Command during the height of the *intifada*. In the latter period of his five-year tenure, he was responsible for drawing up the major security aspects of the Oslo 1 accord, as signed in Cairo on May 4, 1994. These included defining the shared roots, the checkpoints and the road-side security zones in Gaza. Vilna'i is well known for his close relations with troops on the ground, and his attention to detail (which may explain the delays in settling Oslo 1).

On Nov. 24, 1994 he was promoted to Deputy IDF Chief of Staff, serving under his close colleague, Amnon Shahak. Maj.-Gen. Uri Saguy, then head of military intelligence, was apparently the preferred candidate of the outgoing chief of staff, Ehud Barak; but in the end Yitzhak Rabin sided with Shahak's choice. Vilna'i currently monitors the security arrangements which he had recommended, and which, on the whole, have been judged to have been a success. He is also is responsible for the IDF's annual and longer term plans, the implementation of Rainbow 2 (the IDF redeployment operation attached to Oslo 2), and the reduction of the military budget.

To Vilna'i, security lies at the core of Oslo 2, and he is satisfied that it covers all possible problems. He is prepared to help Jewish settlements which want protective perimeter fences. Vilna'i welcomed the change in atmosphere surrounding Oslo 2, as seen in terms of better organization and direct co-operation between Israeli and Palestinian officials on the West Bank. While admitting that Oslo 2 is dauntingly complicated, Vilna'i believes that it has the clear advantage of spelling out modalities for every eventuality, and will reduce the number of IDF personnel in the territories.

Vilner, Meir   Israel

Secretary-General of *Hadash*, Democratic Front for Peace and Equality (*Hadash*). Vilner favours a Marxist solution to Israel's problems, and the establishment of an independent Palestinian state in the West Bank and Gaza. *Hadash* won three seats in the 1992 Knesset elections, and numbers Jews and Arabs as members.

W

Wali, Yusuf Amin   Egypt

Deputy Prime Minister and Agriculture Minister; Secretary-General of the ruling National Democratic Party (NDP); an enthusiast for improved links with Israel. Wali first entered the cabinet as Agriculture Minister in January 1982, when Hosni Mubarak initiated a major reshuffle following the assassination of his predecessor, Anwar Sadat. He was appointed to the NDP political bureau in 1984, and became its secretary-general in September 1985. Also in 1985, he became one of the country's four new deputy prime ministers. Avuncular and loyal to Mubarak, Wali has been entrusted with quietly building up the NDP. In 1986 land reclamation was added to his portfolio. This is now a key plank of Egypt's agricultural policy, and Wali, a life-long advocate of economic reform, sees it as a means of alleviating Egypt's population problem. He also encouraged Israeli scientists to introduce sophisticated water reclamation techniques to Egypt, but this has led some parliamentary foes to criticize him for 'collaborating with Zionists'.

Wattez, Edouard   France

Special Representative in the Jerusalem office of the Programme for Assistance to the Palestinian People (PAPP). PAPP is a UN Development Programme (UNDP) project that has run since 1980. Its current yearly budget is $30 million, and this includes funds from the UNDP and donor countries. Since 1994, PAPP has co-operated with the Palestine National Authority in the fields of water and sanitation, health, agriculture, public administration, education, rural development and women in development.

Wazir, Intissar al-   Palestinian

Minister for Social Affairs in the Palestine National Authority, and widow of the late Khalil al-Wazir (Abu Jihad). Intissar al-Wazir was born in Gaza City. From 1959 she worked as secretary to her cousin, Khalil, who together with Yasser Arafat and three other Palestinian exiles had founded *Fatah* in Kuwait a year earlier. By the time they married, in 1962, Khalil and Intissar al-Wazir had secretly established *Fatah* cells throughout Gaza and the West Bank, ready to be 'activated' whenever so demanded. The couple then moved to Kuwait, and later to Algeria and Syria. In 1966 Syria imprisoned the entire *Fatah* leadership, leaving Intissar as the group's temporary commander until their release. In 1972, she became one of the first two women members of the *Fatah* general conference. She later became Vice-President of the *Fatah* Revolutionary Council, and a member of *Fatah's* top body, the Central Committee, in 1989 (a year after her husband was assassinated in Tunis by an Israeli strike force).

Intissar al-Wazir (known as Umm Jihad) returned to Gaza with Arafat in July 1994. As the only female member of the PNA cabinet, she initially faced some rivalry from Hanan Ashrawi and others. However, she did help to put women's affairs onto the agenda while the PNA set up its infrastructure in Gaza and the West Bank. During her tenure in office, Wazir formed useful ties with her Israeli counterpart, Ora Namir. Her PNA duties have incorporated her work since the early 1960s, of running the Welfare Organization for the Families of Martyrs and Prisoners. She is now the director of a special committee, and disburses funds totalling $60 million to 28,000 cases in the self-rule territories, and 65,000 needy families in Lebanon,

Jordan and Syria. Intissar al-Wazir also campaigns for Palestinian prisoners and detainees still held in Israel.

She says she cannot yet forgive Israel for killing her husband, but believes that it is time for co-operation and co-existence, and for negotiations to 'make real the dream of an independent Palestinian State with East Jerusalem as its capital'. Self-assured and well-groomed in appearance, she is proud of her children's achievements. She believes all Palestinians should have access to education and health care, and also favours a separate department devoted to women's affairs. Wazir enjoys the loyal support of many *Fatah*-supporting Diaspora Palestinians, and, as the heir to Abu Jihad's legacy, she may well play an important role in forthcoming talks with Israel on their future. During the run-up to the Palestine Council election, she campaigned in the Gazan refugee camps; on Jan. 20, 1996, Wazir was placed fourth out of 12 legislators who were elected for the district of Gaza City.

Wazir, Khalil al-   Palestinian

Founder member of *Fatah,* editor of its influential newsletters, and once tipped as successor to Yasser Arafat. Wazir (better known as Abu Jihad) rose to become number two to Yasser Arafat within the PLO hierarchy. In 1974 he voted with Arafat to amend to the PLO's position from 'total liberation', to establishing a state on 'any inch of liberated land'. He had special responsibility for fostering PLO support in the occupied territories. Israeli officials knew that as head of Western Sector he was in charge of all *Fatah* military operations against Israel (including allegedly terrorist ones), and believed he was the mastermind behind the *intifada*. In April 1988 Khalil al-Wazir was assassinated by *Mossad* agents in Tunis. Since then, Abu Jihad has become the *Fatah* martyr *par excellence.* His widow, Intissar al-Wazir, holds the welfare and social affairs portfolio in the Palestine National Authority.

Weiss, Shevah   Israel

Knesset Speaker. Shevah Weiss was born in Borislav, Poland (afterwards part of the USSR), and came to Palestine in 1947. He took a law degree in 1966, and holds a PhD in political science from the Hebrew University. Weiss is a lifelong member of the Labour movement. After serving 12 years on the Haifa municipal council, he entered the Knesset in 1981. As Speaker, Weiss has some influence as the person who sets the agenda for legislation. He also has the deciding voice in the case of a hung vote.

Ezer WEIZMAN

Nationality	Israeli
Religion	Jewish
Place of birth	Tel Aviv
Date of birth	1924
Current position	President of Israel
Previous positions	Long and distinguished military career, ending as head of the Air Force
	Chairman of *Herut* (main component of *Likud*)
	Ministerial posts, including Defence (from 1977–80) under *Likud*
	Founder of pro-peace party, *Yahad,* in 1984
	Co-ordinator of Arab Affairs, 1985
	Minister of Science and Development (from 1988 to 1990) under Labour
Allies	Wide support from across the political spectrum
Position on peace	A veteran albeit maverick dove, Weizman appeared disenchanted with errors in the peace process and blamed PNA for not stopping terror
National political importance	Aims to be a source of national unity, especially after Rabin murder; but criticized by some for exceeding the titular limits of presidency

Ezer Weizman was elected as Israel's seventh President by the Knesset on May 13, 1993, crowning an illustrious career in the military, business and political worlds. Few other leaders in Israel have achieved so much, and few can so readily defy categorization as Weizman. Born in Tel Aviv and raised in Haifa, Weizman is the nephew of Israel's first President, the famous scientist and instigator of the Balfour Declaration, Chaim Weizman. In a sense Ezer Weizman comes as close to royalty as a republic like Israel can allow. The Knesset judged that a man held in such affection and respect was ideal to act as its head of state, especially as the five years of his tenure of office were to coincide with the difficult process of adapting to peace.

Ezer Weizman joined Britain's Royal Air Force during World War II and served in Egypt and India. After the war he flew in the Palestine Jewish community's Air Service. Following Israel's Declaration of Independence, Weizman moulded the service into today's Israel Air Force (IAF). In 1956 he was appointed Commander-in-Chief of the IAF, and ten years later he became head of operations for the IDF. Weizman grasped the potential of air power in modern warfare, and is regarded as the architect of Israel's victory over the Egyptian Air Force during the 1967 Six Day War.

He retired from the IDF in 1969, and immediately embarked on a political career by being appointed Minister of Transport in Levi Eshkol's second national unity government. When the *Gahal* coalition (forerunner of *Likud*) left the government in 1970, Weizman became Chairman of the *Herut* party's Executive Committee for two years (*Herut*, led by Menachem Begin, was a component of *Gahal*). In 1977 he ran the *Likud's* successful election campaign for the ninth Knesset, ensuring the first victory for Begin's supporters since the state was founded.

Begin duly rewarded Weizman with the prestigious post of Minister of Defence. Ezer Weizman was instrumental in the process leading to the peace treaty with Egypt. He fostered close relationships with Egyptian leaders, including his opposite number in the Egyptian Air Force, Hosni Mubarak, who was later to succeed Anwar Sadat as president. However, as the Camp David negotiations continued, it was clear that Weizman and Begin differed over their vision of peace, and how to achieve it. Weizman resigned his cabinet post in 1980, and was subsequently expelled from *Likud*. He left the political arena to set up a business career, but in 1984 returned to the fray as head of a new party, *Yahad*. Its policies reflected his full conversion to the 'peace camp', and in elections held that year it gained three seats.

Weizman join the resultant Labour-*Likud* government of national unity, as Minister without Portfolio. He also served in the inner cabinet, from where, with his military reputation, he helped to oversee Israel's withdrawal from most of Lebanon. In 1985 he was appointed Co-ordinator of Arab Affairs, and worked to improve conditions for Israel's Arab population. After the demise of *Yahad*, Weizman ran Labour's 1988 electoral campaign, and became Minister of Science and Development in the new coalition government. He left the cabinet when Labour pulled out of the coalition in 1990. In February 1992, Ezer Weizman resigned from the Knesset over what he regarded as lack of progress in the Arab–Israeli peace process. Once again 'in the wilderness', Weizman decided to stand for the presidency. In 1993 he defeated fellow political veteran, Lova Eliav, to succeed Chaim Hertzog as state president.

As head of state, Ezer Weizman has proved as much the maverick as he was in the cabinet. He began as an enthusiast for he peace process, and welcomed the Washington Declaration of Principles in September 1993. However, as terror incidents mounted in 1994, Weizman accused the PLO of acting in bad faith, and suggested suspending the peace process. In late 1995 he refused to allow the release of Palestinian prisoners from Israeli jails (one of the stipulations of Oslo 2, or the Interim Agreement, signed between Israel and the PLO). Critics have accused him of abusing his titular prerogative by making political pronouncements. But Weizman and his faithful head of office, Shumer, countered that in a democracy, every citizen has a right to express his or her opinions. On the international front, Weizman has used his charm and copious contacts to further Israel's image. But even here, his frankness has offended some. Speaking to US Jewish communal leaders, he told them not to dictate terms to Israel. If they felt strongly about Zionism, they should immigrate, he said.

Unlike most Israeli government figures, Weizman was a popular visitor to West Bank settlements, while at the same time enjoying good relations with Israeli Arabs. Twice a week he visits people with problems (including Soviet and Ethiopian immigrants, or those living in run-down neighbourhoods or cash-strapped *moshavim*). While critics say he is falsely raising expectations, Weizman counters that his office may be ceremonial, but he has 'the power of influence'. In December 1994 he was accused of playing party politics, when he suggested that opposition parties should join a broader-based government. Perhaps his most testing moment came after the assassination of Prime Minister Yitzhak Rabin on Nov. 4, 1995. Weizman led the funeral orations at Rabin's graveside, and later worked hard to heal the national wounds. There were suggestions that he may run in the first direct elections for prime minister, which are due in 1996 (in the end, he did not do so). Certainly, Weizman is loath to lose his already limited powers, to a prime minister with the mandate of a US president. But Israeli politicians normally end their careers as president, and it is unlikely that Weizman can buck that trend.

Williamson, Molly   USA
Former US Consul General in Jerusalem; since 1994, a deputy assistant secretary of defence, with responsibility for regional security affairs in the the Middle East. Williamson, the daughter of Californian Chinese-Americans, became Consul General in August 1991. She came to the job with 13 years experience in the Middle East, having served in Tel Aviv and Amman. She had close ties Palestinian and Israeli leaders, as well as US Jewish communal leaders, and helped to foster discussions between these parties during the Madrid talks, and the Taba talks after Oslo 1.

Y

Ya'acobi, Gad   Israel
Israeli Ambassador to the United Nations since October 1992. Born in 1935, Ya'acobi was a Labour MK from 1969 to 1992. Ya'acobi advocated negotiations with Palestinians, and wrote about the potential of a peace dividend. However, his pragmatic dovish approach got little hearing when he served in the *Likud*-Labour Government of National Unity, first as Minister for Economics and Planning, from 1984 to 1988, and next as Minister for Communications and Transport, from 1988 to 1990. Instead, he was credited for his innovative new policies, which helped to repair the economic damage caused by the expenses of the Lebanon War.

He planned to run in the 1991 Labour primaries for party leadership, but decided to bow out and support Yitzhak Rabin's candidacy instead. Ya'acobi was placed too far down Labour's electoral list to get elected in 1992. As UN Ambassador, he has defended some of Rabin's more controversial policies (such as the 1992 deportations, and expropriation of parts of Arab Jerusalem). At the same time, he has quietly fostered good ties with Israel's many new friends in the General Assembly, building on the successful record of his predecessor, Zalman Shoval. One of Ya'acobi's goals was to change the UN's stance towards Israel. He welcomed the appointment of Israelis to UN bodies in 1993, for the first time in 30 years. Ya'acobi was also pleased that the UN passed resolutions against terrorism, and explicitly condemned terror attacks on Israelis. But while approving the UN's role in supporting the PNA, he also called for the abolition of special Palestinian bodies at the UN, such as the Special Committeee to Investigate Israeli Practices. In March 1995 Ya'acobi defended Israel's decision not to sign the Nuclear Non-Proliferation Treaty (NPT), saying that it could not do so as long as Iran and Iraq possessed nuclear weapons, and refused to make peace with Israel.

Ya'alom, Moshe   Israel
Chief of Military Intelligence, successor to Uri Saguy. In 1996 Ya'alom testified that Arafat had not done enough to dismantle the infrastructure of *Hamas* and Islamic *Jihad*. Together with Deputy Defence Minister Ori Orr, Ya'alom is planning Israel's counterstrike against the fundamentalists, after the suicide bombings of February and March 1996.

Yahiya, Abed al-Razzaq al-   Palestinian
Director of the Committee to Study Proper Implementation of the Gaza-Jericho-First Agreement. Yahiya was a former commander of the Palestine Liberation Army. As such, he ensured that many PLA troops from Iraq, Jordan and Tunisia would become the rump of the new Palestine National Authority police force. Yahiya negotiated for the PLO on security aspects of Oslo 1 with Israel at Taba, alongside the PLO's chief negotiator at the time, Nabil Sha'ath.

Sheikh Ahmed Ismail YASSIN

Nationality	Palestinian
Religion	Muslim
Place of birth	Gaza
Current position	Official head of *Hamas*; currently held in Israeli prison
Previous position	Muslim preacher in Gaza; Chairman of the Islamic Congress
Allies	Sheikh Shikaki; rumours of ties to *Hezbollah, Ikhwan,* and Iran
Position on peace	Initially strongly opposed; backs Arab Palestine within Muslim Middle East; lately has reportedly spoken of need to come to an accomodation with the PNA and even with Israel
National political importance	Influential despite imprisonment; martyr to young radicals in territories
Prospects	Improve whenever PNA errs; but depends if he is released, and also on whether younger men usurp his role.

Sheikh Ahmed Ismail Yassin of Gaza is the spiritual leader and founder of *Hamas*, the most powerful Islamic fundamentalist group amongst Palestinians, and a rival to the PLO. Although he has been held in an Israeli prison since May 1989, he still wields enormous influence as the founder and spiritual leader of *Hamas*.

For years he was well-known in the Zaitoun quarter of Gaza, but in few areas outside there. Despite a debilitating illness which left him almost totally paralysed, he set up and chaired a group called the Islamic Congress (*Al-Majama al-Islami*), in effect a front for the conservative Egyptian-based Muslim Brotherhood. Sheikh Yassin enjoyed a reputation for expertise on Islamic law amongst a small but devoted coterie of supporters. During the 1980s his sermons became more overtly political and anti-Israeli, although their main thrust remained the religious improvement of Muslims in Gaza.

At first Israeli intelligence supported the *Majama* as a counterweight to Palestinian nationalists in the PLO. Yassin developed the group into *Al-Majahadoun al-Falestiniyoun* in 1982, which planned an armed struggle against the PLO. He called PLO leaders 'pork-eaters', and purged their representatives at Gaza's Al-Azhar Islamic University. Yassin had a particular antipathy towards Arafat. In 1984 he was sentenced to 13 years in prison for arms possession, but was released the following May as part of the Ahmed Jibril prisoner exchange, and came out against a policy of terrorism. He nonetheless told supporters that they had to 'purge rivals from within'. In 1986 he set up the *Hamas* Security Section, to curb drug-dealers and keep tabs on opponents.

However, it was the *intifada* which turned him into a national political figure. Cautious and conservative by nature, Yassin initially resisted attempts by younger disciples to 'politicize' and 'Palestinianize' the Islamic Congress. But in February 1988, faced by the prospect of the rival PLO–influenced United National Command (a secret steering committee for *intifada* activities) undercutting his followers, he relented and formed *Hamas*. The word *Hamas* is an acronym for 'Islamic Resistance Movement', but it also means 'zeal' in Arabic – an appropriate epithet considering the speed with which its message spred throughout Gaza, and soon to Nablus, Hebron and Tulkarm in the West Bank. Yassin was responsible for setting up the *Hamas* network of social help groups and community health centres.

He also wrote *Hamas*'s leaflets, managed financial affairs, and liaised with radical Islamists abroad. Yassin probably directed the *Majd* (an acronym for the Holy War and Sermonizing Group) which later evolved into the military wing, the best-known faction of which is the Izz al-Din al-Qassem Brigade. Lately, though, they appear to be acting independently of the political wing. As the *intifada* unfolded, Yassin countermanded PLO handbills, and deliberately ordered Gazans to strike on different days. He opposed PLO leftists and their plans for civil disobediance, favouring instead self-help, charity drives and discipline. When Arafat won the backing of the Cairo chapter of the Muslim Brotherhood, Yassin drafted his own alternative to the PLO Covenant, in August 1988, which he called the 'Covenant of *Hamas* Palestine'. Ironically, this drawing of the dividing lines also allowed for a partial rapprochement between the two organizations.

Sheikh Yassin was arrested and imprisoned in May 1989. Since then, a new generation of ocal Hamas leaders, including Mahmoud al-Zahar, Abdel Aziz Rantisi, and 'expatriate' eaders, like Ahmed Yousef and Musa Abu Marzouk, have attempted to fill the void. Yassin's absence may explain the apparent diffusion of views within the group; and the evident split between its political and 'military' wings. The ostensible reason for the Beit Lid bomb attack in 1994 was to demand Yassin's release from prison. In late 1995, the Sheikh issued a statement from prison, urging *Hamas* members to consider co-operating with the Palestine National Authority under Yasser Arafat. At the same time, he has not openly condemned terrorist atrocities against Israelis, conducted in the name of *Hamas*. In late 1995, with Yassin's apparent approval, *Hamas* said that it was instituting a political party. In the event, it did not stand in the Palestinian elections of January 1996. A dramatic announcement followed two *Hamas* attacks on Israelis in Jerusalem and Ashkelon, in February 1996, in which Sheikh Yassin was said to have announced a ceasefire with Israel.

Yatom, Danny (Maj.-Gen.)   Israel

Chief of Israeli military intelligence. Military aide to both Yitzhak Rabin and Shimon Peres, and officer in command of the IDF Central Command. Under the Labour-*Likud* coalition, Yatom served as military secretary to Defence Ministers Yitzhak Rabin and Moshe Arens. Maj.-Gen. Yatom played an important role in arranging the transfer of powers from Israel to the PNA in Gaza and Jericho. Yatom, who was 50 in 1995, is allied to the new military Chief of Staff Amnon Shahak. In January 1996 he and IDF Planning head, Eli Dayan, travelled to the Wye Valley Plantation in Maryland, USA, to conduct fruitful talks with their Syrian counterparts. In February 1996 he warned that *Hamas* and the Islamic *Jihad* were planning terrorist acts aimed at large crowds inside Israel, but praised the PNA for pre-empting violent incidents. In June Yatom took over as head of *Mossad*.

Yeltsin, Boris   Russia

President of the Russian Federation since 1991; and together with the USA and Norway, an official co-guarantor of the Israeli–PLO Oslo accords. Despite the latter title, Yeltsin has not been able to wield the influence he may have wished in the Middle East, because of severe political crises on his home soil. Boris Yeltsin was born in 1931 in the Svedlovsk region of Russia, joined the Communist Party in 1961, and rose through its ranks to become head of its regional aparatus in Sverdlovsk in 1976.

Boris Yeltsin was elected President of the Russian Federation in June 1991. Since then, Yeltsin has been dogged by constitutional difficulties, and open warfare in the former Soviet Union, in Armenia, Chechnya and Moldova. He inherited a weaker Russian foreign policy in the Middle East Internal problems led to Boris Yeltsin's long absence from direct involvement in the Middle East in 1995. However, by early 1996, he seemed to reverse this trend, in contradictory ways – he replaced Kozyrev with the dynamic Yevgeny Primakov, an unreformed Communist who backed radical regimes; yet in March he joined Clinton, Arafat, Mubarak and Peres in a display of unity against terrorism, at a large conference in Cairo.

Yilmaz, Mesut   Turkey

Prime Minister of Turkey since March 1996, and leader of *Anap*, the Motherland Party. According to a coalition agreement with the outgoing Prime Minister Tansu Ciller, Mesut would serve for two years, and then Ciller would resume power for another two years. Although their political views are similar, the two are bitter rivals. He became leader of *Anap* in 1991, and is known as a 'technocrat' who favours a policy of free enterprise, secularism, and economic ties with the European Union.

Yosef, Ovadiah (Rabbi)   Israel

Former Chief Sephardi Rabbi of Israel and President of the Supreme Rabbinical Court from 1973 to 1983; and mentor of the ultra-orthodox *Shas* Party. Rabbi Yosef was born in Baghdad, Iraq in 1920, arrived in Palestine the following year. As Chief Rabbi of Israel, Yosef won a reputation for his considered judgements, and his stress on the practical applications of religious law. Since leaving that office, he has maintained his extraordinary influence amongst Sephardi Jews, who take pride in his encyclopaedic talmudic knowledge. He remains close to *Shas* party leader Rabbi Arye Deri, and frequently advises him on matters of policy. In 1989 he ruled that territorial compromise was permissible if it would prevent war, on the talmudic principle of *pikuach nefesh* (preservation of life). In 1990 he and Deri visited President Mubarak in Egypt, to discuss new peace initiatives. After the 1992 elections, he again approved of *Shas* participation in a Labour government. Since then, both pro-and anti-peace factions have tried to sway his opinion. Generally Rabbi Yosef holds a positive outlook on the peace process, well to the left of much orthodox Jewish opinion, although he said he remained 'open to persuasion'. He is currently 'considering the verdict' on whether Israel should withdraw from the Golan Heights. *Shas's* electoral victory in 1996 will boost his influence.

Yusuf, Nasser (General)   Palestinian
PNA military commander of Gaza Strip. He is reputedly on an Islamic *Jihad* 'death list', and has been accused by some Palestinians of being Israel's lackey, for cracking down on *Hamas* dissidents in 1994. Similarly, Palestinian human rights groups have accused him of allowing human rights abuses in Gaza's prisons. Unlike the situation in Jericho, where his counterpart Jibril Rajoub enjoys a near monopoly on Palestinian police power, Yusuf has faced rivalry from a range of 'legitimate armed groups'. Analysts suggested this bore the hallmark of Arafat's 'divide and rule' policy with regard to PLO factions. His chief rival within the PNA is probably Col Dahlan. Yusuf deserves much of the credit for the success of joint Israeli–Palestinian security patrols in Gaza, and for the relative absence of attacks on Jewish settlers in the region. Yusuf's force was significantly expanded under the terms of the Oslo 2 agreement. Many of its core members are former fighters in the Iraqi-trained Palestine Liberation Army. Yusuf oversaw the departure of IDF forces from Jenin in November 1996, and said it was a credit to the memory of the recently assassinated Yitzhak Rabin. After the resumption of *Hamas* bombings in late February 1996, Yusuf will be expected to arrest and 'discipline' many *Hamas* leaders.

Z

Za'noun, Riyad   Palestinian
PNA Minister of Health, head of the Higher Council for Health in Gaza. Za'noun is a physician himself, who has been affiliated with *Fatah* for many years. After just one year of PNA rule, he had managed to double the number of people who received medical insurance cover under Israeli occupation. He also worked to ensure that Gazans continued to have access to Israeli government hospitals. Health Ministry staff numbers rose by 25%, and 60,000 schoolchildren underwent 'health screening'. Za'noun was enthusiastic about the economic progress which the PNA has made. In the Jan. 20 Palestinian Council elections, he was placed fifth out of 12 candidates who were elected to the district of Gaza City (or Central Gaza).

Za'noun, Salim   Palestinian
Speaker of the Palestine National Council (PNC), and its acting Chairman. In November 1995 Za'noun convened the first meeting of a special 'higher committee to defend Jerusalem'. The committee reportedly included three members of the PNA. Its deputy chairman is a former Jordanian cabinet minister, Raef Najm. Za'noun said he would arrange a joint memorandum with other Arab and Islamic leaders, to dissuade US President Bill Clinton from moving his nation's embassy to Jerusalem (as per a vote in Congress). Nonetheless, he defended the PNC's and PNA's decision to postpone talks on Jerusalem until after the final status negotiations.

With the imminent retirement of the 93-year-old official Chairman of the PNC, Abed al-Hamid a-Sayeh, Salim Za'noun acted as the Council's spokesman on the issue of abrogating the Palestinian Charter, as stipulated in Oslo 2. In February 1996 he demanded that Israel should meet three preconditions – it should hand the entire West Bank and Gaza to Palestinian control; release all Palestinian political prisoners; and allow all PNC members to return to the Autonomy as residents, not tourists. Za'noun is an Arafat loyalist, but will still have a considerable task determining the relationship between the long established PNC, and the newly elected Palestinian Council of Gaza and the West Bank.

Zahar, Mahmoud (Dr)   Palestinian
Prominent *Hamas* leader and ideologue in Gaza. Israel arrested him for subversive activities.

following a car-bombing, in 1995, but later released him. Known for his frequent layman's sermons at Gaza City's Palestine Mosque, Dr Zahar is the most vocal *Hamas* leader, and helped to revive the group's infrastructure after the imprisonment of its leader, Sheikh Ahmed Yassin, in 1989. But whether he is more than just a spokesman is unclear. In 1994 he backed an Islamist 'political party' within the PNA. Again, in November 1995 he appeared to endorse a political role for *Hamas* within the peace arrangements, and headed a Conciliation Committee with the PLO. Later he retracted statements backing *Hamas* participation in the forthcoming Palestine Council elections. After the bomb bombings of February and March 1996, Zahar announced that *Hamas* would suspend its attacks 'for the present'. He was later arrested by the PNA police.

Zaideh, Sufyan Abu　　　Palestinian
Prominent *Fatah* activist in Gaza. In March 1994, Abu Zaideh became one of the first *Fatah* members to visit the Israeli Knesset, in the wake of Oslo 1. Abu Zaideh is the head of the Israel desk in the PNA.

Zaki, Abbas　　　Palestinian
PLO veteran who returned to Gaza in 1995. Zaki spoke as the putative heir of his former mentor, Abu Jihad, the chief of PLO military operations, who was assassinated in Tunis in 1988. He won popular support for opposing the rapprochement with Israel, and successfully contested the Jan. 20 1996 Palestine Council elections. After a review of the vote in February, Zaki was declared top of a poll of ten elected candidates in Hebron.

Zakut, Jamal　　　Palestinian
A leader of *Fida*, the Palestinian Democratic Forum. *Fida* was founded by Yaser Abed-Rabbo as a breakaway from the DFLP (Democratic Front for the Liberation of Palestine). Like Abed-Rabbo, Zakut broadly supports the current peace process with Israel. In the early days of the *intifada*, Zakut, a labourer who had received education in Bulgaria, founded a branch of the Unified Leadership in Gaza. His brother-in-law, Mohammed Labadi, was said to be the first real organizer of the *intifada*. Zakut was interrogated and deported. Now he is one of the few members of the Unified Leadership to keep power in the PNA era.

Zayyad, Ziyad Abu　　　Palestinian
Senior Palestinian official, elected as a *Fatah* candidate for Jerusalem, on Jan. 20, 1996. Abu Zayyad said he had participated in 'fruitful yet informal exploratory talks' on the issue of Jerusalem with Israeli officials and academics, prior to the final status talks, which formally began in May 1996. During the election campaign, he was the only candidate to address the issue of abrogating the Palestinian Charter. Ziyad Abu Zayyad was born in Bethany, and graduated in law from Damascus University in 1965. After the Israeli capture of East Jerusalem, Zayyad enrolled on a course to learn Hebrew, and worked as translator for the Palestinian *Al-Quds* newspaper. In 1976 he was detained on charges of belonging to the PFLP. The following year he edited a Hebrew language version of *Al-Fajr*, and in 1986 he set up his own Hebrew newspaper, *Gesher* (Bridge). He was one of the first 'internal' Palestinians to openly advocate a two-state solution, and was criticized by extremists for these views. Zayyad has fostered longstanding ties with Israeli leftists, like Meron Benvenisti and Yossi Sarid; after the Gulf War (in which he opposed the PLO line, yet was detained by Israel) he interceded between Palestinian and Israeli leaders. In 1992 he was the chairman of the Political Committee of Jerusalem, which aimed to form a link between 'the masses', the PLO in Tunis, and the negotiating team in Washington.

Ze'evi, Rechavam　　　Israel
Head of the far right pro-settler *Moledet* Party. Ze'evi advised Prime Minister Rabin from 1974 to 1977 on how to fight terrorism; from 1981 he directed the Land of Israel Museum, and controversially campaigned for the annexation of all Israeli–held territories. Just before the 1988 elections, Ze'evi created *Moledet* (Homeland) which won three seats in the Knesset on a platform advocating 'voluntary transfer' of Palestinians from the territories. In February 1991 he entered government for the first time, as Minister Without Portfolio, despite major qualms from several leading *Likud* politicians. He pulled out of the coalition in January 1992,

together with *Tehiyah,* in protest at the mention of Palestinian autonomy at the Madrid track peace talks. *Moledet* gained an extra seat in the 1992 elections, but the party was deeply split over Ze'evi's increasingly dictatorial style. Since the signing of the Oslo Accords, Ze'evi has joined extra-parliamentary protests led by settlers. He has threatened to shoot any Palestinian policeman who tries to arrest him.

Zibri, Taysir al-   Jordan
Secretary-General of the Jordanian People's Democratic Party (*Hashd*). Zibri's party enjoys strong support amongst Jordanian Palestinians, and it was regarded as an extension of the Democratic Front for the Liberation of Palestine (DFLP). Zibri supports DFLP leader Naif Hawatmeh, a fellow Marxist, and opposes the Israel–PLO agreements.

Zichroni, Amnon   Israel
Leading lawyer, former pacifist, and adviser to Yasser Arafat on economic affairs. Amnon Zichroni was born in Tel Aviv in 1935. He was an ardent follower of Menachem Begin's *Irgun* until he was 16, when the plight of Palestinian refugees altered his political outlook. Two years later Zichroni became Israel's first conscientious objector. After dabbling in journalism, he entered law school and in 1960 became legal advisor to Uri Avneri's dissident *Ha'olam Hazeh* newspaper. In 1977 Zichroni, Avneri and Yair Tsaban founded the pro-peace *Sheli* Party. He virulently opposed the 1986 Israeli law which banned contacts with the PLO. Zichroni's clandestine contacts with the PLO made him a valuable intermediatory in negotiations to free the Western hostages in Lebanon, in 1989. At other times, he has defended an Orthodox Jewish politician accused of corruption, large corporations, workers threatened by dismissal, and alleged Soviet spies. Western multinationals have employed him to negotiate with Third World countries. Most recently, Zichroni agreed to defend Ya'akov Shoval, a police commander accused of negligence after the Rabin assassination. Zichroni believes a strong Palestinian economy is vital to the success of the peace process. His close ties with both IDF Chief of Staff Amon Shahak and PNA President Yasser Arafat has probably cast him as a vital, albeit unofficial, bridge between Israel and the PNA.

Zohar, Gadi   Israel
West Bank Civil Administration head. He negotiated the initial transfer of authority to the PLO in Jericho.

Zuabi, Mahmud   Syria
(See Zu'bi, Mahmoud az-)

Zu'bi, Fawwaz al-   Jordan
Secretary-General of the Freedom Party. Zu'bi is a former Communist, but more recently has tried to fuse aspects of Marxism with Islamic tradition and Jordanian nationalism. Zu'bi backed the peace process, and favours a healthy opposition to 'shadow the government' by monitoring all ministerial projects.

Zu'bi, Mahmoud az-   Syria
Prime Minister of Syria since 1987. Zu'bi has been a lynchpin in the Syrian regime, and a great source of stability, even though he maintains a quiet profile in public. From 1981 to 1987, Zu'bi was the Speaker of Syria's People's Assembly (parliament). His main brief is internal politics, and he has used his training as an agronomist to boost Syria's agricultural performance. In November 1994, he announced a major economic reform package, designed to increase private investment in the Syrian economy.

Zvilli, Nissim   Israel
General-Secretary of the Labour Party. Zvilli originally wanted the Agriculture Ministry, but had to settle for a deputy portfolio in the Finance Ministry in 1992. As party secretary, he has had the arduous task of calming contending factions. Even so, he wields considerable backstage influence in two spheres – drafting the party manifesto (where it is rumoured he may drop Labour's traditional objections to a Palestinian state); and approving new ministers (Zvilli helped usher in Ehud Barak to the cabinet). In early 1995, he said that he favoured accelerating peace talks to the final stage. Zvilli has had a dovish reputation since 1985, when

he founded the *Kfar Hayarok* faction within Labour with fellow MK, Haim Ramon. He also represents the interests of Israel's *moshavim* (semi-communal agricultural settlements). Following the assassination of Yitzhak Rabin in November 1995, and Shimon Peres' assumption of the premiership, Zvilli helped to restore morale in the shocked Labour Party. In January 1996 he and Foreign Ministry Director-General Uri Savir suggested moving forward the national general elections, in a bid to capitalize on Labour's new popularity, and give Peres the mandate needed to achieve a full peace with Syria. Peres accepted this suggestion, and called elections for May 29, 1996, which he narrowly lost.

PART FOUR B

LISTING BY COUNTRY OF BIOGRAPHIES

Australia
Leibler, Isi

Brazil
Koch-Weger, Caio

China
Qichen, Qian

Egypt
Abdel-Meguid, Esmat
Abu Ghazala, Mohammed
Arabi, Nabil al-
Baz, Osama al-
Beltagi, Mamdouh el-
Boutros Ghali, Boutros
Boutros Ghali, Youssef
Fahmi, Nabil
Fatah, Ali Abed al-
Ganzoury, Kamal Ahmad
Gheit, Ahmed Abul
Heikal, Mohammed
Khalil, Mustafa
Moussa, Amr
Mubarak, Hosni
Sadat, Anwar
Sedqi, Atef
Wali, Yusuf Amin

France
Bajolet, Bernard
Kahn, Jean
Mitterrand, Francois
Sibiud, Jean-Luc
Wattez, Edouard

Germany
Kohl, Helmut
Rhein, Eberhard

India
Garg, Prem

Iran
Khameini, Seyed Ali
Mohtashami, Hojatoleslam
Rafsanjani, Ali Akbar H
Shaikholeslam, Hussein
Velayati, Ali Akbar

Iraq
Hussein, Saddam

Israel
Aloni, Shulamit
Alpher, Joseph
Amir, Yigal
Amirav, Moshe
Amital, Yehuda
Arens, Moshe
Asaad, Asaad
Aviram, Ram
Avner, Yehuda
Avneri, Uri
Ayalon, Ami
Bakshi-Doron, Eliahu

Barak, Aharon
Barak, Ehud
Baram, Uzi
Begin, Menachem
Begin, Ze'ev Binyamin
Beilin, Yossi
Ben-Aharon, Yossi
Ben-Ami, Shlomo
Ben-Eliezer, Binyamin
Ben-Elissar, Eliayahu
Ben-Tsur, Eitan
Ben-Yair, Michael
Bin-Nun, Yoel
Biran, Ilan
Biran, Yoav
Brodet, David
Burg, Avraham
Carmon, Yigal
Chazan, Naomi
Cohen, Ruth
Cohen, Ra'anan
Cohen, Ya'akov
Darawshe, Abdul Wahab
Darwish, Abdallah Nimr
Dayan, Eli
Dayan, Moshe
Dayan, Uzi
Dayan, Yael
Deri, Aryeh
Divon, Haim
Domb, Aharon
Dromi, Uri
Drori, Mordechai
Druckman, Haim
Eban, Abba
Eitan, Raphael
Eliav, Arie 'Lova'
Elitzur, Uri
Elon, Benny
Epstein, Haim
Eran, Oded
Feiglin, Moshe
Feldman, Avigdor
Frenkel, Ya'akov
Gal, Yossi
Gazit, Shlomo
Gillerman, Dan
Gilon, Carmi
Ginnosar, Yossi
Golan, Daphna
Goldstein, Baruch
Gonen, Eli
Goodman, Hirsh
Gur, Mordechai
Gutman, Shaul
Haber, Eitan
Hadas, Shmuel
Hadas, Yossi
Ha'etzni, Elyakim
Halevy, Ephraim
Hammer, Zevulun
Hanegbi, Tzachi
Harel, Yisrael

Hareven, Alouf
Harish, Micha
Hendel, Zvi
Hertzog, Haim
Hirsch, Moshe
Hirschfeld, Yair
Ilan, Baruch
Ivri, David
Jubran, Salem
Kahalani, Avigdor
Kahane, Benyamin
Kahane, Meir
Kahane, Shamai
Kashdan, Bruce
Kashriel, Benny
Kattan, Shlomo
Katz-Oz, Avraham
Katzover, Zvi
Kessar, Yisrael
Khalefeh, Khaled
Kinarti, Noah
Kollek, Teddy
Lahat, Shlomo 'Chich'
Landau, Uzi
Lang, Bob
Levin, Aryeh
Levine, Amiram
Levinger, Moshe
Levy, David
Liba'i, David
Lubrani, Uri
Maoz, Moshe
Massalha, Nawaf
Meirom, Hagai
Merhav, Reuven
Meridor, Dan
Merzel, Baruch
Nachman, Ron
Netanyahu, Benyamin
Nevo, Danny
Novick, Nimrod
Ofir, Gabi
Olmert, Ehud
Olmert, Yossi
Orr, Ori
Peled, Rafi
Peled, Matityahu
Peleg, Yisrael
Peres, Shimon
Polisar, Dan
Pundak, Ron
Rabin, Leah
Rabin, Yitzhak
Rabinovich, Itamar
Ramon, Haim
Raviv, Avishai
Rothschild, Danny
Rubinstein, Amnon
Rubinstein, Elyakim
Saguy, Uri
Samiah, Yom Tov
Sandler, Deborah
Sarid, Yossi

Savir, Uri
Schach, Eliezer
Segev, Gonen
Shachor, Oren
Shahak, Amnon
Shahal, Moshe
Shamgar, Meir
Shamir, Shimon
Shamir, Yitzhak
Sharansky, Natan
Sharon, Ariel
Shek, Danny
Shetreet, Shimon
Shevis, Shimon
Shohat, Avraham
Shoval, Zalman
Singer, Joel
Sneh, Ephraim
Somekh, Sasson
Spiegel, Baruch
Tsaban, Yair
Tsedakah, Binyamin
Tsur, Ya'akov
Tzilker, Tzvi
Vilna'i, Matan
Vilner, Meir
Weiss, Shevah
Weizman, Ezer
Ya'acobi, Gad
Ya'alom, Moshe
Yatom, Danny
Yosef, Ovadiah
Ze'evi, Rehavam
Zichroni, Amnon
Zohar, Gadi
Zvilli, Nissim

Italy
Annielli, Suzanna
Ayyash, Yehiya

Japan
Ogata, Sadako

Jordan
Abbadi, Abd as-Salam
Arabiyat, Abd al-Latif
Awad, Marwan
Ayoub, Fouad
Badran, Mudar
Bani-Hadi, Muhammad
Farhan, Ishaq
Gammo, Sami
Haddadin, Munther
Hahsana, Duryad
Hassan ibn Talal
Hussein ibn Talal
Jaber, Kamal Abu
Kabariti, Abdul-Karim
Khader, Asma
Khawaja, Azmi Abdul Aziz
Khreisheh, Mijhim al-
Kuwar, Samir
Majali, Abd al-Salam al-

Majali, Abd al-Hadi al-
Muasher, Marwan
Mufleh, Jhassan
Nabulsi, Muhammad al-
Nahhas, Salem
Najm, Raef
Qassim, Marwan al-
Ragheb, Ali Abu al-
Rawabdeh, Abdul Raouf al-
Rifa'i, Abdul-Monem
Saket, Bassam as-
Shaker, Zaid ibn
Tarawneh, Faiz
Zibri, Taysir al-
Zu'bi, Fawwaz al-

Lebanon
Aoun, Michel
Berri, Nabih
Boueiz, Fares
Chamoun, Dory
Dalloul, Muhsin
Dib, Roger
Din, Muhammad Shams ad-
Dirani, Mustafa
Fadlallah, Muhammad
Fayyad, Sharif
Geagea, Samir
Hariri, Rafiq
Hobeika, Elie
Hrawi, Elias
Jumblatt, Walid
Khalil, Joseph Abu
Khoury, Michel Bechara
Lahad, Antoine
Lahoud, Emile
Makkawi, Khalil
Nasrallah, Hassan
Obeid, Abd al-Karim
Sa'ade, George
Sfeir, Nasrallah Pierre
Shaban, Sayed
Shamas, Suheil
Tufeili, Subhi

Libya
Ghaddafi, Muammar

Luxembourg
Jacques Santer

Morocco
Azoulei, André
Filali, Abdelatif
Hassan II

Netherlands
Serri, Robert
Van den Broek, Hans

Norway
Aas, Evn
Egeland, Jan
Godal, Bjorn Tore
Heiberg, Marianne

Holst, Johan Jorgen
Juul, Mona
Larsen, Terje Rod
Stoltenberg, Thorvald

Oman
Alawi, Yusuf bin

Palestinians
Abbas, Mahmud Zaidan
Abdul Hadi, Mahdi
Abdullah, Samir
Abed-Rabbo, Yasser
Abideen, Abdel-Qadir
Abu Adib [see Za'anoun]
Abu 'Ala [see Qurei]
Abu al-Mundhir [see Qirsh]
Abu Ammar [see Arafat]
Abu as-Said [see Hassan, K]
Abu Ayyash [see Ayyash]
Abu Bakr, Tewfiq
Abu Iyad [see Khalaf]
Abu Jihad [see Wazir, K.]
Abu Libdeh [see Libdeh]
Abu Lutf [see Qaddumi]
Abu Marzak [see Marzouk]
Abu Mazen [see Abbas, M.]
Abu Musa [see Muragha]
Abu Nidal [see Banna]
Abu Samer [see Labadi]
Abu Tayeb [see Natur]
Abu Za'im [see Attala]
Abu Zaideh [see Zaideh, S.]
Abu Zayyad [see Zayyad]
Abul Abbas, Muhammad
Abul Razak, Hisham
Abyad, Darwish
Agazarian, Albert
Agha, Zakaria al-
Ahmed, Abd al-Aziz
Aker, Mamdouh al-
Alami, Maher al-
Alami, Sa'ad al-Din al-
Aloul, Mahmoud al-
Amla, Muhammed Yusuf al-
Amr, Yasser
Arafat, Fat'hi
Arafat, Souha
Arafat, Yasser
Asfour, Hassan
Ashhab, abd al-Hafiz al-
Ashkar, Ihab al-
Ashrawi, Hanan
Attala, Attala Muhammad
Atrash, Ziyad al-
Awad, Mubarak
Awartani, Hisham
Aynan, Sultan Abu al-
Ayyash, Radwan Abu
Balawi, Hakam
Banna, Sabri Khalil al-
Barghouti, Bashir al-
Barghouti, Hassan

Bargouthi, Marwan
Barghouti, Mustafa
Besseiso, Fuad Hamadi
Birnawi, Fatmeh
Dahlan, Muhammad
Daoudi, Muhammad Omar
Darwish, Mahmoud
Elmusa, Sharif S.
Erakat, Sa'eb
Faluji, Imad
Fattah, Zia Abd al-
Freij, Elias
Ghosheh, Samir
Ghussein, Jawid
Habash, George
Hamad, Ghazi
Hanieh, Akram
Hassan, Hani al-
Hassan, Khalid al-
Hawatmeh, Naif
Hindi, Amin al-
Hulleileh, Samir
Husseini, Faisal al-
Hut, Shafiq al-
Ishaq, Jad
Ismail, Mahmoud
Ja'abari, Muhammed Amin
Ja'abari, Suleiman al-
Jaber, Hajj Ismail
Jarrar, Bassam
Jauda, Hisham
Jibril, Ahmed
Jiryas, Sabri
Kamail, Ahmed Awad
Kamal, Sa'id
Kamel, Zahira
Kana'an, Sameh
Kanafani, Marwan
Karas, Attar Abu
Kassem, Anis
Kassis, Nabil
Khader, Husam
Khalaf, Salah
Khaled, Leila
Khalidi, Rashid
Khalil, Samiha
Khalili, Saleh al-
Khatib, Ghassan
Kidra, Khalid al-
Kidwa, Nasser al-
Kilani, Sami
Kleibo, Mounir
Kurd, Maher al-
Kuttab, Daoud
Kuttab, Jonathan
Labadi, Mohammed
Libdeh, Hasan Abu
Ma'aruf, Lamia
Malki, Riyad Najib al-
Mansour, Camille
Maqdah, Mounir
Marzouk, Musa Abu
Masri, Munib Sabih

Medein, Freih Abu
Medhat, Kamal
Moddalal, Sa'id
Muragha, Sa'id Musa
Musallum, Sami
Musamih, Sayyid Abu
Mustafa, Abu Ali
Najjab, Suleiman an-
Nashashibi, Muhammad
Nasser, Maha
Natsheh, Mustafa
Natur, Muhammed a-
Nazzal, Muhammed
Nofel, Mahmoud
Nusseibeh, Sari
Odeh, Abd al-Aziz
Qaddumi, Farouk
Qirsh, Subhi Abu
Qurei, Ahmed
Rahim, Tayyeb Abd al-
Rahman, Ahmed Abd al-
Rahman, Hassan Abd al-
Rajoub, Jibril
Rantisi, Abd al-Aziz
Rashid, Muhammed
Sabbah, Michel
Sabri, Ikirmeh
Sadi, Ghazi al-
Safieh, Afif
Said, Edward
Saleh, Abdel Jawad
Sarraj, Iyad
Sawalha, Kasem
Sayeh, Abed al-Hamid a-
Sha'ath, Nabil
Shafi, Haidar Abd al-
Shafi, Khaled Abd al-
Shahid, Leila
Shaiah, Khalil
Shaka'a, Bassam al-
Shaka'a, Ghassan al-
Shallah, Ramadan A
Shanab, Ismael Abu
Sharif, Bassam Abu
Sharif, Mohiedin
Sharif, Nabil
Shawwa, Mansour Aoun al-
Shawwa, Rashad
Shehadah, Raja
Shehadah, Samir
Shiqaqi, Fat'hi
Shiqaqi, Khalil
Shtayyeh, Muhammed
Shueibi, Azmi
Shukeiri, Ahmed
Siam, Walid
Siniora, Hanna
Sourani, Raji
Souss, Ibrahim
Sultan, Khaled
Surani, Jamal as-
Tahboub, Hassan
Tamari, Salim

Tamimi, Asa'ad Bayoud al-
Tarbuk, Ahmad
Tarifi, Jamil al-
Terzi, Zehdi Labib
Tibi, Ahmad
Umm Jihad [see Wazir, I.]
Wazir, Intissar al-
Wazir, Khalil al-
Yahiya, Abed al-Razzaq al-
Yassin, Ahmed Ismail
Yusuf, Nasser
Za'noun, Riyad
Za'noun, Salim
Zahar, Mahmoud
Zaideh, Sufyan Abu
Zaki, Abbas
Zakut, Jamal
Zayyad, Ziyad Abu

Qatar
Thani, Hamed bin J al-

Russia
Bessmertnykh, Alexander
Gorbachev, Mikhail
Kozyrev, Andrei
Primakov, Yevgeny
Yeltsin, Boris

Saudi Arabia
Abdullah ibn Aziz ibn Saud
Bandar ibn Sultan al-Saud
Fahd ibn Aziz ibn Saud
Saud al-Faisal ibn Saud

Spain
González Marquez, Felipe
Juan Carlos
Marín Gonzales, Manuel

Sweden
Andersson, Sven
Lidbom, Carl

Syria
Alaf, Muwafak
Assad, Hafez al-
Jazzar, Majdi
Jinnah, Zuheir
Kenaan, Ghazi
Khaddam, Abd al-Halim
Mu'alam, Walid
Salman, Muhammad
Shar'a, Farouq ash-
Shihabi, Hikmat
Tlass, Mustafa al-
Zu'bi, Mahmoud az-

Tunisia
Ben Ali, Zide el-Abidine

Turkey
Cetin, Hikmet
Ciller, Tansu
Guvendiren, Ekrem Esat

Turkmen, Ilter
Yilmaz, Mesut

UK
Craig, James
Dalton, Richard John
Green, Andrew
Hurd, Douglas
Major, John
Manning, David
Sacks, Jonathan Henry
Thatcher, Margaret Hilda

USA
Albright, Madeline
Baker, James
Bentsen, Lloyd
Brown, Ron
Bush, George
Carter, Jimmy
Chomsky, Noam
Christopher, Warren

Clayman, David
Clinton, Bill
Coopersmith, Esther
D'Amato, Alfonso
Djerejian, Edward
Dole, Bob
Glaspie, April
Goldman, Nahum
Gore, Albert R
Grossman, Steve
Haass, Richard
Indyk, Martin
Jahshan, Khalil
Jones, Richard
Kantor, Micky
Kissinger, Henry
Kurtzer, Dan
Lake, Anthony
Le Baron, Richard
Linowitz, Solomon
Miller, Aaron

Pelletreau, Robert
Perry, William
Powell, Colin
Pressburg, Gail
Preston, Lewis
Rabie, Mohammed
Reagan, Ronald
Ross, Dennis
Rothermel, Timothy
Schultz, George
Speth, James Gustave
Vance, Cyrus
Williamson, Molly

Vatican
Celli, Claudio Maria
John Paul II

Yemen
Iryani, Abdul-Karim al-

PART FIVE

CURRENT DEVELOPMENTS AND THE FUTURE

Review of 1996

In less than five months, the Middle East peace process has undergone a number of twists and turns, making it an extraordinarily eventful slice of history.

JANUARY

Palestinians hold Legislative Council and Presidential elections, Israel and Jordan conclude final enabling agreements, and international donors pledge millions to Palestinians.

FEBRUARY

A new pro-peace cabinet takes power in Jordan, Peres calls early elections, and *Hamas* launches a bombing campaign in Israel.

MARCH

Palestinians inaugurate their Legislative Council, 27 nations attend an anti-terrorism conference at Sharm el-Sheikh, Israeli–Syrian talks on the Golan are suspended, and Israel imposes a tight closure on the territories.

APRIL

Israel counters *Hezbollah* attacks with Operation Grapes of Wrath in Lebanon, the USA brokers a ceasefire, and the Palestine National Council amends its Covenant.

MAY

Israel and the PLO officially begin their 'final status talks', multilateral negotiations on water resume in Tunisia, and Israelis vote for a *Likud*-led government in closely fought national general elections.

In a speech to foreign journalists, former Israeli Prime Minister Shimon Peres related the story of an army instructor who was teaching new recruits how to swim across the Sea of Galilee. The officer's advice was simple — by the time you get to the middle, you will be tired; but rather than swim back, it makes as much sense to go on towards the other side. Using this as a metaphor for the peace process, Peres was acknowledging how repeated setbacks (most recently, the bomb attacks in Jerusalem and Tel Aviv) had made the Israeli public understandably weary of the peace. Yet by the same token, so much had been achieved already that it made no sense to 'go back' to the past.

The surprise election of Benjamin Netanyahu as Prime Minister of Israel, on May 29, 1996, revived doubts about the future of the peace process. Narrow though his margin of victory was, it did mark a clear sign that Israelis felt the sacrifices for peace were not worth the benefits. While not rejecting peace *per se*, they indicated that it was time to slow down the process, and take stock of its achievements. To extend Peres's metaphor, it is tempting to see Netanyahu as a swimmer who is happy to tread water, and wait for the coast to come to him.

Shimon Peres' analogy had a two-fold moral: by its very nature, a 'peace process' is something dynamic, so it is futile to ask at some interim stage whether it has succeeded or not. At the same time, to judge by statements from Peres, Arafat and even Netanyahu, it has passed the point of no return. While no-one knows exactly how it will end, we do know what the major issues are. This section provides a brief overview of those issues, and illustrates how they are so vitally inter-related.

Chapter 19　Issues in final status talks

*Israel and the PLO agreed to launch final status talks, but this could only take place after certain conditions had been reached, as stipulated in the Interim Agreement (Oslo 2). Firstly, Israeli troops would redeploy from major West Bank cities (defined as zone A). Secondly, Palestinians would hold elections on 20 January, 1996. Thirdly, Israel would release more Palestinian political prisoners. And fourthly, the Palestine National Council (PNC) would rescind aspects of the Palestine National Charter which called for the destruction of Israel. After this final milestone was achieved in April, full talks on final status topics began on schedule in the first week of May 1996. If all goes according to the timetable, these talks will be concluded in or by 1999. The nature of the talks have been profoundly effected by the results of the Israeli elections held at the end of May 1996. Nonetheless, on paper, the Netanyahu administration is committed to continuing with negotiations. The main topics in question are: **Refugees, Settlers, Water, Borders and the future status of Jerusalem.***

Refugees

BACKGROUND

The issue of Palestinian refugees goes to the heart of the Arab–Israeli dispute [for background details, see p18, p23, p25, p26, p113, p158]. The first Arab–Israeli war of 1948–49 led to a majority of Palestine's Arab population leaving their homes. According to UN Security Council Resolution 194 of 1949, Palestinian refugees were entitled to return to their homes in what was now Israel. The first Israeli government under David Ben-Gurion did allow a few thousand to return under 'family reunification', but talks about implementing UN 194 foundered at the Laussane Conference. UN General Assembly Resolution 301 (IV) of 1949 established the United Nations Relief and Works Agency for Palestinian Refugees in the Near East (UNRWA). Since 1950 UNRWA has educated and cared for the one-third of Palestinian refugees who live in 61 purpose-built camps in Jordan, Syria, Lebanon, the West Bank and Gaza. As of early 1996, UNRWA decided to relocate from its headquarters in Vienna to the Gaza Strip, where it is deeply involved in joint projects with the PNA. It plans to dissolve itself by May 1999, corresponding to the scheduled end of the final status talks.

UN 242 (1967) and UN 338 (1973) reaffirmed the provisions of UN 194, but Syria and the PLO rejected both these latter resolutions, as they ignored Palestinian political rights by over-emphasizing the refugee nature of the 'Palestinian problem'. The Madrid and Moscow peace tracks (1991 and 1992) established a multilateral working group to discuss the refugee issue; in time the group included Israeli, Palestinian and Jordanian negotiators. Under the terms of Oslo 1, the PLO and Israel both accepted UN 242 and UN 338, and their stipulations on refugees.

There remains a wide conceptual gulf between Israeli and Palestinian views on the issue. The PLO is still officially committed to a Law of Return for all Palestinian refugees (corresponding to the Jewish Law of Return in Israel). Israel rejects this formulation, certainly regarding its own land; but conceivably such a Law may be restricted to Palestinian-ruled areas. Israelis have also spoken of a 'double refugee scenario': if Palestinians were forced to leave Israel/Palestine, then equal numbers of Oriental Jews (*Sephardim* or *Mizrachim*) were forced to leave Arab states — a depiction which most Arab states reject.

DEFINITIONS AND STATISTICS

Additional complexities arise from definitions of 'who is a refugee?'. Not all Palestinians outside Israel are refugees — wealthier families have often integrated into other Arab societies. Approximately 2/3 of those registered as refugees, and holding UN travel permits, live outside actual refugee camps. In 1991, UNRWA listed some 354,000 refugees in Gaza and the West Bank (refugees form a majority of the Palestinian population in the former, and a minority in the latter). Latest estimates suggest there are 2.5 million registered refugees; within this figure are some 300,000 'displaced persons' who fled after the 1967 war. If one includes unregistered refugees, the total may be as high as four million. Finally, in some cases

Palestinians have become refugees twice over — in 1970–1, many fled from Jordan to Lebanon in the wake of fighting between the Hashemite Kingdom and the PLO; others became internal refugees during the Lebanese civil war; about 350,000 Palestinian expatriate workers (most originally from Jordan) had to flee from Kuwait, Saudi Arabia and other Gulf States after the Gulf War of 1991; and about 30,000 Palestinians were forced out of Libya in 1995.

FORUM FOR DISCUSSION

In practice, the multilateral talks have concentrated on what may be called the 'operational level' — improving conditions for existing refugees on a day-to-day basis. The final status talks will probably address the broader and more sensitive political and strategic level. Between these two polarities, another institution is already playing a crucial role — the Quadrilateral Commission, consisting of Israeli, Palestinian, Egyptian and Jordanian officials, which was set up with US encouragement after the Israel–Jordan treaty of 1994. In April 1995 the commission set up a committee of experts in Amman, which met two months later in Beersheva, Israel, to discuss displaced persons. The Israel–Jordan peace treaty of 1994 also commits both nations to a resolution of the refugee problem under international law (some 1.2 million Palestinians live in 12 Jordanian refugee camps, of which Baq'a outside Amman is the largest in the world).

Until recently, the Palestine National Council (PNC) has represented the interests of the Palestinian diaspora, and, *inter alia*, the Palestinian refugees. Despite the creation of the Palestine Legislative Council in 1996, the PNC may indeed increase its authority as a *de facto* forum for their concerns. Many refugees in Lebanon, Syria and Jordan, oppose the current peace process because they fear that the PLO has 'abandoned' their rights in exchange for achieving territorial rule over a smaller Palestine. Hence the refugee issue became intimately connected with the debate over the Palestinian Charter [see below]. However, refugees within 'historic Palestine' (such as those from Balata camp outside Nablus, Deheishe near Bethlehem, or Khan Yunis in Gaza) have a slightly different perspective. Many of them voted for *Fatah* in January 1996; yet they can just as easily withdraw their support if Arafat does not heed their immediate needs. In short, it is in their interests to make the PNA work.

MAJOR PLAYERS

Several names are mentioned as possible negotiators. Amongst Palestinians, there is the sociologist Dr Salim Tamari, and Dr Zuhari Zaid, who led a delegation to the 1995 Quadripartite talks. Shamai Kahane led Israel's team at the multilateral talks in 1992; while Israel's former Foreign Ministry Director-General, Dr Yosef Hadas, led Israeli delegates in 1995. Hadas' group included Autonomy Department Director Baruch Ilan and the Coordinator of the Multilateral Working Group on Refugee Affairs, Danny Nevo. The Jordanian and Egyptian delegations were led by Abdallah Matzdehah and Bader Hamam respectively. There may be arbitrating roles for UN High Commissioner on Refugees, Sadako Ogata, Crown Prince Hassan of Jordan, and UNRWA director, Ilter Turkmen. Finally, external PLO leaders will contribute on issues concerning 'the diaspora'.

ACHIEVEMENTS TO DATE/ SCENARIOS FOR THE FUTURE

Israel allows refugees from Lebanese camps to pay special visits to their former homes in Israel. In precedents set by Oslo 2, Palestinians can (with Israeli security clearance) 'return' to Nablus or Ramallah, on the West Bank, but not to Haifa, in Israel. Under Labour rule, Israel granted more permits for family reunification, and it appeared to be on the brink of announcing a deal for the 'displaced persons' of 1967. However, in June 1996, Dore Gold, chief aide to the victorious Benjamin Netanyahu, signalled a firmer Israeli line on the question. He explicitly warned against 'Judea and Samaria' (the territories) being 'flooded with four million refugees'. This was the main reason why *Likud* rejected Palestinian statehood, and demanded Israeli control of international borders.

The Palestinian position is likely to be found somewhere between a maximalist demand for a Law of Return, and a minimalist demand for compensation in lieu of return. The 'compensation option' faces three distinct obstacles: the emotional surrender of the absolute right to return for Palestinians; the apparent need for Israel, the Arab states, or both, to 'admit guilt' for the refugee crisis in the first place; and the logistics of who will pay. Other questions remain. Will Israel adhere to UN 194? And will refugees in Lebanese camps and elsewhere accept a ruling from a PLO now firmly based in Gaza and the West Bank? Some solutions may emerge 'laterally': Jordan has pledged its support for Palestinian refugees, and Prince Hassan has suggested a new definition of nationality which could encompass refugees. If peace does become truly regional, there may be scope for a broader project, which takes into account the separate demands of Palestinians from 1948, alongside Palestinians from Kuwait, Kurds, Oriental Jews, Marsh Arabs and political refugees generally.

Settlers

BACKGROUND

Jewish settlers are a minority within the West Bank (there are between 122,000 and 140,000 of them, compared to 1.3 million Palestinian Arabs, according to July 1995 estimates). They form an even smaller minority within the Israeli population of some 4.5 million. Between 75% and 90% of them live on only 11% of the West Bank. In Gaza, there are barely 5,000 Jewish settlers, compared to 813,000 Palestinians. Yet their numbers belie their importance, for the following reasons.

In Palestinian eyes, the presence of Jewish settlers on 'Palestinian soil' is an unacceptable reminder of the occupation. They also accuse the Israeli government of favouring the human rights of settlers over those of indigenous Palestinians, on matters ranging from the right to bear arms, to electrification and access to limited water supplies. Palestinian lawyers assert that settlement of land occupied in war is forbidden by the Fourth Geneva Convention. Hence the official PLO position has been that the settlements should be dismantled. By the same token, many Palestinians consider that the 144,000 Jewish inhabitants of East Jerusalem should also be regarded as settlers, and thus deserve similar treatment.

Within Israel itself, the settlers issue has been controversial for a generation of politicians. It is related to issues of guaranteeing the state's security, and the popular attachment to *Eretz Yisrael,* the biblical Land of Israel, as constituted by the West Bank. Broadly, the Labour government until 1977 tried to limit the number of civilian (as opposed to military) settlements in the West Bank and Gaza. Thereafter, various *Likud* and *Likud*-led governments encouraged new settlements as the apotheosis of Zionism; but they stopped short of actually annexing the occupied territories to Israel. Since 1992, Yitzhak Rabin froze new 'ideological settlements'; yet left-wing Israelis and Palestinians say he allowed his advisor, Noah Kirnarti, and Housing Minister Ben-Eliezer to fund the expansion of existing settlements (like Efrat, near Bethlehem) through the backdoor. Even so, Rabin's policy of territorial compromise did throw the settlers' future into doubt. This bred feelings of insecurity and, in turn, antagonism towards both Palestinians and the Israeli establishment.

While secular elements in *Likud* and *Tsomet* believed that settlements guaranteed Israel's strategic depth', Labour politicians, including the late Yitzhak Rabin, began to regard settlers more as a security liability. The 1994 peace treaty with Jordan further undermined settlers' claims that they represented a vanguard against invasion from the east. Most worryingly, the 'settler issue' became conflated with the emotionally fraught debate between secular and religious Jews within Israeli domestic politics; in particular, the National Religious Party became closely associated with groups like *Gush Emunim, Zo Artzeinu* and even *Eyal*. Fringe elements have even supported actions like the Hebron massacre (1994) and the murder of Rabin (1995); while certain radical rabbis have sanctioned civil disobediance and armed defiance of the peace process.

DIVISION IN SETTLER RANKS

The Rabin assassination shocked many formerly radical settlers into re-assessing not only their methods in opposing the Labour-backed peace process, but even their opposition to the interim Agreement (Oslo 2) itself. The official settlers representative body, *Yesha,* was split when the mayors of major settler towns, including Ariel, Karnei Shomron and Alfei Menashe, opened talks with the newly appointed PLO-backed mayors of neighbouring Palestinian towns. Meanwhile, top *Yesha* figures remain adamantly opposed to Oslo 2. Broadly, the division mirrors that between the generally more moderate and less ideological 'commuter belt' settlers, and more extreme messianic religious settlers, as epitomized by the strongholds of Kiryat Arba, Tapuach and Hebron itself.

CHANCES FOR COMPROMISE

There is a suggestion that the PLO has softened its position, by acknowledging that not all settlers would have to leave. One option is to nominally nationalize the land, but allow settlers to stay on as expatriate citizens of Israel. The issue is intimately connected with that of borders, and during secret talks held between Abu Mazen and Yossi Beilin, it was suggested that Israel might annex 11% of the West Bank, containing 90% of the settlers, and leave the remaining land to the Palestinians, as the basis for a state.

Clearly, most settlers opposed such changes, as does the current *Likud* government. If ultimately Palestinian rule encompasses existing settlements, some settlers may choose to leave. But to date the Israeli government refuses to pay compensation (although a secret Housing Ministry fund apparently exists for such an exigency). Most settlers would probably remain if their security could be guaranteed. Finally, a militant minority which is wedded to the idea of Jewish sovereignty over all of *Eretz Yisrael*, vows to fight eviction, or the imposition of Palestinian rule. The Olso 2 Accords stipulated Jewish right of access to about a dozen sites of religious importance, many of which reside in Palestinian-controlled areas. The two best known sites are Rachel's Tomb near Bethlehem, and the Tomb of the Patriarchs in Hebron. Israeli and Palestinian security officers are co-operating to reduce the chances of clashes in these sensitive areas. Yet even before *Likud's* victory in May 1996, many Palestinian sceptics saw signs that settlements were to be permanent: why else, they asked, would Israel build perimeter security fences and expensive bypass roads for the settlers?

FORUM FOR DISCUSSIONS/MAJOR PLAYERS

During the Israeli election campaign, Benjamin Netanyahu promised to spend $3.6 billion towards expanding settlements. Nonetheless, talks on settlements remain on the agenda, and Netanyahu pledged to abide by the provisions of Oslo 2 and its monitoring committee. Figures who may play a role include: Khalil Shiqaqi, Director of the Centre for Palestine Research and Studies, in Nablus, who favours compromise and possible co-operation between moderate economically productive settlers in commuter-belt settlements, and surrounding Arab towns; Ehud Sprinzak, the Hebrew University's expert on the far right; Rabbi Yoel Bin-Nun, who submitted his own maps for an accomodation with Palestinians; Yisrael Harel and Aharon Domb of *Yesha*, who are determined to resist further concessions; Ron Nachman, Mayor of Ariel; Rabbi Shlomo Riskin of Efrat; and Rabbi Yehuda Avital, who acted as a ministerial 'bridgehead' to the settlers after the Rabin assassination.

Water

Water is the most precious commodity in the Middle East, and on several occasions it has been a source of war, or potential war. By the same token, solving the 'water issue' would be the ultimate 'confidence-building measure' to ensure a solid regional peace. Furthermore, it would guarantee a sound basis for the area's economy, without which peace cannot be sustainable.

OPERATIVE REALITIES

The water issue has many dimensions — regional and local, political and technological, economic and moral. As a region, the Middle East is the first in the world to suffer an absolute water deficit. Diminishing supplies and rising populations has meant that by 1990 it needed twice as much water as was available to meet its strategic needs (this may rise to a 4:1 disparity within three decades). Agriculture uses up most water, invariably in the form of irrigation, as rainfall is so sparce.

With respect to Israelis and Palestinians, what is in dispute is water sources which all originate in the Jordan River Valley (JRV). Israel gets about a third of its water from two surface supplies, the Sea of Galilee and the northern reaches of the Jordan River. Throughout the early 1960s, Israel and the Arab states accused each of trying to divert the river's headwaters. Until the 1967 war, most of Israel's water came via a National Water Carrier, an integrated network of canals, pipelines and reservoirs which transfers water from the comparitively water-rich north to the arid south. Today, fully 60% of Israel's water derives from two aquifers (underground water tables): 35% from the Western aquifer, most of which originates in the West Bank; and 25% from the Eastern aquifer, located on the Khor plateau in the West Bank. Currently, agriculture consumes 70% of water in the West Bank, where groundwater from aquifers yields 630 million cubic metres per annum (compared to just 42 million in Gaza). Smaller amounts come from natural springs and boreholes.

The abiding problem remains one of scarcity. There are broadly three approaches to tackling this:

- Changing the distribution of existing resources between and within nations and populations;
- Finding ways of importing water and building cross-border pipelines;
- Making the usage of water more efficient.

DISTRIBUTION

There is tremendous confusion over what legal principles apply to equitable distribution of water. In *realpolitik* terms, state possession of land carries much weight. This becomes more complicated when, according to the Fourth Geneva Convention, the land in question is 'occupied after war' (such as the West Bank, Gaza and Golan Heights); or when one of the negotiating parties (ie the PNA) is not a state. There are also considerations of riparian rights: downriver states fear that upriver states may 'cut off' the supply (hence Syrian, Jordanian and Israeli worries over Turkey's control of river sources). Certain vague principles apply, as expounded in the technically defunct Johnson Plan for the Jordan River Valley in 1954; a more liberal principle of direct users' rights emerged from the International Law Association's Helsinkii Accords in the mid-1970s. But there is still no universal standard.

Water also looms large in bilateral discussions over borders. Israel's 'security zone' in southern Lebanon affords it access to the Litani River, which it would be loathe to lose if it withdrew. Similarly, Syria's broader definition of the Golan Heights area (which it seeks to recover from Israel) would give it access to the Sea of Galilee. In the Israeli–Palestinian context, the water issue is bound up with that of settlers, who use up to six times as much per capita as their Palestinian neighbours. Palestinians accuse Israel of confiscating Arab boreholes by military edict. Excessive Israeli pumping, they say, has raised the salinity of Gazan wells to dangerous levels. Israel counters that its water extraction technology has helped Palestinians since 1967; further, it allocated an extra 28 million cubic litres to Palestinians under Oslo 2, and acknowledged their rights to water. Yet many are wary of dependence upon Israeli largesse. In short, 'water ownership' remains part of the problem. Below are other concepts, which suggest more equitable solutions.

IMPORTATION AND PIPELINES

External sources of water would negate the need to quarrel over limited shared sources. In Israel's case, water could be literally imported, from Europe or Turkey, by ships dragging huge plastic containers of fresh water. More realistic are plans for pipelines, and there are several ideas afoot:

- President Sadat's El-Salaam (Peace) Canal of 1979, to conduit water from the Nile to Jerusalem. The Nile's flow is 100 times stronger than the Jordan's, so Egypt is self-sufficient in water, despite its high population. In 1993 Mubarak proposed a variant of Sadat's plan, which would reach Rafah, a town that straddles the Egyptian-Gazan border. Presumably, the PNA would then allocate or sell water to Israel. But siphoning more water

from the Nile means less for Egypt itself. This entails domestic political risks, as well as retaliation from upriver states, Ethiopia, Sudan and Uganda.
- A Turkish pipeline, taking water from the Seyhan and Ceyhan Rivers (which currently empty up to 39 million cubic meters into the sea each day) down to Amman, via Syria and Iraq. The original plan, mooted by former Turkish Prime Minister Turgut Ozal, was costed at $8.5 billion. Given the political will, for another $1 billion it could be extended to the JRV peoples.
- A Red Sea – Mediterranean canal ('Red-Med'), an approach particularly favoured by Gazan Palestinians and devised by an Israeli engineer, Shlomo Gur. It would have the additional advantage of exploiting the gradient difference to generate much-needed hydro-electric power for the region.

EFFICIENCIES

Efficiencies are vital in a region where 75% of rainwater is lost to evaporation, and 15% of water supply leaks away. From 1986 to 1994, Israel reduced its water consumption from 2 to 1.6 billion cubic litres a year, through strict 'water management' techniques, like drip irrigation, recycling wastewater, protecting boreholes, desalination, and restricting supply to farms. While Palestinians have not benefited directly, this trend may yet help them: it frees up shared water resources in the territories, and offers a model for similar efficiencies in the PNA. Over the past 12 months, Israel has exported its expertise in cloud-seeding, arid zone agriculture, hothouse environments and countering 'desertification' to Mauretania and Tunisia, in one of the less trumpeted byproducts of the Mideast peace process.

PROJECTS ON THE TABLE/ MAJOR PLAYERS

The PNA is currently seeking investment for a range of projects to improve its water infrastructure. These include: a National Bulk Water Utility Company (NBWUC), a Regional Water Company (RWC), a Technical Support and Research Company, and a Middle East Water Training Centre. In addition, it is discussing with Israel and Jordan three joint projects: the development of the Jordan River Basin, the Red-Med Canal (see above), and a Water Carrier from the West Bank to Gaza. Meanwhile, the UN's Programme of Assistance for the Palestinian People (PAPP) has spent 15 years building sewage collection systems for northern Gaza, and water supply networks for 500,000 Palestinians in the territories

Since 1995 Ram Aviram has steered Israel's policy formulation at the multilateral level. Palestinians are represented by Water Commissioner Nabil Sharif, while academics like Jonathan Kuttab and Jad Ishaq of the Applied Research Institute, while Sharif Elmusa of the Institute of Palestine Studies in Washington DC, have delivered papers on water. As of June 1996, it appears that the veteran *Likud* hardliner, Ariel Sharon, intends having the last word on water usage in the territories due to his appointment as Israel's new Minister for National Infrastructure.

ACHIEVEMENTS TO DATE

The multilateral working group on water provides an important forum for discussing new ventures (see p. 111). One instance is an Israeli–Omani desalination project, which set a precedent for wedding Israeli expertise with Gulf State capital. The latest round of the working group opened in Hamamat, Tunisia, on May 15 1996; some 40 nations were represented. The multilaterals have provided interstitial local solutions, such as joint projects in the JRV, and improving sewage systems in Gaza. Together with US and UK academics in MEWIN (Mideast Water Information Network), they have begun collecting vital data on water resources (the lack of which had stymied previous projects). Ultimately, the multilaterals hope to spawn a regional water treaty. As a first step towards this, on February 14, 1996, Israel, the PLO and Jordan signed a Declaration of Principles on new and additional water sources, in Oslo, after multilateral negotiations steered by USA, Russia and Norway. But until Lebanon and Syria sign up, it will be hard to implement it over the whole JRV.

The crucial issue of distributing water between states, on a strategic level, remains firmly within the ambit of bilateral talks; most specifically, final status talks between Israel and the

PLO, and talks between Israel, Lebanon and Syria. Initially, the Israel–Jordan peace treaty of 1994 was seen as paradigm of how to solve water disputes through negotiation. Under the treaty, Israel agreed to grant Jordan a greater share of the River Jordan's headwaters; the terms were further amplified at the Baqura meeting of June 1995. Yet there have been persistent problems, not least, the unexpectedly prohibitive cost of pumping water to Jordan. This was one of the issues which forced Israel's Foreign Minister Ehud Barak to meet King Hussein in London, in May 1996.

A CONCEPTUAL SHIFT?

Many academics believe the Middle East needs a radical conceptual shift in tackling its water problem. Starting from the premise that the area will never be self-sufficient in food (at least not economically so) they favour switching water usage from 'inefficient' agriculture to 'efficient' consumer and industrial sectors. The economic benefits of healthier industry and a happier urban populus, will more than outweigh any damage done to farming communities. So argues Prof Tony Allan of London University's School of Oriental and African Studies, who adds that importing food from rain-rich countries represents 'virtual water' for the whole region. Hence global trade patterns would determine water's availability, rather than fruitlessly trying to find new local replenishable sources.

Privatization represents another such 'lateral' approach, according to a MIT/Harvard team. Taking water out of governments' hands, costing it as a resource, and leaving it for a holding company to sell (an annual stock of just $200 million, says one estimate), would at a stroke obviate the relevance of borders, and make water distribution simply a matter of market forces, not armed might. Yet there are large obstacles to both approaches. 'Virtual water' runs counter to the cherished national goal of agricultural self-sufficiency, and ignores the strategic importance of water; while privatization appears to offer little protection to poorer consumers, and hence merely shifts the dispute from the political to the economic arena, with the same people suffering.

Palestinian Borders and Constitution

The issue of borders is inextricably bound up with that of the future of the settlements, but it also touches on the nature of the ultimate Palestinian entity. The Israeli Labour Party abandoned its 'Jordanian option', after the peace treaty with Jordan of 1994; and appeared to accept the possibity of a State of Palestine (which is the PLO's goal). Shimon Peres preferred a completely demilitarized entity, possibly in some loose confederation with Jordan. Yet there was a schism within Labour: Peres wanted Israel to maintain its 'security border' along the Jordan River Valley, while Yossi Beilin felt this was unnecessary because of Israel's new friendship with Jordan. *Likud*, meanwhile, said Labour wanted to return Israel to its pre-1967 borders. Netanyahu is officially committed to 'maximum Palestinian autonomy with a minimum of Israeli interference'. But Israel would retain control of 'security' in the territories, and the PLO would have no independent foreign policy.

Within the Palestinian camp, 'rejectionists' or 'maximalists' oppose the notion of a ministate, which recognizes Israel's existence in the rest of 'historic Palestine'. However, in the wake of Yasser Arafat's success at the extraordinary PNC session, in April 1996, it appears that the minimalists currently have the upper hand. According to Omar Massalha, the PLO's representative to UNESCO, 1980–1993, the PNC's 'Declaration of Independence' in 1988 has a certain legal veracity in international law, regardless of whether there is immediate possession of land. Arafat still wants Jerusalem to be capital of a Palestinian state, which will be a major consideration for 'final borders'.

Aside from questions of status, where would the borders lie? When in 1995 Police Minister Moshe Shahal proposed a costly security fence to 'seal' the territories, *Likud* opposed it as it risked formalizing the borders of a potential Palestinian state. Since then, Shimon Peres responded to *Hamas* bombings by re-introducing a 'separation policy' with his 'security seam' and one-mile 'exclusion zone', again broadly dovetailing with the old Green Line. In the longer term, if final status talks are frozen, the PNA may be left with Areas A and B; but more than 70% of the West Bank (Area C) will stay in Israeli hands. To Palestinian opponents of

Oslo 2, the resultant cluster of non-contiguous Palestinian 'blocs' is merely a 'bantustan': unsustainable and weak. Finally, there remains the issue of a corridor connecting Gaza to the West Bank, as agreed to in the Declaration of Principles. Arafat favours a physical link, but this would necessarily mean severing the geographical integrity of Israel, which few Israelis would accept.

HUMAN RIGHTS AND A PALESTINIAN CONSTITUTION

In 1995, Amnesty International issued separate reports which criticized Israeli and PNA records on human rights. It charged the PNA of running night-courts without due process of law, and of infringing the independence of the judiciary. In addition, it accused the PNA of torturing Palestinian dissidents in detention, police harassment, and suppressing free speech (accusations previously leveled at Israel). Since then, there have been reports of the continued persecution of the human rights activist, Iyad Sarraj, and curbs on press freedom, including the brief imprisonment of the newspaper editor, Maher al-Alami, during the Legislative Council election campaign.

However, on 23 Feb. lawyers drafted a Basic Law for Palestine, which guarantees pluralism, human rights, womens' rights, and free speech. This may be the forerunner of a full Palestinian constitution, to succeed the Charter; seven draft plans are now being considered. Aside from moral concerns, the issue of human rights assumes even greater importance for the PNA, as the US Congress insists on compliance with human rights as a precondition for granting it further aid (according to the PLO Commitments Compliance Act, PLOCCA, of 1989; and the Middle East Peace Facilitation Act, MEPFA, of 1993). Important players on the Palestinian side include Justice Minister Freih Abu Midein, Attorney General al-Khidra, human rights activists, Iyad Sarraj and Bassam Eid and Mamdouh al-Aker, and, 'from the inside', newly elected Council MPs, Hanan Ashrawi and Haidar Abd al-Shafi.

Jerusalem

Of all the issues concerned with the peace process, the future of Jerusalem is the most emotional and potentially divisive. It probably played a decisive part in the defeat of Peres in the 1996 Israeli elections. Jerusalem (*Yerushalayim*, City of God's Peace in Hebrew) has generated much rhetoric and is suffused in legal intricacies. As we go to print, Israel denies that it is an issue for discussion; while Palestinians say that a State of Palestine without Jerusalem as its capital is inconceivable. Even so, analysts on both sides have hinted that 'the Jerusalem issue' is far from intractable.

HISTORICAL BACKGROUND

All three monotheistic faiths have profound ties to Jerusalem, which gives it a truly international dimension. For Jews, it is the only capital city in their history, the site of the two Temples and Mount Zion, and a symbol of Return from Exile ('If I forget thee, O Jerusalem, may my right hand wither' — Psalm 137). For Christians, it was where Jesus Christ preached and was crucified, a Crusader kingdom during the Middle Ages, and a place of pilgrimage. For Muslims, Jerusalem (in Arabic, *Al-Quds*, The Holy Place) is where Muhammed ascended to heaven; it is the third holiest site in Islam after Mecca and Medina, and was under Islamic rule for some 11 centuries. In this century, Jerusalem acquired a political dimension, too, as it became a microcosmic, though intensified, version of the broader Arab–Israeli dispute. Jerusalem also has a local, municipal dimension, as the nexus of a battle for influence between rival ethno-religious communities.

Jerusalem's modern history can be divided into three epochs:

- 1920–1948   British Mandate — failed attempts to balance rival claims
- 1948–67   Divided between Israel and Jordan
- 1967–present   Reunited under Israeli law

In 1920, 1929 and 1935, Jerusalem was at the centre of violent clashes between Jews and Arabs. The most contested area was the Temple Mount, or Haram al-Sharif, in the Old City, with its famous mosques perched on top of the Jewish Western (or Wailing) Wall. In 1947–8, Israeli forces lost the Old City to Jordanian troops, as well as the enclave of Mt Scopus, site of the Hebrew University; however, the Jewish state took over several formerly Arab neighbourhoods (Katamon, Baqa'a). For 19 years the city was divided. In 1950, Jordan annexed East Jerusalem along with the West Bank, and it became the capital of a governorate within Jordan. But only Pakistan and the UK recognized the annexation, and real authority resided in Amman. Officially, the Hashemites were holding Jerusalem 'in custodianship' for the Palestinians; they took over the *waqf* (religious endowments body) and have spent up to £500 million on the mosques' upkeep. In 1964, the PLO was launched in East Jerusalem, which signified a specifically Palestinian claim to the city.

Meanwhile, West Jerusalem was developed as the site of the Israeli Knesset and government bodies. New immigrants took over abandoned Arab neighbourhoods (according to the absentee property laws of 1949). Teddy Kollek was elected Mayor of West Jerusalem in 1965. Two years later he became Mayor of a 're-united city' after the Six Day War. His East Jerusalem counterpart, Ruhi al-Khatib, fled into exile; thousands of Jerusalem Arabs became 'displaced persons' overnight. The Arab Moghrabi area in the Old City was cleared to afford Jews access to the Wall (denied since 1948). However, Kollek sought a *modus vivendi* with the Arab community; and while no Arabs stood in municipal elections, many chose to vote (invariably for Kollek). Others served as municipal officials. Kollek also aimed at equality of treatment for the three faiths; but politically, he stood by Israeli sovereignty over the whole city. Since 1967, Jews have settled in new suburbs 'over the green line': Gilo, French Hill, East Talpiot, and Pisgat Ze'ev.

DEMOGRAPHIC CHANGES, DUBIOUS 'UNIFICATION'

Demography has been a major weapon in Jerusalem's recent history. According to Israeli sources, Jews became a relative majority in 1830, an absolute majority in the early 20th century, and even a majority of east Jerusalem in 1989. At the turn of the century, Jerusalem had three distinct communities: Jewish, Muslim and Christian. However, since the 1920s the Christian proportion has declined; and Bernard Wasserstein of Oxford University now speaks of a new tripartite dispensation.

In early 1995, the population was:

- Palestinian (mainly Muslim, with 15,000 Christians) Arabs   160,000
- Secular and 'modern' Orthodox Jews   290,000
- Ultra-Orthodox Jews   130,000

Of these three groups, the Palestinians and Ultra-Orthodox Jews are growing fastest. . An alliance of right-wing secular Jews and the ultra-Orthodox, combined with a boycott by Arab voters, saw *Likud's* Ehud Olmert defeat Labour's Teddy Kollek in the mayoral elections of September 1992. (In a sense, this coalition's success was a harbinger for Netanyahu's narrow victory in May 1996). Yet if Wasserstein's thesis holds water, there is no monolithic 'Jewish vote'; indeed, given the ultra-Orthodox's traditional lack of enthusiasm for the Zionist state, it is not inconceivable that they may desert *Likud* and side with East Jerusalem Arabs if it serves their community's interests.

In theory, Jerusalem was united under Israeli rule after 1967; a Knesset Basic Law formally annexed East Jerusalem on 22 July, 1980. Yet in practice, it remains very much a divided city. There are certain mixed neighbourhoods (like Abu Tor); and instances of Jews living in Muslim areas for political reasons (Ariel Sharon's house in the Old City, or Orthodox Jews in Arab Silwan). But these exceptions prove the rule. More than anything else, the *intifada* re-imposed a *de facto* bifurcation of the city in 1988. Matters worsened in 1990, when 17 Muslim protesters were killed by police on the Temple Mount; there followed a spate of *Hamas* stabbings of Jews. Virtually no East Jerusalemites have adopted Israeli citizenship, nor do they abide by Israel's Muslim courts.

PRELIMINARY BATTLE OF SYMBOLS

Palestinians wanted the Madrid/Moscow multilateral track to set up a special working group on Jerusalem in 1992, but Israel rejected this. Shamir even barred East Jerusalem Palestinians from talks, so as not to 'cede Jewish sovereignty' over the city. Rabin was more amelioratory, and the Israeli–PLO Declaration of Principles in 1993 decreed that Jerusalem would be an issue in the final status talks. Until then, the PLO was barred from opening offices in the city. Yet in a letter to his Norwegian counterpart, Jorgen Holst, Foreign Minister Peres promised that Israel would honour 'Palestinian interests' in the city.

Since Oslo 1, Israel and the PLO have engaged in a war of symbols over Jerusalem. In 1994, Faisal al-Husseini became (unofficially) Minister for Jerusalem within the PNA cabinet, after setting up a Jerusalem National Council-Palestine with Mahdi Abdul-Hadi the previous November. Husseini regularly hosts foreign leaders in the PLO's Orient House, which angered most Palestinians (see pages 100–101), in East Jerusalem. Yasser Arafat called for a *'jihad* to liberate Jerusalem', which infuriated Israelis. Israel's response took many forms. The Jordanian treaty of 1994 appeared to grant the Hashemite family 'special interests' in Jerusalem . While Israel has turned a blind eye to the PLO's presence at the Temple Mount mosques (presumably in preference to *Hamas*), Ehud Olmert has repeatedly threatened to shut down Orient House. In September 1995, Police Minister Moshe Shahal forced three Palestinian institutions to close. This followed an attempt by Israel to 'confiscate' some acres of Arab land in the city, aborted after international protests. At the same time, Olmert launched Jerusalem 3000. Originally conceived by his predecessor, Teddy Kollek, as a multi-cultural festival to commemorate the founding of the City of David three millenia ago, it was widely condemned as a political ploy, to publicize Israel's claim on sole sovereignty over Jerusalem. To counter this, and a Congressional vote to move the US embassy to Jerusalem, PNC Speaker Salim al-Za'noun convened a Higher Committee to Defend Jerusalem, in Jordan in November 1995.

Even so, events have forced concessions on all sides. Police units from the PNA operate in East Jerusalem, in contravention of Oslo 1, but with the tacit approval of Jerusalem Police Chief Ariyeh Amit. Abu Mazen and Yossi Beilin discussed Jerusalem in secret throughout 1995, while PLO official Ziyad Abu Zayyad held parallel talks with Israeli academics. Many Arab leaders ignored strictures on visiting 'occupied Jerusalem', to attend Yitzhak Rabin's funeral in the city on Nov. 5, 1995. Less than three months later, Israel allowed Jerusalem Arabs to vote in the Palestine Council elections — a tacit acknowledgement that they were part of the Palestinian community, and not in any sense 'Israeli Arabs'. But the *Hamas* bus bombings in February and March deliberately targeted Jerusalem, and led Israel to extend the closure of the territories to the city itself.

OPTIONS FOR A SOLUTION

At the time of writing (early June 1996), Jerusalem's future remains a matter of speculation. The Israeli Institute for Jerusalem is presently considering 77 plans for reaching some Israeli–Palestinian accomodation. Plans include: two capitals within one city (Afif Safieh); cantons (Teddy Kollek); shared sovereignty with Palestinian symbolic authority over the Temple Mount (Shimon Shamir and Meron Benvenisti); expanding city boundaries to incorporate Jewish settlements like Ma'ale Adumim, and Arab towns like Abu Dis, then dividing it between Jewish and Arab communities (variants by Bernard Wasserstein, Hana Siniora and Meir Amirav). Some, like Prof Avishai Margalit, even want to revive the *corpus separandum* idea enshrined in UN 181 (II) of 1947, of making Jerusalem an 'international city'. Initially accepted by Israel but rejected by Palestinians, the plan was overtaken by the 1948–9 war, and fell into abeyance after a few abortive UN conferences in the mid-1950s.

Israel's new Prime Minister Netanyahu accused Shimon Peres of being prepared to 'surrender' East Jerusalem to the Palestinians. Yet his unwillingness to even discuss the issue would appear to contradict the terms of the Oslo Accords. For his part, Yasser Arafat met King Hussein and President Mubarak on June 2, and said he may unilaterally declare Jerusalem as the 'capital of Palestine'. This, too, appears to contradict the Oslo terms. In a worst case scenario, such a 'breach of signed agreements' may give Israel's new government the pretext to suspend final status talks with the PLO. Nonetheless, there are signs that *Likud* may not be as adamant as it implied it was during the election. A fortnight after the election, the *Likud* Mayor of Tel Aviv, Ronnie Milo, opened talks with Faisal Husseini. Judging from this scant evidence, it appears that the Israeli right is at least prepared to debate an inter-communal, municipal solution. If this bears fruit, the more contentious question of Jerusalem's *political* future may yet be back on the agenda by 1999.

Chapter 20   Further developments

Palestinian Council elections and changes to the Charter

The elections to a Palestine Legislative Council were probably the most tangible sign of the peace process to date. They were held on January 20 1996 throughout the territories, and were open to all Palestinians over 18 living in Gaza, the West Bank and East Jerusalem (see p 90 and p 165). Altogether, there were 16 multi-member constituencies: 11 in the West Bank (Qalqilyah, Jericho, Salfit, Tubas, Jenin, Nablus, Tulkarm, Ramallah, Hebron, Bethlehem and Jerusalem); and five in Gaza (North Gaza, Gaza City, Deir al-Birah, Khan Yunis, and Rafah, or South Gaza). This yielded a Council of 88 seats. There was a separate poll for the President, whose new cabinet would replace the existing Executive of the Palestine National Authority (PNA).

CAMPAIGN

The PLO tried to persuade opposition groupings (*Hamas*, the PFLP and DFLP) to participate; apart from *Fida*, a moderate wing of the DFLP, most did not do so. *Fatah's* own procedure of chosing candidates proved controversial: many familiar local figures were dropped in favour of 'external' PLO veterans, despite many of the local figures having already been nominated in party primaries. Several consequently ran as independents. On election day, East Jerusalem voters protested against what they saw as heavy-handed policing by Israel. (They needed special arrangements to vote, including ballot stations outside the city borders). The police retorted that they were just obeying the terms of Oslo 2, and were protecting voters from protests by settlers.

Aside from these setbacks, the three-week campaign saw enthusiastic canvassing in towns and refugee camps. Most significantly, Samiha Khalil, a veteran women's rights worker on the West Bank, decided to challenge Yasser Arafat for the Presidency. This was a double relief for Arafat: an opponent would prove his democratic credentials, yet he also did not want to compete with someone who would pose a serious threat. In an echo of Jordan's electoral system, the PNA allocated specific seats for minority Christian and Samaritan communities. Former Portuguese President Mario Soares (on behalf of the EU) and former US President Jimmy Carter oversaw a 200-strong team of foreign election monitors. While some criticized Arafat's 'dictatorial tendencies', and objected to sporadic violence (one monitor was killed), on the whole they were satisfied with the conduct of the campaign.

RESULTS

The results confirmed Yasser Arafat's political dominance: in the presidential poll, he won more than 88% of the vote cast, while *Fatah* won 66 of the 88 Council seats. However, there were a few surprises. Of *Fatah's* tally, 16 had run as *Fatah* 'Independents'. And figures who had made their name during the *Intifada* and the Madrid talks, like Hanan Ashrawi in Jerusalem and Dr Haidar Abd al-Shafi in Gaza, polled amongst the highest of any candidates. In addition, several *Hamas* supporters ran as independent Islamists; four were elected, notably Imad Falluji. Overall, electors tended to choose figures with a proven record or high academic achievement, rather than vote along clan affiliations, as was originally predicted. A boycott campaign by *Hamas* and the PFLP appeared to fail. Up to 70% of eligible voters turned out (90% in Gaza and 68% in the West Bank); although tensions in Jerusalem and Hebron led to lower figures (35% and 50% respectively).

The Muslim fasting month of Ramadan commenced immediately after the elections, which allowed President Arafat a period of grace to choose his cabinet. The PNA released a revised version of the results on February 12, which coincided with Arafat's swearing in as President in the new Council Chamber in Gaza City. The revisions were said to be necessary because of certain disputed results; however, critics alleged that Arafat had amended the popular verdict. Ahmed Qurei (Abu 'Ala) was named as the Council Speaker at its inaugural session on March 7.

REVOCATION OF THE CHARTER

Before final status talks could proceed, Israel demanded (according to the original Declaration of Principles) that the PLO remove aspects of its Palestinian Charter (or Covenant) which called for the destruction of the state of Israel. This required an extraordinary convention of the Palestine National Council (PNC), or PLO 'parliament-in-exile'. The convention raised a number of constitutional challenges for both Israel and the PLO. In order to facilitate the meeting, Israel had to grant special permission for the return to the territories of PNC members whom it had hitherto regarded as terrorists (including PFLP leader George Habash, DFLP leader Naif Hawatmeh, PLF leader Abul Abbas, and the former PFLP hijacker, Leila Khaled; Habash and Hawatmeh declined the invitations).

Within the Palestinian community, there was some ambiguity about the future of the PNC, and, indeed, the entire 'external' PLO. Officially, the newly elected Legislative Council represented a minority of the PNC's total of 669 members (roughly corresponding to the percentage of Palestinians worldwide who lived in the territories). In reality, the Oslo peace process has made Arafat and his Council the effective centre of political power. Thus many analysts saw the convention as the last chance for 'external' PNC members to assert their diminishing authority, by voting down Arafat's proposals for amending the Charter. Leading Palestinians demanded that the Charter remain intact, until Israel granted further concessions (for instance, by vacating Hebron, addressing the Jerusalem issue, releasing all political prisoners, evacuating settlements and recognizing Palestinian statehood). These included liberals like Hanan Ashrawi and Dr Haidar Abd al-Shafi, PNC veterans like Abdullah al-Hourani, and younger radicals like Riyad al-Malki. The convention was held on 22–25 April, during the height of Israel's military incursion in Lebanon, which seemed to further reduce Arafat's chances of success.

In the event, Arafat confounded his sceptics with an historic victory. Of the 572 delegates present, 504 voted in favour of amending the charter, 54 voted against, and 14 abstained. The essence of the deal was an acknowledgement that the existing agreements with Israel (DOP, the Paris Protocol on Economic Affairs, Oslo 1 and Oslo 2) had rendered the anti-Israeli terms of the Charter redundant. Arafat and Peres probably decided on this formulation just before the convention met. The PNC were now given six months to draft a new charter, and the PNA Attorney General Khalid al-Kidra is currently considering seven plans. Shimon Peres welcomed the vote, and set the wheels in motion for the final status talks, on 4 May. Not surprisingly, right-wingers in the *Likud*, especially Benny Begin, saw the vote as a bluff which had not really altered the Charter at all. For its part, *Hamas* mocked this act of PLO democracy as fickleness; the *Hamas* "Charter" of 18 August, 1988, was 'sanctioned by Allah' through the *ulema* (clergy), and was immutable.

Palestinian economy

For Palestinians, economic strength is not an incidental by-product of peace, but a prerequisite for political autonomy. The PLO's UK delegate, Afif Safieh, explained: 'We must move from our current dependency on Israel to full economic independence. Only then should we talk of economic interdependence'. However, this required good planning in three stages:

- Short term   international aid to rehabilitate economy and set up infrastructure
- Medium term   encouragement for private investment, and co-operation with Israel
- Longer term   supporting projects from own tax regime

Currently about 90% of food and goods consumed in the territories comes from Israel. While access to the well-developed Israeli economy since 1967 had boosted standards of living for Palestinians, it also stymied nascent Palestinian industries. Israeli hyper-inflation in the early 1980s hit the territories particularly badly. Palestinian sources accuse Israel of 'under-investing' in the territories; although Israel refutes this, pointing to the new hospitals, schools and colleges built there since 1967.

However, the most serious effect on the Palestinian economy has been the repeated closure of the territories, for reasons of security, such as after the *Hamas* bomb attacks in 1996. They have prevented aid and goods from entering the territories, and stopped Palestinian workers from earning their living. Between 1992 and 1995, the numbers of Palestinians working in Israel fell from 116,000 to 29,500. Figures released by the World Bank in February 1996 illustrate the effect: GDP in the West Bank and Gaza grew by an impressive 7.3% in real terms in 1994, and by an estimated 3.5% in 1995; but Gross National Product (which includes external income) fell by up to 3% in 1995. Coupled with a population rise of 4%, this meant a fall in per capita income of nearly 7%. Despite this, there were some unexpected successes. Whereas in 1995, the PNA projected a budget deficit of $228m in 1995, at the January 1996 Paris meeting of donors (the Ad Hoc Liaison Committee) they required just $75m (in addition to the recurrent investment figure of $550m), thanks to better revenue generation. In the event, 50 nations pledged $865m, which resulted in an 'overshoot'. (Of this total figure, the EU pledged $120m, South America $100m, World Bank $90m, USA $71m, and Japan $63m).

INTERNATIONAL AID – AN IMPROVED REGIME

In 1993, Yasser Arafat estimated that it would cost $5 billion over three years to rebuild the Palestinian economy ($2.4 bn was actually pledged in 1993). In the interim period, much of this was to come from international aid. Initially, there were lots of problems (see Chapters 9 and 14). However, by 1996 the mechanisms for aid disbursement and allocation had been better streamlined:

* EAP   Emergency Assistance Programme, within which there is:
* ERP   Emergency Rehabilitation Programme, disbursements of $53.7m
* TAP   Technical Assistance Programme, including a TATF(Technical Assistance Trust Fund) of $25m. This will come on line particularly as the new Council sets up operations.
* EHRP   Education and Health Rehabilitation Project, becoming effective in September 1996; $100m in co-financing sought by PECDAR
* Holst Fund   24 donors have currently pledged $215m, and $157m has been disbursed

SUCCESS IN BUILDING INFRASTRUCTURE

In addition, the World Bank has devised new programmes with the PNA to benefit the private sector and infrastructure. These include: Municipal Infrastructure Development, Water and Sanitation Services, Housing Finance Project, Electricity

Approximately 50% of West Bank Palestinians are unemployed, and up to 58% of Gazans. Therefore one of the prime aims of the PNA is to develop labour-intensive public works projects which can also meet urgent social needs. Among the projects on the drawing boards are: a hospital and university in Jerusalem, regional training centres, a Palestinian Securities Exchange Market, housing schemes in Al-Addassah, Beit Hanina and Al-Istiklal City. Additional plans include improvements in the transport and energy sectors (especially a 240 MW independent power plant, costing $170m to build, and using imported Egyptian gas). In addition tourism could bring much needed revenue and employment.

A solid legal framework is another prerequisite for economic progress. In April 1995 the PNA passed its Law for Encouraging Investment, which provides a sliding scale of incentives for investors, including tax holidays and exemptions from duties, according to how much money is invested, and how many Palestinians are employed in the new enterprizes. The law guarantees against nationalisation and allows full repatriation of capital. Its primary emphasis is on export-orientated businesses. However, the law will only take full effect once (or if) PNA rule extends to more land in the West Bank. The passage of an important bylaw on foreign investment in Jordan, on December 15, 1995, was thought to benefit investment opportunities and trade in Palestinian areas.

Amongst new institutions, two of the most important are the Palestine Monetary Authority (PMA) and the Palestine Economic Council for Development and Reconstruction

(PECDAR) (see Chapter 14). The PMA has a triple role as:

1. a 'bank of banks', supervising banking activities and issuing banking permits;
2. a financial consultant to the PNA; and
3. the body which maintains the PNA's foreign currency reserves.

There has been close co-operation between the PMA Director Dr Fuad Bseisso, and the Governor of the Bank of Israel, Ya'akov Frenkel.

FORUM FOR DISCUSSION AND MAIN PLAYERS

Until his replacement in January 1996 by Kemal Dervis, from Turkey, the main external authority on aid to Palestinians was the Brazilian, Caio Koch-Weser, the World Bank's Vice-President in charge of Middle East and North Africa. The EU's chief co-ordinator on policy pertaining to Israel and the territories is Eberhard Rein. More locally, chief planners have included the Director General of the Israeli Finance Ministry David Brodet, Crown Prince Hassan of Jordan, and Sami Abdallah of PECDAR.

Regional trade and investment

From Israel's perspective, Middle Eastern peace has bolstered chances for trade. But as Hebrew University's Prof Ephraim Kleiman maintains, much of this will pay off in terms of trade with the Far Abroad (Asia and Europe; Japan has opened its stock market to Israeli firms, for instance), and the Near Abroad (Gulf States) rather than with Jordan, Syria or the PNA. However, there are opportunities for Israeli manufacturers to 'outsource' production to neighbouring countries, where wages and costs are cheaper. This has already started in the garments industry.

Eberhard Rein, the EU's chief co-ordinator on policy pertaining to Israel and the territories, believes the Middle Eastern regional economy is standing at a crucial historical juncture. Four years of negotiations in various forums have given birth to a plethora of new institutions, with vastly increasing opportunities for trade and development. However, firstly certain obstacles must be addressed. These include: dealing with the issue of water, improving security structures, reducing military budgets, improving coherence between economic organizations, giving the Arab League a role, eliminating tariff barriers, and accelerating negotiations between Israel, Syria and Lebanon to arrive at a stable peace.

What has been achieved so far? The Regional Economic Development Working Group (REDWG) of the multilateral talks has already convinced Egypt, Jordan, Israel and the Palestinians to integrate their electricity grids, form a joint business council, reduce trade barriers, and join MEMITTA (the Middle East/Mediterranean Travel and Tourism Association, which has met in Casablanca, Tunis, Beersheva and Bethlehem) [for further details, see pp 111–2; for bilateral trade deals, see Chapters 9, 10].

Running in parallel with the multilateral talks are the Middle East/North Africa (MENA) economic summits: the third is scheduled for Cairo in November 1996. A permanent Economic Summit Executive Secretariat is now located in Rabat, Morocco from where MENA runs a website, MENA net, three dedicated programmes: a Science and Technology Exchange (STE), an Investment Promotion Programme (IPP), and Energizing Business Actors (EBA) to help small firms to network. At the Amman summit, Italy, Greece, Holland and Austria were involved in setting up a MENA Development Bank in Cairo. (Although larger EU countries favoured the existing European Investment Bank as a conduit for funds to the Middle East). In another step towards institutionalization, REDWG established a permanent secretariat in Amman.

US policy in the region both competes with and complements the EU initiative. Under the late Trade Secretary, Ron Brown, and his successor since April 1996, Mickey Kantor, the USA has encouraged private investment in the region. Much of this is channelled through a US Federal Agency, OPIC (Overseas Private Investment Corporation). Given the political climate in the US, the Clinton Administration prefers this path to asking Congress for more aid grants; however, given the tense political climate in the Middle East, investors are often loathe to risk their capital.

In January 1995, participants at the multilateral talks agreed to build 13 cross-border highways; although these adventurous schemes await significant political breakthroughs before they can be implemented.

Planned road links in the Middle East

North-South

- Adana (Turkey) → Latakia (Syria) → Beirut (Lebanon) → Haifa (Israel) → Tel Aviv (Israel) → Gaza (Palestine) → Rafah (Egypt) → El-Arish (Egypt) → Ismailia (Egypt) → Cairo (Egypt).
- Jenin (Palestine) → Ramallah (Palestine) → Jerusalem (Israel) → Hebron (Palestine) → Dhahiriya (Palestine) → perhaps also extended to Eilat (Israel).
- Magdal Angar (Israel) → En Sheya (Israel) → Bet She'an (Israel) → Jericho (Palestine) -Sedom (Israel) → Eilat (Israel).
- North Al-Shuna (Palestine) → South Al-Shuna (Palestine).
- Rafah (Egypt) → Bir Muran (Egypt) → Taba (Egypt).
- As Safawi (Jordan) → Al-Azraq (Jordan) → Al-Janubi (Jordan) → Al-Qatrana/Maan (Jordan) → Al-Mudawwara (Jordan) → Tabuk (Saudi Arabia).

East-West

- Haifa (Israel) → Irbid (Jordan) → Al-Mafraq (Jordan) → Al-Traybeel (Jordan) → perhaps ultimately extended to Baghdad (Iraq).
- Tel-Aviv (Israel) → Jerusalem (Israel) → Jericho (Palestine) → Amman (Jordan).
- Ashdod (Israel) → Jerusalem ring road.
- Gaza (Palestine) → Hebron (Palestine) . . . [traversing Israel].
- Cairo (Egypt) → Ismailia (Egypt) → Nizzana (Israel) → Tel Alim (Israel) → Dimona (Israel) → El-Safi (Jordan) → Karak (Jordan) → En-Yahav (Jordan).
- Cairo (Egypt) → Ismailia (Egypt) → Al-Nahl (Egypt) → Eilat (Israel) → Aqaba (Jordan) → Haql (Saudi Arabia) . . . [including building a causeway over the Strait of Tiran which separates the Sinai and Arabian peninsulas].
- Cairo (Egypt) → Suez (Egypt) → Nabq (Egypt) → Ras Qisbah (Saudi Arabia) → Ash Saih (Saudi Arabia) → Humayd (Saudi Arabia).

Security, Arms Control and Terrorism

'Peace with security' was one of the slogans which won Benjamin Netanyahu the Israeli prime ministership on May 29. Indeed, for most Israelis security was the litmus test by which they would judge the success of the peace process. With the renewed violence from *Hamas* and *Hezbollah* in the first half of 1996, many doubted whether the much-vaunted co-operation between Israeli and Palestinian security forces (as enshrined in Oslo 1 and 2) was working. By the same token, the assassination of Yitzhak Rabin in November 1995 showed that there were serious holes in Israel's own General Security Services (GSS). This led to the resignation of GSS Chief Karmi Gilon, who was replaced by Ami Ayalon, on 14 January 1996.

A REGIONAL PERSPECTIVE

However, the safety of individual Israelis is only one aspect of the region-wide question of arms and security. For most of the post-war period, the Middle East was caught up in the superpower conflict between the USA and USSR. Each side had its 'client states'; broadly, the USA supported Israel and some conservative Arab states, like Saudi Arabia; the USSR supported the PLO, and 'radical' states, like Syria and Egypt. By the end of the 1970s, however, two new factors began to alter the picture: the peace treaty between Israel and Egypt placed Cairo more firmly in the 'American camp', and this also started to erode the once monolothic Arab opposition to Israel; while the ascent to power of Ayatollah Khomeini in Iran introduced a third force to challenge the influence of the superpowers, namely revolutionary Islamic fundamentalism. The final breach began with the collapse of the Communist eastern bloc in 1989, and culminated in the triumph of the US-led coalition against Saddam Hussein's Iraq, in 1991. Yet with the average mid-east state still spending proportionately three times more on defence than western states, the potential for renewed wars remains high.

NEW ALLIANCES

More then five years have elapsed since the end of the Gulf War, and during that period, the peace process has begun to change the military dispensation in the Middle East. But as of June 1996, it is hard to say exactly what shape this realignment will take. Significant recent trends include:

- Israeli military co-operation with Jordan, since late 1995; Israeli and Jordanian officers have trained together, and Israel interceded with the USA for more arms and warplanes to Jordan
- Israeli military mutual assistance accords with Turkey, signed after President Suleyman Demirel's visit to Israel in March 1996
- Syria's consequent fear of being caught in a pincer from Israel and Jordan in the south, and Turkey in the north (Turkey blames Syria for sponsoring PKK Kurdish rebels in eastern Anatolia; while Iraq and Syria may consider joint action against Turkey over its plans to dam the Tigres and Euphrates Rivers)
- Jordan's growing ire at alleged Syrian sponsorship of terrorism in the Kingdom
- Israel's armed response to *Hezbollah* in Operation Grapes of Wrath (see below), a warning to Syria
- Egypt's campaign against Israel's reluctance to sign the Nuclear Non-Proliferation Treaty; in December 1995, Shimon Peres admitted that Israel had a nuclear arsenal; afterwards Israeli Defence Ministry Director General David Ivri described plans for Israel's strikeback facility
- Fears of Iranian, Iraqi and Syrian acquisition of nuclear and chemical weapons
- The role of Iran, Sudan and Afghan war veterans behind groups like *Hezbollah* and *Hamas*; criticism of Teheran's alleged support for terrorism formed the centrepiece of the 'Conference of Peacemakers', held at Sharm el-Sheikh on 13 March
- Resurgent Russian influence in the region, under new Foreign Minister Yevgeny Primakov

---

Operation Grapes of Wrath and aftermath

On 11 April, 1996, Israel launched its biggest incursion into Lebanon since 1982. The short-term aim was to end *Hezbollah's* campaign of *katyusha rocket* attacks on northern Israel; in the longer term, it appeared that Israel wished to eradicate *Hezbollah* altogether, or at least force Damascus and Beirut to curb the militia's activities, as a precondition for further negotiations on the Golan Heights. In purely political terms, commentators noted that the Labour government wished to re-assert Israel's regional military superiority, put into practice the commitments of the Sharm el-Sheikh conference, and silence *Likud* critics who had blamed Shimon Peres for lax security after the earlier *Hamas* bombings in Israel. In many respects, Grapes of Wrath resembled 1993's Operation Accountability. Once again, Israel used the ploy of displacing Lebanese civilians as a means of pressurizing the Beirut government to deal with *Hezbollah*. The operation was again almost entirely aerial, with no major troop incursions. However, Israel also bombed Beirut in the first few days, and appeared to target Lebanese economic infrastructure by destroying an electricity power generation plant, and blockading Lebanese ports. At the end of 17 days' fighting, the USA managed to broker a new set of agreements between Israel, Lebanon and Syria. But as a military exercise, Grapes of Wrath was not an unqualified success. Katyushas continued to reign down on northern Israel during the fighting, and Israel lost much public sympathy in the West for the numbers of civilians who were killed in the crossfire. The most serious incident occurred at Qana, a UNIFIL base, near which Hezbollah had placed its rocket launchers. In total 102 refugees who were sheltering at the base, died in the attack. The agreements which came into force on April 28 committed *Hezbollah* and Israel to refrain from attacks on civilians. To this end, Israel was 'entitled' to remain in its southern security zone, while *Hezbollah* was 'allowed' to attack IDF troops stationed there, but not in Israel proper. Shimon Peres publicly offered to recompense the Lebanese government for war damage, although Beirut did not take this up. Paradoxically, the war boosted Prime Minister Hariri's prestige as a 'national leader' and helped him win more concessionary aid from donor states. Meanwhile, Peres drafted plans to improve defences and shelters in some 100 Jewish and Arab towns in northern Israel, and named the area the 'Confrontation Zone'. More than anything else, this preparation for future conflict probably symbolized the stopgap nature of the peace agreements.

CONFLICTING TRENDS TOWARDS A SOLUTION

Multilateral arms control talks produced the idea of regional conflict prevention centres, in Tunisia, Oman and Jordan. Yet the conflict in Lebanon has proven how ineffective such mechanisms still are. Ultimately, outside powers (notably the USA) had to intervene to end the fighting, which suggested that little had changed since 1991. Possibly the creation of a ceasefire monitoring committee, involving Israel, Syria and Lebanon, with US and French guidance, may offer a new forum for local 'self-regulation'.

During the Peres government, US Defence Secretary William Perry had discussed a formal strategic alliance with Israel. There were pros and cons on both sides: the USA would have a base in Israel, more secure than its bases in Saudi Arabia, but might thereby antagonize new allies like Syria; Israel would gain security, but lose its autonomy of action. In the end, Perry and Peres signed a less ambitious 'co-operation pact' on 28 April, 1996.

Netanyahu's victory in May 1996 has introduced an important new variable into the regional equation. From June 21–24 1996, for the first time since Iraq's invasion of Kuwait in 1990, the Arab League convened major Arab leaders (apart from Iraq) in Cairo to warn against the new Israeli government's peace policy. Even Arafat and Assad staged a rapproachement. Paradoxically, Israel's strong tactics may be having a reverse effect to that intended: a re-forging of Arab unity against Israel. The USA is reconsidering its plans in this context.

THE FIGHT AGAINST TERRORISM

Between Oslo 1 and Oslo 2, some 149 Israelis had died in terrorist attacks. In total, 62 were killed in the four suicide bombings in February and March, 1996, in Ashkelov, Jerusalem and Tel Aviv. In point of fact, while the death toll from terrorism increased in 1996, there were actually fewer attacks than in previous years. According to Israel's GSS Chief Ami Ayalon, co-operation between Israeli and PNA forces had prevented many bombings. Since March, the PNA rounded up *Hamas* and *Jihad* officials on orders from Israel (*Jihad's* number two, Hassan Salameh, was caught on 18 May). In accordance with Oslo 2, Israel's Co-ordinator for Military Activities in the Territories, Oren Shachor, and the PLO's Jamil Tarifi, held regular consultations. Yet the perception of Israeli vulnerability persisted, and helped to defeat Peres at the polls. Meanwhile, Palestinians grew frustrated at what they saw as Israeli 'collective punishment' (via 'closures') for the actions of a few extremists.

It appears that Israel's anti-terror strategy is now changing under *Likud*, from co-operation with the PNA while imposing a closure, to possibly lifting restrictions, but reserving the right to take unilateral action in Gaza and the West Bank. PLO officials warn that their forces will resist any such intervention. There were even hints of a resurgent *intifada*, as Palestinians stepped up 'drive-by' shootings of settlers after the Israeli elections. Once more, the security issue is poised on a knife-edge, and threatens to undermine the whole peace process.

Israel-Syria Negotiations

Negotiations between Israel and Syria resumed after the assassination of Yitzhak Rabin (see Chapter 12). Shimon Peres broadened the terms of the talks to include full diplomatic relations, and go beyond merely issues of security around the Golan Heights. As it transpired, the Golan Heights remained the crucial issue, and, until it could be resolved, Peres had to shelve his plans for a broader peace deal. Talks had broken down in 1995 over Israel's demand for early warning stations on the Golan. So Peres deliberately played down this issue, and saw the stationing of US or UN peace-keepers as a compromise solution.

However, a new question arose over the delimitations of the borders themselves. Israel held to pre-1967 *de facto* borders; Syria spoke about 'international borders' as defined at the Israel-Syrian armistice agreement of 1949. The actual difference is small – a matter of a few square kilometres – but Syria's definition of the Golan Heights would give it access to the Sea of Galilee, something which Israeli Foreign Minister Ehud Barak was set against. Syria's 'maximalist' claims may also upset Palestinians, who had hoped to win control over the Hamat Gadar area in the southern Golan. In addition, many Labour supporters did not want to see the Golan returned to Syria, as this would deprive them of their most popular tourist destination (with 1.75 million visits a year). Finally, there were questions over the future of 14,000 Jewish Israeli Golan settlers (also mainly Labour supporters) and 17,000 Golani Druze (who had remained after 1967 from an original population of 60,000). Some settlers were willing to move if it led to real peace; but most backed The Third Way, or *Likud*, whose slogan was *Am Yisrael Im Ha-Golan*, the Israeli People with the Golan.

CENTRALITY OF THE US ROLE

The USA has played a central role in the latest phase of Syrian-Israeli talks, both as a facilitator and a potential guarantor of agreements. Bill Clinton believed that an Israel-Syria peace treaty could help his bid for re-election in late 1996. The US Secretary of State Warren Christopher, had by now made 20 trips to Jerusalem and Damascus, signalling his personal interest in the initiative; Dennis Ross, the USA's 'co-ordinator for the peace process', was his chief aide. However, there were risks attached: the influential conservative Senator Jesse Helms opposed US peace-keeping troops on grounds of cost, and his mistrust for Syria.

Talks took place at the Aspen International Centre at the Wye River Valley, in Maryland, USA. There were three sessions in all – 28 December 1995 to 5 January 1996; 24 to 31 January 1996; and 28 February to 4 March 1996 – when talks were suspended after the terror attacks in Israel. The two main protagonists, Israel's Shimon Peres and Syria's Hafez al-Assad, did not meet at a proposed summit, as was originally predicted. At one level below them, however, Syria's Foreign Minister, Farouk a-Shar'a and Israel's Foreign Minister, Ehud Barak, had met at the Barcelona conference on Mediterranean affairs, in early December 1995.

At an 'operational' level, the negotiating teams were initially led by the Director of the Israeli Foreign Ministry, Uri Savir, and the Syrian Ambassador to the USA, Walid Mu'alem. Later, Israel's Ambassador to the USA, Prof Itamar Rabinovich, led the Israeli delegation, and was joined by senior military personnel, Danny Yatom and Uzi Dayan. Prof Moshe Maoz, head of the Truman Institute at the Hebrew University, was tipped to become the first Israeli Ambassador to Damascus if peace was finalized. Finally, a 'troika' of foreign ministers from EU countries (Ireland, Spain and Italy) offered Syria economic inducements in exchange for progress at the negotiating table. They felt confident of success, as they were seen as less 'pro-Israeli' than the USA. But lack of co-ordination over the Lebanese crisis in April (when French Foreign Minister Herve de Cherette flew to Damascus, Beirut and Jerusalem) merely re-emphasized the fact that they had no effective common foreign policy.

PROGRESS TO DATE

Shimon Peres' 10-point plan was an advance on Yitzhak Rabin's 'four legs of a table'. It called for negotiations without preconditions, differentiation between issues of contention, like the border, and 'those requiring resolution', like security arrangements and water issues. It also aimed at turning the Golan Heights from an area of military confrontation into a centre of economic co-operation, and stressed the need for peace in Lebanon. In response, Farouq a-Shar'a spoke of Syria's desire for 'a deep and comprehensive peace', and said it would be harder gained, and thus more genuine, than the peace which Jordan had signed with Israel. Several Arab states (Tunisia, Morocco, Qatar, Oman and Yemen) said that they would sign full peace treaties with Israel, but only when Syria did so. Thus a Syrian-Israeli peace would generate a regional settlement, and also lead to Syrian and Lebanese participation in the multilateral peace talks.

There were initial hints of progress, but by 1996 the talks stalled over questions of interpretation, and the extent of the 'mandate' of Syrian negotiators to address issues like diplomatic relations, trade, and water. Despite Syrian Foreign Minister Farouq a-Shar'a's strong hints that Syria would curb *Hezbollah* attacks on Israel, these actually increased in February 1996. Israel accused Syria of acting in bad faith, and responded with Operation Grapes or Wrath (see above). Israel and Syria agreed to new 'understandings' after the war. With US and French backing, they set up a committee to monitor the agreement. France (on behalf of the EU), and Jordan (an Arab ally of Israel) gained a role on the committee. So did Lebanon itself, which meant that after a two year lull, it had an official forum within which to negotiate with Israel. But the war cast a pall on diplomatic relations in the 'northern Levant triangle' (Israel, Syria and Lebanon). Benjamin Netanyahu's refusal to cede an inch of the Golan to Syria, has, in the short term at least, frozen talks with Syria.

Israeli general elections

BACKGROUND

Elections must be held in Israel every four years, unless the Prime Minister decides to call an early poll. November 1996 was thus the latest possible date for an election after the one held in 1992. Shimon Peres assumed the premiership after the assassination of Yitzhak Rabin in November 1995, and initially chose to serve the remainder of his allotted office (ie 12 months). The Labour Party secretary Zvilli wanted him to call an early poll, to capitalize on increased sympathy for Labour, and thus give himself a clear mandate for carrying on with the peace process. But Peres preferred to 'go to the people' with a Syrian peace treaty to his credit. When talks with Syria failed to bear fruit, on 11 February 1996, Shimon Peres announced elections for the end of May.

The timing seemed propitious – despite warnings of violence from Jewish and Muslim extremists, the Palestinian election (of 20 January 1996) was judged to be a relative success. During four years in power, Labour had overseen an economic boom and prevented inflation. However, within a fortnight of calling the polls, there was a spate of *Hamas* and Islamic *Jihad* bomb attacks on Israeli targets. Almost overnight, Shimon Peres's 20–30% lead in the opinion polls over Benjamin Netanyahu evaporated. The government's tough response (total closure of the territories and tightened security) managed to restore some public confidence in Israel. But by apparently undermining the authority of Yasser Arafat, it also cast doubt on the future of the peace process, the cornerstone of Labour's policies.

The subsequent Sharm el-Sheikh conference endorsed Peres and the Labour Party, although domestically many Israelis viewed the event as little more than a media opportunity. More Israelis were initially impressed by the vigour of their government's response to incessant *Hezbollah katyusha* rocket attacks on northern Israel. Known as 'Operation Grapes of Wrath', the 17-day campaign ended with a new set of arrangements to guarantee Israeli security (see boxed text on p. 418). But *Hezbollah* remained intact, and the operation was judged to be only a partial success.

CONSTITUTIONAL CHANGES

According to a law passed in 1992, the elections after the June 1992 poll would have two ballots – one for party lists in the *Knesset*, and the other for a directly elected prime minister. Whoever won would be called on to form the next government over the next 45 days (in the past, the president would ask the leader of the largest party to form a government). It was hoped that the reform would reduce the disproportionate influence of smaller parties, and facilitate a more assertively presidential style of politics in Israel. Yet as events in 1996 transpired, the law had a reverse effect. Smaller parties started striking deals with prime ministerial candidates before the polls, instead of afterwards. In addition, during the actual elections, voters tended to vote 'nationally' in the prime ministerial poll, but according to particular interests, (and hence for minority parties) for the *Knesset*.

Presidential-style elections tend to favour a two-horse race; with this in mind, the right chose to unite behind one candidate, Benjamin 'Bibi' Netanyahu, leader of *Likud*, for the prime ministership. To win their full backing, however, Netanyahu struck a controversial deal with Raphael Eitan, leader of the more extreme *Tsomet* Party, and later with David Levy of the breakaway *Gesher* group. This guaranteed the smaller parties higher places on a joint electoral list, which in effect displaced a number of *Likud* stalwarts.

CAMPAIGN

Both major parties sought the broad centre, with Labour moving rightwards, promising to guarantee Jerusalem's 'indivisibility' and tighter security, and *Likud* moving leftwards, embracing the main tenets of Oslo 2 as a *fait accompli*. Mindful of the violent repurcussions of strong political rhetoric (which arguably inspired the assassination of Rabin), both parties avoided invective. For its part, Labour deliberately chose not to play the 'Rabin card', although in retrospect this 'statesmanlike' approach was probably a miscalculation. The party also suffered through bad co-ordination between its prime ministerial campaign (led by Ehud Barak) and its *Knesset* campaign (led by Haim Ramon). This led to what many called a 'lacklustre campaign', but the high voter turnout shows how important Israelis considered the poll to be.

NETANYAHU AND PERES ON THE PEACE PROCESS

Within those parameters, however, each camp held to distinctly different views of Israel's future in the Middle East. For the first time, the Labour platform did not rule out the possibility of a Palestinian state, while Likud planned to freeze talks with Syria on returning the Golan Heights, and furthermore promised to invest $3.6 billion on new 'settlements' including in the territories. Whereas Peres stressed the battle against 'Islamic fundamentalism' (where Israel could find common cause with its Arab neighbours), Netanyahu said that Israel's chief threat came from 'Arab dictatorships'. According to some interpretations, this meant that Jerusalem could never build strong ties with Syria or the PLO. Ariel Sharon, *Likud's* veteran right-wing standard-bearer, promised that a *Likud* administration would interpret the Oslo Accords so narrowly as to effectively freeze negotiations on substantive issues with Palestinians. Netanyahu only grudgingly agreed to meet Arafat, something he had never done as Leader of the Israeli Opposition.

Through careful rhetoric, Netanyahu claimed to support 'the peace process'. Thus 'floating voters' could assuage themselves that by voting for Netanyahu, they were not necessarily voting 'against peace'. But it would be 'peace with security' (*shalom beto'ach*) and his administration would not yield an inch of Israeli soil. He would 'not return to Gaza', but, by the same token, he said 'Gaza would not return to Israel' [in the form of *Hamas* terror attacks]. Netanyahu did not rule out redeploying Israeli troops in autonomous West Bank areas, if he considered it necessary. Palestinians believed this transgressed the terms of the two Oslo Accords. During the campaign, Netanyahu deliberately scared Jewish voters by suggesting that Peres was prepared to 'divide Jerusalem'. In their face-to-face eve-of-election television debate, Netanyahu used the word 'fear' 11 times. His 'big idea' was for a grand Middle East conference: in effect, a 'second Madrid'.

ANALYSING THE OUTCOME – TRIUMPH OF THE SMALLER PARTIES

In the *Knesset* election, there was a strong trend away from support for the two main blocs, Labour and *Likud*, and a corresponding trend towards the smaller parties:

- Of the two main parties, *Likud* was probably worst hit, as its pre-election alliance committed it to reserving seats on its joint list to coalition partners, *Tsomet* and *Gesher*. Labour remained the largest single party, but its lacklustre campaign, and schisms between factions, were blamed for its poor showing.
- On the left, *Meretz* defied predictions of a wipeout. Both of the traditionally Arab or Arab-dominated parties, *Hadash* and the United Arab List (UAL), registered increased votes, which testified to an unusually strong interest by Arab voters in the 1996 elections. It was also the first time that candidates backed by the 'fundamentalist' Islamic Movement (including the UAL's new leader, Abdul-Malik Dahamshe) were elected to the *Knesset*. Most Arabs supported Peres for Prime Minister.
- On the right fringe, *Moledet* did slightly worse than in 1992. *Tsomet's* vote was subsumed within the *Likud-Tsomet-Gesher* joint list, but can be assumed to have attracted fewer voters than its impressive performance in 1992.
- In the centre of Israeli politics, two new parties scored well: The Third Way (essentially a right-wing breakaway from Labour) won four seats, indicating concern for the retention of the Golan Heights. Likewise, Natan Sharansky's *Yisrael B'Aliyah* formed a strong bloc for immigrants' rights, and attracted at least half of the 400,000 voters from the former Soviet Union.

1996 ISRAELI ELECTION RESULTS

Some 3,135,000 Israelis, representing 79.7% of the Israeli electorate, voted on Wednesday, May 29, 1996. This was 2.5% higher than the turnout figure for the 1992 elections. Approximately 80% of Jewish voters and 77.4% of Arab voters participated. The Jewish settlers of Gaza and the West Bank registered the highest turnout. of 89.4%

Prime ministerial election

Most attention was focused on the prime ministerial race, which was extremely close. Polls closed on Wednesday, and initial exit polls indicated a Peres victory. Counting continued into Friday, and the definitive result was only known after 150,000 absentee ballots were accounted for, representing the votes of soldiers, diplomats and hospital patients. Binyamin Netanyahu won with 1,501,023 votes (50.5% of the total); Shimon Peres received 1,471,566 votes (49.5%).

Knesset election

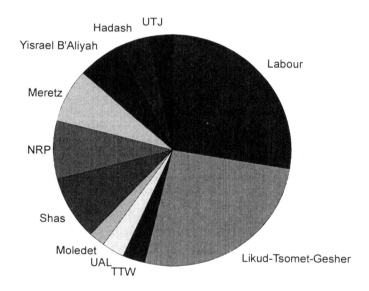

Parties	Percentage of vote	Seats 1996	Seats 1992
Labour	26.8	34	[44]
Likud-Tsomet-Gesher	25.1	32	[31]
Shas	8.5	10	[6]
NRP (National Religious Party)	7.8	9	[6]
Meretz	7.4	9	[12]
Yisrael B'Aliyah	5.7	7	–
Hadash	4.2	5	[4]
UTJ (United Torah Judaism)	3.2	4	[4]
TTW (The Third Way)	3.1	4	–
UAL (United Arab List)	2.9	4	[2]
Moledet	2.3	2	[2]

Note: Tsomet won 8 seats as a separate party in 1992; thus the figure for Likud-Tsomet-Gesher in 1992 really applies to Likud alone. Only 23 actual Likud MKs were returned in 1996, nine less than in 1992. Technically, the UAL did not exist in 1992, so the two seats ascribed to it went to the Arab Democratic Party, its largest constituent grouping. Likewise, Yisrael B'Aliyah and the Third Way did not exist in 1992.

● The most remarkable feature of the 1996 elections was the revival in fortunes of the religious parties, which as a bloc increased from 16 seats to 23, its largest size in Israeli history. *Shas* benefited from a Sephardi 'protest vote' on social issues; while the NRP successfully harnessed a new assertiveness amongst religious Zionists, and in particular the settler movement. This was all the more noteworthy, because only six months earlier, extreme elements in the NRP had been roundly blamed for spawning the atmosphere which led to Rabin's assassination. An estimated 90% of religious Jewish voters backed Netanyahu.

Future prospects for the peace process

PERES' CONTRIBUTION TO PEACE

During his six months as Prime Minister, Shimon Peres registered important gains for the peace process. Relations with Jordan improved with King Hussein's triumphal state visit to Israel, and open military co-operation. Mauritania had become the third Arab state to open full diplomatic relations with Israel, in late 1995, and contacts increased in 1996. In January, Peres met Yemeni President Ali Abdullah Saleh in Paris; in April he paid his first official visit as Prime Minister to Oman and Qatar; in May, Israel and Tunisia opened mutual interest offices. Trade with Morocco increased to several million dollars in a few months, and Turkey and Israel signed a defence accord. For the first time Israelis joined the boards of UN bodies; and the prospect of a gas deal with Egypt helped to defuse earlier problems. Closer to home, Peres kept rigorously to the Oslo 2 schedule: troops redeployed by the end of 1995, Palestinian elections were held on January 20, 1996, and final status talks with the PLO began on May 4. Peres co-ordinated with Arafat over aid to the PNA; and Israeli officials witnessed the opening of Gaza's first international airport, at Rafah.

Yet Peres' tenure will equally be remembered for his failures: deadlock in the talks with Syria; inability to prevent *Hamas* suicide bombings; closure of the territories which undermined the Palestinian economy; the repeated delays in deploying from Hebron; and the ill-considered Operation Grapes of Wrath, which failed to end attacks on Israeli troops, and whose civilian casualties embarassed Israel's allies. In the end, Peres failed to convince Israeli voters that his vision of peace could work.

CHANGE UNDER NETANYAHU

By mid-June, as Prime Minister Benjamin Netanyahu prepared to take power in Israel, the future success of the peace process hangs in the balance. Officially, Netanyahu believes in peace, and restated his call for a new round of regional negotiations in his acceptance speech. But the terms which he is demanding seem unacceptable to most Arabs. During the election campaign, he ruled out withdrawal from Hebron, and vowed to close down Orient House, the PLO's *de facto* headquarters in Jerusalem. Netanyahu has had to choose his cabinet from a *Knesset* which is more fractured than ever before. Pessimists say that he is beholden to right-wingers, like Raphael Eitan and Ariel Sharon, who wish to return Israel to pre-1991 days. Significantly, Netanyahu rejects the 'land for peace' formulation which underlies the Oslo Accord.

On the other hand, some observers see signs for cautious optimism. The very narrowness of his victory testifies to the residual strength of the pro-peace lobby in Israel. Immediately after his election was confirmed, Netanyahu instructed his chief aide and peace talks advisor, Dore Gold, to contact Abu Mazen, the Speaker of the Palestine Legislative Council, and leader of the Palestinian delegation at the final status talks. Behind his rhetoric Netanyahu is seen as a pragmatist, who keenly appreciates the importance of US support for Israel. Mindful of Shamir's experience, he would be unwilling to risk jeopardizing US loans by immediately expanding settlements. Given Bill Clinton's and Warren Christopher's past commitments, the results of the US presidential election in November 1996 will have a strong bearing on the Middle East peace process.

CAUTIOUS REACTIONS AND NEW FACES

Despite fears of a new *Intifada* breaking out, most of the Palestinian leadership appears to have accepted the new dispensation with stoicism and a pragmatic willingness to 'do business'. In the two weeks after the Israeli elections, Arab leaders (Yasser Arafat, Hosni Mubarak, King Hussein, Hafez al-Assad and Saudi King Fahd) held three summit meetings, with the goal of presenting a 'united front' to support the continuation of the peace process.

Netanyahu's first public speech as prime minister aimed at reconciliation within Israel ('peace must begin at home'), and drawing Arab states into the 'circle of peace'. His government is legally commited to honour the agreements which his predecessors signed, and which have been counter-signed by the USA, Russia and the EU, and are binding in international law and endorsed by several UN resolutions. Having said that, he is sure to replace many of the leading figures of the old peace process, like Ambassador Rabinovich in Washington, and Oslo 2's architect, Uri Savir. Their departure would represent an inevitable breach of continuity, and it will take time to restore the strong personal bonds between Israeli, Palestinian, Syrian and Jordanian negotiators which underpinned the peace process to date.

By the same token, many feel that the Peres-Rabin-Arafat initiative faltered precisely because it was a 'peace between leaders', and not a 'peace between peoples'. On both sides, military, political and diplomatic elites dominated the proceedings. There was comparitively little involvement from other important consitutencies: community and religious leaders, women, youth, business directors, educationalists, Israel's own Arab Community, and, most of all, the peace activists who had kept channels of communication open during four decades of Israeli–Arab belligerancy. Even so, the Madrid, Moscow and Oslo peace tracks have at least provided the infrastructure within which to conduct future negotiations. Two trends appear irreversible: Israel's economic integration into the region, and Palestinian acquisition of the instruments of statehood. Given the vicissitudes of the past few years, it would be a rash person who would pass judgement on the ultimate state of the Mideast peace process.

Cabinet approved by Israel's 14th Knesset, on June 18, 1996

Benjamin Netanyahu (*Likud*) Prime Minister, Minister of Housing, and Religious Affairs
Rafael Eitan (*Tsomet*) Deputy Prime Minister, Minister of Agriculture and Environment
Zevulun Hammer (NRP) Deputy Prime Minister, Minister of Education and Culture
Moshe Katsav (*Likud*) Deputy Prime Minister, Minister of Tourism
David Levy (*Gesher*) Minister of Foreign Affairs
Yitzhak Mordechai (*Likud*) Minister of Defence
Ze'ev Benjamin Begin (*Likud*) Minister of Science
Yuli Edelstein (*Yisrael B'Aliyah*) Minister of Immigrant Absorption
Ariel Sharon (*Likud*) Minister of National Infrastructure
Avigdor Kahalani (Third Way) Minister of Public Security
Tzachi Hanegbi (*Likud*) Minister of Health
Rabbi Yitzhak Levy (NRP) Minister of Transport and Energy
Limor Livnat (*Likud*) Minister of Communications
Dan Meridor (*Likud*) Minister of Finance
Ya'akov Ne'eman (non-party appointment) Minister of Justice
Natan Sharansky (*Yisrael B'Aliyah*) Minister of Trade and Industry
Eli Suissa (Shas) Minister of the Interior
Eliyahu Yishai (Shas) Minister of Labour and Social Affairs

Index

The following index includes names, treaties, organizations and selected places. It covers the whole book, apart from the Biography Section (Part IV). Bold numbers refer to special or more detailed sections on the subject in question.